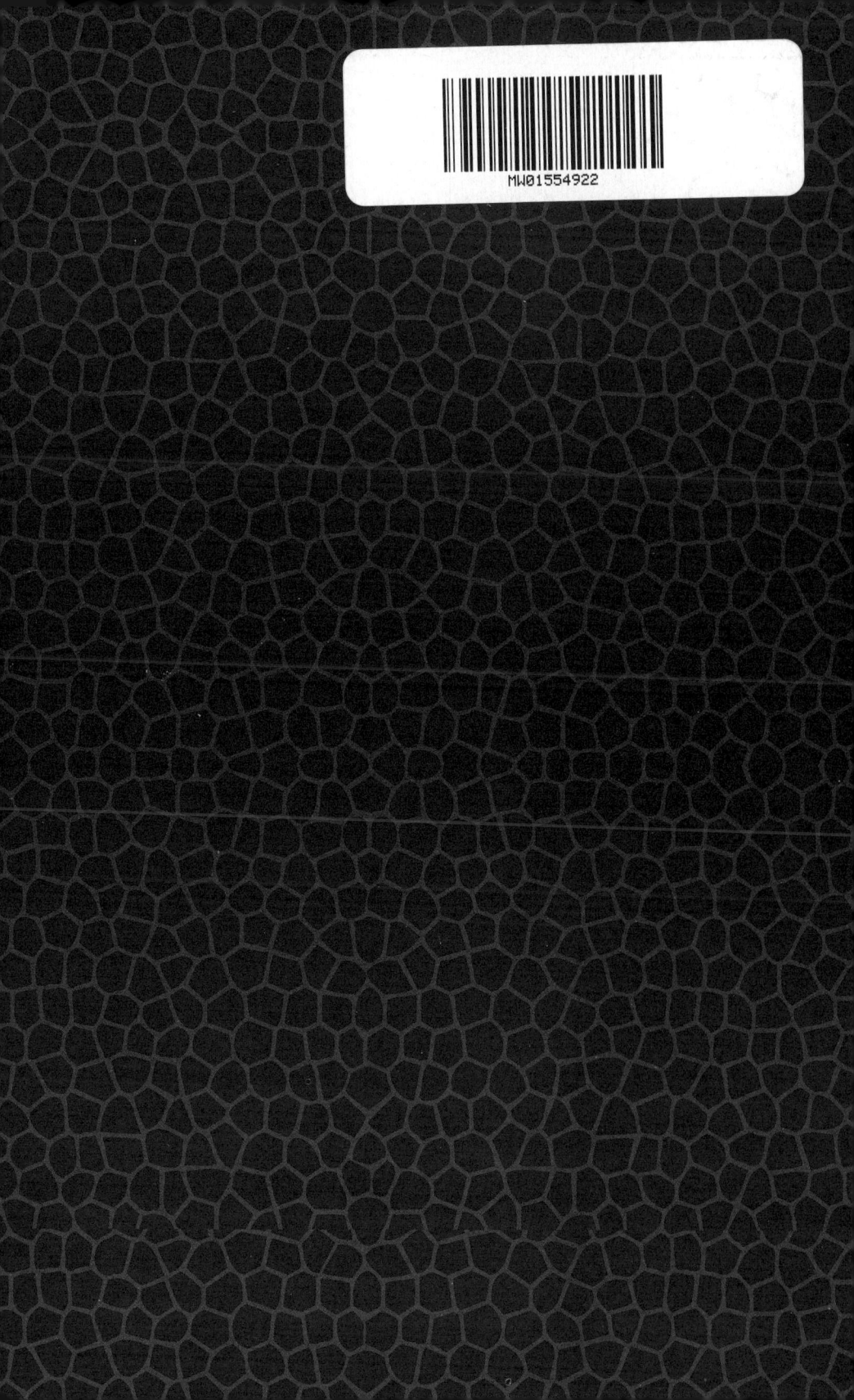

ספר
עיונים בהלכה
הלכות המזון
food
A Halachic Analysis

INSIGHTS INTO HALACHA

ספר
עיונים בהלכה
הלכות המזון

food
A Halachic Analysis

RABBI YEHUDA SPITZ

Copyright © 2021 by Mosaica Press

ISBN: 978-1-952370-06-9

All rights reserved. No part of this book may be used or reproduced or transmitted in any form or by any means, electronic or mechanical, including photocopying, recording, or by any information storage and retrieval system, without written permission from the publisher.

Published by Mosaica Press, Inc.
www.mosaicapress.com
info@mosaicapress.com

Dedicated in honor of our remarkable children

RABBI YEHUDA AND MIRIAM SPITZ

the author and his wife
for their tireless devotion to *harbotzas Torah* and for being
exemplary role models to their wonderful children

*Mordechai Zev, Avigayil, Chaim Aryeh, Rivky,
Elisheva, and Eliezer Meir*

May Hakadosh Baruch Hu continue to grant them *koach*
and *gezunt* in their *avodas hakodesh*.

Also dedicated in honor of our parents

BERNARD AND RUTH SPITZ

and in memory of
our parents

**RABBI YAAKOV ELIEZER
AND HADARA BAKER**

uncle

DR. LARRY SPITZ

and sister

SHOSHANA LEAH KAGAN

RABBI MANISH AND ROCHEL SPITZ

This *sefer* is dedicated in loving memory
of our grandparents

RABBI JACOB L. AND REBBETZIN HADARA BAKER

הרב יעקב אליעזר בן אברהם יצחק זצ״ל
נפטר י״ט טבת תשס״ו

הרבנית דרייזא ליבא (הדרה) בת ר' גרשון ז״ל
נפטרה י״ט מרחשון תשנ״ז

An illustrious *talmid chacham*, spiritual leader, and renowned *chazan*, Rabbi Baker and his rebbitzen served communities throughout the United States, mainly in the Bronx, New York. In their later years, they fulfilled their lifelong dream by moving to Kiryat Telz-Stone, Israel, and establishing a shul.

Rabbi Baker wrote a memorial book describing the 1941 massacre that took place in his hometown of Jedwabne, Poland. The revelation that the murders were committed by his Polish neighbors caused an international uproar. Eventually, the Polish people accepted the blame and publicly apologized for their deeds. They honored him for his efforts, with their country's highest honor,

the "Jan Karski Award."

The years that Rabbi Baker learned in the renowned Łomza Yeshiva set him on a lifelong path of piety and scholarship. He and his rebbetzin established a home filled with Torah, which their descendants have emulated, following their example.

May their memory be a blessing.

ת.נ.צ.ב.ה.

THE KAGAN, KAPLAN, BAKER, MILLER, AND SPITZ FAMILIES
Children, Grandchildren, and Great-grandchildren

In loving memory of our grandparents

ELTER BUBBY AND ZAIDY GRAFF

סימא בת ברוך פרץ ע״ה

אשר זעליג בן זאב ע״ה

Mrs. Sima Graff, a scion of the distinguished Meltzer family from Kletzk, cultivated a loving relationship with each grandchild, even from a distance. She took great pride in their accomplishments, complimenting their creativity, and reveling in their success. Bubby connected strongly to *Torah* and *Tefilla*, and appreciated hearing *Torah* ideas and inspiration.

Mr. Arthur Graff, American born and bred, led the family with wisdom and his ever-present sense of humor. Employed by the Department of Defense, Zaidy was an engineer who worked on rockets, yet his down-to-earth values and relationships kept him strongly involved in his children and grandchildren's lives. His *hakaras hatov* was legendary, as throughout his ninety-four years, he never stopped marveling at the *brachos* with which Hashem had blessed him, and expressed his appreciation at every opportunity.

BUBBY AND ZAIDY LIEBERMAN

רבקה בת זלמן שבח ע״ה

משה בן יעקב צבי ע״ה

Hailing from Rochester, NY, Mrs. Ruth Lieberman was a paragon of *chessed* and community activism. She stood loyally behind the building of her shul, quietly ensuring its continued existence. Her cheerful nature and the smile that lit up her face made her home a welcome place to visit for grandchildren and guests alike, as all were greeted with a hearty meal and a listening ear. Bubby was a beloved teacher, and she loved to learn, teach, and explore new frontiers together with her students and grandchildren.

Growing up in America during challenging times for Orthodox Jewry, Mr. Murray Lieberman's *shemiras Shabbos* never wavered, as he struggled to support his family by working in the public-school system. Zaidy honored Shabbos through singing *zemiros* and studying the weekly *parashah*, strongly adhering to tradition, and was grateful to see his grandchildren following his path. As president of their shul, as well as a respected *chazan*, Zaidy's shul, Khal Adath Yeshurun of the Bronx, remained the central pillar in their lives.

May their memory be a blessing.

ת.נ.צ.ב.ה.

In memory of

BURTON HUTMAN M.D.

בנימין שמשון בן חיים ע"ה

נפטר כ"ד כסלו תשע"ז

Beloved husband, father, and grandfather

Humble

"וילמד ענוים דרכו" (תהלים כה:ט)

Hardworking

"בכל ביתי נאמן הוא" (במדבר יב:ז)

Honest

"וכל מעשהו באמונה" (תהלים לג:ד)

May his memory be a blessing.

JACQUELINE
WAYNE AND ELITE
NOAH AND CHERIE
BERNIE AND SUSAN
MICHAEL AND BRETTE

לע"נ
עטרת ראשינו

ר' מאיר ב"ר דוד הכהן אונגר
MR. ALEX UNGAR
נפטר כ"ט טבת, תשע"ז

מאת
משפחת אונגר
משפחת ווינטרויב
משפחת קאלווריא

ת.נ.צ.ב.ה.

Dedicated in loving memory of
CHANA SILVERBERG
EDITH SEIF
CANTOR ABRAHAM SEIF
RABBI YOSSI HEBER
ROCHEL (SHELLY) SEIF
GOLDA SEIF
ALAN SEIF
JACK PERLSTEIN
ETHEL PERLSTEIN

HOWARD AND DENA SEIF

שלחו מתם איזהו בן העולם הבא ענוותן ושפל ברך שייף עייל שייף ונפיק וגריס באורייתא
תדירא ולא מחזיק טיבותא לנפשיה (סנהדרין פ״ח ע״ב)
לזכר נשמת
אאמו״ר ר' זעליג פסח בן ישעי' זאב הלוי ארץ ז״ל
נלב״ע כ״ט אלול תשס״ט (ערב ר״ה)
למעלה מיובל שנים למד ולימד שמר עשה והחזיק והעמיד תלמידים לאלפים ורבבות, והכל
יפה עשה בדרכי נועם ובעין טובה להפליא

Dedicated by
YITZCHOK AND TOBY ORATZ AND FAMILY
Marlboro, NJ

לע"נ
צבי הערש בֶּן ישראל

ישראל מאיר ווקם

This wonderful book is sponsored
in loving memory of
our mother and grandmother

MRS. EDITH (BRACHA) KLEIN

לע"נ

אמי מורתי מרת ברכה בת ר' דוד ע"ה הכ"מ
נלב"ע מוצאי יוה"כ תשע"ח
ת.נ.צ.ב.ה.

REUVEN CHAIM AND SHIRA YAEL KLEIN
BINYAMIN ELIEZER, ELIMELECH, MASHI, AND DOVID KLEIN
Beitar Illit, Israel

Dedicated to the multi generations of

KAGAN, BAKER, MINKOWITZ, AND HOLCZER FAMILIES

on all continents, who stand fast in their belief of G-d, Torah, and the Jewish Nation

GAMLIEL AND TERRI KAGAN

In honor of my dear friend

RABBI YEHUDA SPITZ, *SHLITA*

May you always have the strength and peace of mind to continue doing great things.

YITZY WEINBERG

In memory of our fathers

TIMOTHY ELLIOT RAPHAEL JACOBS

ר׳ עלי רפאל בן חזקיה צבי הלוי ע״ה

and

AVRAHAM ISAAC LEVIN

ר׳ אברהם יצחק בן משה הלוי ע״ה

RICHARD AND VANINA JACOBS

Dedicated *l'iluy nishmas*

משה ליברמן ע״ה
Throughout his life, he was devoted to and strongly supported Torah scholarship endeavor—intensively as a student, committedly as a teacher.

רבקה ליברמן ע״ה
Communicated her love for being and acting Jewish by unwavering enthusiasm and unstinting community volunteer leadership work.

Both took great pride in all their grandchildren's Jewish educational projects and achievements, and would be proudly doing so as well today for this new *sefer*.

With best wishes for much *hatzlachah* for Rabbi Spitz ahead,

THEIR DAUGHTER, SANDRA
THEIR GRANDSON, YISROEL YONASAN

In memory of

MAX AND ANITA KARL

ERNESTO AND MARIA SECOMANDI

DRS. ROBERT AND NILZA KARL, DANIEL KARL, LARA STREIGHT AND KEVIN KARL

In honor and
appreciation of

**RABBI
YEHUDA SPITZ**

May you continue your
avodas hakodesh for many
years to come.

Your *talmidim*,
SHMULY BOTNICK AND
DOVID SKLARZ

L'iluy nishmas

**ELIEZER
AVROHOM
TZVI** BEN
PSACHYA LEIB

Dedicated by
SHLOMO AND NAOMI
RADNER AND FAMILY

לע"נ
מו"ר הרב הגאון הצדיק

ר' יונה בן
ר' ישראל הלוי
פארסט זצ"ל

תלמידו
שמואל דוד הערצאג

In loving memory of our parents

יהודה בן יהושע הלוי

שפרינצא בת

הרב יששכר דוב

**JULES
AND JANET
GLOGOWER,**
A"H

They exemplified the virtues of humility,
truthfulness, and loving kindness.
May their memory be a blessing.

THE GLOGOWER FAMILY

In memory of
ALFRED AND
EDITH GROSS

אברהם ויהודית גרום ע״ה
of McKeesport,
Pennsylvania

THEIR CHILDREN,
IRA AND TMIMA GROSS

לעילוי נשמת
אסתר בת **מאיר**
ו**בערל** בן **אברהם**

In memory of our beloved parents
and grandparents
**SHLOMO CHAIM (SOL)
AND MALKA RIVKA
(MARLENE) KALCHMAN**

Dedicated by
YECHEZKEL KALCHMAN AND HIS
DEAR CHILDREN, SHLOMO, DAVID,
MOSHE, AND NAOMI

L'iluy nishmas
MOSHE BEN YAAKOV TZVI
RIVKA BAS ZALMAN SHEVACH
ZLATA FREIDA BAS R' YOSEF
CHAIM AVROHOM
CHAIM BEN R' YAAKOV
YERACHMIEL YISROEL DOV
BEN MOSHE AHRON
Dedicated by
AHRON AND ESTY LIEBERMAN

In memory of and
L'iluy nishmas avi mori
R' HERSHEL
BEN **MICHEL**, Z"L

His children,
YAKOV AND CHUMIE VANN

To my good friend
and *marbitz Torah*,
RAV YEHUDA SPITZ

From a dedicated reader,
JOEL SCHNUR

לזכר נשמת
הילד רפאל ברוך דוב ע״ה
בן **אשר צבי האפט** נ״י

In loving memory of our fathers

ר' **מיכאל** בן יוסף וויים ז״ל
MICHEL WEISS

ר' **בנימין יצחק** בן מאיר ראם ז״ל
BINYOMIN YITZCHAK ROSS

MR. AND MRS.
MENASHE REUVEN WEISS

L'iluy nishmas

DEVORAH ITA
BAS PESACH

L'zecher nishmos

RAV YITZCHAK ARYEH
BEN HARAV CHAIM MOSHE

REB BINYAMIN
BEN R' SHMUEL

In honor of and as a *zechus* for
our children

YOSEF BORUCH,
MEIR SIMCHA, AND
YEHUDA LEIB, BA"H

BINYOMIN AND BROCHI RADNER

In honor of my good friend

RABBI JEFF SEIDEL

DAVID SULTAN

In memory of my mother

RACHEL BAS YOSEF, A"H

ELI WEISS

Dedicated in memory of my mother
ZLATA FREIDA BAS R' YOSEF CHAIM
AVROHOM, Z"L

In honor of my dear *mechutanim*
R' YAACOV TZVI AND REBBETZIN
LIEBERMAN

In honor of my children
R' AHRON AND ESTY LIEBERMAN,
CHAIM, AND MOSHE

YITZCHOK PORTNOY

לעילוי נשמות

רחל בת תנחום ע״ה • משה מתתיהו בן מאיר
הכהן ע״ה • שרה נחא בת שאול זאב ז״ל
אפרים בן אהרן ז״ל • מינה שרה בת תנחום ז״ל
יעקב בן מרדכי פיטל ע״ה • שיינע ליבע בת נתן
מנחם ז״ל • חיים יהושע בן שאול ז״ל • אריה לייב
בן אברהם ע״ה • יהושע בן מאיר הכהן ע״ה
לוסי בת אברהם ע״ה • מורנו הרב שלמה
בן זאב יעקב ז״ל

לע"נ
שושנה לאה
בת ר' יעקב אליעזר
קגן ע"ה

לז"נ
התינוקת רחל ע"ה
בת ר' בנימין ניסן נ"י

Dedicated by Yitzchok Lewis in memory of
FRANK STERN
אפרים בן ירמיהו ע"ה
and the *kedoshei haShoah*
Also in honor of
RABBI SPITZ
for his assistance with the
Hilchos Shabbos Semicha test

לע"נ
ישראל אליעזר
בן זאב שפיץ ע"ה

L'iluy nishmas the Rosh Yeshiva
RAV MENDEL WEINBACH, ZT"L
הרב חנא מנחם מנדל
בן ר' יחזקאל שרגא זצ"ל
One of the fathers of *kiruv*
and founders of Ohr Somayach
Guiding light to thousands
ת.נ.צ.ב.ה.

L'iluy nishmas the unforgettable
REB CHAIM (M'YERUSHALAYIM) DASKAL, ZT"L
ר' חיים ברוך יהודה
בן ר' דוד צבי זצ"ל
נלב"ע מוצאי שבת פר' קרח תשע"ד
"זאת חוקת התורה"
ת.נ.צ.ב.ה.

לזכות ולהצלחת
שירה יפה בת רחל מרים
וכל יוצאי חלציה

אשר זעליג וייס
כגן 8
פעיה"ק ירושלם ת"ו

בס"ד

בס"ד
כ"ב תמוז ע"ח

זה שנים רבות שמכיר אני את מחבר ספר יקר זה, תלמידי אהובי וידיד נפשי הרה"ג ר' יהודה בצלאל שפיץ מרביץ תורה ומורה הוראה בחסד. הרבה דן לפני בהלכה וראיתי את כשרונותיו הברוכים ושכלו הישר בנוסף על בקיאותו הגדולה במקורות ההלכה.
הרב שפיץ כבר הוי"ל ספרים חשובים ועתה עומד לצאת ספר חשוב בירורי הלכה בשפה האנגלית לתועלת הרבים. כמעשהו בראשונים כך גם ספר זה, דברים בהירים וברורים בישרות ובהיקף, ובטוחני שרבים יהנו לאורו של ספר חשוב זה.
ברכתי שיזכה תמיד להגדיל תורה ולהאדירה בשמחה ושלוה כאות נפשו הטהורה.

באהבת איתן,
אשר זעליג וייס

**RABBI
MORDECHAI FRIEDLANDER**
Rav of Kiryat Shomrei Hachomos
Ramat Shlomo, Jerusalem
Rosh Yeshiva Ohr Chodosh

מרדכי פרידלנדר
רב קריית שומרי החומות
רמת שלמה
מו"צ העדה החרדית
פעיה"ק ירושלים תובב"א
ראש ישיבת אור חדש

ד' תמוז תשע"ד

ראיתי תחריכי כתבי עם בירורי הלכה בהרבה מקצועות שבתורה, פרי עמלו ועטו של הרב הגאון ר' יהודה בצלאל שפיץ שליט"א, נו"נ בכולל הלכה אור לגולה שע"י ישיבת אור שמח ירושלים עיה"ק.

ושמחתי לראות קנקן חדש מלא ישן, הן בהבנה הן בהיקף ידיעתו לברר הלכות החמורות כקלות בטוב טעם ודעת דבר דבור על אופניו, וכבר העידו עליו רבותיו הגאונים על כל הנ"ל. וראיתי לכבוד התורה לחזק את ידו שיעלה ויצמח כגן רוה להגדיל תורה ולהאדירה למעלה למעלה וישזכה לישב באהלה של תורה מתוך הרחבת הדעת דקדושה להעמיד הדינים לתורה ולהוראה.

בברכת כל טוב סלה,
ידידו מוקירו,
מרדכי פרידלאנדר

בס"ד

Rabbi Ephraim Greenblatt
5556 Barfield Road
Memphis, TN 38120

הרב אפרים גרינבלאט
רב ושו"ב במעמפיס
מח"ס שו"ת רבבות אפרים ח"ח וענה"ת

טלפון: (901) 682-3291   Telephone: Fax: (901) 685-0258 :פקס

ד' מנחם אב תשע"ג

הרב ר' יהודה שפיץ שליט"א עומד להוציא לאור את ספרו שדן בעניינים רבים, ועייינתי בספרו החשוב וראיתי חידושים נפלאים.
לכן הנני נותן לו <u>הסכמה</u> על ספרו, וספרו ראוי לעלות על שלחן מלכים.
ובברכה שיזכהו השם יתברך שילך מחיל אל חיל, ולהוציא עוד ספרים חשובים.
ובאתי בזה על החתום בירושלים עיה"ק תובב"א,
הרב אפרים גרינבלט

*יצוין כי ככל הידוע הסכמה זו היא האחרונה שיצא מתח"י הגאון זצ"ל
*As far as this author is aware, this is the final *haskama* that Rav Greenblatt *zt"l* wrote before his passing several months later.

YISROEL REISMAN
1460 EAST 19TH STREET
BROOKLYN, NY, 11230

ישראל רייזמאן
ישיבה תורה ודעת
אגודת ישראל בפלאטבוש

ב' תמוז תשע"ח

כבוד ידידי הרב יהודה שליט"א

שמחתי (ונהנתי) לראות שעתה מכין לדפוס את פרי עמלך בסוגיות הנוגע
למאכלים. יודעני רוב העמלות שעתה שוקע בהלכה, והכל רואים את גודל
השמחה וה"געשמאק" דשעתה שעתה בא ללמד הענינים. ויש לך במיוחד,
הכח לברר—הן ההלכה והן המציאות. הגר"א על משלי מסביר שדיין "הדן
דין אמת לאמיתו וכו'", שיש שני גדרי אמת—האמת בהלכה והאמת בבירור
המציאות. ומה שכתב לענין דיינים, כן הוא בכל עניני הלכה. ובזה כוחך גדול.

יהי רצון שהעולם התורה יזכו ל"טעמו וראו"—לטעום ממתיקות בירור
ההלכה שבספרך. ואני מקוה שיבואו עוד ספרים על הרבה סוגיות בהלכה
שזכית לברר.

בידידות וכבוד רב,
ישראל רייזמאן

בית המדרש להוראה "תורת שלמה"
ע"ש הר"ר שלמה בהר"ר ששכר דוב ברומן ז"ל
בנשיאות הגאון רבי משה שטרנבוך שליט"א, ראב"ד פעיה"ק ירושלים

[מכתב בכתב יד]

כ"ב תמוז תשע"ב,

שמחתי לראות פרי עמלו של תלמידי הוותיק, תלמיד המחכים את רבו, הרב יהודה בצלאל שפיץ שליט"א, אשר למד אצלינו יו"ד הלכות איסור והיתר (בשר בחלב, תערובות, ומליחה), וגם נתעטר בסמיכת חכמים על ידי נשיאנו הגאון רבי משה הלברשטאם זצ"ל, ויבדלחי"ט הגאון רבי משה שטרנבוך שליט"א, ראב"ד פעיה"ק. ומאז התעמק בהלכות אלו, וגם מזכה את הרבים במאמרים בעניני כשרות להלכה ולמעשה בירחונים בארץ ובחו"ל.

וידוע אני מד ערכי, ולא באתי להיות שר המסכים, שלא הגעתי למצב זה כלל וכלל, בכל זאת מצאתי לנכון להעיד על הרב המחבר שיגע ועמל בעניני כשרות בשו"ע ונושא כלים, ועל ידי זה זכה לברר וללבן ענין שני כלים שנגעו זה בזה (יו"ד סוף סימן צ"ב וצ"ג) ועוד עניינים בטוב טעם ודעת. ויהא רעוא שימשיך ללמוד וללמד ולזכות את הרבים.

הכותב וחותם לכבוד התורה ולומדיה,

יוסף יצחק לרנר

בס"ד

Rabbi Zev Leff
Rabbi of Moshav Matityahu
Rosh HaYeshiva—Yeshiva Gedola Matityahu

הרב זאב לף
מרא דאתרא מושב מתתיהו
ראש הישיבה—ישיבה גדולה מתתיהו

D.N. Modiin 71917   Tel: 08—976—1138 טל'   Fax: 08—976—5326 פקס'   ד.נ. מודיעין 71917

Dear Friends,

    I have read many portions of the manuscript "Insights into Halacha – Food! A Halachic Analysis" by my talmid, friend, and colleague, Rabbi Yehuda Spitz Shlit"a.

    Many of these halachic essays were originally installments to Ohr Someach's Parsha Sheet – Ohrnet. Rabbi Spitz is an accomplished Talmid Chochom with a keen talent for presenting Halachic issues in a comprehensive, lucid and interesting manner. He is also a pundit (no pun intended) at presenting this information with entertaining wit.

    The vast array of topics covered by this book and the thoroughness of each individual presentation is truly impressive.

    This work will be a true aid to those who want to gain a solid understanding of these Halachic issues and contribute in general to one's understanding of the Halachic process.

    I commend Rabbi Spitz, son of my illustrious colleague Rabbi Manish Spitz of South Florida, for following in his Father's footsteps, and presenting the community with a truly quality work.

    I pray that Hashem grant him and his family life and health and the wherewithal to continue to merit the community in his many and varied ways.

                                                      Sincerely,
                                                      With Torah blessings

                                                      Rabbi Zev Leff

בס"ד

Ohr Lagolah
HERTZ INSTITUTE
FOR INTERNATIONAL
TEACHER TRAINING

*A Torah Corps
Training Program
for Educators and
Communal Leaders*

an affiliate of
OHR SOMAYACH
Tanenbaum College

POB 18103
Jerusalem, 91180 Israel
Tel: 02-581-0315
Fax: 02-581-2890
lagolah@ohr.edu

21 Sivan 5778
June 04, 2018

It has been both a pleasure and an inspiration working together with Rabbi Yehuda Spitz at Yeshivas Ohr Somayach's Hertz Ohr Lagolah Institute. His encyclopedic mind and ability to intelligently analyze difficult situations have clarified many a problem.

A number of years ago, Rabbi Spitz began writing weekly analyses of *halachic* issues, and the result has been a collection of articles that present issues of interest in a lucid, comprehensive, and informative manner. I have often used his essays in explaining intricate matters in clear and concise terms.

I look forward to the publishing of the book so that the general public will gain the benefit of his scholarship.

Best wishes for *Hatzlocha*.

Rabbi Shmuel Bloom

Dean,
Ohr Lagolah
Hertz Leadership Institute

Executive Vice President Emeritus,
Agudath Israel of America

Table of Contents

Foreword XXXI
Preface XXXIII
Acknowledgments XXXVI

Part 1
Bassar B'chalav: Milk and Meat

CHAPTER 1: The Importance of a *Diyuk* 3
CHAPTER 2: *Maaseh Avos = Halacha Lemaaseh: Hekker, Shomer,*
   and *Maris Ayin* 16
CHAPTER 3: To *Bentch* or Not to *Bentch* (between Milk and Meat)?
   That Is the Question...25
CHAPTER 4: Weighty Waiting Options 31
CHAPTER 5: Hard Cheese Complexities 47
CHAPTER 6: The Great Dishwasher Debate 59
CHAPTER 7: The Ins and Outs of "*Shnei Keilim Shenagu*" 72

Part 2
Meat, Chicken, and Fish

CHAPTER 8: The Lox and Cream Cheese Dilemma 83
CHAPTER 9: Genetically Engineered Meat......................97
CHAPTER 10: Buffalo Burgers and the Zebu Controversy 133
CHAPTER 11: The *Gid Hanasheh* Incongruity...................145
CHAPTER 12: The Erev Pesach Meat Scandal 154

CHAPTER 13: Salting with Sugar?! 166
CHAPTER 14: Fish with Legs?! 177

Part 3

Famous Foods

CHAPTER 15: The Great Cholent Challenge 187
CHAPTER 16: The Chicken Bone 'n' Cholent Commotion 200
CHAPTER 17: The *Halachic* Adventures of the Potato 206
CHAPTER 18: The Odd Account of the Overnight Onion. 225
CHAPTER 19: The Quinoa-*Kitniyos* Conundrum 235
CHAPTER 20: The Coca-Cola Kashrus Controversy 256
CHAPTER 21: Of Bull's-Eyes, the *Korban* Cheesecake,
and Dairy Bread. 269

Part 4

Washing and *Pas*

CHAPTER 22: The Colored Water Caper 281
CHAPTER 23: The Parameters of *Pas Palter* 289
CHAPTER 24: *Mayim Acharonim, Chova?* 308

Part 5

Key Concepts

CHAPTER 25: *Chodosh* in *Chutz La'aretz* 325
CHAPTER 26: *Chatichah Hareuyah L'Hischabed*: All about Honor . . 351
CHAPTER 27: Margarine, Misconceptions, and *Maris Ayin* 360
CHAPTER 28: Leeuwenhoek's *Halachic* Legacy: Microscopes
and Magnifying Glasses 368
CHAPTER 29: The *Halachic* Discourse of Louis Pasteur:
Is Wine Fine? 378
CHAPTER 30: *Chalav Yisrael*: A *Halachic* History 394
CHAPTER 31: *Kashering* Teeth?! 439

ADDENDUM: Additions 445
APPENDIX: The Evolution of "Kosher" Gelatin in America........455
Index..476

Foreword
by Rabbi Yitzchak A. Breitowitz
Rav, Kehillas Ohr Somayach, Yerushalayim

FOR MANY YEARS RABBI YEHUDA SPITZ has authored a *halacha* column for the Ohr Somayach newsletter and website. At the urging of many, including myself, he has finally agreed to assemble these columns into a book or more accurately, a series of books, so that his penetrating insights would reach a wider audience.

The first in this projected series contains more than thirty chapters devoted to a wide variety of *halachic* complexities pertaining to food—the reader will encounter discussions of *Bassar B'chalav*, artificial meat, *chodosh*, buffalo burgers, cooking on Shabbos, *Chalav Yisrael*, overnight onions, *Yayin Nesech*, and many other fascinating topics.

As a longtime fan of Rabbi Spitz's outstanding articles, let me point out several notable features of his work:

- Accuracy: many *halachic* works, both in English and in Hebrew, will quote or paraphrase sources based on how those sources are cited in earlier works without bothering to verify the original source. More than once, this has led to the widespread perpetuation of error, as a mistake or omission by one author gets automatically followed by later authors, as each one uses the predecessor text as the source. Rabbi Spitz has gone to great effort to trace every quoted *psak* and *sevara* to its original source, and does not rely on secondary quotations or paraphrases. And if there is ambiguity in the reports, he will note it.

- Completeness: When Rabbi Spitz addresses a topic, he will give you all the views on the topic. He does not limit himself to a selection of the views he finds most persuasive. He includes many oral *psakim* that cannot always be found in writing and carefully documents the source of them as well.

- Clarity and organization: Rabbi Spitz not only gives you the rules, but explains the background and the underlying reasons in a clear, organized manner. He will typically choose an interesting contemporary topic (e.g., stem cell meat) or historical topic (e.g., the kashrus of Coca-Cola) as a hook for his analysis, and he will embellish his detailed and comprehensive analysis with flashes of humor and occasional references to popular culture. These quickly capture the reader's attention and stimulate his interest.

Whether you are a beginner or even a seasoned *talmid chacham*, you will gain a richer understanding of the topic because of his lucid explanations as well as the copious references. May Rav Yehuda continue to have much *hatzlacha* in his endeavors *l'hagdil Torah U'lehadira*.

Preface

DEAR READERS,

Shehechiyanu v'kiyimanu, v'higiyanu lazman hazeh. This book, or more accurately, *sefer*, that you hold in your hands, featuring over thirty chapters of *halachic* exposition related to food, is the culmination of thousands of hours over more than a decade of learning, researching, teaching, elucidating, and writing of *halachic inyanim*. The importance and centrality of *halacha* in Jewish life cannot be overstated; as the well-known Talmudic dictum of R' Chiya bar Ami in the name of Ulla (*Brachos* 8a) stresses, "*Miyom shecharav Beis Hamikdash ain lo l'Hakadosh Baruch Hu b'olamo ela arba amos shel halacha bilvad*—From the day the Beis Hamikdash was destroyed, Hashem's presence dwells exclusively in the four *amos* of *halacha*."

Yet, in modern times, it often seems that there is somewhat of a lacuna in the appreciation and application of this core concept. Many feel that *halacha* is dry and unapproachable, some may even find it bewildering at times, or simply think that "everything is a *machlokes*." As the expression goes, "Perhaps something is lost in the translation," or to be more precise, the presentation.

This *sefer* sets out to try to change that perception, by clarifying the *halacha* in an interactive and enjoyable, albeit comprehensive, manner. Each chapter and topic is structured in a manner that allows the layman to gain clarity, and aids in understanding the step-by-step intricate and complex *halachic* process utilized by a *Posek* to arrive at a *halachic* conclusion, from the background sources all the way up to contemporary authorities.

The encouragement received by the overwhelming feedback for my "Insights into Halacha" column for Ohr Somayach, as well as the *halachic* articles featured in many major international *frum* publications and media over the years, demonstrates that this approach is indeed highly valued. The enthusiastic response made publishing this *sefer* the next logical step, in order to be able to reach a wider audience, and hopefully exemplify the Gemara's dictum (*Brachos* ibid.) of "*Oheiv Hashem she'arim hametzuyanim b'halacha.*" It is very gratifying that I have been able to be *zocheh* in benefitting the Torah world by endeavoring to make authentic *halacha* readable and accessible to all. I *daven* that this *sefer* adequately serves this purpose.

THIS SEFER, THE FIRST IN this projected series, focuses on *halachos* related to food. Not just due to its relevance in all of our lives, as we all need food for nourishment, but the Torah teaches us that we are truly not primarily sustained by the material, but rather by Hashem's blessings: "*Ki lo al halechem levado yichyeh ha'adam*—Man does not live by bread alone" (*Parashas Eikev, Devarim* Ch. 8:3; see *Ibn Ezra* and *Daas Zekeinim* ad loc.).

The *Kli Yakar* (*Parashas Haazinu, Devarim* Ch. 32:1, s.v. *v'yeish*) explains that there is a message implicit in these words. Many ask how the world can subsist if we are otherwise busy and engaged with spiritual pursuits. He explains that the response is, "*B'zechus HaTorah ha'omedes b'makom matar v'tal*—In the merit of the Torah which stands in place of rain and dew." When we perform the will of Hashem, the heavens will remain silent and hearken to His bidding, guaranteeing us sustenance.

This idea is further developed by the *Malbim* (*Yeshaya* Ch. 55:1), who draws a fascinating parallel between the food and drinks that are necessities of life, and Torah and Mitzvos. Water, which is essential for life, is abundant and free and hence, akin to the Mitzvos of *Emunah* and *Hashgacha* of Hashem, inherent in everyone. Bread, which is also necessary—but not as much as water, and costs money but is not expensive—is similar to the Mitzvos of *limud HaTorah*, Shabbos, and *Tefilla*, which are constant Mitzvos that are the hallmarks of a believing Jew. Other Mitzvos are similar to milk, and others wine.

In a similar vein, my ancestor and namesake, the *Maharal M'Prague* (*Nesivos Olam, Nesiv Ha'Avodah* Ch. 17; explaining the Gemara *Pesachim* 118a) clarifies why bread was singled out as an example of an important food by the Torah. He explains that as bread requires intellect, creativity, and consciousness in order to produce it, it signifies man's unique abilities and purpose to improve, perfect, and refine the natural world. [See also *Midrash Tanchuma* (*Tazria* 5), detailing Rabbi Akiva's similar rejoinder to Turnus-Rufus regarding Bris Milah, *shibolim* and *gluska'os*.] Hence, bread is the perfect food for the Torah to showcase mankind's need for physical nourishment, yet cautions that the spiritual nevertheless trumps it in actual significance.

The key point is that there is a direct connection and correlation between the food we eat for physical sustenance, and the Torah and Mitzvos we perform for spiritual sustenance.

My *tefilla* is that this *halacha sefer* should serve as an aid in elucidating the spiritual content pertaining to food, elevating and uplifting the mundane by providing insight into the myriad details that encompass ensuring the *halachic* permissibility of the foods we eat.

IMPORTANT NOTE: The *halacha* presented in this *sefer* is simplified to present the issues in a comprehensible manner, so that the reader may gain an appreciation for and understanding of the *halachic* process, and is not intended to convey final *psak halacha*. Therefore, one must make sure to ask a competent *halachic* authority for guidance in each individual situation or in case of an actual *sheilah*.

Acknowledgments

FIRST AND FOREMOST, I WOULD like to take the opportunity to acknowledge the constant goodness bestowed upon me and my family by Hakadosh Baruch Hu. The unending *hashgacha pratis* and *siyatta diShmaya* we receive cannot begin to be adequately expressed. I am especially and eternally grateful to Him for being given the incredible twin privileges of being numbered among the *yoshvei Beis Midrash* and raising my family in Eretz Yisrael. May we be *zocheh* to continually serve Him properly and always give Him *nachas ruach*.

In his introduction to his magnum opus *Even Ha'Azel* (vol. 6, *Avodah* vol. 2; see the introduction to *Mori v'Rabi* Rav Yosef Yitzchok Lerner's *Sefer HaBayis* pg. 22-23), Rav Isser Zalman Meltzer writes that in *Mizmor shir chanukas habayis* (*Tehillim* Ch. 30), Dovid HaMelech is imparting an invaluable message to us. When one is *zocheh* to build a house and wishes to express his gratitude to Hashem, it is not sufficient to thank Hashem for his current wealth that enabled him to do so. Rather, he should remember all that has occurred to him along the way leading up to this fateful moment, and offer thanks to Hashem for it all, even if he has done so previously.

In this vein, especially as the journey of publishing this *sefer* has been a long one, I wish to express my appreciation and pay tribute to the many individuals along the way to whom I owe much gratitude. I ask forgiveness in advance from anyone whose name has been unintentionally omitted.

Growing up in Miami Beach, I attended Rav Yochanon Zweig's Mesivta of Greater Miami and Talmudic University of Florida, which transmitted essential foundations in *Yiddishkeit* and taught us "how to learn." Special thanks are due to my dedicated *Rabbeim*, Rav Yisroel Moshe Janowski and Rav Akiva Zweig, for their encouragement.

I later attended Yeshiva Gedolah and Rabbinical College Ateres Mordechai of Greater Detroit under the tutelage of the Rosh Yeshiva, Rav Leib Bakst zt"l. I owe sincere *hakaras hatov* to my devoted *Rabbeim* there over the years, Rav Shimon Goldberg, Rav Yitzchok Kahan, Rav Odom Ribiat, Rav Binyomin Sendler, and Rav Menachem Butrimovitz, and especially the current Roshei Yeshiva, Rav Yehuda and Rav Mayer Simcha Bakst, who personally "warmed-up" the frigid Midwest winters for an out-of-town *bochur* from Miami, and for immersing us in the depths of the *Yam HaTalmud*.

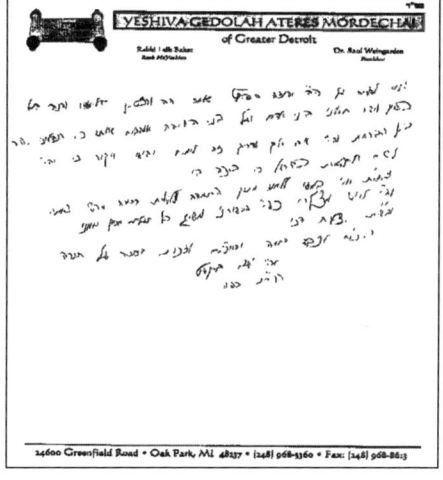

A special note of appreciation is due to my secular studies principal in *yeshiva*, Mr. David J. Wayntraub, who, after my valedictory address upon graduating *yeshiva* high school, informed me in no uncertain terms that he was of the firm opinion that I would utilize my secular studies education in my intended "career" in *Klei Kodesh*. Well, it seems he certainly won that bet.

Onto Eretz Yisrael, where I had the great *zechus* to learn for many years, including later in *Kollel*, in the renowned Mir Yeshiva, under the guidance of the Rosh Yeshiva, Rav Nosson Tzvi Finkel, zt"l. Deserving of special mention are Rav Nissan Kaplan (currently Rosh Yeshiva of Daas Aharon) and Rav Peretz Tarshish, *Rabbeim* who give their all to their *talmidim*. I credit Rav Tarshish, not only as a *rebbi*, but also a mentor and neighbor, for his astute advice and encouragement to study *halacha b'iyun*.

After years of learning in the Mir Kollel, I was accepted into Rav Yosef Yitzchok Lerner's Beis Midrash L'Horaah Toras Shlomo, described by some as the "Harvard of *Semicha Kollelim*," and others simply as "Rabbinic Boot-camp." I owe Rav Lerner, a true *Talmid Chacham par excellence*, tremendous *hakaras hatov*, not only for imparting to me a proper *derech halimud* in *halacha*, but also a *mesoras hapsak*, culminating in *Semicha*. I owe him much gratitude for continually encouraging me in my rabbinic pursuits, including penning a *haskama*.

I later studied other *Inyanei Halacha* with and received *shimush* from Rav Yonason Wiener, *Moreh Tzedek* on the She'aris Yisrael Beis Din, *Posek* for Ohr Somayach, and renowned expert on *Hilchos Nida*. I am truly grateful for the opportunity, as well as for his continued wisdom, guidance, and friendship over the years.

Although the last place in Yerushalayim one might expect to find a group of American *yungerleit* would be in the home of one of the senior *dayanim* of the *Badatz Eidah Hachareidis*, yet, amidst the hustle and bustle of the busy Yerushalmi household of Rav Yaakov Blau, *zt"l*, head of the *Badatz's* kashrus *hashgacha*, as well as their chief *Eruvin* and Finance/Business *halacha* expert, the American expatriate *avreichim* doing *shimush* held a special place. Interestingly, Rav Blau, notwithstanding his position or scholarship, felt that he had a unique opportunity to pass on his *mesorah* to *avreichim* who would likely become future leaders in the Diaspora. He spent many a Friday morning debating, clarifying, *paskening* and explaining the *sheilos* that had been brought to him, all the while cognizant of the fact that what he taught would serve as the next link in the chain of *mesorah* for many communities in *Chutz La'aretz*. In fact, among the only letters he would sign was a *ksav hamlatza*, a letter of approbation, for one who was fortunate to have performed *shimush* by him. *Baruch Hashem*, I had the privilege of being one of the select few. I am honored to include in this *sefer psakim* that I personally clarified with Rav Blau, *zt"l*.

In the years following, I have had the *zechus* to develop a *kesher* with Rav Asher Weiss, *Gaavad* of *Darchei Torah* and the renowned *Minchas Asher*. I am deeply grateful for his encouragement and opportunity to "talk in learning" to someone of his stature—asking complicated *sheilos* and receiving clarity, *sevara yeshara*, and *Daas Torah* in return, as well as for Rav Weiss generously writing *haskamos* for my *sefarim*.

Aside from my aforementioned *Rabbeim*, I am also privileged to be *b'kesher* with a "*chevra*," of sorts, of *Rabbanim* and *Poskim* around the world who aid in clarifying *halachic inyanim* that arise. I would like to acknowledge these *Rabbanim*'s wealth of Torah knowledge, keen insights, and invaluable contributions, not only to this *sefer*, but also to my daily living. They include (in alphabetical order) Rav Yitzchak Breitowitz, Rav Mordechai Frankel, Rav Yitzchok Dovid Frankel, Rav Binyomin Forst, Rav Yirmiyohu Kaganoff, Rav Mordechai Kuber, Rav Efraim Landy, Rav Zev Leff, and Rav Doniel Neustadt. Worthy of special mention are longtime *Rav* of Maalot Dafna and *Talmid Muvhak* of Rav Yosef Shalom Elyashiv, *zt"l*, Rav Nochum Eisenstein; Rav Breitowitz, who graciously agreed to pen the foreword for this *sefer*; and Rav Leff, who provided a *haskama* as well. *Ashreihem v'ashrei chelkam*.

A special note of gratitude is deserved to my former boss, mentor, advisor, and friend, Rabbi Richard Jacobs, who hired me as *Sho'el U'Meishiv*, and later *Rosh Chabura*, of the Ohr Lagolah Halacha Kollel at Yeshivas Ohr Somayach in Yerushalayim. Without his leadership, it is doubtful that I would have been able to remain in Eretz Yisrael in such a position of being *Marbitz Torah*. In addition, this *sefer* has largely been brought to print through his devotion, time, efforts, and unique diplomacy.

Hakaras hatov is due to the Ohr Somayach Roshei Yeshiva, Rav Mendel Weinbach, *zt"l*, and *yblch"t* Rav Nota Schiller, for their faith in me and my abilities, and entrusting to my responsibility the running of their *Halacha Kollel* and guiding *avreichim* for *Semicha*. Other noteworthy *yeshiva Rabbanim* include Rav Moshe Lazerus, Rav Shmuel Bloom, Rav Yehuda Samet, Rav Zvi Wainstein, Rav Moshe Pindrus, Rav Avraham Reisman, Rav Nachshon Schiller, Rav Yehonaton Peretz, Rav Avraham Rockmill, Rav Mordechai Perlman, Rabbi Yaakov Meyers, Rabbi Shlomo

Simon, Rabbi Alter Klein, Rabbi Yaakov Lubow, Rabbi Dr. Guy Matalon, Rabbi Moshe Dovid Butrimovitz, Rabbi Aharon Fine, Rabbi Yisroel Leskin, Rabbi Pesach Feldman, Rabbi Eli Merl, Rabbi Yitzchak Botton, and Rabbi Yisroel Booth. Thank you for your continued friendship over the years.

Soon after I started my roles in the *yeshiva*, Rav Yisroel Reisman, in town for his annual summer Yerushalayim learning schedule, advised me to take on additional roles of *Harbotzas HaTorah*. At the time, I often would correspond with authors of *halachic* articles, and at times offer my source-based opposing viewpoint, with varied results. Quite often, I would disappointedly find that the authors would not deign to respond, and if they did, would sometimes try to shirk out of the important issues raised. However, after I sent a four-page sourced query to Rabbi Donneal Epstein of the OU regarding a "Kashrus Kaleidoscope" article he penned for *Hamodia* back in 2009, not only did he agree with my points, but suggested that I write *halacha* articles for *Hamodia* as well. At his urging, I subsequently authored several for them, which, based on the feedback received, turned out to be pretty popular. I am grateful to Rav Reisman, Rabbi Epstein, and *Hamodia* for kick-starting my "English *halacha* writing career." Rav Reisman also later agreed to write a *haskama* for this *sefer*, a fitting conclusion for a journey he helped start.

Another important step along the way was former *talmid* Rabbi Yehuda Goldman, currently CEO of EarthKosher, who at the time was affiliated with a small website titled "Close to Torah." He invited me to pen *halacha* articles for them, which were B"H well-received. Subsequently, I was contacted to write for other *frum* media outlets, including VINNews, Matzav.com, and *Ami Magazine*. Soon after, Ohr Somayach asked me to author a dedicated "Insights into Halacha" column for their website, as they wanted me to write for the "home team." This later led to Rabbi Pinchos Lipschutz of the *Yated Ne'eman* requesting that I pen an ongoing *halacha* column for his respected newspaper. It is gratifying to see how the numerous articles that I have been *zocheh* to write have been effective in clarifying many *halachic inyanim*, and well-received by the broader public world-wide. I am greatly thankful to Rabbi Lipschutz, and all those involved in the disseminating of my "Insights into Halacha."

A special note of thanks is particularly due to my devoted proofreader in Ohr Somayach, Mrs. Rosalie Moriah, as well as the *OHRNET* general editor, Rabbi Moshe Newman.

I would also like to thank historian Roger Horowitz for providing me with hard-to-find *kisvei yad* and *teshuvos* of *Rabbanim* from the 1930s, as well as encouraging me to further my research into the *halachic* histories of gelatin and glycerin in America, even when my findings and conclusions did not necessarily mirror his own.

Thanks are also due to the Mosaica Press team for seeing this complicated project through to completion. Of special note are editors Rabbi Reuven Butler and Mrs. Sherie Gross, and graphic artist Mrs. Rayzel Broyde.

I would like to take this opportunity to thank the many individuals, friends, and *chaveirim*, who have assisted me each in their own way over the years: Rabbi Yosef Radner, R' Zvi Ryzman, R' Chezky Adler, Rabbi Yaakov Skoczylas, Rabbi Yitzchok Aharon Kramer, Rabbi Dr. Eliezer Brodt, Rabbi Aver Jacobs, Rabbi Arnie Wittenstein, Rabbi Binyomin Povarsky, Rabbi Menashe Svei, Rabbi Noach Sosevsky, Rabbi Reuven Chaim Klein, Rabbi Mordechai Zev Trenk, R' Avrohom Yitzchok Shulman, R' Tzvi Price, Rabbi Moshe Wachsman, Rabbi Yishai Greenwald, R' Peysi Adlerstein, Rabbi Matis Friedman, Rabbi Elchanan Shoff, Rabbi Abbish Rand, Rabbi Daniel Freedman, R' Yehoshua Burnham, Rabbi Ari Glatstein, several individuals who requested not to be named, my brother Dov, my brother in-law Rabbi Ezra Carter, my longtime *chavrusa* Rabbi Jeff Seidel, and our mutual friend Asher David Milstein. I would also like to personally thank the many individuals who assisted in sponsoring this *sefer* and furthering *Harbotzas HaTorah*. May Hakadosh Baruch Hu reward them all commensurately for their support.

Heartfelt *hakaras hatov* is due to my parents-in-law, Rabbi Yaacov Tzvi and Rochel Lieberman of Far Rockaway, for giving us their *bracha* way back when, upon our moving 6,000 miles away soon after marriage. Their steadfast encouragement in our *Avodas Hashem*, *Harbotzas*

HaTorah, and our raising their grandchildren far away, in Eretz Yisrael, is always much appreciated. May you continue to have much *nachas* from all of your children and their families.

I would like to express my sincere gratitude to my Zaidy and Bubby, Bernard and Ruth Spitz, originally of Cincinnati, Ohio. Their shining character and and sterling qualities continually inspire us all, and set a stellar example for their children, grandchildren, and great-grandchildren. May Hashem bless them with long and happy years of health and *nachas*.

No words can express my deep *hakaras hatov* to my dear parents, Rabbi Manish and Rochel Spitz, of Miami Beach, known by all to be *rosh v'rishon l'chol davar shebekedusha*. Their years of self-sacrifice, dedication, and devotion to the *klal* in being *mezakeh* the *rabbim*, have guided and inspired me in all my endeavors *l'sheim Shamayim*. I would also like to express my heartfelt appreciation for their constant input and encouragement. May Hashem grant you many more years of health and *Yiddishe nachas* from all of your descendants.

Special mention is due to the strongest person I know, my dear sister, Shira Lebovic, who serves as a constant inspiration and beacon of light, despite extremely difficult circumstances. May Hakadosh Baruch Hu grant her and her family tremendous *hatzlacha* in all of their endeavors.

Acharon acharon chaviv, words fail me when it comes to thanking my remarkable *eishes chayil*, Miriam. Chazal teach us (*Bava Metzia* 59a) that *bracha* is only bestowed upon a home in a wife's merit. This certainly holds true regarding my incredible partner, collaborator, adviser, enthusiast, and sometimes editor. Her unwavering dedication, support, encouragement, loyalty, and moral compass have immensely contributed to my continued success. She serves as an exemplar and true role model for our entire family. In many ways, the credit for this *sefer* belongs to her. To quote Rabbi Akiva (*Kesuvos* 63a and *Nedarim* 50a), "*Sheli v'shelachem shela hi*."

May Hashem shower our home with abundant blessing and may we be *zocheh* to continue to raise our family *b'derech HaTorah u'mitzvos*. May our wonderful children, Mordechai Zev, Avigayil, Chaim Aryeh, Rivky, Elisheva, and Eliezer Meir continue to grow in their own *Avodas*

Hashem, and be true guardians of the Torah and a source of *nachas ruach* for the Eibeshter and Klal Yisrael as we *daven* for them to be.

I conclude by *davening* to Hashem, echoing the wise words of Rabbi Nechunia ben Hakanah (*Brachos* 28b), that nothing I have written should be a source of error or misunderstanding and that I may continue to serve Him by learning and teaching His Torah.

Yehuda Spitz
Adar 5780
Givat Zev

Part 1

BASSAR B'CHALAV:
MILK AND MEAT

Chapter 1

The Importance of a *Diyuk*

WHEN LEARNING, WE WILL OFTEN make some sort of *diyuk*. This is basically an inference to understand the intent of the text, derived from the precise choice of words used. These *diyukim* are sometimes theoretical, but every now and then an innocuous looking line might have significant practical *halachic* ramifications.

Two prime examples of this are based in *Parashas Mishpatim*, where we find the first of the three times that the Torah mentions the prohibition of *Bassar B'chalav*—mixing milk and meat. From the fact that this proscription is mentioned three separate times,[1] the Gemara teaches us that there are really three separate Biblical prohibitions involved:[2]

- cooking milk and meat together;
- eating milk and meat that was cooked together;
- deriving benefit (*hana'ah*) from this forbidden mixture.[3]

---

1 "*Lo Sevashel G'di Ba'chaleiv Imo*"—*Parashas Mishpatim* (*Shemos* Ch. 23:19), *Parashas Ki Sisa* (*Shemos* Ch. 34:26), and *Parashas Re'eh* (*Devarim* Ch. 14:21).

2 There is, however, some debate as to how many of the 613 Mitzvos this prohibition counts as. The *Rambam* (*Sefer HaMitzvos, Lo Sa'aseh* 186 and 187) and the *Sefer Hachinuch* (Mitzva 92 and 113) count it only as two Mitzvos. The *Tashbetz* (*Zohar HaRakia, Azharos HaRashbag* 197–200), however, counts it as three full separate Mitzvos, while the *BeHa"G* (*Seder Minyan HaMitzvos, Lavin* 58) counts it as only one Mitzva. See Rabbi Yitzchak Aharon Kramer's recent *Arichas Hadaas* (on *Hilchos Bassar B'chalav* and *Taaruvos*, Ch. 1, footnote 4) for more on this issue.

3 *Chullin* (115b), "*Tanna D'vei Rabbi Yishmael*" as the Biblical source for this

4 *Food: A Halachic Analysis*

Rabbinically, even eating chicken and milk together is prohibited.[4] Due to the nature and potential for possible mix-ups, Chazal made several other *takkanos*[5] to ensure that "ne'er the twain (milk and meat) shall meet" (or is it "meat"?), including:

- Forbidding people eating meat and milk at the same time at the same table;[6]
- Mandating a waiting period after eating meat prior to eating dairy;
- Requiring rinsing, washing, and palate cleansing after eating dairy products prior to partaking of meat.[7]

---

prohibition. See *Rashi's* commentary to *Mishpatim* ibid. (end s.v. *lo sevashel*) and *Tur* and *Shulchan Aruch* (Y.D. 87:1). The *Baal HaTurim*, in his commentary to *Devarim* ibid (s.v. *lo sevashel*; although this author finds it curious that he only elucidates this in his commentary on the third, and final, mention of this prohibition in the Torah) brings proof to this source, as the *Gematria* of the words "*lo sevashel*" (do not cook) equals that of the words—"*Issur achila u'bishul v'hana'ah*" (prohibited for eating and cooking and deriving benefit), 763.

4   *Tur* and *Shulchan Aruch* (ibid). The *Rambam* (*Hilchos Mamrim* Ch. 2:9) goes as far as to say that anyone who claims that a chicken and milk mixture is *Biblically* prohibited violates the Biblical prohibition of *Bal Tosif*, adding on to the Torah's commandments (*Devarim, Parashas Re'eh* Ch. 13:1; see *Sefer Hachinuch* ad loc. Mitzva 454). This is the normative *halacha*, following the *Rambam, Rif*, and *Rosh's* understanding of the Mishnah in *Chullin* 113a, and not like Rashal (*Yam Shel Shlomo, Chullin* Ch. 8:100) and *Bach* (Y.D. 87:2) who hold like *Tosafos'* (*Chullin* 113a s.v. *bassar*) understanding of the Mishnah; see also *Shach* (ad loc. 4).

5   Gemara *Chullin* (114b). *Rashi* (ad loc. s.v. *aval hacha*) understands this to mean that it is all considered one *Gezeira*. However, the *Taz* (Y.D. 88:1) seemingly understands that this case is an exception and posits that Chazal actually made a *Gezeira L'Gezeira*. See *Pri Megadim* (ad loc. M.Z. 1; based on *Lechem Mishneh, Hilchos Maachalos Assuros* Ch. 9:20, and *Knesses Hagedolah*, Y.D. 88, *Hagahos* on the *Tur* 3), *Chochmas Adam* (40:11), *Yad Avraham* (ad loc.), and *Aruch Hashulchan* (ad loc. 3).

6   See *Tur* and *Shulchan Aruch* (Y.D. 88:1 and 2), based on Mishnah and Gemara *Chullin* (103b-104a and 107b).

Diyuk Discussion

The first Mishnah in the chapter in *Maseches Chullin*[8] dealing with the laws of *Bassar B'chalav* states: "*Kol Habassar assur l'vashel b'chalav…v'assur l'haalos im hagevina al hashulchan*—All meat (except for fish and grasshopper/locust)[9][10] is forbidden to cook in milk…and it's forbidden to place (this meat together) with cheese on the table."

---

7   See *Tur* and *Shulchan Aruch* (Y.D. 89), based on Gemara *Chullin* (105). These issues will be discussed at length in the coming chapters.

8   *Chullin* (103b-104a).

9   The permissibility of eating fish with meat and/or milk is addressed at length in an upcoming chapter titled "The Lox and Cream Cheese Dilemma." Regarding eating grasshoppers or locusts, although there is discussion in the Mishnah and Gemara (*Chullin* 59a and 65a-b) about how to identify kosher locusts' *simanim*, it seems that a true *mesorah* of identifying which species are kosher has mostly been lost over the centuries, save for certain Yemenite and Sefardic communities, and they have not been eaten for centuries by mainstream Judaism. The need for a *mesorah* in addition to *simanim* regarding locusts is mandated by many Rishonim, including the *Rashba* (*Chullin* 65a s.v. *l'inyan*), *Ran* (ad loc. 23a s.v. *Rabbi Yosi*, in the *Rif's* pagination), *Meiri* (ad loc.), and *Rosh* (ad loc. 66), all of whom imply that they personally did not have the *mesorah* but noted other communities that did. This is also the *halacha lemaaseh*, as codified by the *Tur, Shulchan Aruch*, and *Levush* (Y.D. 85:1). Indeed, the question was recently raised in an *Ami Magazine* feature ("Looking for Kosher Locusts," issue 293; Nov. 2016): "How come locusts are yummy to Yemenites, but gross to Galitzianers, *chaloshes* to Chassidim, and loathesome to Litvaks?" And although there are those who nowadays posit that the only reason Ashkenazic Jews don't have a *mesorah* on locusts is because it's extremely rare to find locusts in Europe, and suggest that identifiably kosher locusts should therefore be permitted to eat [see, for example Rav Yitzchak Ratzabi's *maamar* on topic in *Kovetz Tenuvas Sadeh* (vol. 23; Nissan-Iyar 5759; pg. 33-39); although in all honesty, this author finds his rationale, that if mainstream Judaism relies on Teimanim for a kosher *mesorah* regarding *esrogim* we must do so as well for locusts, non-compelling, especially as this exact logic was previously unsubstantiated in *Shu"t Pe'as Sadecha* (vol. 1:62, pg. 112 and 114), differentiating regarding the requirements of *mesorah* between the same species sporting slightly different characteristics and an entirely different species], conversely, many great Ashkenazic (and several

Sefardic) authorities over the centuries, including the *SMa"K* (Mitzva 208), *Bach* (Y.D. 85 s.v. *umashekasav*), *Taz* (ad loc. 1), *Knesses Hagedolah* (*Hagahos* on *Beis Yosef* ad loc. 3), *Lechem Hapanim* (ad loc. 1), *Beis Lechem Yehuda* (ad loc. 1), *Pri Megadim* (S.D. ad loc. end 1; although he maintains that this is *m'Toras safek* and not *vaday*), *Yad Avraham* (ad loc.), *Chochmas Adam* (39:1), *Zivchei Tzedek* (ad loc. 1), *Aruch Hashulchan* (ad loc. 5), *Me'orei Ohr* (*Kitzur Shulchan Aruch on Yoreh Deah* ad loc. 1), and *Kaf Hachaim* (ad loc. 4), expressly prohibited its consumption, due to the fact that we do not have a *mesorah* as to which locusts are indeed kosher, nor the expertise to properly identify them. In fact, dating back almost a millennium, *Rashi* (*Parashas Shemini, Vayikra* Ch. 11:21 s.v. *m'maal*) already declared that locusts' *simanim* are confusing and *"ain anu baki'in bahen"* and *"ain anu yodim lehavdil beineihem."* So did Rav Chaim ben Attar, the *Ohr Hachaim Hakadosh* (*Parashas Shemini* ad loc.) in the mid-1700s, who was not of Ashkenazic origin, but Sefardic. In fact, and quite tellingly, in his commentary on *Yoreh Deah* (*Pri Toar* 85:1), he uses quite strong terms calling such a *"mesorah"* among Moroccan Jewry a tragic mistake, explaining that they historically exclusively ate locusts in times of famine simply to avoid succumbing to starvation. He anecdotally tells that when he was Rav in Morocco, he publicized awareness of the *issur* of eating locusts, and in that *zechus* Morocco was spared by its otherwise quite common plague of locusts for over twenty years. [On the other hand, it is known that several other *Rabbanim* of his time argued quite strongly against his locust proscription. See Rav Moshe Toledano's *Meleches Hakodesh* (*Vayikra* Ch. 11:21; *"mitzva l'achalam"*), Rav Pesachya Mordechai Berdugo's *Shu"t Nofes Tzufim* (Y.D. 13), and Rav Kalifa ben Moshe's *Rach V'Tov*. In fact, due to the strength of Rav Kalifa's arguments, the Chida, in his *Machzik Bracha* (Y.D. 85:1 and *Kuntress Acharon* ad loc.) seems to reverse his original prohibitive *psak*, and Rav Dovid Pinto, in his introduction to his grandfather, Rav Dovid Pardo's *Mizmor L'Dovid*, approvingly cites it as the epitome of a properly worded *machlokes*. Nonetheless, and unbeknownst to many, in his later *Kaf V'Naki* (pg. 318–319), Rav Kalifa briefly addressed the topic once more, ultimately concluding that although he had disproven the *Pri Toar's* arguments, he would still not partake of locust, as *"chosheshani m'Chatas l'achlam,"* that he was concerned that he might be obligated in bringing a *Korban Chatas* due to the possible transgression of eating them.] More contemporarily, in the words of Rav Chaim Kanievsky (*Kuntress Karnei Chagavim* Ch. 7 and in his *Biurim* to *Hilchos Chagavim* 11, both published in his *Siach Hasadeh* vol. 2), Rav Yisrael Pesach Feinhandler (*Shu"t Avnei Yashpei* vol 8:116), Rav Menashe

The famed *Rashash*, Rav Shmuel Strashun of Vilna (1794–1872),[11] notes that when it comes to the prohibition of cooking milk and meat, the Mishnah used the same words as the Torah—milk and meat. Yet, when it came to the Rabbinical injunction of not placing them both on the same table, instead of "milk," the Mishnah switched to the word "cheese." To explain the Mishnah's choice of words, the *Rashash* makes three *halachic diyukim* (inferences) in three separate aspects of this law—just from this one line of Mishnah!

The three inferences are:

Rinsing after Milk

1. The *halacha* mandates that one who has partaken of milk products must perform a three-step process: *kinuach*—palate cleansing by eating a hard food item (e.g., cracker); *rechitza*—handwashing;[12]

Klein (*Shu"t Mishnah Halachos* vol. 16:8), Rav Yisroel Belsky (*Shu"t Shulchan Halevi* Ch. 19:1), and the *Yalkut Yosef* (*Issur V'Hetter* vol. 2, pg. 280–283, and *Kitzur Shulchan Aruch*, Y.D. 85:2 and 3): "although the *Teimanim* have their *mesorah*, since we [Ashkenazim; although Rav Yitzchak Yosef avers the same for Sefardim] do not, and our *minhag* is not to eat locusts, it is prohibited to change our custom."

10 This author is aware of two very different extensive treatments on the topic of kosher locust identification: Rav Chaim Kanievsky's *Kuntress Karnei Chagavim* and Prof. Zohar Amar's *Ha'Arbeh B'Mesoret Yisrael*. Rav Chaim (ibid. Ch. 1), maintains that according to the *Rambam* (*Hilchos Maachalos Assuros* Ch. 1:1 and *Sefer HaMitzvos*, *Mitzvos Asei* 151) [see also *Sefer Hachinuch* (*Parashas Shemini*, Mitzva 158) and *Yalkut Yosef* (ibid.)], one fulfills a *Mitzvas Asei* in attempting to identify kosher locusts. Hence, although it may not appear practical in terms of permitted cuisine for the most of us (as detailed at length in the previous footnote), nonetheless, there still may be a Mitzva in the detective work necessary in identifying them.

11 *Rashash's* commentary to the aforementioned Mishnah (*Chullin* 103b).

12 Although the *Shulchan Aruch* (Y.D. 89:2) personally writes that only at night is handwashing mandated, and otherwise a visual inspection for cheese residue is sufficient, nonetheless, the *Shach* (ad loc. 9) cites Rabbeinu Peretz (originally brought in the *Tur* ad loc.), who maintains that nowadays washing is the proper recourse, day or night, as well as the *Levush* (*Ateres Zahav* ad loc.), who

8 *Food: A Halachic Analysis*

and *hadacha*—rinsing out of the mouth, before being able to eat meat.[13] The *Rashash* infers from our Mishnah's switching to the word cheese, that it is emphasizing that this three-step *halacha* only applies to eating actual cheese, since it is likely to leave some residue in the mouth. However, drinking good ol' fashioned plain liquid milk (which does not crumble or leave a sticky residue) would only require mouth rinsing (*hadacha*). Most authorities follow the *Rashash's diyuk* and rule this way as well.[14]

---

asserts *"v'chein nohagin."* See also *Pri Megadim* (ad loc. S.D. 9), *Chochmas Adam* (40: end 12), and *Aruch Hashulchan* (ad loc. 8).

13   See *Tur, Shulchan Aruch*, and main commentaries to *Yoreh Deah* (89:2). Remarkably, there is some debate on the nuances of how to properly perform this *kinuach* and *hadacha*. Although there are several authorities who maintain that it is preferable to perform the *kinuach* before the *hadacha* to ensure that any left over crumbs from the *kinuach* will be washed away as well, nevertheless, the majority consensus is that one may indeed perform the *hadacha* prior to the *kinuach* if he so wishes. Another interesting *shittah*, stated by the *Tur* (ad loc.) and several others, is that one may first soak his bread in wine or water and then chew and swallow it, thus performing both *kinuach* and *hadacha* in one fell swoop. However, others are wary of this method, as perhaps it will not clean the palate as well as performing each action separately. Another debate among the Acharonim is whether one must actually swallow the *kinuach* after chewing or the *hadacha* after rinsing, or if one accomplished these as well if one spits out the chewed food or drink. A corollary of this *machlokes* is if one decided to perform *kinuach* or *hadacha* in this manner by spitting out, if he is considered to have violated the prohibition of being *"mafsid ochlin"* (a.k.a. *Bal Tashchis*), wasting edible food [see *Parashas Shoftim* (*Devarim* Ch. 20:19) and *Sefer Hachinuch* (ad loc. Mitzva 529)]. For several contemporary approaches to these debates, see *Shu"t Hisorerus Teshuva* (vol. 1:62), *Shu"t Mishnah Halachos* (vol. 16:9), and *Shu"t Yashiv Yitzchak* (vol. 7:17).

14   See *Darchei Teshuva* (89:2 and 31) who cites this rule with no dissenting opinion, adding that the *Yafeh Lev* (vol. 8) asserted that even the Arizal, who was known to be personally very *machmir* regarding waiting between milk and meat (which will be discussed in upcoming chapters), would nonetheless certainly agree that *"lekuli alma b'hadachas hapeh sagi,"* a mouth rinse alone

Washing after Cheese

2. As mentioned above, one of the steps needed after eating a milk meal before eating something meaty is *rechitza*—washing hands to make sure no residue remains. The *Rashash* learns from the Mishnah's stressing of the word "cheese" that this handwashing is only necessary if one ate cheese—a dairy food product that is commonly held in one's hands to facilitate eating. This would exclude actual milk, since it can not be held in one's hands, but rather requires a container or cup to be able to drink it.

Furthermore, in view of the fact that one's hands remain clean after drinking milk, he opines that *rechitza* is not *halachically* required, similar to the *Pri Chodosh's* ruling that one who eats cheese with a fork (and thereby keeping his hands clean) does not have to wash his hands before partaking of meat. Although the basic *halacha* seems to follow the *Rashash*,[15]

---

is sufficient after simply drinking milk prior to eating meat. Although the *Badei Hashulchan* (89:43) feels that one should be stringent with this based on the words of the *Issur V'Hetter* (40:8), see, however, *Zer Hashulchan* (Y.D. 89, Pnei Hashulchan 78), who refutes this logic. Similarly, even though the *Divrei Malkiel* (Shu"t vol. 5:47) advises not to rely on this (for a different reason), Rav Ovadiah Yosef (*Shu"t Yabia Omer* vol. 6, Y.D. 7: end 1 and *Shu"t Yechaveh Daas* vol. 3:58, in the footnote) challenges his reasoning and concludes that the *ikar* follows the *Rashash* on this. Similarly, Rav Moshe Sternbuch (*Shu"t Teshuvos V'Hanhagos* vol. 2:390) and the *Yalkut Yosef* (*Issur V'Hetter* vol. 3:89, end 46 and 56) also rule this way, that the *halacha* in this case follows the *Rashash's* rule.

15 Including the *Pri Chodosh* (Y.D. 89:20), *Shulchan Gavoah* (ad loc. 8), *Ba'er Heitiv* (ad loc. end 13) and *Aruch Hashulchan* (ad loc. 8). Rav Yaakov Emden (*Mor U'Ketziah* 158 end s.v. *v'ha*) writes similarly regarding the handwashing required prior to eating a food item that was dipped into a liquid, that those who are eating with a fork or spoon are not required to wash their hands. Many other authorities rule this way about a *maachal hateebulo b'mashkeh* that is always eaten with a spoon, including the *Taz* (O.C. 158:9), *Shulchan Aruch Harav* (ad loc. 3), *Derech Hachaim* (*Din Netillas Yadayim L'Seudah* 5), *Chayei Adam* (vol. 1, 36:8), *Magen Giborim* (*Shiltei Hagiborim* 7), *Aruch Hashulchan*

(ad loc. 12), and *Mishnah Berurah* (ad loc. 26). However, the *Kaf Hachaim* (ad loc. 23) cites several authorities who differ and rules that even though there is what to rely upon, he nevertheless advises that one should be stringent and wash his hands. Rav Emden a.k.a the Yaavetz (*Mor U'Ketziah* end 181 s.v. *daf*), continues *leshittaso* regarding *Mayim Acharonim* as well, maintaining that one who eats with cutlery and did not actually touch his food has no need to wash *Mayim Acharonim*. However, the *Kaf Hachaim* (ad loc. 27) cites several authorities who do not agree with the Yaavetz's leniency and concludes *leshittaso*, that even if one ate exclusively with utensils, he must still wash *Mayim Acharonim*. This topic is discussed at length in an upcoming chapter titled "*Mayim Acharonim, Chova*?" Interestingly, this *machlokes* seems to be originally based on different understandings of a debate amongst Tannaim (*Nedarim* 49b; thanks are due to R' Baruch Ritholtz for pointing this out) regarding whether it is more proper to eat *die'sah* (porridge) with one's fingers or a "*hutza*, a sliver of wood." The Yaavetz understood that this topic was only relevant in their time, as they apparently did not have proper eating utensils. Accordingly, nowadays, when everyone uses cutlery, this debate would seem somewhat irrelevant. Others, however [see *Maharsha* and *Ben Yehoyada* (ad loc.), and *Bnei Tzion* (vol. 3, O.C. 181:9; from Rav Ben Tzion Lichtman, Chief Rabbi of Beirut, Lebanon, approximately seventy-five years ago)], seem to understand that the Tannaim did generally have spoons, but in that instance they did not have them readily available. Thus, the Gemara's discussion was only regarding when spoons were not available, debating whether it was preferable to use fingers or a wood chip in such an instance. Following the latter approach would seemingly unsubstantiate the Yaavetz's proof from this Gemara. Remarkably, the earliest use of forks as cutlery in Rabbinic literature seems to be from Rabbeinu Chananel (990–1053) in his commentary on *Bava Metzia* (25b s.v. *pirush homnick*), which was first published as part of the famous Vilna Shas by the Brothers Romm, in the 1870s and 1880s. To describe the Gemara's "*homnick*" (or perhaps "*hemnick*"), he explains that it is a two-pronged fork, similar to a "*mazleig*," which he elucidates is a three-pronged fork that "*Bnei Yavan*" use to hold pieces of meat and help cut them with a knife, as an aid for eating without touching the food with one's hands. As implied from Rabbeinu Chananel's terminology that using a fork was a novelty even in his days, it seems that his phraseology can be used as proof to Rav Yaakov Emden's understanding of the Tannaic debate in the Gemara *Nedarim*, some 700 years later. Thanks are due to Rabbi Reuven Chaim Klein for pointing out the location of this comment of Rabbeinu Chananel's.

many authorities advise that nevertheless, one should still wash his hands after drinking a milk product or eating a dairy product with a fork, as handwashing does not usually entail much effort.[16]

Hekker for Milk?

3. It is well known that if two people are eating together at a table and one is eating meat and the other dairy, they must place something between them to remind them not to share food with one another and *chas v'shalom* transgress the prohibition of eating milk and meat together.[17] This is called a *hekker*. Typical examples of such a *hekker* are the use of separate placemats, or putting something distinctive on the table that is not usually between them when eating. The *Rashash* writes that the Mishnah's emphasis on the word "cheese" impacts this area as well: The requirement of a *hekker* is dependent on the possibility of the food getting mixed up, with the one eating cheese ending up eating meat, or vice versa. Therefore, if one is merely drinking milk from a cup, there already is a built in *hekker*: the cup itself! Without the aid of the cup, the milk would not even be able to be drunk, let alone be possibly mixed up with the meat on the table. Therefore, he posits, if one is drinking milk at the same table with someone eating meat, no further *hekker* is required. The basic *halacha* also seems to follow the *Rashash* in this case,[18]

---

16 Including the *Pri Megadim* (Y.D. 89, S.D. 20), *Pischei Teshuva* (ad loc. 4), Chida (*Shiyurei Bracha* ad loc. 15), *Atzei Ha'Olah* (Hilchos Bassar B'chalav 3:12 and *Chukei Chaim* 9; he maintains that a fork is actually worse that a cup, as one might use his hands to push the food onto the fork) [the *Darchei Teshuva* (ibid.) implies this way as well], *Ben Ish Chai* (Year 2, *Parashas Shlach* 14), *Kaf Hachaim* (Y.D. 89:34), and *Me'orei Ohr* (*Kitzur Shulchan Aruch* on *Yoreh Deah*, 89:1).

17 See *Tur* and *Shulchan Aruch* (Y.D. 88:2; based on Gemara *Chullin* 104b), and main commentaries.

18 See *Aruch Hashulchan* (Y.D. 88:6).

though several contemporary authorities aver that it is worthwhile to be stringent, based on people's propensity to "dunk" their biscuits into their coffee,[19] and the common occurrence of cups of coffee spilling.[20]

---

19 See *Shu"t Maadanei Melachim* (77), explaining the reason he wrote to be *machmir lechatchilla* in his *Maadanei Hashulchan* (88:3).

20 See Rav Yosef Shalom Elyashiv's *He'aros B'Maseches Chullin* (103b s.v. *v'assur*) and *Shaarei Shalom* (on *Piskei Ben Ish Chai*, Y.D. 88:1,1), based on the *Meleches Shlomo* in his commentary to *Mishnayos Chullin* ad loc. (s.v. *ha'of*); similar to the *Yad Avraham*'s (ad loc) *shittah*, that open containers of milk or meat require extra vigilance due to their propensity to spill. Indeed, the *Meleches Shlomo*, as does Rav Dovid Pardo (*Shoshanim L'Dovid*, *Chullin* Ch. 8:1 s.v. *im*), makes the exact opposite *diyuk* of the *Rashash* regarding this case. They both maintain that the Mishnah switched to *"gevina"* regarding *ha'alah* (placing on the table at the same time) as it did not need to explicitly mention milk, as milk would certainly be *assur* to place on the table alongside meat, *"mipnei shehu karov sheyitafteif al habassar she'ochel chaveiro,"* it is almost a given that it will drip on the meat his friend is eating. An interesting minority opinion on this is that of the *Badei Hashulchan* (88:6 and *Biurim* ad loc. s.v. *al*), who feels that one must be stringent with this, based on his own *diyuk* in the opinion of the *Ran*, that the issue that we are concerned with is that one might even eat whatever is on the table, and rules that it forbidden to have even a *sealed* container of milk on a table while eating meat. Interestingly, the *Chayei Halevi* (*Shu"t* vol. 5:59:2) later reversed his lenient decision upon seeing the *Badei Hashulchan*'s ruling and instead determined to be *machmir* as well. However, aside from the fact that the *Aruch Hashulchan* explicitly ruled to be lenient as per the *Rashash*, it is noteworthy that the other *machmirim* did as well and only advised to be stringent *lechatchilla* based on the tendency of an *open* cup to spill. It also remains unclear to this author how apt a concern it would be, even according to the *Ran's shittah*, for one to be *nichshal* by somehow unintentionally opening a sealed container of milk expressly to eat together with meat or vice versa, without it being considered an additional *Gezeira L'Gezeira*. See also Rabbi Yaakov Skozylas' *Ohel Yaakov* on *Issur V'Hetter* (88: footnote 6) who cites Rav Chaim Kanievsky's ruling, that there is no *halachic* issue with having a meat meal with a sealed bag of milk on the table.

Chewing It Over

Another excellent example of a related *diyuk* which has great *halachic* relevance is based on the wording of the *Rema*. The *Shulchan Aruch* rules that after eating meat one must wait six hours before eating dairy.[21] He then adds, based on the *Rambam*,[22] that this waiting period even applies to one who merely chewed meat without actually swallowing it. In his glosses to this *halacha*, the *Rema* writes with a slight variation, that it is proper to wait six hours "after eating meat" before cheese.

Rav Akiva Eiger[23] infers from the *Rema's* choice of words "after *eating* meat" (and the fact that the *Rema* didn't explicitly mention chewing), that he did not mean to fully concur with the *Shulchan Aruch's* assessment, but rather meant to dispute the *Shulchan Aruch's* ruling on chewing. He maintains that the *Rema's* intent was to rule that only after actually eating meat would one need to wait six hours. On the other hand, after merely *chewing* meat (without swallowing), one would *not* have to wait the full six hours, rather only the *ikar din* of one hour before being allowed to eat milk products.[24]

---

21 *Shulchan Aruch* (Y.D. 89:1). How much time one must wait after eating meat before eating dairy, and the various common *minhagim*, are addressed at length in an upcoming chapter titled "Weighty Waiting Options."

22 *Rambam* (*Hilchos Maachalos Assuros* Ch. 9:28). This ruling is also cited by the *Tur* (Y.D. 89:1). See *Taz* (ad loc. 1) and *Pri Megadim* (ad loc. M.Z. 1).

23 *Rema* (Y.D. 89:2); Rav Akiva Eiger (ad loc. 2).

24 The various *shittos* of how long one must wait after eating meat before partaking of *milchigs*, including the *Rema's* opinion of the *ikar din* being one hour but preferentially waiting the full six hours, are discussed over the next several chapters. An additional common case of the *ikar din* of a one-hour waiting period being invoked by no less than the *Chasam Sofer* (*Shu"t* Y.D. 73, cited *lemaaseh* by the *Pischei Teshuva* Y.D. 89:3), is regarding a *choleh* (*ketzas*), one who is ill, as well as a *yoledes*, a woman who recently gave birth. Others extend this dispensation to *meinikos*, nursing mothers, and *meubaros*, pregnant women. Although some authorities maintain that this *hetter* only applied with "*Meimei Chalav*" (a milk by-product via straining that *halachically* does not fully constitute real milk, as the *Chasam Sofer* himself only mentioned "*Meimei Chalav*;" see *Ikrei HaDa"T, Ikrei Dinim* 10:4) and prior to eating

Even though many authorities do not agree with this inference, and rule that even after chewing meat one has to wait the "full count,"[25] nevertheless several authorities do indeed follow Rav Akiva Eiger's understanding of the *Rema's* position, and allow leniency for one who simply chewed meat[26] — which may come in handy in the kitchen.

---

fowl (and not actual bovine meat; see *Daas Kedoshim* ad loc. 1), and others opine that it is still preferable to wait two, three, or four hours respectively, nonetheless, in all the above cases, the common contemporary consensus, even among Sefardic *Poskim* who generally mandate a six hour waiting period *me'ikar hadin*, is that if dairy products are necessary, those in this category are only required to wait one hour after eating any type of *fleishigs*, and not the usual six. See *Chochmas Adam* (40: end 13), *Atzei Ha'Olah* (*Hilchos Bassar B'chalav* 3:8 and *Chukei Chaim* ad loc. 7), *Aruch Hashulchan* (Y.D. 89:7), *Sfas Emes* (*Likutei Shu"t* 23), *Zivchei Tzedek* (89:11), *Ben Ish Chai* (Year 2, *Parashas Shlach* 11), *Shu"t Salmas Chaim* (vol. 2:4; new edition 416), *Kaf Hachaim* (Y.D. 89:21), *Me'orei Ohr* (*Kitzur Shulchan Aruch* on *Yoreh Deah*, 89:1), *Shu"t Shoel V'Nishal* (vol. 2, Y.D. 26), *Shu"t Pe'as Sadecha* (vol. 3, Y.D. 30), *Shu"t Shevet Halevi* (vol. 2:32), *Emes L'Yaakov* (on *Tur* and *Shulchan Aruch*, Y.D. 89, footnote 36), *Pischei Halacha* (on *Hilchos Kashrus*; *Teshuvos* of the *Ba'er Moshe* #5), *Shu"t Even Yisrael* vol. 9:126, 5), *Shu"t Yechaveh Daas* (vol. 3:58 s.v. *v'da*), *Shu"t Eimek Hateshuva* (vol. 6:314), *Shu"t Shulchan Halevi* (Ch. 22:10, 4), *Shu"t Ohr Yitzchak* (vol. 1, Y.D. 4:4), *Piskei Halachos* (of Rav Elyashiv; pg. 53:7), *Orchos Rabbeinu* (new edition; vol. 4 pg. 25:3 and pg. 297:28), *Kovetz M'Beis Levi* on *Yoreh Deah* (pg. 34:4), and *Nishmas Avraham* (vol. 2-Y.D. 89:1). This *psak* is echoed in several contemporary *sefarim* dealing with the *halachos* pertaining to women, including *Koh Somar L'Beis Yaakov* (Ch. 22, pg. 142, footnote 20; citing Rav Yonason Steif and Rav Yaakov Kamenetsky), *Halichos Baysa* (Ch. 12, pg. 109:28), and *Halichos Bas Yisrael* (Ch. 10, end footnote 32, s.v. *agav*).

25 Including the *Pri Toar* (89:3), *Pri Megadim* (ad loc. M.Z. 1; due to a *lo plug*), *Pischei Teshuva* (ad loc. 1), Chida (*Shiyurei Bracha*, ad loc. 12), *Atzei Ha'Olah* (*Hilchos Bassar B'chalav* 3:2), *Zivchei Tzedek* (89:4), *Ben Ish Chai* (Year 2, *Parashas Shlach* 19), *Yalkut Me'am Loez* (*Parashas Mishpatim*, pg. 890), *Shu"t Kapei Aharon* (30), *Kitzur Shulchan Aruch* (46:9), *Me'orei Ohr* (*Kitzur Shulchan Aruch* on *Yoreh Deah*, 89:1), and *Kaf Hachaim* (Y.D. 89:4).

26 Including the *Yad Yehuda* (89, *Peirush Ha'aruch* 1 and *Peirush Hakatzer* 3), *Aruch Hashulchan* (ad loc. 4), *Shu"t Pe'as Sadecha* (vol. 3, Y.D. 31), and *Badei Hashulchan* (ad loc. 38). See also *Maadanei Hashulchan* (ad loc. 4), who

As the *Chofetz Chaim* was wont to stress, albeit regarding the significance of *Shemiras Halashon*, we should never underestimate the *(halachic)* importance of even just one word.

---

concludes that in a case of need, an Ashkenazi definitely has what to rely upon. On the other hand, and in somewhat of a similar scenario, if one merely tasted *fleishig* food with his tongue and spit it out (commonly performed while making soup), the *halachic* consensus follows the ruling of Rav Shlomo Kluger (*Hagahos Maharshak* on the *Pri Megadim* ad loc.) that *l'kuli alma* there is no waiting period mandated (and *kinuach/hadacha* will suffice).

Chapter 2

Maaseh Avos = Halacha Lemaaseh: Hekker, Shomer, and *Maris Ayin*

WHEN IT COMES TO THE *parshiyos* of *Sefer Bereishis*, many people mistakenly kick back, relax, and go on "cruise control." They think that now is the time for stories, not actually actively learning any "real *halacha*" from the *Chumash*.

However, this is the wrong approach. There is a plethora of relevant information that we can and should glean and learn, *lishmor v'laasos*, from the actions of our great forefathers, the Avos and Imahos. This does not only fall into the realm of proper conduct, *midos tovos* and *maasim tovim*, but even *halacha lemaaseh*.

Hashomer Malachim Anochi?

One prime example can be seen in *Parashas Vayera*. But first a little background. As mentioned in the previous chapter, the *halacha* states[1] that if two people are eating at a table, and one is eating meat and the other dairy, they have to place something between them to remind them not to share food with one another and possibly transgress the prohibition of *Bassar B'chalav*, eating milk and meat together. This is known as a *hekker*.[2] Typical examples of such a *hekker* are the use of

---

1 See *Shulchan Aruch* (Y.D. 88:2; based on Gemara *Chullin* 104b and *Shabbos* 13a).
2 However, there are certain notable exceptions to the rule. For example, if the two people hate each other to the extent that they made a *neder* (vow) not to accept any benefit from each other, then they may sit at the same table,

one eating dairy and the other meat, without a *hekker* [see *Rosh* (*Nedarim* 41b s.v. *v'ochel imo*), *Minchas Yaakov* (77:21), *Pri Megadim* (Y.D. 88, M.Z. 2; adding "*upashut hu*"), *Pischei Teshuva* (ad loc. 3), *Zivchei Tzedek* (ad loc. 8), *Aruch Hashulchan* (ad loc. 2), *Atzei Ha'Olah* (*Bassar B'chalav* 2, 88:3 and *Chukei Chaim* ad loc. 3), and *Kaf Hachaim* (ad loc. 11), and not like the *Yad Yehuda* (ad loc. *Peirush Ha'aruch* 3 and *Peirush Hakatzer* 5) who holds a *hekker* is still needed]. This is because there is absolutely no chance that they would possibly eat from each other's plates. Similarly, if one was eating at the same table as a non-Jew who was eating noticeably non-kosher food, a *hekker* would not be required for the same reason [see *Ba'er Heitiv* (Y.D. 88:2; citing *Shu"t Beis Yaakov* 12), *Kreisi U'Pleisi* (ad loc. *Kreisi* 1), *Pri Toar* (ad loc. 1), and *Yad Yehuda* (ad loc. *Peirush Ha'aruch* 2; who adds that in his opinion, if they become good friends it can then become problematic)]. One the other hand, if one would make a *neder* not to eat a certain food item, most *Poskim* assert that this would not be sufficient, as if one was really hungry, his personal vow would not be enough of deterrent [see *Shach* (ad loc. 2), *Minchas Yaakov* (ibid.), *Pischei Teshuva* (ad loc. 2), *Pri Megadim* (ad loc. S.D. 2), Chida (*Shiyurei Bracha* ad loc. 3), *Yad Avraham* (ad loc.), *Zivchei Tzedek* (ad loc. 9), *Yad Yehuda* (ad loc. *Peirush Ha'aruch* 2 and *Peirush Hakatzer* 3), and *Kaf Hachaim* (ad loc. 12), and not like the *Chaguras Shmuel* (on the *Levush*; ad loc. 2) and Maharsham (*Daas Torah* ad loc. end s.v. *v'ayin Tosafos*), who maintain that a personal *neder* should be sufficient and possibly even a stronger deterrent.] The rule governing this topic is "*kamah badil inish m'zeh*," how far would one go to avoid the food under discussion. A related and quite contemporary question is how to categorize one with a severe life-threatening milk allergy (i.e. anaphylactic to milk). If he would be sitting at the same table, merrily munching his meat sandwich, while his friend is eating dairy, would a *hekker* be required for him? Several years back, this author asked Rav Feivel Cohen, noted author of the *Badei Hashulchan*, his thoughts on the matter. Rav Cohen remarked that in his opinion, a *hekker* would still be required, as this case is akin to one where someone is on a diet, that he would still use full-fat milk in his coffee if a low-fat alternative was not available. Moreover, he said that as the case of one with a milk allergy is a rare exception, in his opinion, a "*lo plug*—a Rabbinic proscription across the board," was in effect, as is mentioned by the *Taz* (Y.D. 88:2). This was also the opinion of Rav Yisrael Pesach Feinhandler (author of *Shu"t Avnei Yashpei*, in an as-yet unpublished *teshuva*; thanks are due to R' Betzalel Bresler for providing this author with this *teshuva*). However, in this author's estimation, this argument seems non-compelling (indeed, Rav

separate placemats, or putting something distinctive on the table that is not usually there when eating.

There is a *halachic* disagreement between two of the preeminent commentators on the *Shulchan Aruch*, Rav Akiva Eiger (d. 1837) and

---

> Cohen and I respectfully concluded to "agree to disagree"), as in the aforementioned cases we clearly see that the majority of the *Gedolei* Acharonim did not indicate a *lo plug* in their arguments, but rather addressed each individual topic on merit alone, in each specific case, whether or not it was considered "*badil inish m'zeh*." Moreover, as explained by Rav Levi Rabinowitz (*Shu"t Maadanei Melachim* 80), although the *Taz* does cite a *lo plug*, on the other hand, a careful reading shows that he only invokes this rule in regard to a case where there is still somewhat of a possibility that they might come to eat from each other. However, when it is apparent to all that there is no such possibility [the example Rav Rabinowitz gives is *"makirim umisbayshim,"* people so embarrassed of each other that there is no chance that they will eat from each other], a *hekker* is not required. It certainly stands to reason that in a case of a life-threatening allergy, as opposed to someone on a diet, or even one who is lactose intolerant, since it is a matter of *sakanas nefashos*, "*ain badil inish yoseir m'zeh*, there is nothing in the world this person would stay far away from more than this item," and in spades. As such, a *hekker* should not be required, because it would not be any worse than those who made a vow against each other, as there is no *sakanos nefashos* in that case. Indeed, after hearing this argument, Rav Ezriel Auerbach agreed that this is indeed correct, and not as he was quoted in *Kashrus in the Kitchen Q & A* (pg. 218; *Teshuvos* Rav Ezriel Auerbach). As later attested to by both by its author, Rabbi Avi Wiesenfeld, as well as *Mori v'Rabi* Rav Yonason Wiener upon consultation with Rav Ezriel, the confusion relating to his *psak* seems to have stemmed from the common Hebrew translation of the word "allergy,"—"*regishut*," which can also mean "sensitivity," ostensibly referring to one who is lactose intolerant. In such a case, Rav Ezriel was indeed *machmir* that a *hekker* would still be required, as there is still a possibility that he might come to eat dairy products. Yet, when he later heard that the author's intent was regarding a severe life-threatening milk allergy, he ruled that certainly a *hekker* would not be required. Although this indeed seems to be the *halacha lemaaseh*, the merit of nonetheless placing a *hekker* in such a situation can still be debated, albeit due to a different potential concern, that of *Maris Ayin*. The *machlokes* whether or not *Maris Ayin* is applicable regarding *Issurei Derabbanan* is addressed at length in a later chapter titled "Margarine, Misconceptions, and *Maris Ayin*."

the *Pischei Teshuva*, Rav Avraham Tzvi Hirsch Eisenstadt (d. 1868),[3] as to whether appointing someone to stand watch over the two people eating to ensure that they do not eat from each other's plates (a *shomer*) is effective. The question is: May one rely on someone standing there watching instead of a *hekker* to allow them to eat together? To simplify: Can a *shomer* take the place of a *hekker*?

- Rav Akiva Eiger, citing the *Ginas Veradim*,[4] maintains that a *shomer* should be considered *halachically* ineffective to permit partaking of milk and meat at the same table, as such an undertaking would require a constant conscious awareness to ensure no inadvertent mixing occurs. In their opinion, however helpful a watchman may be, he would still come up short in this category.
- On the other hand, the *Pischei Teshuva*, citing the *Maseis Binyomin*,[5] maintains that since the purpose of the *hekker* is to serve as a constant reminder, the presence of a watchman should certainly seem sufficient to prevent a kashrus mix-up, as his just being noticeable at the table might be akin to an ad hoc *hekker*.

Interestingly, many *halachic* authorities through the ages have taken stances on both sides of this debate, with no clear-cut consensus.[6]

---

3   The entirety of the issue is obviously far more complicated that how it is summarized and presented here, but this is the basic *machlokes*. It seems to be based on their disparate understandings of the purpose of a *hekker*, how it exactly works *halachically*, and whether *daas* is necessary or not.

4   Rav Akiva Eiger (Glosses to Y.D. 88:1), citing *Shu"t Ginas Veradim* (*Gan Hamelech*, end 71).

5   *Pischei Teshuva* (ad loc. 4), citing *Shu"t Maseis Binyomin* (112).

6   For example, the *Atzei Ha'Olah* (*Hilchos Bassar B'chalav, Klal* 2, 88:6 and *Chukei Chaim* ad loc. 5), *Dalsei Teshuva* (Y.D. 88:1), *Darchei Teshuva* (ad loc. 6), and the *Machaneh Yehuda* (*Shu"t* 41) all rule like Rav Akiva Eiger, while the *Yad Efraim* (Y.D. 88), *Chochmas Adam* (40:11; who maintains that a *hekker* would work for even one eating by himself), and the *Yavin Daas* (*Shu"t*, *Chiddushim* to Y.D. 88:2) *pasken* like the *Pischei Teshuva*. Although the *Matteh Reuven* (184) and *Badei Hashulchan* (Y.D. 88, pg. 46, *Biurim* s.v. *im asu*) question the *Pischei Teshuva's* application of the *Maseis Binyomin's* rule, as they maintain that he

However, what is most fascinating is that the *Lev Aryeh, Ben Ish Chai*, and the *Me'am Loez*,[7] all separately bring proof to this issue from *Parashas Vayera*. The *pasuk* states that upon welcoming the three disguised angels, Avraham Avinu serves them a meal fit for a king, made up of both meat and dairy ingredients (tongue, as well as butter or cream).[8] The verse continues "And he stood over them, under the tree, and they ate." The aforementioned commentators, as well as later, Rav Yosef Shalom Elyashiv,[9] raise the question of why the Torah specifically stated that Avraham Avinu "stood over them." Why was this detail necessary for the Torah to add?

These authorities understood that these extra words indicated that while some of the angels were eating dairy, the others were eating meat. By "standing over them," Avraham was actually acting as their self-appointed *shomer*, to ensure that "ne'er the twain shall meet." This is cited as a proof to the *Pischei Teshuva's* position that a *shomer* can indeed work in place of a *hekker* between meat and milk. In fact, based on

---

never meant to apply it to *Hilchos Bassar B'chalav*, but was rather referring to *Hilchos Harchakos*, nevertheless, with the recent publishing of *Pischei Teshuva Hashaleim*, along with the reprinting of his sources in their original, history has disproven this claim, as the *Maseis Binyomim* explicitly uses this logic to allow eating milk and meat together at the same table with others acting as watchmen, adding that there is no *"hefsek gadol yoseir m'zeh."* The *Maadanei Hashulchan* (ad loc. 2) characteristically concludes that since this is a *Machlokes HaPoskim*, it is preferable not to rely upon it barring extenuating circumstances. However, in his later *Shu"t Maadanei Melachim* (75 and 76), he strongly defends the position of the *Pischei Teshuva*, concluding that in his opinion, it is *halachically* correct and a *shomer* is indeed sufficient.

7   *Lev Aryeh* (in his commentary to *Chullin* 104b s.v. *u'vazeh*), *Ben Yehoyada* (*Yoma* 28b s.v. *sham kayam*), and *Yalkut Me'am Loez* (*Parashas Mishpatim* pg. 892).

8   *Bereishis* (Ch. 18:8). See *Rashi* (ad loc. verse 8 s.v. *chemah*, and verse 7 s.v. *bakar*), based on Gemara *Bava Metziah* (86b).

9   Both, in his commentary to Gemara *Chullin, He'aros B'Maseches Chullin* (104b s.v. *gezeira*), as well as in his commentary to *Chumash, Kovetz He'aros shel HaGri"sh* (pg. 16 s.v. *v'af*). The *Midrash Hagadol* (*Toldos* 26:5) implies this way as well.

this proof, Rav Elyashiv actually rules this way *lemaaseh*, that a *shomer* is akin to a *hekker* in this regard.

Angelic Deception

In a related idea, the *Talilei Oros,* quoting the *Meilitz Yosher,* asks why the *pasuk* emphasized that the angels ate, especially as *Rashi,* quoting the Midrash and Gemara,[10] maintains that angels cannot actually eat, but rather that these angels gave the appearance of eating. The difficulty with this explanation is that the Midrash[11] teaches that at the time of receiving the *Torah,* the angels did not want to "release it" to Moshe Rabbeinu. The angels were informed that they were undeserving of receiving the Torah, as they had previously shown that they had not observed its laws, for they ate milk and meat together at Avraham's house! Yet, according to *Rashi,* they did *not* actually eat! So why then did all "angelkind" lose the privilege of keeping the *Torah*?

The *Meilitz Yosher* answers that even though the angels did not actually eat, the *Torah* still refers to their actions as eating. Why? To indicate the power of *"Maris Ayin,"* a Rabbinic enactment that prohibits taking actions which are permitted according to the letter of the Law, but nevertheless give onlookers the impression of doing something *halachically* forbidden. The basic idea of *Maris Ayin* is that we have an obligation to act in a manner that will not cause observers confusion between what is permitted and forbidden.[12] Therefore, since the *Malachim* gave the

---

10 *Talilei Oros* (vol. 1, pg. 175; quoting the *Meilitz Yosher*), *Rashi* (*Parashas Vayera* ad loc. s.v. *vayocheilu*; quoting the *Midrash Rabbah, Bereishis* 48:14, and Gemara *Bava Metziah* 86b).

11 *Midrash Shochar Tov* (8) and in *Pesikta Rabassi* to *"Aseir Te'aser";* cited by the *Shittah M'Kubetzes* (*Bechoros* 6b:2). There are many different ways to understand this Midrash, including how exactly Moshe Rabbeinu was able to sway the *Malachim* with his logic regarding their eating *Bassar B'chalav* at Avraham Avinu's house. For an interesting explanation relating to whether or not *Malachim* possess a *Yetzer Hara,* see Rav Moshe Yekusiel Kaufman-Cohen's *Chukei Chaim* (*Os Shin,* 2, *Dinei Chag HaShavuos,* pg. 111b).

12 See *Yoreh Deah* (87:3 and 4), and relevant commentaries. This topic is

appearance of eating milk and meat, even though they may not have actually done so, they lost the opportunity to claim the *Torah* for themselves. The popular expression might be "looks may be deceiving," but even so, everyone (apparently inclusive of angels) must make sure not to engage in questionable activities, or even questionable-looking ones.

That's Not All, Folks…

In fact, from just this single episode, many *halachic* commentators and authorities glean various possible *halachos*, including the proper order of eating—dairy before meat;[13] the importance of wiping and rinsing out one's mouth (*kinuach v'hadacha*) in between a dairy and a meat course;[14] the idea that one should perform the aforementioned *kinuach* exclusively with bread;[15] tongue meat's elevated status in *halacha* vis-à-vis its nullification;[16] special *halachic* dispensation given regarding invited guests, even those who are viewed as "charity cases";[17] the proper

---

addressed at length in the chapter titled "Margarine, Misconceptions, and *Maris Ayin*."

13   See *Midrash Leket Tov* (ad loc.).

14   See the *Chasam Sofer's Toras Moshe* (*Parashas Vayera* s.v. *shalosh*); cited in Rabbi Yitzchak Aharon Kramer's *Arichas Hadaas* (Ch. 3: end footnote 27). According to this interpretation, the *Malachim* ate the dairy foods before the meat, yet neglected to do the required *kinuach*, *rechitza*, and *hadacha* between them. The importance of these required actions was addressed in the previous chapter.

15   See the Maharam Schiff's glosses to Gemara *Chullin* (105a), based on the *Midrash Rabbah* (ad loc.).

16   See *Taz* (Y.D. 101:8), quoting the Rashal (*Yam Shel Shlomo*, *Chullin* Ch. 7:53). This is because tongue is a dish to serve important guests; as such, it is considered a *Chatichah Hareuyah L'Hischabed* and cannot be nullified. This is fully addressed in the chapter titled "*Chatichah Hareuyah L'Hischabed*: All About Honor."

17   See *Soles L'Mincha* (15:3), arguing on the premise of the *Toras Ha'Asham* (ad loc.); cited in *Pischei Teshuva* (Y.D. 69:13). See also the *Chofetz Chaim's Ahavas Chessed* (vol. 3: Ch. 1 s.v. *v'da*) and Rav Moshe Halberstam's *Shu"t Divrei Moshe* (42:2). This issue is also discussed in the chapter titled "*Chatichah Hareuyah L'Hischabed*: All About Honor."

way of sending a *"kos shel bracha"* to one's wife after *Birkas Hamazon*;[18] the significance of eating *"chullin b'taharah"*;[19] the problem of burning meat and milk together (as a form of cooking);[20] the kashrus status of an animal created via *Sefer Yetzira*;[21] and possibly not having to wait the full amount of time after eating meat on Shavuos.[22]

---

18 *Shu"t Sheilas Yaavetz* (vol. 1:126); based on *Ritva's* commentary to *Bava Metziah* (87a). *Rashi* (Ch. 18:9 end s.v. *vayomeru*) also cites this briefly. See also *Gur Aryeh* (ad loc. 33) for an explanation.

19 See *Rashi* ad loc. (s.v. *vayikach*), based on Gemara *Bava Metziah* (87a). As discussed in a recent article titled *"Pie Crusts, Pas Palter and the Aseres Yemei Teshuva"* (*Yated Ne'eman*, 24 Elul 5774/September 19, 2014), and online at: https://ohr.edu/this_week/insights_into_halacha/4893), this *inyan* of eating *chullin b'tahara* is one of the *mekoros* for being *makpid* on *Pas Yisrael* during the Aseres Yemei Teshuva. See Rabbi Dr. Eliezer Brodt's *Bein Kesseh L'Assor* (Ch. 2 and 3) at length.

20 See the Steipler Gaon's *Birchos Peretz* (ad loc.), cited in *Talilei Oros* (vol. 1, pg. 174), based on the comments of the *Shittah M'Kubetzes* on *Bechoros* (6b:2). According to this explanation, the *Malachim* actually did eat *Bassar B'chalav* and their internal fire cooked them together, transgressing what would have been a Biblical prohibition of cooking *Bassar B'chalav*, had they been Jewish human beings.

21 See the *Malbim's HaTorah V'HaMitzva* (*Parashas Vayera* Ch. 18:8) who explains that the *"ben habakar asher **assah**"* was meant literally—that Avraham Avinu created the calf using the *Sefer Yetzira*, and is therefore essentially pareve. According to this explanation, that is why he was able to serve the visiting Angels a meal containing both milk and meat; the meat was truly pareve, as he created it that day. A similar explanation can also be found in the *Pirkei D'Rabbi Eliezer* (cited in *Yalkut Reuveini* on *Parashas Vayera*) and by the *Chessed L'Avraham* (ancestor of the Chida; *Ein Mishpat, Nahar* 51). The *Pardes Yosef* cites this as well (*Parashas Vayera* Ch. 18, pg. 115, end first paragraph and *Parashas Vayeishev* Ch. 37, pg. 268, end first paragraph). See also *Darchei Teshuva* (87:29). The idea and application of creating meat using the *Sefer Yetzira* is discussed at length in the chapter titled "Genetically Engineered Meat."

22 See *Noam Elimelech* (end *Parashas Mishpatim* s.v. *lo sevashel*). There are many explanations as to his intent (see for example *Piskei Teshuvos*, end 494; who opines that the *Noam Elimelech* generally would not eat meat and dairy on

24 Food: A Halachic Analysis

In conclusion, we see not to take the conduct of the Avos lightly. Aside from the well-known effect of *"Maaseh Avos Siman L'Banim"*—in which a unique form of spiritual DNA is transmitted to us, their children[23]—even just a small act on the part of the Avos imparts to us a treasure trove of *hanhaga, hashkafa,* and yes, even *halacha*.

---

the same day—except for Shavuos), and many authorities do not agree with his logic in this scenario as *halacha*. Yet, fascinatingly, and although certainly not the normative *halacha*, there is a minority opinion who does hold this way—the *Kol Bo* (106 s.v. *v'achar* and in *Orchos Chaim* vol. 2, *Hilchos Issurei Maachalos* pg. 335:73 s.v. *v'yeish*) and *Elyah Rabba* (O.C. 494: end 10) write that if one ate *fleishigs* at the Shavuos morning *seudah*, he may eat *milchigs* at the later evening one, even if six hours has not yet elapsed. However, this opinion was clearly not accepted. See *Magen Avraham* (O.C. 494:6), *Pri Megadim* (ad loc. E.A. 6), *Chok Yaakov* (ad loc. 11), *Aruch Hashulchan* (ad loc. 5), *Mishnah Berurah* (ad loc. 17), *Darchei Teshuva* (89:19), and *Shu"t Mishnah Halachos* (vol. 7:70).

23 See *Ramban* (*Parashas Lech Lecha*, Ch. 12:6 and introduction to *Sefer Shemos*). According to the *Ramban*, based on the *Midrash Tanchuma* (*Parashas Lech Lecha* 9) and cited by many later authorities [see, for example, *Kli Yakar* (*Parashas Toldos* Ch. 26:19 and *Parashas Vayeishev* Ch. 38:18), *Maharsha* (*Chagigah* 5b and *Avodah Zarah* 8b), and *Shu"t Sheilas Yaavetz* (vol. 1:75)], the purpose of showcasing the actions of the Avos is to demonstrate that a physical action, small as it may be, serves as a conduit to actualize and channel a Divine decree, in this case creating and enabling abilities in future generations.

Chapter 3

To *Bentch* or Not to *Bentch* (between Milk and Meat)? That Is the Question

PREVIOUS CHAPTERS TOUCHED UPON THE topic of what needs to be done after one ate dairy food items before he is permitted to eat meat. *Halacha*[1] mandates one who has partaken of milk products to perform a personal three-step process: *kinuach*—palate cleansing by eating a hard food item (e.g., cracker), *hadacha*—rinsing out of the mouth, and *rechitza*—handwashing[2]—as well as removing any remnants and leftovers of the dairy meal[3]—all before being able to have a meat meal.

---

1 *Shulchan Aruch* (Y.D. 89:2 and 4).

2 As most civilized people generally use utensils such as forks and knives to eat and their hands remain clean, they therefore may not actually require handwashing according to many authorities, including the *Pri Chodosh* (Y.D. 89:20), *Shulchan Gavoah* (ad loc. 8), *Ba'er Heitiv* (ad loc. end 13), *Rashash* (*Chullin* 103b), *Mor U'Ketziah* (end 181), and *Aruch Hashulchan* (Y.D. 89:8). Nevertheless, many authorities maintain that since handwashing involves minimal effort, one should still do so, even after eating dairy items with proper utensils (cheesecake, anyone?). These *Poskim* include the *Pri Megadim* (Y.D. 89 S.D. 20), *Pischei Teshuva* (ad loc. 4), Chida (*Shiyurei Bracha* ad loc 15), *Atzei Ha'Olah* (*Hilchos Bassar B'chalav* 3:12 and *Chukei Chaim* 9), *Ben Ish Chai* (Year 2, *Parashas Shlach* 14), *Kaf Hachaim* (Y.D. 89:34), and *Me'orei Ohr* (*Kitzur Shulchan Aruch on Yoreh Deah*, 89:1). See also *Chaguras Shmuel* (ad loc. 25) who maintains that even when one eats with a fork it is inevitable that some residue will remain on his hands. This issue, relevant to different *inyanei halacha*,

Yet, that is all that the *Shulchan Aruch* necessitates. If so, why do many people additionally wait half an hour before eating anything meaty? And, why are many people particular to also recite *Birkas Hamazon* between eating any dairy and a meat meal?

Zohar Zehirus

The answer to the first question actually predates the *Shulchan Aruch* by quite a bit and lies in a cryptic comment found in the *Zohar*, the classic text of *Kabbalah* (loosely translated as "Jewish Mysticism") attributed to the great *Tanna* Rabbi Shimon Bar Yochai.[4] The *Zohar* writes that everyone should wait between dairy and meat meals "one meal or one hour," (or else suffer potentially dire consequences). Although there are many interpretations offered for this enigmatic remark,[5] the most common one is that "one hour" is referring to mandating a waiting period of one hour even after eating dairy.[6] Several authorities, including the

---

is addressed in several chapters of this book, including "The Importance of a *Diyuk*" and "*Mayim Acharonim, Chova?*"

3   *Shulchan Aruch* (Y.D. 89:4). See also *Aruch Hashulchan* (ad loc. 15) and *Shu"t Igros Moshe* (Y.D. vol. 1:38).

4   *Zohar* (*Parashas Mishpatim* pg. 125:1), cited by the *Beis Yosef* (O.C. 173 s.v. *v'yeish*) and *Biur HaGr"a* (Y.D. 89:11).

5   See *Chemdas Hayamim* (*Shabbos* Ch. 8, *Sod Seudas Shabbos*, end s.v. *u'mah*), *Levush* (O.C. 173:1), *Pri Toar* (89:6), *Kreisi U'Pleisi* (ad loc. 89:3), and *Chaguras Shmuel* (ad loc. 18), each of whom have a completely different approach to understanding the *Zohar's* intent. Interestingly, Rav Chaim Vital is quoted as holding that one must wait six hours after consuming dairy before partaking of meat, and there are those who opine that this is ostensibly based on a different version of the *Zohar's* statement—"*b'seudasa chada*," meaning that one may not eat milk and meat during a period of one *seudah*—meaning six hours. See the recent *Shulchan Aruch HaZohar* (Y.D. vol. 1:89, footnotes 4 and 5; explaining the *Ohr Hachama's* citing of Rav Chaim Vital). Thanks are due to to my *talmid*, R' Yitzchak Rubin, for pointing out this fascinating source.

6   See *Beis Yosef* (O.C. 173 s.v. *v'yeish*), *Shach* (Y.D. 89:15), *Pri Chodosh* (ad loc. 6), *Biur HaGr"a* (ibid.), *Chida* (*Shiyurei Bracha* ad loc. 6 s.v. *v'ani* and *Kikar L'Aden* 5, *Likutim* 8), and *Ikrei HaDa"T* (*Ikrei Dinim* Y.D. 10:5).

Pri Chodosh, actually rule this way,⁷ and the *Shulchan Aruch* himself, in his *Beis Yosef* commentary,⁸ implied this way as well. Yet, when it came down to the actual practical ruling, the *Shulchan Aruch* did not mandate following the *Zohar's* view.

That is why, according to the basic *halacha*, no actual waiting period is required after partaking of dairy foods. Nevertheless, there are those who try to take the *Zohar's* opinion into account and at least "meet him halfway," as we find the Talmudic dictum of *"m'palga karov karu lei*—from halfway is already considered close," meaning, that in our case, by waiting at least a half hour, it is "as if" one waited an hour. Some suggest that the *Zohar* did not intend a full, actual hour but rather a short but specific waiting period.⁹ In any event, as an added stringency,

---

7   *Pri Chodosh* (ibid.). Other authorities who rule this way include the *Shlah* (*Shavuos, Ner Mitzva* 8), *Pri Toar* (ibid.), *Elyah Rabba* (O.C. 173:2), *Shulchan HaTahor* (O.C. 173:2), *Shu"t Kol Gadol* (64), and *Kaf Hachaim* (O.C. 173:2, 494:61; and Y.D. 89:10). See also *Shiyurei Bracha* (Y.D. 89:13), *Darchei Teshuva* (ad loc. 19), *Shu"t Teshuvos V'Hanhagos* (vol. 2:390), and *Shu"t Chayei Halevi* (vol. 5:60, 11) who cite waiting an hour as a proper *minhag*. The *Darchei Halacha* (*Bassar B'chalav* 89:3, pg. 29) cites a responsum of the *Chasam Sofer's* son-in-law, Rav Zalman Spitzer, *Av Beis Din* of Vienna (originally published in *Kovetz Ha'Ohel*; Kislev 5632) who mandates an hour waiting period after dairy products, based on the *Zohar*. Rav Aharon Pfeiffer's *Kitzur Shulchan Aruch* (*Bassar B'chalav*, Ch. 11:5, pg. 116) refers to this as *"Minhag Chassidus."* It is noteworthy that several authorities, including the *Pri Chodosh* (ibid.), *Pri Toar* (ibid.), *Yaavetz* (*Mor U'Ketziah*, end 173), and *Aruch Hashulchan* (Y.D. 89:11) qualify this ruling, that the one hour waiting period does not apply before eating fowl.

8   *Beis Yosef* (O.C. 173 s.v. *v'yeish machmirin*).

9   Gemara *Kiddushin* (12a). There are many authorities who apply this dictum to waiting a half-hour after eating *milchigs* or suggest that the *Zohar* did not mean a full, actual hour but rather a short but specific waiting period [see *Tosafos* (*Sota* 11a s.v. *Miriam*) for a possible precedent]. See *Matteh Reuven* (186), *Shu"t Maharshag* (vol. 1, Y.D. 13 s.v. *amnam*), *Shu"t Divrei Chachamim* (Y.D. 1:3; quoting Rav Yaakov Kamenetsky), *Shu"t Teshuvos V'Hanhagos* (vol. 2:390), *Shu"t Shraga HaMeir* (vol. 7:105, 2), *Nitei Gavriel* (*Shavuos* Ch. 31:5), *Shu"t Maadanei Melachim* (85:3), *Shu"t Mishnah Halachos* (vol. 10:135),

a custom has developed among many to wait half an hour between a dairy meal and a meat one.

Bentching Brouhaha

The matter of whether *Birkas Hamazon* is also required after a dairy meal is addressed by the *Magen Avraham* in *Hilchos Shavuos*.[10] Since it is customary on the holiday of Shavuos to eat dairy (aside from the traditional meat *seudah*),[11] a common question is whether one may have them as part of the same meal, by merely doing the basic rinsing, washing, and palate cleansing mandated by the *Shulchan Aruch*, or whether one must have the *milchig* and *fleishig* courses each as part of a separate *seudah*.

The *Magen Avraham* rules that unless one ate hard cheese, which would require a full six-hour wait, one need not have the dairy dishes and subsequent meat foods as part of separate meals. Thus, no *bentching* is actually required, just the three-step process described above. Many authorities follow the *Magen Avraham*'s ruling and do not require *Birkas Hamazon* between a dairy and a meat meal.[12]

However, many other authorities, including the *Knesses Hagedolah* and *Shlah*, strongly disagree and mandate *bentching*. The *Be'er Mayim Chaim* even maintains that the *Magen Avraham*'s opinion must have been a printing mistake and avers that certainly one may *not* eat milk

---

Halichos Shlomo (*Moadim* vol. 2, Ch. 12, footnote 49), *Kovetz M'Beis Levi* on *Yoreh Deah* (pg. 35:15), and *Minhag Yisrael Torah* (O.C. vol. 3, 494:8 s.v. *v'hinei*).

10 *Magen Avraham* (O.C. 494:6).

11 Especially according to the *shittah* of the *Rema* (ibid.), *Machatzis Hashekel* (O.C. 494:7 s.v. *hu hadin b'Shavuos*), and Rav Moshe Feinstein (*Shu"t Igros Moshe* O.C. vol. 1:160) regarding the proper way of having both *milchigs* and *fleishigs* on Shavuos. See also *Darchei Teshuva* (89:19) at length. This topic is discussed at length in the chapter titled "Of Bull's-Eyes, the *Korban* Cheesecake, and Dairy Bread."

12 Including the *Levush* (ad loc.), *Matteh Yonason* (ad loc.), and *Machatzis Hashekel* (O.C. 494:6). See also *Shu"t Rivash* (384; cited in *Shaarei Teshuva*, O.C. 206: end 1).

and meat as part of the same meal. To add another wrinkle, anyone who follows the *Zohar*'s view of waiting even after dairy would undoubtedly require *Birkas Hamazon* as well, as he mandates a higher degree of separation.[13] Therefore, many later and contemporary authorities rule that one should indeed *bentch* after *milchigs* if at all possible, even though it may not be required by the strict letter of the law.[14]

Still, others ardently defend the *Magen Avraham*'s position, and refer to this *bentching* as a "*chumrah yeseirah*."[15] Additionally, if it were truly a printing mistake, the *Magen Avraham*'s son-in-law, Rav Moshe Yekusiel Kaufman-Cohen, would have corrected it in his comprehensive *sefer* on *halacha* and *minhag*, *Chukei Chaim*. Yet, instead he rules exactly as his father-in-law did, with no requirement to *bentch* between *milchigs* and *fleishigs* (with the exception of one who ate hard cheese).[16] This is also the final ruling of both the *Aruch Hashulchan* and *Mishnah Berurah*—that one is *not required* to make two separate meals out of his different dishes unless one ate hard cheese.[17]

---

13   Including the *Shiyarei Knesses Hagedolah* (O.C. 493:3; cited in *Darchei Teshuva*, Y.D. 89:14), *Shlah* (*Shavuos*, *Ner Mitzva* 8), and *Be'er Mayim Chaim* (*Parashas Vayera* Ch. 18:8; cited in *Pischei Teshuva* vol. 3:287, 1). Other authorities who rule this way include the *Minchas Yaakov* (76:5), *Pri Chodosh* (Y.D. 89:6), *Pri Megadim* (ad loc. S.D. 6 and 15), *Elyah Rabba* (O.C. 173:8 and *Elyah Zuta*, O.C. 494:6), *Kitzur Shulchan Aruch* (46:11), *Kaf Hachaim* (Palaji; Ch. 24:25), and *Kaf Hachaim* (Sofer; O.C. 494:61).

14   See *Shu"t Maharshag* (ibid.), *Shu"t Vayaan Dovid* (vol. 1, Y.D. 115), *Shu"t Beis Yisrael* (O.C. 97), *Shu"t Maharsham* (vol. 3: end 126 s.v. *u'mah*), *Kaf Hachaim* (O.C. 173:2; 494:61 and Y.D. 89:10), *Darchei Teshuva* (89:19), *Shu"t Igros Moshe* (O.C. vol. 1:160, who writes that it is "*yoser tov*" to *bentch* in-between), *Shu"t Teshuvos V'Hanhagos* (ibid.), *Shu"t Az Nidberu* (vol. 4:42), *Shu"t Avnei Yashpei* (vol. 7:70, 3), and *Nitei Gavriel* (*Shavuos* Ch. 31:1).

15   Including the *Matteh Reuven* (187), *Shu"t Melamed L'Ho'eel* (vol. 2-Y.D. 23), *Shu"t Keren L'Dovid* (140), *Shu"t Mishnas Sachir* (vol. 1:29), and *Shu"t Yad Yitzchak* (vol. 3:189).

16   *Chukei Chaim* (*Os Shin*, 2, *Dinei Chag HaShavuos*, pg. 112a): "*d'eino tzarich lehafsik b'Birkas Hamazon im aino ochel gevina kasheh, v'yizaher likach mapah acheres*."

17   *Aruch Hashulchan* (Y.D. 89:9) and *Mishnah Berurah* (494:15). The *chumrah*

Food: A Halachic Analysis

In the final analysis, it appears that all one needs to do after partaking of a standard dairy item is the rinsing, washing, and palate cleansing prescribed in *halacha*. One is not required to wait an extra hour, half-hour, or *bentch* before eating *fleishigs*.

Nevertheless, many have the custom do some or all of the enumerated above, and to go "above and beyond" the letter of the law to properly ensure that their meat and milk stay distinctly separate without "meat-ing." But it is equally important that one should never lose sight of what is actual codified *halacha* and what is truly a *chumrah*.[18]

---

to *bentch* after *milchigs* is also noticeably absent from the *Chochmas Adam*, who only cites the lenient *ikar din*. Other contemporary authorities who were lenient include the *Chazon Ish* and Steipler Gaon (cited in *Darchei Halacha* on *Kashrus Habayis*, Ch. 4, footnote 22; citing Rav Chaim Kanievsky), the *She'arim Metzuyanim B'Halacha* (vol. 1:46, 6), Rav Chaim Kanievsky himself (cited in *Kuntress Maaneh Ra"ch* pg. 54:446–447), the *Badei Hashulchan* (Y.D. 89:75), and Rav Mordechai Eliyahu (*Darchei Halacha* glosses to the *Kitzur Shulchan Aruch* 46:8).

18 Indeed, the Vilna Gaon (*Biur HaGr"a* Y.D. 89:11) refers to keeping this *hanhaga* of the *Zohar's* as a "*chumrah al davar hamuttar*." See also Rav Ovadiah Yosef's *Shu"t Yabia Omer* (vol. 6, Y.D. 7:4 and 5) and *Shu"t Yechaveh Daas* (vol. 3:58) at length, who explains that going above 'the letter-of the-law' in this case is certainly considered a *chumrah*.

Chapter 4

Weighty Waiting Options

AS MENTIONED IN A PREVIOUS chapter, we often find that the Torah's description of even simple actions of our great forefathers impart to us a treasure trove of *hanhaga, hashkafa,* and even *halacha.* Sometimes though, it is the exact opposite: a *halacha* is gleaned from the acts of those far from being paragons of virtue or exemplars of excellence. Indeed, sometimes we learn fascinating *halachic* insights from people whom we would not consider role models by any stretch of the imagination.

Double Agents

Every Tisha B'Av, and every time we read *Parashas Shlach*, we are reminded of the grave sin of the *Meraglim*, the spies whose evil report about Eretz Yisrael still echoes, with repercussions felt until today.[1] Of the twelve spies sent, only two remained loyal to Hashem: Yehoshua bin Nun and Calev ben Yefuneh.[2] The other ten chose to slander Eretz Yisrael instead and consequently suffered immediate and terrible deaths. Due to their vile report, the Jewish People were forced to remain in the desert an additional forty years, and eventually die out before their children ultimately were allowed to enter Eretz Yisrael.

---

1 See *Taanis* (26b and 29a), that this, the first of five tragedies, occurred on Tisha B'Av.

2 Calev's father's real name was actually Chetzron. See *Divrei Hayamim* I (Ch. 2:18) and *Sota* (11b).

Hashem called this rogues' gallery of spies an *"eidah,"*[3] literally, "a congregation." The Gemara[4] famously derives from this incident that the minimum requirement for a *minyan* is a quorum of ten men, since there were ten turncoat "double-agents" who were contemptuously called "a congregation." If ten men can get together to conspire and hatch malevolent schemes, then ten men can assemble to form a congregation for *devarim shebekedusha,* sanctified matters. This exegesis is duly codified in *halacha,*[5] and all because of the dastardly deeds of ten misguided men.[6]

Covetous Carnivores

Another prime example of *halacha* being set by the actions of those less than virtuous,[7] [8] is the tragic chapter of the rabble-rousers who

---

3   *Bamidbar (Parashas Shlach,* Ch. 14:27).

4   *Megilla* (23b), *Brachos* (21b), and *Sanhedrin* (74b). See *Rashi al HaTorah* (ad loc. s.v. *l'eidah*).

5   *Rambam (Hilchos Tefilla* Ch. 8:5), *Tur* and *Shulchan Aruch* (O.C. 55:1 and 69:1), *Aruch Hashulchan* (O.C. 55:6), and *Kitzur Shulchan Aruch* (15:1). Many authorities cite this as the source for this law, including the *Bach* (O.C. 55:1), *Taz* (ad loc. 1), *Levushei Srad* (ad loc. 1), *Chida* (*Birkei Yosef* ad loc. 3), *Shulchan Aruch Harav* (ad loc. 2), *Mishnah Berurah* (ad loc. 2), and *Kaf Hachaim* (ad loc. 6).

6   For a full treatment of the *Meraglim* and their intentions, see relevant commentaries to *Parashas Shlach,* as well as Rabbi Moshe M. Eisemann's excellent *"Tear Drenched Nights—Tish'ah B'Av: The Tragic Legacy of the Meraglim."*

7   Another interesting example of this is a potential *halacha* we glean from Bilaam. The Gemara *(Brachos* 7a) explains that Bilaam knew the exact millisecond each day that Hashem "gets angry" and knew how to properly curse during that time. *Tosafos* (ad loc. s.v. *she'ilmalei* and *Avodah Zarah* 4b s.v. *rega*) asks what type of curse was possible to utter in such a limited time frame (a fraction of a second!) and gives two answers: **1)** the word *"kaleim,* destroy them" **2)** once Bilaam started his curse in that exact time frame, he "locked it in" and can continue as long as it takes, since it is all considered in that exact time. The *Aruch Hashulchan* (O.C. 110:5), the Butchatcher Rav (*Eishel Avraham* O.C. 104), and the *Yid Hakadosh* of Peshischa (cited by the Kozoglover Gaon in his *Shu"t Eretz Tzvi,* end 121 s.v. *v'amnam*), take the second approach a step

further and apply this idea to *Tefilla B'Zmana*. As long as one starts his *Tefilla* before the *Sof Zman*, it is considered that he "made the *zman*", even if the majority of his *Tefilla* actually took place after the *Sof Zman*. Not everyone agrees with this, though. Indeed, many *Poskim*, including the *Magen Avraham* (O.C. 89:4 and 124:4), *Pri Megadim* (O.C. 89, E.A. 4 and 110, E.A. 1; note however, that in the beginning of O.C. 620, in his *Eishel Avraham* commentary, he accepts this understanding regarding *Mussaf* on *Yom Kippur* prior to the seventh hour), and *Mishnah Berurah* (58:5 and 89: end 5), are *makpid* that one must **finish** his *Tefilla* before the *Sof Zman*. Nevertheless, a similar logic (based on Bilaam) is presented by the *Machatzis Hashekel* (O.C. 6: end 6), quoting the *Beis Yaakov* (*Shu"t* 127) in the name of the Arizal regarding *Tefillas HaTzibbur*. [There is precedent to this understanding in the *Yerushalmi* (*Brachos* Ch. 4, *Halacha* 1 and *Taanis* Ch. 4, *Halacha* 1). See also *Gilyonei HaShas* (*Brachos* 54) and *She'arim Metzuyanim B'Halacha* (vol. 1, 18:2 and *Kuntress Acharon* 2). Indeed, on a practical level, although the *Pri Megadim* (O.C. 109, E.A. 2) and seemingly followed by the *Mishnah Berurah* (66:35 and 109, *Biur Halacha* s.v. *hanichnas*; however, see 14 ad loc.), implies that one is only considered to have davened *Tefilla B'Tzibbur* if he **starts** his *Shemoneh Esrei* at the exact same time as the *chazan* and congregation (see *Brachos* 21b, and *Tur* and *Shulchan Aruch* and main commentaries to O.C. 109:1), nonetheless, numerous contemporary *Poskim*, including Rav Moshe Feinstein (*Shu"t Igros Moshe*, O.C. vol. 3:4 s.v. *uvadavar echad*), the *Chazon Ish* (cited in *Orchos Rabbeinu*, new edition, vol. 1, pg. 118:55), Rav Shlomo Zalman Auerbach (*Halichos Shlomo, Tefilla*, Ch. 8:7), and Rav Yosef Shalom Elyashiv (cited in *Avnei Yashpei* on *Tefilla*, Ch. 6, footnote 22), maintain that if one starts soon after, while the *Tzibbur* is still davening *Shemoneh Esrei* (preferably while still in the first *bracha*), one still "made" *Tefilla B'Tzibbur*. See also *Chayei Adam* (vol. 1:19, 8), *Aruch Hashulchan* (O.C. 109:5 and 12), *Shu"t Ba'er Moshe* (vol. 4:11), *Shu"t B'tzeil Hachochma* (vol. 4:3), *Shu"t Yabia Omer* (vol. 2, O.C. 7; who rules that the same applies in reverse, that if one starts his *Shemoneh Esrei* before the *Tzibbur* and continues along with them, it is still considered *Tefilla B'Tzibbur*), and *Ishei Yisrael* (Ch. 12:8).] If such design worked for one as despicable and reprehensible as Bilaam to enable him to curse us, how much more so should it work for us regarding *Tefilla B'Tzibbur* which is an *eis ratzon*!

8   An interesting *hanhaga* we learn from Bilaam is that an '*Adam Chashuv*' should not travel without having two assistants. See *Rashi* (*Bamidbar* Ch. 22:22 s.v. *ushnei*), quoting the *Midrash Tanchuma* (*Parashas Balak* 8). An additional example of a *halacha* gleaned from the wicked actions of Bilaam is that

lusted after meat, and disparaged Hashem's gift of the Heavenly bread called manna (*munn*), chronicled at the end of *Parashas Beha'aloscha*.[9] The *pasuk* states that "the meat was still between their teeth" when these sinners met their untimely and dreadful demise.[10] The Gemara extrapolates that since the Torah stressed that there was meat between their teeth, it means to show us that meat between the teeth is still considered tangible meat and requires one to wait before having a dairy meal afterward.[11]

There are actually several different ways to understand the Gemara's intent, chief among them *Rashi's* and the *Rambam's* differing opinions:[12]

---

of *Tzaar Baalei Chaim*, causing living creatures unnecessary pain. Although the Gemara (*Bava Metzia* 32a-b) debated whether this *halacha* is *Deoraysa* or *Derabbanan*, according to most authorities, including the *Rambam* (*Hilchos Rotzeach* Ch. 13:13; see also *Kessef Mishneh* ad loc. 9), *Rif* (*Bava Metzia* 17b), *Rosh* (ad loc. 30), *Mordechai* (end *Maseches Shabbos*, 448), *Sefer Hachinuch* (Mitzva 451, end s.v. *kasav*), *Tur* (C.M. 272:11), *Rema* (ad loc. 9), *Bach* (ad loc. 5), Vilna Gaon (*Biur HaGr"a* ad loc. 11), *SM"A* (ad loc. 15), *Kitzur Shulchan Aruch* (191:1), and *Aruch Hashulchan* (C.M. 272:2), as well as the *mashmaos* of the Gemara *Shabbos* (128b; see also *Rashi* ad loc. s.v. *tzaar*, as well as *Chiddushei Chasam Sofer* on *Bava Metzia* 32), and *Shulchan Aruch* (O.C. 305:18; as otherwise dismounting from an animal on Shabbos is an *Issur Derabbanan*, and he nonetheless rules that *Tzaar Baalei Chaim* supercedes it, implying that it is *Deoraysa*; thanks are due to Rav Yirmiyohu Kaganoff for pointing this out), *Tzaar Baalei Chaim* is indeed *Deoraysa*. According to the *Midrash Hagadol* (*Parashas Balak* 22:32), *Rambam* (*Moreh Nevuchim* vol. 3: end Ch. 17), and *Sefer Chassidim* (666) this can be gleaned from Bilaam's actions of hitting his donkey. In fact, they maintain that since Bilaam remarked that if he had a sword in his hand he would have killed his donkey on the spot, this is why he eventually was slain specifically by sword! Thanks are due to Rabbi Shimon Black of the KLBD for pointing out several of these sources.

9   *Bamidbar* (*Parashas Beha'aloscha* Ch. 11).

10 Ad loc. verse 33.

11 Gemara *Chullin* 105a, statements of Rav Chisda.

12 There are however, other opinions. For example, the *Kreisi U'Pleisi* (89, *Pleisi* 3) and *Chochmas Adam* (40:13) posit that the waiting period is actually dependent on digestion.

- The *Rambam* writes that meat tends to get stuck between the teeth and is still considered meat for quite some time afterward.[13]
- *Rashi* however, doesn't seem to be perturbed about actual meat residue stuck in the teeth, but simply explains that since meat is fatty by nature, its taste lingers for a long time after eating.[14]

In any case, regarding the general separation necessary between meat and milk, the Gemara itself does not inform us what the mandated waiting period is. Rather, it gives us several guideposts that the Rishonim use to set the *halacha*. The Gemara informs us that Mar Ukva's father would not eat dairy items on the same day that he had partaken of meat, but Mar Ukva himself (calling himself "vinegar the son of wine") would only wait *"m'seudasa l'seudasa achrina*—from one meal until a different meal."[15] [16] The various variant *minhagim* that Klal

---

13   *Rambam* (*Hilchos Maachalos Assuros* Ch. 9:28).

14   *Rashi*, in his glosses to Gemara *Chullin* (105a s.v. *assur*). However, *Rashi* would still agree that any meat found in the oral cavity even after six hours must be removed and *kinuach* and *hadacha* required.

15   Although the *Aruch Hashulchan* (Y.D. 89:4) maintains that the waiting period starts from when one finishes the *seudah* that he partook of meat, nevertheless, most authorities, including many contemporary authorities, follow the *Dagul Mervavah* (ad loc. 1), and are of the opinion that the waiting period starts immediately after one finishes eating the actual meat product and not the entire *seudah*. These *Poskim* include the *Erech Hashulchan* (ad loc. 3), *Darchei Teshuva* (ad loc. 4), *Atzei Ha'Olah* (*Hilchos Bassar B'chalav*, 3:1), *Shu"t Moshe Ha'Ish* (Y.D. 16), and the *Kaf Hachaim* (ad loc. 9), as well as Rav Yosef Shalom Elyashiv (cited in *Piskei Halachos*, Y.D. *Bassar B'chalav* 8, pg. 54), Rav Shmuel Halevi Wosner (*Kovetz M'Beis Levi* on *Yoreh Deah, Bassar B'chalav* 2, pg. 33), the Debreciner Rav and Rav Asher Zimmerman (both cited in *Rayach Habosem* on *Bassar B'chalav* Ch. 3, Question 28), Rav Chaim Pinchas Scheinberg (cited in *Shu"t Divrei Chachamim*, Y.D. Ch. 1, Question 6), Rav Chaim Kanievsky (cited in *Doleh U'Mashkeh* pg. 257), Rav Menashe Klein (*Shu"t Mishnah Halachos* vol. 5:97, 2), the *Rivevos Efraim* (*Shu"t* vol. 5:516), and Rav Shalom Krauss (*Shu"t Divrei Shalom* on Y.D. 25).

16   For an elucidation of what exactly Mar Ukva and his father disagreed upon, see the *Tosafos Yom Tov's Toras Ha'Asham* (76, s.v. *v'kasav d'nohagin*).

Yisrael keep related to waiting after eating meat are actually based on how the Rishonim understood this cryptic comment.

Six Hours

This, the most common custom, was first codified by the *Rambam*. He writes that meat stuck in the teeth remains "meat" for up to six hours, and mandates waiting that amount. This is the *halacha* as codified by the *Tur* and *Shulchan Aruch*,[17] as well as the vast majority of authorities. The *Rashal*, *Chochmas Adam*, and *Aruch Hashulchan*[18] all write very strongly that one should wait six hours. The mandated six hours seemingly comes from the many places in Rabbinic literature where it mentions that the "meals of a Torah scholar" are six hours

---

17 *Tur* (Y.D. 89:1 and O.C. 173) and *Shulchan Aruch* (Y.D. ad loc. 1). As the renowned *talmid* of the Maharam M'Rothenburg, the *Shaarei Dura* (end 76) already put it in the late 1200s: "*Ha'olam nahagu k'psak HaRambam shetzarich sheish sha'os bein seudas bassar l'seudas gevina.*" According to the *Tur*, *Shach*, and *Taz* (Y.D. ad loc. 1), this *halacha* is based on the fact that we *pasken* following both *Rashi's* and the *Rambam's shittos lemaaseh*. See also *Pri Megadim* (ad loc. M.Z. 1).

18 The *Rashal* (*Yam Shel Shlomo*, *Chullin* Ch. 8:9; quoted *lemaaseh* by the *Shach* in Y.D. 89:8) writes that anyone who has even a "*Rayach HaTorah*, a scent of Torah" would wait six hours. The *Chochmas Adam* (ibid.) writes that whoever doesn't wait six hours violates "*Al Titosh Toras Imecha*" (*Mishlei* Ch. 1:8). The *Aruch Hashulchan* (Y.D. 89:7) writes that whoever doesn't wait six hours is in the category of "*poretz geder*" who deserves to be bitten by a snake (*Koheles* Ch. 10:8). See also *Kanfei Yonah* (ad loc. pg. 65a-b) and *Pri Toar* (ad loc. 5) for similar assessments. The *Shlah* (*Shaar Ha'Osiyos*, *Kedushas Ha'achilah* 95, *Hagahah*) wrote to his son that he does not view the *minhag* of waiting only one hour in a positive light, indeed referring to it as "*Ra b'einai me'od*," and as most of the Rishonim, including the *Rambam*, *Rosh*, and *Rashba*, mandated waiting six hours, he exhorted him "*al tifnu l'minhag artzachem b'zeh*," not to follow the lenient view.

19 See, for example, the Gemara in *Shabbos* (10a) and *Pesachim* (12b), *Ritva* (*Chullin* 105a s.v *bassar bein*), *Rosh* (ad loc. end 5), *Rashba* (*Toras Habayis*, *Bayis* 3, *Shaar* 4), *Baal Ha'Itur* (*Shaar* 1, *Hilchos Bassar B'chalav* 13a-b), *Lechem Mishneh* (on the *Rambam* ibid.), *Tur* and *Shulchan Aruch* and main

apart.[19] Therefore, this fits well with Mar Ukva's statement that he would wait from one meal until the next after eating meat, meaning six hours.

Five Hours and Change

The idea of waiting five hours and a bit, or five and a half hours, is actually based on the choice of words of several Rishonim, including the *Rambam* and *Meiri*, when they rule to wait **six** hours. They write that one should keep *"k'mo sheish sha'os," approximately* six hours.[20] Several contemporary authorities maintain that "six hours" does not have to be an exact six hours—that waiting five and a half or the majority of the sixth hour (or according to some even five hours and one minute) is sufficient, as it is almost six hours.[21] However, it should be noted

---

commentaries (O.C. 157:1), *Biur HaGr"a* (Y.D. 89:2), *SM"A* (C.M. 5:10), and *Mor U'Ketziah* (184 s.v. *v'chein*).

20 *Rambam* (ibid.), *Meiri* (*Chullin* 105a s.v. *v'hadar*; however, in a separate *sefer*—*Magen Avos*, beg. *Inyan* 9, he explicitly writes that one may wait five hours—"*sheish sha'os oh chameish*"), *Agur* (Hilchos Seudah 223 and *Hilchos Issur V'Hetter* 1242), *Kol Bo* (106 s.v. *v'achar bassar*; and in *Orchos Chaim* vol. 2, *Hilchos Issurei Maachalos* pg. 335:73 s.v. *v'achar*).

21 Several authorities make this *diyuk*, including the *Minchas Yaakov* (*Soles L'Mincha* 76:1), Butchatcher Rav (*Daas Kedoshim* Y.D. 89:2), and the *Aruch Hashulchan* (ad loc. 2). Authorities who relied on not needing a full six-hour wait include the *Divrei Chaim* of Sanz (cited in *Shu"t Siach Yitzchak* 399 and *Shu"t Divrei Yatziv*, *Likutim V'Hashmatos* 69; however, see also *Shu"t Yashiv Yitzchak* vol. 5:14 and *Shu"t Mishnah Halachos* vol. 12:11), Rav Chaim Soloveitchik of Brisk (cited in *Torah L'Daas* vol. 2, *Parashas Beha'aloscha* pg. 229, Question 5), Rav Seligman Baer (Yitzchak Dov) Bamberger (the renowned Würzburger Rav and author of *Shu"t Yad Halevi*; cited in *Kovetz Hame'ayen*, Teves 5739, pg. 33, and later in *Nishmas Avraham*, third edition, Y.D. 89, footnote 1), the *Matteh Efraim* (Ardit; pg. 28:4), Rav Aharon Kotler (cited in *Shu"t Ohr Yitzchak* vol. 1, Y.D. 4), Rav Shlomo Zalman Auerbach (*Kovetz Moriah*, Teves 5756, pg. 79), Rav Yosef Shalom Elyashiv (*Shu"t Yissa Yosef* O.C. vol. 2:119, 5), Rav Ovadiah Yosef (*Shu"t Yabia Omer* vol. 1, Y.D. 4:13 and vol. 3, Y.D. 3; although in his earlier *teshuva* he only mentions being lenient after eating chicken, in his later *teshuva* he adds that he holds the

that not everyone agrees to this, and many maintain that the six hours must be exact.²²

---

same dispensation applies equally after eating meat, and not as some mistakenly suggest as to his intent), and Rav Moshe Sternbuch (*Shu"t Teshuvos V'Hanhagos* vol. 6:171 s.v. *ul'atzmi*; although he personally is stringent, he holds that one may indeed be lenient on five and a half hours). See also Rav Eitam Henkin *H"yd*'s defense of the *minhag* of waiting five hours and a bit, in his comprehensive *maamar* in *Kovetz Beis Aharon V'Yisrael* (vol. 141, pg. 71–76; also citing the *shittos* of his father, Rav Yehuda Herzl Henkin—the "*Bnei Banim*," and his great-grandfather, Rav Yosef Eliyahu Henkin).

22 Including Rabbeinu Yerucham (*Sefer Ha'Adam*, *Nesiv* 15, vol. 2:27, pg. 137), *Chamudei Daniel* (*Taaruvos* vol. 2:15), *Shu"t Ginas Veradim* (*Gan Hamelech* 154), *Perach Shoshan* (1:1), *Mikdash Me'at* (on *Daas Kedoshim* ibid. 2), *Yalkut Me'am Loez* (*Parashas Mishpatim* pg. 889–890 s.v. *shiur*), *Yad Yehuda* (89, *Peirush Hakatzer* 1), *Chofetz Chaim* (*Nidchei Yisrael* Ch. 33), Rav Yisrael Yaakov Fischer (*Shu"t Even Yisrael* vol. 9:126, 5), Rav Chaim Kanievsky (cited in *Doleh U'Mashkeh* pg. 257), and the *Badei Hashulchan* (Y.D. 89:8 and *Tziyunim* ad loc. 14). Several other contemporary authorities maintain that one should strive to keep the full six hours *lechatchilla*, but may be somewhat more lenient in times of need, and not wait an exact six hours. These include Rav Moshe Feinstein (cited in *Shu"t Divrei Chachamim* Y.D. 1:1; and in private conversation with Rav Moshe's grandson Rav Mordechai Tendler, author of *Mesores Moshe*), Rav Yosef Shalom Elyashiv (cited in *Shu"t Avnei Yashpei* vol. 5:101, 3 and 4 and *Ashrei Ha'Ish* O.C. vol. 3, pg. 441:10), Rav Shmuel Halevi Wosner (*Kovetz M'Beis Levi on Yoreh Deah*, pg. 34:3 and footnote 3), and Rav Menashe Klein (*Shu"t Mishnah Halachos* vol. 5:97, 3; see also vol. 7:70 and vol. 12:11, where he strongly urges to wait a full six hours). The *Pe'as Sadecha* (*Shu"t* vol. 3, Y.D. 29 s.v. *amnam*) posits that this *machlokes* of whether or not six complete hours is mandated, might depend on a different *machlokes* whether a *Talmid Chacham's seudah* is supposed to be at the beginning or the end of the sixth hour [see *Beis Yosef* (C.M. 5:3), *Drishah* (ad loc. 7), *Bach* (ad loc. 7 s.v. *ela*), *SM"A* (ad loc. 10), *Shach* (ad loc. 6), *Magen Avraham* (O.C. 157:2), *Elyah Rabba* (ad loc. 1), *Pri Megadim* (ad loc. E.A. 2), *Ba'er Heitiv* (O.C. 157:2), *Mishnah Berurah* (ad loc. 3), and *Aruch Hashulchan* (O.C. 157:2 and C.M. 11; who maintains that this is not necessarily a *machlokes*, but rather that the whole sixth hour is considered "*zman achilas Talmid Chacham*")].

Four Hours

Waiting four hours is first opined by the *Pri Chodosh*, who comments that the six hours mandated are not referring to regular "sixty-minute" hours, but rather *halachic* hours, known colloquially as *"sha'os zmanios."* This complicated *halachic* calculation is arrived at by dividing the amount of time between sunrise and sunset into twelve equal parts. Each of these new "hours" are *halachic* hours and are used to calculate the various *zmanim* throughout the day. The *Pri Chodosh* asserts that in the height of winter when days are extremely short, it is possible that six *halachic* hours can turn into a mere four actual hours![23] Although several authorities rule this way, and others say one may rely on this exclusively in times of great need,[24] nevertheless, his opinion here is rejected out of hand by the vast majority of authorities, who maintain that the *halacha* follows six true hours.[25] The *Yad Efraim* points out that

---

23 *Pri Chodosh* (Y.D. 89:6). Others who rely on his opinion include the *Gilyon Maharsha* (ad loc. 3), *Ikrei HaDa"T* (*Ikrei Dinim* 10: end 5) and *Minchas Yaakov* (*Soles L'Mincha* 76: end 1). Rav Aharon Wirmush, renowned *talmid* of the *Shaagas Aryeh*, in his *Me'orei Ohr* (vol. 7, *Chullin daf* 105 s.v. *chala bar chamra*) writes that *"peshita sheyeish lismoch alav* (the *Pri Chodosh*) *b'shaar maachalei chalav, afilu baal nefesh, meshum shelo nizkar b'Talmud rak gevina shemosheich taam v'nidbak bein hashinayim*—certainly even the scrupulous may rely upon the *Pri Chodosh's* opinion regarding waiting time mandated prior to consuming milk and most dairy products, as the Gemara only singled out (hard) cheese, due to its meat-like characteristics of lingering taste and palate clinginess." The issue of hard cheese, its properties, and *halachic* status, is discussed at length in the next chapter, titled "Hard Cheese Complexities."

24 Including the *Yad Efraim* (Y.D. 89:1), *Yeshuos Yaakov* (ad loc. *Peirush Hakatzer* 1), *Maharsham* (*Daas Torah* ad loc.), and the *Zeicher Yehosef* (*Shu"t* end 196), who allow one to rely on the *Pri Chodosh* only if one is sick or in times of great need. See also *Darchei Teshuva* (ad loc. 21).

25 Including the *Knesses Hagedolah* (Y.D. 89, *Hagahos* on *Tur*, ad loc. 6–7), *Maharach Algazi* (*Ba'ei Chayei* ad loc. pg. 39b), *Pri Megadim* (ad loc. M.Z. 1), *Pischei Teshuva* (ad loc. 3), *Kreisi U'Pleisi* (ad loc. *Pleisi* 3), *Chochmas Adam* (40:12), *Chida* (*Shiyurei Bracha*, Y.D. 89:3–4), *Zivchei Tzedek* (ad loc. 2), *Chaguras Shmuel* (ad loc. 8), *Ben Ish Chai* (Year 2, *Parashas Shlach* 9), and *Me'orei Ohr* (*Kitzur Shulchan Aruch on Yoreh Deah*, 89:1; by Rav Yitzchak Isaac

if one follows "*sha'os zmanios*" in the winter, then he must also follow it during the summer, possibly needing to wait up to eight hours!

One Hour

Waiting only one hour between meat and dairy, mainly germane among Jews in and/or from Amsterdam, is codified by the *Rema*, citing common custom, based on several great Ashkenazic Rishonim, including the Maharil and Maharai (author of the *Terumas Hadeshen*).[26] The *Rema* himself, though, concludes that it is nevertheless proper to wait six hours.

Three Hours

Interestingly, and shocking to some, the common German custom of waiting three hours does not seem to have an explicit *halachic* source.[27]

    Schorr, *Av Beis Din* of Bucharest), who adds that one must wait six hours after eating meat, "*bein b'kayitz, bein b'choref*," winter and summer alike. See also *Darchei Teshuva* (ad loc. 6 and 20).

26 *Rema* (Y.D. 89:1), Maharai (*Hagahos Shaarei Dura* 76:2; although according to his *talmid* in *Leket Yosher*, vol. 1, pg. 35:2, he personally waited six hours), Maharil (*Minhagim, Hilchos Issur V'Hetter* 5, s.v. *achal*; although he refers to waiting six hours as "*Minhag Chassidim*") and *Issur V'Hetter* (40:4). In *Shu"t Maharam M'Rothenburg* (Lvov [Lemberg] edition; 552, Question 2), there is a *teshuva* from Rav Avigdor Ben Rav Elya Hakohen stating that the Maharam was of this opinion as well, that one must only wait a '*sha'ah kalah*' between meat and milk. Although the Rashal (ibid.) and *Taz* (Y.D. 89:2) cast aspersions on this custom, the Vilna Gaon (*Biur HaGr"a* ad loc. 6) defends it as the *Zohar's minhag* as well, to wait an hour between all milk and meat meals [this is addressed at length in the chapter titled "To *Bentch* or Not to *Bentch*?...That is the Question"]. Relevant to the proper custom in Amsterdam, see *Minhagei Amsterdam* (pg. 20:24 and pg. 52), *Shu"t Yashiv Yitzchak* (vol. 13:25), and *Shu"t Shav V'Rafa* (vol. 3:114).

27 There is no mention of a three hour wait in any traditional *halachic* source, save for one. And, although the *Badei Hashulchan* (*Miluim* to Y.D. 89) and several others cite Rabbeinu Yerucham's *Kitzur Issur V'Hetter* (39; found at the end of his main *sefer*) as a possible source for this *minhag*, as it does mention waiting '*Gimmel Sha'os*' [using the letter '*Gimmel*'], it is important to note that

In fact, one who delves into the *sefarim* of great *Rabbanim* who served throughout Germany, from Rav Yonason Eibeshutz to Rav Samson Raphael Hirsch, will find that they all recommended keeping the full six hours! Yet, there are several theories explaining how such a widespread custom came about:[28]

---

this is an apparent misprint, as in the full *sefer* itself (*Sefer Ha'Adam*, *Nesiv* 15, vol. 2:27, pg. 137) Rabbeinu Yerucham spells out unequivocally that one must wait *"lechol hapachos sheish sha'os*, at least **six hours!**" Additionally, the source he cites for his three hour quote is Rabbeinu Peretz, who also actually mandates waiting six hours (*Hagahos* on *SMa"K* 213:8). Furthermore, the actual quote is waiting *"Gimmel Sha'os k'Rashi*," three hours as per *Rashi's shittah*. As the Chida (*Shiyurei Bracha*, Y.D. 89:2 s.v. *gam*) points out, there is no record of *Rashi* holding such an opinion; rather the opposite in *Sefer Ha'Orah* (110), that one must wait *"Shiur Seudasa Achariti"* between eating meat and cheese. Moreover, it seems likely that Rabbeinu Yerucham is not the author of the *Kitzur Issur V'Hetter* attributed to him (see Rabbi Yisrael Ta-Shma's article in *Kovetz Sinai*, Shvat-Adar 5729). For more on the topic of Rabbeinu Yerucham and three hours, see Rav Moshe Sternbuch's *Orchos Habayis* (Ch. 7, note 45), Rav Chaim Kanievsky's opinion cited in *Kovetz Nitzotzei Aish* (pg. 860:32), and Rav Asher Weiss' *Shu"t Minchas Asher* (vol. 1, 42:2, s.v. *u'mkivan*). Renowned *Rabbanim* who served throughout Germany who wrote to keep six hours include Rav Yonason Eibeshutz (*Kehillas AH"U*; *Kreisi U'Pleisi* 89:3), the *Pri Megadim* (*Kehillos* in Berlin and Frankfurt; Y.D. 89, M.Z. 1), Rav Yosef Yuzpa Koschmann (*Noheg K'tzon Yosef-Minhag Frankfurt*, *Hilchos Seudah* pg. 120:4), the Würzburger Rav, Rav Seligman Baer (Yitzchak Dov) Bamberger (cited in *Kovetz Hame'ayen*, ibid. and later in *Nishmas Avraham* ibid.; although, as mentioned previously he held *"chameish sha'os u'mashehu"* was sufficient to be considered six hours), and Rav Samson Raphael Hirsch (*Chorev* vol. 4, Ch. 68, pg. 30). [In an interesting counter-point, in his English translation of *Chorev*, titled *"Horeb*," Dayan Dr. Isidor (Yishai) Grunfeld added a footnote (pg. 327, par. 453, footnote 2) supporting the "widespread *minhag*" in "western countries" of "waiting only three hours."]

28   *Mizmor L'Dovid* (Y.D. 89:6). Rav Hamburger's explanation was written in a letter to *Mori v'Rabi* Rav Yonason Wiener (dated Rosh Chodesh Tamuz, 5765). See *Shu"t Nachlas Pinchas* (vol. 1:36, 7) for a similar assessment. An additional rationale was posited by Rabbi Shimon Silver in his recent *Talei Oros* (*Redes HaTal, Inyanei Chag HaShavuos*). He cites that regarding certain *halachos*, we

- One, by the *Mizmor L'Dovid*, is that it is possibly based on the *Pri Chodosh's* opinion of *sha'os zmanios*. He posits that if in the middle of winter, three hours is deemed sufficient waiting time, it stands to reason that it should suffice year-round as well.
- Another hypothesis, by Rav Binyomin Hamburger, author of *Shorshei Minhag Ashkenaz* and head of *Machon Moreshes Ashkenaz*, is that their original custom was to wait only one hour like the basic *halacha* cited by the *Rema*, following the majority of Ashkenazic Rishonim. Yet, when the six hours mandated by the *Rambam* and other Rishonim became more widespread, those in Ashkenaz decided to meet the rest of the world halfway, as a sort of compromise. According to this explanation, it turns out that waiting three hours is intrinsically a *chumrah* on waiting one hour.
- An additional possible theory is that since many in Germany were accustomed to eating five light meals throughout the day, as opposed to the current common three large ones, their interpretation of *"m'seudasa l'seudasa achrina"* would be waiting the three hours they were accustomed to between their meals.[29]

---

find that between one set meal and the next, there should be three hour wait. For example, the *halacha* states that on Erev Shabbos, one may not start a *seudah* after the ninth hour—which is three (*halachic*) hours before the onset of Shabbos, as then he will enter Shabbos too full to be able to accord the proper honor and respect due a Shabbos *seudah* [see Gemara *Pesachim* (99b), and *Beis Yosef* and *Shulchan Aruch* (O.C. 249:2)]. Hence, he posits that this possibly is the Gemara in *Chullin's* intent with waiting *"m'seudasa l'seudasa achrina,"* meaning the amount of time in between set meals necessitated in other places in *Shas*, which is three hours. For other *sevaros*, see Rabbi Yaakov Skoczylas' *Ohel Yaakov* (on *Bassar B'chalav*, 89, end footnote 1; quoting Rav Shimon Schwab) and *Shu"t Mishnah Halachos* (vol. 16: end 9).

29 This author has seen this theory posited by both Rav Yisroel Belsky and Rav Binyomin Hamburger. Thanks are due to Dr. Steven Oppenheimer, who related that his mother described her meals in Germany exactly this way. Rav Moshe Sternbuch (*Shu"t Teshuvos V'Hanhagos* vol. 6:171 s.v. *v'nireh*) implies this as well; explaining that the common German *minhag* is most likely based

Bentch and Go

Another opinion, and one not accepted *lemaaseh*, is that of *Tosafos*,[30] who posits that "from one meal to another" means exactly that. As soon as one finishes his meat meal, clears off the table and recites *Birkas Hamazon*, he may start a new dairy meal. Some add that this includes washing out the mouth and cleansing the palate (*kinuach* and *hadacha*). This is actually even more stringent than Rabbeinu Tam's opinion, that all one needs is *kinuach* and *hadacha*, and then one may eat dairy—even while part of the same meal![31] It is important to realize that his opinion here is categorically rejected *lemaaseh* by almost all later authorities.

A Day Away

The most stringent opinion is not to eat meat and milk on the same day (some call this a full twenty-four hours, but it seems a misnomer according to most authorities' understanding). First mentioned by Mar Ukva as his father's personal *hanhaga*, several great *Rabbanim* through the ages, including the Arizal, have been known to keep this. Interestingly, this custom is cited by Rav Chaim Palaji[32] as the proper

---

on *Tosafos'* shittah (see next paragraph above) and therefore dependent on actual meals, which in Germany would have commonly been lunch, or to be more precise, "*Gabelfrühstück*," a second light breakfast or brunch, three hours after breakfast.

30 *Tosafos* (*Chullin* 105a s.v. *l'seudasa*), *Ravyah* (1108; cited by the *Rosh* and *Hagahos Ashri* to *Chullin* Ch. 8:5), *Rema* (Y.D. 89:1).

31 Rabbeinu Tam's opinion is found in *Tosafos* (*Chullin* 104b s.v. *of*). Other Ashkenazic Rishonim who wrote similarly include the *BeHa"G* (*Hilchos Brachos*, end Ch. 6, pg. 9b, bottom right column s.v. *amar Rav Chisda*), *Sefer Yereim* (149), and the *Baal Hama'or* (in his glosses to Gemara *Chullin*, pg. 37a in the *Rif's* pagination, s.v. *Rav Yitzchak*). It is noteworthy that the Maharam M'Rothenburg, a bastion of Ashkenazic *psak* who is considered lenient regarding this topic, is quoted (*Shu"t Maharam M'Rothenburg*, Lvov [Lemberg] edition; 552, Question 2) as explicitly rejected this *shittah*, explaining that the Gemara is teaching that one may not simply perform *kinuach* and *hadacha* to eat cheese after meat.

32 *Kaf Hachaim* (Palaji; Ch. 24:25–26). This was known to be the Arizal's custom

one, and in his opinion, only those who are not able to stick to it can rely upon a "mere" six hours.

Just Sleep on It

Another remarkable, albeit not-widely accepted custom is that of sleeping after eating a meat meal. The proponents of this, including Rav Yosef Shalom Elyashiv and Rav Yaakov Yitzchak Ruderman, Rosh Yeshivas Ner Yisrael, maintain that sleeping causes the food to digest quicker, thereby lessening the required waiting period.[33] It is told that the *Chasam Sofer* wanted to start relying on this leniency, but upon awakening, every time he tried drinking his coffee (presumably with milk) it would spill. He concluded that this *hetter* must not have been

(*Taamei HaMitzvos* of Rav Chaim Vital, *Shaar HaMitzvos, Parashas Mishpatim*). See also *Shulchan HaTahor* (173:2), *Ben Ish Chai* (Year 2, *Parashas Shlach* 15), *Shu"t Torah L'Shma* (212), and *Shu"t Shraga HaMeir* (vol. 7: end 105). Some say (see *Piskei Teshuvos*, end 494) that based on his writings to *Parashas Mishpatim* (s.v. *lo sevashel*), the *Noam Elimelech* must have also generally kept this stringency (except for an allowance on Shavuos). However, it is known that there were several *Gedolim* who understood this to mean to wait an actual full twenty-four hours after eating meat before allowing milk products, including the *Shlah* (cited by his *chaver* Rav Yosef Yuzpa Haan-Norlingen in his *Yosef Ometz*, 137; remarkably, Rav Haan adds that he personally could not keep it and instead waited a mere twelve hours!) and the *Reishis Chochma* (in his *Totzaos Chaim, Shaar* 2, *Hanhaga* 45, pg. 32). Interestingly, the *Darchei Teshuva* (89:2) cites that the *Yafeh Lev* (vol. 8) asserted that the Arizal was only this stringent regarding eating dairy and meaty *foods*. Yet, he would certainly agree that *"lekuli alma b'hadachas hapeh sagi,"* a mouth rinse alone is sufficient after simply drinking milk prior to eating meat, and not mandate a long waiting period. Thanks are due to Rabbi Dr. Eliezer Brodt for pointing out several of these sources.

33 See *Daas Kedoshim* (Y.D. 89:2), *Vayaas Avraham* (of Tchechnov; pg. 333:51 and *Ateres Zekainim* ad loc. 155), *Piskei Teshuva* (vol. 3:285), *Piskei Halachos* of *HaGri"sh Elyashiv* (Y.D. Bassar B'chalav pg. 53:6; see also *Shu"t Yissa Yosef*, O.C. vol. 2:119, 6 and *Ashrei Ha'Ish*, O.C. vol. 3 pg. 442:15, who claim that Rav Elyashiv only intended to rule leniently after chicken and not actual meat). Rav Ruderman's predilection for this *shittah* was related to this author by his noted *talmid*, Rav Shmuel Bloom.

accepted in Heaven.[34] The majority of contemporary authorities as well do not rely on sleeping as a way of lessening the waiting time.[35] The Steipler Gaon is quoted as remarking that this leniency was the exclusive domain of Rav Elyashiv, as most people sleep six hours a night and he only slept three hours nightly.

Although there are many different and widespread opinions about the proper amount of time one is required to wait after eating meat, and everyone should follow his or her proper family *minhag* as per the dictum *"minhag avoseinu Torah hi,"*[36] nevertheless, it is interesting to

---

34   The story about the *Chasam Sofer* is cited in *Zichron L'Moshe* (pg. 79), *Shu"t Divrei Yisrael* (vol. 2, pg. 28, footnote) and in *Shu"t Siach Yitzchak* (399).

35   Including *Shu"t Siach Yitzchak* (ibid.), *Shu"t Teshuvos V'Hanhagos* (vol. 1:431), *Kovetz M'Beis Levi on Yoreh Deah* (pg. 34, 5; citing the opinion of Rav Shmuel Halevi Wosner), *Shu"t Beis Avi* (vol. 3, Y.D. beg. 108), *Shu"t Mishnah Halachos* (vol. 7.70), *Shu"t Shulchan Halevi* (Ch. 22·10, 1), *Doleh U'Mashkeh* (pg. 257-258 and footnote 15; citing the opinion of Rav Chaim Kanievsky, as well as his father, the Steipler Gaon). This leniency is also conspicuously absent from the vast majority of earlier authorities.

36   *Tosafos* (*Menachos* 20b s.v. *v'nifsal*). See also *Shorshei Minhag Ashkenaz* (vol. 1, pg. 18) citing the late great Ponovezher Rosh Yeshiva, Rav Elazar Menachem Mann Shach, on the importance of keeping family *minhagim*, even if it runs contrary to accepted convention. Indeed, in his letter cited previously, Rav Binyomin Hamburger adds that this was also the view of the *Chazon Ish*, Rav Shlomo Zalman Auerbach, and Rav Yaakov Kamenetsky. Nonetheless, there were/are several contemporary *Poskim*, including Rav Yosef Shalom Elyashiv (*He'aros B'Maseches Chullin* 105b s.v. *v'ha*), Rav Shmuel *Halevi* Wosner (cited in the aforementioned letter), Rav Menashe Klein (*Shu"t Mishnah Halachos* vol. 16: end 9), Rav Shimon Schwab (cited in the aforementioned letter), Rav Chaim Kanievsky (*Teshuvos* printed in *Kashrus in the Kitchen Q & A*, pg. 209), and Rav Yitzchak Yosef (*Yalkut Yosef, Issur V'Hetter* vol. 3, 89:17), who when asked, were known to have shown predilection for telling those who normally waited less than six hours due to family *minhag*, that they should start keeping the full six if at all possible. For further discussions on this topic, see *Shu"t Pe'as Sadecha* (vol. 3, Y.D. 29; thanks are due to R' Sam Neufeld for pointing out this source), *Shu"t Minchas Asher* (vol. 1, 42:2), Rav Aharon Pfeiffer's *Kitzur Shulchan Aruch* (*Bassar B'chalav*, Ch. 10:16), *Maadanei Asher*

note that the core requirement of waiting is based on the actions of those with less than perfect intentions. As it states in *Pirkei Avos*, "Who is wise? One who learns from everyone."[37]

(*Issur V'Hetter*, 41:3 s.v. *ul'dina*), *Mesores Moshe* (vol. 2, pg. 176:26), *Shu"t Yashiv Yitzchak* (vol. 13:25), *Shu"t Shav V'Rafa* (vol. 3:114), *Kuntress Yad Dodi* (*Kashrus*:#32a-b, and *Klalim/Minhagim*:#5a-b, 15, and 17), and Rav Herschel Schachter's *maamar* titled "*Hashbeia Hishbea*" (*Kovetz Beis Yitzchak* vol. 39, 5767; pg. 516:5; thanks are due to Rabbi Yisroel Israel and Rabbi Dr. Eliezer Brodt for providing this source).

37   *Avos* (Ch. 4, Mishnah 1).

Chapter 5

Hard Cheese Complexities

THE ONE DAIRY ITEM THAT requires a six-hour wait after consumption before eating meat is hard cheese. This prohibition, although not mentioned in the Gemara, nevertheless dates back to the days of one of the greatest Ashkenazic Rishonim, Rav Meir ben Rav Baruch, the renowned Maharam M'Rothenburg (1215–1293).[1] It seems that a while after he ate a piece of hard cheese, he reported that he still felt cheese residue in his mouth. He concluded that hard cheese shares similar properties with meat, and therefore maintained that it is proper to

---

1   *Shu"t Maharam M'Rothenburg* (Lvov [Lemberg] edition; 552, Question 1). This also cited by the *Mordechai* (*Chullin* 627) and the *Hagahos Ashri* (Glosses to the *Rosh* on *Chullin* 105:5). On a historical sidenote, the Maharam M'Rothenburg was *niftar* in captivity after being unjustly imprisoned for seven years in Ensisheim Fortress, in order to force the resident Jews to pay an exorbitant ransom to fill the king's (Rudolf I of Germany) depleted coffers. The Maharam refused to allow himself to be ransomed, fearing that it would set a dangerous precedent of rulers holding *Rabbanim* captive and forcing the unfortunate Jews to pay the price. Indeed, a short while after his passing, the king attempted to do the same for the Maharam's prized pupil, the *Rosh*, who only narrowly avoided capture, escaping to Spain. Tragically, the Maharam's body was only allowed to be buried fourteen years later, when a ransom was paid by Alexander ben Shlomo Wimpfen, who was subsequently laid to rest beside the Maharam, in the Jewish cemetery of Worms, Germany (also known as *"Heiliger Sand"*), nowadays commonly considered the oldest surviving Jewish cemetery in Europe.

wait a corresponding amount of time after eating such cheese before partaking in a meat meal, as one normally would do after eating meat. Although some authorities, including the Maharshal (who was very adamant that no one else should have to wait due to the Maharam's anecdotal account),[2] felt that the Maharam only mandated this for himself as a personal stringency, nevertheless, most authorities understood that the Maharam was introducing a new *halacha*, meant for all of Klal Yisrael.[3] In fact, this is how the *Rema* rules practically.[4] Followed by virtually all later authorities,[5] the *Rema* wrote that it is appropriate to wait a commensurate amount of time after eating hard cheese as one would wait after eating meat.[6] However, it is important to note that the

---

2   *Yam Shel Shlomo* (*Chullin* Ch. 8:6).

3   *Issur V'Hetter* (40:8 s.v. *vay*), *Beis Yosef* (O.C. 173 s.v. *v'yeish machmirim*), *Darchei Moshe* (Y.D. 89:2), *Shach* (ad loc. 17).

4   *Rema* (Y.D. 89: end 2).

5   Including the *Shach* (Y.D. 89:15), *Taz* (ad loc. 4), *Pri Chodosh* (ad loc. 16), *Levush* (ad loc. 2), *Pri Megadim* (ad loc. M.Z. 4 and S.D.15 and 16), Chida (*Shiyurei Bracha* ad loc. 13), *Machatzis Hashekel* (ad loc. 15), *Chochmas Adam* (40:13), *Yad Yehuda* (89, *Peirush Hakatzar* 26), *Atzei Ha'Olah* (*Bassar B'chalav* Ch. 3:16), *Chaguras Shmuel* (Y.D. 89:18), *Kitzur Shulchan Aruch* (46:11), *Zivchei Tzedek* (89:27), *Aruch Hashulchan* (ad loc. 11), *Mishnah Berurah* (494, *Shaar Hatziyun* 15), *Kaf Hachaim* (Y.D. 89:46 and 47), and *Me'orei Ohr* (*Kitzur Shulchan Aruch* on *Yoreh Deah*, 89:1; by Rav Yitzchak Isaac Schorr, *Av Beis Din* of Bucharest). On the other hand, Rav Aharon Wirmush, renowned *talmid* of the *Shaagas Aryeh*, in his *Me'orei Ohr* (vol. 7, *Chullin daf* 105 s.v. *chala bar chamra*) offers a notable dissenting opinion. He vehemently argues on all the above, claiming that the *Shach* and *Taz* misunderstood the *Rema's* intent, and that the *Rema* was only mandating waiting *an hour* after hard cheese, following the *Zohar's* precedent (as discussed in previous chapters). He adds that the Maharshal truly understood the Maharam's *chumrah* correctly, that he meant it only for himself, citing proof from the *Terumas Hadeshen's* (end 101) brief discussion of the topic. The *Me'orei Ohr* concludes reserving very strong terms for those who wait six hours after hard cheese, calling it *"chumrah yeseirah v'taus, b'chlal yuhara u'minus."*

6   Since the whole waiting period after hard cheese is based on the waiting

Rema himself[7] qualifies that this *halacha* is intrinsically a *chumrah*, and concludes that "one may not chastise anyone who does not follow it."[8]

Defining Hard Cheese

What exactly constitutes "hard cheese," and thus necessitates a waiting period? As with many other *halachic* issues, this is debated by the authorities. The accepted conclusion is that if the cheese in question fits into one or more of the following categories, then it would be considered "hard cheese" and thus requires a full waiting period:

- It is aged at least six months[9] (Parmesan would usually fit this category).
- It is "holey"[10] as a result of production (as in "holey Swiss cheese!").
- It is extremely fatty and greasy[11] (making the taste linger much longer).

---

period after meat, one may not wait less time after eating meat than he would after eating hard cheese—*Shach* (Y.D. 89:17).

7   Interestingly, and although the *Rema* rules that this hard cheese rule applies equally whether waiting to eat meat or fowl, the Maharam M'Rothenburg himself (*Shu"t* ibid.), who is the *mekor* of this *halacha*, did not mandate a waiting period between eating hard cheese and poultry, but rather only prior to eating real meat. The *Beis Yosef* (ad loc.) wrote similarly to the *Rema's psak*, adding that if the Maharam would have seen the *Zohar* (discussed in previous chapters), he would have ruled stringently regarding consuming fowl after hard cheese as well. Yet, inexplicably, in his later authoritative *Shulchan Aruch*, the *Beis Yosef* made no mention of this ruling. Although beyond the scope of this discussion, this intriguing issue is addressed at length in this author's *M'Shulchan Yehuda*.

8   There are several *halachic* dispensations due to this. See for example, *Maadanei Hashulchan* (Y.D. 89, *Mataamei Hashulchan* 11).

9   *Issur V'Hetter, Shach, Pri Chodosh, Pri Megadim, Machatzis Hashekel, Chaguras Shmuel* (ibid.), *Ben Ish Chai* (Year 2, *Parashas Shlach* 15). See *Shu"t Shulchan Halevi* (Ch. 22:1 s.v. *u'be'air*).

10 *Issur V'Hetter, Taz, Pri Megadim, Atzei Ha'Olah, Zivchei Tzedek, Kaf Hachaim* (ibid.), *Chasam Sofer* (Glosses ad loc. on the *Taz*).

- It is very strong and sharp[12] (Limburger would be a good example of this).

Any cheese that does not meet at least one of these requirements, for all intents and purposes, is considered soft cheese and would only entail rinsing and cleaning of the mouth and hands before eating meat. As detailed in previous chapters, this is the *halachically* mandated three-step process of *kinuach*—palate cleansing by eating a hard food item (e.g., cracker); *rechitza*—handwashing; and *hadacha*—rinsing out of the mouth.[13]

There are other customs as well:

- There are those who follow the standard understanding of the *Zohar* and wait one hour after eating *any* dairy product.[14]
- Others wait half an hour, even though there is no actual specific known source for this. There are different rationales offered to explain this custom, most based on the Talmudic dictum of *"m'palga karov karu lei*—from halfway is already considered close,"[15] meaning by waiting at least a half hour, it is as if one waited an hour.
- Additionally, there are those who are also strict with making *Birkas Hamazon* between a dairy and a meat meal. This is a tremendous dispute among *halachic* authorities, whether *Birkas*

---

11 *Aruch Hashulchan* (ibid.).

12 *Taz, Pri Megadim, Chaguras Shmuel,* and *Kitzur Shulchan Aruch* (ibid.). However, see *Chasam Sofer, Atzei Ha'Olah,* and *Yad Yehuda* (ibid.).

13 *Yoreh Deah* (89:2); as discussed at length in previous chapters.

14 As discussed in a previous chapter, the *Zohar* (*Parashas Mishpatim* pg. 125:1; cited by the *Beis Yosef*, O.C. 173 s.v. *v'yeish* and *Biur HaGr"a*, Y.D. 89:11) writes that everyone should wait between dairy and meat meals "one meal or one hour." Although there are many varying interpretations offered for this enigmatic remark, the most common one is that "one hour" is referring to mandating a waiting period of one hour even after eating dairy.

15 *Kiddushin* (12a). There are many authorities who apply this *klal* to waiting a half hour after eating *milchigs*.

Hamazon is required after eating dairy foods before being allowed to eat meat. However, everyone agrees that it is indeed *required* if one ate actual hard cheese.[16]

American and Yellow Cheese

The standard everyday cheeses used for grilled cheese, cheese toasts, pizza etc., [American, Yerushalayim, Mozzerella, Achuza, Gush Chalav etc.] would not seem to fit any of the above criteria and thus would not require a waiting period. In fact, the majority of contemporary authorities including the *Chazon Ish*, Rav Aharon Kotler, Rav Yosef Eliyahu Henkin, and Rav Moshe Feinstein,[17] rule that they are not considered *halachic* hard cheese. Rav Aharon related that most people nowadays do not know what real hard cheese is—a cheese that needs a *"rib-eisen"*

---

16 These issues are detailed at length in a previous chapter titled "To *Bentch* or Not to *Bentch*?...That is the Question."

17 These *Gedolim* include the *Chazon Ish* (cited in *Orchos Rabbeinu* vol. 3, pg. 77:34; new edition vol. 4, pg. 25:1 and in *Maaseh Ish* vol. 5:pg. 22; he held that the cheese must be aged for a full year to be considered hard cheese; for a possible explanation see *Shu"t Maadanei Melachim* 87 and 88), Rav Aharon Kotler (cited in *Kitzur Shulchan Aruch*, Pfeiffer; on *Bassar B'chalav*, vol. 1, *Kuntress Habiurim* pg. 138), Rav Yosef Eliyahu Henkin (*Shu"t Gevuros Eliyahu* vol. 2-Y.D. 13; he holds that one only needs to wait one hour), Rav Moshe Feinstein (cited in *Shu"t Mishnah Halachos* vol. 16:9), the Debreciner Rav (*teshuva* printed in *Pischei Halacha* on *Hilchos Kashrus* pg. 108), Rav Yisrael Yaakov Fischer (*Shu"t Even Yisrael* vol. 9:68), Rav Moshe Halberstam (cited in *Shu"t Shav V'Rafa* vol. 2:26), Rav Ben Tzion Abba-Shaul (cited in *Sefer Hakashrus* Ch. 10, footnote 122; he holds that one only needs to wait one hour), Rav Chaim Pinchas Scheinberg (cited in *Shu"t Shav V'Rafa* vol. 2:26; but maintains that this *hetter* is *"b'dieved"*), Rav Chaim Kanievsky (cited in *Nezer Chaim, Devarim Nochachim* 124; who rules like his uncle, the *Chazon Ish*), Rav Moshe Sternbuch (*Shu"t Teshuvos V'Hanhagos* vol. 6:171 s.v. *lefi aniyus daati*; he writes that although he personally is *machmir* to wait six hours, nonetheless waiting one hour along with *kinuach* and *hadacha* is indeed sufficient), Rav Ovadiah Yosef (*Shu"t Yabia Omer* vol. 6, Y.D. 7:4 and *Shu"t Yechaveh Daas* vol. 3:58; he maintains that the whole *din* is essentially a *chumrah*), the *Rivevos Efraim* (cited in *Yagel Yaakov* footnote 247), Rav Yisroel Belsky (*Shu"t Shulchan Halevi* Ch. 22:1; see also his

(sharp grater or possibly a hacksaw) to cut off pieces, as the old-time hard cheese wheels sold in Europe did. This would exclude our common cheeses, which can easily be pulled apart with our bare hands.[18]

However, if it's so simple, why are there people who claim that one must wait after eating any sort of semi-hard cheese? Some even take this a step further and assert that it is "*Minhag Eretz Yisrael*" to wait a *full six hours* after eating pizza! What is the basis for such a position?

Authentic European hard cheeses. Note the actual crust that is characteristic of these hard cheeses (picture courtesy of SPAR, Davos Dorf, Switzerland).

Minhag Eretz Yisrael?

The answer is based on a few enigmatic statements and responsa by several contemporary *Gedolei Eretz Yisrael*—Rav Shlomo Zalman Auerbach, Rav Yosef Shalom Elyashiv, and Rav Shmuel *Halevi* Wosner:

- Rav Shlomo Zalman Auerbach is quoted as ruling that one must wait the "full count" after eating the Israeli "yellow cheese" (Yerushalayim, Achuza, Gush Chalav, etc.).
- Rav Elyashiv and Rav Wosner both wrote responsa asserting similarly, that although not truly fitting the "hard cheese" criteria established by earlier authorities, nevertheless, one should still wait after these cheeses.
- Following their lead, several other authorities rule stringently as well.[19]

---

earlier *teshuva* in *Kovetz Mesorah* vol. 20, pg. 91–92; Adar 5764), Rav Asher Weiss (*Minchas Asher al HaTorah, Shemos* 61:2), Rav Shmuel Kamenetsky (*Kovetz Halachos, Shavuos* pg. 135), and Rav Dovid Feinstein (cited in *Shu"t Vidibarta Bam* vol. 1:212, pg. 561 s.v. *v'shamaati* and *Kuntress Yad Dodi*, Y.D. Kashrus, Question 26).

18 See *Megillas Sefer* (on *Bassar B'chalav* 89:5 s.v. *u'vagvinos*) who proves this from Gemara *Shabbos* 121b.

19 Including the *Maadanei Hashulchan* (89:30 and *Shu"t Maadanei Melachim* 89 and 90), the *Mishnah Halachos* (*Shu"t* vol. 16:9), the *Mishnas Yosef* (*Shu"t*

- Consequently, many people, especially in Eretz Yisrael, wait six hours after eating these cheeses.

Yet, if one would properly and thoroughly analyze the actual responsae of these *Gedolim*, he might conclude rather differently:

- Finding out Rav Shlomo Zalman Auerbach's authentic opinion is easier said than done. His opinion is quoted in no less than six separate *sefarim* (!), each relating conflicting and contradictory accounts of what his ruling actually was.[20] The varied accounts include a lenient ruling on this topic, namely that these "yellow cheeses" are not considered hard cheese at all. It would therefore seem incongruous to be stringent exclusively on account of his reportedly *machmir* opinion.
- Rav Wosner wrote his responsum on this topic approximately fifty years ago, stating that he personally was stringent, as (at the time) it was impossible to tell how long the cheeses were aged, since there was no manufacturer's dating code printed on it. Since it was possible that the "yellow cheese" sold was aged

---

vol. 9:184), and the *Avnei Yashpei* (*Shu"t* vol. 6, 112:2), all of whom say that they follow the *psak* and rationales of these *Gedolim* to rule stringently with "yellow cheese." The *Minchas Yitzchak* was also quoted as saying *"yeish makom lehachmir"* (cited in *Shu"t Teshuvos V'Hanhagos* vol. 2:388 and vol. 6:171).

20 *Sefer Hakashrus* (Ch. 10:50, footnote 126) quotes Rav Shlomo Zalman as being stringent as the high fat percentages used in modern day "yellow cheese" causes the taste to linger much longer, similar to real hard cheese. Yet, *Me'or HaShabbos* (vol. 3, *Teshuvos*, 38:1) cites a different (albeit ultimately erroneous; as soon explained) reason entirely why Rav Shlomo Zalman was *machmir*, as nowadays, with modern day chemicals etc., cheese can be "aged as if six months" in a relatively short time, and therefore the common "yellow cheese" is considered as if it was already aged six months. Yet, two other reliable sources, Rav Aharon Pfeiffer's *Kitzur Shulchan Aruch* (on *Bassar B'chalav*, vol. 1, *Kuntress Habiurim* pg. 138), and in *Kovetz Moriah* (Teves 5756; *Piskei Halachos shel HaGaon Rav Shlomo Zalman*) both report that Rav Shlomo Zalman maintained that "yellow cheese" is not considered hard cheese, and no waiting period is required. However, they relate that he personally was indeed stringent. *Halichos Shlomo* (*Moadim* vol. 2, Ch. 12; 13, footnote 50) tries to

for six months, he was *machmir*. However, nowadays, with the actual manufacturing date printed on every package, one can easily see if this cheese was aged for six months or not. In fact, more recent accounts of Rav Wosner's opinion are that one does not have to wait after eating these "yellow cheeses."[21]

---

synthesize all these accounts and opines that Rav Shlomo Zalman originally only mandated waiting after *real* hard cheeses. But, in his later years, after "it became difficult to tell the differences between cheeses," he became more stringent and ruled as well for others. The only problem with this is that in *Shu"t Shav V'Rafa* (vol. 2:26), Rav Shmuel Auerbach is quoted as saying that his father, Rav Shlomo Zalman, held that there is absolutely no reason to be stringent with "yellow cheeses" at all. This is also similar to what Rav Shlomo Zalman's son-in-law, Rav Zalman Nechemiah Goldberg, personally told this author, that his *shver* was only *makpid* on real 'Kashkeval' cheese, and not the "yellow cheeses" at all. This was further confirmed to this author by his son, Rav Aharon Goldberg, who actually stayed and ate with Rav Shlomo Zalman in his final years. On the other hand, to further complicate matters, Rav Ezriel Auerbach was quoted as saying that his father always waited six hours after eating "yellow cheeses." Quite fascinatingly, in the recently published *Maadanei Shlomo* (on *Dalet Chelkei Shulchan Aruch*, pg. 242:5), Rav Shlomo Zalman's *talmid*, Rav Yerachmiel Fried (author of *Yom Tov Sheini Kehilchaso*) writes that he noted to Rav Shlomo Zalman in his lifetime that there were differing accounts of his true *psak* [which he writes was that Rav Shlomo Zalman really held that there is no issue but nevertheless the *minhag* in his house was indeed to wait], and concludes that Rav Shlomo Zalman did this on purpose; that he did not want to take a public stance and be *machria* one way or the other.

21 *Shu"t Shevet Halevi* (vol. 2:35). See *Shu"t Mishnah Halachos* (ibid. s.v. *uvadavar*) who although ruling to be *machmir* like Rav Elyashiv and the *Shevet Halevi's psak*, nevertheless concludes that if there are manufacturing dates printed on the cheese packaging, one may indeed rely on them. See also *Kovetz M'Beis Levi* (vol. 6, 5755; from Rav Wosner's Beis Midrash) who concludes that one does not need to wait after "yellow cheese." This is also corroborated (in *Shu"t Shav V'Rafa* ibid.) by Rav Shlomo Berman, (the Steipler Gaon's son-in-law, and Rosh Yeshivas Ponovezh) who related that Rav Wosner told him explicitly that one does not have to wait after such cheeses.

- As for Rav Elyashiv's responsum, he definitely does rule that one must wait after eating such cheese.[22] However, his reasoning has puzzled many. Rav Elyashiv writes that one must be stringent, for the taste of these "yellow cheeses" is *"charifah v'chazakah*—sharp and strong," terms which many would only associate with such strong cheeses as Limburger, Gold Cheddar, and Roquefort.
- Several later authorities, including Rav Yisrael Yaakov Fischer, *Raavad* of the *Badatz Eidah Hacharedis* of Yerushalayim, have been perplexed by Rav Elyashiv's words, since "yellow cheese" as we know it is neither sharp nor strong tasting.[23] Interestingly, Rav Elyashiv's *talmid muvhak*, Rav Yosef Efrati, writes that Rav Elyashiv was stringent on "yellow cheese" only due to *chumrah* and *minhag*, but held that *me'ikar hadin* one does not need to be stringent, and especially not in *Chutz La'aretz*. A similar sentiment was expressed by Rav Elyashiv's son-in-law, Rav Ezriel Auerbach, that even though *me'ikar din* one does not have to wait six hours for such cheeses, nevertheless, the *minhag* is still to wait.[24]
- Additionally, over a hundred years ago, the *Ben Ish Chai* related that *Minhag Yerushalayim* is to be lenient with such "hard cheeses."[25] Moreover, as mentioned previously, the great *Chazon Ish*, final arbiter for much of Eretz Yisrael,[26] ruled that nowadays,

---

22 *Kovetz Teshuvos* (vol. 1:58, 2). This *teshuva* is originally from 5744/1984, and was reprinted in *Kovetz B'Nesiv Hachalav* (vol. 1; Tishrei 5763, pg. 97).

23 *Shu"t Even Yisrael* (vol. 9:68, 2), *Shu"t Shulchan Halevi* (Ch. 22:1), and *Shu"t Shav V'Rafa* (ibid. quoting *Mori v'Rabi* Rav Yonason Wiener).

24 *Shu"t Yissa Yosef* (O.C. vol. 2:120). Rav Ezriel Auerbach's opinion is cited in *Kuntress Sheilos U'Teshuvos Ketzaros B'Inyanei Issur V'Hetter* (pg. 20:26).

25 *Ben Ish Chai* (Year 2, *Parashas Shlach* 15).

26 Cited in *Orchos Rabbeinu* (vol. 3, pg. 77:34; new edition vol. 4, pg. 25:1) and *Maaseh Ish* (vol. 5, pg. 22). The *Chazon Ish's* nephew (and Rav Elyashiv's son-in-law), Rav Chaim Kanievsky (cited in *Nezer Chaim, Devarim Nochachim* 124)

unless a cheese is aged *for a full year*, it is not considered "hard cheese"—and our "yellow cheeses" most definitely do not meet that criterion.

In conclusion, although many in Eretz Yisrael are indeed stringent, the claim that the prevailing custom in Eretz Yisrael is to wait after "yellow cheese," seems unsubstantiated. In fact, to quote *Mori v'Rabi* Rav Yaakov Blau *zt"l* of the *Badatz Eidah Hacharedis* (to this author) on this topic, "to wait after yellow cheese is a *chumrah bli taam* (a stringency without reason)."

Quick Age?

One of the recent *sevaros* that justify being *machmir* on this subject is that nowadays, with modern day chemicals etc., cheese can be "aged as if six months" in a relatively short time, and therefore the common "yellow cheese" is considered *as if* it was already aged six months, and consequently is *halachic* hard cheese.

The only problem with this idea is that it…is not exactly true!

Several years ago, this author visited Tnuva's main cheese-making factory in Israel with three renowned kashrus and *halachic* experts, Rav Yonason Wiener, Rav Mordechai Kuber, and my father, Rav Manish Spitz.[27] The Tnuva factory cheese specialists explained that this rationale does not hold water, and no additional chemicals or enzymes are used to "speed up" the basic cheese process, which is pretty much the same as it always was—sitting and aging in a "salt water bath" for varying periods of time.

This is echoed by renowned kashrus expert and chief *Posek* for the OU, Rav Yisroel Belsky, who uses very sharp terms to disprove the claims of the *machmirim* based on this erroneous rationale.[28]

---

rules this way as well. See *Shu"t Maadanei Melachim* (87 and 88) for a possible explanation.

27 This factory inspection was part of an Ohr Lagolah Kashrus 'field trip' to train budding *Semicha* students with practical kashrus experience.

28 *Shu"t Shulchan Halevi* (Ch. 22:1, *Hosafa* s.v. *gam*).

The Tnuva expert also informed us that the "yellow cheese" average processing time is only eighteen days! This was later confirmed to this author by *Mori v'Rabi* Rav Yaakov Blau *zt"l*, who headed the *hashgacha* department of the *Badatz Eidah Hachareidis*. He added that standard "yellow cheese" is not aged for more than twenty-five days—nowhere near the six-month mark. So even if "yellow cheese" continues to age in the fridge and on the store shelf, it still has a long way to go to reach six months. This is why Rav Blau called waiting after its consumption a *"chumrah bli taam."*[29] A similar ruling was issued by Rav Yisrael Yaakov Fischer—after he learned the actual ins and outs of "yellow cheese" processing—that there is no requirement to wait six hours after its consumption.[30]

A Cheesy *Hetter*

Pizza and other melted-cheese favorites actually have an additional consideration to be lenient, even if actual hard cheese is used. The *Yad Yehuda* rules that if hard cheese is melted, it no longer retains the status of hard cheese and one is not required to wait after eating it.[31]

Although not unanimously accepted, (as the cheese's taste remains unchanged even in its melted form),[32] and there is some contemporary debate as to his exact intent (whether he was referring to cheese melted

---

29 Interestingly, Rav Blau related that he personally was stringent on waiting six hours since his *rebbi* did, and therefore he was beholden to as well, even though he held that there was no *halachic* reason to do so.

30 As cited in *Halichos Even Yisrael* (on *Moadim* vol. 1, pg. 230, footnote 21 s.v. *v'seeper*). This was seemingly the basis of his *psak* in *Shu"t Even Yisrael* (vol. 9:68).

31 *Yad Yehuda* (89, *Peirush Hakatzar* 26). However, there is some contemporary debate as to his exact intent. See Rav Doniel Neustadt's *The Daily Halachah Discussion* (pg. 238:22), Rav Binyomin Forst's *Pischei Halacha: The Laws of Kashrus* (Ch. 8:2, 96), and *Kovetz Ohr Yisroel* (vol. 6:pg. 89, s.v. *ulam*).

32 Including the *Ben Ish Chai* (ibid.), Rav Yosef Shalom Elyashiv (ibid.), *Badei Hashulchan* (pg. 63, *Biurim* s.v. *v'chein*), *Avnei Yashpei* (ibid.), and *Maadanei Melachim* (*Shu"t* 91). They all write that there should be no difference between melted or solid hard cheese concerning the waiting period.

into or onto a food), nevertheless, several later authorities follow this ruling as well.³³ They assert that one may definitely rely on this leniency regarding pizza since it is made with *melted* Mozzarella or "yellow cheese."³⁴

In conclusion, although there are those who are stringent, there is very strong basis for the generally accepted custom of not waiting six hours after grilled cheese or pizza.

Still, these days, when it's popular to use all types of exotic ingredients in gourmet cooking, it may be worthwhile to check your cheese packaging carefully, to ascertain whether it might possibly be a true "six-hour cheese."

---

33 Including the *Atzei Ha'Olah* (*Bassar B'chalav* 3:17, *Chukei Chaim* 16), Rav Dovid Feinstein (cited in *Shu"t Vidibarta Bam* vol. 1: end 212, s.v. *v'shamaati*), Rav Ezriel Auerbach (cited in Rabbi Avi Wiesenfeld's *Kashrus in the Kitchen* Q & A, *Teshuvos* pg. 216), Rav Yisroel Belsky (*Shu"t Shulchan Halevi* ibid. s.v. *zos*), and Rav Chaim Kalman Guttman (*Kovetz Pri Temarim* vol. 5, pg. 128:82).

34 An additional current issue is that of enzyme modified cheese (EMC): cheese that is modified to create a much stronger taste in a smaller amount of time. Generally, this is then mixed and essentially diluted with other bulkier ingredients, such as whey or blander cheese powders, to create cheese sauces, etc. According to www.cheesescience.net, EMCs are only available as pastes or dried to form powders; in other words, they are almost impossible to eat or even obtain by themselves. EMCs, which may have approximately fifteen to thirty times the flavor intensity of natural cheese, are used to give a cheese flavor note to products such as processed or analogue cheese, cheese powders, soups, sauces, dips, crackers, salad dressings, and in coatings for snack foods. In volume, the other ingredients constitute the majority of the seasoning. Since the cheese actually remains a soft cheese (albeit with a very strong flavor), once it is diluted to become a fraction of the seasoning, it stands to reason that one would not have to wait after eating it, especially according to the *Yad Yehuda*, as it is technically not a true hard cheese, but rather a seasoned soft cheese.

Chapter 6

The Great Dishwasher Debate

ALTHOUGH WE LIVE IN A world of technological advancements and achievements, and their impact on *halacha* can seem complicated and confusing, *baruch Hashem* Klal Yisrael has been blessed through the ages with *Poskim* who have enlightened us as to the practical application of *halacha* in new and developing areas.

Rav Shlomo Zalman Auerbach in particular, among other *Gedolei* and *Poskei Yisrael*, was known to relish hearing about technological advances and demonstrating how the *halacha* still applied to them, for as we know, "*Ain kol chodosh tachas hashemesh*—There is nothing new under the sun."[1] In this spirit, this chapter will focus on the intricacies, as well as the issues the *Poskim* deal with, in deciding the *halachic* status of a not-so-recent technological advancement: the dishwasher.

Theoretical questions:

- Do I really need separate dishwashers for my meat and milk dishes?
- By accident, my dishwasher washed my *milchig* and *fleishig* dishes together! Do I need to throw everything out?

Assuming your dishwasher is not your significant other (read: your spouse), in which case one should suffice to wash all of your dishes (of course not together), these are somewhat complicated questions, and in order to properly answer them, we must first gain at least a basic understanding of the complex *halachic* issues involved.

---

1   *Koheles* (Ch. 1:9).

Nat Bar Nat (or Not Bar Not)

Not (no pun intended) the name of someone mentioned in the Gemara, nor the latest Jewish music song (yet!), this is actually the term used to define indirect taste transfer. *Nat Bar Nat* stands for "*Nosein Taam Bar Nosein Taam.*" A *Nosein Taam* refers to a direct transfer of taste. For example if one would cook a nice, hefty cholent with meat inside, the meat would transfer direct taste into the rest of the cholent, rendering the entire cholent *fleishig* (unless of course the chef was a little too stingy in the meat department and the minuscule piece was *battel b'shishim*, and *halachically* considered nullified).[2] A *Nosein Taam Bar Nosein Taam* refers to indirect, or secondary, transfer.

Case in point:

If one would use a clean, *ben yomo* (used within the last twenty-four hours) *fleishig* pot to cook macaroni, and subsequently placed the macaroni on a plate and then mixed them with cheese—is that considered *Bassar B'chalav*?

The answer is no. It is one-hundred percent permissible to eat, for there was no direct contact between the meat and the cheese, only a weak secondary contact. This is known as *Nat Bar Nat*. In order for this *hetter* to occur, the meat and milk must be at least twice removed from each other. (Think of the branches on a family tree; Uncle Earl might be directly related to you, but that does not really make him related to Cousin Edna.)

There is the transfer of:

1. The *bliyah* (imparted taste) of meat (absorbed) into the pot.
2. The *bliyah* from the pot into the macaroni.
3. The *bliyah* from the macaroni into the cheese.

Therefore, the macaroni and cheese is not considered *Bassar B'chalav*, since there are (at least) two degrees of separation in between them.

---

2   See *Shulchan Aruch* and main commentaries to *Yoreh Deah* 98. Barring specific circumstances, this is the standard rule of nullification in *halacha*. If there is present sixty times the amount of non-kosher, it is considered nullified. This rule of thumb and its various exclusions are discussed throughout the book.

Please note that this *hetter*, however, only applies by *Bassar B'chalav*; it does not apply by *bliyos* of *issur* or *treif* (actual non-kosher).³

There is much discussion in the *Poskim* as to the parameters of this *din*:

- The *Shulchan Aruch* rules that *Nat Bar Nat* is a *hetter* even *lechatchilla* (intentionally).
- The *Rema* argues that one may only rely on this dispensation *b'dieved* (post facto).⁴

That means, according to the *Shulchan Aruch*, (back to our example) if one would use a clean, *ben yomo fleishig* pot to cook macaroni, and subsequently placed the macaroni on a plate, then he would now be allowed to mix cheese into the macaroni.⁵ According to the *Rema*, however, only if one already mixed in the cheese would it be permissible to eat; if he had not yet done so, it would be forbidden to mix them together in order to eat the macaroni with cheese.

"O.K. While it is always nice to be enlightened about a *halachic* concept," one might say, "what does this have to do with dishwashers?"

The answer is—everything!

---

3   Important note: There are numerous scenarios and similar sounding cases in which the *din* may be very different (for example, many *Poskim* are *machmir* that there is no *hetter* of *Nat Bar Nat* applicable regarding roasting and there is also much debate among the Acharonim whether *Nat Bar Nat* applies *b'shaas bishul*); therefore, one may certainly not *pasken* for oneself based on this chapter. The *halacha* presented here is simplified to present the issues in an understandable manner. One must ask a competent *halachic* authority for guidance in case of an actual *sheilah* in this and all other *halachic* matters.

4   *Shulchan Aruch* (Y.D. 95:1) and *Rema* (ad loc. 2).

5   Although there is some debate, this description follows the basic understanding of the *Shulchan Aruch's* true opinion *lemaaseh*, as per the majority of authorities, including the *Issur V'Hetter* (34:1), *Shach* (Y.D. 95:3), *Taz* (Y.D. 94, Daf Acharon* s.v. *assur*), *Pri Chodosh* (Y.D. 95:1) *Ba'er Heitiv* (ad loc. 5), *Kreisi U'Pleisi* (ad loc. 1), *Beis Lechem Yehuda* (ad loc. 3), *Knesses Hagedolah* (ad loc. *Hagahos* on *Beis Yosef*, end 20), *Pri Megadim* (ad loc. M.Z. 4, end s.v. *ul'inyan*), *Erech Hashulchan* (ad loc. 5), *Kehillas Yehuda* (ad loc.), *Zivchei Tzedek* (ad loc. 2), and *Kaf Hachaim* (ad loc. 1). This follows the precedent of several Rishonim, including the *SMa"K* (213), *Hagahos Maimoniyos* (*Hilchos Maachalos Assuros*

Washing Dishes = *Nat Bar Nat*?

A few paragraphs later, the *Shulchan Aruch*, following the lead of several Rishonim, including the *Rosh*, *Ramban*, and *Rashba*,[6] equates our case of macaroni to washing dishes. He states that even if one washed milk and meat dishes together, as long as the dishes themselves were clean of actual pieces or *mamashos* (literally, substance), there would not be a transfer of taste, for this too would be considered a *Nat Bar Nat* occurrence, and therefore permitted.

Ch. 9:23), Rabbeinu Yerucham (*Sefer Ha'Adam*, Nesiv 15, vol. 5:28; pg. 137, fourth column), and the *Mordechai* (*Chullin*, 708 and 754). Accordingly, even though the *Shulchan Aruch* would hold that *Nat Bar Nat* is *lechatchilla*, he was referring to once the cooking was already done, that now it comes into play and one may then rely on it *lechatchilla*. However, one may still not cause a *Nat Bar Nat*. A good example would be to cook macaroni in a *fleishig ben yomo* pot in order to later mix it with cheese, will still be prohibited; but if it was already cooked in such a pot, the *Shulchan Aruch* would hold that one may now mix in cheese. On the other hand, there are several contemporary Sefardic *Poskim*, most notably Rav Ovadiah Yosef (*Shu"t Yabia Omer* vol. 8, Y.D. 43:1–5) and Rav Shlomo Amar (*Shu"t Shama Shlomo* vol. 1, Y.D. 2, and vol. 2, Y.D. 5), who maintain that the *ikar* intention of the *Shulchan Aruch* (as per his *Bedek Habayis* amendments to his *Beis Yosef* commentary, beg. Y.D. 95 s.v. *kasav rabbeinu*) is to allow one even to be *"gorem Nat Bar Nat lechatchilla."* Others who rule this way include the *Tefilla L'Moshe* (vol. 3:12) and *Yalkut Yosef* (*Issur V'Hetter* vol. 3, pg. 30–31 and 420–425). Conversely, other *Poskim*, including Rav Shalom Messas (Meshash) (*Shu"t Mizrach Shemesh* 98; *Shu"t Shemesh U'Magen*, Y.D. 8; and his responsa published in *Shu"t Shama Shlomo* vol. 2, Y.D. 4 and 6) and Rav Mordechai Eliyahu (cited in *Ikarei Hashulchan* on *Bassar B'chalav* pg. 225; see also *Shu"t Vayaan Yitzchak*, Y.D. 4, who rules similarly), argue that the *halacha* follows the majority opinion of the Acharonim in their understanding of the *Shulchan Aruch's shittah*. Although for Ashkenazim this *machlokes* yields no practical difference, on the other hand, as the *Shulchan Aruch's* true intent is debated by contemporary Sefardic *Poskim*, a Sefardi must ascertain from his own knowledgeable *Posek* which opinion to follow *lemaaseh*.

6   *Shulchan Aruch* (ad loc. 3), based on the *Rosh* (*Chullin* 112a: end 29), *Ramban* (cited by the *Ran* in his glosses to *Chullin* 41a in the *Rif's* pagination), and *Rashba* (*Toras Habayis*, Bayis 3, Shaar 4).

The *Rema*, however, following precedent of other Rishonim, including the *Sefer HaTerumah*, *Ran*, *Mordechai*, and *Tosafos*, argues that since the dishes would be sitting together in the same boiling water at the same time while washing, there *will* be a direct transfer of *taam*. He therefore rules that this case would *not* fall under the category of the *hetter* of *Nat Bar Nat*, and the dishes would be considered non-kosher.[7]

Nevertheless, the *Rema* does allow room for leniency if these clean dishes were washed in the same water one *after* each other. He maintains that since there is no actual mixing of absorbed taste of meat and milk simultaneously, it would be considered *Nat Bar Nat*, and consequently the dishes would be permitted. The basic *halacha* follows the *Rema* on this.

That said, even though the *Shulchan Aruch* was referring to washing *clean* dishes in boiling water, this *halachic* debate still applies to our common dishwashers.

Dishwashing *Din*

Rav Moshe Feinstein, rules in numerous *teshuvos*[8] that one may use the same dishwasher for both *milchig* and *fleishig* dishes, provided that it not be used for both types of dishes at the same time and that it is cleaned out (along with an empty rinse cycle) in between uses. He also

---

7 *Rema* (ad loc. and *Darchei Moshe* ad loc. 3). See *Tur* (ad loc. 3; citing the *Sefer HaTerumah*, 61), *Ran* (*Chullin* 41a in the *Rif's* pagination; see also *Chiddushei Anshei Sheim* ad loc. 1, explaining why the *Ran* agrees with the *Sefer HaTerumah*), *Mordechai* (*Chullin* ad loc. 710), and *Tosafos* (*Chullin* 111b-112a end s.v. *hilchasah*). This understanding is followed by many other Rishonim including the *SMa"K* (213), *SMa"G* (*Mitzvos Lo Sa'aseh* 140 and 141), *Shaarei Dura* (57), *Terumas Hadeshen* (vol. 2-*Psakim U'ksavim* 97), and *Issur V'Hetter* (34:16 and 17). This *shittah* is also the *Haskamas HaPoskim*. See *Yam Shel Shlomo* (*Chullin* Ch. 8:64), as well as the main commentaries to *Yoreh Deah* 95:3, including the *Shach*, *Taz*, *Biur HaGr"a*, *Ba'er Heitiv*, *Chavaas Daas*, *Pri Megadim*, *Chochmas Adam*, and *Aruch Hashulchan*.

8 *Shu"t Igros Moshe* (O.C. vol.1:104 s.v. *uvadavar*; Y.D. vol. 2:28 and 29; Y.D. vol. 3:10, 2 and 11 and O.C. vol. 3: 58 s.v. *v'chein*).

requires one to maintain separate dish racks, one for the exclusive use of the dairy dishes and one for the exclusive use of the meat dishes.[9]

He maintains that since the *hetter* of *Nat Bar Nat* applies by dishes being washed consecutively even in the same water, accordingly, the *hetter* certainly applies to dishwashers, where the second set of dishes is washed in separate clean water. Additionally, there will always be *shishim* (sixty times the amount) of water against any actual food residue, so one does not have to worry about the food leftovers actually making the dishwasher *assur*. Therefore, as long as one sticks to these important details, Rav Moshe maintains that one may use the same dishwasher for both meat and milk dishes separately.

Contemporary Concerns

Still, many contemporary *Poskim* expressed reservations about Rav Moshe's *psak* for various reasons:[10]

- Rav Moshe does not mention filters. Unless one constantly changes or at least cleans out the filters between loads, the dishwasher may be cooking that food residue into the next load of

---

9   The need for a second set of racks according to Rav Moshe's *shittah* is due to the fact that the dirty dishes sit directly on the racks. It stands to reason that these racks will consequently more readily absorb direct *taam* from the food residue. Therefore, if one would place dirty *milchig* and *fleishig* dishes on the same rack (even in two separate cycles), this may result in the racks absorbing both meat and dairy taste. This then transmits together to the dishes in a subsequent load as *taam Bassar B'chalav*.

10 See *Shu"t Ba'er Moshe* (vol. 7:60), *Shu"t Beis Avi* (vol. 2:93), *Shu"t Avnei Yashpei* (vol. 3:71; citing Rav Yosef Shalom Elyashiv), *Kovetz M'Beis Levi* (vol. 1, *Hakashrus Hamitbach* pg. 30:7, footnote 6), *Shu"t Eimek Hateshuva* (vol. 6:318), *Shu"t Chayei Halevi* (vol. 5:62, 5), *Rayach Habosem* (Ch. 3, footnote 34, pg. 89; quoting Rav Yosef Eliyahu Henkin and Rav Asher Zimmerman), *Yalkut Yosef* (*Issur V'Hetter* vol. 3 pg. 491, s.v. *ulam*), *Badei Hashulchan* (Y.D. 95:81; *Biurim* pg. 309, s.v. *u'linyan*), *Kitzur Shulchan Aruch* (Pfeiffer; on *Bassar B'chalav* vol. 2, *Kuntress Habiurim* 6), *Sefer Hakashrus* (Ch. 1, pg. 75–76), *Sefer Kashrus V'Shabbos B'Mitbach Hamoderni* (pg. 114), *Ohel Yaakov* (on *Hilchos Issur V'Hetter*, first edition pg. 296–297:26, footnotes 52 and 53; second

dishes, thereby creating a potential kashrus concern. (However, it must be noted that it is possible that when Rav Moshe wrote his *teshuvos* on this topic over forty-five years ago, filters may not have been standard on dishwasher models).
- There is always the possibility that actual food residue will remain on the dishes even after the wash cycle. This residue might have imparted a direct infusion of taste into either the walls of the dishwasher and/or into the next set of dishes placed inside when they will be washed, thus possibly causing the dishes to become *assur*.
- One of Rav Moshe's provisos is that there must always be *shishim* (sixty times the amount) in the water against the collected amount of food residue and particles on all the dishes. However, this might not always prove true, especially with the smaller dishwasher models available these days. Additionally, even in larger models, some dishwashers slowly fill up and empty out with boiling hot water. The question of whether there is sixty times the amount of residue might actually depend on where the water level is at that time as it slowly fills up or empties out.
- Rav Moshe writes that a dishwasher, "even while in the boiling water...is not considered actual cooking, for the water enters from another place." This implies that he holds that the level of *bishul* of the water is only a *kli sheini* (a secondary vessel on which something hot was only placed, not actually cooked in), which according to the *ikar din*, is not considered actual *bishul*.[11] However, many current models first fill up with cold water and only afterward heat up the water, making the dishwasher a *kli rishon* (the vessel in which something *was* actually cooked, similar to a pot on the fire), which *is* considered *bishul* according

---

edition pg. 374–375, footnotes 51 and 52), and *Pischei Halacha: The Laws of Kashrus* (pg. 258–262).

11 For example, see *Shulchan Aruch* and *Rema* (O.C. 318:9–13; Y.D. 68:11; 95:3; and 105:2).

to all opinions, thus increasing the likelihood of an impending kashrus risk.

- Considering how important the details and caveats are, many people do not understand the different nuances and fine distinctions in *halacha* and may very well come to being *nichshal* (unintentionally negligent and possibly transgress) by using the same dishwasher for both sets of dishes.

As a result of the *halachic* issues raised, many contemporary authorities, including Rav Yosef Shalom Elyashiv, Rav Shmuel *Halevi* Wosner, and the Debreciner Rav, maintain that as a safeguard to lessen the probability of a potential kashrus pitfall, one is required to purchase two separate dishwashers or dedicate the use of the dishwasher exclusively for either milk or dairy dishes. One may not use the same dishwasher for both sets of dishes, even consecutively.[12]

Ashes Attack

"Wait a minute," one may ask. "What about the dishwashing detergent (or soap)? Doesn't that help out to make this whole issue less of a problem? In the very next paragraph after the discussion of washing dishes, the *Shulchan Aruch* rules that if ashes are added to the boiling water, then it renders the *taam* disgusting or at least unpalatable (known as *pagum*), and it actually prevents the transfer of taste—even regarding meat and dairy dishes at the same time.[13] Shouldn't I be able to rely on this? Aren't ashes equivalent to soap?"

Before we get to soap, it is important to note that the ashes issue is not so clear-cut. While the leniency of ashes is correct according to the *Shulchan Aruch* and other *Poskim* who defend him,[14] many

---

12   As mentioned in a previous footnote. The majority of *Poskim* rule this way, that although one may rely on Rav Moshe's ruling *me'ikar hadin*, nevertheless, if at all possible, one should have separate dedicated dishwashers for meat and for dairy dishes.

13   *Shulchan Aruch* (Y.D. 95:4).

14   Including the *Kreisi U'Pleisi* (95:4; and in *Matteh Yonason* ad loc. s.v. *yireh*), *Chacham Tzvi* (*Shu"t* 101), the Yaavetz (*Hagahos* on Y.D. 95 s.v. *yireh*), *Pri Toar*

authorities, most notably the *Shach* and *Taz*,[15] maintain that there is no valid basis for such a ruling, and as such disagree with his *hetter*. Due to the staunch opposition to the *Shulchan Aruch*'s reasoning, some authorities only endorse the *hetter* in extenuating and difficult circumstance, or in case of great financial loss.[16] It would seem that in accordance to this, one should not rely on this dispensation by a dishwasher *lechatchilla*.

Soapy Surprise

Yet, the *Yad Efraim*, the *Pri Megadim*, and other authorities qualify the issue. They maintain that the above *machlokes* is only referring to mixing ashes into the boiling water. They explain that the dissenters are of the opinion that ashes do not do an adequate job of imparting unpalatable taste and rendering *pagum*. [If you think about it, it makes sense. We eat bread and eggs dipped into ashes on Erev Tisha B'Av

---

(ad loc. 6), *Knesses Hagedolah* (ad loc. *Hagahos* on *Beis Yosef* 46), *Damesek Eliezer* (cited by *Knesses Hagedolah* ibid.), *Knesses Yechezkel* (*Shu"t* 28), *Tzemach Tzedek* (*Shu"t* 91), *Shoel U'Meishiv* (*Shu"t Mahadurah Telita'ei* vol. 2:148 s.v. v'hinei b'shnas), *Minchas Yaakov* (55:20), *Imrei Baruch* (Y.D. 95), *Levush* (ad loc. 4), *Chida* (*Shiyurei Bracha* ad loc. 4), *Beis Dovid* (*Shu"t* Y.D. 41), *Shaagas Ayreh* (cited in *Midei Chodesh B'chodsho* vol. 2, *Piskei Halachos* pg. 93), *Erech Hashulchan* (Y.D. 107:1), *Shulchan Gavoah* (ad loc.), *Zivchei Tzedek* (95:38), *Eidus B'Yehoseif* (42), *Matteh Yehuda* (452:5), and *Kaf Hachaim* (Y.D. 95:56).

15 Including the *Shach* (Y.D. 95:21), *Taz* (ad loc. 15), *Rashal* (*Yam Shel Shlomo*, *Chullin* Ch. 8:94), *Levushei Srad* (*Chiddushei Dinim* Y.D. 135), *Biur HaGr"a* (Y.D. 95:24), and *Mishmeres Shalom* (Y.D. 92, M.Z. 24:4).

16 Including the *Pri Chodosh* (Y.D. 95:19), *Pri Megadim* (ad loc. S.D. 21, s.v. *ayin*), *Chavas Daas* (ad loc. *Chiddushim* 2), and *Chochmas Adam* (42:17). Several of these *Poskim* (as well as Rav Akiva Eiger, Y.D. 92:17), point out that the *Minchas Yaakov* himself later retracted his lenient position, as in (57:26) he concludes "*tzarich iyun lemaaseh*" on whether one may rely on ashes being *pagum*. There are also those who only allow use of the ashes leniency in very specific circumstances, implying that one may not rely on their use as a *davar pagum lechatchilla*—see *Pischei Teshuva* (Y.D. 95:6), *Yad Yehuda* (ad loc. *Peirush Ha'aruch* 33 and *Peirush Hakatzer* 37), *Ben Ish Chai* (Year 2, *Parashas Bechukosai* 12), and *Aruch Hashulchan* (Y.D. 95:24).

without too many side effects.] On the other hand, since "our soap" does a much better job, as it most definitely is stronger and better at cleaning than ashes, everyone would agree that soap has the ability to prevent the infusion of *bassar* and *chalav* taste to each other, thus averting any possible kashrus problem.[17]

Rav Ovadiah Yosef cites this reasoning for his own *psak* on dishwashers. He rules that although *lechatchilla*, if at all possible, one should wash the meat and milk dishes separately, however, if one cannot, he may use the same dishwasher for both meat and milk dishes—*even at the same time*.[18] He maintains that dishwashing detergent most definitely is strong enough to be considered *pagum* according to all opinions, and he feels that the contemporary *Poskim* who are *machmir* did not take the *pagum* factor into account.

Although other authorities, including his own son, the current *Rishon L'Tzion* and Chief Rabbi of Israel, Rav Yitzchak Yosef, employ similar logic and allow washing both types of dishes in the same dishwasher, they are of the opinion that one may utilize this *hetter* of dishwashing detergent exclusively for separate cycles.[19] Meaning, even though the detergent renders the water foul-tasting enough to prevent actual *issur* from occurring, one is still required to wash the milk dishes and the meat dishes separately.

Nevertheless, other *Poskim* are unconvinced by this reasoning and are reluctant to use the *hetter* of detergent. They maintain that if there are large quantities of leftover food on the plates (more than a few crumbs or grease), then even after a full wash they remain intact and edible. Additionally, even with smaller amounts of food residue, the plates do not always come out of the washer squeaky clean. This proves that the

---

17 *Yad Efraim* (Y.D. 92:4), *Pri Megadim* (ibid.), *Yad Yehuda* (ibid.), *Chasam Sofer* (*Shu"t* O.C. 120 s.v. *uvchol*), *Mishmeres Shalom* (Y.D. 95, M.Z. 15:1), *Aruch Hashulchan* (ibid.), and *Shu"t Yabia Omer* (vol. 6, Y.D. 10: end 1).

18 *Shu"t Yabia Omer* (vol. 10:4). His opinion is also cited in *Hakashrus B'Halacha* (pg.165) and *Sefer Hakashrus* (Ch. 10, footnote 137).

19 *Yalkut Yosef* (*Issur V'Hetter* vol. 3, 89:86; and pg. 491–492) and *Shu"t Ohr Yitzchak* (vol. 1, Y.D. 4 s.v. *madeyach keilim*).

detergent does not always render the item *pagum*.[20] Others maintain that running both types of dirty dishes together and relying on the detergent to do its job by preventing the *issur* from occurring, falls under the category of "*Ain Mevattlin Issur Lechatchilla*," the prohibition of actively nullifying non-kosher ingredients in a kosher mixture,[21] and it therefore becomes forbidden to do so.

In the final analysis, although there undeniably is what to rely upon if stuck in a situation with one dishwasher, and especially *b'dieved* (and even if they were washed together, according to some *Poskim*), at the same time, most contemporary authorities advise that if at all possible, one should endeavor to procure two separate dedicated dishwashers, one for milk and one for meat, in order to prevent potential kashrus pitfalls.[22] If that's not possible, there is always the good old fashioned

---

20 *Shu"t Ba'er Moshe* (ibid.). This is also the opinion of Rav Ezriel Auerbach (cited in *Kuntress Shu"t Ketzaros B'Inyanei Issur V'Hetter* pg. 26:13).

21 See *Shulchan Aruch* and commentaries to Y.D. (99:5) at length for the parameters of this rule. "*Ain Mevattlin Issur Lechatchilla*" is referring to a case where although if a non-kosher substance would accidentally fall into kosher food (as long as there was the prerequisite sixty times the amount of non-kosher that fell in) it would be permitted to drink, nonetheless, if one would add it on purpose with the express intention of nullifying it, the entire mixture becomes forbidden for the person who transgressed and for whomever he intended to benefit from it. Several *Poskim*, including the *Beis Avi* (ibid.) apply this dictum to washing dairy and meat utensils in a dishwasher together. On the other hand, Rav Ovadiah argues that it is not applicable to a dishwasher, as one's intent is to get his dishes clean and not at all on potentially "cooking" *Bassar B'chalav* together in a dishwasher. This is based on another complicated *Machlokes HaPoskim* regarding the parameters of *Ain Mevattlin Issur Lechatchilla*. This author addressed this issue in a recent *maamar* in *Techumin* (vol. 35; 5775, pg. 194–195), "*Bassar M'ta'i Geza*." An in-depth discussion of this topic is presented in the chapter titled "The Coca-Cola Kashrus Controversy."

22 As mentioned previously. Additionally, many of the authorities who rule leniently in this manner, including Rav Ovadiah Yosef maintain that it is still preferable not to "come into" the *sheilah* and have to rely upon the *hetterim lechatchilla*.

do-it-yourself "elbow grease" in the kitchen sink. You never know, this might also be the reason why disposables were created.

Postscript: Don't Try This at Home?

After completing this chapter, this author received a fascinating communication from R' Shragi Kahana, who used to drive Rav Moshe's brother-in-law, Rav Nechemia Katz, Rav in Toledo, Ohio, for many years, to visit Rav Moshe. He wrote that over forty years ago he asked Rav Moshe several of the aforementioned concerns about his dishwasher leniency.

In his words: "Rav Moshe answered that his entire *teshuva* was misunderstood. The *teshuva*, he explained, only addressed commercial dishwashers, not residential ones. To describe the difference for anyone who has not seen a commercial dishwasher: in a commercial dishwasher, the bottom is open. The dishes are rinsed by a strong heavy spray, and the dirty water drains off entirely with the residue. There is no accumulation of water at the bottom. In such a case, Rav Moshe said, it is obviously permitted to use the same equipment for both *milchig* and *fleishig*, but the racks, which come in direct contact with the food, must be changed. But in a residential dishwasher, there is potential '*mamashos*' (food residue) sitting at the bottom, which floats up next time the tub is filled with water for the next load. That, Rav Moshe specifically said, is absolutely a problem, and one should not *lechatchilla* use the same unit for *milchigs* and *fleishigs*. The easier way to describe the difference between the two may be this: a commercial dishwasher is akin to a shower, whereas a residential dishwasher is more like a bathtub. So it turns out that in a commercial dishwasher, which is open at the bottom with no recirculation of the water, it is *muttar lechatchilla* if one uses separate racks, and there would be no reason to be *machmir*. On the other hand, in a residential dishwasher where there is generally residue on the bottom around the filter, it would not be *muttar lechatchilla*. *B'dieved*, though, due to the other factors, it would not make the dishes *treif*."

If so, there is ample reason to be stringent, certainly *lechatchilla*, regarding using the same dishwasher for both milk and meat dishes.[23]

---

23 However, in this author's estimation, it is important to note that Rav Moshe wrote several *teshuvos* on the topic of dishwashers over the years (as mentioned in a previous footnote). In some, [compare, for example *Shu"t Igros Moshe* (Y.D. vol. 3, 10:2 and 11], Rav Moshe seems to specifically address commercial dishwashers, implying that his other rulings were referring to residential dishwashers. Likewise, in the recently published *Shu"t Vidibarta Bam* vol. 2 (244 s.v. *v'shamaati*), the author quotes Rav Dovid Feinstein as clarifying his father, Rav Moshe's position, as addressing residential dishwashers, and not only commercial ones. He explains that even if the dishwasher would be considered a *kli rishon*, nonetheless, regarding the *bliyos*, *Nat Bar Nat* would apply. Regarding potential *mamashos*, generally there is a *shishim* against them. Even if there isn't, it would still be *pagum*, and there would not be an actual mixture of *bassar* and *chalav*. Hence, maximum, there would be at least a constant *sfek sfeika*, and therefore permitted.

Chapter 7

The Ins and Outs of *"Shnei Keilim Shenagu"*

WHAT EXACTLY IS *"shnei keilim shenagu"*?[1]
How does it affect my life?
Does it affect my life?
In typical Jewish fashion I will attempt to answer these questions with another, a quite common kitchen question:

> *I was cooking macaroni and cheese in one pot on the stove, while in another pot my cholent was simmering. I accidentally knocked one pot into the other, and they were touching for at least ten seconds before I realized and moved them apart. Did I just make my pots non-kosher? Can I still eat the food? Help!!*

The *Psakim* Children Say

Many years ago, my wife actually asked several of my young children this above question. What did they think the actual *halacha* was?

- Child #1: They both become pareve.
- Child #2: They both got dead.
- Child #3: It depends on which pot was bigger. The bigger pot would change the kashrus status of the smaller pot to match it.

---

[1] *"Shenagu"* means "that touched," and not, as some may mistakenly think, a type of massage. As far as this author is aware, that is *"shiatsu."*

Although they all received an A+ for effort, unfortunately my budding *talmidei chachamim* were are all mistaken as to the proper *halacha*.

The *Rema*[2] in two *simanim* of *Hilchos Bassar B'chalav*, briefly addresses this topic, writing that the *din* of "*shnei keilim shenagu,*" or two pots of opposite types (meaning one dairy and one meat) that touched each other, even while both are boiling hot and on the fire, is that they are permitted *b'dieved*. In layman's terms: "no harm, no foul!" Therefore, in the aforementioned case, everything is still kosher and all the food may be eaten (of course not together; that would be violating the prohibition of *Bassar B'chalav*).

The only issue with this ruling of the *Rema* is that it's a bit vague and does not address other factors in the equation, nor does it set parameters. For example:

- Does this still apply if there is moisture in between the pots?
- What about *chometz* pots hitting Pesach pots?
- Or non-kosher pots hitting kosher ones?
- Does this mean that the handle of a pot is considered a separate pot?

What exactly are the boundaries and guidelines of this *halacha*?

The following, after extensive, exhaustive research, are my conclusions and findings on this topic:[3]

1. In the case of two dry, hot pots that touch each other, whether one is dairy and one meat,[4] or whether one is kosher and one non-kosher,[5] or whether one was *chometz* and one kosher for

---

2   *Rema* (Y.D. 92: end 8; and end of 93:1).

3   This is by no means a complete, comprehensive, and authoritative guide, but rather a brief summary, adapted and summarized from this author's original Hebrew exhaustive *Kuntress B'Inyan Shnei Keilim Shenagu Zeh B'Zeh Vehagderosav*.

4   *Mekorei Hadin*: *Mordechai* (*Chullin* pg. 8:690), quoting *Sefer HaTerumah* and the Maharam, who infers this from *Tosafos* (*Chullin* 108a s.v. *tipas chalav*); and *Hagahos Maimoniyos* (*Maachalos Assuros* Ch. 9:3) quoting Rabbeinu Shimshon (cited in *Toras HaChatas* 55:5).

Pesach,[6] and even while steaming upward,[7] the bottom-line *halacha* is that no harm was done, the food and the pots were unaffected, and the kosher ones remain kosher. This applies even if the pots are ceramic[8] and even if the pots contain greasy absorbed taste.[9] However, it is commendable to refrain whenever

---

5   *Issur V'Hetter* (38:16), *Knesses Hagedolah* (Y.D. 92, *Hagahos* on *Beis Yosef* 71), Rashal (*Yam Shel Shlomo*, *Chullin* Ch. 8:45), and *Shach* (Y.D. 105:22).

6   *Shu"t Maharam M'Lublin* (106), *Magen Avraham* (O.C. 451:44), *Taz* (ad loc. 28), *Biur HaGr"a* (ad loc. 22 s.v. *v'assur*), *Chok Yaakov* (ad loc. 63), *Pri Chodosh* (ad loc. s.v *u'mah shekasav assur*), *Elyah Rabba* (ad loc. 45), *Ba'er Heitiv* (ad loc. 49), *Chok Yosef* (ad loc. 54), *Pri Megadim* (ad loc. M.Z. 28), *Machatzis Hashekel* (ad loc. 44 s.v *midofen*), *Ateres Zekeinim* (ad loc. 22), *Maamar Mordechai* (O.C. 447:10, 22 s.v. *amnam*), *Chayei Adam* (vol. 2, 125:2) *Shulchan Aruch Harav* (O.C. 451:41 and 67), *Aruch Hashulchan* (ad loc. 44), *Mishnah Berurah* (ad loc. 136), and *Kaf Hachaim* (ad loc. 267 and 272) all maintain that the same *halachos* of *shnei keilim* apply to Pesach as well. [Not like the minority opinion of Rav Hirsh Shorr (cited by the *Bach*, O.C. 447, and the *Knesses Hagedolah* ad loc. *Hagahos* on *Beis Yosef* 23), and the *mashmaos* of the *Yad Shaul* (Y.D. 92, also alluded to in his *Shu"t Shaul U'Meishiv, Telita'ei* vol 1:174), who maintain that the laws of Pesach are more stringent.]

7   *Pri Megadim* (Y.D. 92, M.Z. 29), who infers this from the *Toras HaChatas* (56:8), *Zichron Avraham* (ad loc.), *Maharsham* (*Shu"t* vol. 3:236), *Zivchei Tzedek* (92:78), and *Kaf Hachaim* (ad loc. 102).

8   As per the *Beis Yosef* (Y.D. 122:8 s.v. *kasav*) that standard vessels are ceramic, and especially here, for the *Taz* (Y.D. 97:3 and O.C. 451:28), *Magen Avraham* (O.C. 451:44), *Yad Efraim* (Y.D. beg. 97), and Yaavetz (*Shu"t Sheilas Yaavetz* vol. 1:93) write explicitly that our case is referring to a *kli cheres*. This is also the opinion of the *Birchos Moshe* (*Shu"t* 8 and 9), *Rav Dovid Sperber* (*Chiddushei HaGra"d Sperber*, end of Y.D. 92), *Sdei Chemed* (vol. 6, *Maareches Bassar B'chalav* 16), *Pri Hasadeh* (*Shu"t* vol. 2:100), and *Netta Sorek* (*Shu"t* Y.D. 35a s.v. *avakesh*). This is also the conclusion of the *Darchei Teshuva* (92:180 and 181) who agrees with the *Birchos Moshe* that by this *halacha* one may not differentiate between a metal vessel and a ceramic one. [Not like the minority opinion of the Maharsham (*Shu"t* vol. 3:236; *Daas Torah*, end of Y.D. 92; and *Techeiles Mordechai*, vol. 2, *Parashas Hachodesh*) who makes a distinction between a ceramic vessel that is new and one that was used in the last twenty-four hours.]

possible, not to cook using these kinds of pots together on a stove, to avoid any potential kashrus concerns.[10]

My Pot Runneth Over! Does that change the status?

2. If there is moisture between the touching hot pots, many authorities contend that the liquid will allow transfer between the pots and will render the pots and the food non-kosher.[11] Other authorities maintain that if there is only a minute amount of liquid (with the pots being sixty times its amount), then it can still be considered dry and everything will still be kosher.[12]

---

9   *Pri Chodosh* (Y.D. 105:28), *Pri Megadim* (ad loc. S.D. 22), *Chavas Daas* (ad loc. Biurim 15), *Imrei Baruch* (Y.D. 92), *Ksav Sofer* (*Shu"t* Y.D. 54), *Birchos Moshe* (*Shu"t* 9; quoting Rav Baruch Tzvi Hirsch Rosenblum, *Av Beis Din* of Pietrikov), *Yad Yehuda* (92, *Peirush Ha'aruch* 56), *Tehilla L'Dovid* (30), *Mishmeres Shalom* (Y.D. 94, M.Z. 7:3), *Aruch Hashulchan* (Y.D. 92:54), and *Kaf Hachaim* (Y.D. 105:82). See also *Ohr Somayach* (*Maachalos Assuros* Ch. 9:19 s.v. *v'hinei*) who implies this. [Not like the minority opinion of the *Toras Yekusiel* (105:8), *Divrei Yosef* (621:4 s.v. *v'nirah li*; brought in *Darchei Teshuva* 92:180), and the *mashmaos* of the *Kanfei Yona* (Y.D. 92; cited by the *Yad Shaul*, Y.D. 92) that by greasy absorbed taste the taste does transfer.] The *Darchei Teshuva* himself concludes *lemaaseh* that even if the pot contains greasy absorbed taste one should not be stringent, and "*chalilah* to be *mechadeish* a new *din* against the *halacha* that was already decided by the *Rema* and the *Avos Horaah*."

10 *Yad Yehuda* (92, *Peirush Hakatzer* 73) and *Ksav Sofer* (*Shu"t* Y.D. 54).

11 *Taz* (Y.D. 92:29; according to many *Poskim*), *Yad Yehuda* (ad loc. *Peirush Ha'aruch* 56), *Divrei Yosef* (621:6), *Zichron Avraham* (end Y.D. 92 s.v. *u'mashekasav b'shnei*), *mashmaos* of Rav Akiva Eiger (Y.D. 93:3) and Rav Shlomo Kluger (*Shu"t Tuv Taam V'Daas*, *Telita'ei*, vol. 1:185), *Chochmas Adam* (46:5), *Chemed Moshe* (O.C. 451:8), *Beis She'arim* (*Shu"t* Y.D. vol. 1:160 s.v. *amnam*), and is the opinion of Rav Shlomo Zalman Auerbach (cited in *Shu"t Maadanei Melachim* 109).

12 *Chavas Daas* (Y.D. 92, Biurim 20), *Yad Efraim* (Y.D. 76: end 1), *Beis Yitzchak* (vol. 2, *Akeres Habayis*, *Bassar B'chalav* 92, Ch. 4:8, A.Z. 39–40), *Atzei Ha'Olah* (*Bassar B'chalav* Ch 5:25), *Yad Yosef* (*Shu"t* Y.D. 47), *Chukosai Tishmoru* (Ch. 17:13, 18; who cites proof to this from several Rishonim), *Zer Hashulchan* (Y.D. 92:110; that there is no transference of *bliyos* without "*rotev mamash*"),

Others maintain that in the aforementioned case, only the food remains kosher, but the pots will need to be *kashered*.[13] Ask your local knowledgeable *halachic* authority for guidance.

Say Cheese!

3. If, however, there was hot cheese between the pots at the point of contact, and there is sixty times its amount in the pots, then the food remains kosher, but the pots need *kashering*.[14]

Clothes = Pots

4. For all intents and purposes, clothes would have the same *halacha* applicable to them as pots do.[15] Therefore, if hot milky coffee spills and gets absorbed into a shirt, and then the shirt touches a hot meat pot, everything is still fine. (Except that now you need to clean your shirt. Oh well, at least coffee stains come out in the wash.)

---

and is the opinion of Rav Shmuel *Halevi* Wosner (cited in *Kovetz M'Beis Levi on Yoreh Deah, Hilchos Hachsharas Kli* pg. 38–39:4). See also *Nochach Hashulchan* (Y.D. 92, *Tziyunim* 181) and *Yevakesh Torah* (*Shu"t* vol. 3:11, 1) who hold this way, but due to different *sevaros*.

13   Maharsham (*Shu"t* vol. 1:217 and vol. 3:236) and *Maadanei Hashulchan* (Y.D. 92, *Mataamei Hashulchan* 53).

14   *Shu"t Maadanei Melachim* (108 and 109) and *Halichos Shlomo* (*Moadim* vol. 2, Pesach, Ch. 12, 11, footnote 13), based on the *Shulchan Aruch* (Y.D. 94:8) [as well as the *Shach* (ad loc. 34; although the *Chazon Ish*, Y.D. 22:6 questions this application), *Pri Megadim* (ad loc. M.Z. 16), and *Aruch Hashulchan* (ad loc. 33)], that cheese, due to its nature, can only absorb and *assur* another item *kdei klipah* (a fingernail's thickness).

15   Maharshak (*Shu"t Ha'Elef Lecha Shlomo*, Y.D. 150, and in *Hagahos Chochmas Shlomo*, Y.D. 105), *Shu"t Pischa Zuta* (Y.D. 27) and *Shu"t Maharsham* (vol. 3:205). However, the Maharsham maintains that there must also be sixty times in the vessel against the amount of *issur ba'ein* inside the holes of the garment.

Get a Handle on It

5. If non-kosher hot liquid falls on the handle of a pot, some authorities maintain that the food in the pot is unaffected, for the handle (since it's only attached by screws) would be considered a different vessel.[16] Others maintain that, practically, it is all considered one vessel, and it therefore will affect the food.[17] However, all agree that if the handle was actually welded on, it would be considered one vessel, and that would thus affect the kashrus status of the food.[18] One should contact his local knowledgeable *halachic* authority for guidance.

Pareve Pots

6. If one of the pots is pareve and the other is either dairy or meat, it's permissible for them to come into contact with each other, even *lechatchilla*[19] (as long as they are clean at the point of contact).

---

16 Rav Akiva Eiger (O.C. 451:12, 10), *Imrei Baruch* (*Hagahos HaGaon Rav Baruch Frankel* to the *Magen Avraham*, ad loc. 25), *Zer Zahav* (on the *Issur V'Hetter* 39:8, 3), *Atzei Ha'Olah* (*Bassar B'chalav* Ch. 7:6, and in *Chukei Chaim* ad loc. 7), Yaavetz (*Mor U'Ketziah* end 451), Maharash Engel (*Shu"t* vol. 7:2), *Yad Yehuda* (92, *Peirush Ha'aruch* 36), and *Aruch Hashulchan* (ad loc. 52), that since the handles are only connected via screws, they are still considered separate vessels. See also *Shu"t Maaseh Chosheiv* (vol. 7:8, 11), who utilizes this *shittah* as a *snif* to be lenient.

17 Radbaz (*Shu"t* vol. 6:62 [1038]), *Chasam Sofer* (*Shu"t* O.C. 130; who maintains that the leniencies of *shnei keilim* only apply when there is space separating the vessels), *Chavas Daas* (Y.D. 92, *Chiddushim* 17), *Arugos Habosem* (*Shu"t* O.C. 98), Maharsham (*Shu"t* vol. 3:112), Maharshak (*Shu"t Tuv Taam V'Daas*, Telita'ei 247), and *Darchei Teshuva* (92:122). See also *Shu"t Minchas Yitzchak* (vol. 5:81, 11 and vol. 7: end 56 s.v. *v'kol*).

18 *Mashmaos* of the *Taz* (O.C. 451:18), *Zer Zahav* (on the *Issur V'Hetter* 39:8, 3), *Atzei Ha'Olah* (*Bassar B'chalav* Ch. 7:6, and in *Chukei Chaim* ad loc. 7), *Chok Yaakov* (O.C. 451:41), *Mishnah Berurah* (ad loc. 76), and *Badei Hashulchan* (Y.D. 92, *Biurim* pg. 178).

19 See *Chikosai Tishmoru* (Ch. 17:18, 24) and *Darchei Halacha* (on *Kashrus Habayis*, Ch. 20, *B'Teshuva*), However, Rav Shmuel Halevi Wosner (*Shu"t*

Counter Attack!

7. If someone is cooking in a dairy pot and wishes to take it off the fire, and there is nowhere to place it except on the counter that is usually reserved for meat items, one may nonetheless place it there.[20] Nevertheless, since the issue is not as clear-cut as it's being presented, it is preferable not to do so,[21] but rather

---

Shevet Halevi vol. 11:67, 5) maintains that it is still preferable not to let them touch *lechatchilla*.

20   *Ksav Sofer* (*Shu"t* Y.D. 54; *b'sevara* but not *lemaaseh*), *Yaavetz* (*Shu"t Sheilas Yaavetz* vol. 1:93), *Yad Avraham* (Y.D. beg. 88), *Atzei Ha'Olah* (*Bassar B'chalav* Ch. 1:46), *Divrei Yosef* (621:3 s.v. *amnam*), *Shu"t Igros Moshe* (Y.D. vol. 3:10), and *Shu"t She'ilei Tzion* (*on Shabbos, Eruv, and Pesach*, 20: end 3). This is also the *mashmaos* of the *Radbaz* (*Shu"t* vol. 2:621), the *Tzemach Tzedek* (*Shu"t* O.C. 43), and the *Soles Lemincha* (76:7, 17). This is also *the mashmaos* of many *Poskim* (including the Maharam M'Lublin, *Magen Avraham*, *Pri Megadim*, *Yad Yehuda*, and *Zivchei Tzedek*) who maintain that the *din* of *shnei keilim* to be *machmir lechatchilla* only applies when there is a *chashash* of *ba'ein* between the vessels. Although the *Badei Hashulchan* (92, *Biurim*, pg. 215) and several others attack Rav Moshe's position, based on their understanding of the *Chochmas Adam's shittah* (74:4) regarding a *chatzuvah* (a sort of metal tripod stove), nevertheless, in this author's estimation, it seems that Rav Moshe (ibid. and *Shu"t Igros Moshe* Y.D. vol. 1:59 and O.C. vol. 1: end 124 s.v. *uvadavar*) was indeed correct in his assessment (as well as of the *Chochmas Adam's* view; see the *Chochmas Adam's* actual rulings regarding pots touching in 50:2 and 57:7; noticeably absent from *Badei Hashulchan* and the others' comments), as his stance is based on and shares broad support among the Acharonim. Although the intricacies and nuances involved in this debate are beyond the scope of this discussion, this issue is elucidated at length in this author's *Kuntress B'Inyan Shnei Keilim Shenagu Zeh B'Zeh Vehagderosav* (end *anaf* 10 and *anaf* 11), and recent *maamar* published in *Kovetz Moriah* (Elul 5774; #391–393, pg. 284–287) titled *"B'Inyan Hishtamshus B'Chatzuvos B'Bassar B'chalav U'vPesach."*

21   *Taz* (Y.D. 92:29 and 97:3 and O.C. 451:28), *Ksav Sofer* (*Shu"t* Y.D. 54; conclusion), *Aruch Hashulchan* (Y.D. 88:10), *Yalkut Me'am Loez* (*Parashas Mishpatim* pg. 890 s.v. *vehadavar harishon*), *Toras Yekusiel* (105:8), and *Darchei Teshuva* (95:91; quoting the Rashal). This is also the opinion of Rav Yosef Shalom

The Ins and Outs of "Shnei Keilim Shenagu" 79

one should place another layer of separation down first[22] (for example, a board, towel or aluminum foil) in order to satisfy all opinions.

These are just a few basic guidelines—an introductory overview—of the *halacha* of *"shnei kelim shenagu."* Of course, one should not compare similar cases in order to *pasken* one's own *sheilos*, but should refer his questions to a competent *halachic* authority.

Elyashiv (originally cited in this author's *Kuntress B'Inyan Shnei Keilim Shenagu Zeh B'Zeh Vehagderosav, anaf* 12 s.v. *hereisi* and *v'HaGri"sh*; and later in Rabbi Chaim Gross' *Hashulchan V'Hakeilim*, 92: pg. 76–77; Rabbi Yaakov Skoczylas' *Ohel Yaakov* on *Hilchos Issur V'Hetter*, expanded edition, 92: end footnote 82, pg. 311–312; and *Ashrei Ha'Ish*, Y.D. vol. 1, Ch. 5:35), that since the whole *din* is *muttar* anyway *b'dieved*, and the *machlokes* is only regarding the permissibility of placing on an opposite counter *lechatchilla*, therefore one should be *machmir* if at all possible.

22 *Shu"t Beis Hayotzer* (20) and *Noam Halacha* (*Piskei Halachos Bassar B'chalav* Ch. 17:21). See also *Shu"t Shevet Halevi* (vol. 11:67, 5) and *Shu"t Chayei Halevi* (vol. 2, E.H. 78:51 s.v. *v'od*).

Part 2

MEAT, CHICKEN, AND FISH

Chapter 8

The Lox and Cream Cheese Dilemma

Bris Brouhaha?

THE NEXT TIME YOU ARE at a *bris*, as you are about to smear a nice dollop of cream cheese on your bagel and add the lox (obviously not at the *fleishig brissos* that are common in Eretz Yisrael),[1] look around and see if others are doing the same. You might just find that certain people (probably Sefardic or Chassidic) will refrain from adding cream cheese to the lox bagel. Aside from those who are allergic to fish or can't stand

---

1 Which is a topic for a discussion in its own right. Although there certainly is support to make a *milchig Bris seudah* [for example, see *Shu"t Chasam Sofer* (O.C. 69), *Shu"t Maharam Schick* (366), and *Aruch Hashulchan* (Y.D. 265:17)], and all the more so with fish [see *Yerushalmi* (*Pesachim* Ch. 4, Halacha 1), *Rashi* (*Parashas Pinchas* Ch. 29:36; citing the *Midrash Tanchuma* ad loc. 17, who implies that fish is considered *chashuv* for a *seudah*; thanks are due to kashrus expert Rav Mordechai Kuber for pointing this out), and *Magen Avraham* (O.C. 533:8 and 552:2)], nevertheless, all things being equal, it seems that if at all possible, optimally, it would be preferable that a *Bris seudah* be *fleishig*. See *Mordechai* (*Taanis*, end 638), *Shu"t Chavos Yair* (end 178), *Magen Avraham* (O.C. 249:6; citing the *Maharash M'Lublin*), *Machatzis Hashekel* (ad loc.), and more contemporarily, *Shu"t Shevet Halevi* (vol. 3:18) and *Shu"t Teshuvos V'Hanhagos* (vol. 2:282 and vol. 3:294). This topic was addressed in previous articles titled "Meat for Breakfast?!" (https://ohr.edu/

it, there is a large portion of observant Jewry who will not eat a fish and milk combination.

"Hold your horses!" one might exclaim. "I've never seen any mention of this in my Chumash, or even *Shulchan Aruch*! Not only that, the *Shulchan Aruch*[2] states that the exact converse is true—that one *may* cook milk and fish together, for there is no *issur* involved, even *Derabbanan*! Is this the new *chumrah* of the week? And how exactly am I expected to go to a *Bris* and not have bagels with lox and cream cheese? It just wouldn't seem Jewish!"

Actually, although this is not a new *chumrah*, indeed there is no mention of such a *halacha* in the *Shulchan Aruch* at all. To better understand where such a *shittah* comes from, one must first understand the *halachos* of mixing fish and **meat**.

Tzara'as Tzaros

The *Shulchan Aruch* writes that one must be careful not to eat meat and fish together for this mixture may cause *tzara'as* (very loosely translated as leprosy).[3] It is generally accepted that this prohibition includes chicken, turkey, and all other fowl as well.[4]

This is also the reason that between meat and fish courses, for example on Shabbos after the gefilte fish, we rinse our mouths (or drink a

---

this_week/insights_into_halacha/4851) and "Meat on Rosh Chodesh Av" (*Yated Ne'eman*, 1 Av 5776/August 5, 2016) and online at: (https://ohr.edu/this_week/insights_into_halacha/7441).

2   *Shulchan Aruch* (Y.D. 87:3).

3   *Shulchan Aruch* (Y.D. 116:2), based on Gemara *Pesachim* (76b).

4   See *Shu"t Shvus Yaakov* (vol. 2:104), *Pischei Teshuva* (Y.D. 116:2), Chida (*Shiyurei Bracha* Y.D. 116:8), *Atzei Ha'Olah* (*Devarim Ha'assurim Meshum Sakana, Chukei Chaim* 2), *Ben Ish Chai* (Year 2, *Parashas Pinchas* 8), *Kitzur Shulchan Aruch* (33:1), *Aruch Hashulchan* (Y.D. 116:10), and *Kaf Hachaim* (O.C. 173:5). The *halachic* consensus does not follow the minority opinion of the *Beis Yehuda* (*Shu"t* Y.D. 24) and *Ikrei Dinim* (*Ikrei HaDa"T* 14:3) who maintain *"ain limchos b'yad hameikilim, u'kvar nahagu ha'olam lehakel"* regarding mixing fish and chicken.

l'chaim)⁵ and eat something—*kinuach v'hadacha*. Sefardic custom is to also wash hands in between.⁶ Some maintain it is preferable to have the fish course (usually the appetizer) before the meat course, as well.⁷ All this—to maintain a separation between the two, and to make sure that at the time of eating one, there should not remain even a trace or residue of the other—comes from the Talmudic dictum, "*Chamira*

---

5   Although there appears to be no exact source for the general *minhag* of drinking specifically a shot of whiskey between eating fish and the Friday night chicken, the *She'arim Metzuyanim B'Halacha* (33:2) posits that it is possible that this custom stems from the words of *Tosafos* (*Moed Kattan* 11a s.v. *kavra*), who exhorts us not to drink water after eating fish due to possible *sakana*. As *Tosafos'* assertion is cited *lemaaseh* by the *Kessef Mishneh* (*Hilchos Dei'os* Ch. 4:18), Rav Akiva Eiger (Y.D. 116:5), *Aruch Hashulchan* (ad loc. 10), and *Kaf Hachaim* (O.C. 170:79), he posits that this might explain why whiskey has long since become the preferred drink after fish at the *Leil Shabbos seudah*. Rav Nissim Karelitz is also quoted (*Chut Shani* on *Hilchos Shabbos* vol. 4, *Kovetz Inyanim*, pg. 399) as favoring this background. See also *Shemiras Haguf V'Hanefesh* (vol. 1:1, footnote 33).

6   See *Shulchan Aruch* (O.C. 173:2 and Y.D. 116:3) and *Rema* (Y.D. ad loc.). See also *Pri Toar* (116:4), *Shiyurei Bracha* (ad loc. 116:8), *Noheg K'tzon Yosef* (*Hilchos Seudah* pg. 120:3 and *Hilchos Sakana* pg. 122:2), *Shu"t Sheilas Shalom* (*Tinyana* 165), *Yeshuos Chochma* (33:2), *Beis Lechem Yehuda* (Y.D. 116:4), *Shulchan Chai* (1:15), *Chochmas Adam* (68:1), *Lechem Hapanim* (Y.D. 116:3), *Shu"t Dvar Shmuel* (367), *Ben Ish Chai* (Year 2, *Parashas Pinchas* 8), *Darchei Teshuva* (116:30 and 32), *Mishnah Berurah* (173:4 and *Shaar Hatziyun* ad loc. 2), *Divrei Yoel* (*Parashas Vayishlach* pg. 177b), and *Orchos Rabbeinu* (new edition; vol. 4, pg. 44:27 and 28; that the *Chazon Ish* and Steipler Gaon were *makpid* on washing hands in between like the *Shulchan Aruch*, and not lenient like the *Rema* on this).

7   Regarding which is better to eat first, although there are those who mention eating fish after meat (see for example *Kitzur Shulchan Aruch* 33:22), nonetheless, several authorities, including the *Aruch Hashulchan* (O.C. 173:2), *Yafeh Lalev* (O.C. vol. 1, 157:2), and *Kaf Hachaim* (ad loc. 38), cite a possible source for preference for first eating fish and only then meat. The *Rambam* (*Hilchos Dei'os* Ch. 6:7) writes that when eating one should first eat a "lighter food (*davar hakal*)" before a "heavier food (*davar hakaved*)." See also *Shu"t Nishmas Shabbos* (vol.1:130) and *Kovetz M'Beis Levi* (vol. 3, pg. 45).

Sakanta Mei'Issura."[8] This means that something that involves a severe health risk is considered more stringent than regular prohibitions. A fine example of this involves the *halacha* of *bittul* (nullification):

- In a normal scenario where one encounters something non-kosher which might have accidentally fallen into a kosher mixture, the *halacha* in most cases, maintains that if there is present sixty times the amount of kosher against the non-kosher, the non-kosher product is considered nullified, and one is permitted to partake of the mixture.
- However, in a case of a severe health risk, many hold that *halachically* there is no nullification,[9] as *halacha* is extremely cautious when it comes to people's health.

However, our situation may not be the standard one, for some opine that there are plenty of people in the world who do mix meat and fish, and there has not been any recent news of leprosy outbreaks!

---

8   *Chullin* (10a), cited *lemaaseh* by the *Shulchan Aruch* (O.C. 173:2) and *Rema* (Y.D. 116:5).

9   *Taz* (Y.D. 116:2), citing proof from the *Mordechai, Ohr Zarua* (both cited by the *Issur V'Hetter* 23:7), Issur V'Hetter (ibid.), and Maharil (*Hilchos Issur V'Hetter* pg. 526). Conversely, the *Shach* (*Nekudos Hakessef* ad loc.) argues, maintaining that "*Chamira Sakanta Mei'Issura*"—having no nullification—only applies in that exact case cited by the Gemara, of snake venom. However, in other potential cases of *sakana*, he avers that the laws of nullification are still in effect. Many authorities, including the *Pri Chodosh* (ad loc. 4), *Pri Toar* (ad loc. 4, end s.v. *v'davka*), *Shvus Yaakov* (*Shu"t* vol. 2: end 104), *Chavos Yair* (*Shu"t* 64; and in his *Shu"t Chut Hashani* 67), *Chochmas Adam* (61:1), and *Aruch Hashulchan* (Y.D. 116:10), agree with the *Shach's* assessment. On the other hand, other authorities, including Rav Shlomo Kluger (*Shu"t Tuv Taam V'Daas, Mahadura Telita'ei*, vol. 2:10), the *Shoel U'Meishiv* (*Shu"t Mahadura Revii*, vol. 1:28), and the *Pischei Teshuva* (Y.D. 116:2; although he is lenient with fish and meat) agree with the *Taz's* assessment, that nullification is not applicable to matters of *sakana*. The *Darchei Teshuva* (ad loc. 21) as well, cites other *Poskim* who also follow the *Taz's mehalech*.

Environmental Enigma

The *Magen Avraham* actually addresses this concern and advances the notion that the *teva* (roughly translated as environmental conditions) has since changed and therefore one no longer has to be concerned about this issue. Other notable authorities, including the *Aruch Hashulchan* and the *Mishnah Berurah* seem to accept his argument as *halacha*. Furthermore, as the *Chasam Sofer* noted, there is no mention of this danger of eating meat and fish together in any of the works of "*Gadol HaRofim*," the *Rambam*, the best-known Jewish doctor in history.[10]

However, most *halachic* authorities do not agree with this *chiddush* and maintain that the basic *halacha* follows the *Shulchan Aruch* and that this mixture remains forbidden.[11]

Yet, many authorities do take the lenient opinion into consideration to allow for some leniency in certain questionable situations.[12] They

---

10 *Magen Avraham* (O.C. 173:1), *Bach* (ad loc.), *Shu"t HaMaharshdam* (vol. 4:124; citing the *Sefer Hakaneh*), *Aruch Hashulchan* (O.C. 173:2), and *Mishnah Berurah* (ad loc. 3). Moreover, there is no mention of a *sakana* with mixing meat and fish in the authoritative works of the *Rif* and *Rambam*. There are also those who maintain that said *sakana* does not apply with every type of fish, but rather only specific types. See *Shu"t Be'er Sheva* (35), *Shu"t Ezras Yisrael* (85, Hagahah), *Shu"t Chasam Sofer* (Y.D. 101; explaining the *Rambam's shittah*), *Shu"t Tuv Taam V'Daas* (Mahadura Telita'ei vol. 2:10), *Shu"t Beis Shmuel* (173), *Rashash* (*Chullin* 97a), *Shu"t Chelkas Yaakov* (vol. 1:109), *Otzar Yad Hachaim* (217), and *Shemiras Haguf V'Hanefesh* (vol. 1:1, footnotes 1 and 2).

11 Including the *Noheg K'tzon Yosef* (*Hilchos Seudah* 120:3), who strongly argues that the opposite should hold true, that if anything the *teva* has since changed for the worse, not the better, and this has to be assessed in every land separately. Others who disagreed with the *Magen Avraham's* supposition include the *Yafeh Lalev* (O.C. 173:2), *Malbushei Yom Tov* (54), *Shvus Yaakov* (*Shu"t* vol. 3:70), *Sdei Chemed* (vol. 3, Klalim, Maareches Tes, Klal 5), Maharam Schick (*Shu"t* Y.D. 244), *Shulchan Aruch Harav* (*Shemiras Guf V'nefesh* 9), *Chochmas Adam* (68:1), *Yad Efraim* (Y.D. 116:3), *Kitzur Shulchan Aruch* (33:1), *Kaf Hachaim* (O.C. 173:9), and *Divrei Yoel* (ibid.).

12 See, for example *Shu"t Chasam Sofer* (ibid.), *Shu"t Shvus Yaakov* (ibid.), *Yad Efraim* (ibid.), *Pischei Teshuva* (Y.D. 116:3), *Shu"t Divrei Malkiel* (vol. 2:53), *Shu"t Tiferes Tzvi* (91), *Shu"t Shevet Halevi* (vol. 6:111, 3), and *Shu"t Shulchan*

therefore maintain that nullification is applicable here, as it is not considered a true case of *sakana*.[13] In fact, the OU designates certain

---

Halevi (Ch. 23:1). This is also the conclusion of the *Darchei Teshuva* (116:16) that we may rely on the *Magen Avraham's shittah*, of environmental change, but only as a *snif lehakel*. For example, there are *Poskim* who are of the opinion that although we generally hold that *Ain Mevattlin Issur Lechatchilla*—it is prohibited to actively nullify non-kosher ingredients in a kosher mixture, nevertheless, if a small amount of fish got mixed in with meat or vice versa, one may purposely nullify it among the rest of the mixture, as it is not a true *issur*. Although, other authorities do not agree with this leniency, and others conclude *tzarich iyun*, nonetheless, we see that many authorities maintain that this case is somewhat more lenient than other *issurim*. Another example with practical application is whether one may serve fish and meat at the same time at the table or whether a *hekker* would be required, as it is regarding milk and meat [as discussed in previous chapters]. Although the *Kehal Yehuda* (Y.D. 88) is cited as being *machmir* (see *Kaf Hachaim* Y.D. 116:13; however, as pointed out in *Shemiras Haguf V'Hanefesh* vol. 1:1, 3 footnote 3, the *Kaf Hachaim* in O.C. 173:6 seems to rule leniently) nonetheless, the vast majority of *halachic* authorities rule leniently, that one may indeed serve fish and meat at the same time. However, in places where they might get mixed up (for example *"musaka,"* which can be mistaken for a chicken loaf, or serving both herring and *fleishig* cholent at the same time at a *kiddush*), it is nonetheless advisable to avoid doing so in order to mitigate potential *halachic* mishaps.

13   Including the *Knesses Hagedolah* (Y.D. 116, *Hagahos* on *Beis Yosef* 21), *Pri Chodosh* (ad loc. 4), *Pri Toar* (ad loc. 4), *Beis Lechem Yehuda* (ad loc. 3), *Pischei Teshuva* (ad loc. 3), *Erech Hashulchan* (ad loc. 3), *Chochmas Adam* (68:1), *Chasam Sofer* (*Shu"t* Y.D. 101), Maharsham (*Shu"t* vol. 3:288), *Aruch Hashulchan* (Y.D. 116:10), *Kaf Hachaim* (ad loc. 12), Rogatchover Gaon (*Shu"t Tzafnas Pane'ach* 264), *Chelkas Yaakov* (*Shu"t* vol. 2:10), and Rav Ovadiah Yosef (*Shu"t Yabia Omer* vol. 1, Y.D. 7). See also *Shemiras Haguf V'Hanefesh* (vol. 1:1, 4 and footnote 5) who cites a long list of authorities, to prove that *rov Poskim* are of the opinion that such a *taaruvos* will indeed be *battel b'shishim*. This certainly would hold true according to the authorities who followed the *Shach's shittah* that the laws of nullification are in effect for every *sakana*, except for snake venom. On the other hand, the renowned Rav Tzadok Hakohen M'Lublin, in his *Tiferes Tzvi* on *Yoreh Deah* (116), has a different understanding of the issues at hand. He explains that according to the laws of nature, there certainly is no danger involved with eating fish and meat together, as for physical danger we

Worcestershire sauces with an "OU Fish" designation, denoting that the fish content within is *not* nullified, and one may not serve it on meat. If it contains sixty times the fish content, they consider it nullified and do not designate it as "OU Fish."[14]

The bottom line is that if meat and fish would not be actually cooked together in the same pot, the majority of *halachic* authorities would permit it to be eaten. In fact, one may cook fish in a meat pot, as long as no actual meat remains in the pot.[15] The same would apply to cooking fish in a meaty oven.[16]

---

certainly may rely on the wisest of doctors, the *Rambam*. However, he opines that the danger here is not merely physical, but rather a spiritual danger, such as *Ruach Ra'ah* (see the chapter titled "The Odd Account of the Overnight Onion" for more on this topic). As it is well known that the *Rambam* seems not to have been concerned with this issue [see for example, his *Shu"t Pe'er Hador* (146) and *Shu"t Maharam Alshaker* (79)], Rav Tzadok asserts that we cannot simply rely on his expertise as a doctor to avoid this spiritual danger, and we therefore must still remain vigilant not to mix meat and fish. Yet, he nonetheless concludes that *'b'makom Mitzva ul'tzorech Shabbos V'Yom Tov'* we can be *meikil*, even if there is no *shishim* to nullify the mixture, as it is stated in *Koheles* (Ch. 8:5): *"Shomer Mitzva lo yeida davar ra."*

14 *Shu"t Shulchan Halevi* (Ch. 23:1), from the OU's chief *Posek*, Rav Yisroel Belsky. This is the OU's official position as well; see: https://oukosher.org/halacha-yomis/many-worcestershire-sauces-contain-anchovies-permissible-add-worcestershire-sauce-meat and https://oukosher.org/blog/industrial-kosher/all-ou-symbols-explained. The Star-K (see Rabbi Tzvi Rosen, "The Secret Ingredient," *Kashrus Kurrents*, Spring 2012) holds similarly, that only if there is more than 1.6% (a sixtieth of) anchovies in the Worcestershire sauce's blend does it need to be labeled "Kosher-Fish." However, not every *hashgacha* agrees with this assessment, and in fact, both the KLBD (see the United Synagogue's *Daf HaShavua, Parashas Yisro* 5775/2015, pg. 4) and the KF (see my former *talmid*, Rabbi Josh Bennett of the KF's article printed in "Oneg Shabbos," *Parashas Vayakhel–Pekudei* 5775/2015, pg. 3) in England mandate that even if there is a tiny amount of fish in a product's make-up, it nevertheless requires a special "Fish" designation to indicate that it should not be eaten with meat.

A Milky Mix-Up?

"That's all fine and dandy," one might exclaim, "but what does that have to do with mixing fish and **milk**?" The answer to this lies in the *Beis Yosef*, the *Shulchan Aruch's* commentary on the *Tur*. For in *Yoreh Deah* 87[17] the *Beis Yosef* writes that "one should not eat fish and milk together because of the danger involved, as it is explained in *Orach Chaim* 173." A number of *Poskim* follow this

---

15 Although the *Tur* (Y.D. 116) and the *Issur V'Hetter* (39:26) cite opinions that "*yeish lehachmir lechatchilla*" regarding cooking fish in meat pots and pans, nonetheless, the fact that this is not cited by the *Beis Yosef, Shulchan Aruch*, or their main commentaries speaks volumes. In fact, the vast majority of Acharonim rule that it is indeed permitted, even *lechatchilla*. These include the Rashal (*Yam Shel Shlomo, Chullin*, Ch. 7:15), Taz (Y.D. 95:3), *Chavos Yair* (*Shu"t Chut Hashani* 67), *Minchas Yaakov* (57:1), Rav Shlomo Kluger (*Shu"t Ha'Elef Lecha Shlomo*, O.C. 312 and 313), *Chochmas Adam* (68:1, *Hagahah*), *Mor V'Ohalos* (*Shu"t, Ohel Brachos V'Hoda'os* 43, pg. 41), *Yad Yehuda* (95, *Peirush Hakatzer* 4), *Zivchei Tzedek* (95:5), *Darchei Teshuva* (116:27), *Kaf Hachaim* (ad loc. 20), and on a more contemporary note, the *"Leshem Shevo V'achlamah"* (in a *teshuva* printed in his grandson, Rav Yosef Shalom Elyashiv's *Kovetz Teshuvos* vol. 4:244, pg. 297–298), Rav Moshe Feinstein (cited in *Mesores Moshe* vol. 1, pg. 217:27), and Rav Shmuel *Halevi* Wosner (*Shu"t Shevet Halevi* vol. 6:111, 4 s.v. *uv'inyan*; although he cites that the *"medakdekin"* maintain separate fish pots). On the other hand, it is known (*Orchos Rabbeinu*, new edition vol. 4, pg. 43:24, and as related to this author by *Mori v'Rabi* Rav Yonason Wiener, who received a personal letter from Rav Chaim Kanievsky attesting to this) that the *Chazon Ish* and Steipler Gaon were extremely *makpid* with this, even mandating separate silverware for fish and meat. An interesting side issue, although beyond the scope of this discussion, and one that is debated extensively by later authorities as to whether one may indeed rely on this *hetter* or not, is that there are even those who extend this *"bliyos hetter"* to a case if one accidentally cooked meat and fish together, maintaining that the pot does not require *kashering*. This issue was addressed at length in a *maamar* on topic in this author's *M'Shulchan Yehuda*, titled *"Gidrei Hadin Shel Achilas Dagim B'chalav V'hamista'ef."*

16 For more on this topic, see: www.dinonline.org/2011/01/30/meat-and-fish-in-same-oven.

17 *Beis Yosef* (Y.D. 87:3 s.v. *dagim*).

The Lox and Cream Cheese Dilemma 91

ruling, and likewise maintain that one should not eat a combination of milk and fish, based on the statement and reasoning of the *Beis Yosef*.[18] However, many authorities point out that the location the *Beis Yosef* referenced for his *halachic* decision to be *machmir* is referring to eating fish with **meat**, not *milk*. They therefore maintain that this issue is a case of mistaken identity (a misprint) and that eating fish with milk should truly be one hundred percent permissible.[19] Some add that if the *Beis Yosef* truly intended to rule stringently in this matter, he would not have only mentioned it in his commentary, but rather would have written it as an official *psak halacha* in the *Shulchan Aruch*.[20]

Cool Off!

On the other hand, many authorities hold that there is still a *sakana* involved in eating fish and milk, but it's not a *halachic* issue, rather a medical one. They maintain that since both fish and milk serve to cool down the human body, when they are ingested together it can create

---

18 Including the *Levush* (*Ateres Zahav* Y.D. 87; according to the basic understanding of his *lashon*), *Zivchei Tzedek* (ad loc. 18), *Shu"t Beis Dovid* (Y.D. 33), *Pachad Yitzchak* (*Maareches Beis*, 69b, *erech Bassar Dagim*), *Ikrei HaDa"T* (Y.D. 14:5), and Rav Ovadiah Yosef (*Shu"t Yechaveh Daas* vol. 6:48).

19 Including the *Rema* (*Darchei Moshe* Y.D. 87:4; who writes, seemingly somewhat in jest, that it seems the *Beis Yosef* essentially made a *"Taaruvos* of *Bassar V'Chalav"*), *Shach* (ad loc. 5), *Taz* (ad loc. 3), *Pri Chodosh* (ad loc. 6), *Magen Avraham* (beg. O.C. 173), *Chida* (*Machzik Bracha* Y.D. 87:4), *Prishah* (ad loc. 5), *Chaguras Shmuel* (ad loc. 7), *Elyah Rabba* (O.C. 173:9), *Shulchan Gavoah* (ad loc. 11), *Ba'er Heitiv* (Y.D. 87:5), *Be'er Sheva* (*Shu"t* 35 s.v. *nishalti*), *Be'eros Hamayim* (*Shu"t* Y.D. 1), *Yaavetz* (*Mor U'Ketziah* 173), *Imrei Binah* (Y.D. 87:6), *Aruch Hashulchan* (Y.D. 87:15), and *Darchei Teshuva* (116:14).

20 *Aruch Hashulchan* (ibid.). However, in this author's estimation, this assertion would not be problematic according to Rav Ovadiah Yosef's *Klalei Horaah* (printed at the end of the older editions of *Shu"t Yechaveh Daas* vol. 6; *Klalei Shulchan Aruch* 33, 38, and 39). This is because he maintains that although a *psak* written in the *Shulchan Aruch* would *halachically* trump a comment its great author, Rav Yosef Karo himself wrote earlier in the *Beis Yosef*, nevertheless, if there is no specific ruling directly arguing against a comment in the *Beis Yosef*, then it is presumed that Rav Karo meant for that (ruling

bodily harm.[21] This, they hold, is the reason the *Beis Yosef* intended when stating not to eat them together, and not because of *tzara'as*. While these *Poskim* do cite this logic and say one should therefore refrain, many authorities, most notably the *Chasam Sofer*,[22] argue that this cannot possibly be true, for we see many people eating them together and not becoming (noticeably) sick.[23] Also, the greatest Jewish doctor,

---

in the *Beis Yosef*) to be his final word on the subject. As such, we can easily explain his cryptic comment as meaning that although there should not be any intrinsic prohibition with eating milk and fish together, nonetheless it preferably should still be avoided, due to the *chashash* of *tzara'as*. Accordingly, we can defend the *Beis Yosef*'s presumed position from the *Aruch Hashulchan*'s difficulty.

21 Including one of the Rishonim, Rabbeinu Bachya (*Parashas Mishpatim* Ch. 23:19 s.v. *lo sevashel*; however, he writes that the *sakana* is due to both reasons). However, there seems to be a difference of opinions among the Acharonim as to how they understood his *lashon*. For example, the *Aruch Hashulchan* (ibid.) wrote that Rabbeinu Bachya only proscribed eating fish with cheese, but not milk, whereas the *Pischei Teshuva* (Y.D. 87:9) understood that he was stringent with fish and milk as well. Other authorities who cite this rationale include Rav Yitzchak Lampronati (*Pachad Yitzchak, Maareches Beis*, pg. 69b; who was also renowned as a doctor in his time), the *Knesses Hagedolah* (Y.D. 87, Hagahos on *Beis Yosef* 19; citing the *She'aris Yehuda*), the *Beis Lechem Yehuda* (ad loc. 4), Rav Yaakov Emden (*Mor U'Ketziah* end 173), *Gilyon Maharsha* (Y.D. 116:2; citing the Maharam M'Krakow), *Chinuch Beis Yehuda* (*Shu"t* 61; who posits that this was the *Levush*'s true reasoning for ruling stringently), *Adnei Paz* (*Shu"t* 42), *Pri Megadim* (Y.D. 89, M.Z. 3; who concludes *yeish lizaher*), and *Ben Ish Chai* (Year 2, *Parashas Beha'aloscha* 15 and in *Shu"t Rav Pe'alim* vol. 1, Y.D. 10). There are those who make a case that *Rashi* held this way as well, as in his responsa (*Teshuvos Rashi* 326) he implies to be *machmir* for this scenario, but for a very different reason, involving the *"chashash shel shamnunis b'ke'arah."*

22 *Shu"t Chasam Sofer* (Y.D. 101).

23 Including the *Pischei Teshuva* (Y.D. 87:9), *Yad Efraim* (ad loc.), *Aruch Hashulchan* (ibid.), and *Badei Hashulchan* (ad loc. 33), akin to the reasoning of the *Shaarei Teshuva* (O.C. 171:1), that in situations such as these, when we see that

the *Rambam*, makes absolutely no mention of this danger, either,[24] and neither do any contemporary medical authorities.

Still, others maintain that this depends on the time and place.[25] Just because someone won't get sick from it in New York, there is no assurance that the same would be true in Kabul, Afghanistan. (Although I am assuming that if one is in Kabul he has other *sakanos* to worry about...)

A Fishy Conclusion

The outcome of this *halachic* debate is that different *minhagim* developed over time among different segments of Jewry. An oversimplified generalization is that Sefardim (since they follow the *psakim* of the *Beis Yosef*) should be *machmir* and Ashkenazim can be *meikil*.[26] Indeed, this is the common custom.

However, there are Sefardic *Poskim* who rule that a Sefardi can be lenient (some hold only *b'dieved*,[27] while others hold even *lechatchilla*),[28]

---

nowadays many do so and do not get harmed ("*dashu bei rabbim*"), it must be *muttar*.

24 See *Rambam* (*Hilchos Maachalos Assuros* Ch. 9:5). This is also the opinion of other Rishonim, including the *Ran* (*Chullin* 37a in the *Rif's* pagination) and *Rashba* (*Toras Habayis Ha'aruch, Dinei Bassar B'chalav*, Bayis 3, Shaar 4, pg. 82b), following the basic understanding of the Mishnah and Gemara in *Chullin* (103b), that if it is permitted to cook milk and fish together, it stands to reason that eating them together is also permitted.

25 Including the *Yad Yehuda* (87, *Peirush Hakatzer* 6), *Atzei Ha'Olah* (*Devarim Ha'assurim Meshum Sakana, Chukei Chaim* 6), and *Kaf Hachaim* (Y.D. 87:24 and O.C. 173:3).

26 See *Shu"t Yechaveh Daas* (vol. 6:48, *sikum*).

27 *Shu"t Zivchei Tzedek* (vol. 3:143), *Shu"t Yechaveh Daas* (ibid. *Hagahah*), *Yalkut Yosef* (*Issur V'Hetter* vol. 3, 87:83, and pg. 311 s.v. *ulefi aniyus daati*).

28 Including the *Pri Chodosh* (Y.D. 87: end 6), Chida (*Machzik Bracha* ad loc. 4), *Shulchan Gavoah* (ad loc. 11), and more contemporarily, Rav Shalom Messas (Meshash) (*Shu"t Shemesh U'Magen* vol. 4, Y.D. 12), the *Birkas Yehuda* (*Shu"t* vol. 2, Y.D. 5), and the *Ya'alas Chein* (*Shu"t* Y.D. 2). It seems that this Sefardic allowance of eating fish and milk *lechatchilla* seems to be much more prevalent among those of Moroccan descent.

and there are Ashkenazic *Poskim* who maintain that even an Ashkenazi should be *machmir*.[29]

---

29 Ashkenazic authorities who advise stringency include the *Levush* (ibid.), *Pri Megadim* (ibid.), *Atzei Ha'Olah* (Y.D. 116:8), *Shulchan HaTahor* (from the Kamarna Rebbe; 173:5), as well as implied by the Yaavetz (*Mor U'Ketziah* ibid.) and *Gilyon Maharsha* (ibid.). On a more contemporary note, it is known that Rav Shlomo Zalman Auerbach (*Halichos Shlomo, Moadim* vol. 2, Pesach Ch. 12, footnote 48) was personally stringent about not eating fish and milk together. Rav Yosef Shalom Elyashiv (*He'aros B'Maseches Chullin*, 104a s.v. *chutz*; and as attested to this author by his *talmid* Rav Nochum Eisenstein) held that one should not cook milk and fish together *lechatchilla*. This author has heard a similar assessment from *Mori v'Rabi* Rav Yaakov Blau of the *Eidah Hachareidis*, that although a fish and milk mixture is not truly *assur*, nevertheless there is an old Yerushalmi *minhag* not to eat it, with the exceptions of butter and *shmetinin* (see next footnote). This was also the custom of Rav Moshe Aryeh Freund (*Mara D'Shmaatsah* 387). Rav Aharon of Belz was known to have been stringent with this and therefore many Belzer Chassidim are *makpid* as well (cited in *Damesek Eliezer Doleh U'Mashkeh* on *Hilchos Bassar B'chalav*, pg. 50, footnote 100; "*u'mikol makom minhageinu lehakpid bazeh*"). The Karlsburger Rav, Rav Yechezkel Roth (*Shu"t Eimek Hateshuva* vol. 6:308) concludes that "*Kol Batei Yisrael*" should be careful not to eat fish and milk together. Rav Yosef Lieberman (*Shu"t Mishnas Yosef* vol. 6:61 and vol. 11:131) writes regarding Ashkenazim who are *machmir*, "*tavo aleihem bracha*." On the other hand, *Orchos Rabbeinu* (ibid. footnote 24) relates that the *Chazon Ish* and Steipler Gaon were certainly more lenient regarding fish and milk than they were with fish and meat. As noted previously they were *makpid* with not even using meaty silverware for fish and vice versa, so they instead used milky silverware for the fish course! There is an interesting *shittah* attributed to the *Tzemach Tzedek* of Lubavitch (as pointed out by Rabbi Gedalya Oberlander, editor of *Kovetz Ohr Yisroel*, this is cited briefly in the *Reshimas Ha'Admor M'Lubavitch, Choveres* 185) that optimally one should follow the stringency of the *Beis Yosef*. However, as it seems there is a mistake in his words, this requirement is only applicable to the actual 'letter of law.' Hence, as the *Beis Yosef* only wrote not to eat "fish with milk," all other milk products and by-products, including cheese, would be permitted to be eaten with fish. This does seem to be the common Lubavitch *minhag*. On the other hand, it should be noted that the *Ben Ish Chai* (ibid.) understood the *Beis Yosef's* fish exhortation to include cheese and other milk products as well.

A remarkable side point is that most of the authorities who are *machmir* when it comes to mixing fish with milk and/or cheese, including Rav Ovadiah Yosef, are nevertheless lenient when it comes to mixing fish with butter.[30] This *hetter* of butter also includes "*shmetinin*," the layer of fat skimmed off of the top of milk.

However, it should be noted that the famed *Ben Ish Chai*, Rav Yosef Chaim of Baghdad, disagreed and was *machmir* with butter as well. Interestingly, his *Rebbi* and preceding Chief Rabbi of Baghdad, the *Zivchei Tzedek*, Rav Ovadiah (Abdallah) Somech, answering a query posed to him by Sefardim living in Bombay, India (now Mumbai), cited many proofs that one who does not have a stringent custom may at least be lenient with butter and fish, and is not required to follow his disciple's *machmir* stance.[31] Of course, there is also the majority opinion that the whole issue is a non-starter and there is no problem whatsoever, even with a tuna melt.

So, back at that *Bris*, whether you decide to take a bite of your Bagels and Lox Deluxe or not, at least you now have some food for thought.

Postscript: Butter in Baghdad?

This author recently spoke with Rav Yaakov Hillel, Rosh Yeshivas Ahavat Shalom, author of *Shu"t Vayashav HaYam*, and renowned expert

---

30 See *Shu"t Chinuch Beis Yehuda* (ibid. citing the Maharam M'Krakow), *Beis Lechem Yehuda* (ibid.), *Shu"t Adnei Paz* (ibid.), *Pri Megadim* (ibid.), *Yad Yehuda* (ibid.), *Yad Dovid* (Y.D. 87:14), *Zivchei Tzedek* (ad loc. 18), *Gilyon Maharsha* (Y.D. 116:2), *Atzei Ha'Olah* (Y.D. 116:8), *Shulchan HaTahor* (173:5), *Kaf Hachaim* (ibid.), *Shu"t Yechaveh Daas* (ibid.), *Halichos Olam* (vol. 7, pg. 20), and *Yalkut Yosef* (ibid.); and not like the *Ben Ish Chai* (ibid.) who forbade cooking fish with milk by-products, including butter. See next footnote.

31 *Ben Ish Chai* (ibid.), who forbade cooking fish with all milk by-products, including butter. The *Zivchei Tzedek* (*Shu"t* vol. 3:143; cited in *Yalkut Yosef* ibid.) proves that the Chida's ruling (ibid.) should be the *ikar* for Sefardim, as "*M'Yosef ad Yosef lo kam K'Yosef*," and concludes that even for those from Bombay, who generally follow Minhag Baghdad [see *Shu"t Rav Pe'alim* (vol. 3, Y.D. 17)], can cook their fish with butter, and are not required to follow his

on the rulings of the *Ben Ish Chai*, about which Sefardic *Minhag Baghdad* is customarily followed.

Generally speaking, the *Ben Ish Chai* and his *Rebbi*, the *Zivchei Tzedek*, concurred about what constituted *Minhag Baghdad*. Rav Hillel told this author that as seldom as it may be, if there was ever a difference of opinion between the two luminaries, as the *Ben Ish Chai* was the later *Posek (Basrai)*, then his *shittah* would be followed. This case, on the other hand, is unique, as the *Zivchei Tzedek's* counter-ruling was not published in his earlier *sefarim* on *Yoreh Deah*, but rather in his responsa printed at the end of his life, after the *Ben Ish Chai's psak* in this matter was already printed and well known. As such, it might truly be considered the *"psak basra."*

Rav Hillel concluded that if there is someone of Iraqi or Indian descent whose family *minhag* was to allow cooking fish in butter, as per the *Zivchei Tzedek*, he may certainly continue doing so. However, as far as he was aware, the general *minhag* was to follow the *Ben Ish Chai's* more stringent ruling in this matter and forbid cooking fish in butter.

This seems to be further attested to by Rav Mordechai Eliyahu, former *Rishon L'Tzion* and Sefardic Chief Rabbi of Israel, in his *Darchei Halacha* glosses to the *Kitzur Shulchan Aruch*,[32] who states matter-of-factly that *"anu nizharim shelo le'echol dagim im chalav oh gevina*, we are careful not to eat fish with milk or cheese," citing the *Ben Ish Chai's* precedent, implying that the more common Sefardic *minhag* follows the *Ben Ish Chai*.

---

talmid, the *Ben Ish Chai's*, more stringent ruling of prohibiting even fish and butter.

32   *Darchei Halacha* glosses on the *Kitzur Shulchan Aruch* (33:1).

Chapter 9

Genetically Engineered Meat

SEVERAL YEARS AGO, THE BBC broke an exclusive story[1]—one that many claim has potential to change the world. In a press conference held in London on August 5, 2013, Professor Mark Post of Maastricht University in the Netherlands revealed that he had done the impossible. Employing cutting-edge stem-cell biotechnology, he created the world's first laboratory-grown hamburger. While news of this $325,000 hamburger was welcomed by environmentalists, animal-rights activists, and doom n' gloom predictors alike—with others defining it as "just plain weird"—our concern is how such a creation would be viewed through the lens of *halacha*.

Frankenburgers?

This hamburger was created by extracting stem cells (the body's master cells; templates from which specialized tissue develops) from a living cow's neck muscle tissue via a small syringe. The stem cells (or to be more specific, myosatellite cells, a kind of stem cell that repairs muscle tissue) were then separated from the other cells in the tissue sample and were cultured and grown in-vitro in a bio-reactor, multiplied utilizing nutrients and growth-promoting chemicals, and later coalesced, forming tiny strips of muscle fiber. Approximately twenty thousand of these strips were needed to create just one hamburger.[2]

---

1   BBC: http://www.bbc.co.uk/news/science-environment-22885969.
2   See Post M.J. "Cultured Beef: Medical Technology to Produce Food," in *Journal of the Science of Food and Agriculture* (April 1, 2014; vol. 94:6, pg. 1039–1041).

It is important to note that although there are now quite a few companies working on developing the science and applying it for the commercial use of synthetic meat in the near future, nonetheless, with the current price tag of test-tube beef being in the six figures, its mass production unrealistic in the foreseeable future, and the exact scientific process kept under wraps, this *halachic* discussion is primarily academic and firmly entrenched in the realm of theory—and perhaps even science-fiction. If and when lab-grown burgers become affordable and mainstream, their status would need to be appraised by the expert *Rabbanim* of the time, based on the actual *metzius*, or facts on the ground, of how these burgers are made.

Still, over the last few years, several *Rabbanim* have tackled the topic, attempting to define how these lab-grown burgers should be considered from a *halachic* standpoint. Yet, based on different precedents cited, their theorized conclusions are quite diverse.[3] Would this man-made

---

According to Mosa Meat, the Dutch company, Dr. Post founded to produce this "meat" (www.mosameat.com), the process for producing cultured, or "clean" meat, is to take muscle tissue from animals under anesthesia using a biopsy probe. Cells from this tissue are then induced to revert to myosatellite stem cells, which are the embryonic precursors to muscle cells. These cells are placed in a carefully controlled nutrient serum in a bioreactor, where they proliferate. When enough cells are grown, the nutrients are reduced, causing the cells to differentiate and form a primitive muscle tissue called myotubes. They are then transferred to a hydrogel medium to help them form into muscle fibers by the thousands until, after suitable infusion with myoglobin-like substances to give them the proper color and after being ground, they resemble hamburger or sausage meat. The company claims it could make up to eighty thousand quarter pounders from a single sample.

3   See, for example, this Jerusalem Post article from 2013: http://www.jpost.com/Jewish-World/Jewish-News/Orthodox-groups-debate-kashrut-of-lab-grown-meat-322642. Since then, the issue of stem cell meat and its kashrus status has been discussed and debated by various *Rabbanim* (including this author) in several volumes of *Techumin* (vol. 34–36; 2014–2016), *Tradition* (46:4; Winter 2013), the (RJJ) *Journal of Halacha and Contemporary Society* (vol. 72; Succot 5777/Fall 2016), *Headlines* (*Halachic Debates of Current Events*; vol. 1), Machon HaTorah V'Ha'aretz (www.toraland.org.il), *Kovetz*

Genetically Engineered Meat 99

and modified meat be considered kosher or *treif*? Pareve or *fleishig*? Let's address the various potential *halachic* possibilities.

Magical Mystery Meat

In truth, meat created from non-traditional sources has a tradition and precedent, and is already mentioned in the Gemara—once regarding meat that came down from the Heavens, and again concerning meat that was created using the *Sefer Yetzira*, "the Book of Creation" attributed to Avraham Avinu.[4]

Hame'ayen (Teves 5776), *B'sod Siach* (Sivan 5776), *Contemporary Halakhic Problems* (vol. 7), *Hakirah* (vol. 24; Spring 2018), and most recently in the OU's *Daf HaKashrus* (vol. 27, issues 3 and 4; March-May 2019). This author was recently featured on the "Headlines" radio show (07/22/2017) discussing this topic. A recording of the show may be accessed at: http://podcast.headlinesbook.com/e/72217-self-driving-cars-in-halacha-staying-spiritually-safe-in-the-workplace-and-on-business-trips-stem-cell-meat-in-halacha/

4   *Sanhedrin* (59b and 65b). However, it must be noted that on a practical level there are differences between these two *Maasei Chazal*. The Gemara in *Menachos* (69b) deals with whether the *Mincha* for a *Korban* can be brought from "wheat that came down from the clouds," as the Torah mandates it be from *"moshvoseichem*, your dwelling places" (*Vayikra, Parashas Emor* Ch. 23:17). *Rashi* (ad loc. s.v. *sheyardu*) understands this case to mean that the clouds sucked in wheat from a wheat-laden ship in the ocean, and when raining, some wheat kernels rained down along with the rain. Yet, *Tosafos* (ad loc. *chittin*) maintains that this was an actual *neis*, meaning a genuine miracle. Indeed, the *Rambam* (*Hilchos Tamidin U'Mussafin* Ch. 8:3) concludes that although the Gemara leaves the issue as an *"eebaui delo ifshitta"* (meaning, it did not rule conclusively whether cloud based grain truly constitutes *"mimoshvoseichem"*), still, such wheat is at least *kosher b'dieved* for *Korbanos*. Several contemporary authorities, including the Kozoglover Gaon (*Shu"t Eretz Tzvi* vol. 2:9), Rav Betzalel Stern (*Shu"t B'tzeil Hachochma* vol. 6:99 s.v. *v'acharon*), and Rav Nosson Gestetner (*Shu"t Lehoros Nosson* vol. 7:11, 9) explain that when the item in question is a result of a *neis* from Hashem, it maintains all the attributes of a natural item of the same, as technically speaking, "nature" is also a G-d given miracle. Yet, if it was a man-made item, then it would be exempt from all natural attributes and obligations of a similar natural item. Hence, meat that came down from the Heavens and

The *Malbim* writes that meat created using the *Sefer Yetzira* is essentially pareve. That, he posits, is the reason is why Avraham Avinu was able to serve the visiting angels a meal containing both milk and meat; the meat was truly pareve, as Avraham created it that day!⁵ The *Cheshek Shlomo, Av Beis Din* of Vilna in the nineteenth century, extrapolates further. He posits that it stands to reason that milk from a cow created via the *Sefer Yetzira* should not be truly *milchig*, but rather pareve too.⁶

---

man-made meat via *Sefer Yetzira* may not necessarily share the exact *halachos*. This author has seen a recent discussion by Rabbi Avraham Maimon in *Kovetz Ohr Torah* (Teves 5759; 32, pg. 268–279) regarding what the proper *bracha* would be, and whether a *bracha* is even mandated, regarding this "magical meat," based on the famous discussion regarding the *munn*, manna that came down from Heaven. The *Ram"a M'Fano* is even quoted as mandating "*Hamotzi lechem* **min hashamayim**" for *munn*. Certainly, as per Gemara *Brachos* (48b), *Birkas Hamazon* was mandated for eating the *munn*. [See Rav Nissan Kaplan's *Shalmei Nissan* (on *Perek Keitzad Mevorchin* pg. 304–305; who cites many *shittos* on topic) at length.] Rabbi Maimon opines that the same should apply to meat created via *Sefer Yetzira*, as by eating it one is still receiving *"hana'ah min ha'olam"* as per Gemara *Brachos* (35b), and therefore a *bracha* would be required, presumably *Shehakol*. This question was also briefly addressed, with no compelling rationale either way, in *Shu"t Vayaan Shaul* (Y.D. end 8). Thanks are due to R' Eliezer Freimark for pointing out several of these interesting sources.

5   *Malbim* (*HaTorah V'HaMitzva, Parashas Vayera* Ch. 18:8). A similar explanation can also be found in the *Pirkei D'Rabbi Eliezer* (cited in *Yalkut Reuveini* on *Parashas Vayera*) and by the *Chessed L'Avraham* (ancestor of the Chida; *Ein Mishpat, Nahar* 51). The *Pardes Yosef* cites this as well (*Parashas Vayera* Ch. 18, pg. 115, end first paragraph and *Parashas Vayeishev* Ch. 37, pg. 268, end first paragraph). See also *Darchei Teshuva* (87:29). There are many other interpretations of how to understand Avraham Avinu's actions. This was discussed in a previous chapter titled "*Maaseh Avos = Halacha Lemaaseh: Hekker, Shomer*, and *Maris Ayin.*"

6   *Cheshek Shlomo* (end Y.D. 98, s.v. *v'da*). He is attempting to resolve the *Kreisi U'Pleisi's* question (81:7; at length) on the Gemara *Bechoros* (6b), why it did not cite Avraham Avinu's serving of milk as proof that milk is not considered *Aver Min Hachai* (see *Shulchan Aruch* Y.D. 81:5), which would be prohibited even for non-Jews as it is one of the Seven Mitzvos of Bnei Noach (see *Rambam, Hilchos*

If so, some opine that our test-tube burger should be considered not only kosher, but pareve as well, due to this precedent regarding items created from non-traditional sources.[7]

Melachim Ch. 9:10 and *Aruch Hashulchan* Y.D. 62:4 and 5). A similar solution is offered by Rav Yitzchak *Halevi* Horowitz of Hamburg in his *Metaamei Yitzchak* glosses to the *Kreisi U'Pleisi* (ad loc.). It is also worthwhile to see the *Chasam Sofer's* (*Shu"t* Y.D. 73 s.v. *vl'shleimus ha'inyan*) interesting alternate approach to the *Kreisi U'Pleisi's* question, although it is not directly related to this discussion. On the topic of the Seven Mitzvos of Bnei Noach, see Rav Yirmiyohu Kaganoff's fascinating treatment titled "Noahide Halacha 101 or Meet the Adams Family," in his recent English *sefer From Buffalo Burgers to Monetary Mysteries*, and online at http://rabbikaganoff.com/noahides-halacha/.

7   Although Rabbi Menachem Genack, CEO of the OU, had previously asserted in an *Ami Magazine* interview (issue 342, pg. 188; Nov. 15, 2017; available on the OU's website) that this is indeed his personal opinion, according to a more recent *New York Times* article (Sep. 30, 2018; titled "The Incredible New Kashrut: Meat Labs Pursue a Once-Impossible Goal: Kosher Bacon"), and perhaps due to the compelling arguments presented herein (full disclosure: this author sent an earlier version of this chapter to Rabbi Genack), he has since changed his mind, as well as set the OU's policy accordingly. To cite the *New York Times*, Rabbi Genack, "initially thought clean meat could be pareve, based on his belief that clean meat was created from an animal's genetic code. But because the process involves an animal cell, replicating itself millions of times, he now believes the product should be thought of as meat." As such, *shechita* would be required. As the article reports, Rabbi Gavriel Price of the OU told the biotech companies that the original cells that go into the solution would have to be kosher, "from an animal that was properly slaughtered and not scraped off a live animal. (There is a Jewish law against eating live animals.) This was not well received by some of the clean meat companies, which want to produce something that does not involve killing any animals." Indeed, in a recent *Daf HaKashrus* (vol. 27, issue 4; April-May 2019; "Halachic Perspective on Cell-Based Meat") Rabbi Eli Gersten of the OU explicitly writes that "to grow cultured meat, the living cells would have to be extracted and isolated, and the effect of these cells would be apparent as they grow. At that point, we would recognize them as being living meat cells...As such, cells extracted from a live or unslaughtered animal would be *treif*, even though they were not initially visible. Cells from a kosher slaughtered animal would be treated as *fleishig*...If non-kosher stem cells are used, the resulting product

However, it is important to note that even according to this theory, in order for the burger to receive this *halachic* status, the cow that the stem cells were harvested from would need to have had a proper *shechita*, precluding a biopsy from a live cow. Although meat created utilizing the *Sefer Yetzira* should not technically need ritual slaughter (as it was not truly alive),[8] nevertheless, *shechita* still would be mandated due to the Rabbinic injunction of *Maris Ayin*.[9] The basic definition of this law is the prohibition of taking actions which, although strictly speaking are

> would be non-kosher…If the [kosher animal] was not *Shechted*, these cells would be *Bassar Min Hachai* and forbidden."

8   *Shlah* (*Shnei Luchos Habris* vol. 2, *Torah She'bichsav*, *Parashas Vayeishev*), explaining that this was what the *Shevatim* were eating that Yosef *HaTzaddik* wrongly assumed was *Aver Min Hachai*. See also *Shu"t Lehoros Nosson* (vol. 7:11) who cites this *Shlah lemaaseh*, that an animal created via *Sefer Yetzira* would be exempt from many related Mitzvos. Interestingly, the *Shlah* continues that when Yosef suspected his brothers of *Giluy Arayos*, it was really a female Golem they created *"letayel imah."* Fascinatingly, the *Chofetz Chaim*, in his *Shemiras Halashon* (vol. 2, Ch. 11, end s.v. *vayavei Yosef*), cites this as the *pashut pshat*.

9   *Pischei Teshuva* (Y.D. 62:2). A similar assessment is given in *Mili D'Abba* (on *Sanhedrin* 65b), that *me'ikar hadin* such an animal would not need *shechita*, and only does due to *Maris Ayin*. See also *Darchei Teshuva* (ad loc. 6). However, see *Shu"t Rivevos Efraim* (vol. 7:385; in a *teshuva* from Rav Yosef Binyomin Tzarfati of Antwerp) at length, who posits that such an animal created with *Sefer Yetzira* would have the full status of a real animal and would need *shechita m'dina*. He explains that the main reason why a man-made Golem would not be able to be counted for a *minyan*, according to the majority consensus, is that it lacks the ability of speech. In order to be considered having a *neshama*, a creation needs to have the potential for speech [see, for example the *Ramban's* commentary to *Parashas Bereishis* (Ch. 2:7; based on *Targum Onkelus* ad loc.)], an attribute a Golem sorely lacks. See *Shu"t Sheilas Yaavetz* (vol. 2:82), *Maharsha* (*Sanhedrin* 65b, *Chiddushei Aggados* s.v. *v'lo*), *Shu"t Yehuda Yaaleh* (vol. 1, O.C. 26), *Shu"t Afraksta D'Anya* (vol. 4:388 s.v. *puk*), the Radzhiner Rebbe's *Sidrei Taharos* on *Maseches Ohalos* (pg. 5a, *Peirush Ha'aruch*) and *Chazon Ish* (Y.D. 116:1). Accordingly, in layman's terms, a Golem is technically considered "an animal in human form" and therefore *lemaaseh* cannot be counted for a *minyan*. [This was discussed at length in an article titled "Of

permitted according to *halacha*, nevertheless give onlookers the impression that we are doing something *halachically* forbidden.[10] Accordingly, the same would apply to our home-grown hamburger, and *shechita* would be required.

On the other hand, on a practical level, as Rav Asher Weiss noted in a recent responsum on the topic, it would be tenuous at best to cite precedent from rationales offered as simple exegesis (*drush v'aggada*) as *halachic* proof. Moreover, it seems quite incongruous to suggest that *Sefer Yetzira* or other miraculous food creations that appeared out of thin air should affect our discussion at all, as lab-developed meat is not "*maaseh nissim*" ("miracle meat"), but rather meat that was scientifically harvested, grown, and multiplied from its own original minuscule stem cells.[11]

Elul, L'Dovid, and Golems" (*Yated Ne'eman*, 10 Elul 5774/September 5, 2014; and online at: http://ohr.edu/this_week/insights_into_halacha/4886)]. However, conversely, an animal never has the potential for speech, and therefore a man-made animal should intrinsically have the same status of a regular animal; ergo, *shechita* would be mandated. Obviously, this logic would not be in concurrence with the *Shlah* and those who rule like him (see previous footnote). For more on issues related to animals created via *Sefer Yetzira*, see *Pardes Yosef* at length (*Parashas Vayeishev* Ch. 37, pg. 267–269), as well as *Shu"t Lehoros Nosson* (vol. 7:11), *Chashukei Chemed* (*Sanhedrin* 65b), *Kovetz Ohr Torah* (Teves 5759; 32, ibid.), and *Shu"t Avnei Chein* (Cohen; vol. 3:12–14).

10 This issue is addressed at length in the chapter titled "Margarine, Misconceptions, and *Maris Ayin*." See also *Shu"t Maadanei Melachim* (67:1), citing precedent from the *Ben Ish Chai* (*Ben Yehoyada*, *Sanhedrin* 65b s.v. bram), who maintains that although this *sheilah* is not applicable nowadays, nevertheless, the prohibition of *Maris Ayin* would not be applicable to eating meat created using *Sefer Yetzira*, and it is permissible to eat with milk. He explains that since this meat has no blood, nor taste, and is not physically satiating for the body, that is its own built-in *hekker* that it is not true meat, "*hein b'mareh, hein b'taam.*"

11 Rav Weiss' (as yet unpublished) *teshuva* titled "*B'Inyan Bassar Sintetti* (Concerning Synthetic Meat)." Indeed, this lab-grown meat is not "*yeish m'ayin*" (something created from nothing) but "*yeish m'yeish*" (something created from something), just originally a "microscopic *yeish*." Similarly, in

Gelling Together

Another possible precedent posited was to compare the lab burger's status to that of gelatin, which is a whole separate discussion in itself. Already controversial when cited in *halachic* literature over a century ago, gelatin's kashrus status is still being debated today.

Gelatin is a translucent, colorless, and flavorless solid protein-based substance, derived from collagen obtained from various animal by-products, mainly the bones and skin of cows and/or pigs. It is the gelling agent that makes marshmallows and "gummy bears" gummy.

The process to make gelatin is an interesting one: the collagen in the bones and skin of the animals is converted into ossein by soaking them in hydrochloric acid. Then it is soaked in lime for about a month, followed by a wash in sulfuric acid.[12] (Do not try this at home!)[13]

Contemporary authorities debate gelatin's *halachic* status. Although Rav Chaim Ozer Grodzenski and Rav Simcha Zelig Rieger, *Dayan* of Brisk, permitted gelatin made utilizing hard cow bones, and Rav Ovadiah Yosef even allowed gelatin made from cow skins,[14] nevertheless, when

---

a recent "Headlines" radio show dedicated to this topic (aired 07/22/2017), the host, Dovid Lichtenstein, retorted that "Respectfully, it seems almost a foolish comparison...somebody taking something that is here and growing it through a scientific method is not *Sefer Yetzira*...there is nothing miracle about it, it's science...honestly, a pretty *na'arish* comparison."

12 As per Rabbi Eliezer Eidelitz's *Is It Kosher?* (pg. 122). See also Rav Zushe Yosef Blech's exhaustive *Kosher Food Production* (pg. 369–375; "Will These Bones Live?").

13 I still remember the poem my high school chemistry teacher, Mr. Ezra Roberg, drilled into us regarding the potential dangers of sulfuric acid: "Johnny was here yesterday; today he's here no more. For what he thought was H_2O, was H_2SO_4."

14 *Shu"t Achiezer* (vol. 3:33, 5) and *Shu"t Yabia Omer* (vol. 8, Y.D. 11). Rav Simcha Zelig's responsum, dated 5698, was well known, but was only first published in Elul 5775 (*Kovetz Moriah*, issue 400–402, pg. 76–77). One of the primary points for permitting is that of "*Panim Chadoshos*, that it is considered a brand new entity." The source for this leniency is the opinion of Rabbeinu Yonah, cited by the *Rosh* in *Brachos* (Ch. 6:38) regarding the status of musk. During

this *sheilah* arose in the 1950–60s, most *Gedolim* based in America, including Rav Aharon Kotler, Rav Eliezer Silver, Rav Moshe Feinstein, and Rav Yosef Eliyahu Henkin (as well as most later *Poskim* in Eretz Yisrael) all unequivocally prohibited gelatin,[15] unless it was derived

---

the process of producing gelatin, the original bones are completely destroyed by the various acids et al., and the inedible gelatinous results bear no resemblance, not even by taste nor form to the original, and would therefore be considered a completely new item. This would be similar to the rule of *Or Hakeiva* that has become as hard as wood losing its status of meat (see *Rema* Y.D. 87: end 10). However, Rav Chaim Ozer's and Rav Simcha Zelig's allowance for gelatin was based on certain processes of the day (processed from hard cow bones, as they wrote, which are not intrinsically *assur*). It is highly doubtful that if they had seen gelatin produced from pig flesh they would have still maintained the same *hetter* (see next footnote). The issue of "hard" versus "soft" (edible) bones is based on a *machlokes* between the *Minchas Yaakov* (*Shu"t* 15) and *Pri Megadim* (Y.D. 87, S.D. 22) how to understand the *Shulchan Aruch's* choice of words (Y.D. 87:7) defining bones' halachic status, as well as the *Shach* and other commentaries in *Hilchos Taaruvos* (Y.D. 99:1). There were other *Poskim* who permitted gelatin over the years, including Rav Yosef Konvitz (*Shu"t Divrei Yosef* vol. 2:6), Rav Shmuel Aharon *Halevi* Pardes (in several *teshuvos* over the years in his renowned Pardes Torah Journal and in his posthumously published *Avnei Shmuel, Birurei Halacha* 19), Rav Moshe Nosson Nota Lemberger (*Shu"t Ateres Moshe* Y.D. vol. 1:42 and 43), Rav Eliezer Yehuda Waldenberg (in the preface to his *Shu"t Tzitz Eliezer* vol. 4, published along with Rav Yechezkel Abramsky's original *teshuva*, and vol. 20:34), and Rav Ben Tzion Abba-Shaul (*Shu"t Ohr L'Tzion* vol. 1, O.C. 34, pg 90); yet, several of them, including Rav Dovid Tzvi Hoffman of Berlin (*Shu"t Melamed L'Ho'eel* vol. 2, Y.D. 35), Rav Tzvi Pesach Frank (*Shu"t Har Tzvi* Y.D. 83), and Rav Yechezkel Abramsky (*Chazon Yechezkel, Zevachim, Shu"t* 5), qualified their permissive rulings, stating that only *b'dieved* or for a *choleh* (a sick person) may dispensation be given.

15 Rav Aharon Kotler (*Shu"t Mishnas Rabbi Aharon* 16 and 17), Rav Moshe Feinstein (*Shu"t Igros Moshe* Y.D. vol. 2:27), and Rav Yosef Eliyahu Henkin (*Eidus L'Yisrael* pg. 177; and in his recent posthumously published *Shu"t Gevuros Eliyahu* vol. 2-Y.D. end 16–23). Rav Silver's *shittah* is well known; aside from publicizing a letter in 1951 against a *hechsher* certifying a well-known gelatin product (Jell-O), he has written at least two separate *teshuvos* on topic: one to Rav Zelig Reuven Bengis of the *Eidah Hachareidis* in Yerushalayim—reprinted

in *Kovetz Yeshurun* (vol. 12, pg. 241), and another in *Kovetz Kerem* (Year 2, vol. 1, pg. 5; Tishrei 5713), in which he decried the state of gelatin production in his day, averring that the process that Rav Chaim Ozer was referring to was not the actual current process of his day, which utilized the flesh and skins of *neveilos*, *treifos*, and even pigs. In his opinion, partaking of such gelatin was transgressing a *safek Deoraysa*, and asserted that certainly his *Rebbi*, Rav Chaim Ozer, would have agreed. [Rav Moshe Feinstein is also quoted as asserting similarly in the recently published *Mesores Moshe* (vol. 2, pg. 186:46): *"d'hayom gam ha'Achiezer yodeh, dehalo osim mei'oros im bassar."*] Rav Silver lists over twenty-five well-known *Rabbanim* and *Poskim* of his day who agreed with his stringent *shittah*. Similarly, in *Avnei Shmuel*, the editor, Rav Simcha Elberg, author of *Shalmei Simcha* and long time editor of *Kovetz HaPardes*, after the founding editor Rav Shmuel Aharon *Halevi* Pardes was *niftar*, published his original extensive *Kuntress* on Gelatin that he wrote in the 1950s, concluding that the only *hetter* for granting *hashgacha* on gelatin was when the process was performed exclusively using hard bones, but not with skins and flesh of *neveilos*—and certainly not pigs. Other *Poskim* who ruled this way include the *Chazon Ish* (Y.D. 12:7), the *Minchas Yitzchak* (*Shu"t* vol. 5:5), Rav Yosef Shalom Elyashiv (*Kovetz Teshuvos* vol. 1:73, 3), Rav Shmuel *Halevi* Wosner (*Shu"t Shevet Halevi* vol. 7:135), Rav Moshe Sternbuch (*Shu"t Teshuvos V'Hanhagos* vol. 2:381), Rav Menashe Klein (*Shu"t Mishnah Halachos* vol. 3:111), and Rav Yechezkel Roth (*Shu"t Eimek Hateshuva* vol. 3:67). One of their main points of contention is questioning the application of "*Panim Chadoshos*" to gelatin, as the collagen which is the basis for the gelatin, was part and parcel of the original bones and skin the whole time [see, for example, *Shu"t Even Yikara* (vol. 2:140); cited in *She'arim Metzuyanim B'Halacha* (47:5), who makes this distinction in the *shittos* of Rishonim regarding honey manufactured by a non-Jew]. Additionally, the fact that one wants to use it as a food item might make it considered "*Achshevei.*" This means that one's intention to eat it, although currently inedible, would *halachically* return it to its original status, reconsider it a food item, and thus, in our case, be rendered *treif*. [For an example of how this might work, see *Rosh* (*Pesachim*, Ch. 2: end 1), *Taz* (O.C. 442:8), *Minchas Chinuch* (Mitzva 261:5), and *Shu"t Shaagas Aryeh* (75).] Moreover, nowadays pig by-products (hides and skins, etc.) are often used in making gelatin, and the *Rambam* (*Hilchos Maacholos Assuros* Ch. 4:21) states that the hides of domesticated pigs have the *halachic* status of meat, and are considered edible and are most definitely not kosher. Thus, even those who argued that gelatin made from the hides of (non-*halachically shechted*) beef

from properly *shechted* kosher animals.[16] Nowadays, although the Israeli Chief Rabbinate permits gelatin as kosher and has a distinct designation, *"kosher l'ochlei gelatin,"* on the other hand, no *Mehadrin* kashrus agency or *Badatz* in Eretz Yisrael, nor any mainstream certifying agency

---

or from bones is still *me'ikar hadin* kosher, would nevertheless have a harder time defending that position in regard to porcine (pig-based) gelatin. It is worthwhile to read Rav Yirmiyahu Cohen, *Dayan* in Antwerp and later *Av Beis Din* of Paris' *Shu"t Veheirim Hakohen* (vol. 2:31), who details at length the processes of both types of dedicated gelatin lines from a plant in Belgium; one using only dried-out bones and the other utilizing skins and fresh bones etc. from *neveilos*. He concludes that although "we personally do not rely on either one" as kosher gelatin, nevertheless, the line of gelatin processed exclusively out of dried out bones is exactly as Rav Chaim Ozer described in his *teshuva*, and one who is *"somech atzmo al hetter hana"l b'Taaruvos, yeish lo al mi lismoch."* This heavily implies that other common types of processed gelatin would not fit under Rav Chaim Ozer's *hetter*.

16 In a fascinating historical sidenote, the aforementioned *sheilah* addressed by Rav Aharon, Rav Moshe, and Rav Silver in the early 1960s was sent by Rav Nochum Tzvi Kornmehl, Chief Rabbi of Albany, New York and *Rav Hamachshir* for Barton's Candy. He wanted to know their opinions on the permissibility of utilizing gelatin to manufacture marshmallow-covered chocolates and if kosher gelatin produced from properly *shechted* animals would be considered *fleishig* or pareve. Their *psak* of using exclusively kosher *shechted* animals for gelatin was later confirmed by the *Vaad HaRabbanim* of the *Agudas Yisrael* in Yerushalayim, and signed by Rav Yitzchak Flakser (Rosh Yeshivas Sfas Emes and author of the seventeen-volume *Shaarei Yitzchak* on *Shas*), Rav Aharon Bernstein, and Rav Yisrael Grossman. Rav Kornmehl actually published an entire treatment on the topic (titled *"Kuntress B'Inyan Gelatin"*) in the beginning of his first volume of responsa, *Shu"t Tiferes Tzvi*, including in it the *teshuvos* of the aforementioned *Gedolim*. Indeed, for many years Barton's was widely known for their strict adherence to *halacha*, and only used gelatin made from *glatt* kosher beef hides in producing their confections. Later on, in the 1980s and 90s, the renowned Rav Shimon Eider was involved in kosher animal-based gelatin production, ensuring the availability of one hundred percent kosher, real bovine-derived gelatin (dubbed "Kolatin") for the kosher consumer.

in America considers real gelatin kosher,[17] unless it is produced from properly *shechted* kosher animals.

Back to our test-tube burger, if it can be compared with gelatin, as it is essentially a meat-based product that has undergone extreme change via chemicals, its *halachic* status could depend on the above *machlokes*:

- According to those who rule leniently even with gelatin that is not kosher-based, an argument can be made that the same dispensation could be given to our Petri-dish patty and the actual source of the original stem cells should not trouble us too much.[18]
- Yet, according to the mainstream opinion that kosher gelatin must originate from a *shechted* kosher animal, the same would certainly apply to our lab-created burger and be mandated for it as well.

---

17 I used the term "real gelatin," as nowadays kosher "gelatin" made from agar-agar (seaweed) or from fish is quite commonplace, and does not have these same *halachic* issues as true gelatin made from possible *neveilos u'treifos*.

18 Rav Shlomo Aviner (*Torat Harav Aviner*, 12 August, 2013, "Kashrut of Laboratory-Grown Hamburger") seems to be a proponent of this theory. He writes that "this 'meat' undergoes many changes to the point that its entire identity is different. This is the same as gelatin from non-kosher animals. The bones undergo so many changes that the product is considered an entirely new creation. While some authorities are strict about this issue, the basic *halacha* is that gelatin is kosher (See *Shu"t Yabia Omer* 8:11)." Rav Aviner's assessment can be accessed at http://www.ravaviner.com/2013/08/kashrut-of-laboratory-grown-hamburger.html?m=1. Thanks are due to Rabbi Anthony Manning for providing this source. Rabbi Yuval Chernow, co-founder of the controversial Tzohar Rabbinical Organization, took this leniency a "giant leap" further and made headlines when he recently announced that in his opinion, this would even apply to pigs. He stated that when the "cell of a pig is used and its genetic material is utilized in the production of food, the cell loses its original identity and therefore cannot be defined as forbidden for consumption. It wouldn't even be meat, so you can consume it with dairy." However, opposition was not long in coming, and most rabbis have essentially labeled this new kashrus revelation as "nothing but hogwash." [See for example, http://www.5tjt.com/tzohar-rabbi-is-incorrect-cloned-pig-meat-is-not-kosher/, http://thejewishvoice.com/2018/03/26/nothing-kosher-cloned-pig/,

An interesting outcome of this *machlokes* is actually another *machlokes*. Even amidst the mainstream ruling regarding gelatin, there are differences between the opinions:

- For example, Rav Moshe and several other *Poskim* held that real kosher gelatin made from *shechted* cows is considered completely pareve.
- Rav Aharon Kotler, however, was of the opinion that *lechatchilla* one should still consider it somewhat *fleishig* and not mix it with milk, unless the gelatin content would be less than one-sixtieth of the final product.

If we use gelatin as our *halachic* springboard, one could make a case that the same debate can also technically apply to our home-grown hamburger:

- Accordingly, those who follow Rav Moshe's *psak* regarding kosher gelatin being pareve (for example, the OU), may perhaps also assume that the lab burger is pareve as well.
- On the other hand, those who follow Rav Aharon's *shittah* should still ensure that no milk is mixed amid the man-made modified meat.

However, it is important to note that the comparison to gelatin is not exactly comparable, as during the process of producing gelatin, the

---

and https://www.torahmusings.com/2018/04/cloned-pigs-arent-kosher/.] Moreover, even regarding "pork" created via *Sefer Yetzira*, already in the late 1800s Rav Avraham Palaji, Chief Rabbi of Izmir and one of the *Gedolei Hador* wrote (*Vayikra Avraham, Parashas Vayikra, Parashah* 3, *Piska* 12, end s.v. *nissim*; thanks are due to R' Eliezer Freimark for pointing out this source) that it is highly doubtful that such "pork" would be permitted to be eaten. Any rationale for proscription would certainly apply to "pork" grown in a lab utilizing a pig's own stem cells. To sum it up, practically, although the media seems to have enjoyed the paradoxical discussion about kosher pig meat, however, the consensus is that this lab-grown pig meat is certainly forbidden for multiple reasons, many which are delineated in this chapter. All potential *halachic* issues relevant to utilizing stem cell cow meat, and then some, would undoubtedly apply to using porcine stem cells to "grow meat."

original bones are completely destroyed by the various acids and chemicals, and the inedible gelatinous results bear no resemblance—not by taste or form—to the original.

On the other hand, regarding the stem-cell burger, the chemicals are used to enhance and grow its original meaty essence, not break it down to convert it to a different substance. In other words, in the case of synthetic meat, as opposed to gelatin, the product remains edible throughout the process. Accordingly, this seems to mark its *halachic* similarities to gelatin as quite questionable, and consequently, the above theoretical discussion not very pertinent to its status on a practical level.

Permitted Patties?

Recently, there have been several *Rabbanim* who would categorize all stem-cell meat as non-problematic from a *halachic* standpoint due to several interesting precedents.[19] Regarding pregnancy, Chazal refer to a fetus prior to reaching forty days after conception as *"maya b'alma,"* just plain water; meaning that it has not yet reached a stage where it is actually considered a living person.[20] There are various *halachos* based

---

19 See R' Zvi Ryzman's original *maamar* in *Techumin* vol. 34 (5774) at length, his responses to both this author's and Rav Yaakov Ariel's refutations in *Techumin* vol. 35 (5775) and vol. 36 (5776), as well as Rabbi Zev Weitman of Tnuva's brief *maamar* in *Techumin* (vol. 36 ad loc.). Rav Dov Lior of Kiryat Arba is quoted as holding similarly (*Kashrus Magazine*, March 2019, pg. 29–30), that "because it is microscopic, it has taken on a new identity and would not be considered meat, and is clearly pareve" (although admitting that "I don't know how it's done)." Rav Shlomo Aviner (*Torat Harav Aviner* ibid.) writes similarly, as a *tziruf* of several *sevaros lehakel*: "In sum: It seems that a lab-grown burger is not *Treif*, not considered a limb taken from a living animal and is Parve (although it is not vegetarian) based on three reasons: A. It is not created in the regular process as the creation of meat. B. It has undergone many changes to the point that its entire identity is different. C. The stem cells from which it is taken cannot be seen by the human eye." Yet, he concludes "However, since this is a new creation, the great Torah scholars must decide on the matter."

20 See Mishnah (*Nida* 30a) and accompanying Gemara, as well as Gemara (*Yevamos* 69b).

on this, mainly relevant to a *Korban Yoledes*, miscarriages, and whether a *Bas Kohen* may partake of *Terumah*. It stands to reason, they maintain, that the same should apply with the stem-cell burger. At the time of removing the actual stem cell, it is still microscopic. Aside from the fact that *halachically* speaking, anything non-visible to the naked eye is not considered substantial or even as existing on a level to be able to cause prohibition,[21] a microscopic stem cell would certainly not be considered any more of an issue than a fetus at the first stages of pregnancy, which according to Chazal is deemed *"maya b'alma."* Yet, even at that early stage a fetus contains stem cells. Additionally, even if we would consider the actual stem cell if it was taken from a living cow as non-kosher, shouldn't that minuscule cell be nullified in the final product, which has well more than the standard sixty times *issur* needed? Therefore, they opine, the source of the stem cell should be irrelevant, and hence the lab-grown hamburger is intrinsically kosher, and even pareve.

Meaty Possibilities

On the other hand, although it would seem improbable at best to consider microscopic cells removed from a cow's shoulder and undergoing chemical treatment as a potential violation of the Biblical prohibition of eating actual *"Aver Min Hachai*, a limb from a live animal,"[22] nonetheless,

---

21 See *Shu"t Tuv Taam V'Daas* (*Tinyana, Kuntress Acharon*, 53), *Binas Adam* (34; on *Chochmas Adam* 38), *Tiferes Yisrael* (*Avodah Zarah* Ch. 2: Mishnah 6, Boaz 3), and *Aruch Hashulchan* (Y.D. 84:36). This ruling, that anything non-visible to the human eye has no *halachic* bearing, was almost-universally accepted by later and contemporary authorities. This issue is discussed at length in the chapter titled "Leeuwenhoek's *Halachic* Legacy: Microscopes and Magnifying Glasses."

22 See *Tur* and *Shulchan Aruch* (Y.D. 62 and 81) at length. Although there is some debate whether a limb that does not contain actual *bassar* can be considered *Aver Min Hachai* [see *Rambam* (*Hilchos Maachalos Assuros* Ch. 5:2) and *Darchei Teshuva* (62:2 s.v. *v'gam*)], nonetheless, it seems that either way, it would still not be applicable to our case of stem cells. The reason why it cannot be considered as such is that in order to be considered an *"Aver"* or even *"Bassar*

there still seems to be strong basis to consider our homegrown hamburger meaty.

The Mishnah in *Bechoros* teaches that "*Hayotzei min hatamei, tamei, v'hayotzei min hatahor, tahor*—Anything that comes out of (or is derived from) a non-kosher animal is deemed non-kosher and anything that comes out of (or is derived from) a kosher animal is deemed kosher."[23] This is the reason why milk that comes from a non-kosher species is also *halachically* non-kosher. Although many might mistakenly assume that this *halacha* is only referring to actual secretions, such as milk and brine,[24] actually, the case the Mishnah began with was a kosher animal that was born from a non-kosher one, whose own meat is still rendered non-kosher.

If so, there certainly seems like there is room to classify this stem-cell grown meat that was extracted from an actual cow, as a "*Yotzei*." Consequently, if it was taken from a live or even a dead but not properly *shechted* cow, it should be considered non-kosher.

However, even if we would classify a stem cell as a *Yotzei*, it still might not be significant enough to rule that if it was extracted from a properly *shechted* animal, it would be deemed actual meat. For example, the

---

Min Hachai," it would need to physically constitute at least a minimal *shiur*. In fact, to be *chayav malkus* it would need to be at least a *kezayis* [see *Rambam* (ad loc. 3 and 4) and *Sefer Hachinuch* (*Parashas Re'eh*, Mitzva 452; see also *Minchas Chinuch* at length)] and although for the *issur* itself even far less would still be considered *Aver Min Hachai* [see *Tur* and *Beis Yosef* (Y.D. 62)], nevertheless, it still would need to have an actual physical presence. A microscopic stem cell would certainly not be considered any more of an "*Aver*" than a fetus at the first stages of pregnancy, which according to the Gemara is not considered as such, but rather "*maya b'alma*." Yet, even at that early stage a fetus contains stem cells. Therefore, it seems abundantly clear that it would be quite a stretch to label our stem cell burger as actual *Aver Min Hachai*. For more on this, see R' Zvi Ryzman's recent *maamar* in *Techumin* vol. 34 (5774), "*Bassar M'ta'i Geza*" (pg. 103).

23 *Bechoros* (5b).

24 See *Bechoros* (6b-7a), *Chullin* (112b, 116b, and 120a), and *Tur* and *Shulchan Aruch* (Y.D. 81:1).

Rambam codifies that although it is forbidden to eat extraneous parts of a non-kosher animal (such as skin, bones, horns, and hooves), nevertheless, these same parts of a kosher animal, even when cooked in milk, are not considered actual *Bassar B'chalav*, as they are not considered actual meat.[25] Accordingly, as opposed to one who eats actual non-kosher meat, one who eats a non-kosher *Yotzei* is not *chayav malkus* (liable to punishment by lashes).

On the other hand, Rav Chaim Soloveitchik of Brisk makes an important distinction. He explains that although the *Rambam* distinguished

---

25 See *Rambam* (*Hilchos Maachalos Assuros* Ch. 3:6; 4:18, and 9:7) and *Shulchan Aruch* (Y.D. 87:7). Accordingly, and as opposed to one who eats actual non-kosher meat, one who eats a non-kosher *Yotzei* is not *chayav malkus*. In fact, several Acharonim explicitly differentiate between a *Yotzei* and actual meat, including Rav Yonason Eibeshutz (*Kreisi U'Pleisi*, Y.D. 81:1, who explains that for a *Yotzei* to be *assur* it must be normally edible), the *Chelkas Yoav* (*Shu"t* Y.D. 15), Rav Chaim Soloveitchik (cited in *Chiddushei HaGri"z* on *Nazir* 50a; see also *Chiddushei HaGri"z*, Stencils on *Bechoros* ad loc.), the *Ohr Somayach* (on *Hilchos Maachalos Assuros* Ch. 4:20), Rav Aharon Kotler (*Shu"t Mishnas Rabbi Aharon* 16, 17, and 18), and the *Chazon Ish* (Y.D. 12:3). Interestingly, *Tosafos* (*Chullin* 64a s.v. *she'im rikma*) does not seem to agree to this distinction and implies that one who eats a *"Yotzei Min Ha'Issur"* would be liable to *malkus*. However, as cited above, that does not seem to be the normative *halacha*. Yet, even so, the *halachos* of a *Yotzei* are not necessarily uniform and certain *Yotzeis* may have different *halachos*. We find that regarding the *mei raglayim* of a donkey, the Gemara (*Bechoros* 7a-b) cites two *lashonos*, whether it is permissible or not. The *Rosh* (*Bechoros* Ch. 1:7) and *Tur* (Y.D. 81), maintain that drinking it is an *Issur Deoraysa*, while the *Rambam* (*Hilchos Maachalos Assuros* Ch. 4:20) rules it is permissible. Although in his *Beis Yosef* commentary (ad loc.) he seems to side with the *Rosh*, nonetheless, when he codified the *halacha* in the *Shulchan Aruch* (Y.D. 81:1), he cites both opinions without a definitive ruling. The *Bach* (ad loc. s.v. *u'mashekasav d'mei*) and *Kreisi U'Pleisi* (ad loc. 1) rule like the *Rambam*, however, the Maharshal (*Issur V'Hetter* 65), *Shach* (ad loc. 2), *Chaguras Shmuel* (ad loc. 2), and *Aruch Hashulchan* (ad loc. 8; however in the next *se'if kattan* he offers an explanation for the *Rambam's shittah*), strongly argue, that certainly it is *assur*. The Mahari Chagiz (*Shu"t Halachos Ketanos* 207; cited in *Ba'er Heitiv* ad loc. 1) makes an allowance exclusively for a *"choleh mesukan,"* yet the *Knesses Yechezkel* (*Shu"t* 29; cited in *Pischei Teshuva* ad loc. 2)

between a *Yotzei* and actual meat, that rule applied exclusively when said *Yotzei* was not actual meat (e.g., eggs, milk, skin, bones, etc.). Yet, he avers, in a case such as the Mishnah's, a kosher animal that was born from a non-kosher one, where its meat is rendered non-kosher akin to the mother animal, certainly one who partakes of its meat would be liable for *malkus*, as it is still a "*min bassar*," a type of actual meat, and is considered "*issur machmas atzmo*," inherently prohibited.[26] Similarly, although not expressing this exact distinction, several other Acharonim who explain the *Rambam's* differentiation between a *Yotzei* and actual meat, including the *Chelkas Yoav* and *Chazon Ish*, seemingly agree to this understanding.[27] Moreover, both Rav Shlomo Zalman Auerbach and Rav Eliyahu Bakshi-Doron expressly prohibit genetic engineering, gene splicing, and/or grafting of kosher with non-kosher animals based on this precedent.[28]

---

and *Pri Megadim* (ad loc. S.D. 2) maintain that even for *choleh she'ain bo sakana* we may be *meikil*. Interestingly, the *Pri Megadim* later seems to retract his lenient position (Y.D. 103, S.D. 2 s.v. *v'da*), concluding *tzarich iyun*. Additionally, there are those [see *Pri Chodosh* (ad loc. 2), *Pri Toar* (ad loc. 1, s.v. *ul'inyan*), and *Chochmas Adam* (37:1)] who differentiate between the *mei raglayim* of a donkey and that of other animals; regarding a donkey one must be stringent due to the strength of the *Rosh's* arguments, however by other animals one many be more lenient, possibly even for a *choleh she'ain bo sakana*. For more on this topic, see R' Zvi Ryzman's *maamar* in *Techumin* vol. 34, "*Bassar M'ta'i Geza*" (pg. 101 -102), the recent book *Headlines* (vol. 1, pg. 390–391), and this author's recent *maamar* in *Techumin* vol. 35 (5775), "*Bassar M'ta'i Geza*."

26   *Chiddushei Rabbeinu Chaim Halevi al HaRambam* (*Hilchos Maachalos Assuros* Ch. 3:11).

27   Both the *Chelkas Yoav* (*Shu"t* Y.D. 15) and the *Chazon Ish* (Y.D. 12:3) when explaining the *Rambam's shittah* write that a standard *Yotzei* is more lenient as it is not "*shayach l'guf habriya*" and is not "*bassar gamur*." Therefore, it seems that they would both agree to Rav Chaim's distinction regarding a *Yotzei* that is actual meat, that it would be *Assur M'Deoraysa* and *chayav malkus*.

28   *Shu"t Minchas Shlomo* (vol. 2:97, 27) and *Shu"t Binyan Av* (vol. 4:43, 3). For possible precedents, see *Tzafnas Pane'ach* (*Hilchos Maachalos Assuros* Ch.1:1) and *Mishnas Yaavetz* (Y.D. 6).

In light of this theory, it stands to reason that regarding a harvested stem-cell hamburger which was extracted and developed from the meat itself, and has the same physical and chemical properties as meat, these Acharonim would be of the opinion that this *Yotzei* would not be considered a standard *Yotzei*, but rather still a *"min bassar"*—a type of meat itself. If so, even if it originated from a *shechted* kosher animal, and would be deemed kosher, it would still be considered *fleishig* and forbidden to be eaten or cooked with dairy products.[29]

Moreover, regarding scientists grafting plants on a microscopic, genetic level, Rav Shlomo Zalman Auerbach avers that it still violates the prohibition of *Kilayim*. He explains that although the cells are not visible to the human eye, nevertheless, as to these scientists that fact is negligible, as they are still able to graft under these conditions, it is clear that in this case it is still *halachically* considered "*Nireh L'Einayim*" (literally, "able to be seen"), meaning it no longer maintains a *halachic* dispensation of being microscopic. A similar sentiment can be expressed by our lab-grown meat, which although started from a microscopic stem cell,

---

29 In Rav Asher Weiss' words (in his recent *teshuva* titled "*B'Inyan Bassar M'turvat*"): "*u'mistavar d'lekuli alma dino k'bassar l'chol davar.*" Indeed, this 'meaty' designation is not just compelling from a *halachic* standpoint, but it is even expressed by the involved scientists themselves. For example, in a recent Wired.co.uk article (available at: https://www.wired.co.uk/article/scaling-clean-meat-serum-just-finless-foods-mosa-meat), Michael Selden, CEO of lab-grown fish startup Finless Foods, was quoted as stating that "all the startups working in this nascent industry are doing is growing meat in roughly the same way that animals do, but without having a living body wrapped around it. Everything animals eat is going to bone formation, blood formation, brain formation, and muscle. This is a more streamlined way of bringing these nutrients into meat that people want to eat. And, unlike plant-based meat alternatives, lab-grown meat doesn't just taste like real meat. It *is* real meat." Similarly, in a recent interview with *The Times of Israel* (Dec. 16, 2018; available at https://www.timesofisrael.com/israeli-test-tube-steak-smells-real-feels-real-and-may-even-be-kosher/), Israeli startup Aleph Farms Ltd. CEO and co-founder Didier Toubia, who made global headlines when he announced that they have created the first "test-tube" steak, added his perspective on its kashrus status as well. "I believe that technically it is a meat

the scientists are nonetheless able to cultivate it and eventually form a complete hamburger.[30] Accordingly, the origin of the harvested stem cell should determine its final *kashrus* status. As such, if the stem cell was extracted from a live animal, it may still qualify as the prohibited "*Bassar Min Hachai*."

Growth Spurts?

Additionally, we find an enlightening rule regarding growths from *issur*. The Mishnah in *Terumos* and as elucidated by the *Yerushalmi*,[31]

---

product, because it is made from cells and we reproduce the same taste and texture. Some rabbis think it should be pareve, but we don't necessarily agree. Obviously, to be kosher, the cells need to come from an animal that is considered kosher—so no pig meat would be allowed yet. Other considerations that need to be taken into account when considering kosher consumption is where the cells are taken from. If they come from a slaughtered animal, then the slaughtering process should have been a kosher process. Also relevant is how the cells are cultured; all the added ingredients must be kosher." On the other hand, as pointed out by Dr. John D. Loike in his recent article on topic titled "Pareve Cloned Beef Burgers: Health and Halakhic Considerations" (*Hakirah* vol. 24 ibid.), theoretically, if science can find a way to process the stem cell burger from a kosher, properly *shechted* cow, exclusively utilizing the stem cells from the *skin*, and not actual flesh (and assuming that there are no other *halachic* issues with the process), a compelling case can be made for considering that lab grown burger as pareve, as the source "meat" would not be *halachically* meaty, but rather a *Yotzei* from an extraneous part of a kosher animal. Interestingly, as per a recent article in *Frontiers in Sustainable Food Systems* ("Tissue Engineering for Clean Meat Production," June 18, 2019), there are researchers opining that from scientific and humanistic perspectives this is actually the preferred method for the future of lab-grown meat.

30   *Shu"t Minchas Shlomo* (*Tinyana* 100:7 s.v. *b'inyan*). Rav Yaakov Ariel (in his *maamar* in *Techumin* vol. 35; 5775) emphatically sets Rav Shlomo Zalman's *klal* as precedent to this case to explain why microscopic stem cells are not grounds to be lenient by the lab grown burger. The OU as well, in a recent *Daf HaKashrus* (vol. 27, issue 4; April-May 2019; "Halachic Perspective on Cell-Based Meat") likewise cite and agree with this assessment *lemaaseh*.

31   *Terumos* (Ch. 9: Mishnah 6) and elucidated by the *Yerushalmi* (ad loc. Halacha 2).

teaches regarding prohibited produce—such as *Tevel, Terumah, Maaser,* or *Sheviis,* that later sprouts and sustains further growths that utilized the original prohibited produce as its source material—that these later growths are intrinsically permitted, as they are not considered part and parcel of the original prohibited produce. Yet, there is an important exception: when referring to produce that is *"Aino Zaro Kala,"* when the original prohibited item's essence is still extant in some form or another, then even *Gidulei Gedulim*—the growths of the growths, are nevertheless prohibited.

Although this *halacha* practically affects disparate types of *issur* differently, nonetheless, the rule holds true.[32] As such, regarding our lab-grown burger, it would seem quite tenuous to assume that the original prohibited cell (if taken from a non-kosher source) would be nullified by the end product, as those cells and all later cells are grown from the original prohibited stem cell.

Rather, it would stand to reason that they should instead be considered *"Giddulei Issur"* as the Mishnah indicates. While immersion in the

---

32 See Mishnah *Terumos* (ibid. as well as Ch. 7:7), *Yerushalmi* (*Terumos* ibid.), Gemara *Nedarim* (57b-58a), Gemara *Pesachim* (34a), *Rambam* (*Hilchos Maaser* Ch 6:6), *Merkeves HaMishnah* (*Hilchos Terumos* Ch. 11: *Halacha* 22), *Pe'as Hashulchan* (Ch. 23 or *Sheviis* Ch. 4:4 and 5), *Aruch Hashulchan Ha'Asid* (*Hilchos Shemittah V'Yovel* 22:11 and *Hilchos Terumos* 83:9–16), *Kuntress Tosefes Sheviis* (pg. 36a s.v. *v'ap"y*; printed at the back of the *Beis Ridbaz* version of the *Pe'as Hashulchan*), *Chazon Ish* (*Sheviis* Ch. 8:1 and 2; especially brackets in s.v. *hachi*), and *Derech Emunah* (vol. 2, *Hilchos Terumos* Ch. 11:132 and *Tziyun Hahalacha* 361 and 362). Although the *halacha* is more lenient regarding *Sheviis*, as such an eventuality would be rare and only regarding the Rabbinically prohibited *Sefichin*, and by *Tevel* after three (or four) separate growths we are lenient, conversely, regarding *Terumah* it remains prohibited even after a hundred separate individual growths. The *Rash M'Shantz* explains a Mishnah in *Kilayim* (Ch. 1:9 s.v. *v'lo meshum Sheviis* and *v'lo meshum Maaser*) in a similar manner to the aforementioned Mishnah in *Terumos.* The Mishnah writes succinctly (and somewhat ambiguously) that if one buries a turnip or radish underneath a grapevine, as long as some of the leaves are still "revealed" (meaning not buried along with the majority and roots of the plant), he does not need to be concerned with the potential prohibitions of

chemicals may create a temporary *shishim* (sixty times the original *issur* and hence render it nullified), they do not survive. The final product does not contain *shishim* of *hetter*, but rather, we seem to simply have an *issur* that has grown thousands of times larger over the course of time, as the minuscule meat cell just kept growing, magnifying, and splitting.[33]

Kilayim, Sheviis, or *Maasros*. As opposed to the *Rambam's* explanation (*Peirush HaMishnayos* ad loc.) that growths from these turnips do not constitute true *"zera ha'aretz"* as the vegetable was not entirely submerged underground and therefore this situation is an exception to the usual rules, the *Rash* takes an alternate approach. He understands that the Mishnah was referring to a case where the vegetable's growths only appeared in the following *halachic* agriculture year than the turnip was buried. As such, the Mishnah was not questioning whether or not these *halachos* apply, but rather which year's rules. He cites two examples, when the turnip was buried in the second year when *Maaser Sheini* applies, but the growths only appeared in the following year when *Maaser Ani* applies, and a similar case when said turnip was buried in the sixth year but the growths made their appearance in the seventh year, *Shemittah*. The *Rash* explains that the Mishnah is teaching us that in both of these cases [he seems to understand the *Kilayim* exemption akin to the *Rambam*] the growths on these turnips still maintain the *halachic* status of the root vegetable, and are considered part and parcel of the original vegetable for all intents and purposes since part of the root vegetable stayed "revealed," even though the new growths were never submerged with the rest of the plant and are entirely new growths of the following agriculture year. Hence, *Maaser Sheini*, and not *Maaser Ani*, would be required of the growths, and in the second case, they would still be considered *Shishis* produce and not the forbidden *Sefichin* of *Sheviis* [this topic was addressed at length in an article titled: "*Shemitta Sheilos*: The Case of the Contraband Carrots" (*Yated Ne'eman*, 25 Sivan 5775/June 12, 2015; and online at https://ohr.edu/this_week/insights_into_halacha/6349)]. According to the *Rash's* understanding, it would stand to reason that the same would hold true regarding meat grown from a stem cell, that it would maintain the status of the original root animal.

33   See also Rav Chizkiyahu Yosef Cohen's *Shu"t Avnei Chein* (vol. 3:14, 5 s.v. *u'lemaaseh*; see also 12 and 13) who, after an extensive *halachic* analysis of clones, Siamese twins, Golems, creations via *Sefer Yetzira*, and other esoteric oddities, concludes similarly [without citing these sources], that it is *"mistaver b'yoseir"*

Furthermore, the comparison to a fetus prior to forty days does not seem compelling vis-à-vis the aforementioned precedents, as *halachically*, "*maya b'alma*" is not necessarily a statement that an item is not considered "meat"; it is a statement that said fetus is not yet considered a living person. As previously mentioned, this rule has classically been invoked regarding a *Korban Yoledes*, miscarriages, and whether a *Bas Kohen* may partake of *Terumah*. We do not find it being used to set *halachic* precedent for other issues not related to the establishment of viable human life, and not even for other creatures.

It also does not seem to preclude the possibility that a similar object may still be considered meat. More importantly, in our case, the originating cell is not a new creation created by the fusion of male and female chromosomes. It is a cell taken from a fully developed animal. As such, and in any case, even if the fetus analogy would be deemed accurate, our stem cell should certainly be considered more than forty days after fertilization, and hence meaty.

Catalyst Conundrum

Aside from these possibilities, there is an important additional factor to take into account which might render our in-vitro burger meaty as well.

Halachically speaking, as mentioned previously, a prohibited ingredient that is present in minute quantities in a mixture is generally considered nullified as long as there is at least a sixty-to-one ratio against it (*battel b'shishim*).[34] Although this would imply that the Petri-dish patty

---

that any growth utilizing stem cells still maintains the status of a growth of its "root tree"—"*k'zera ilan l'chol davar.*" In his closing words: "*kol sheba b'derech toladah m'guf chai...nagdir es oso 'ta' k"zera ikar" shenisorer shelo k'derech hateva lehafros toladah.*" What is most remarkable to this author, is that this responsum, mainly grounded in the realm of the hypothetical, theoretical, and purely conjectural, was written over a decade before Professor Mark Post's groundbreaking press conference, at a time when most of the world viewed such topics as pure fantasy. Thanks are due to R' Eliezer Freimark for providing this fascinating source.

34 As discussed several times throughout this book, this is the standard rule

would be considered kosher even if it was harvested from a non-kosher source because the final patty has twenty thousand muscle fibers grown from a few stem cells, on the other hand it is not so simple, as every rule has its exceptions.

One of the exceptions to the nullification rule is a case of a *Davar HaMaamid*, an essential ingredient in the makeup of a product that establishes its form. This catalyst impacts it tremendously, far greater than its size belies. A prime example of a *Davar HaMaamid* is the small amount of a calf's stomach lining (rennet) placed in a huge vat of milk that turns it to cheese.[35] The *halachic* status of a non-kosher *Davar HaMaamid* is that it cannot be nullified, no matter how infinitesimal it seems compared to the final product.[36]

It is entirely possible that the same rule should apply to our lab burger. Since the whole hamburger's essence, as well as the entire development of the meat, "stems" from those original minuscule meaty stem cells, it is highly feasible that they would have the *halachic* status of a *Davar HaMaamid*. If so, and they were harvested from a non-kosher animal, it might just deem the final product non-kosher as well. However, if these cells would be extracted from a properly slaughtered kosher animal, then the lab-grown burger would be considered kosher,[37] and most likely *fleishig*, if the cells are reckoned substantial enough to be considered meaty.

On the other hand, sometimes even the exceptions have exceptions. For example, a product produced via a non-kosher *Davar HaMaamid* can

---

of nullification in *halacha*. If there is present sixty times the amount of non-kosher, then it is considered nullified. See *Shulchan Aruch* Y.D. 98.

35 OK, one might ask, then how did they make kosher cheese before synthetic rennet was discovered, if the real rennet is never *battel*? For a start, see *Shach* (Y.D. 87:30), *Shu"t Rabbi Akiva Eiger* (vol. 1:207), *Shu"t Chasam Sofer* (Y.D. 81), *Matteh Yonason* (Glosses to Y.D. 87:9), and *Pischei Teshuva* (Y.D. 87:19).

36 See *Shulchan Aruch* Y.D. 87:11 and relevant commentaries.

37 See *Shulchan Aruch* Y.D. 87:11 and relevant commentaries. The basic rule is that a kosher *Davar HaMaamid* would indeed be *batel b'shishim* as opposed to a non-kosher one.

still sometimes be permitted if there is also a kosher catalyst involved in the production of the item. This is termed *"Zeh V'Zeh Gorem,"* meaning that both catalysts caused the production. This terminology refers to a product that was not manufactured exclusively using a non-kosher *Davar HaMaamid*, but rather utilized it as a combination catalyst complementing another kosher one.

The *halacha* in cases deemed a *"Zeh V'Zeh Gorem"* is that the basic rules of *battel b'shishim* are back in effect, and only sixty times the original non-kosher catalyst in its makeup is mandated in order to permit the final product.[38] It is possible that there are additional kosher *Devarim HaMaamidim* used in the manufacture of the man-made burger. If so, and there is present a ratio of sixty times against the original meaty stem cells, it might be deemed pareve and possibly permitted.

Yet, to further complicate matters, many authorities maintain that in order for combination catalysts to qualify as a *"Zeh V'Zeh Gorem,"* the non-kosher catalyst must not have the strength to fully impact and establish the item's form, but only work in tandem as a "tag-team" of sorts, with the kosher catalyst. Otherwise, according to these authorities,[39]

---

38 See *Shulchan Aruch* (Y.D. 142:11) and *Rema* (Y.D. 87:11), based on the *Mordechai* (*Chullin*, Ch. 8:733 and 761). On a more contemporary note, Rav Eliyahu Bakshi-Doron (*Shu"t Binyan Av* vol. 4:43, 2), in a somewhat similar case to ours, rules that utilizing a different product's genes to enhance another item's abilities (e.g., genetically modified wheat) would be permitted even if the source of the gene is technically prohibited for consumption, due to the rule of *"Zeh V'Zeh Gorem."* However, he concludes that it would nevertheless be preferable to use genes of permitted origin.

39 Including the *Taz* (Y.D. 87:13), *Shach* (ad loc. 36; although he concludes *tzarich iyun*), *Pri Chodosh* (Y.D. 87:31), *Kreisi U'Pleisi* (ad loc. *Kreisi* 25 and *Pleisi* 21), *Ba'er Hagolah* (ad loc.), *Pri Megadim* (ad loc. M.Z. 13), *Mishnah Berurah* (442:25 and *Shaar Hatziyun* ad loc. 45), and *Aruch Hashulchan* (Y.D. 87:42), citing *Tosafos* in *Avodah Zarah* (68b s.v. *l'Rabbi Shimon*) as proof. However, the *Yad Yehuda* (ad loc. *Peirush Ha'aruch* 54 and *Peirush Hakatzer* 26) argues that *"Zeh V'Zeh Gorem"* applies even when the non-kosher catalyst has enough strength by itself to affect the required change. He maintains that since the whole issue of *Davar HaMaamid* not being nullified is not so clear-cut in the earlier *Poskim*

it would still maintain its *Davar HaMaamid* status and deem the final product non-kosher as well, due to its inability to be nullified.

Moreover, the *Gadol Hador*, Rav Chaim Ozer Grodzenski, ruled that in order to be considered a *"Zeh V'Zeh Gorem,"* both catalysts—the kosher and non-kosher—must be performing the exact same action. The example he gives is fermenting bread utilizing both sourdough that is *Chullin* and sourdough that is *Terumah*, that this combination qualifies as *"Zeh V'Zeh Gorem."* However, if there are two different *maamidim* present performing independent actions, although their combined efforts jointly effect a desired result, that is not considered *"Zeh V'Zeh Gorem,"* but rather two independent, full-fledged *Maamidim*.[40] The same argument would apply with stem-cell meat as well. Although growth factors and nutrients are necessary to trigger and support the cell's growth, they do not accomplish the same function as the cells, which

---

[for example, Rabbeinu Tam (*Sefer Hayashar* 53:5), the *Baal Hama'or* (in his glosses to *Chullin* 42b-43a in the *Rif's* pagination s.v. *u'mi*; arguing on the Ri Migash's two *kushyos*), *Tur* (Y.D. 87:11), and Rashal (*Yam Shel Shlomo, Chullin* Ch. 8:106) are all of the opinion that *Davar HaMaamid* is *battel b'shishim*; in fact, the *Yad Yehuda* (ad loc. *Peirush Ha'aruch* 25) goes to great lengths to prove that most Rishonim held this way, contrary to how others present their opinions], and that the *Mordechai* (who first makes this dispensation), and later the *Rema*, make no mention of such a proviso, [he also gives several other *halachic* rationales], *"Zeh V'Zeh Gorem"* will even apply when the non-kosher *Davar HaMaamid* can impact the item sufficiently by itself, as long as a kosher *Davar HaMaamid* is present.

40   *Shu"t Achiezer* (vol. 4:31); also printed in *Kovetz Moriah* (vol. 165–166; Shvat 5746, pg. 35–36, "*B'din Mitz Oros Keivos Neveilos U'Treifos*," in the brackets), citing precedent from *Shu"t Minchas Baruch* (*Nachalas Baruch, Din Zeh V'Zeh Gorem*, 1: *Anaf* 2; 3: *Anaf* 1; and 5, at length.) The OU's recent *Daf HaKashrus* (vol. 27, issue 4; April-May 2019; "Halachic Perspective on Cell-Based Meat") cites this ruling as precedent for their assessment of cell-based meat, explaining why if non-kosher stem cells are used in creating this burger, the resulting product would be non-kosher. They add that the original cell is not simply a *gorem*, but "rather, when a cell divides, the new cells are expansions of the original cell. If the original cell is non-kosher, then all expanded cells will be non-kosher as well."

make up the lab-grown burger's actual essence. Accordingly, a stem cell would certainly seem a true *Davar HaMaamid*, and if not sourced from a *shechted* kosher animal, may quite possibly not be nullified, and is liable to deem the final product non-kosher as well.

Additionally, to use a non-kosher *Davar HaMaamid lechatchilla*, even if it is considered a *"Zeh V'Zeh Gorem,"* might nonetheless transgress the proscription of *"Ain Mevattlin Issur"* and be prohibited.[41] This refers to the concept that following the basic rules of nullification, if a non-kosher substance would accidentally fall into kosher food (as long as there was the prerequisite sixty times the amount of non-kosher that fell in) it would still be permitted, nonetheless, if one would add the non-kosher item on purpose with the express intention of nullifying it, the entire mixture becomes forbidden for the person who transgressed and for whomever he intended to benefit. Rav Akiva Eiger, citing precedent from the *Rivash*, rules that this prohibition applies equally in a commercial setting, maintaining that such products become forbidden for consumer purchase.[42]

---

41   It is important to note that even if the item meets the requirements of *"Zeh V'Zeh Gorem,"* it is by no means a blanket *hetter*. The *Avnei Miluim* (vol. 2, Shu"t 6) explains at length (see also *Darchei Teshuva* 87:153) that it is only a *hetter b'dieved*. To use a non-kosher *Davar HaMaamid lechatchilla*, even if it is considered a *"Zeh V'Zeh Gorem,"* would nonetheless transgress the prohibition of *"Ain Mevattlin Issur"* and would be prohibited. [Even so, according to the *Imrei Binah* (*Dinei Bassar B'chalav V'Taaruvos* end 6) a *kenass* would not be mandated, as opposed to a traditional *"Ain Mevattlin Issur,"* as a *"Zeh V'Zeh Gorem"* qualifies as *K'Mevattel Issur*).]

42   Rav Akiva Eiger (Y.D. 99:4), citing precedent from the *Rivash* (Shu"t 498 s.v. v'af al pi). He is arguing on the *Taz* (Y.D. 99:4), who cites precedent from the Rashal (*Yam Shel Shlomo, Chullin* Ch. 7:59) that the prohibition only applies to the nullifier's family and/or if the person whom the nullification was performed on his behalf knows about it and wanted it done. Although other Acharonim are divided as to whom the *halacha* follows with no clear-cut consensus, and some argue that the precedents are not entirely accurate, nevertheless, many later authorities exhort caution with purchasing such products, following the ruling of Rav Eiger. Furthermore, it can be argued

Non-Jewish Nullification

Although some might justify the process, claiming "*Ain Mevattlin Issur*" should not be a factor, as the burger is currently being produced by non-Jews (who obviously cannot be considered transgressors of a Rabbinic decree), it turns out that this is also not a simple solution. Already in the 1500s, the *Radbaz* made a distinction between a scenario where a non-Jew nullifies a non-kosher ingredient in a kosher product, where he permits a Jew to partake of the mixture, as opposed to where a non-Jew is selling such a product, where he rules that it is forbidden for a Jew to purchase.[43] He maintains that when a Jew is purchasing the item, it is as if he himself nullified it, and therefore it becomes prohibited for him to eat.

Many *halachic* authorities concurred with this reasoning and likewise forbade a Jew from purchasing items that had a non-kosher ingredient nullified inside of them. However, the majority of *Poskim* disagreed with this rationale, concluding that it is improbable to make such a distinction,[44] as the *Rambam* himself held that it is acceptable to procure

---

that granting a *hashgacha* on such a product and thereby targeting the Jewish consumer as a potential customer, creates a situation in which it would be considered that the nullification is being carried out expressly for the benefit of the Jews. It stands to reason that in such a scenario, it would forbidden for the kosher consumer to benefit from said product, even according to the *Taz's* understanding of the proscription.

43 This, and related issues, are thoroughly addressed in the chapter titled "The Coca-Cola Kashrus Controversy."

44 *Shu"t Maharam M'Lublin* (104), *Minchas Yaakov* (35:2), *Shu"t Noda B'Yehuda* (*Tinyana* Y.D. 56 and 57), *Shu"t Beis Yitzchak* (Y.D. vol. 1:142, 8 and *Kuntress Acharon* 31), *Shu"t Chasam Sofer* (Y.D. 82), *Shu"t Ksav Sofer* (O.C. 87), *Shu"t Imrei Binah* (*Dinei Bassar B'chalav V'Taaruvos* 14; although he concludes that it is preferential to be *machmir* in both instances), *Erech Hashulchan* (Y.D. 99:8), *Zivchei Tzedek* (ad loc. 36), and *Shu"t Beis Shlomo* (O.C. 97), that whatever was produced by a non-Jew is already considered '*b'dieved*' and therefore permissible for purchase. Most contemporary authorities concur with this assessment, including Rav Eliyahu Gutmacher (*Shu"t Mahar"a Gutmacher* Y.D. 32), Rav Henoch Padwa (*Shu"t Cheishev Ha'Eifod* vol. 2: end 104, s.v. *v'ata*),

such items as long as the nullification was performed by a non-Jew.[45] They maintain that such a product is suitable for purchase.

However, to further complicate our case, the *Tashbetz* made a further qualification to this permissible ruling, following the precedent of the *Rashba* and *Raavad*.[46] They aver that although one may rely upon a non-Jew's nullification for purchase in infrequent circumstances, conversely, if the non-Jew is doing it for his job, or on a frequent basis, then certainly it is considered as if the Jew himself nullified it. Several *Poskim* agreed to this decision as well.

In fact, based on this debate, one of the most famous responsa in the annals of American history was written in 1935 by Rav Tuvia (Tobias) Geffen, Chief Rabbi of Atlanta Georgia in the 1930s and 1940s. He had to decide whether or not to grant Coca-Cola a *hashgacha*, as it turned out that there was a non-kosher ingredient (animal based glycerin) in its makeup, but only present in minute quantities. Therefore, although technically it would be permitted to drink, for the non-kosher ingredient was *battel b'shishim*, and therefore considered nullified, nevertheless, it was potentially a violation of "*Ain Mevattlin Issur*," as the Coca-Cola Company was obviously putting this non-kosher ingredient in the batch purposefully, since it was part and parcel of the Coke everyone knew and loved.

Rav Moshe Feinstein (*Shu"t Igros Moshe* Y.D. vol. 1:62 s.v. *u'mdin*, and 63; Y.D. vol. 2:32 and 41), Rav Betzalel Stern (*Shu"t B'tzeil Hachochma* vol. 4:89, 13 and 14; and 104, 18), his brother, the Debreciner Rav (*Shu"t Ba'er Moshe* vol. 3:109, 21), and Rav Ovadiah Yosef (*Shu"t Yabia Omer* vol. 7, Y.D. 7).

45 *Rambam* (*Hilchos Maachalos Assuros* Ch. 3:13). This is also the ruling of his *rebbi*, the *Ri Migash* (cited by the *Ran* in *Avodah Zarah*, 13b in the *Rif's* pagination, s.v. *v'hisi'u ledavar achar*).

46 *Shu"t Tashbetz* (vol. 3:10), *Shu"t HaRashba* (vol. 3:214; cited by the *Beis Yosef*, Y.D. end 134 s.v. *chometz*, and by the *Magen Avraham* O.C. 442: end 1), and *Raavad* (cited by the *Ran* and *Beis Yosef* ibid). A case can be made for positing that this is also the *Ran's* opinion, as he concludes his passage with the words of the *Raavad*.

In the end, Rav Geffen did the unexpected: he asked the Coca-Cola executives to change their formula. The administration listened, and the company removed the problematic ingredients and substituted them with kosher alternatives, making the soft drink kosher *lechatchilla* for everyone.

Rav Geffen later published the whole account, as well as the *halachic* reasoning behind his actions, in his responsum.[47] Later *halachic* authorities as well ruled similarly to Rav Geffen's sound logic and reasoning, maintaining that although there is what to rely upon regarding purchasing, nevertheless, when it comes to granting *hashgacha*, a Rabbinic authority should not give a seal of approval to an item that contains nullified *issur*. In fact, Rav Moshe Feinstein classified doing so (if that is the only justification they are relying upon to proclaim the product kosher) as "*mechuar hadavar*, utterly disgraceful or disgusting."[48]

It is due to this that the fact that the nullification is being performed by non-Jews may still not allow this man-made burger, even if eventually deemed technically kosher, to be sold publicly as kosher.

Kosher Cheeseburgers?

However, it is important to note that even following one of the premises that lab-created meat would maintain a pareve status, it still would not necessarily denote a kosher cheeseburger. The permissibility of such would depend on the laws of *Maris Ayin*.

As mentioned previously, the most basic definition of this law is the prohibition of taking actions that, strictly speaking, are actually permitted according to *halacha*, but nevertheless give onlookers the impression that we are doing something *halachically* forbidden. In other words, although an observer has an obligation to judge others

---

47 The *halachic* and historical account of this story is discussed at length in the chapter titled "The Coca-Cola Kashrus Controversy."

48 See Rav Moshe Feinstein's *Shu"t Igros Moshe* (Y.D. vol. 2:41 s.v. *v'im*), Rav Moshe Sternbuch's *Shu"t Teshuvos V'Hanhagos* (vol. 1:440), Rav Menashe Klein's *Shu"t Mishnah Halachos* (vol. 7:113, 2), and Rav Shmuel Halevi Wosner's *Shu"t Shevet Halevi* (vol. 9:165).

favorably (*dan l'kaf zechus*),⁴⁹ nevertheless we still have an obligation not to perform actions that might raise an observer's suspicions. The common expression might be that "looks can be deceiving," but even so, one must make sure not to engage in questionable activities or even questionable-looking ones.

Hence, it seems that even if this lab-grown burger would prove kosher, one may still not eat it with cheese, due to the proscription of *Maris Ayin*.⁵⁰ Although practically this *halacha* depends on how common an item is, on the other hand, with a $325,000 price tag, a potential kosher cheeseburger is still a long way off! This is because even if they manage to mass produce said burger and bring the price down ten-thousandfold,⁵¹ it would still have to be common enough that the average Joe would not readily assume that it is a real meat hamburger served with the actual cheese—quite an unlikely eventuality for something that expensive to produce.

This especially holds true as studies have shown that ninety-six percent of Americans eat and enjoy fast-food meats and believe that

---

49 See Gemaros *Shabbos* (127b) and *Shavuos* (30a), and Rabbeinu Yonah's *Shaarei Teshuva* (*Shaar* 3:218 s.v. *v'hinei*).

50 This issue is addressed at length in the chapter titled "Margarine, Misconceptions, and *Maris Ayin*." Indeed, according to the aforementioned recent *New York Times* article (Sep. 30, 2018), "Eitan Fischer, the chief executive of Mission Barns (one of the companies working on clean meat), said he was hopeful that through some creative chemistry, his company could grow pork that would get a kosher designation. 'If we can create kosher bacon one day, as weird as that sounds, I think there is going to be so much excitement around that,' he said. Rabbi (Gavriel) Price (a certifying rabbi for the OU) was cautious. In addition to the kosher laws, there are Jewish rules that warn against doing anything that would make people look as though they were violating the rules. The rabbi added that there are religious texts that discuss the possibility of kosher pigs, once the Jewish messiah arrives and ushers in an age of universal peace. But he is skeptical. 'I'm looking around, and I don't see much evidence we are in messianic times,' he said."

51 Indeed, according to an ABC (Australian Broadcasting Corporation) News/ AM Radio interview with Prof. Mark Post himself in 2015 [available at http://

www.abc.net.au/am/content/2015/s4205857.htm], "After further development, Dr. Post estimates it's possible to produce lab-beef for $80 a kilo—and that within years it will be a price-competitive alternative." Yet, at the same time he admitted that "it will still be another twenty to thirty years before it's commercially viable." However, as recently reported by the *Wall Street Journal* (July 17, 2018; accessible at: https://www.wsj.com/articles/startup-producing-cell-grown-meat-raises-new-funding-1531738800), due to a recent massive influx of investment funding to the tune of $8.8 million dollars (!!) by German pharmaceutical giant Merck KGaA and top European meat processor, Switzerland-based Bell Food Group, in addition to Google founder Sergey Brin's initial €1 million euros, among others, Dr. Post's company, Mosa Meats, now claims that lab-grown burgers could potentially be on restaurant menus in three years. They say that this capital will be used to enable them to develop an end-to-end process for cultured meat production that will hit the market by 2021, with a cost per burger of €9 ($10; this actually comes out roughly the same as the aforementioned $80 per kilo, as the average hamburger is a "quarter pounder," and a kilo is approximately 2.2 pounds) when the process is scaled to industrial size. They now estimate that with efficiency improvements, there is hope for further price reductions within the following seven years. A competing company, Hampton Creek/JUST, Inc. recently announced that they will be the first to get "clean meat" to consumers, by 2019 [!], but it will be turkey or chicken, as opposed to bovine meat. According to Paul Mozdziak, poultry science professor at North Carolina State University, (as cited in a Jan. 02, 2018 online article: https://motherboard.vice.com/en_us/article/3k5ak3/chicken-might-be-the-first-lab-grown-meat-to-make-it-to-your-grocery-store; excerpting Paul Shapiro's recent book, *Clean Meat*) this is because "from a technological standpoint, chicken and turkey cells are much easier to work with, as they grow a lot better in culture than mammalian cells do. They have better plasticity—you can get them to do what you want much more easily." Indeed, he and physiology graduate student Marie Gibbons grew the first-ever cultured turkey nugget, "and for only $19,000 (a giveaway compared to [scientist Mark] Post's $330,000 burger [in 2013])...Perhaps even more impressive is that Gibbons can send any academic scientist a vial of her starter cells and they'd be able to grow their own turkey nuggets in just two weeks." On the other hand, even if this scientific breakthrough does become available in the near future, its popularity and commercial viability, and hence its *halachic* status vis-à-vis the prohibition of *Maris Ayin*, remains to be seen. Indeed, there is staunch opposition to any lab-grown meat being considered

plant-based meat does not adequately mimic the taste, convenience, or barbecuing potential of animal-based meats.⁵² Currently, cultured meat (although animal derived) has not yet proven to possess the same taste or ability to be barbecued or cooked without losing its quality and texture as plain old-fashioned animal meat.

Moreover, recent studies suggest that lab-grown meat may not truly be any better for the environment than classic beef.⁵³ Hence, clean meat may not necessarily become the "wave of the future" it is touted to be.

"meat" at all. Although the United States Department of Agriculture (USDA) and Food and Drug Adminisrtration (FDA) recently agreed to jointly regulate and oversee the cultured meat industry, thereby potentially speeding up government approval, on the other hand, as the State of Missouri officially passed a bill in May, 2018 prohibiting plant-based products as well as lab-grown meat—which may hit market shelves in the future—to use the "meat" moniker, and the US Cattlemen's Association (USCA) petitioning the USDA for a similar outcome (and referring to it as "fake meat"), it seems it will be an uphill battle to woo the masses.

52 See Hopkins, P. and Dacey, A. (2008) "Vegetarian Meat: Could Technology Save Animals and Satisfy Meat Eaters?" in *Journal of Agricultural and Environmental Ethics* (vol. 21:6, pg. 579–596). Yet, there still may be hope for veggie burgers. In a press report on May 23, 2018 (accessible at: https://www.jta.org/2018/05/23/news-opinion/impossible-burgers-now-kosher-pareve), it was announced that the "Impossible Burger," a meatless patty that has made waves for how similar it tastes to real beef, was just certified kosher and pareve by the OU. "Impossible Burgers are different from traditional veggie burgers because they are made directly from proteins and other ingredients including wheat protein, potato protein, and coconut oil. The key ingredient, according to the company, is a protein called heme that gives the burgers their meaty taste and texture. [Although heme is generally found in blood, Impossible Foods sources their heme from the nitrogen-fixing root nodules of legumes, where it's a component of the oxygen-carrying protein "leghemoglobin"—kind of like hemoglobin, for beans.] Impossible Burgers are known for "bleeding" just like a normal burger-and tasting awfully close to one as well." If deemed accurate, and the "Impossible" becomes not only possible, but popular, this might well be the future of cutting edge "tech meat," and not the more *halachically* problematic stem-cell meat, at least for the kosher consumer.

Inconclusive Conclusion?

So, which of the *halachic* precedents detailed in this chapter pertain to our lab-grown burger? Although it certainly seems that the stronger of the arguments is that it would retain the status of its source meat, practically, as stated previously, this cutting-edge scientific discussion of genetically engineered beef is currently purely academic for the kosher consumer. This is due to the fact that until the entire process is made public knowledge, all we can do is conjecture as to the potential *halachic* possibilities.

It is remarkable that paradigms of such technological advances were to some degree foreshadowed thousands of years ago by the wisdom of our Sages, discussing meat created via unconventional means. Who would have thought that seemingly "magical meat" would become practically relevant to our daily lives? Time and technology have once again proven wrong those who might scoff at our Aggadic Mesorah!

Postscript: After initially writing about this subject, this author was notified by noted food scientist Arlene Mathes-Scharf of Kashrut.com that an additional factor in the production of the lab-grown burger was

---

53 "Climate Impacts of Cultured Meat and Beef Cattle" (*Frontiers in Sustainable Food Systems*, February 19, 2019; by John Lynch and Raymond Pierrehumbert of the Department of Physics at the University of Oxford). This study led to several chagrined headlines, including "Is Lab-Grown Meat Actually Worse for the Environment? A New Study Raises Uncomfortable Questions" (accessible at: www.vox.com/future-perfect/2019/2/22/18235189/lab-grown-meat-cultured-environment-climatechange) and "Well, Dang, Lab-Grown Meat Might be Bad for the Planet Too" (accessible at: https://earther.gizmodo.com/well-dang-lab-grown-meat-might-bad-for-the-planet-too-1832783987). Although theoretically cultured meat reliance will certainly decrease the need for cattle and their natural but harmful methane emissions—which can last in the atmosphere up to a dozen years, conversely, it appears that the process of lab-produced meat will increase deleterious carbon dioxide emissions, which can remain extant for almost a century. Hence, clean meat may not practically turn out to be the much-hyped environmentally-friendly "miracle meat" as originally advertised. Thanks are due to David Lederman for pointing out this important information.

Genetically Engineered Meat   131

made public: growing this "meat" involved using fresh calf blood as the growth medium.[54] If so, it definitely might change the lab burger's potential kashrus status. First of all, if it is soaking directly in blood for more than twenty-four hours straight, it might be considered *kavush k'mevushal* ("pickling" via soaking, which is somewhat akin to cooking) and prohibited (at least Rabbinically).[55]

---

54 http://www.nbcnews.com/science/lab-grown-meat-here-will-vegetarians-eat-it-6C10830536. However, Mrs. Mathes-Scharf later reported that she attended a seminar by Professor Mark Post himself, who explained that as they are positioning this product as an animal cruelty free-way to produce meat as well as a way to produce meat using fewer resources, they are working on developing animal-free nutrient solutions for the cells. Still, she concluded that this technology has a long way to go before it is feasible. See http://www.kashrut.com/articles/IFT2015. Indeed, according to a recent report on NewAtlas.com (July 18, 2018; https://newatlas.com/lab-grown-burgers-market/55505/), Dr. Post's "company says that the biggest challenge at present is to find a substitute for the fetal bovine serum currently used as a nutrient because it negates the whole no-animals-needed thing. The hope is to find an economical substitute." According to a recent Wired.co.uk article titled: "The Clean Meat Industry is Racing to Ditch its Reliance on Foetal Blood" (available at https://www.wired.co.uk/article/scaling-clean-meat-serum-just-finless-foods-mosa-meat), "unless the clean meat industry can solve the serum question, not a sliver of lab-grown meat will ever make its way into our kitchens. "There's absolutely no way you can have a viable product that has serum," says Michael Selden, CEO of lab-grown fish startup Finless Foods." In the words of a tech article available at https://www.fastcompany.com/3044572, "among the hurdles still left to overcome: figuring out how to produce test-tube meat at scale, and coming up with a way to produce it that doesn't use fetal calf serum (currently, cells are grown in the serum, which is taken from cow fetus blood). And, of course, there's the biggest hurdle of all: convincing people to eat lab-grown meat."

55 An object that is immersed in liquid and soaks for twenty-four hours straight is considered to have been somewhat "cooked" and there is a transfer of *bliyos*. If it is soaked in brine, or a salty or spicy liquid, this effect occurs much quicker, generally accepted at eighteen minutes (although there is a minority opinion that maintains that this effect occurs in as fast as six minutes; see *Darchei Teshuva* 105:42). For the parameters of the *halachos* of *kavush k'mevushal*, see

Additionally, if blood is used as an actual growth medium, it would seem to be a *Davar HaMaamid* and would never be *battel*. Furthermore, even if it might qualify as a *"Zeh V'Zeh Gorem,"* nonetheless, if it is considered such an integral part of the growth process, presumably at no time would there be present a ratio of sixty against it. Consequently, if proven accurate, use of blood as the growth medium can complicate matters, and would seemingly make production of the Petri-dish patty highly problematic.[56]

Just another excellent reason why it is necessary to ascertain the actual *metzius* when viewing innovation via the lens of *halacha*.[57]

Tur, *Shulchan Aruch*, and main commentaries to *Yoreh Deah* (105:1) at length. On the other hand, in a recent responsum titled *"B'Inyan Bassar Miturbat,"* Rav Asher Weiss argues that in his opinion, if blood serum (meaning, the blood plasma without white blood cells, red blood cells, or fibrinogens; in short, it is "blood" with all cellular components removed) as opposed to blood itself, is used exclusively in the process, *"yeish sevara lomar"* that it may not maintain the *halachic* status of the prohibited "blood." However, as mentioned previously, he is of the opinion that in order for this meat to be considered kosher, the stem cells must be harvested from a properly *shechted* kosher animal.

56   An additional concern this author has seen raised was that once the tissue sample has been extracted from the cow, it should need to be either salted or broiled to remove the prohibited blood [this topic is discussed at length in the chaper titled "Salting with Sugar?!"], both processes that would destroy the muscle stem cells. However, it is likely that this is not an actual *halachic* issue, as Rav Moshe Feinstein (*Shu"t Igros Moshe*, Y.D. vol. 2:23 s.v. *aval*) explains that the blood inside meat that necessitates removal is considered a *bliyas issur*, thus not allowing the meat to be eaten without first performing *melicha* or *tzliyah*, nonetheless, this only applies at the time when said meat would be *raui l'achila*, edible. Hence, regarding the minuscule tissue sample containing the stem cells, a strong case can be made that as at the time of its extraction from the cow it is inedible, *melicha* would not be mandated at that time.

57   This author wishes to thank former *talmidim* Rabbi Yisroel Meir Wachs and Chaim Orelowitz for their impetus in my interest and research in this topic, as well as Rav Yitzchak Breitowitz for helping review this topic.

Chapter 10

Buffalo Burgers and the Zebu Controversy

PARASHAS SHEMINI DISCUSSES AND SPECIFIES the requirements and parameters for determining the kosher status of members of the animal kingdom. For example:

- Fish need to have fins and scales.[1]
- Domestic land animals (*beheimos*) must chew their cud (be ruminant) and have completely cloven (a.k.a. "split") hooves.[2]
- Non-domestic land animals (*chayos*) share the same basic set of rules to be considered kosher, but have slightly differing *halachos*. Some of the more well-known ones include that they do not have the prohibition of eating forbidden fats (*cheilev*) that a domestic land animal does, but there is a requirement to cover its blood immediately after slaughtering (*kisui hadam*), similar to a fowl but unlike a *beheimah*.[3]

---

1 *Parashas Shemini* (*Vayikra* Ch.11:9–13). The specifics of defining and discerning which fish are considered kosher are also presented in *Parashas Re'eh* (*Devarim* Ch. 14:9–10). This topic is discussed at length in the chapter titled "Fish With Legs?!"

2 *Vayikra* (*Parashas Shemini* Ch. 11:1–3) and *Devarim* (*Parashas Re'eh* Ch. 14:6).

3 See *Vayikra* (*Parashas Acharei Mos* Ch. 17:13) and Mishnah and Gemara *Chullin* (83b and 89b).

Buffalo Burgers

What is buffalo considered? Can we partake of a nice juicy buffalo burger? Although the *Shulchan Aruch* himself rules that a buffalo is considered a kosher *beheimah*,[4] it is quite certain that he was not referring to our American buffalo—which was unknown at the time and is truly a bison—but rather the Asian water buffalo.[5]

Still, it is clear that the American buffalo/bison chews its cud and has split hooves, the signs of a kosher animal. Surely that should be enough to let us start grilling!

But, if so, why is its meat not more common? And, on an anecdotal level, this author has never seen buffalo (bison) burgers advertised in Eretz Yisrael in any *Mehadrin* supermarket, butcher, or even fast-food joint! So, as the expression goes, "Where's the beef?"

Cryptic Comments and Fowl Play

The reason for the lack of American buffalo (bison) meat is based on a cryptic comment of the *Shach*, where he compares the kashrus status of the *chaya* to that of fowl.

---

4   *Shulchan Aruch* (Y.D. 28:4). The *Rema* (ad loc.) however, is unsure and classifies it as a possible *chaya*. The main difference between these two positions is whether one should cover its blood after slaughter without a *bracha*.

5   The *Ba'er Hagolah* (ad loc. 9) traces this to the *Agur* (1099) citing Rav Yeshaya Ha'acharon of Italy. This buffalo is also mentioned by *Tosafos* (*Zevachim* 113b s.v. *orzulaya*), the *Mordechai* (*Chullin* 653), the *Shach* (Y.D. 80:3), and *Aruch Hashulchan* (Y.D. 80:12). In Italy "buffalo" is still used to refer to the water buffalo. It would be hard to imagine that these early authorities were referring to the American bison which was completely unknown at the time of writing their *sefarim*. See Rabbi Dr. Ari Z. Zivotofsky's excellent article on www.kashrut.com titled "Kashrut of Exotic Animals: The Buffalo." Rav Shlomo Miller of Toronto, in his second *teshuva* on topic (titled "Zebu and Bison 2," available on his Kollel's website-www.kollel.org), maintains that as we are uncertain whether bison is a *beheimah* or *chaya* (or possibly the fabled *koy* or *kviy*), even if one holds that it is permitted to be eaten, it nonetheless requires *kisui hadam* and it may not be bred.

The Torah enumerates twenty-four various non-kosher "birds."[6] Since so many thousands of avian species exist, Chazal specify four necessary anatomical indicative features (*simanim*) that identify a specific type of fowl as kosher: an extra toe, a crop, a peelable gizzard (meaning the gizzard's inner lining can be peeled from the outer muscle wall), and being non-predatory (*doreis*).[7]

However, as the exact translation of the non-kosher birds listed in the Torah is unknown, as well as the fact that we cannot be assured of the absolute non-predatory nature of any given species of bird, many early authorities contend that we do not rely on our understanding of these *simanim*, but rather we only eat fowl when we have a tradition (*mesorah*) that this specific species is indeed kosher. Indeed, *Rashi* cites precedent from the case of the "Swamp Chicken" (*Tarnegolta D'Agma*), with which even Chazal made a mistake, not realizing at first that it is truly predatory in nature (*doreis*) and therefore non-kosher.[8] He therefore maintains that since we are not experts, we additionally need a *mesorah* to allow fowl to be eaten. The *Rema*, in fact, and concurred by virtually all *halachic* authorities, definitively rules this way *lemaaseh*, that we may not eat any species of bird without a *mesorah*.[9]

Concerning the laws of a kosher *chaya*, the *Shulchan Aruch* discusses the different types of horns which distinguish a *chaya* from a *beheimah*.[10] The *Shach* enigmatically comments that "I did not elaborate,

---

6 *Vayikra* (*Parashas Shemini* Ch. 11:13–24) and *Devarim* (*Parashas Re'eh* Ch. 14:11–21).

7 Mishnah and following Gemara (*Chullin* 59a-61b). There is much debate among the Rishonim how to properly define these *simanim*, especially a "non-*doreis*," as well as if the Gemara's intent was that all four features are necessary to render a bird kosher, or if the three physical characteristics are sufficient proof that the fowl is non-predatory and therefore kosher.

8 Gemara *Chullin* (62b) and *Rashi* (ad loc. s.v. *chazyuha*).

9 *Rema* (Y.D. 82:3). The *Shulchan Aruch* (Y.D. 82:2) actually rules this way as well, but allows several more leniencies (see ad loc. 82:3) than the *Rema's* stronger language.

10 *Shulchan Aruch* (Y.D. 80:1). Speaking of horns, for a fascinating discussion of

since nowadays we only use what we received as a *mesorah*, similar to the laws of kosher fowl."[11] The basic understanding seems to be that the *Shach* is implying that just as for a bird to be considered kosher it needs to have a *mesorah* even if it fits all other requirements, so too a *chaya* would also need to have a *mesorah* to allow it to be eaten, even though it is technically kosher! This would imply that the American bison would be on the verboten list. As it was an unknown animal, by definition it could not have had a *mesorah*.

Mandating *Mesorahs*?

The *Pri Megadim*, foremost commentary on the *Shach*, categorically rejects such a possibility, as it would run counter to the Gemara's ruling that identifying features are sufficient to determine a *chaya's* kashrus status.[12] Additionally, there is no mention of such a requirement in any of the early authorities. He concludes that the *Shach* must have meant something else entirely, namely, regarding the differences between a *beheimah* and a *chaya*: Since the defining distinctions between a *beheimah* and a *chaya* are often unclear, one should not eat the *cheilev* of any species (permissible by a *chaya*, prohibited by a *beheimah*) unless we have an oral tradition that said species is indeed a kosher *chaya*.[13] In other words, the *Shach* was referring to the need of a *mesorah* to allow

---

what a unicorn might be considered, see *Pri Chodosh* (Y.D. 80:2) and *Shu"t Beis Yaakov* (41).

11 *Shach* (Y.D. 80:1). See also the *Ibn Ezra's* commentary to *Parashas Re'eh* (*Devarim* Ch. 14:5) who likewise writes an ambiguous comment related to *beheimos* and *chayos* which can also possibly be interpreted in both of these different manners. It is worth noting that Rav Yisroel Belsky (*Shu"t Shulchan Halevi* Ch. 19:1 s.v. *u'mah*) writes that it is abundantly clear that the *Ibn Ezra* did not intend to get involved in the practical *halacha* of defining said animals, but is rather simply stating that he is aware that there are other kosher animals extant, yet is uncertain how to properly identify them. In other words, he is merely pointing out that these other animals were not common in his time and place (1100s' Spain).

12 *Chullin* (59b).

13 *Pri Megadim* (Y.D. 80, S.D. 1).

a *halachic* detail, but not in actually identifying a kosher animal. The majority of later authorities agree with the *Pri Megadim's* understanding of the *Shach's* comment and rule likewise—that *mesorah* plays no factor in whether or not an animal (domestic or not) may be eaten; the only necessary requirements being that it chews its cud and has split hooves.[14] This would mean that buffalo burgers can be on the menu!

However, before you get that grill fired up, you might want to "hold your horses (er...buffalo)." Two major later authorities, the *Chochmas Adam* and the *Aruch Hashulchan* both seem to accept the *Shach's* words at face value, and not like the *Pri Megadim's* interpretation, implying that an oral tradition *is* needed to allow any land animal to be eaten.[15]

In fact, the renowned *Chazon Ish* ruled this way explicitly in 1950, regarding the importing of the zebu ("Indian humpbacked cow") to Israel, stating that the *Chochmas Adam's* interpretation of the *Shach's* comment is the correct one! He therefore maintained that any "new" land animal may not be eaten unless there is a *mesorah*. He added that since the *sefer Chochmas Adam* was considered in Lithuania (Lita) as the authoritative work on *Yoreh Deah*, we must follow his ruling relating to this.[16] The *Chazon Ish* concludes that the only known animals that we

---

14 Including the *Kreisi U'Pleisi* (ad loc. 2), *Pischei Teshuva* (ad loc. end 1; he is arguing on the *Beis Yaakov* ibid. s.v. *v'gam*, who opines that a *chaya* must have another *siman* in order to be considered kosher: horns; the *Beis Yaakov's* opinion is rejected by many, if not all, *halachic* authorities), *Beis Yitzchak* (ad loc. *Amudei Zahav* 3), *Mishmeres Shalom* (ad loc. S.D. 1), *Darchei Teshuva* (ad loc. 3), and *Kaf Hachaim* (ad loc. 5).

15 *Chochmas Adam* (36:1) and *Aruch Hashulchan* (Y.D. 80: end 10).

16 The *Chazon Ish's* brother-in-law, the Steipler Gaon (see *Orchos Rabbeinu*; new edition, vol. 4, pg. 91:20) also held this way, that Rav Avraham Danzig's classic *halachic* works, *Chayei Adam* on *Orach Chaim* and *Chochmas Adam* on *Yoreh Deah* were "*sifrei yesod lehoraasav v'hanhagosav*." His son, Rav Chaim Kanievsky, follows this as well, telling people who were *nichshal* in a *Bassar B'chalav* matter, to relearn and review the *halachos* with the *Chochmas Adam*. See *Doleh U'Mashkeh* (pg. 258–259), and Rabbi Yaakov Skoczylas' *Ohel Yaakov* (on *Hilchos Issur V'Hetter*, revised edition pg. 222, footnote s.v. *v'shamaati*).

eat are "cows, sheep, and goats."[17] This understanding would obviously not permit the buffalo/bison either.

In fact when the "New Zebu Controversy" broke out in 2004, many wished to have zebu meat banned (which would logically be extended to buffalo as well), based primarily on the *Chazon Ish's* strongly worded ruling from over fifty years prior.[18]

---

17   *Chazon Ish* (Y.D. 11:4 and 5), *Kovetz Igros Chazon Ish* (vol. 1:99; vol. 2:83; and vol. 3:113), and in the recent *Shu"t V'Chiddushim Chazon Ish* (130 and 131). These writings of the *Chazon Ish* were actually a series of correspondence between himself and the Chief Rabbi of Israel, Rav Yitzchak Isaac *Halevi* Herzog. Rav Herzog wrote a *Kuntress* on the topic, titled *"Kuntress Pnei Shor"* (printed in his responsa as *Shu"t Heichal Yitzchak* Y.D. vol. 1:20) concluding that the zebu is permitted to be eaten. He also maintained that there was a *mesorah* in India and other countries going back centuries that the zebu was considered a kosher cow. He suggests that anyone who argues that a *mesorah* is required is possibly violating the Biblical prohibition of *Bal Tosif*, adding on to the Torah's commandments (*Devarim, Parashas Re'eh* Ch. 13:1; see *Sefer Hachinuch* ad loc. Mitzva 454). See also *Pe'er Hador* (of the *Chazon Ish*; vol. 4, pg. 226–230), and *Orchos Rabbeinu* (new edition; vol. 4, pg. 9–16), which cite and summarize the correspondence. Rav Chaim Kanievsky was recently quoted (*Doleh U'Mashkeh* pg. 255–256) regarding the *"Bor Hahodu Shehaya B'zman HaChazon Ish,"* as expressing very strongly that he considers it one hundred percent non-kosher. The *Beis Halevi* is quoted as being of the same opinion as the *Chazon Ish*—see *Contemporary Halakhic Problems* (vol. 5, pg. 255, footnote 15).

18   See *Orchos Rabbeinu* (new edition; vol. 4, pg. 9–16) at length. Likewise, Rav Shlomo Miller wrote a strongly worded *teshuva* on topic dated 8 Shvat 5766 (titled "Zebu and Bison," available on his Kollel's website-www.kollel.org) stating that although there are kashrus agencies who grant *hashgacha* to zebu and/or bison meat, nevertheless the *psak* of the *Chazon Ish* was already accepted, and based on this, Rav Elyashiv and other *Poskim* of Eretz Yisrael prohibited this meat, and therefore it should not be eaten. However, in a later (albeit undated) *teshuva* on topic (titled "Zebu and Bison 2," also available on his Kollel's website) and possibly due to the arguments raised above, Rav Miller backtracks somewhat on his prohibitory *psak*, writing that his intention is simply to raise awareness for those who follow the *Chazon Ish*, that nowadays they should not eat zebu and bison, as the same issues should still apply.

Grounds for Leniency

However, several contemporary authorities pointed out many potential flaws with making such an argument,[19] including:

- If the *Shach* truly meant to qualify the permissibility of eating a *chaya*, he would have written it in the previous *siman* (*Yoreh Deah* 79), which discusses which animals are kosher, and not where he actually commented, where only identifying features were being discussed.
- The *Chochmas Adam* and *Aruch Hashulchan* are not really any clearer in their ruling than the *Shach* himself, thus allowing their comments to be interpreted like the *Pri Megadim's* opinion as well.[20]
- The *Chazon Ish* himself only restricted an animal that is considered a "new species"; it has since been proven that the zebu has been eaten and considered kosher for a long time in many different countries.[21] In fact, due to this reasoning, the *Chazon Ish*

---

19 Including Rav Yitzchak Isaac *Halevi* Herzog (ibid.), Rav Meshulam Roth ("The Hordonka *Iluy*"; *Shu"t Kol Mevasser* vol. 1:9), Rav Shalom Krauss (*Shu"t Divrei Shalom* vol. 7:38), Rav Shmuel *Halevi* Wosner (*Shu"t Shevet Halevi* vol. 10:114), Rav Yisroel Belsky (*Shu"t Shulchan Halevi, Chelek Birurei Halacha* 19), Rav Yechezkel Roth (*Shu"t Eimek Hateshuva* vol. 6:305), and Rav Asher Weiss (*Minchas Asher al HaTorah, Parashas Shemini* 14). Although not all bring the same arguments, nevertheless, each of these authorities cites at least one of these reasons. This was also the opinion of Rav Moshe Feinstein (see *Mesores Moshe* vol. 1, Y.D. 13, pg. 211 and footnote 22, and vol. 2, Y.D. 15, pg. 169), that the *ikar* is to follow the *Pri Megadim's* understanding and that buffalo is indeed considered a kosher animal. See also Rabbi Dr. Ari Z. Zivotofsky's article on topic published in *Kovetz Hame'ayen* (Teves 5768, vol. 48:2, pg. 16–18).

20 See for example, the *Beis Yitzchak* (ibid.) and *Kaf Hachaim* (ibid.), who cite their opinions this way as basic understanding.

21 In fact, as recently pointed out to this author by David Hojda, according to recent studies, it seems that zebu was actually originally indigenous to the Middle East. Moreover, and quite interestingly, zebu is prominently featured in the figurative wall paintings of the Dura-Europos ancient synagogue in

himself ate turkey, the quintessential "New World" fowl, based on a responsum of his father's, Rav Shemaryahu Yosef Karelitz.[22]

Syria (dating back to 244 C.E.) that were uncovered by archaeological dig in 1932 (in the painting depicting the "*Avodah* in the *Beis Hamikdash*").

22 See *Shu"t Meishiv Davar* (Y.D. 22). Although referring to the turkey, the symbolic New World fowl which the vast majority of world Jewry eats, even though a *mesorah* pre-Columbus would be a seeming impossibility, nonetheless, the *Netziv* permits it to be eaten on this basis, that it has been eaten for a long time and is now considered having a *mesorah*. For more on the topic of the kashrus status of turkey, and its more kashrus-wise complicated companion fowl, the Muscovy Duck, Posen Hen, Guineafowl, and/or Cochin, and how they are/were viewed from a *halachic* perspective through the ages, see *Nachal Eshkol* (on the *Sefer Ha'Eshkol*, *Hilchos Beheima*, *Chaya*, *v'Of* 22:10; he understands there to be an Indian *mesorah* on the turkey), *Knesses Hagedolah* (Y.D. 82:31), *Shu"t Shoel U'Meishiv* (*Mahadura Telita'ei* vol. 1:149 and *Mahadura Chamisha'ah* vol. 1:69), *Shu"t Chasam Sofer* (Y.D. 74), *Shu"t Divrei Chaim* (O.C. 9 and Y.D. vol. 2:45–48), *Shu"t Maharam Schick* (Y.D. 98–100), *Shu"t Tuv Taam V'Daas* (*Mahadura Telita'ei* 150–152), *Shu"t Ha'Elef Lecha Shlomo* (Y.D. 111), *Shu"t Beis Yitzchak* (Y.D. vol. 1:106), *Shu"t Yehuda Yaaleh* (vol. 1, Y.D. 92–94), *Shu"t Tzelosa D'Avraham* (7), *Shu"t HaRim* (Y.D. 8), *Shu"t Tzemach Tzedek* (Y.D. 60), *Shu"t She'eilas Shalom* (Y.D. 22), *Arugas Habosem* (*Kuntress HaTeshuvos* 16), *Shu"t Ori V'Yishi* (vol. 1:11), *Damesek Eliezer* (*Chullin* Ch. 3, 51:84 and Ch. 4, 13:73 and 78), *Shu"t Binyan Tzion* (vol. 1:42), *Shu"t Dvar Halacha* (53), Rav Yissachar Dov Illowy's *Shu"t Milchemos Elokim* (pg. 162–165; also citing *teshuvos* from Rav Samson Raphael Hirsch and Rav Nosson Adler, the first Chief Rabbi of England; regarding the Muscovy Duck), *Shu"t Avnei Nezer* (Y.D. 75), *Shu"t Michtav Sofer* (Y.D. 3), *Shu"t Melamed L'Ho'eel* (vol. 2-Y.D. 15), the Maharsham's *Daas Torah* (Y.D. 82:3), *Shu"t Mei Be'er* (19; who opines that the turkey actually came from India and even has a *mesorah* dating back to Moshe Rabbeinu!), *Zivchei Tzedek* (82:17), *Darchei Teshuva* (82:26), Rav Yehuda Leib Tsirelson's *Maarchei Lev* (*Chelek HaTeshuvos*, Y.D. 30; regarding the Posen Hen), *Shu"t Divrei Malkiel* (vol. 4:56), Rav Yosef Aharon Teren of Argentina's *Zecher Yosef* (pg. 1a-6b; regarding the Muscovy Duck), *Shu"t Nishmas Chaim* (Y.D. 63), *Kaf Hachaim* (Y.D. 82:21), *Shu"t Igros Moshe* (Y.D. vol. 1:34; also citing the opinions of Rav Naftali Carlebach and Rav Yosef Eliyahu Henkin; regarding the Posen Hen), *Shu"t Har Tzvi* (Y.D. 75; regarding the Muscovy Duck), *Shu"t Minchas Yitzchak* (vol. 5:31), *Kovetz Mesorah* (vol. 3, pg. 60–65; in a *maamar* from the *Beis Avi*, Rav Yitzchak Isaac Liebes, regarding Rock

- Rav Yaakov Kamenetzky has been quoted as maintaining that the *Pri Megadim* was considered the authoritative work in Lita, and not necessarily the *Chochmas Adam*.[23]
- Even if we would assume that the *Chochmas Adam's* ruling would be binding for those in Lita, it most definitely would not be obligatory to any other communities, who would be free to follow their own *halachic* authorities.
- The *Chochmas Adam* himself writes that deer (venison) is permissible, and as mentioned previously, the *Shulchan Aruch* ruled

---

Cornish Hens), *Shu"t Shulchan Halevi* (Ch. 19:1), Rav Shmuel Salant's posthumously published *Aderes Shmuel* (222; pg. 225–228), *Sichas Chullin* (pg. 429, on *Chullin* 63a; who astoundingly posits that the turkey *mesorah* possibly came from the Ten Lost Tribes who might have been early Native Americans, as per Rav Menashe ben Yisrael's unsubstantiated theory, who then contacted Indian and English *Poskim*!!), and Rav Yaakov Yedidyah Adani's fascinating *halachic* history of the Muscovy Duck, published in *Kovetz Eitz Chaim* (vol. 26; Elul 5776, pg. 430–455). Additionally, and quite interestingly, we find that several Acharonim, including the *Bach* (O.C. 79, s.v. *kasav Beis Yosef*), *Magen Avraham* (ad loc. 14), *Ateres Zekeinim* (ad loc.), *Ba'er Heitiv* (ad loc. 12), *Aruch Hashulchan* (ad loc. 16), and *Mishnah Berurah* (ad loc. 26), understand the *Yerushalmi's* (*Eruvin* Ch. 3, *Halacha* 5) "Red Chickens" (*Tarnegolim Aduma*), which we must distance ourselves from its excrement while davening (see *Shulchan Aruch* ad loc. 6; as opposed to the understanding of red excrement from a chicken), to be referring to a turkey; giving implicit consent that it is indeed a kosher bird (however, and quite interestingly, it remains unclear how an American New World fowl was seemingly extant in Eretz Yisrael at the time of the writing of the *Yerushalmi*). In fact, the *Chazon Ish* himself ate turkey, based on a *teshuva* of his father's, Rav Shemaryahu Yosef Karelitz [this *teshuva* was recently published in *Shu"t V'Chiddushim Chazon Ish* (132)]. See *Orchos Rabbeinu* (new edition; vol. 4, pg. 9:1). The mainstream opinion that turkey is considered an acceptable fowl is also seen by the contemporary *Poskim* who allowed it being eaten on Thanksgiving. This topic was discussed at length in a recent article titled "Thanksgiving: Harmless Holiday or *Chukos HaGoyim*?," accessible at: https://ohr.edu/this_week/insights_into_halacha/6105.

23 *Shu"t Shulchan Halevi* (ibid. pg. 282, s.v. *v'yoser*).

that water buffalo is kosher, proving that the *Chazon Ish's* rule of only eating "cows, sheep, and goats," is not absolute.
- The *Chochmas Adam* and the *Aruch Hashulchan* both wrote explicitly that only a *chaya* needs a *mesorah*, not a *beheimah*. The zebu (being a humpbacked cow) however, is considered a *beheimah*, not a *chaya*, and therefore should not require an oral tradition.
- The Gemara states that kosher and non-kosher species cannot physically crossbreed.[24] Thus, if two species can indeed hybridize and one is known to be kosher, it should be proof positive that the other is kosher as well. As since the time of the *Chazon Ish's* writing both the bison and zebu have successfully been interbred with cattle, this should prove them both as kosher species. Indeed, aside from the known "beefalo," most cows currently extant in Israel have at least a percentage of zebu "*yichus*" (lineage).
- The *Chazon Ish* himself, in a later letter, accepts that the zebu is technically a kosher animal, but reiterates that we need to have a proper *mesorah* to permit it to be eaten. Yet, he concludes that "in our times, with Reform making inroads into authentic Torah Judaism, it is impossible to allow new things to be considered permitted if in the past they were deemed prohibited…as one breach (of tradition) leads to subsequent breaches."[25] Nowadays, it can be debated that this logic might no longer be applicable.[26]

---

24 *Bechoros* (7a) and ruled accordingly by the *Rambam* (*Hilchos Maachalos Assuros* Ch. 1:13), that "*ain min tamei misabeir m'min tahor klal.*" Rabbi Dr. Ari Z. Zivotofsky strongly makes the case for this reasoning in his extensive article on www.kashrut.com titled "Kashrut of Exotic Animals: The Buffalo."

25 Printed in *Pe'er Hador* (ibid. pg. 228–230), and later reprinted in *Kovetz Igros Chazon Ish* (vol. 3:113), *Orchos Rabbeinu* (ibid. pg. 12–13), and *Shu"t V'Chiddushim Chazon Ish* (131).

26 It is worthwhile to note that another of the issues the *Chazon Ish* prohibits for the same reason is slaughtering meat in another country and importing it to Eretz Yisrael. This author is not entirely sure why that proviso is widely ignored (as even the most *Mehudar Badatzim* perform *shechita* in foreign

Buffalo to Go?

Due to these rationales, as well as the facts that currently most milk cows in Israel are descended from zebu, and that many *Tefillin* and *Sifrei Torah* are written on parchment (*klaf*) made from their hides, and although initially reported otherwise,[27] Rav Yosef Shalom Elyashiv, and other contemporary *Poskim*, later concluded that these humpbacked cows are essentially permitted.[28]

Therefore, even if one wishes to be stringent with eating the zebu or buffalo itself (as Rav Elyashiv himself favored), nevertheless, regarding potential related offshoot issues, such as crossbred offspring and the *halachic* status of their milk, as well as *Sifrei Torah* and *Mezuzos* written on their hides, etc., the final *psak* is that these are certainly permitted.

Conclusively Kosher?

All this said, are we going to see "Buffalo Burgers" or "Zebu Zurprize" in our local supermarket any time soon? In America, perhaps. In Israel, probably not.

---

countries), but the zebu issue erupted in renewed controversy, even as both are part and parcel of the same letter the great *Chazon Ish* wrote.

27 "Hoda'ah L'Tzibbur," *b'sheim* Rav Elyashiv and Rav Nissim Karelitz, dated 21 Adar 5764; interestingly signed by three "*Talmidim*": Rav Yitzchak Mordechai Rubin, Rav Dovid Aryeh Morgenstern, and Rav Moshe Mordechai Karp, and not Rav Elyashiv himself; originally published in the Israeli daily *Yated Ne'eman* newspaper on March 19, 2004. See *Orchos Rabbeinu* (ibid.), *Kovetz Yeshurun* (vol. 22, pg. 924 s.v. *uv'gimmel Adar*; although this might not be the exact same letter), Rav Shlomo Miller's first *teshuva* on topic (ibid.), *Contemporary Halakhic Problems* (vol. 5, pg. 260), Rav Yirmiyohu Kaganoff's recent *From Buffalo Burgers to Monetary Mysteries* (pg. 217–218, "Anyone For a Buffalo Burger?"), and *Halachic World* (vol. 2, pg. 162, "Bison Blues").

28 See *Shu"t Shulchan Halevi* (ibid. pg. 284:2), *Minchas Asher* (ibid. pg. 82, s.v. *hinei*), Rav Shlomo Miller's second *teshuva* on topic (titled "Zebu and Bison 2"), and *Shu"t Vidibarta Bam* (vol. 2:235 and 236 s.v. *v'shamaati*; citing Rav Dovid Feinstein). This is because although these animals may not have a true *mesorah*, and according to some, may therefore not be eaten, nonetheless, they still have *simanei kashrus*, and are therefore definitively considered

Even though many contemporary authorities rule that there is no real kashrus issue with them and that they may be eaten by even those stringent on the highest levels of kashrus, on the other hand, authorities maintain that out of respect and in deference to the great *Chazon Ish*, and especially in Eretz Yisrael, "the land of the *Chazon Ish*," it is preferable to abstain from partaking of them.[29] For this reason buffalo/bison burgers apparently won't be found in Israel with a *Mehadrin hashgacha*, although they may be more easily obtainable in the land "where the buffalo roam."

---

kosher animals. As such, the potential problematic issues with their offspring regarding "*Zera Ha'Av*" (Gemara *Chullin* 79a) should not apply in our case, as there is a *safek Derabbanan* on a disputed prohibition that is clearly at worst, a *minhag*. [See Gemara *Bechoros* (7a), *Rambam* (*Hilchos Maachalos Assuros* Ch. 1:13), *Lechem Mishneh* (ad loc.), *Tosafos* (*Chullin* 58a s.v. m'kaan), and *Shu"t Avnei Nezer* (Y.D. 75:8).] See also *Orchos Rabbeinu* (ibid.) which details several fascinating conversations between its author, Rav Avraham Hurvitz and Rav Ezriel Auerbach, Rav Elyashiv's son-in-law, on this topic. He concludes that *lemaaseh*, Rav Elyashiv held that the Israeli *hashgachos* should not perform *shechita* on zebu to import it *davka* to Eretz Yisrael, as the *ikar hanhaga* should be according to "*Rabban shel Yisrael*" the *Chazon Ish*, but even so, notes that Rav Elyashiv held that the *Chazon Ish's psak* is not the "*psak hakavua b'davar issur achilas beheimos bli mesores*," and therefore was essentially *meikil* regarding other zebu-related issues, such as *chashashos* of offspring, milk, *Sifrei Torah* and *Tefillin*, etc.

29 See *Shu"t Shevet Halevi* (ibid.), *Orchos Rabbeinu* (ibid.), *Minchas Asher* (ibid.), and *Shu"t Vidibarta Bam* (ibid.; citing Rav Dovid Feinstein).

Chapter 11

The *Gid Hanasheh* Incongruity

IN *PARASHAS VAYISHLACH*, AFTER YAAKOV Avinu's epic battle with Eisav's guardian angel[1] during which he gets injured in his hip socket,[2] we are given a Biblical commandment, the third and last of the whole *sefer Bereishis*, that Bnei Yisrael may not partake of the *Gid Hanasheh*, the sciatic nerve, of any animal. Additionally, there is a Rabbinic prohibition on eating from the outer sinew of the animal's thigh tendon.[3] The *Sefer Hachinuch* writes that this Mitzva actually serves as testament to the eternity of the Jewish people and a constant reminder that eventually we will be redeemed from our protracted exile.[4]

---

1 *Bereishis* (end of Ch. 32). This follows *Rashi's* understanding (ad loc. 25, end s.v. *vayei'aveik ish*), based on the *Midrash Rabbah* (ad loc. 77:3) and *Midrash Tanchuma* (ad loc. 8; who adds that the guardian angel of Eisav was Sama-el). However, there is another opinion, cited in *Otzar Hamidrashim* (ad loc.), that it was really the *malach* Michoel that Yaakov fought, and not Eisav's guardian angel, in order to prove to Yaakov that he had nothing to fear from Eisav.

2 Due to the dictum of *"Maaseh Avos Siman L'Banim"* we are still feeling the repercussions of this act nowadays. See *Chofetz Chaim al HaTorah* to *Parashas Vayishlach*. This *inyan* is discussed in the chapter titled *"Chatichah Hareuyah L'Hischabed*: All About Honor."

3 Gemara *Chullin* (91a-93b) and *Shulchan Aruch* (Y.D. 65:8).

4 *Sefer Hachinuch* (Mitzva 3). Several Rishonim, including the *Ramban* (*Bereishis* Ch. 32:26), Rabbeinu Bachya (ad loc.), *Rashba* (*Chiddushei Agados, Chullin* 91a), and *Ra'ah* (*Pekudas Haleviim, Brachos* 33b), as well as the *Midrash Rabbah* (*Parashas Vayishlach* 78:5), also imply this message. See the *Machon Yerushalayim* edition of *Sefer Hachinuch* (Mitzva 3, footnote 3) at length.

To fulfill this Mitzva properly, every last trace of said nerves and the fat covering the sciatic nerve must be removed as well. This act is called *nikkur*, a.k.a. *treibbering*, de-veining, or porging the forbidden nerves and fats,[5] and it takes a true expert to perform it properly.[6]

---

5   See *Shulchan Aruch* and *Rema* (Y.D. 65:13 and 14), and their commentaries. Many communities mandate complete removal of the major arteries and veins as well prior to *kashering* the meat via salting, as part of the *treibbering* process. The salting process is discussed at length in an upcoming chapter titled "Salting with Sugar?!"

6   Indeed, several Rishonim, including the *Rashba* (*Toras Habayis*, *Bayis* 3, *Shaar* 3), the *Hagahos Ashri* (*Chullin*, Ch. 7:16), and the *Agur* (end 1175), emphasize that one should only rely upon the *treibbering* of a known expert, and the *Rema* (Y.D. 64:7 and 65:8; see also *Darchei Moshe* ad loc. 13) points out **twice** that *nikkur* cannot be learned from a text, only through apprenticeship. In fact, due to lack of expertise in *Nikkur Achorayim*, *treibbering* the forbidden fats from hindquarters, already dating back to the 1500s [see *Shu"t HaRadbaz* (vol. 1:162), *Damesek Eliezer* (*Chullin*, pg. 237b and 241b; cited by the *Knesses Hagedolah*, Y.D. 65, *Hagahos* on the *Beis Yosef* 63), and the Maharshal's *Yam Shel Shlomo* (*Chullin* Ch.1:2 and Ch. 7:19; cited by the *Ba'er Heitiv*, Y.D. 65:6), who complained about the problematic state of affairs already in their day, and advised not to partake of such meat], a general Ashkenazic *minhag* of sorts has developed over the years of not eating meat from the hindquarters of the animal. This meat (including prime cuts such as Filet Mignon, Sirloin, and T-bone steak) is rather sold to non-Jews. Although we do find in the works of Ashkenazic Acharonim that hindquarters was eaten with several additional checks in place to ascertain that the *treibbering* was performed properly, on the other hand, they also attest that many communities did not use the hindquarters meat at all, but rather sold it as non-kosher, because they lacked skilled *menakkerim*. See, for example *Shu"t Tzemach Tzedek* (73), *Shu"t Chavos Yair* (178), *Shu"t Noda B'Yehuda* (Tinyana, Y.D. 31), *Shu"t Chasam Sofer* (Y.D. 68), *Yeshuos Yaakov* (Y.D. 64:2), *Shu"t Divrei Dovid* (Meldola; 35 s.v. v'hasheini), and Rav Samson Raphael Hirsch's posthumously published *Shu"t Shemesh Marpeh* (34). In fact, Rav Yonason Eibeshutz writes (*Kreisi* ad loc. end 16) that he would not eat hindquarter meat unless he *treibbered* it himself. As attested to by the *Aruch Hashulchan* (Y.D. 64:54 and 65:31) and *Darchei Teshuva* (65:96), by the late 1800s, in most Ashkenazic communities *treibbering* and eating hindquarters was the exception rather than the norm. More contemporarily, although under extenuating circumstances *Rabbanim* have

ruled that Ashkenazim may partake of *treibbered* hindquarter meat when performed by expert porgers, as it never was truly considered prohibited [for example, when the Polish Parliament (Sejm) outlawed selling kosher *shechted* meat to non-Jews in 1936, the *Gadol Hador*, Rav Chaim Ozer Grodzenski (*Shu"t Achiezer* vol. 3:84), ruled that *Nikkur Achorayim* must be reinstated so the Jews will still have kosher meat to eat], nevertheless, the general Ashkenazic *minhag* has been and currently is not to eat hindquarter meat. See *Shu"t Igros Moshe* (Y.D. vol. 2:42), *Shu"t Teshuvos Vehanhagos* (vol. 1:418–419 and vol. 4:183), *Shu"t Mishnah Halachos* (vol. 10:85), and *Shu"t Shulchan Halevi* (Ch. 18:8). Interestingly, and the *Radbaz's* responsum notwithstanding (as he was based in Sefardic Egypt), Sefardic communities have generally continually performed *Nikkur Achorayim*, relying on their own expertise [see for example *Shulchan Gavoah* (ad loc. 37; who was known as an expert *treibberer*—see ad loc 64:18), who cites much of the above and concludes that nevertheless, he personally relied on the best of his abilities after a thorough examination that said *treibbering* was performed properly].

There is a noteworthy anecdote related about the Arizal (*Ha'Ari V'Gurav*, pg. 217; citing *Meir Einei Hagolah*, 237), that he refused to partake of hindquarters meat, even meat personally *treibbered* by Rav Yosef Karo, the *Shulchan Aruch* himself! In contrast to the above, and as attested to by Rav Avraham Yitzchak Hakohen Kook in a letter to Rav Chaim Ozer Grodzenski (*Shu"t Daas Kohen* 223), and elucidated in great detail in *Toras HaNikkur HaYerushalmi* (published 5702/1942; vol. 1, pg. 26–35), the Ashkenazic *minhag* in Yerushalayim classically was to perform *Nikkur Achorayim* and eat hindquarters meat (and not as believed by the *Darchei Teshuva*, 64:46). This divergence from the Ashkenazic norm was instituted by the *Gedolei* Yerushalayim at the time when Ashkenazic *shechitta* was first allowed by the ruling authorities (Turks/Ottomans), in 5634/1874. These *Gedolim*, including Rav Meir Auerbach (the *Imrei Bina*), Rav Shmuel Salant, and the Maharil Diskin, accepted and continued many of the Sefardic traditions related to *shechitta* that had been the practice until that time, as these *minhagim* dated back to when the *Pri Chodosh* was Rav of Yerushalayim, over 150 years prior. Although this no longer seems to be the case, this author has been told anecdotally more than once by those eating at a restaurant under Rav Shlomo Machpud's "*Yoreh Deah*" Hashgacha, that if one orders the filet mignon or other fancy cut of hindquarter meat, the staff has been trained to ask the patron whether they are Ashkenazi or Sefardi. For additional treatment of this topic, see Rav Yirmiyohu Kaganoff's article titled "May an Ashkenazi Eat Sirloin?" (http://rabbikaganoff.com/

Trouble was the Traveling *Treibberer*

One of the most outstanding experts in *hilchos nikkur* known was Rav Yonason Eibeshutz (1690—1764), one of the greatest *Torah* giants of his period and famed author of eighty-nine (!) works,[7] including the renowned *Yaaros Devash*, *Urim V'Tumim*, and *Kreisi U'Pleisi*. In the latter *sefer*, in his commentary to the laws of *Gid Hanasheh*,[8] Rav Yonason recorded a fascinating historical incident, which posthumously sparked a raging *halachic* controversy.

He related that an expert porger came to town (Prague) claiming that the sinew that Jews have been removing for centuries was the wrong one! This *treibberer* alleged that a different sinew was the true *Gid Hanasheh*. The ramifications of his claim were gargantuan, for if it was deemed accurate, all of World Jewry would have *chas v'shalom* been eating non-kosher from time immemorial!

Rav Yonason writes that he showed this fellow the error of his ways, as the sinew this porger was referring to was found exclusively in male animals and could therefore not possibly be the correct one, for it states in the "*SMa"G* (ostensibly the *Sefer Mitzvos HaGadol* written by Rav Moshe of Coucy in the thirteenth century) that the prohibition of *Gid Hanasheh* applies to both males and females." With his vast knowledge and expertise, Rav Eibeshutz thus averted potential communal disaster. He concludes his passage reiterating the importance and necessity of a porger's proficiency and capability.

Kreisi Controversy

However, as many puzzled people later pointed out, this logic seemed inherently flawed, as this quote does not actually appear in the *SMa"G*! In his actual quote, the *SMa"G* was referring to people, not animals![9]

---

may-an-ashkenazi-eat-sirloin/) and Rabbi Dr. Ari Z. Zivotofsky's article titled "What's the Truth About...*Nikkur Achoraim*?" (originally published in the OU's *Jewish Action Magazine*, Fall 5767/2006 and available online at www.kashrut.com).

7   See preface to *Chacham Harazim—Rebbi Yonason Eibeshutz*.

8   *Kreisi U'Pleisi* (65 *Kreisi* 16).

In other words, he wrote that women were obligated in keeping this prohibition, just as men are.[10] They wondered if it was possible that the great Rav Eibeshutz could have made such a simple mistake? And, if so, what was it that the *Kreisi U'Pleisi* showed this traveling *treibberer* that contradicted his claims and refuted his *taynos*? Many scholars over the years searched for a proper solution to this perplexing conundrum:

- One suggestion was that the porger was unlearned, and Rav Yonason wanted to expose his ignorance and therefore set a trap and easily refute him.[11] The issue with this theory is that by Rav Yonason's own testimony, the porger was a "*Talmid Chacham* and expert," which would negate this solution.
- The *Pischei Teshuva* cites the *Toldos Adam*, who takes a different approach and makes an example out of this story as proof that even *Gedolim* can err[12] Following this would mean that one may not partake in eating said meat without removing *both* sinews. Although the *Toldos Adam*'s intent was merely to uncover the truth, he unwittingly fueled the fires of the *Haskalah*, as one of their primary goals was the undermining of Rabbinic authority.[13] In fact, this author personally heard noted historian Rav Berel Wein aver that the *Haskalah* used this story as propaganda to sway the masses.

---

9 *SMa"G* (*Mitzvos Lo Sa'useh* 139).

10 See for example, the *Baruch Taam*'s glosses to the *Kreisi U'Pleisi* ad loc. Although others, including the *Tzemach Hasadeh* (on Y.D. 65, pg. 41), assumed he meant the *SMa"K*, it is also not found there; neither is it in the *Rambam's Sefer HaMitzvos* (*Mitzvos Lo Sa'aseh* 183). See also Rav Shmuel Ashkenazi's *Alpha Beta Tinyeisa D'Shmuel Ze'ira* (vol. 1, pg. 195–196).

11 See *Hegos B'Parshiyos HaTorah* by Rav Yehuda Nachshoni (*Parashas Vayishlach*, pg. 137).

12 *Pischei Teshuva* (Y.D. 65:2), citing the *Toldos Adam* (Rav Yechezkel Feivel Wolfe of Vilna; vol. 2, Ch. 15, pg. 237).

13 Paraphrase from Professor Shnayer Zalman Leiman's excellent *Rabbi Jonathon Eibeshuetz and the Porger* (pg. 16). Thanks are due to Rabbi Dr. Eliezer Brodt, for providing this important source.

- On the other hand, many Rabbinic luminaries wrote responsae,[14] including a tremendous *pilpul* by the *Chasam Sofer*,[15] not only defending Rav Eibeshutz's words from attack, but actually each citing different proofs and logic how his *shittah* is truly correct, that the *Gid Hanesheh* must be present in both male and female animals.

- Several authorities wrote that it must be a printing mistake and the correct point of reference was S-H-G (סה"ג), referring to the *Sefer Halachos Gedolos* (commonly known as the *BeHa"G*), a ninth century *halachic* code which contains a section on *Hilchos Treifos*,[16] who actually *does* imply that the *Gid Hanasheh* is found in both male and female animals.[17]

---

14 Including the Mahari Assad (*Shu"t Yehuda Yaaleh*, Y.D. 102), Rav Shlomo Kluger (*Shu"t Tuv Taam V'Daas*, *Mahadura Kama* vol. 1:100; see however *Shu"t Even Yisrael*, vol. 7, Y.D. 64) [neither of whom actually approved of the *Chasam Sofer*'s *pilpul*], the Butchatcher Rav (*Daas Kedoshim* Y.D. 65, *Hilchos Giddin Ha'Assurin* 4; see explanation in *Gidulei Hakodesh* there, 1), the *Ginzei Yosef* (*Shu"t* 96:2; quoting the *Einei Yisrael*, *Chullin* 69b), the Mahari Halevi (*Shu"t* vol. 1: end 36 s.v. *mah shetamah*), the *Beis Yitzchak* (*Shu"t* Y.D. vol. 1:98), the *Tzemach Hasadeh* (Y.D. 65), the *Aryeh D'vei Ila'ei* (*Shu"t* Y.D. 4, *Avnei Zikaron*), *Mishnas Eliezer* (*Shu"t Mahadura Tinyana*, *Kuntress Mishnas Chachamim* pg. 32), *Otzar Yad Hachaim* (34), the Maharsham (*Daas Torah*, Y.D. 65:5; citing the *Maharsha*'s explanation of *Tosafos*, *Chullin* 69a s.v. *d'asa*), and the *Arugas Habosem* (*Shu"t* Y.D. 64:4). See also Rav Moshe Yosef Shapiro of Prague's *Bris Avraham* (*Parashas Vayishlach*) who, quite thoroughly argues on the whole premise of those who questioned Rav Eibeshutz, as once the Torah wrote that Bnei Yisrael may not partake of any *Gid Hanesheh*, it is patently obvious that it must occur in all kosher *beheimos*, with no differentiation between male and female. Additionally, as the *Rambam* writes in his preface to his *Peirush HaMishnayos* regarding the Torah's *"Pri Eitz Hadar"* being identified as the *esrog*, once we have a *Mesorah L'Doros* dating back to Moshe Rabbeinu, all other so-called "proofs" to the contrary immediately fall off. Therefore, he asserts, the same would apply here as well regarding the *Gid Hanesheh*.

15 *Shu"t Chasam Sofer* (Y.D. 69), cited approvingly by the *Pischei Teshuva* (ibid.) and *Shu"t HaRava"z* (Y.D. 111). The *Aruch Hashulchan* (Y.D. 65:25; in the brackets) might be referring to this solution as well.

- Others felt that he meant "a *sefer Mitzvos gadol*," meaning a big book of Mitzvos, possibly referring to the *Sefer Hachinuch*,[18] who implies this as well.[19]

"V'Hetzdiku es HaTzaddik"

However, the whole truth did not actually come out until 1930, when a rabbi in Los Angeles, Rabbi Shlomo Michoel Neches, wrote in the *Shaarei Tzion Torah Journal*[20] that he had in his possession an original manuscript of the *Kreisi U'Pleisi*, and the words *SMAG* were crossed out by Rav Yonason Eibeshutz himself, and written on top of them were the

---

16   *BeHa"G* (61, *Hilchos Treifos* pg 129a, right-hand column; exact location cited in *Maadanei Hashulchan*, Y.D. 65, footnote 118; in the 5752 *Machon Yerushalayim* edition, pg. 626). See *Hagahos Rav Ezriel Hildesheimer* to the *BeHa"G* (ad loc.; footnote 48 in the *Machon Yerushalayim* edition), who quite unambiguously understands this to be indicating both male and female animals. Still, others feel that the *BeHa"G*'s words are also not entirely clear that he was referring to female animals. See *Chadrei Deah* (ad loc. 8), *Giluy Daas* (ad loc. 7), and *Daas Yonason* glosses to the recent *Zichron Aharon* edition of the *Kreisi U'Pleisi* (65:16). Several of these authorities maintain that the *BeHa"G* was using the words "male" and female" to actually refer to types of muscles, not the gender of the animals.

17   Including the *Mishmeres Shalom* (Y.D. 65, M.Z.), Rav Avraham Shimon Traub, the Kaidan Gaon, in a new edition of *Sefer Halachos Gedolos* (pg. 296) that he published, the *Ginzei Yosef* (ibid.), and Rav Yosef Adler (cited in *Shu"t Mishnah Halachos* vol. 3:67). The *Tzitz Eliezer* (*Shu"t* vol. 8:25, 2 and vol. 18:63, 6 s.v.*v'ani*) actually prefers this amending to the later one, opining that Rabbi Neches must not have been able to read Rav Yonason's handwriting clearly.

18   *Sefer Hachinuch* (Mitzva 3).

19   See *Shu"t Mishnah Halachos* (vol. 3:68, s.v. *u'mah*). One can also infer this from the *Minchas Chinuch's* comments (Mitzva 3:13).

20   *Shaarei Tzion Torah Journal* (*Choveret HaYovel* 1930:25), under the title "*V'Hetzdiku es HaTzaddik*, The *Tzaddik* Was Justified," (paraphrasing *Devarim* Ch. 25:1); also printed in *HaPardes* journal (vol. 4, Journal 1:10 pg. 18–19). This important historical tidbit is found in *Pardes Yosef* (*Parashas Vayishlach*, 33 s.v. *uv'Kreisi U'Pleisi*), as well as in *Torah Shleimah* (*Parashas Vayishlach* 169), and *Shu"t Tzitz Eliezer* (ibid.). It is also added as an important footnote

letters S-H-N (סה"נ), which stood for *Seder Hilchos Nikkur*, referring to the *Seder HaNikkur* of the *Baal Ha'Itur*.[21] There it was written explicitly that the *Gid Ganasheh* that both men and women are forbidden from consuming is found in both male and female animals. Finally and justly, a *Gadol Hador* was vindicated—165 years after his death![22]

Although we had to wait over a century and a half to attain clarity on this *halachic* mystery, it is imperative that we realize that our true *mesorah* (in this case—all the way back to Yaakov Avinu) is rock solid and our *chachamim* are given special *siyatta dishmaya* to arrive at the correct *halachic* conclusions. It might take a century or even a millennium, but in the end we clearly see why our *chachamim* are called "*Einei Ha'Eidah*."[23]

Postscript: A *Kreisi* Mix-Up?

Interestingly, and quite apropos, this fascinating historical episode has had a recent and equally fascinating addendum. Apparently, many of Rabbi Neches' *sefarim*, including his original copy of the *Kreisi U'Pleisi*, were donated to the UCLA Research Library. Rabbi Yaakov Yitzchak

---

in many recent editions of the *Shulchan Aruch*, some printed with the words "*Mitzva Lifarsem*."

21 *Seder HaNikkur* (*Shaar HaRishon, Hechsher Habassar* 8b—exact location cited in *Maadanei Hashulchan* Y.D. 65, footnote 118), also brought by the *Tur* (end Y.D. 65), as well as Rabbeinu Yerucham (*Sefer Ha'Adam, Nesiv* 15:14, pg. 128b). According to Professor Leiman (cited above) the version Rav Eibeshutz showed the porger was the 1577 edition with the glosses of Rav Tzvi Bochner, a master *treibberer* and contemporary of the *Rema*, as there are those [see *Prishah* (Y.D. 65:56) and *Shu"t Mishnah Halachos* (vol. 3:68 s.v. *bram* and s.v. *mevuar*)] who explain that in other versions, the words "male" and "female" are actually referring to types of muscles, not the gender of the animals.

22 Also thereby proving that Rav Eibeshutz chose the right name for his *sefer*, "*Kreisi U'Pleisi*"—see Gemara *Brachos* (4a) and *Rashi* (ad loc. s.v. *shekorsim*).

23 *Parashas Shlach* (*Bamidbar* Ch. 15:24). Interestingly, this author has seen it stated that history has proven that in the whole *sefer Kreisi U'Pleisi* on all of *Yoreh Deah* only one (!) actual mistake was found, but it turns out that it was clearly an error in geometry—see *Kreisi U'Pleisi* (*Tiferes Yisrael* Y.D. 190:14) and the *Kitzur Shulchan Aruch*'s *Lechem V'Simlah* (ad loc. *Simlah* 11). This *inyan*

Miller of Lakewood, editor of the *Chitzei Giborim Torah Journal*, traveled there to see Rav Eibeshutz's original amendment and came upon an astonishing discovery: It is likely that it was not the handwritten correction of that renowned Rav Yonason Eibeshutz, but that of another, later Rav Yonason Eibeshutz, who lived at least a century after the first.

This second Rav Eibeshutz, a Torah scholar of note, was the *Av Beis Din* of Lashitz, Poland, and author of *Shu"t Tiferes Yonason*. Apparently, this was his personal copy of *Kreisi U'Pleisi*, and he was the one who made the amendment which was later proven accurate in shedding light on the original Rav Yonason's puzzling citation, and not the author himself![24] In any event, and whichever Rav Eibeshutz, we manifestly see the Divine orchestration involved in clearing up this complicated complexity of historical record.

Rabbi Neches' original version of Kreisi U'Pleisi with the handwritten amendment (courtesy of Rabbi Yaakov Yitzchak Miller).

---

was addressed in this author's recent *maamar* in *Kovetz Eitz Chaim* (vol. 29; Nissan 5778) titled "B'Inyan Shiur K'Gris—Birur B'Divrei Ha'Acharonim Hei'ich Lesha'er Hashiur B'Matbei'os Zmaneinu."

24 See Rabbi Yaakov Yitzchak Miller's *maamar* in *Kovetz Hame'ayen* (vol. 215; Tishrei 5776, pg 100–102), with pictures of the title page and amendment of Rabbi Neches' copy of *Kreisi U'Pleisi*. This author wishes to thank Rabbi Miller for allowing his pictures to be republished here. Thanks are also due to R' Moshe Boruch Kaufman and R' Dovid Wasserlauf for first pointing out this startling recent development in the saga of Rav Eibeshutz and the traveling *treibberer* to this author.

Chapter 12

The Erev Pesach Meat Scandal

THE L.A. EREV PESACH MEAT Scandal of 2013 shocked the Jewish world.[1] Featuring a private investigator, hidden cameras, and online videos, this shameful episode had all the makings of a spy novel. One of the main suppliers of kosher meat for one of the largest metropolitan Jewish areas was caught bringing unsupervised packages of meat and/or poultry into his store at a time when he knew that the *mashgiach* was not around. Although consumers might have taken some solace in the fact that it was not horse meat they bought, thus being a step up from much of Europe,[2] nevertheless, the thought that they might have unwittingly and unknowingly eaten non-kosher is a tough pill to swallow.

Unfortunately, such sordid stories have been around for a long time. Over a century ago, the famed *Ridbaz*, Rav Yosef Dovid Willovsky, best known for his seminal commentaries on the Talmud *Yerushalmi*, was chased out of Chicago (on Shabbos yet!) for his attempts to clean up the prevalent fraud perpetrated in the name of "kosher meat."[3] Likewise,

---

1   Not to get confused with the 2006 Monsey Chicken Scandal, which is not the focus of this discussion.

2   As reported by the BBC. See http://www.bbc.co.uk/news/world-europe-21406778.

3   See the introduction to the *Ridbaz's sefer* on Chumash, *Nemukei Ridbaz*, at length, where he decries the deplorable level of kashrus in America at that time. A clear picture of the horrific conditions of Chicago slaughterhouses at that time was showcased in Upton Sinclair's classic *The Jungle*, including a mention of cows "slaughtered in a certain way" labeled by the "kosher rabbi

Rav Yaakov Joseph (R.J.J.), New York's first and only chief rabbi, after being publicly shamed and discredited by the unlearned masses for attempting a similar kashrus clean up in New York in the early 1900s, was forced into early retirement. Even so, every time another scandal occurs, world Jewry collectively cringes.

Three O'Clock?

Yet, with this recent one, many were puzzled by the ruling that was publicized in the aftermath of the scandal by the *Rabbanim* of the certifying kashrus agency after consulting with Rav Yisroel Belsky, Rosh Yeshivas Torah Vodaath and chief *Posek* for the OU. The *Rabbanim* ruled that all meat that was bought in the store before three PM on that day (Erev Erev Pesach) was considered kosher; however, any meats purchased after that time was/would be considered non-kosher.

This fascinating *psak* was the subject of much discussion and was even featured in a Question and Answer article in a major Jewish publication.[4] The much discussed question was where the "magical number" three o'clock came from. Furthermore, if the basis of the *hetter* permitting the meat purchased before that time was due to "*rov*," a simple majority rule, as the owner was caught bringing in eight boxes of unsupervised meat (and/or poultry) while at the same time many other pallets of supervised meat were coming in (approximately three hundred) boxes,[5] shouldn't all the meat be permitted? Why the need for the cutoff time?

---

for the orthodox" (in the same factory as pigs!), with nary a mention of distinction between the kosher and non-kosher. In fact, it was due to the public outcry engendered by this book that the Federal Meat Inspection Act of 1906 was passed. Other American cities at the time were not much better. See *Shu"t Igros Moshe* (Y.D. vol. 2:2) where Rav Moshe Feinstein, in 1962, ruled that the "Kansas City *Takkanah*" made around sixty years prior, stating that due to the rampant kashrus problems of the time any kosher *shechita* performed there needs two qualified *mashgichim* who are also certified *shochtim*, still needed to be upheld.

4 *Ami Magazine* (Issue 114, April 10, 2013, pg. 48).

Let's try to shed some light on the complicated nuances of the *halachos* of *kavua* and *parush* in order to better understand the *Rabbanim's psak*. In the words of Rav Yaakov Emden, who when faced with a similar crisis, wrote "Everything is clearly explained in the *Tur* and *Beis Yosef* and Acharonim, and everyone agrees to the ruling of the *Shulchan Aruch*...there is nothing to question."[6] The same applies here as well.

Pondering *Parush*

There is a famous Talmudic rule "*Kol D'Parush M'Rubah Parush.*" This means that anything that is separated, whose origin is in question, is assumed to come from the *rov*, or majority. An example of this would be if one finds an item lying around and there are several manufacturers of such an item, *halachically* we may assume that its source was "the most likely suspect"—i.e. the majority.[7] Knowledge of this dictum is what caused many to erroneously assume that this is the basis for the *hetter*. Since most people's meat was already bought and taken home, they safely assumed it came from the majority, which in this instance, was kosher meat. This is why they questioned the three o'clock cut off.

Yet, to anyone well-versed in *Hilchos Taaruvos*, a simple *rov* would obviously be insufficient grounds to allow leniency. First of all, according to the *Rema*, whom Ashkenazic practice follows, even large raw pieces of meat (steak, cutlets, brisket, etc.) would fall into the category of *Chatichah Hareuyah L'Hischabed*,[8] a piece fit to be served to an important

---

5   As per the aforementioned interview with the certifying agency's president.

6   *Shu"t Sheilas Yaavetz* (vol. 1:57). He further defends this ruling in the very next responsum (ad loc. 58). The location of the *Tur*, *Beis Yosef*, and *Shulchan Aruch* he was referring to is *Yoreh Deah* (110:5).

7   This *klal* is found throughout *Shas*, including *Brachos* 28a, *Yoma* 24b, *Yevamos* 15b, *Kesuvos* 15a, *Kedushin* 73a, and *Zevachim* 73b. Obviously, when finding unwrapped meat in the middle of the street, it would still be *Assur M'Derabbanan* due to the prohibition of "*bassar shenisalem min ha'ayin*, meat that was hidden from the eye." See *Shulchan Aruch* (Y.D. 63 and 110:3), *Shach* (Y.D. 110:20), and *Ba'er Heitiv* (ad loc. 11). However, in such a case of *parush*, one need not be concerned with *Chatichah Hareuyah L'Hischabed*; see *Shach* (Y.D. 110:16) and *Pri Megadim* (ad loc. S.D. 16).

guest, and are not subject to nullification, even if there is a ratio of a thousand pieces of kosher meat to one *treif* piece. Therefore, in this instance, the mere fact that the majority of the meat was kosher cannot be the grounds to permit the meat already purchased. Although there are authorities who maintain that in a case of extenuating circumstances or great loss (and loss of meat on Erev Yom Tov for an entire community would surely qualify!) one may rely on the *Shulchan Aruch's* opinion that the rule of *Chatichah Hareuyah L'Hischabed* only applies to cooked, ready-to-eat cuts of meat, on the other hand, many other authorities disagree entirely, and others only allow use of this rationale as an additional factor to permit leniency, but not on this basis alone.[9]

---

8   See *Yoreh Deah* 101 at length for the full parameters of this *halacha*. Generally, if a piece of non-kosher food is mixed in with two or more identical pieces of kosher food, it is *battel b'rov*, it becomes nullified within the majority. However, if the non-kosher food is a *Chatichah Hareuyah L'Hischabed*, a piece fit to be served to an important guest, it is not *battel*. Regardless of how many pieces are involved, whether three or three thousand, the entire mixture is forbidden, and none of the pieces may be eaten. This topic is addressed at length in the chapter titled "*Chatichah Hareuyah L'Hischabed*: All About Honor."

9   The *Chasam Sofer* (*Shu"t* Y.D. 91; cited in *Pischei Teshuva* Y.D. 101:4) maintains that since many Rishonim, including the *Rashba* (*Toras Habayis Ha'aruch, Bayis* 4, *Shaar* 1, pg. 13b), *Ran* (*Chullin* 36b s.v. *v'garsinan*), *Ra'ah* (*Bedek Habayis, Bayis* 4, *Shaar* 1, pg. 17a), and *Rambam* (*Hilchos Maachalos Assuros* Ch. 16:5), whom the *Shulchan Aruch* bases his *psak* on, and other *Poskim* including the *Pri Chodosh* (Y.D. 101:12) rule like the *Shulchan Aruch's shittah*, one may therefore definitely rely on the lenient opinion *b'makom hefsed merubah*, if there is any sort of additional *safek* involved. Other Ashkenazic authorities who rule similarly include the *Shvus Yaakov* (*Shu"t* vol. 3:68), Maharsham (*Daas Torah*, Y.D. 49:19), Yaavetz (*Shu"t Sheilas Yaavetz* vol. 1: end 58, s.v. *od*), and *Aruch Hashulchan* (Y.D. 101:15). However, the *Pri Megadim* (Y.D. 101, S.D. end 8 and *Klalei Horaah* 6) is uneasy to accept this leniency and concludes *tzarich iyun*. Other authorities, including the *Pri Toar* (101:6), *Yeshuos Yaakov* (ad loc. 7), and *Chochmas Adam* (53:9), rule exclusively like the *Rema*. Additionally, the *Beis Shlomo* (*Shu"t* Y.D. vol. 1:122), Rav Shlomo Kluger (*Hagahos Chochmas Shlomo* to Y.D. 102), and the *Yad Yehuda* (101, *Peirush Ha'aruch* 9 and *Peirush Hakatzer* 16) all maintain that an Ashkenazi may not rely on the *Shulchan*

Kavua Questions

Additionally, the flip side of the rule of *parush* is that "*Kol Kavua K'Mechtza al Mechtza Dami*,"[10] that as long as the question was born in a place of permanence, majority rule is no longer in effect. The Gemara's example of this is that of "*Teisha Chanuyos*," nine stores selling a kosher item and one store selling a non-kosher version of the same item. In such a scenario, if one would have purchased this item from a store but is unsure from which store he bought it, he would not be allowed to rely on the simple majority. Since there is a permanent store dedicated to the selling of a non-kosher version of the same item, although the majority of stores are selling kosher, nonetheless, this item's *halachic* status is considered 50/50, and is therefore forbidden (the reverse applies as well). So, a simple majority would not be deemed sufficient to allow everyone to eat their Yom Tov roasts.

Yet, there are subtle nuances in the *halachos* of *kavua* which still allow grounds for leniency. There are two main types of *kavua*: *Kavua Deoraysa* (a Biblical case of Permanence) and *Kavua Derabbanan* (a Rabbinic case of Permanence).[11]

Aruch's shittah regarding this *halacha*, even *b'makom hefsed merubah*. See more on this in the chapter titled "*Chatichah Hareuyah L'Hischabed*: All About Honor."

10 As with the Rule of *Parush*, its flip side *psak*, the Rule of *Kavua*, is at least equally represented throughout *Shas*, including *Yoma* 84b, *Pesachim* 9b, *Shekalim* 19b, *Yevamos* 119a, *Kesuvos* 15a, *Kedushin* 73a, *Bava Kama* 44b, *Sanhedrin* 79a, *Chullin* 95a, *Zevachim* 73b, and *Nida* 18a. See also *Shekalim* 19a. The rule of *Kavua* is based on the *pasuk* in *Parashas Shoftim* (*Devarim* Ch. 19:11), "*V'arav lo v'kam.*" The various nuances of these rules are dealt with extensively by the *Tur* and *Shulchan Aruch* and their commentaries in *Yoreh Deah* (110:3–5).

11 There is actually a third type of *Kavua*, that of *Taaruvos Chanuyos*, based on the understandings of the *Rashba* (*Toras Habayis Ha'aruch*, *Bayis* 4, *Shaar* 2, pg. 30a) and *Ra'ah* (*Bedek Habayis*, *Bayis* 4, *Shaar* 2, pg. 29b s.v. *od nirah*). This refers to when one buys a piece of meat from a kosher store, and a *treifa* was later found in one of the stores, but it is unclear which store it is. The *Shach* (ad loc. 14 and 17) ruling akin to the *Bach* (Y.D. 110:6), and based on the

- *Kavua Deoraysa* is when there is an official one hundred percent dedicated non-kosher store operating in the area (think McDonalds).
- *Kavua Derabbanan* is when some non-kosher meat gets mixed up in an otherwise kosher store, creating a *"Taaruvos Chatichos,"* a meat mix-up.

Although there are several differences,[12] one of the hallmark distinctions between the two is whether the rule of *Kavua Lemafraya* applies.

---

above Rishonim, maintains that this case posseses both the *chumros* of *Kavua Deoraysa* and *Kavua Derabbanan*; therefore, the piece would be *assur* since we would apply *Kavua Lemafraya*. On the other hand, the Pri Chodosh (ad loc. 13) argues that this case would maintain the status of *Kavua Derabbanan*. [Interestingly, they both cite the *Rashba's* words as proof to their *shittos*.] The Taz (ad loc. 5; see Pri Megadim's explanation ad loc. M.Z. 5) strongly implies that he considers *Taaruvos Chanuyos* a *Kavua Deoraysa*, with all of its rules. Conversely, the Yad Avraham (ad loc. 3) questions the *Shach's* assertion that this is indeed the *Rashba's shittah*. In a similar vein, the Chavas Daas (ad loc. Chiddushim end 11) writes that he holds that the *Shach's* "*chiddush*" is *tzarich iyun*, and in a standard *Taaruvos Chanuyos*, *Kavua Lemafraya* would not apply. Nevertheless, he concludes that if one knows that he bought it from the store which had the *safek*, *Kavua Lemafraya* would apply and his prior purchase would be *assur*. Although the Chochmas Adam (63:1) seemingly does not take sides in this *machlokes*, in his later Binas Adam (Shaar Hakavua end 4) he writes that he posed this *sheilah* to the Beis Meir who ruled stringently like the Bach, that a *Taaruvos Chanuyos*, has the status of *Kavua Deoraysa* and *Kavua Lemafraya* would therefore apply. The Chochmas Adam concludes that it is difficult to allow any leniency regarding a *Taaruvos Chanuyos*, and even in a case of *hefsed meruba*. However, the Pri Megadim (ad loc. S.D. end 14) rules that *b'makom hefsed meruba* one may rely upon the Pri Chodosh's *shittah*, while the Aruch Hashulchan (ad loc. 42 and end 47) argues that we may not add any more cases to *Hilchos Kavua*, and therefore we may be lenient even without *hefsed meruba*. Similarly, the Yad Yehuda (ad loc. Peirush Ha'aruch 20 and Peirush Hakatzer 28) also argues that we may not add any more cases to *Hilchos Kavua*, but concludes that he does not consider a scenario of *Taaruvos Chanuyos* as a case of *Kavua* at all, and the regular rules of *bittul* would apply.

12 Other potential differences between *Kavua Deoraysa* and *Kavua Derabbanan* that are cited (and debated) by the *Poskim* include whether or not Chazal were

Kavua Lemafraya refers to the retroactive application of the majority-nullifying rule of *Kavua*. In plain English, this means that when *Kavua* applies (therefore prohibiting the meat), meat that has been purchased previously might also be affected. By a *Kavua Deoraysa* the rule is that *Kavua Lemafraya* also applies. Hence, even if the purchased meat was safely in your freezer at the time of the *sheilah* (e.g., the meat has no identifying markings on it and you have no idea or recollection from which store it was purchased), it may still be forbidden.[13]

However, in a situation of a *Kavua Derabbanan*, *Kavua Lemafraya* does not apply. This means that only from the time of the actual *sheilah* will further purchase of meat at the same store be forbidden. That is where three o'clock comes into the picture. According to the aforementioned article, the *Rabbanim* only found out about the surveillance videotapes earlier that same afternoon. They watched them then "until about 2:30," and by 3:00 they decided to remove the *hashgacha* based on the evidence. Since the actual *sheilah* was only made known at that point, it is only then that the rules of *Kavua* took effect.[14]

---

gozer shema yikach min hakavua, the status of *pirush lifaneinu*, and how far the *Kavua* prohibition extends. For example, what the *halacha* is after pieces from a *Kavua* got mixed up in another *Taaruvos* (or more). Additionally, as noted by Rav Yisroel Reisman (see *Taz* ad loc. 3), definition-wise, they are not quite analogous. As mentioned previously, *Kavua Deoraysa* is the flip-side of the rule of *Kol D'Parush M'Rubah Parush*, that when the *sheilah* is born in a place of dedicated permanence, majority rule is no longer in effect. However, *Kavua Derabbanan* is essentially a *chumrah* on the leniency of *rov*, that even though *M'Deoraysa* the cuts of meat in the store with the meat mix-up inside should be permitted due to majority rule, nonetheless, in this case Chazal made a *Gezeira* on the store, and all pieces of meat situated inside after the *sheilah* of the *treif* piece arose are now forbidden, as this situation is somewhat akin to the classic question of *Kavua*.

13 This *psak*, as well as the basic *halacha*, does not seem to follow the notable minority opinion of the *Ran* (*Chullin, Perek Kol Habassar* 33b s.v. *amar Rav*) who maintains that even regarding *Kavua Deoraysa* there is no *din* of *Kavua Lemafraya*.

14 Although some question why this ruling did not take affect from the time of

Since up until that point the store was known as a kosher store, it has

---

the actual surveillance video several weeks earlier, which would potentially have a far greater impact on the kashrus status of many people's meat, as then at the time of the actual ruling, the store may have even been considered the more stringent *Taaruvos Chanuyos* (due to the *safek* regarding the store's reliability, that one may have purchased ostensibly 'kosher meat' from a store that may have already unwittingly been rendered non-kosher by that point) and *Kavua* status applied earlier, *halachically* it would not have. As mentioned previously, even if that was the *psak* of the *shaas noda* [which it is not—see Rav Akiva Eiger (Y.D. 99:7, quoting the *Yerushalmi*, *Orlah* Ch. 2, end *Halacha* 1), *Ha'Aruch M'Shach* (Y.D. 94, s.v. *b'Yerushalmi*), *Yad Yehuda* (99, *Peirush Ha'aruch* 25 s.v. *haRash* and *Peirush Hakatzer* 33), *Darchei Teshuva* (99:97), *Hagahos Chasam Sofer* (ad loc.), and *Shu"t Tuv Taam V'Daas* (*Mahadura Kama*, 156, *Hosafa*) whom, regarding the issue of *chozer v'nayur*, discuss whether one may be lenient by relying on the fact that there was *noda chaveiro*. There are several other discussions related to *noda* of other people, such as of whether we *k'nass* a *shogeg* after *shaas noda* [see *Shu"t Panim Me'iros* (vol. 1:105) and *Pri Megadim* (Y.D. 110, S.D. 33 s.v. *v'adayin* and M.Z. 8 s.v. *kasav*)] and whether if a *baal davar* knows that a reliable Jew somewhere else in the world found out what actually occured, but he personally is unaware of any of the details, if it can create a *kavua* at all [see *Kreisi U'Pleisi* (110, *Pleisi* 12 s.v. *mihu*), *Chavas Daas* (ad loc. Biurim 6), *Pri Toar* (ad loc. end 6), *Pri Megadim* (ad loc. S.D. 14, *Chelek* 2, s.v. *v'ani*), *Binas Adam* (*Shaar Hakavua* 2), *Beis Yitzchak* (*Shaar Hakavua* 1), *Mishmeres Shalom* (Y.D. 110, S.D. 14, *B'emtza Davar* 13), *Yad Yehuda* (ad loc. *Peirush Ha'aruch* 21 and *Peirush Hakatzer* 29), and *Chazon Ish* (Y.D. 37:13 s.v. *b'Chavas Daas*)], yet, to the best of this author's knowledge, we undoubtedly don't find *"noda lehachmir"* based on a random person's knowledge, in order to be *machmir* on a *baal davar*, and especially not retroactively! Moreover, certainly *b'makom hefsed meruba* one may rely on the *Poskim* who rule that we would still consider such a case a *Kavua Derabbanan*, and thus *Kavua Lemafraya* would not apply. Additionally, from a *halachic* perspective, the actual *Baal Davar* in this instance is the certifying agency and not the proprietor, as people were always exclusively relying on the kashrus certification for effecting the meat as kosher, and not the non-religious owner, and rightly so. These issues, as well as whether a non-Jew, or non-reliable Jew can create a *"noda"* at all, and related issues, although beyond the scope of this discussion, were addressed at length in this author's Hebrew *maamar* on topic in his *M'Shulchan Yehuda*, titled *"B'Inyan Parashas Habassar 5773."*

the status of a *Kavua Derabbanan*, and therefore will not affect any meat or poultry previously purchased.[15] As noted by the great Yaavetz, this

---

15 Although some were concerned that there possibly may not have been a *rov* on certain cuts of meat, and wondered how it could be possible that certain parts of the same chickens might have been ruled kosher and other parts *treif*, this question has already been dealt with at length by the *Poskim*. Although based on an interesting story and three-way *machlokes* cited by the *Beis Hillel* (Y.D. 110:1 s.v. *maaseh*; quoting his own opinion and those of the *Birkas Hazevach*—who likewise ruled stringently, and the *Chelkas Mechokek* and Rav Heschel M'Krakow [as recorded in *Shu"t HaGaonim Basrai* (5)]; who both ruled leniently), nonetheless, the *halacha* follows the *Pri Chodosh* (Y.D. 110:23 and *Kuntress Acharon* to Y.D. 110) who ruled that even if this is a potential, if distant, possibility, nonetheless, it does not affect the *halachos* of *Kavua*. What was purchased before the *sheilah* is still permitted and what was purchased afterward is still prohibited. Although questioned by the *Bechor Shor* (in his glosses to *Chullin* 42) *"d'ain lifsok davar taima kazeh,"* and *Beis Lechem Yehuda* (Y.D. 110:21), and the great Rav Shlomo Kluger seems undecided [in his *Mei Nida* on *Maseches Nida* he ruled stringently, yet in his *Avodas Avodah* on *Maseches Avodah Zarah* he ruled leniently, but seemingly later backtracked in his *Shu"t Tuv Taam V'Daas* (*Telita'ei* 207 and 267; see also *Darchei Teshuva* 110:100)], and Rav Isser Zalman Meltzer unconvinced (*Even Ha'Azel*, vol. 9, *Hilchos Ishus* Ch. 10, *Halacha* 15, pg. 47b s.v. *ul'fee mah shebee'arnu*), nevertheless, this *psak* was accepted and echoed *lemaaseh* by the confirmed majority of Acharonim, including the *Minchas Yaakov* (*Soles L'Mincha* 43:1 s.v. *aval*), *Kreisi U'Pleisi* (ad loc. *Pleisi* 13 s.v. *v'hinei*), *Pri Megadim* (Y.D. 110, M.Z. end 5, s.v. *v'hinei*), Rav Yaakov Emden (*Shu"t Sheilas Yaavetz* vol. 1: end 60, s.v. *u'mah*), *Beis Yitzchak* (*Shaar Hakavua* end 55; notwithstanding what he wrote in Y.D. 110: vol. 3, *Tikun Habayis* 2), *Shev Shmaatsah* (*Shmaatsah* 4, end Ch. 4 s.v. *v'yitachein*), *Chemdas Shlomo* (*Shu"t* Y.D. 6; who, although questioning the *Shmaatsah's* application, still agrees to the *klal*), *Nediv Lev* (*Shu"t* vol. 1: end 9), *Levushei Srad* (*Shu"t Neos Desheh* vol. 1:23; at length), *Imrei Baruch* (*Hagahos Baruch Taam al HaKreisi U'Pleisi*, ibid.), *Yad Yehuda* (110, *Peirush Ha'aruch* 24 and *Peirush Hakatzer* 34), *Zivchei Tzedek* (ad loc. 40), *Aruch Hashulchan* (Y.D. 101:49), *Kaf Hachaim* (ad loc. 64), and *Chazon Ish* (Y.D. 37:17 s.v. *b'Pischei Teshuva*). The *Chasam Sofer* (*Shu"t* Y.D. 99), according to the *Pischei Teshuva* (Y.D. 110: end 4, see parenthesis), strongly implies this way as well. The *Shev Shmaatsah* explains the rule as follows (and brings several proofs to this): once the Torah defines a scenario as *Kol D'Parush M'Rubah Parush*, even though it

psak is **the** *halacha* as codified by the *Tur* and *Shulchan Aruch*, with no dissenting opinions.[16] That is why all meat that was bought before that time was considered one hundred percent kosher. This also explains why the new owners *kashered* the store afterward, as all meats remaining in the store after three o'clock were deemed non-kosher.[17]

The purpose of this chapter is to shed some light on the seemingly mysterious three o'clock cutoff time which had many scratching their heads. It should be clear to the reader that this time was far from arbitrary, and was unequivocally based in codified *psak halacha*. There are so many variables and rationales utilized by a *Posek* in arriving at a final ruling, and this author's intention was merely to provide a peek into that process and to provide the reader with an appreciation for the sheer vast breadth of knowledge and ability to apply it that a *Posek* must possess. Undoubtedly, following the directives of our *Rabbanim* and *Poskim*, who toil in the study and teaching of Torah, is always the correct option.[18] May this be the last kashrus scandal that ever needs *halachic* analysis.[19]

---

is not a *vaday* that it is *muttar*, nevertheless, since the Torah permitted it, it is *machria* the *safek* as a *muttar vaday*. However, what was *paskened* as remaining part of the *kavuah* and *assur*, maintains its *safek* status and remains *assur*, even though there might be a possibility that the different pieces technically came from the same animal. The *Shach* (*Nekudos Hakessef* 110:5) also implies similarly.

16   *Tur and Shulchan Aruch* Y.D. (110:5).

17   This author has since heard from Rav Belsky that he never specifically mentioned 3:00 PM in his *psak*, but rather told the *Rabbanim* involved that any meat bought before it is known that the meat had been compromised was permitted. This became translated as 3:00 PM, but he never actually discussed with them the exact time when the meat would become *assur*, be it 2:20, 2:30, 2:45, or 3:00. Thanks are due to Rabbi Yaakov Luban and Rabbi Eli Gersten, Rabbinical Coordinators at the OU, for clarifying Rav Belsky's *psak*.

18   See Gemara *Rosh Hashanah* (25b) and *Rashi's* commentary to *Devarim* (*Parashas Shoftim* Ch. 17:9, s.v. *v'el hashofet*), who explain the need for the Torah to delineate the authority of contemporary leaders.

19   Unfortunately, this wish has not held up, with the startling 2018 Johannesburg

Postscript: Supplemental *Sevaros*

Although the aforementioned rationale is certainly the correct one to explain the ruling, there actually are several other avenues of leniency that seem to be available in this case. For example, no one actually saw what was inside the unsupervised boxes that the proprietor snuck in, and he was recorded taking them from a different store that sold non-*glatt* meat and non-*mehudar* poultry.[20] This creates somewhat of a *safek* (however slight) as to the meat's status and might possibly be considered non-*vaday issur* (non-certain *issur*). In a situation where there is even a slight chance of not *vaday issur*, several prominent authorities, including the Yaavetz, *Kreisi U'Pleisi*, *Chochmas Adam*, and *Aruch Hashulchan* maintain that the "strict" rules of *Kavua* may not apply.[21]

Additionally, it might create a *sfek sfeika* (case of compounded doubt), thereby upgrading the rest of the meat's kashrus status, as the prohibition of *Chatichah Hareuyah L'Hischabed* may no longer be applicable in such a case,[22] and especially *b'makom hefsed merubah*,[23] which this

---

Chicken Scandal, followed by the recent Antwerp and subsequent Liverpool/Manchester scandals. However, this discussion has practically been proven helpful to those in South Africa, as this author has been contacted concerning sharing this analysis to assist the local *Rabbanim* in determining the best plan of action in moving forward.

20 Although the proprietor obviously cannot be trusted that said boxes merely contained a specific brand of non-*mehudar* chicken, especially as the company he specified has not been producing chickens in almost ten years, nevertheless it does create somewhat of a *safek* and might not be *vaday issur*.

21 *Shu"t Sheilas Yaavetz* (vol. 1:58, s.v. *u'va'emes* and *aval*), *Kreisi U'Pleisi* (110, *Pleisi* 12 s.v. *ach*) *Chochmas Adam* (*Binas Adam, Shaar Hakavua* 41), and *Aruch Hashulchan* (Y.D. 110:52).

22 See *Yoreh Deah* 110:9 at length. The *Shulchan Aruch* and *Taz* (ad loc. end 14, s.v. *klal*) maintain that a *safek* by a *treif* piece of meat that gets mixed up in a *Taaruvos* is not considered a *sfek sfeika*, and one may not utilize this rationale to permit the meat. However, the *Rema* (ad loc. 8 and 9), the *Shach* (ad loc. 62 and *Nekudos Hakessef* 15), and *Pri Chodosh* (ad loc. 46) argue that when the reason it is not *battel* is only *M'Derabbanan*, it is considered a *sfek sfeika* and we may rule leniently. [See *Aruch Hashulchan* ad loc. 82 for a *hesber*.] The

undoubtedly was, as we are referring to an entire community, eighteen hours before the onset of Pesach. Rest assured that when the *Rabbanim* wrote that everyone should "enjoy their Yom Tov meat" there was ample *halachic* reason to do so.

Pri Megadim (ad loc. end M.Z. 14 s.v. *u'mah*) and the Yaavetz (*Shu"t Sheilas Yaavetz* ibid. end 58, s.v. *od*) rule that only regarding the more stringent *Davar Sheyesh Lo Mattirin* [an item which although not permitted currently, will become permitted by itself at a later date, for example, an egg that was laid on Yom Tov—its status is that it is only permitted to be eaten after Yom Tov; this is a more stringent category of non-nullifiable items, as one can simply wait until it becomes *muttar* by itself; see *Yoreh Deah* 102 at length], would the *Shulchan Aruch* and *Taz* be *machmir*; yet, if the *safek Derabbanan* we are referring to is the *machlokes Shulchan Aruch* and *Rema* if a raw piece of meat can be considered a *Chatichah Hareuyah L'Hischabed*, then certainly it can be *metztaref* to be considered a *sfek sfeika*.

23 As explained at length in a previous footnote.

Chapter 13

Salting with Sugar?!

ONE OF THE MAIN TOPICS discussed extensively in *Sefer Vayikra* is that of *Korbanos* (loosely translated as sacrifices), one of whose primary functions is to bring us closer to Hashem.[1] Unfortunately, we no longer have the opportunity to experience *Korbanos* firsthand, ever since the time of the destruction of the *Beis Hamikdash,* which resulted in their cessation.

Nowadays, it seems that due to *Korbanos'* complicated nature and exacting minutiae, as well as the relevant *Parshiyos* usually falling out during the hectic pre-Pesach season, many of us regrettably have neither an accurate understanding nor a proper appreciation of their deeper meaning and relevance to our daily lives. Perhaps this is due to the fact that according to the Gemara our daily *Tefillos* are recited in lieu of offering *Korbanos*, and are currently "holding up the world" in their stead.[2]

Contemporary *Korbanos*

Yet, there are still some aspects of *Korbanos* that *do* impact our lives more noticeably. For example, the Mitzva to have salt on the table when having a meal[3] is directly based on the requirement to have salt

---

1   See *Ohr Hachaim* (*Vayikra* Ch. 1:2 s.v. *uvaderech*), *Seforno* (ad loc. s.v. *adam*), and Rav Samson Raphael Hirsch's commentary (ad loc. s.v. *korban*).

2   *Taanis* (27b) and *Megillah* (31b).

3   See *Shulchan Aruch* and *Rema* (O.C. 167:5).

on every *Korban*,⁴ as our tables are compared to the *Mizbe'ach* (Altar) and our food to a sacrifice.⁵

Another practice based on this aspect of *Korbanos* is the proper size of salt needed to salt our meat and chickens when *kashering* them. The *Shulchan Aruch* rules that medium-sized salt should be used.⁶ Rabbeinu Bachya famously comments that this can be inferred from the unique phraseology of the verse regarding the Mitzva of ensuring that all *Korbanos* are salted: *"b'melach timlach,* that you shall salt them with salt."⁷ ⁸ He asserts that the fact that the Torah uses the same word twice

---

4   *Vayikra* (Ch. 2:13).

5   See *Brachos* (55a), *Tosafos* (ad loc. s.v. *haba*), *Hagahos Ashri* (*Brachos, Perek Keitzad Mevorchin* 22), *Beis Yosef* (O.C. 167; quoting the *Shibolei Leket* 141), *Shulchan Aruch* and *Rema* (O.C. 167:5), *Magen Avraham* (ad loc. 15), *Machatzis Hashekel* (ad loc. 15), *Ba'er Heitiv* (ad loc. 7; citing the Arizal), *Chayei Adam* (vol. 1:42, 11), *Kitzur Shulchan Aruch* (41:6), *Aruch Hashulchan* (O.C. 167:12), *Ben Ish Chai* (Year 1, *Parashas Emor* 10), *Mishnah Berurah* (167:30 and 32), and *Kuf Hachaim* (ad loc. 38 and 40). See also *Shlah* (*Shaar Ha'Osiyos, Eimek Bracha* 66), *Kiryas Chana Dovid* (49), *Shu"t Beis Yaakov* (165), and *Halachic World* (vol. 2:pg. 151, "Table Salt"). Practically, the outcome is that although nowadays our bread is *"nekiya"* and we would not have an actual requirement to dip it into salt *me'ikar hadin*, nevertheless, due to the comparison of our tables to the *Mizbe'ach*, one should still have salt on the table while eating. Moreover, having this salt at the table protects us from punishment, as fulfilling this keeps the *Satan* at bay as he cannot claim that we are sitting idle without Mitzvos. As cited by many of the above *Poskim*, Kabbalistically speaking, one should dip his bread into salt three times. See R' Zvi Ryzman's recent *Ratz Katzvi* on *Maagalei Hashana* (vol. 1:3, Ch. 2:10), who adds a potential reason for this based on the *Baal HaTurim* (*Vayikra* Ch. 2:13), regarding the three times that salt is mentioned in said *pasuk*.

6   *Shulchan Aruch* (Y.D. 69:3). See also the main commentaries ad loc. who explain why salt that is too small (e.g., table salt) and salt that is too big (e.g., rock salt) should not be used *lechatchilla* for salting meat and poultry; rather the midsize salt (coarse, a.k.a. "kosher salt") is optimal. However, it should be noted that if midsize salt is unavailable or *b'dieved*, the other salts are acceptable in a pinch.

Food: A Halachic Analysis

to describe this action shows that it should be performed with medium-sized (coarse) salt.[9]

This actually affects everyone's lives, due to the Biblical prohibition against eating blood.[10] As is detailed by the Gemara and codified as

---

7   *Vayikra* (Ch. 2:13).

8   There is another aspect of modern day salting inferred from this verse, by the *Issur V'Hetter* (1:9), and cited in *Ba'er Heitiv* (Y.D. 69:21). The *halacha* states (*Shulchan Aruch* Y.D. 69:6) that in order for the salt to do its job, it must remain on the piece of meat for at least "approximately twenty minutes," *me'ikar hadin*. This is known as "*Shiur Melicha.*" [However, *lechatchilla*, the meat should be covered in salt for a full hour, especially according to Ashkenazic authorities; see *Rema* (ad loc.; citing the *Terumas Hadeshen* 167)]. The *Issur V'Hetter* points out that "*Shiur Melicha*" may be inferred from our *pasuk*, as the word "*b'melach*" has the same *Gematriya* as "*Mil*" (80), the distance that takes "approximately twenty minutes" to walk, known as "*Shiur Hiluch Mil.*" The actual amount of time of "*Shiur Hiluch Mil*" is debated among the Rishonim, whether this translates to eighteen minutes (*Terumas Hadeshen*), twenty-four minutes (*Rambam* and *Bartenura*), or twenty-two-and-a-half minutes (*Gr"a*), [for an understanding in the differences of opinions of the Rishonim see *Chok Yaakov* (O.C. 459:10), *Biur HaGr"a* (ad loc. 5), and *Biur Halacha* (ad loc. s.v. havei)]. There is also some debate among the later authorities how this debate applies to *Melicha*—whether similarly, or as since *Melicha* is *Derabbanan* perhaps we may rely on the most lenient *shittah*, as practically this *shiur* is only invoked *b'dieved* anyway. See *Pri Chodosh* (Y.D. 69:26), *Shu"t Chanoch Beis Yehuda* (60), *Pri Megadim* (Y.D. 69, S.D. 25), *Gilyon Maharsha* (ad loc. 54), *Yad Efraim* (ad loc. s.v. *kdei*), *Chochmas Adam* (39:9), *Ben Ish Chai* (Year 2, *Parashas Tazria-Metzora/Taharos* 17), *Kitzur Shulchan Aruch* (36:11), *Mishnah Berurah* (459:15), *Kaf Hachaim* (Y.D. 69:89), *Chazon Ish* (O.C. 123:1 and Y.D. 10:18), and *Shu"t Tzitz Eliezer* (vol. 12:52).

9   Well, actually not so famous, but it should be. This enlightening comment of Rabbeinu Bachya's (a Rishon!) was first shown to this author way back when, during his *Semicha* test from and by Rav Moshe Halberstam of the *Badatz Eidah Hachareidis* and author of *Shu"t Divrei Moshe*. Rabbeinu Bachya explains that the fact that the Torah stressed a double *lashon* of "salting with salt" (instead of just "salting," which would seemingly indicate either *davka* large or small granules), implies that the salt used should not be too big, nor too small, but just right.

Salting with Sugar?! **169**

halacha,[11] the proper way to remove the blood from a properly slaughtered kosher animal or fowl, thereby rendering it fit for eating, is via this salting.[12] [13] In fact, the methodology and related *halachos* of the process

---

10   See *Vayikra* (*Parashas Acharei Mos*, Ch. 17:10–14), *Rambam* (*Hilchos Maachalos Assuros* Ch. 6:1–4), *Tur* and *Shulchan Aruch* (Y.D. 65–68).

11   This is detailed in Gemara *Chullin* 113a in the statement of Shmuel's, and codified as *halacha* by the *Rambam* (*Hilchos Maachalos Assuros* Ch. 6:10), *Tur* and *Shulchan Aruch* (Y.D. 69:4).

12   There is an additional method available to remove the blood when salting is not an option—"*tzliyah*," or roasting (or broiling) in a very specific manner, "*ad shayazuv kol damo*, until all of its blood has left it," and then it is permitted for cooking. See *Shulchan Aruch* and main commentaries to *Yoreh Deah* 69:21 and 76 as to the details of this process. According to many *Poskim* [see *Taz* (Y.D. 69:54; citing the *Hagahos Shaarei Dura*, 9:10), *Ba'er Heitiv* (ad loc. 54), *Pri Megadim* (ad loc. M.Z. 54), *Chavas Daas* (ad loc. *Chiddushim* 76), *Aruch Hashulchan* (ad loc. end 118), and *Kaf Hachaim* (ad loc. 320)], if one wants to perform this "*tzliyah*" *lechatchilla*, the meat must be roasted until the meat is "*yisyaveish m'bachutz*, dried out from the outside," as only then would all of the prohibited blood be considered completely drawn out *l'divrei hakol*. Indeed, Rav Moshe Halberstam told this author (at the aforementioned *Semicha* Test) that utilizing the broiling *hetter* is not so practical, as after the proper roasting, the meat is somewhat hard (tough) and quite often not so palatable. On the other hand, there is a specific case where "*tzliyah*" is not only optimal, it is *halachically* mandated: regarding liver. As the liver is completely infused with blood, the only way to *kasher* it is via broiling, after cutting it open "*shasi v'arev*," meaning sliced open vertically and horizontally or criss-cross. See *Yoreh Deah* 73 at length for the full details and parameters of the liver-*kashering* process.

13   There is another method of eating a *kosher shechted* chicken—raw! In Aramaic called "*Umtzah*" (see Gemara *Shabbos* 128a), eating a raw chicken, simply rinsed off from external blood, without any salting or roasting necessary, is cited by many Rishonim, including *Tosafos* (*Chullin* 14a s.v. *v'nisbin*), *Rosh* (ad loc. 19), *Ran* (ad loc. 4a in the *Rif's* pagination s.v. *hashochet l'choleh*), *Shaarei Dura* (*Shaar Chamishi*, 9), and the *Tur* (Y.D. 67:2), as perfectly acceptable, and is the *halacha pesuka* of the *Shulchan Aruch* (ad loc. 2). On the other hand, there are several good reasons why we don't see this option performed or even really discussed. First of all, the *Rambam* (*Hilchos Maachalos Assuros*

Ch. 6:12) argues that this is not a viable option, but rather ruling that salting is necessary. Second, the *halacha* is (see *Shulchan Aruch* and *Rema* Y.D. 69:1) that any time raw meat is cut, the new exposed face needs a proper washing from the blood. There is a *machlokes* between the *Shach* (ad loc. 3) and the *Pri Chodosh* (ad loc. end 4) whether the same applies when raw meat is cut by hand (a.k.a. ripped). Although many *Poskim* follow the *Shach's* more lenient approach, on the other hand, the *Darchei Teshuva* (ad loc. 12) and the *Kaf Hachaim* (ad loc. 7) conclude with opinions that it is proper to be *machmir* like the *Pri Chodosh*. To further complicate matters, the *Chavas Daas* (ad loc. Biurim 3; cited briefly by the *Pischei Teshuva* ad loc. 3) raises the issue that certainly teeth are more akin to knives regarding cutting meat. Hence, how is there ever a *hetter* of "*Umtzah*," if with every bite of raw meat, one's teeth cut into it, releasing blood? It seems improbable to suggest that the dispensation of eating raw meat is only regarding swallowing it whole without chewing. Although the *Chavas Daas* concludes *tzarich iyun* on the matter, the *Imrei Baruch* (Glosses to the *Chavas Daas*, ad loc. 2) states that this issue is probably the reason why the *Rambam* did not allow this *hetter*. Moreover, as cited by the *Darchei Teshuva* (67:10), quoting several Acharonim, including the *Arugas Habosem*, *Beis Yehuda*, and *Mor V'Ohalos*, this is a "*kushya atzuma*" and it is "*tzarich iyun* to be lenient with eating raw meat." The *Pri Megadim* as well (O.C. 308, M.Z. 20 s.v. ul'inyan) states that a lenient reading is untenable, as "*zeh aino, shelemaaseh afilu b'bar avza* (that is tender and assumed to have much less blood than *bassar beheimah*), *mikol makom bli hadacha rishona ee efshar*" to chew it. Additionally, the *Kaf Hachaim* (ad loc. 8) adds that anyone who ruled like the *Pri Chodosh* regarding meat ripped by hand, would certainly need to be *machmir* regarding meat cut by teeth. Although there are those who differentiate, including the *Yad Yehuda* (67, *Peirush Ha'aruch* 5 s.v. u'mah), who explains that when one cuts meat with his teeth, it has the status of a knife; yet if this is performed while chewing, this is called "*derech achilah*" and would not fall into the prohibited category, but rather is the permitted "*Umtzah*," nonetheless others do not agree. Indeed, the *Marcheshes* (*Shu"t* vol. 1:28, 1) rules that such a case is prohibited and the permitted "*Umtzah*" is referring to one swallowing (without chewing) small pieces of raw meat that have already been properly washed. And although the *Seridei Aish* (new edition; vol. 2:16) seems to accept the position of the *Yad Yehuda* in the *Chavas Daas' kushya*, at least for a *choleh* [the *Shulchan Aruch Harav* (O.C. 308:68) and *Mishnah Berurah* (ad loc. 125) imply this way as well, that chewing raw meat would not violate the "blood prohibition," at least *mei'ikar hadin*; thanks are

of the proper salting of animals, referred to simply as "*Hilchos Melicha*," comprise an entire body of study in *Issur V'Hetter* of its own right.[14]

Sugar = Salt?

However, over the years, there were several *Poskim* who furthered the connection between the laws of salting a *Korban* and our salting of meat. Rav Yaakov Chagiz (1620–1674; a.k.a. Mahari Chagiz, renowned as the *Baal Halachos Ketanos*), in his *Shu"t Halachos Ketanos*, addresses

---

due to my son Mordechai Zev for pointing this out], conversely, Rav Moshe Feinstein wrote (*Shu"t Igros Moshe*, Y.D. vol. 1:67 s.v. *u'mashekasav*) similarly to the *Marcheshes*' conclusion, that only swallowing without chewing is "*Muttar B'Umtzah*" according to all opinions. Hence, after all is said and done, eating a chicken raw is clearly not a common viable option, but rather a possible rare exception. It is told of the renowned *Gadol*, Rav Yisrael Zev Gustman, *Dayan* in Vilna and later Rosh Yeshivas Netzach Yisrael, that when he was escaping the Nazis through a forest during the Holocaust, he caught and *shechted* a wild chicken. As he obviously had no kashering salt with him and could not risk broiling the chicken and thus sending smoke into the air, he ate it raw. And although he had no other choice in the face of *pikuach nefesh*, it is said that he was always worried about the possibility that he did not perform a *halachically* sufficient job on the chicken. Thanks are due to Rabbi Yosef Mendelson for sharing this fascinating anecdote.

14 *Yoreh Deah* (69–78). Optimally, this *halachic* process must commence within seventy-two hours after the animal is *shechted* (and before the meat is frozen, chopped, or ground), since it is assumed that the blood would be too congealed and set in the meat after this period for the salt to be effective enough to remove it. When necessary, this period may be extended by properly soaking the meat before the seventy-two hours have elapsed, thereby allowing for an additional seventy-two hours before salting will be required. Performing the actual *Melicha* process *lechatchilla* is time consuming and consists of rinsing off the meat well (from the outer blood sitting on it), soaking it in water for a half-hour and letting it drip dry a bit afterward, covering every inch of the piece of meat with salt, and letting it sit in its salt for a full hour in a manner where the blood can drain off freely, followed up with a rinse off, and washed three times (meaning three full dunks in different containers of water) to properly ensure the removal of the residual blood-infused salt. After that, the meat is ready for cooking.

the issue of whether sugar can be used as a substitute to "salt" a *Korban*. He maintains that it is indeed permissible to use sugar, as, although sugar is sweet, nevertheless, since it can be used as a preservative, it is considered a true salt.[15]

Rav Daniel Tirani (d. 1814), Chief Rabbi of Florence, Italy, and author of *Ikrei HaDa"T*, takes this comparison a step further, noting that sugar in his time was in fact called by many "Indian salt." Interestingly, he concludes that just as sugar may be used to salt a *Korban*, so too, if one has no salt available to *kasher* his meat, he may use sugar instead![16]

Several authorities, ruled similarly, allowing sugar as a substitute for *kashering* their chickens.[17] The *Avnei Nezer* even testified that the *Gaon* from Lisa, Rav Yaakov Loberbaum, better known as the *Chavas Daas* and *Nesivos Hamishpat*, once used sugar to salt his meat![18] In fact, the venerated Rav of Yerushalayim of the late 1800s, Rav Shmuel Salant, once publicly ruled to allow meat that was "salted with sugar" to be eaten at a wedding.[19]

---

15 *Shu"t Halachos Ketanos* (vol. 1:218).

16 *Ikrei Dinim* (O.C. 14:36). This widely quoted commentary was standard in all older editions of the *Shulchan Aruch*. He writes that if salt is unavailable, one can use sugar instead, without a second's hesitation. See also *Darchei Teshuva* (69:328).

17 See *Shu"t Beis Yitzchak* (Danzig; vol. 2, Y.D. 27), *Shu"t Maaseh Avraham* (Y.D. 30), *Misgeres Hashulchan* (Y.D. 69:21), *Mizmor L'Dovid* (116), *Shu"t Mei Noach* (29), and *Shu"t Menachem Meishiv* (vol. 1:24).

18 *Shu"t Avnei Nezer* (O.C. 532). However, the *Piskei Teshuva* (pg. 71) posits that it is possible that the *Chavas Daas* wasn't referring to our commercial sugar which "obviously cannot be considered salt." Others claim that this had to have been a one-time occurrence and possibly only *b'shaas hadchak*. See also *Pardes Yosef* (Vayikra Ch. 2:13) and *Darchei Teshuva* (69:328) for more on this topic. The *Avnei Nezer* added that he heard from the *Av Beis Din* of Łodz that in "*Sifrei HaRofim*" (Medical texts) sugar is categorized as a type of salt.

19 See the recently published *Aderes Shmuel* (Hanhagos U'Psakim of Rav Shmuel Salant; *Hilchos Dam U'Melicha* 226, pg. 230–232) at length. Rav Shmuel is reported to have said that "the same way salt draws out blood so does sugar." However, in the footnotes (ad loc. 261 s.v. *ulam*), the author/compiler opines

Not Worth Its Salt

On the other hand, many authorities vehemently argued against permitting sugar for salting. Their main objection was that equating the salt of *Korbanos* to the laws of salting our meat was a tenuous comparison. They explained, that even if sugar fits into the salt category as a preservative to allow it to be offered on the Altar,[20] nevertheless, in order to be used as salt to *kasher* our meat and chickens, its proficiency in drawing out blood on an equal level as salt would have to be proven!

Due to these concerns, the majority of Acharonim who addressed this topic, including the *Divrei Chaim* of Sanz, the Maharshak (Rav Shlomo Kluger), the *Ksav Sofer*, the *Shoel U'Meishiv*, and the *Ben Ish Chai*,[21] unequivocally forbade salting meat or chicken with sugar as a salt substitute.

Many contemporary *Poskim* as well, including Rav Yosef Chaim Sonnenfeld, Rav Ben Tzion Chai Uziel, Rav Moshe Feinstein, the Klausenberger Rebbe, Rav Shmuel *Halevi* Wosner, the *Tzitz Eliezer* (who adds that the rumor that Rav Tzvi Pesach Frank permitted meat "salted

---

that it is possible that Rav Shmuel only ruled to be lenient in that specific case, as a wedding *seudah*, especially during that period of rampant poverty in Yerushalayim, would certainly be considered *shaas hadchak*.

20 This is also not so clear-cut, as honey is also a great preservative, yet is banned from being considered a salt substitute on the Altar [see *Vayikra* (Ch. 2:11)]. It is worthwhile to read Rav Samson Raphael Hirsch's commentary to this verse.

21 *Shu"t Divrei Chaim* (vol. 1, Y.D. 25), *Shu"t Tuv Taam V'Daas* (*Mahadura Kama* 111), *Shu"t Ksav Sofer* (Y.D. 37), *Shu"t Shoel U'Meishiv* (*Mahadura Kama* vol. 1:141 and 142), *Shu"t Rav Pe'alim* (vol. 2, Y.D. 4), and *Ben Ish Chai* (Year 2, *Parashas Tazria* 22). Other authorities who forbade salting with sugar include the Maharash Engel (*Shu"t* vol. 3:121, 2), the *Chessed L'Alafim* (*Shu"t* 72), Rav Chaim Palaji (*Ruach Chaim*, Y.D. 69:5; although he does at first seem to accept this *hetter*, nonetheless reversed his *psak* when he realized that sugar does not draw out blood as salt does), the *Chessed L'Avraham* (Teumim; Y.D. 32), the *Arugas Habosem* (Y.D. 69:17), the Maharam Brisk (*Shu"t* vol. 1:7), and *Kaf Hachaim* (Y.D. 69:322). The *Minchas Chinuch* (end Mitzva 119) writes that the Mahari Chagiz's *chiddush* is not a *"davar barur,"* as we generally do not invoke the dictum of *"Asei Docheh Lo Sasei"* in regard to the *Beis Hamikdash*

with sugar," is *"eidus sheker*, blatantly false"), and Rav Ovadiah Yosef, write very strongly that salting with sugar is not a viable option.[22] Several authorities maintain that if one transgresses, he might even be required to *kasher* his utensils used.[23]

Sugary Circumstances

However, and although it is not the normative *halacha*, there have been those who gave dispensation in extremely extenuating circumstances.[24] In fact, Rav Moshe Halberstam of the *Badatz Eidah Hachareidis* and

---

(see Gemara *Zevachim* 96b). The *Beis Yitzchak* (*Shu"t* Y.D. 7; cited by the *Darchei Halacha* on *Issur V'Hetter* 69:3, s.v. *b'davar*; presumably a different *Beis Yitzchak* than the one who allowed it), when faced with a complicated *sheilah* which could easily have been ruled permitted if he would have accepted that sugar works as salt, simply replied that it is too much of a *chiddush* and the *hetter* had to be based on other factors. It should also be noted that the Mahari Chagiz himself was unwilling to make that much of a jump in logic, and only would allow sugar-salted meat if it was nullified with 60 times against it. The *Yad Yehuda* (69, *Peirush Ha'aruch* 97) even recorded that when he asked scientists whether sugar can draw out blood as salt does, he was laughed at.

22 *Shu"t Salmas Chaim* (old print; vol. 2:3), *Shu"t Mishpetei Uziel* (*Tinyana* Y.D. 8:1), *Shu"t Igros Moshe* (Y.D. vol. 3:23), *Shu"t Divrei Yatziv* (vol. 2:14 and 15), *Shu"t Shevet Halevi* (vol. 2:24 and 26), *Shu"t Tzitz Eliezer* (vol. 9:35), and *Shu"t Yabia Omer* (vol. 4, Y.D. 2 and 3). See also *Bris Melach* (Ch. 8:6, pg. 69a) and *Shu"t Ba'er Chaim* (72).

23 Including *Shu"t Rav Pe'alim* (ibid.), *Arugas Habosem* (ibid.), *Shu"t Kol Mevasser* (vol. 2:15), and *Shu"t Tzitz Eliezer* (ibid.). See also *Shu"t Yabia Omer* (vol. 4, Y.D. 3), and Rabbi Yaakov Skoczylas' *Ohel Yaakov* (on *Hilchos Issur V'Hetter*, second edition pg. 22–24) on this topic.

24 See *Shu"t Rivevos Efraim* (vol. 7:388) who allows salting with sugar for a sick person who cannot have salt. However, the *Shevet Halevi* (ibid.) sharply disagrees and prohibits this even *"b'shaas hadchak gadol"*; he instead allows *chalitah* [sort of flash-searing; which ordinarily is not permitted for *kashering* purposes—see *Shulchan Aruch* (Y.D. 73:2), *Rema* (Y.D. 67:6), *Shach* (Y.D. 67:13 and 73:10), Rav Akiva Eiger (Y.D. 73:2), and *Mishnah Berurah* (454:11 and *Biur Halacha* 454 s.v. *layka*)]. This is also the opinion of the *Minchas Yitzchak* (*Shu"t* vol. 9:73) and the *Shemiras Shabbos Kehilchasa* (Ch. 40:87; new edition

author of *Shu"t Divrei Moshe*, once informed this author that there even was a historical precedent where this was performed *b'shaas hadchak*: During the 1948 Israeli Independence War, in certain places where the Jews were cut off from supply lines with no other viable alternative, they were forced to rely upon sugar for salting their meat!

In the final analysis, nowadays, most of us would consider this whole issue to be moot, as our meat and chickens, although not actually "grown on the supermarket shelf," are still generally pre-salted prior to purchase. Yet, the next time we add a "spoonful of sugar" (or a "salt substitute" substitute) into our coffee, or acknowledge the salt placed on our table at mealtimes, we can remind ourselves of the intricacies of the *Korbanos* that are woven into our daily lives. We hope and pray that we will soon merit actually attaining the closeness to *Hashem* engendered by bringing *Korbanos* in the rebuilt *Beis Hamikdash, bimheirah b'yameinu*.

Postscript: Sugary Substitutions

Although as detailed, most authorities do *not* allow sugar replacing salt for salting meat, nevertheless, there are several situations where a sugar substitution is *halachically* acceptable. For example, Rav Yaakov Emden accepts that sugar is considered a type of salt regarding *bishul* on Shabbos. The *She'arim Metzuyanim B'Halacha* posits that based on this, if one does not have salt on his table, he can fulfill the Mitzva of *"bris melach"* by having sugar on his table instead. For if the table is akin to the *Mizbe'ach*, and sugar would work in place of salt for an actual *Korban*, then certainly sugar can replace salt for this purpose. In fact, the *Ben Ish Chai*, although rejecting the idea of sugar for use as salt

---

Ch. 40:100; quoting *Shu"t Yeshuos Moshe* 47). See also *Shu"t Yad Yitzchak* (vol. 2:164, 1), *Shu"t Maharash Engel* (vol. 3:121, 2), *Shu"t Tirosh V'Yitzhar* (178), *Shu"t Har Tzvi* (Y.D. 66), and *Darchei Halacha* (on *Issur V'Hetter* 69:3, s.v. *b'davar*) for various scenarios of mixtures that some authorities allow if sugar was substituted. See also Rav Yosef Shalom Elyashiv's *He'aros B'Maseches Chullin* (113a), who does not rule conclusively on this topic.

to *kasher* meat, nonetheless, in *Shu"t Torah L'Shma* (which is generally attributed to him) he accepts sugar's use as salt for dipping.[25]

However, the *Kaf Hachaim* argues on the use of this leniency, and writes that the sugar would not satisfy the requirement of salt for dipping after *Hamotzi*, either. He avers that Kabbalistically it would actually be preferable to dip the bread into another slice of bread, as the words "*melach*" and "*lechem*" share the same letters. He maintains that only on *Rosh Hashanah*, and only after first dipping his bread into using salt, may one afterward dip his bread into sugar to "sweeten his *din*."[26]

Although this might sound astounding to some, there are also those who dip their *challah* and/or apple into sugar instead of honey on *Rosh Hashanah*. This is colloquially known as the *Ben Ish Chai's minhag*, and is generally followed by certain Sefardic sects.[27] I guess this just goes to show that *halachically*, a little bit of sugar goes a long way.

---

25   *Mor U'Ketziah* (318 s.v. *k'yotzai*), *She'arim Metzuyanim B'Halacha* (41:4), *Shu"t Rav Pe'alim* (vol. 2, Y.D. 4), and *Shu"t Torah L'Shma* (500).

26   *Kaf Hachaim* (O.C. 167:37). For more on this topic, see R' Zvi Ryzman's recent *Ratz Katzvi* on *Maagalei Hashana* (vol. 1; 3, Ch. 3 and 4) at length.

27   See *Ben Ish Chai* (Year 1, *Parashas Nitzavim* 4), *Shu"t Torah L'Shma* (ibid.), *Yafeh Lalev* (vol. 2, pg. 118b:2), *Shu"t Maaseh Avraham* (Y.D. 30), and *Kaf Hachaim* (O.C. 583:4).

This *minhag* was personally hammered home to this author some years back, when my *chavrusa*, the indefatigable Rabbi Jeff Seidel, requested our hosting several secular youth for a *Rosh Hashanah* meal. One stood out in particular, due to his gargantuan buff size as well as his every movement screaming military. This tattoo-sporting former U.S. soldier, in Jerusalem discovering his roots after returning from a tour of duty in Afghanistan, was very *makpid* to dip his *Rosh Hashanah challah* exclusively into sugar. In his trademark Western drawl and measured tone brooking no room for dissent, he explained, asserting rather emphatically, that "us *Sefaradim* follow all *minhagim* of the *Ben Ish Hai*."

Chapter 14

Fish with Legs?!

IN *PARASHAS NOACH* WE READ about how Hashem brought the *Mabul* (Great Flood/Deluge) and destroyed all living creatures, save for those inside *Teivas Noach* (Noach's Ark).[1] Additionally, we find that the fish in the oceans were spared as well.[2] It would be fascinating to find out on which side of the Ark a "fish with legs" would have been. Would it have been considered a fish, and therefore spared, or an animal, in which two (or perhaps seven pair) might have been sheltered inside while the rest of the species were wiped out?

A Fishy Tale?

Far from being a theoretical question, this issue was actually brought up almost four hundred years ago, when a certain Rabbi Aharon Rofei (perhaps Rabbi Dr.?)[3] placed such a fish, known as a *Stincus Marinus*, in front of the then *Av Beis Din* of Vienna, the famed Rav Gershon Shaul Yom Tov Lipman Heller, author of such essential works as the *Tosafos Yom Tov*, *Toras Ha'Asham*, and *Maadanei Yom Tov*,[4] and asked for his

---

1   *Parashas Noach* (*Bereishis* Ch. 7:21–23).

2   *Midrash Rabbah* (*Bereishis* 32:9), cited by *Rashi* (*Noach* Ch. 7:22 s.v. *asher*).

3   The *Lev Aryeh* (*Chullin* 66b, end s.v. *b'Gemara*) and *Pri Megadim* (Y.D. 83, M.Z. 2) seem to understand that the questioner was indeed a doctor and the moniker given was not actually referring to his name.

4   There is a famous quote attributed to the renowned author of the *Shu"t Imrei Yosher*, Rav Meir Arik, [originally printed in *Zer Zahav* (Tziternbaum; published in 5693), and later cited in the introduction to *Machon Yerushalayim's*

opinion as to the kashrus status of such a "fish," unknowingly sparking a *halachic* controversy.

What is a (Kosher) Fish?

This was no simple *sheilah*. It is well known that a kosher fish must have both fins and scales.[5] This so-called "fish" presented actually had scales, but legs instead of fins. Yet, technically speaking, would that astonishing characteristic alone be sufficient to prove it as non-kosher?

Chazal set down a general rule that "whatever has scales has fins as well,"[6] and should still be presumably kosher. This means that if one would find a piece of fish that has scales noticeably present, one may assume that since it has scales, it must therefore have had fins as well, and is consequently considered kosher. This ruling is codified as *halacha* by the *Rambam*, as well as the *Tur* and *Shulchan Aruch*.[7]

As for our *Stincus Marinus*, which had scales but legs instead of fins, the *Tosafos Yom Tov* averred that this "fish" cannot be considered kosher, as the aforementioned ruling was referring exclusively to actual fish and not sea creatures. Since the *Stincus Marinus* has legs instead of fins, it could not be considered a true fish, but rather some other sort of hybrid or sea creature, and must therefore not be kosher.[8]

Many authorities, including the *Knesses Hagedolah*, the Mahari Chagiz, Rav Yaakov Emden, the *Malbim*, and the *Aruch Hashulchan*, agreed to this ruling and considered the *Stincus Marinus* an aquatic creature and not a true fish, and thus decidedly non-kosher.[9] This fits

---

recent *Chiddushei Maharal M'Prague* on *Bava Metzia* (pg. 14, footnote 1)] that "it is unknown whether the Maharal M'Prague actually created a Golem. However, to have 'created' a *talmid* of the stature of the *Tosafos Yom Tov*, is certainly a greater wonder!"

5   *Parashas Shemini* (*Vayikra* Ch.11:9–13) and *Parashas Re'eh* (*Devarim* Ch. 14:9–10).

6   Mishnah *Nida* (51b) and Gemara *Chullin* (66b).

7   *Rambam* (*Hilchos Maachalos Assuros* Ch. 1:24), *Tur* and *Shulchan Aruch* (Y.D. 83:3).

8   *Maadanei Yom Tov* (*Chullin* 66b:5).

well with the terminology of the *Rambam*, that "anything that doesn't look like a fish, such as the sea lion, the dolphin, the frog, and such, is not a fish, kosher or otherwise."[10]

However, the *Pri Chodosh* rejected the opinion of the *Tosafos Yom Tov*, maintaining that Chazal's rule that "whatever has scales also has fins, and is presumed kosher," applies equally to all sea creatures, not just fish, and actually ruled that the *Stincus Marinus* **is** indeed kosher, regardless of whether or not it is considered a true fish.[11]

The *Tevuos Shor* wrote that in his assessment, this whole disagreement was seemingly born of a colossal misunderstanding, and that all opinions would agree to an alternate interpretation. He opined that although it would be classified as a sea creature, the *Stincus Marinus* should still indeed be considered kosher for a different reason. As although this "fish" has no true fins, still, its feet are the equivalent of fins,[12] and accordingly, it still fits the *halachic* definition of a fish![13]

Rule of Thumb (or Fin)

The renowned Rav Yonason Eibeshutz, although agreeing in theory with the *Pri Chodosh* that Chazal's rule meant to include all aquatic life and not just fish, conjectured that perhaps the rule was not meant to be absolute; rather it was meant as a generality. Generally speaking, if a fish has scales, one may safely assume that it also has fins; however, this does not exclude the possibility of ever finding one fish which does not. According to this understanding, the *Stincus Marinus* would apparently be considered an exclusion to the rule and therefore non-kosher.

---

9   *Knesses Hagedolah* (Y.D. 83, *Hagahos* on *Tur* 6), *Shu"t Halachos Ketanos* (vol. 1:255, and vol. 2:5; cited in *Shiyurei Bracha*, Y.D. 83:1), *Siddur Yaavetz* (*Migdal Oz*, *Dinei Dagim* 8 and 9; quoted in the *Darchei Teshuva* 83:27–28), *Malbim* (*Parashas Shemini*, 80; he writes that a sea creature with four legs is not considered a fish, rather a non-kosher "*Chai HaYam*"), and *Aruch Hashulchan* (Y.D. 83:10).

10 *Rambam* (*Hilchos Maachalos Assuros* Ch. 1:24).

11 *Pri Chodosh* (Y.D. 83:4).

This is also the understanding of several other authorities including the *Yeshuos Yaakov*, the *Shoel U'Meishiv*, and *Haksav V'Hakabbalah*.[14]

In strong contrast to this understanding of Chazal's statement, the *Taz* emphatically declared, "No fish in the world has scales but no fins," meaning that Chazal's rule *was* meant to be unconditional, and consequently, by definition there cannot be an exception. Most authorities agree to this understanding, with several of them, including the *Pri Chodosh*, the Chida, and the *Kaf Hachaim* ruling accordingly that the *Stincus Marinus* was indeed kosher based on this, since it did actually have scales.[15] [16]

---

12   There seemingly is precedent for such a theory, based on the words of several Rishonim describing the *Pelishti Avodah Zarah* "*Dagon*" (*Shmuel* I Ch. 5:2–7), which many commentaries, including *Rashi* (ad loc. 2 s.v. *eitzel*), the *Raavad* (in his commentary to *Avodah Zarah* 41a), R' Menachem Ibn Saruk (*Machberes Menachem*; London, 1854 edition, pg. 61–62), and the *Metzudas Dovid* (*Shmuel* I ibid. 4 s.v. *rak*), describe as a "fish-god," meaning an idol in the shape of a fish. Yet, the *Navi* explicitly writes that the idol had "hands" (that were cut off). This implies that a fish's flippers or fins can indeed justifiably be called a "*yad*" in the Torah. On the other hand, there are other interpretations given by the *Radak* (*Shmuel* I Ch. 5:4), Donash Ibn Librat (*Teshuvos Donash al Machberes Menachem*, London, 1855 edition, pg. 58), as well as Rabbeinu Tam (*Hachraos Rabbeinu Tam* ad loc.), *Ralbag* (*Shmuel* I ibid. 1), and Abarbanel (ad loc. 4), including that "*Dagon*" was an idol in human form, and alternatively, a hybrid half-man-half-fish idol, in which case, as the top half was in human form, would have had human hands. According to either of these latter interpretations, this passage would not yield any proof to the *Bechor Shor*'s assessment. See Rabbi Reuven Chaim Klein's recent excellent *GOD versus gods: Judaism in the Age of Idolatry* (pg. 318–320, "*Dagon*"), for more on this interesting tangent.

13   *Bechor Shor* (in his commentary to *Chullin* 66b; cited by the *Darchei Teshuva* ibid).

14   *Kreisi U'Pleisi* (83:3), *Yeshuos Yaakov* (ad loc. 2), *Shu"t Shoel U'Meishiv* (*Mahadura Kama* vol. 3:54), and *Haksav V'Hakabbalah* (in his commentary to *Vayikra* Ch. 11:9).

Scientifically Speaking

A scientific study published in 1850 by Rav Avraham Zutra (Sutro) of Münster identified the *Stincus Marinus* as a relative of the scorpion, or a type of poisonous lizard.[17] Similarly, the *Chasam Sofer* wrote that he accepted the findings of "expert scientists" who confirmed that the *Stincus Marinus* is not actually a sea creature at all. Rather, it lives on the shore and occasionally jumps into the water, similarly to the frog.[18] According to both of these *Gedolim*, our "fish" was most definitely not a fish, rather a *sheretz* (non-kosher crawling land animal)! This would make the entire preceding *halachic* discussion irrelevant, as the *Stincus*

---

15 *Taz* (Y.D. 83:3), *Pri Chodosh* (ibid.), Chida (*Machzik Bracha*, Y.D. 83:7 and *Shiyurei Bracha* ad loc. 1; also mentioned in his *Shu"t Chaim Sha'al* vol. 2:19), and *Kaf Hachaim* (Y.D. 83:6 and 15).

16 The *Pri Megadim* (Y.D. 83, M.Z. 2; also writing that this seems to be the *Prishah's shittah* (ad loc. 7) as well; see however *Mishmeres Shalom*, *B'emtza Davar* 3, who attempts to answer the *Pri Megadim*) and the Maharam Schick (in his commentary on the Mitzvos, Mitzva 157, cited by the *Darchei Teshuva* ibid.) maintain this way as well; however they do not definitively rule on the kashrus status of this so-called "fish." The *Aruch Hashulchan* (Y.D. 83:5) as well as his son, the *Torah Temima* (*Shemini* Ch. 11:9, 32), also held this way, that this rule is *Halacha M'Sinai*, yet, the *Aruch Hashulchan* himself, still ruled that this specific "fish" is non-kosher, as he considered the *Stincus Marinus* a sea creature, not a fish, like the *Rambam*. The *Eretz Tzvi* (as discussed further) as well, although maintaining that it is not kosher for a different reason, writes emphatically that this rule of Chazal is absolute, and is even testimony to the Divinity of the Torah.

17 *Shomer Tzion HaNe'eman* (vol. 91, pg. 182), cited by the *Darchei Teshuva* (ibid.) without quoting the author, as well as cited in *Kolmus* (R' Eliezer Eisikovits, "Fish Story", Pesach 5769, English edition) without citing the source. As pointed out by Rabbi Richard Jacobs of Ohr Lagolah, this is especially interesting as entymologically speaking, the scorpion is not remotely related to a lizard. The former is a predatory arachnid and the latter a squamate reptile.

18 *Chasam Sofer* (*Chullin* 66b s.v. *shuv*). He identifies it as a type of small crocodile. He posits that this crocodile is the same one that Rabbeinu Chananel maintained was the Biblical *Tzfardaya*. See *Ibn Ezra* (*Parashas Va'era* Ch. 7:27), *Abarbanel* (ad loc.), and *Haamek Davar* (ad loc. 29).

Marinus would not fall under the category of *Chazal*'s statement and would thereby be one hundred percent non-kosher. The Kozoglover Gaon actually uses this "fish" as a testament to the Divinity of the Torah, as the only known exception to *Chazal*'s rule turned out to be not a fish at all, but rather a type of lizard![19]

On the other hand, not only does the *Darchei Teshuva* not accept Rav Avraham Zutra's scientific study, but even writes a scathing response that he does not understand how one can place these findings from non-*halachic* sources between *teshuvos HaGaonim* without a clear proof from *Chazal* or *Poskim* "*sherak mipihem anu chayim*—whose words we live by."[20] Accordingly, this opinion of the *Darchei Teshuva* would also unsubstantiate the conclusion of the *Chasam Sofer*, for although the *Chasam Sofer* agreed to the *Tosafos Yom Tov*'s conclusion that the *Stincus Marinus* is not kosher, his claim that it is not a true sea creature is based on "scientific experts." Therefore, this scientific analysis that the *Stincus Marinus* be considered a lizard may not actually be acknowledged by all.

Practical Impracticality

The Gemara questions *Chazal*'s rule that scales suffice to render a fish kosher, "Why then does the Torah mention fins altogether? The Gemara answers in an extremely rare fashion: "*l'hagdil Torah ulha'adirah*—To magnify and enhance the Torah."[21]

The *Magen Avraham*, in his commentary to the *Yalkut Shimoni*, takes this a step further. He writes that *l'hagdil Torah ulha'adirah* was not limited to the topic of fins and scales; rather, it was also referring to our exact case of the *Stincus Marinus*. It is stated in the famous last Mishnah in *Makkos* that Hashem wishes to grant Klal Yisrael extra reward and He therefore added effortless *Torah* and Mitzvos. *Rashi* comments that this includes refraining from eating repulsive creatures that one

---

19 *Eretz Tzvi* on *Moadim* (*Yalkut Ha'Emuna, Maamar Sheini, Inyan Sheini* pg. 251–252).

20 *Darchei Teshuva* (83:28).

21 *Nida* (51b) and *Chullin* (66b). For an interesting explanation of this dictum, see *Lev Aryeh* (*Chullin* 66b s.v. *v'ulam*).

wouldn't want to eat anyway.²² The *Magen Avraham* explains that this certainly applies to our "fish"; since the *Stincus Marinus* is poisonous, one wouldn't have any sort of desire to eat it, thus potentially taking it out of the realm of practical *halacha*. Nevertheless, this whole issue of finding out its kashrus status was meant for us to delve into exclusively to get rewarded in the Next World; an infinitely more appealing approach.²³

So was the strange looking sea creature swimming in the ocean outside the *Teivah* or was it found within? It seems like we probably will never fully know the answer, although it certainly is fascinating that it seemingly would depend on how the *Stincus Marinus* is classified *halachically*!

Postscript: Swimming in Sand

Scientifically, it appears that the classification *Stincus Marinus* is somewhat of a misnomer, as it is categorized as a lizard from the skink family, known as a *Scincus Scincus*, or a sandfish lizard.²⁴ In a recent published study by Daniel I. Goldman in the prestigious *Science* journal,²⁵ it has been proven utilizing high speed X-ray imaging, that although non-aquatic, when below

Stincus Marinus/Scincus Scincus/ sandfish lizard

---

22 Gemara *Makkos* (23b) and *Rashi* (ad loc. s.v. *l'zakos*).

23 *Zayis Raanan* (*Parashas Shemini*, commentary on the *Yalkut Shimoni*; explanation on pg. 146a). The *Lev Aryeh* (*Chullin* 66b, end s.v. *b'Gemara*) explains that it seems from the *Magen Avraham*'s elucidation that he seems to agree with the opinion of Rav Yonason Eibeshutz that Chazal's fish rule was not meant to be absolute. For, if it was, why would the Gemara conclude that extra reward is given for staying away from a poisonous *Stincus Marinus* that would technically have been kosher? *L'hagdil Torah ulha'adirah* would only have been applicable if this "fish" turned out to be the exception to the rule, and even though it had scales was still not kosher. Accordingly, although we would avoid this "fish" because it was poisonous, we would nonetheless still attain *sechar* for doing so, as it would not have been deemed kosher.

24 For example, see http://runeberg.org/nfcd/0703.html.

the surface the sandfish lizard no longer uses limbs for propulsion but "generates thrust to overcome drag by propagating an undulatory traveling wave down the body." In other words, although deemed a lizard, it does possess fish-like characteristics, as it "swims" through the sand beneath the surface.[26]

Scientists are even trying to understand and mimic its unique abilities to help search-and-rescue missions.[27] So it is quite understandable how many of the aforementioned *Gedolim* felt that the *Stincus Marinus* was a fish or aquatic creature, even though current science has sided with the *Chasam Sofer*'s conclusion that it is truly a *sheretz ha'aretz*.

---

25 *Science* (vol. 325; July 17, 2009; "Undulatory Swimming in Sand: Subsurface Locomotion of the Sandfish Lizard").

26 A clip showcasing the sandfish lizard's amazing ability is available at: https://www.youtube.com/watch?v=P4bxRj-BjFg, as well as a picture of several of them preserved in a German Museum: http://i0.wp.com/themuseumtimes.com/wp-content/uploads/2014/12/IMAG1193.jpg.
Thanks are due to R' David Hojda for providing these fascinating links. This topic was recently featured on Rabbi Yosef Wikler's "Kashrus on the Air" radio show and is accessible at: https://soundcloud.com/jroot-radio/yosef-wikler-oct-22.

27 As detailed in this clip:
https://www.youtube.com/watch?v=Xzt1iJbwNXEandspfreload=10.
Also known as the "medicinal skink," as already attested to in Rav Zutra's study in 1850, the *Stincus* is known for its medicinal properties and pharmacodynamic effects and was used over the years in various tonics and potions. Recent studies have shown that the sandfish lizard actually has a cholesterol-lowering and hypotriglyceridemia effect.

Part 3

FAMOUS FOODS

Chapter 15

The Great Cholent Challenge

Cholent Is Its Name

AHH! NOTHING SMELLS MORE *GESHMAK* than the awesomely redolent aroma emanating from the kitchen and wafting throughout the house on a Shabbos morning. If you are like most of us, you just can't wait until you sink your teeth into that piping hot, special-for-Shabbos delicacy, cholent. This exceptional meat, potato, barley, and bean (and whatever else you decide to throw in) concoction of a stew has been around for a very long time. In fact, the eminent *Ohr Zarua*, Rav Yitzchak of Vienna, already mentioned cholent by name in the mid-1200s![1]

Etymologists have a difficult time figuring out where the name comes from. There are several hypotheses regarding cholent, including the Hebrew/Aramaic *"shelan"* (food that rested overnight), *"shaluk"* (thoroughly cooked), from the German *"shul ende,"* referring to a food for after *shul*, and a combination of the French words *"chaud"* (hot) and *"lent"* (slow). However, most Sefardim stick to the name given to a hot Shabbos food by the Mishnah,[2] *"chamin"* or *"hamin."*

The origins of this humble dish lie in the words of the renowned *Baal Hama'or*, Rav Zerachiah Halevi of Gerona, who lived in the mid-1100s. He writes that it is a *Takkanas Chachamim* (Rabbinic decree) to enjoy the

---

1   *Ohr Zarua* (vol. 2, Shabbos, *Hilchos Erev Shabbos*, end 8).
2   *Shabbos* (36b).

Shabbos with a hot dish. He adds that whoever does not do so is suspect of being a *"Min"* (heretic; a.k.a *Apikores*)![3]

His reason for the strong language was because the heterodox *Kara'im* (Karaites), who denied the Rabbinic *Mesorah*, prohibited eating any hot food on Shabbos due to their rejection of *Torah She'Baal Peh* (the Oral Law) coupled with their literal interpretation of the *pasuk*, *"Lo seva'aru aish bechol moshvoseichem b'Yom HaShabbos*, You shall not kindle fire in any of your dwellings on the Shabbos day."[4] The *Baal Hama'or* explains that one who refuses to eat a hot dish on Shabbos (cooked before Shabbos; as per the Oral Law), is suspect of following their heretical interpretation of the Torah and not those of our *Chachmei Hadoros*.[5]

On the other hand, the *Baal Hama'or* assures that whoever makes sure to cook, heat up (before Shabbos), and eat a hot dish on Shabbos will merit seeing "the end of days." Quite a large reward just for eating cholent. And this is not just a minority opinion; his words are codified in *halacha* by the *Rema* as a "Mitzva" and eating cholent on Shabbos is considered *"Minhag Yisrael"* by the *Mishnah Berurah*.[6] In fact, I know of a certain well-known rabbi who, although not enamored of cholent, nonetheless makes sure to "eat one bean every Shabbos," and that way fulfill *"Mitzvas Cholent."*

Serving Up

However, getting the cholent from a bubbling pot on a *blech* (a simple sheet of metal placed on the gas burners) onto our plates presents several *halachic* challenges, as in our zeal to fulfill this gastronomical Mitzva, we certainly do not want to unintentionally desecrate the

---

3   *Baal Hama'or* (in his glosses to Gemara *Shabbos*, *Perek Kira*, *Ma'or Hakattan* end 16b in the *Rif's* pagination, end s.v. *v'im*); also cited by the *Orchos Chaim* (*Hilchos Shabbos* 72) and the *Kol Bo* (31, pg. 32a).

4   *Shemos*, *Parashas Vayakhel* (Ch. 35:3).

5   For an expanded explanation and the parameters of this Mitzva, see *Shu"t Ba'er Moshe* (vol. 1:1, 2) and *Chut Shani* (*Shabbos* vol. 2, pg. 147, Ch. 28:12).

6   *Rema* (O.C. 257: end 8), *Darchei Moshe* (O.C. 259:2), and *Mishnah Berurah* (ad loc. 49).

Biblical prohibition of *"Bishul,"* cooking on Shabbos. Aside from the issues of *Shehiya*, placing a food on the fire before Shabbos until the time it is being served on Shabbos, and the more stringent *Chazara*, returning food to the flame on Shabbos, there is also a separate issue of *Maygis*, stirring, which one might possibly violate by doing the simple innocuous actions of lifting the lid off of the simmering cholent pot and replacing it,[7] or just ladling out some Friday night *"To'ameha"* cholent.[8]

Therefore, in order to serve our *"Mitzva Cholent"* properly, without *chas v'shalom* unwittingly transgressing any Shabbos prohibitions, authorities have come up with a five-point plan that enables us to serve a steaming, savory cholent, and allows us to return it to the flame for seconds (more Mitzvos!).

Note: this follows the widespread Ashkenazic practice that one must first remove the pot from the fire in order to serve.

Here are the five steps:

1. The pot of cholent must be sitting on a covered flame, as a reminder that we cannot adjust the flame on Shabbos.[9] In

---

[7] See *Bartenura* (*Shabbos* Ch. 7: Mishnah 2, s.v. *ha'ofeh*), *Shulchan Aruch* (O.C. 254:4 and 257:4), *Mishnah Berurah* (254:23 and *Biur Halacha* 257 s.v. *gorem*), *Mekor Chaim* (318:18), *Shvisas HaShabbos* (*Mevashel* 26:81), *Ketzos Hashulchan* (124), *Shu"t Igros Moshe* (O.C. vol. 4:74, *Bishul* 10), *Chut Shani* (*Shabbos* vol. 2, pg. 197), *Shu"t Titz Eliezer*, (vol. 7:15), *Shu"t Teshuvos V'Hanhagos* (vol. 1:207, 3), and *Shemiras Shabbos Kehilchasa* (new edition Ch. 1:41).

[8] There is an *inyan* of tasting the Shabbos food on Erev Shabbos *l'kavod Shabbos*, to ensure that it is properly cooked, as well as over Shabbos itself. This is referred to as *"To'ameha."* See *Machzor Vitry* (191), *Arizal* (*Shaar Hakavannos, Drushei Seder Shabbos*, 1), *Magen Avraham* (250:1), *Elyah Rabba* (ad loc. 6), *Shulchan Shlomo* (ad loc. 1), *Shlah* (*Shabbos, Ner Mitzva* 31), *Shulchan Aruch Harav* (O.C. 250:8), *Mishnah Berurah* (ad loc. end 2), and *Kaf Hachaim* (ad loc. 5).

[9] For the basic discussion, see *Rashi* (*Shabbos* 36b s.v. *ad sheyigrof*), *Tosafos* (ad loc. s.v. *lo*), *Rambam* (*Hilchos Shabbos* Ch. 3:4), *Rif* (16a in his pagination), and *Ran* (15b in the *Rif's* pagination, s.v. *oh ad*). This is based on the famous *machlokes* (*Shabbos* 36b) between Chananya and the Rabbanan regarding placing partially cooked food on a fire before Shabbos. The Rishonim and *Poskim*

differ in their understandings as to what exactly they were disputing, as well as whom the *halacha* follows [see for example *Ba'er Hagolah* (O.C. 253:10), *Pri Megadim* (ad loc. M.Z. 1), *Hagahos Rabbi Akiva Eiger* (ad loc. 5), and the *Mishnah Berurah's* introduction to O.C. 253]. The *halachic* bottom line is that making sure the flame is covered is a prerequisite for committing *Chazara* on Shabbos in a permitted manner; see *Shulchan Aruch* and *Rema*, *Orach Chaim* 253 and main commentaries at length. Additionally, although the *ikar minhag* is to be lenient regarding *Shehiya* once it is cooked at least *shiur maachal Ben Derosoi* (which is at least a third or half cooked) before Shabbos that *Garuf V'Katum* is not necessitated [following the opinion of many Rishonim, as well as the *Yeish Omrim* in the *Shulchan Aruch* and the *Rema* (ibid.; who writes "*v'nahagu lehakel k'sevara acharonah*"), and the *Shulchan Aruch Harav* (ad loc. 9)], nevertheless, several Acharonim, including the *Machatzis Hashekel* (ad loc. 15 s.v. *v'yeish*; who explains this as the *Magen Avraham's* intent, that he was uneasy relying on the more lenient *Yeish Omrim*; on the other hand, it must be noted that the *Pri Megadim*, in his *Mishbetzos Zahav* ad loc. 15, did not understand the *Magen Avraham's* comment in this context), the Maharsham (*Daas Torah* ad loc. s.v. *v'nahagu*; he comments strongly, citing precedent that anytime a ruling is referred to as "*nahagu*," it reflects how the *hamon am* commonly act, but not necessarily deciding the proper *halacha*, which in this case would be to only allow *Shehiya* when the fire is *Garuf V'Katum*), the *Mishnah Berurah* (*Biur Halacha* ad loc. s.v. *vinahagu*; based on the *Rosh*—*Shabbos* Ch. 3: end 1; who concludes that "*b'shvil shrabu dei'os b'hai piska, v'Yisrael adukin b'Mitzvas Oneg Shabbos,* **v'lo yishma'u lehachmir, hanach lahem k'minhag shenahagu** *al pi haposkim k'Chananya*") and *Chazon Ish* (O.C. 37:3; on the other hand, see *Orchos Rabbeinu*, new edition vol. 1, pg. 197:6) maintain that *lechatchilla* it is preferable even regarding *Shehiya* that one should still ensure that his fire is *Garuf V'Katum* before Shabbos, unless he is certain that his cholent fulfills the requirement of *metztamek v'ra lo*. Additionally, even though technically one may put the food on a fire raw right before Shabbos (called *Kedaira Chaysa*) [see Gemara *Shabbos* (18b), *Rambam* (*Hilchos Shabbos* Ch. 3:8), *Shulchan Aruch* (O.C. 253:1), and *Magen Avraham* (ad loc. 15; who writes that this is actually the preferred option as it is *lechatchilla l'kulei alma*)] and one won't be *nichshal* by adjusting the flame, nevertheless, nowadays several authorities frown upon relying on this, as our stoves and ovens cook much quicker and the cholent will be ready long before the Shabbos day *seudah*. Additionally, how raw the meat must be right before Shabbos is also debated. Therefore, optimally, the preferred option is to ensure that the cholent is fully cooked before Shabbos

Mishnaic and Talmudic terms this is referred to as "*Garuf V'Katum*," meaning the coals in the ovens were pushed to the side and/or covered up. There is a famous *machlokes* Rishonim whether the key reason for doing this is so there will be a reminder that it is prohibited to stoke the coals and make the food cook faster and better, or whether it is meant to actually lessen the cooking heat. Making sure the flame is covered is a prerequisite for performing *Chazara* on Shabbos in a permitted manner. A *blech* on the stovetop is the most commonly known example of this.[10] [11]

2. The cholent must be fully cooked.[12]
3. It must still be hot or at least warm.[13]
4. One must take it off the fire in order to serve it.[14] If one wants to keep it hot for later (*fleishig Shalosh Seudos*, anyone?) he must have in mind when taking the pot off the fire to serve that he is planning on returning it to the fire.[15]
5. One must have his hand on it the whole time.[16]

However, in extenuating circumstances, even if one was not planning to return it to the flame, as long as his hand was still on it, he may nevertheless do so. Similarly, if he placed it on the counter (i.e., in order to serve the cholent), but still intended to return it to the fire, according to the majority consensus, he is permitted to return it to the *blech*.[17]

Sefardic Style

Common Sefardic practice follows the opinion of the *Shulchan Aruch* based on his understanding of the *Rambam*, that once the cholent is fully cooked, scooping out from the pot no longer constitutes *Maygis*.

---

for these reasons as well. See *Elyah Rabba* (O.C. 253:2), *Mishnah Berurah* (ad loc. 11), *Biur Halacha* (ad loc. 1 s.v. *maysiach*), *Sfas Emes* (*Shabbos* 18b), *Chazon Ish* (O.C. 37:22), Rav Yosef Eliyahu Henkin's *Shu"t Gevuros Eliyahu* (vol. 1-O.C. 58:2 and 67, 68, 69, and 70), Rav Shlomo Zalman Auerbach's *Shu"t Minchas Shlomo* (Tinyana 12:4), and Rav Ben Tzion Abba-Shaul's *Shu"t Ohr L'Tzion* (vol. 1, O.C. 21).

10 Although there are those, most notably the *Chazon Ish*, who are stringent that a *blech* does not qualify [see *Chazon Ish* (O.C. 37:9 and 11) as well as his *teshuva* printed in *Shu"t Shevet Halevi* (vol. 1:91), *Orchos Rabbeinu* (new edition; vol. 1, pg. 196, 2), and *Chut Shani* (*Shabbos* vol. 2, pg. 11, *Shaar Hatziyun* 35); in fact, *Peninas HaShabbos* (vol. 1, Ch. 9, pg. 14–19) spends considerable length and detail on trying to understand the main reasons as to the *Chazon Ish's* stringent *shittah* regarding a *blech*; see also *Shu"t Panim Meiros* (vol. 1:84; cited in *Shaarei Teshuva* O.C. 254:8), *Shu"t Maharsham* (vol. 3:165), and *Shu"t Levushei Mordechai* (O.C. Mahadura Telita'ei 37) who are *machmir* regarding a similar sounding case, with a rudimentary heat source used for making tea that will be hot and ready Shabbos day], nonetheless, nowadays the vast majority of contemporary authorities, based on the *Magen Avraham* (253:31), *Chayei Adam* (vol. 2:20, 11), *Mishnah Berurah* (253:81), and *Kaf Hachaim* (ad loc. 11), maintain that this *din* translates to a *blech*. See *Shu"t Maharam Schick* (O.C. 117), *Shu"t Maharshag* (vol. 2:50), *Shu"t Maharam Brisk* (vol. 2:76; who adds that the aforementioned *Gedolim* who were *machmir* regarding the tea and heat source was only due to the fact that they held that that heat source did not qualify as a true *blech*; conversely, if a real *blech* would be placed between the heat source and the tea, "*ain kaan shum pikpuk l'kuli alma*"), *Shu"t Igros Moshe* (O.C. vol. 1:93), *Shu"t Gevuros Eliyahu* (vol. 1-O.C. 67, 68, and 96), *Shu"t Shevet Halevi* (ibid.), *Shu"t Yaskil Avdi* (vol. 3, O.C. 10:2, 6), *Shu"t Tzitz Eliezer* (vol. 7:15), *Moadim U'Zmanim* (vol. 7:143), *Shu"t Teshuvos V'Hanhagos* vol. 1:207, 2), *Shu"t Yabia Omer* (vol. 6, O.C. 32:4), *Shu"t Ohr L'Tzion* (vol. 2, Ch. 17:2), *Yesodei Yeshurun* (vol. 4:18 and 19), *Halichos Even Yisrael* on *Hilchos Shabbos* (vol. 1, Ch. 31:3), *Shemiras Shabbos Kehilchasa* (new edition Ch. 1:20, 5 and footnote 54), and *Kovetz Kol HaTorah* (vol. 42, Nissan 5757, pg. 14:4; "*Leket M'Hanhagos V'Hora'os HaGaavad zt"l [Minchas Yitzchak] B'Inyanei Hilchos Shabbos*"; adding that "*shekein hayah mekubal b'dor shelifnei hamilchamah*"). Indeed, the *Me'or HaShabbos* (vol. 2, Ch. 10, pg. 286) notes regarding a *blech* that the "*de'ah hamekubeles b'tzibbur b'derech klal, lehachshiva k'aish mechuseh*." Several authorities, including Rav Moshe Feinstein (ibid.), Rav Moshe Stern (the Debreciner Rav; in a *teshuva* printed in *Kovetz Am HaTorah* vol. 13, pg. 21, s.v. *v'od d'halo* and later in *Shu"t Ba'er Moshe* vol. 7, *Kuntress Electric* vol. 2:3), and Rav Shmuel *Halevi* Wosner (*Shu"t Shevet Halevi* ibid.) maintain that it is preferable to cover the oven knobs as well. However, if this was not done, Rav Shlomo Zalman Auerbach, Rav Yisrael Yaakov Fischer, and Rav Ben Tzion Abba-Shaul held [see *Me'or HaShabbos* (vol. 2, *Peninei Hama'or*, pg. 628 and 666), *Shu"t Even Yisrael* (vol. 8:20, 4), *Shu"t Ohr L'Tzion* (ibid.), *Shemiras*

Shabbos Kehilchasa (new edition Ch. 1:20, 5, footnote 63), and *Halichos Even Yisrael* (ibid. 4)] that one may still consider his fire *garuf*. Interestingly, Rav Aharon Kotler is quoted (see Rav Shimon Eider's *Halachos of Shabbos* pg. 338, *Ofeh*, end footnote 800 s.v. *shamaati*) as maintaining that covering the knobs is the *ikar* of making a *blech* considered *Garuf V'Katum*, while covering the fire only preferable, concluding that in a situation where it is difficult to cover the fire with a *blech* or *b'dieved*, one may rely on covering the knobs as deeming the stove *Garuf V'Katum*. Thanks are due to my father, renowned kashrus expert Rav Manish Spitz, for pointing out this invaluable source.

11   Regarding the Shabbos hot plate (*plata*), another common method to keep food warm on Shabbos, most contemporary authorities, including Rav Tzvi Pesach Frank (*Shu"t Har Tzvi* O.C. 136), Rav Moshe Feinstein (*Shu"t Igros Moshe* O.C. vol. 4:74, *Bishul* 35), Rav Shlomo Zalman Auerbach (cited in *Shemiras Shabbos Kehilchasa* new edition Ch. 1: footnote 83), Rav Ovadiah Hadaya (*Shu"t Yaskil Avdi* vol. 7, O.C. 28:8 and 44, *Sheilah* 15:3; retracting from original proscription in vol. 5, O.C. 34 and vol. 6, O.C. 15), the Debreciner Rav (*Shu"t Ba'er Moshe* vol. 6, *Kuntress Electric* vol. 1:1 and 2 and vol. 7, *Kuntress Electric* vol. 2:3), Rav Yisrael Yaakov Fischer (cited in *Me'or HaShabbos* vol. 2, pg. 656 and *Halichos Even Yisrael* on *Hilchos Shabbos* vol. 1, Ch. 31:9), Rav Yitzchak Zilber (*Shu"t Az Nidberu* vol. 1:79, 88, pg. 157 and vol. 8:15), Rav Eliezer Yehuda Waldenberg (*Shu"t Tzitz Eliezer* vol. 8:26), Rav Ben Tzion Abba-Shaul (*Shu"t Ohr L'Tzion* vol. 2: Ch. 17, end footnote 1), Rav Shmuel *Halevi* Wosner (*Shu"t Shevet Halevi* vol. 5: end 30), Rav Ovadiah Yosef (*Shu"t Yabia Omer* vol. 6, O.C. 32:5 and *Shu"t Yechaveh Daas* vol. 2:45), and Rav Yitzchak Yosef (*Yalkut Yosef, Shabbos* vol.1, pg. 90 and *Kitzur Shulchan Aruch*, O.C. 253:1) maintain that it is has the *halachic* status of a *blech*, since its temperature cannot be changed, and it is only meant to keep food warm, and not actually cook. However, it should be noted that several of these *Poskim* maintain that this *halachic* dispensation only applies if one is actually unable to cook on the *plata*. Other authorities feel that even if one can actually cook on said hot plate, the *din* still applies as it is not the *derech* to cook on a hot plate, and therefore no issue of *Mechzei K'mevashel* arises. Several authorities, on the other hand, including the *Chazon Ish* (see O.C. 37:9 and 11; cited in *Orchos Rabbeinu* vol. 1, pg. 102:11; new edition vol. 1, pg. 196:3), Rav Yosef Shalom Elyashiv (cited in *Shvus Yitzchak* on *Inyanei Shehiya* Ch. 8, pg. 91) and Rav Nissim Karelitz (*Chut Shani, Shabbos* vol. 2, pg. 114)], are stringent that a *plata* does not constitute a true covered flame, due to a *lo plug*. Rav Moshe Sternbuch (*Shu"t Teshuvos V'Hanhagos* vol. 1:207, 6) rules that only

b'shaas hadchak may one be lenient to perform *Chazara* onto a *plata*. See also *Me'or HaShabbos* (vol. 2: Ch. 10, footnote 26), who discusses this *machlokes* at length. Due to this debate, several authorities maintain that it is preferable to place a layer of thick aluminum foil on the *plata* before Shabbos, in order to satisfy all opinions; see *Shu"t Shemesh U'Magen* (vol. 1:56), *Shvus Yitzchak* (ibid. 12), *Chut Shani* (Shabbos vol. 2, pg. 116 s.v. *u'mikol makom*), *Halichos Even Yisrael* (ibid.), and *Orchos Shabbos* (vol. 1: Ch. 2, 13).

12   "*Nisbashel Kol Tzorcho.*" See *Rambam* (*Hilchos Shabbos* Ch. 9:3), *Ohr Zarua* (vol. 2:62), *Tur* (O.C. 318:4), *Beis Yosef* (O.C. 253:2 s.v. *umashekasav Rabbeinu*), *Shulchan Aruch* (O.C. 318:4), *Rema* (O.C. 253:2), *Taz* (ad loc. 10), *Biur HaGr"a* (to O.C. 318:4), *Shulchan Aruch Harav* (ad loc. 18), *Chayei Adam* (vol. 2:20, 9), *Mishnah Berurah* (ad loc. 61 and *Biur Halacha* ad loc. s.v. *v'davka* and 318:4 s.v. *afilu*), and *Kaf Hachaim* (ad loc. 45). Although there are many Rishonim who hold that *Chazara* would be permitted once the food is cooked at least *shiur maachal Ben Derosoi* (if all of the other criteria are met), nevertheless, in the words of the *Mishnah Berurah* (*Biur Halacha* ibid.): "*kasheh lehakel d'hu nogeya b'inyan Deoraysa*" and "*ain lazuz lemaaseh m'psak HaShulchan Aruch, uv'prat shehu M'Deoraysa.*" However, the lenient opinions are taken into account, and *b'dieved*, if one performed *Chazara* onto a heat source that was *Garuf V'Katum*, as long as the cholent was cooked *shiur maachal Ben Derosoi* (although not fully cooked), the cholent is still permitted to be eaten on Shabbos. See *Biur Halacha* (318 ibid.), citing precedent from the *Pri Megadim* (ad loc. E.A. 10).

13   See *Shulchan Aruch* (O.C. 253:2), *Rema* (ad loc. 15), *Magen Avraham* (ad loc. 19), *Tosefes Shabbos* (ad loc. 23), *Ba'er Heitiv* (ad. loc. 12), *Shulchan Aruch Harav* (ad loc. 18), *Mishnah Berurah* (ad loc. 24 and 54), and *Kaf Hachaim* (ad loc. 53). Although this is essentially a *machlokes* between the *Shulchan Aruch* and *Rema*, with the *Shulchan Aruch* only permitting *Chazara* when the pot still maintains the heat level of *Yad Soledes Bo* (approximately 113°F or 45°C), nonetheless, the Ashkenazic *psak* follows the *Rema* who allows leniency as long as the pot has not cooled off entirely. Accordingly, the *Yalkut Yosef* (Shabbos vol. 3, pg. 216 and *Kitzur Shulchan Aruch*, O.C. 318:59) maintains that a Sefardi should not personally be *meikil* to perform *Chazara* once the heat level of the cholent has cooled off and is no longer *Yad Soledes Bo*. However, he qualifies that a Sefardic *bochur* in an Ashkenazic Yeshiva need not complain if it is customary in the Yeshiva to be *meikil* with performing *Chazara* with lukewarm cholent, and even if they are doing so specifically to serve the Sefardic *bochurim*.

14   The issue with serving from on the fire is *Maygis*, stirring, which might

technically be an *Issur Deoraysa* of *Bishul*; see Gemara *Beitza* (34a) and *Rambam* (*Hilchos Shabbos* Ch. 9:4). Although in our case we are referring to serving cholent that is fully cooked, and therefore according to most authorities stirring should no longer be an issue [see *Beis Yosef* (O.C. 318:18), *Shu"t Ridbaz* (vol. 3:411), *Maamar Mordechai* (318:20), *Eglei Tal* (*Ha'Ofeh* 17), and *Shu"t Avnei Nezer* (O.C. 59], nevertheless, the *Rema* (O.C. 318:18; citing the Mahari Weil, *Dinin V'Halachos* 30), *Elyah Rabba* (ad loc. 40; citing the *Kol Bo*, 31), *Magen Avraham* (ad loc. 42), *Chayei Adam* (vol. 2:20, 9), *Shulchan Aruch Harav* (O.C. 318:30), *Tosefes Shabbos* (ad loc. 56), *Shvisas HaShabbos* (*Mevashel* 26), *Mishnah Berurah* (ad loc. 113), and Rav Moshe Feinstein (*Shu"t Igros Moshe*, O.C. vol. 4:61 and 74, *Bishul* 9; citing the *Tiferes Shmuel's* glosses to the *Rosh*, *Shabbos* Ch. 3:15), are *machmir* that one should only ladle out the cholent when it is fully cooked *and* also off the fire. Although one may infer from the Mahari Weil and Rema's wording that this action may be problematic as well, nonetheless the vast majority of *halachic* authorities, including the *Shulchan Aruch* (O.C. 318:18), *Taz* (ad loc. 23), *Magen Avraham* (ad loc. 44; referring to beans), *Pri Megadim* (ad loc. M.Z. 23), *Elyah Rabba* (ibid.), *Chayei Adam* (ibid.), *Shulchan Aruch Harav* (ad loc. 30), *Aruch Hashulchan* (ad loc. 56), *Mishnah Berurah* (ad loc. 117 and *Biur Halacha* s.v. *af*), and *Kaf Hachaim* (ad loc. 177), rule that this is the preferred method of serving cholent on Shabbos, (unless you can just pour out directly from the pot) and does not constitute *Maygis*.

15 Gemara *Shabbos* (38b), *Tur* (O.C. 253:2), *Rema* (ad loc.), *Shulchan Aruch Harav* (ad loc. 19), *Mishnah Berurah* (ad loc. 56 and *Biur Halacha* ad loc. s.v. *v'daato*).

16 See *Tur* (O.C. 253:2), *Shulchan Aruch* (ad loc.), *Rema* (ad loc.), *Magen Avraham* (ad loc. 20), *Shulchan Aruch Harav* (ad loc. 19), and *Mishnah Berurah* (ad loc. 55 and *Biur Halacha* ad loc. s.v. *v'lo*). This *halacha* is based on a dispute between the *Shulchan Aruch* and *Rema*, which stems from a *machlokes* Rishonim whose origins lie in the Gemara's *safek* (*Shabbos* 38b) whether specifically placing the pot down on the floor is what no longer allows for *Chazara* (*shittah* of the *Shulchan Aruch*) as it is "*mevattel daato lehachzir*," or if the pot specifically needs to be "*odeh b'yado*" to allow *Chazara* (*Rema*'s *shittah*). Many contemporary authorities maintain that the pot does not need to be held suspended while ladling out cholent; it may be allowed to rest upon a surface (table, counter; certainly not being placed on the floor) as long as the pot is still being held by the handle. See *Shu"t Igros Moshe* (O.C. vol. 2:69 and vol. 4:74, *Bishul* 33), *Shemiras Shabbos Kehilchasa* (new edition Ch. 1:20, 4, footnote 60; quoting Rav Shlomo Zalman Auerbach), *Shvus Yitzchak* (ibid. Ch. 14; quoting

Accordingly, one may scoop out and serve cholent directly from the pot after it is fully cooked, even while it is still on top of the *blech*.[18]

Rav Yosef Shalom Elyashiv), *Chut Shani* (*Shabbos* vol. 2, pg. 123:3), and *Orchos Shabbos* (vol. 1 Ch. 2:47). However, it is important to note that there are contemporary *Poskim*, including the *Minchas Yitzchak* (*Kovetz Kol HaTorah*, Nissan 5757, pg. 15:7, "*Leket M'Hanhagos V'Hora'os HaGaavad zt"l* [*Minchas Yitzchak*] *B'Inyanei Hilchos Shabbos*"), the *Ba'er Moshe* (*Kovetz Am HaTorah, Maharura Tinyana*, vol. 1, pg. 14 and 15), the *Shevet Halevi* (*teshuva* originally printed in *Orchos Shabbos* vol. 1, pg. 516:3 and later in *Shu"t Shevet Halevi* vol. 11:67, 3), Rav Ben Tzion Abba-Shaul (*Shu"t Ohr L'Tzion* vol. 2: Ch. 17, 6), and Rav Shmuel Auerbach (cited in *Orchos Shabbos* vol. 1: Ch. 2, footnote 76), who hold that placing the pot on the counter nowadays is akin to placing it on the floor in the olden days, as that is how cooked food is currently commonly served. As such, they maintain that once one does that, he may no longer perform *Chazara* as it was "*mevattel daato lehachzir*." Therefore, several *Poskim* opine that if one needs to place the cholent pot down on a counter in order to serve, it is preferable to do so only partially, while still supporting its weight in one's hand. In this manner the counter is only being utilized as an aide, and should therefore be *muttar l'divrei hakol*. See *Shvus Yitzchak* (ibid. pg. 161), *Kovetz Am HaTorah* (ibid.), *Kovetz Beis Talmud L'Horaah* (vol. 3:pg. 155, 22 citing the Karlsburger Rav, Rav Yechezkel Roth), and *Peninas HaShabbos* (vol. 1: Ch. 29, 2, pg. 506–507).

17 See *Mishnah Berurah* (253:55 and 56 and *Biur Halacha* ad loc. s.v. *v'daato* and *v'lo*), *Chazon Ish* (O.C. 37:12; who is even more lenient, allowing *Chazara* if the pot was placed on a table, even if one did not have specific intention *lehachzir*; however, it must be pointed out that *leshittaso*, on a practical level, as the *Chazon Ish* did not consider either a *blech* or *plata* to be considered *Garuf V'Katum*, this dispensation would not be so *nogeya*), *Me'or HaShabbos* (vol. 2, Ch. 10:4), *Shemiras Shabbos Kehilchasa* (new edition Ch. 1:21), and *Orchos Shabbos* (vol. 1, Ch. 2:43 and 47), as well as previous footnote.

18 See *Shu"t Yabia Omer* (vol. 10, O.C. 55, *Kovetz He'aros* on *Shu"t Rav Pe'alim*, O.C. vol. 3:44, 35), *Chazon Ovadiah* (*Shabbos* vol. 4, *Mevashel* 14, pg. 362), and *Yalkut Yosef* (*Shabbos* vol. 3:318, 43, pg. 187 and *Kitzur Shulchan Aruch*, O.C. 318:46), based on the *Beis Yosef* (O.C. 318:18; who is *medayek* from the *lashon* of the *Rambam*), *Radbaz* (ibid.), and *Chida* (*Machzik Bracha*, O.C. 318:7). This is also stated as the basic Sefardic *psak* by the *Ben Ish Chai* (*Shu"t Rav Pe'alim* vol. 3, O.C. 44[b]).

However, it should be noted that the *Ben Ish Chai* and later, Rav Ben Tzion Abba-Shaul[19] qualified this leniency, explaining that one should only rely on this *"L'tzorech Mitzva"*; otherwise, they maintain that one must take the pot off of the fire before ladling out. Interestingly, the *Tzitz Eliezer* maintains that Yeshiva *bochurim* raiding the cholent pot on a Friday night in order to learn, qualifies as *L'tzorech Mitzva*. Rav Ovadiah Yosef added that if the *bochurim* in question were trying to save time in order to hurry back to their learning, then certainly even the *Ben Ish Chai* would agree that it is considered *L'tzorech Mitzva* to allow serving while still on the fire.[20]

When in Bnei Brak...

A third opinion is that of the *Chazon Ish*. His was a dissenting opinion regarding the permissibility of relying on using a *blech*, explaining that since a *blech* does not sufficiently lessen the fire's heat level, as well as merely acting as a cover for the fire, it is not considered a true covered flame. Therefore, he held that one may not put the pot back on a *blech* on Shabbos. Consequently, he maintained that in order to keep cholent hot after serving, it is permissible to scoop out cholent while the pot was still on the fire, provided that the cholent was fully cooked and one took care not to actively stir the pot. His brother-in-law, the Steipler Gaon, followed this as well.[21] According to this ruling, once the cholent is fully cooked, one need not take the pot off the fire in order to serve.

---

19 *Shu"t Rav Pe'alim* (ibid.) and *Shu"t Ohr L'Tzion* (vol. 2: Ch. 30, 15, pg. 238). Interestingly, the *Kaf Hachaim* (O.C. 318:171, 173, and 177) also seems to conclude stringently, akin to the Ashkenazic *psak*.

20 *Shu"t Tzitz Eliezer* (vol. 7:15) and *Shu"t Yabia Omer* (ibid.). This assessment fits well with the *Mishnah Berurah's* statement (*Biur Halacha* 342 s.v. *muttar bein*) that anything that is a *"Tzorech Shabbos,"* even if not truly necessary but rather simply adds *"oneg,"* is still considered a *"Tzorech Mitzva."*

21 *Chazon Ish* (O.C. 37:9, 11 and 15) and *Orchos Rabbeinu* (vol. 1, pg. 149; new edition vol. 1 pg. 280–281:16). There is precedent from a similar *shittah* of the *Avnei Nezer* (*Shu"t* O.C. 59; see also his *Eglei Tal*, *Meleches Ha'Ofeh* 17), who maintains that once the cholent is *Nisbashel Kol Tzorcho* and *Metztamek V'ra Lo*, *"yeish lismoch l'hetter"* to scoop out from the pot on the fire, that *"ikar*

Although, as mentioned previously, most contemporary Ashkenazic authorities did not allow one *lechatchilla* to scoop out of a hot pot while still on a *blech*, there is one scenario in which many contemporary authorities rule leniently (relying on the *Chazon Ish's shittah*): if the pot is too heavy to move off of the fire. A prime example of this would be the giant cholent pot found in many a Yeshiva kitchen.

Many decisors, including the *Minchas Yitzchak*, Rav Yosef Shalom Elyashiv, Rav Shmuel *Halevi* Wosner, and Rav Moshe Sternbuch, allow one to scoop and serve the cholent without taking the pot off the *blech* if it is too heavy to move off the flame. However, it should be noted that Rav Moshe Feinstein was not inclined to rule leniently in scooping out cholent from a pot on the fire, even if the pot was too heavy to move.[22] Rather, he mandated that several people move it together in order to properly serve the cholent from off of the fire, or at least move the pot to a place on the *blech* that does not have fire directly underneath it and

---

l'halacha" it is not considered *Maygis*. The Steipler Gaon is quoted (*Orchos Rabbeinu* ibid.) as remarking that since he is *machmir* regarding *Shehiya* and *Chazara* (as per his brother-in-law, the *Chazon Ish*), he must be lenient regarding *Maygis*; otherwise he would not be able to fulfill the Mitzva of eating *Chamin* on Shabbos.

22 See *Shu"t Minchas Yitzchak* (vol. 5:127, 6), *Shvus Yitzchak* (Hilchos Bishul Ch. 41:2, 2, citing Rav Elyashiv's opinion), *Shu"t Shevet Halevi* (vol. 10:11, 2), *Shu"t Teshuvos V'Hanhagos* (vol. 1:207, 4), *Shu"t Az Nidberu* (vol. 5:13, 1), *Shu"t Tzitz Eliezer* (vol. 7:15, 5), *Shu"t Mishnah Halachos* (vol. 7:51), and *Shemiras Shabbos Kehilchasa* (new edition Ch. 1:32). Rav Moshe Feinstein's dissenting *machmir* opinion is found in *Shu"t Igros Moshe* (O.C. vol. 4:74, *Bishul* 9 and 11). [Thanks are due to Rav Yitzchok Dovid Frankel and R' Yochonon Donn for pointing out several important nuances.] Quite fascinatingly, it turns out that concerning the simple-sounding, yet quite complicated *halachic* topic of serving cholent on Shabbos, the perceived "*Meikil*," Rav Moshe Feinstein, who allows *Chazara* onto a *blech*, is actually the most *machmir*, as even regarding an industrial-sized cholent pot, he only allows the cholent to be served when it is off of the direct fire. On the other hand, the perceived "*Machmir*," the *Chazon Ish*, who in practice forbids *Chazara* on Shabbos nowadays, is practically more *meikil*, as *lemaaseh*, once the cholent is fully cooked, he allows it to be scooped out and served from the pot while still on the fire. Food for thought.

there is no chance of the cholent cooking further if it remains there (even if that part of the *blech* is still hot), and serve from there.

Although these procedures and nuances may seem complicated, they are but a small sampling of the numerous intricate *halachos* that pertain to the prohibition of cooking on Shabbos. It behooves us all to make sure that we are serving our cholent in the proper *halachic* way, as aside from the earthly reward of eating cholent on Shabbos, the taste of its Mitzva is eternal.

Chapter 16

The Chicken Bone 'n' Cholent Commotion

APPROXIMATELY FORTY YEARS AGO, SEVERAL students attending a Yeshiva in Eretz Yisrael engaged in a typical Shabbos nocturnal activity: the raiding of the Yeshiva cholent pot.[1] Yet, as these *bochurim* followed the proper laws of scooping cholent out from a pot on Shabbos,[2] their innocuous actions on this Friday night unwittingly sparked a *halachic* firestorm between two of the preeminent *Gedolei Hador*, Rav Moshe Feinstein and Rav Shlomo Zalman Auerbach, *zichronom l'vracha*.

Them Bones...

While partaking of their savory stew, these *bochurim* realized that although the cholent itself was fully cooked (one of the prerequisites for allowing cholent to be returned to the fire *lechatchilla*[3] in order to be

---

1 Which, interestingly, as mentioned in the previous chapter, "The Great Cholent Challenge," the *Tzitz Eliezer*, and agreed to by Rav Ovadiah Yosef, maintains that as long as it was done to help the *bochurim* learn, qualifies as *L'tzorech Mitzva* (!) This assessment fits well with the *Mishnah Berurah's* statement that anything that is a *"Tzorech Shabbos,"* even if not truly necessary but rather simply adds *"oneg,"* is still considered a *"Tzorech Mitzva."*

2 As detailed at length in the previous chapter.

3 An extensive treatment on the conditions permitting the serving and returning of cholent to the flame is discussed in great length in the previous chapter, "The Great Cholent Challenge."

served to the whole Yeshiva on Shabbos morning), the chicken bones inside the cholent were not yet thoroughly cooked. Uncertain whether this changed the cholent's status and possibly affected its permissibility to be served, they decided to send their question after Shabbos to two of the foremost *Gedolei Hador*, Rav Moshe Feinstein, who resided in America, and Rav Shlomo Zalman Auerbach, who lived in Yerushalayim, who took opposing positions as to bones' *halachic* status pertaining to the cholent.

Bones Are Inedible

Rav Moshe Feinstein maintained that since any bones found inside a cholent are not actually meant to be eaten, but are rather placed there as a filler, their presence will not adversely affect the cholent's status.[4] This means that as long as the edible part of the cholent is fully cooked, one is allowed to scoop out cholent and return it to the *blech* (via proper *Chazara*). He also does not consider sucking the marrow out from bones as eating, as no one would eat the bones themselves. Consequently, the fact that the bones were not cooked is entirely irrelevant, according to his view.[5]

Let Them Eat Bones...

Rav Shlomo Zalman Auerbach, on the other hand, took the opposing viewpoint. He agreed with Rav Moshe that the presence of meat bones from cattle, which are very thick and quite inedible, do not *halachically* influence the cholent's status. Yet, he stressed that the question asked by the *bochurim* was regarding chicken bones, which, in Eretz Yisrael are commonly placed in the cholent *to be eaten* along with the rest of the

---

4   Obviously, Rav Moshe and the other *Poskim* mentioned in this chapter offer much more *halachic* rationale and proofs to their opinions. However, the main thrusts of their views are presented here. Regarding the marrow bones, Rav Moshe maintains that they are akin to a vessel which simply holds the marrow, which people need to break open to suck out the marrow, and therefore are not included in the *Bishul* prohibition as no one would eat the bones themselves.

5   *Shu"t Igros Moshe* (O.C. vol. 4:76, 1 and 77).

cholent. He explained that this category of edible "soft" chicken bones (wings, legs, etc.) are considered like part and parcel of the cholent, and therefore must also be fully cooked to allow one to return the pot to the fire after serving.[6]

Bare Bones Cholent

Both of these luminaries later shared correspondence on this topic, writing responsa to each other, each citing *halachic* rationale in support of his opinion. Rav Moshe was astounded to hear that anyone would eat any type of bone,[7] and ruled that in America where this is entirely unheard of, one would not need to take the bones' cooking status into account regarding the permissibility of *Chazara*. Yet, he concluded, regarding those who live in Eretz Yisrael, he deferred to Rav Shlomo Zalman's ruling, as he was the "*Baal Horaah Gadol*" of Eretz Yisrael.

However, this does not mean that Rav Moshe and Rav Shlomo Zalman actually agreed with each other's rulings. On the contrary:

- According to Rav Shlomo Zalman, even if most do not eat chicken bones as part of their cholent in America, it should still be an *issur Derabbanan* to perform *Chazara* while there still are uncooked chicken bones in the cholent. Since he viewed them as edible, even if no one would actually eat them, by performing *Chazara* it would be considered a *psik reisha* (an act that will inevitably lead to a forbidden result) of further cooking them on Shabbos.
- According to Rav Moshe, technically speaking, even in Eretz Yisrael, even if most people do eat the chicken bones, one would still be allowed to do *Chazara*, as he held that only the extremely

---

6   Rav Shlomo Zalman's opinion is cited briefly in *Shemiras Shabbos Kehilchasa* (old print Ch. 1:18 and footnote 56; new edition Ch. 1:20, 1 and footnote 56); and fully in *Shu"t Minchas Shlomo* (*Kama* 6 and *Tinyana* 11),

7   Rav Moshe's astonishment is quite understandable to this author. As an American expatriate, this author had quite a culture shock upon his arrival in Eretz Yisrael many moons ago, attending the largest Yeshiva in the world, and finding the cholent serving bowl filled with chicken bones!

indigent would enjoy eating any sort of bones, even if they are soft. Consequently, they still would not truly be considered a food item in his opinion.[8]

Boning Up on *Chazara*

Several other contemporary authorities later addressed this issue, with some ruling like Rav Moshe's view, including Rav Chaim Pinchas Scheinberg, Rav Moshe Aryeh Freund, Rav Yisrael Yaakov Fischer, Rav Meir Bransdorfer, the Strasbourger Rav, and the *Megillas Sefer*,[9] while others, including the *Minchas Yitzchak*, and Rav Moshe Sternbuch, followed Rav Shlomo Zalman's opinion.[10] Most agreed that the *halacha* would depend on whether chicken bones are commonly eaten as an essential part of the cholent served in the location of the questioner.[11]

---

8   It is only due to the great deference and honor that these contemporary *Gedolim* showed for each other, exuding from their *teshuvos*, that allows such a *halachic* conclusion.

9   Rav Chaim Pinchas Scheinberg's relevant *teshuva* was printed in *Kovetz Zichron L'HaGaon Rav Betzalel Zolty* (pg. 643; Rav Shlomo Zalman's later *teshuva* printed in *Shu"t Minchas Shlomo, Tinyana* 11, was addressed to him), Rav Moshe Aryeh Freund's opinion is printed in his *haskama* to *Me'or HaShabbos* (vol. 1) and in *Mara D'Shmaatsah* (123), *Shu"t Even Yisrael* (vol. 8:16), Rav Meir Bransdorfer's opinion is cited in *Me'or HaShabbos* (vol. 2, pg. 241), *Shu"t Kinyan Torah B'Halacha* (vol. 3:37, 5), and *Megillas Sefer* (on *Hilchos Shabbos*, 3, 22 s.v. *ululei*). The *Megillas Sefer* maintains that since no one actually cooks plain edible bones by themselves to eat, but rather exclusively as part of a cholent, this proves that they are not really considered a food item. See also *Shu"t Avnei Yashpei* (vol. 1:84, footnote, and endnote from Rav Mordechai Gross on pg. 400).

10 *Shu"t Minchas Yitzchak* (vol. 8:25) and *Shu"t Teshuvos V'Hanhagos* (vol. 1:217) Yet, there are differences. The *Minchas Yitzchak* ruled entirely like Rav Shlomo Zalman, while Rav Moshe Sternbuch, although citing a strong rationale to permit *Chazara* on chicken bones, as a *tziruf* that the chicken bones should certainly already be cooked *kdei maachal Ben Derosoi* (which is at least a third- or half-cooked) at the time when the rest of the cholent is fully cooked (see *Biur Halacha* 318:4 s.v. *afilu*), similar to Rav Fischer's *psak*, nevertheless concludes that optimally, one should be *machmir*.

Additionally, several authorities rule stringently if one personally eats his chicken bones as part of his cholent, even if it is uncommon in his locale.[12] For example, Rav Shmuel *Halevi* Wosner, although ruling similarly to Rav Moshe in a published responsum,[13] later qualified his ruling that if someone actually does eat the bones in the cholent, *Chazara* would be prohibited for him until they are thoroughly cooked.[14]

Bone-Appetit?

This ruling of Rav Moshe's is quite interesting, as the upshot is that whether or not one can do *Chazara* on his pot of cholent might just depend on where he is living. If one would be living in America, even if he personally might like to eat chicken bones in his cholent, he would still follow the *minhag* there. And even though (in his mind) his edible chicken bones were not fully cooked, he would still be allowed to take some Friday night "*To'ameha*" cholent[15] and return it to the

---

11   See *Toras HaMalachos* (vol. 2, *Ofeh*, 22) and *Me'or HaShabbos* (vol. 2, Ch. 9:10) at length, as well as *Orchos Shabbos* (vol. 1, Ch. 1:33 and footnote 75) and *Peninas HaShabbos* (*Hilchos Shehiya* and *Chazara*, vol. 2, Ch. 40).

12   See *Shu"t Az Nidberu* (vol. 9:13, 1 and vol. 14:36), who rules that this *din* depends on the individual person's intent whether he planned on eating bones (retracting from an earlier stringent ruling in *Shu"t Az Nidberu* vol. 3:12, 1). Rav Nissim Karelitz (*Chut Shani* on *Hilchos Shabbos* vol. 2, Ch. 26, pg. 107 s.v. *atzamos*) also defines this rule as depending on whether people commonly eat chicken bones in their cholent; however, he disagrees with Rav Moshe regarding sucking on marrow bones, which he considers akin to eating. He also differentiates regarding someone who personally eats the chicken bones, as he maintains that *Chazara* is *assur* for him until those chicken bones are fully cooked. Rav Ben Tzion Abba-Shaul (*Shu"t Ohr L'Tzion* vol. 2, Ch. 17:9) also makes a distinction regarding covering the pot on the fire, based on whether or not one's intent is to eat the chicken bones in the cholent.

13   *Shu"t Shevet Halevi* (vol. 3:93, 2).

14   *Kovetz M'Beis Levi* (vol. 6, *Dinei Shehiya V'Chazara* 13).

15   As discussed in the previous chapter, there is an *inyan* of tasting the Shabbos food before Shabbos *l'kavod Shabbos*, to ensure that it is properly cooked, as well as over Shabbos itself. This is referred to as "*To'ameha.*"

fire. Whereas someone living in Eretz Yisrael who might personally detest chicken bones in his cholent, nonetheless, out of deference to Rav Shlomo Zalman's *psak*, would need to make sure that they are fully cooked before partaking of (and performing *Chazara* with) his weekly gastronomic delight.

One effect is abundantly clear. Although two of the greatest *Gedolim* of recent history had quite a big difference of opinion on a topic that has great ramifications for many of us, nevertheless, the honor and respect they showed for each other while agreeing to disagree, seems, in this author's estimation, to jump off the written page and should stand out as lesson for us all—no bones about it.[16]

---

16 The possible distinction between "hard" and "soft" bones potentially has ramifications in other areas of *halacha*, including *bitul issur* and the kashrus status of gelatin. This topic is discussed in the chapters titled "The Coca-Cola Kashrus Controversy" and "Genetically Engineered Meat."

Chapter 17

The *Halachic* Adventures of the Potato

ALTHOUGH NOWADAYS WE ALL TAKE the potato for granted, it actually has a fascinating history: one which not only has impacted *halacha*, but due to its travels, enshrined its "discoverer," Sir Francis Drake, as one of the *Chassidei Umos Ha'Olam* (righteous gentiles of the world)![1] In this chapter, we will explore the *halachic* impact the potato has made in several different areas.

Ever since first "making the scene" via the victorious Spaniards shipping them from the conquered Incas to their own colonies and armies throughout Europe in the late 1500s, the ubiquitous potato has been a considerable mainstay on the world stage. From circumnavigating the globe with Sir Francis Drake, to famed French physician Antoine Parmentier waxing poetic about this nightshade's nutritional value, to Queen Marie Antoinette wearing a headdress of potato flowers at

---

1 According to the *Tiferes Yisrael* (*Avos* Ch. 3: Mishnah 14, *Boaz* Beg. 1), this act by Sir Francis Drake of introducing potatoes to the European continent, merited him to be classified as one of the *Chassidei Umos Ha'Olam*, as over the centuries potatoes have saved countless lives from starvation. Others included on this exclusive list include Johannes Guttenberg, who invented the printing press and thus enabled the dissemination of Torah on a mass scale, Johann Reuchlin, who defended the Talmud from being burned in numerous debates against the apostate Pfefferkorn, and Edward Jenner, creator of the modern smallpox vaccine, saving "tens upon tens of thousands" of people. Thanks are due to Rabbi Elchanan Shoff for pointing out this fascinating source.

a fancy ball (obviously while she still had her head), by the 1770s the potato had become a staple crop throughout Europe.

What other vegetable has been credited with helping facilitate such diverse events as the Industrial Revolution, the Great Irish Famine of 1845 (due to their susceptibility to blight), Russia's proclivity for vodka, a U.S. vice president's public spelling debacle, and a themed toy version of itself so popular that it was inducted into the National Toy Hall of Fame? Yet, aside from the tuber's worldly presence, it also holds a unique place in the annals of *halacha*, and not just by its significance in latkes, cholent, Pesach cooking, and fresh hot potato kugel.

Bracha Brouhaha—Mind Your K's and T's

If one were to take a poll as to the potato's proper *bracha* the vast majority would respond that since the potato is a vegetable and grows and gets its nourishment from the ground, its proper *bracha* is "*Borei Pri Ha'adama*."[2] Yet, although this seems clear-cut, interestingly, there are those who make a different blessing: *Shehakol*, usually reserved for food items not naturally grown.

The source of this remarkable ruling seems to be an enigmatic translation by the *Aruch*, Rav Nosson M'Romi (literally, of Rome; d. 1106), a contemporary of *Rashi*.[3] When referring to the proper *bracha* of mushrooms and other food items that do not actually get their nourishment from the earth and consequentially their *bracha* being *Shehakol*,[4] the *Aruch* translates them as "***Tartuffel***." Not familiar with the archaic word, the famed *Yismach Moshe* maintained that the *Aruch* must have been referring to "***Kartuffel***," colloquially known as the potato.[5] He added that the great Rav Naftali of Ropshitz made a *Shehakol* on potatoes as well.

---

2 *Brachos* 35a and *Tur* and *Shulchan Aruch* (O.C. 203).

3 See *Rashi* (*Shabbos* 13b s.v. *ha'ochel*), where he quotes the *Aruch*.

4 See *Brachos* 40b.

5 *Aruch* (*Erech Petter*), cited in *Tehilla L'Moshe* (*hakdama* to *Yismach Moshe al Tanach*, vol. 3:pg. 12a). See *She'arim Metzuyanim B'Halacha* (118: end 4).

This rationale is also found in several other *sefarim*, and there are prominent authorities who therefore made a *Shehakol bracha* on potatoes.[6] In fact, Sanz, Bobov (which is a branch of the Sanz dynasty), and Kamarna Chassidim among others, follow this custom to this day.[7]

The Klausenberger Rebbe, the Tzehlemer Rav, and Rav Shraga Feivel Schneebalg staunchly defend the practice of making a *Shehakol* on potatoes.[8] The Klausenberger Rebbe adds a reason to do so: since one can make flour out of potatoes and potatoes satiate and are filling, it might be considered in the same category of rice, whose proper *bracha* is *Mezonos*.[9] The rule is that if one is unsure what the proper *bracha*

---

6   *Likutei Mahariach* (vol. 1, *Seder Birkas Hanehenin* pg. 182b), *Maharam Ash* (*Zichron Yehuda* pg. 23b s.v. *al esrog*), *Shulchan HaTahor* (204:3 and *Zer Zehav* 2), *Otzar Hachaim* (*Parashas Vayelech, Mitzvas Birkas Hanehenin*), *Pischa Zuta* (*Birkas HaPesach* 12:3), *Minhagei Kamarna* (pg. 25:97).

7   An interesting upshot of this *shittah* is that generally speaking, these Chassidim, following the *Yismach Moshe*, will use a vegetable other than a potato for *Karpas* at the Pesach Seder as they hold it is not a true *Ha'adama* vegetable. Thanks are due to Rabbi Nosson Wimer of Kiryat Sanz, Netanya, for pointing this out.

8   *Shu"t Divrei Yatziv* (O.C. vol. 1:82), *Shu"t Migdalos Merkachim* (O.C. 18), and *Shu"t Shraga HaMeir* (vol. 6:119).

9   There is precedent for such rationale regarding *"dochen"* and other satiating foods from *Talmidei Rabbeinu Yonah* (*Brachos* 26a in the *Rif's* pagination s.v. *v'gaon* and *hinei*) and the *Shiltei Hagiborim* (ad loc. 4). Although there is some debate as whether our rice is the rice mentioned by the Gemara and what the proper *bracha* should be [see *Biur Halacha* (208:7 s.v. *ad*) for a synopsis of opinions], and the *Bach* (O.C. 208, *se'if* 7 s.v. *ha'ochel*), *Shulchan Aruch Harav* (O.C. vol. 1, *Seder Birchos Hanehenin* Ch. 1:11), *Kitzur Shulchan Aruch* (52:17), and *Likutei Mahariach* (vol. 1, *Seder Birchos Hanehenin* pg. 183a) write that a *Yarei Shamayim* should only eat it as part of bread meal (and therefore not to have to make a *bracha* on it), and if not, should make a *Shehakol*, and the *Kaf Hachaim* (O.C. 208:38 and 39) concludes whatever *minhag* one follows is fine, nevertheless, the vast majority of *Poskim* rule that the proper *bracha* to make on our rice is indeed *Mezonos* (but its after-*bracha* is still *Borei Nefashos* as it is not one of the five grains). See *Maaseh Rav* (71), *Birkei Yosef* (O.C. 208:6), *Ben Ish Chai* (Year 1, *Parashas Pinchas* 18), *Aruch Hashulchan* (O.C. 208:21),

on a food item is, a *Shehakol* should be made. He therefore opines that potatoes should also be *Shehakol*.

On the other hand, it must be noted that the Steipler Gaon strongly disagreed with this reasoning, maintaining that the Gemara[10] expressly singled out rice for this special *halacha* of making a *bracha* of *Mezonos*, and that it therefore does not apply to any other foods, no matter how satiating they may be.[11]

R' Chaim Safrin, the Kamarna Rebbe of Yerushalayim's son, personally told this author a similar reasoning to the Klausenberger Rebbe's of why Kamarna Chassidim make a *Shehakol*.[12] He added that anyway if one makes a *Shehakol* on any food he is *yotzei b'dieved*, so *kol shekein* one may do so by a potato when many great *Rabbanim* have said to do so.

However, the facts do not seem to corroborate that potatoes should be classified in the same category of mushrooms, as potatoes not only grow and root in the ground, but they also get their nourishment from the ground, as opposed to mushrooms and their ilk. Several contemporary authorities point out that it is highly unlikely, if not outright impossible, for the *Aruch*, who lived in Europe in the eleventh century, to have been referring to "*Kartuffel*" (potatoes) as the proper translation for mushrooms, as tubers were unknown on that continent until almost five hundred years later![13] Therefore, the vast majority of

---

Mishnah Berurah (ad loc. 25 and *Shaar Hatziyun* 31), *Shu"t Igros Moshe* (E.H. vol. 1:114, end s.v. *b'inyan habracha*), *Halichos HaGr"a U'Minhagav* (pg. 167), *Dinim V'Hanhagos Chazon Ish* (Ch. 7:1), *Shoneh Halachos* (vol. 1, 208:24), *Shu"t Ohr L'Tzion* (vol. 2, Ch. 14:22), *Yalkut Yosef* (*Kitzur Shulchan Aruch*, O.C. 208:10; he adds an interesting mnemonic to remember the *halacha*: *Amen—Orez, Mezonos, Nefashos*), and Rav Mordechai Eliyahu's *Darchei Halacha* glosses to the *Kitzur Shulchan Aruch* (52:18).

10 *Brachos* (36b-37a).

11 *Kraina D'Igresa* (vol. 2:88 s.v. *v'hadavar*).

12 See *Shulchan HaTahor* (204:3 and *Zer Zehav* 2), *Otzar Hachaim* (*Parashas Vayelech, Mitzvas Birkas Hanehenin*), and *Minhagei Kamarna* (pg. 25:97).

13 *Shu"t B'tzeil Hachochma* (vol. 4:83), *Shu"t Mishnah Halachos* (vol. 6:39 and 40), and many of the *Poskim* whose *teshuvos* on topic are printed in the recent

authorities rule that the proper blessing on the potato is indeed *"Borei Pri Ha'adama."*[14]

Kitniyos Conflict

Another interesting issue related to the potato is its exclusion from the Ashkenazic prohibition of eating *kitniyos* on Pesach. It is well known that the actual prohibition of *chometz* on Pesach pertains exclusively to leavened products produced from the five major grains: wheat, barley, oats, spelt, or rye.[15] Yet, already in place from the times

---

Teshuvos HaPoskim (11; pg. 143–170). See *Shu"t Igros Moshe* (O.C. vol. 3:63), who also defines the potato as such. Interestingly, although another famous Ashkenazic Rishon, the Maharil (*Hilchos Erev Yom Kippur, Seudah Hamafsekes*, 8; cited by the *Elyah Rabba*, O.C. 608:9, and *Kaf Hachaim*, ad loc. 41), quoting his *Rebbeim*, mentions that a good way to cool off and get nutrition before a fast day is by soaking a so-called *"erd-apple,"* another common colloquialism used for the potato, in water and eating it, he could not possibly have been referring to our potatoes which were not extant in Europe for another several hundred years. Additionally, he refers to it as a *"pri,"* and not a vegetable. As an aside, soaked raw potatoes also does not seem to be one of the usual manners which potatoes are nowadays enjoyed.

14   Including the Yaavetz (*Siddur Beis Yaakov* pg. 108b, *Birkas Hanehenin, Os Kuf*: 18), *Shu"t Imrei Yosher* (vol. 2:113, 2), *Likutei Mahariach* (vol. 1, *Seder Birkas Hanehenin* pg. 182b; who cites both sides but concludes that potatoes are indeed *Ha'adama*), *Mishnah Berurah* (202:40), *Kraina D'Igresa* (vol. 2:88), *Shu"t Igros Moshe* (O.C. vol. 1:60), *Shu"t B'tzeil Hachochma* (vol. 4:83), *Shu"t Rivevos Efraim* (vol. 3:124), *Shu"t Mishnah Halachos* (vol. 6:39 and 40), *Shu"t Az Nidberu* (vol. 11:48), *Orchos Chaim* (Spinka; 204:2), *Darchei Chaim V'Shalom* (Munkacs; 293), *Shvilei Dovid* (O.C. Klalei Brachos, 5, Ch. 2:14), *Yalkut Yosef* (Kitzur Shulchan Aruch O.C. 203:10), *Shalmei Nissan* (on *Perek Keitzad Mevorchin, He'aros* 99:pg. 314–315), and Rav Asher Weiss, in personal conversation. See also the recent *Teshuvos HaPoskim* (11; pg. 143–170) who prints the actual *teshuvos* from many contemporary *Poskim*, including Rav Shlomo Zalman Auerbach, whom the vast majority conclude that the proper *bracha* on the potato is indeed *Ha'adama*.

15   *Mishnah Pesachim* (Ch. 3:1), Gemara *Pesachim* (42a-43a), *Rambam* (*Hilchos Chometz U'Matzah* Ch. 5:1). These are also the only grains with which one may fulfill his obligation of *Achilas Matzah*; see Mishnah in *Pesachim* (35a),

of the Rishonim,[16] there was an Ashkenazic[17] prohibition against eating

---

Rambam (*Hilchos Chometz U'Matzah* Ch. 6:4), and *Tur* and *Shulchan Aruch* (O.C. 453:1).

16 See for example *Mordechai* (*Pesachim* 588), *SMa"K* (222), *Raavad* (*Hilchos Chometz U'Matzah* Ch. 5:1), *Hagahos Maimoniyos* (ad loc.), *Ohr Zarua* (vol. 2:256, pg. 59, third column), Rabbeinu Manoach (Glosses to the *Rambam* ad loc.; cited in *Biur Halacha* 453:1 s.v. *v'yeish*), *Maharil* (*Minhagim, Hilchos Maachalos Assuros B'Pesach* 16), *Terumas Hadeshen* (113 and 133), *Ritva* (*Pesachim* 35a s.v. *hani*), and *Tur* (O.C. 453). Not that they all upheld the prohibition of *kitniyos*, but they all mention it. See also the *Pri Megadim's* Introduction to *Hilchos Pesach* (vol. 2, Ch. 2:6) and the Chida's *Tov Ayin* (18).

17 The *Rambam* (*Hilchos Chometz U'Matzah* Ch. 5:1) explicitly permitted *kitniyos*, the *Ritva* (*Pesachim* 35a s.v. *hani*) writes that the "*minhag pashut b'chol Sefard*" is to eat cooked rice on Pesach, and even the *Beis Yosef* (O.C. 453) refers to it as a strictly Ashkenazic issue. Interestingly, and although not *me'ikar hadin*, there are some Sefardim who are stringent as well, especially with rice; on this topic, see *Knesses Hagedolah* (O.C. 453, *Hagahos al HaTur* 2; citing the Mahari Halevi 38), *Pri Chodosh* (ibid.), the Chida's *Tov Ayin* (9:6), *Shulchan Melachim* (O.C. 453:1), *Ben Ish Chai* (Year 1, *Parashas Tzav* 41), *Shu"t Rav Pe'alim* (vol. 3, O.C. 30), *Kaf Hachaim* (O.C. 453:10), *Shu"t Yabia Omer* (vol. 5, O.C. 37:5), *Shu"t Yechaveh Daas* (vol. 1:9), *Shu"t Ohr L'Tzion* (vol. 3, Ch. 8:15), Rav Mordechai Eliyahu's *Darchei Halacha* glosses to the *Kitzur Shulchan Aruch* (117:2), *Chazon Ovadiah* (*Hilchos Pesach*, pg. 82–86), and *Yalkut Yosef* (*Kitzur Shulchan Aruch* O.C. 453:1). The *Ben Ish Chai* adds that in his opinion one who is *machmir* not to eat rice on Pesach may not cook nor even serve rice to someone who does. [However, see *Sdei Chemed* (*Maareches Chometz U'Matzah* 6:6) and *Kaf Hachaim* (O.C. 453:16) for alternate views.] The *Kaf Hachaim* (ad loc. 10) cites the *Pekudas Elazar* (51, pg. 64b) who writes that in his day, the Sefardim in Yerushalayim were *noheg* to prohibit *kitniyos*. [However, the *Kaf Hachaim* adds that by his time that was no longer the case, but rather each *Kehillah* kept their own *minhagim*.] In a similar vein, seemingly regarding Sefardim and *kitniyos*, Rav Avraham Azulai, ancestor of the Chida, in his Kabbalistic *sefer Maaseh Chosheiv* (which was first printed from a manuscript in 5752; end *Rimon* 13, *B'Inyan Chag HaPesach V'Yetzias Mitzraim* s.v. *matzasi*) writes briefly that he found written in the name of the Arizal, "*Shekol hamishamer Pesach karui b'chol inyanav shehu to'eles l'nefesh l'chol hashana, v'Hachaveirim* (a term generally used to refer to the Arizal and his *talmidim*) *hayu machmirin*

kitniyos (legumes; ostensibly based on its semi-literal translation: "little things") on Pesach, except in times of famine or grave need.[18] Although several authorities opposed this prohibition,[19] nonetheless it is binding on Ashkenazic Jewry in full force, even today.[20]

---

k'minhag Ashkenazim, ad kan matzati." Thanks are due to to my *talmid*, R' Yitzchak Rubin, for pointing out this fascinating source.

18 *Chayei Adam* (vol. 2, 127:1; and *Nishmas Adam, Hilchos Pesach* Question 20), *Mor U'Ketziah* (beg. 453), *Shu"t Teshuva Mei'ahava* (259), *Shu"t Chasam Sofer* (O.C. 122), the *Maharatz Chiyus' Kuntress Minchas Kina'os* (6; printed in *Kol Sifrei Maharatz Chiyus*, vol. 2, pg. 1029), *Mishnah Berurah* (453:7 and *Shaar Hatziyun* 6), and *Aruch Hashulchan* (ad loc. end 5). For a discussion on what is considered great need in order to allow *kitniyos*, see *Shu"t Zeicher Yehosef* (O.C. 157), *Shu"t Shoel U'Meishiv* (Mahadura Tinyana vol. 4:128) and *Shu"t Divrei Malkiel* (vol. 1, 28:20). On the other hand, the Vilna Gaon is quoted (*Maaseh Rav* 184) as being extremely *makpid* with *kitniyos*, even *"b'shnas b'tzores."*

19 As mentioned previously, the *Rambam* (*Hilchos Chometz U'Matzah* Ch. 5:1) explicitly permitted *kitniyos*. See also *Beis Yosef* (beg. O.C. 453), quoting Rabbeinu Yechiel, as well as Rabbeinu Yerucham, who called the *kitniyos* prohibition a *"minhag shtus*, ridiculous custom." The prohibition is also strongly rejected by the *Tur* (O.C. 453), who writes that abstaining from rice and *kitniyos* on Pesach is a *"chumrah yeseirah, v'lo nahagu kein."* The Yaavetz (*Mor U'Ketziah* beg. 453), quoting his father, the great *Chacham Tzvi*, famously declared that if he had the ability to cancel the *kitniyos* prohibition he would, as it mostly affects the poor. The controversial *sefer Shu"t Besamim Rosh* (348) even posits that the *kitniyos* prohibition was started by Karaites (!) and should not be followed. On the other hand, several authorities, including the *Beis Meir* (O.C. 453), *Shaarei Teshuva* (ad loc. 1), and Maharsham (*Daas Torah* ad loc. 1) counter his words, with the Maharsham emphatically declaring that *"ain lanu ela minhageinu, v'chalilah lishmoa eilav."* He then cites the Maharil (*Minhagim, Hilchos Maachalos Assuros B'Pesach* 16, quoting the *Maharash*; also cited by the *Shaarei Teshuva*) that anyone who transgresses the prohibition of *kitniyos, "d'kol d'gazru Rabbanan ha'over alav chayav misah, v'over al lo sasur min hadavar asher yorucha."*

20 *Rema* (O.C. 453:1 and *Darchei Moshe* ad loc. 2), *Levush* (ad loc. 1), *Bach* (ad loc.) *Pri Chodosh* (ad loc. 1; he cites a *mekor* from the Gemara—*Pesachim* 40b), Vilna Gaon (*Biur HaGr"a* ad loc. and *Maaseh Rav* 184; citing the same source), *Shulchan Aruch Harav* (O.C. 453:3–5), *Chayei Adam* (vol. 2, 127:1), *Shaarei*

Although referred to slightly differently by our great luminaries—e.g., the *Kitzur Shulchan Aruch* references the *kitniyos* restriction as an *"issur,"* the *Mishnah Berurah* as a *"chumrah,"* the *Aruch Hashulchan* as a *"geder,"* Rav Tzvi Pesach Frank as a *"gezeira,"* Rav Moshe Feinstein as a *"minhag,"* and the Klausenberger Rebbe as a *"takkanah,"* nonetheless, they all maintain that the *kitniyos* prohibition is compulsory on all Ashkenazic Jewry.[21] In fact, the *Aruch Hashulchan* avers that "once our forefathers have accepted this prohibition upon themselves, it is considered a *'geder m'din Torah'* and one who is lenient is testifying about himself that he has no fear of Heaven." He adds, echoing Shlomo *HaMelech's* wise words in *Koheles* regarding a *"poretz geder,"* that one who breaks this prohibition deserves to be bitten by a snake.[22]

Several reasons are given for the actual prohibition[23] including that *kitniyos* often grow in close proximity to grain; are commonly stored together with grain and actual *chometz* might actually end up mixed

---

Teshuva (ad loc. 1), *Kitzur Shulchan Aruch* (117:4), *Mishnah Berurah* (453:6 and *Biur Halacha* ad loc. s.v. *v'yeish*), and *Aruch Hashulchan* (453:4 and 5). See also the Maharsham's *Daas Torah* (ad loc.), the Chida's *Tov Ayin* (18), as well as the Maharatz Chiyus' *Kuntress Minchas Kina'os* (6; printed in *Kol Sifrei Maharatz Chiyus*, vol. 2, pg. 1029), *Shu"t Chasam Sofer* (O.C. 122), *Shu"t Tzemach Tzedek* (Hachadoshos; O.C. 56), *Shu"t Maamar Mordechai* (32), *Shu"t Maharam Brisk* (48), and *Shu"t Divrei Malkiel* (vol. 1:28), all of whom discuss the strength of this compulsory prohibition. Rav Elazar Flekles (*Shu"t Teshuva Mei'ahava*, vol. 2, on O.C. 459), prime disciple of the *Noda B'Yehuda*, avers rather strongly, that there is not a *Beis Din* in the world that can abolish the *kitniyos* prohibition, not even that of "Shmuel HaRamasi v'Eliyahu (HaNavi) u'Beis Dino, v'chol Gedolei Yisrael af imaheim," since it was already accepted *"b'chol arei Ashkenaz, Tzarfas, Polin-Gadol V'Kattan, Lita, Russia…Ungaren…,"* etc.

21 *Kitzur Shulchan Aruch* (117:4), *Mishnah Berurah* (453:6), *Aruch Hashulchan* (ad loc. 4 and 5), Rav Tzvi Pesach Frank (*Mikra'ei Kodesh*, *Pesach* vol. 2, 60:2), Rav Moshe Feinstein (*Shu"t Igros Moshe* O.C. vol. 3:63), and the Klausenberger Rebbe (*Shu"t Divrei Yatziv* O.C. vol. 2:196).

22 *Koheles* (Ch. 10:8).

23 See *Beis Yosef* and *Rema* (O.C. 473:1) and major commentaries, including the *Biur HaGr"a* (ad loc. 5), *Shulchan Aruch Harav* (ad loc. 3, 4, and 5), *Chok Yaakov*

inside the *kitniyos* container; cooked dishes made from grain and *kitniyos* look similar; and that *kitniyos* can likewise be ground up into flour—a "bread" of sorts can actually be made from them. Since there are many who will not be able to differentiate between them and their Biblically forbidden *chometz* counterparts, *kitniyos* were likewise prohibited.

A Hot Potato?

So how do our spuds measure up? It would seemingly be quite difficult for anyone to mix up potatoes with *chometz* grain, so that rationale to regard potatoes as *kitniyos* is out. But, potatoes can be and are made into potato flour and potato starch, and there are those who do bake potato "bread!" If so, why would potatoes *not* be considered *kitniyos*? According to this, shouldn't they be forbidden for Ashkenazim to partake of on *Pesach*?[24]

In fact, and not widely known, the *Chayei Adam* seemingly considered potatoes *kitniyos*, and the *Pri Megadim* mentioned that he knows of such a custom to prohibit potatoes on Pesach as a type of *kitniyos*.[25] However, the vast majority of authorities rule that potatoes are not any form of *kitniyos* and are permissible to all on *Pesach*.[26]

(ad loc. 5 and 6), *Shaarei Teshuva* (ad loc. 1), and *Mishnah Berurah* (ad loc. 6, and *Biur Halacha* ad loc. s.v. *v'yeish*).

24 This author was recently interviewed on the "Kashrus on the Air" radio show, discussing the topic of *kitniyos* and potatoes, as well as whether quinoa should be considered *kitniyos*. A recording of this show may be accessed at: https://soundcloud.com/jroot-radio/yosef-wikler-apr-07?in=jroot-radio/sets/kashrus-on-the-air.

25 The *Chayei Adam* (*Nishmas Adam*, *Hilchos Pesach*, Question 20) tells a *Maaseh Shehaya* that in the city of Fiyorda (Fürth), Germany in 5531–5532, due to starvation conditions their *Beis Din* allowed them to eat potatoes on Pesach those years, although they normally forbid it due to potato flour being produced there; see also *Chayei Adam* vol. 2, 127:1, where he avers that the biggest *kitniyos* issue is the potential for flour mix-up with grain flour. The *Pri Megadim* (O.C. 453, M.Z. 1) mentions that he knows of such a *minhag*, nevertheless the vast majority of *Poskim*, including the *Pri Megadim* himself (O.C. 464, E.A. 1) rule that potatoes are not considered *kitniyos*. See next footnote.

The Halachic Adventures of the Potato 215

One of the main reasons for this is that at the time when the Ashkenazic *Rishonim* established the decree prohibiting *kitniyos*, potatoes were completely unknown! It is possible that had they been readily available they might have found themselves on the "forbidden list" as well! Yet, since they were never included, as well as since they do not fit most of the *kitniyos* criteria, contemporary authorities could not add "new types" to the list.[27]

However, it must be noted that there are other important reasons as well why potatoes were excluded. Of the four criteria given for the

---

26 The vast majority of *Poskim*, including the *Pri Megadim* himself (O.C. 464, E.A. 1), rule that potatoes are not considered *kitniyos*. Others who explicitly write that potatoes are not *kitniyos* include the *Shu"t Sheilas Yaavetz* (vol. 2:147, 4 s.v. *u'vhiyosi*), *Shu"t Divrei Malkiel* (vol. 2: end 112; he adds an additional reason to be lenient: potato flour doesn't look like grain flour and has a different consistency, therefore mitigating potential mix-ups), *Shu"t Yad Aharon* (16:5), *Aruch Hashulchan* (O.C. 453:5; he adds that with the advent of potatoes one should never have to rely on the *hetter* of permitting *kitniyos b'shaas hadchak*), *Shu"t Levushei Mordechai* (O.C. vol. 1:127), *Kaf Hachaim* (O.C. 453:21), *Shu"t Igros Moshe* (O.C. vol. 3:63), *Halichos Shlomo* (ibid.), *Shu"t Vayaan Yosef* (*Mishpatecha L'Yaakov*, O.C. 41), and *Shu"t Chelkas Yaakov* (new edition, O.C. end 207). It is widely quoted that the famed *Divrei Chaim* of Sanz questioned how the *Chayei Adam* could possibly have forbidden potatoes on Pesach when his *sefer* is titled "*Chayei Adam*," literally "The Life of Man" and potatoes are one of the necessities of life.

27 *Shu"t Sheilas Yaavetz* (vol. 2:147, 4 s.v. *u'vhiyosi*), *Shu"t Levushei Mordechai* (O.C. vol. 1:127 s.v. *v'hinei*), *Shu"t Igros Moshe* (O.C. vol. 3:63), and *Shu"t Chelkas Yaakov* (new edition, O.C. end 207), similar to the rule set by the *Chok Yaakov* (O.C. 453:9). Others who cite this *sevara* include the *Melamed L'Ho'eel* (*Shu"t* vol. 1:87 and 88), and *Seridei Aish* (*Shu"t* vol. 2:37, 2; new edition vol. 1:50). The first mention of such a *sevara* seems to be the *Zeicher Yehosef* (*Shu"t* O.C. 157), who writes that *b'shaas hadchak* one may eat "*she'u'it*, green beans," on Pesach due to this logic. [However, it is important to note that he only utilized this *sevara* to be lenient in extenuating circumstances. Also, the *Shaarei Teshuva* (453:1) seemingly directly argues, writing simply that they are *kitniyos* and thereby prohibited.] See *Vayaged Moshe* (17:7) quoting the *Tiferes Shlomo* (*Ohel Shlomo* vol. 1, pg. 35), that we should give *hoda'ah* for the fact that potatoes were discovered after the *Gezeiras HaGaonim*.

Gezeira of *kitniyos*, potatoes only fit one—that they can be made into flour and a "bread" of sorts can be baked from them. No one would mix up a potato with a grain kernel![28]

As Rav Shlomo Zalman Auerbach noted, Klal Yisrael never accepted the *kitniyos* prohibition to include potatoes.[29]

Cooking Quarrel

The potato was viewed quite differently by many, respective of the time and place. For example, as noted previously, it was prized by French nobility in the 1770s. Yet, by the mid-1800s, tubers were

---

[28] See *Shu"t Levushei Mordechai* (O.C. vol. 1:127) and *Halichos Shlomo* (*Moadim* vol. 2, *Pesach* Ch. 4, *Dvar Halacha* 28). This is a very important factor, as the *Levushei Mordechai* writes that although there are several reasons mentioned for the *kitniyos* ban, the most important one is that *Kitnyos* look similar to grain and get mixed up. This would obviously exclude potatoes from the *kitniyos* category. To paraphrase the *Pri Megadim* (O.C. 464, E.A. 1), no one, not even a blind person, would mix up a potato with a grain kernel!

[29] *Halichos Shlomo* (*Moadim* vol. 2, *Pesach* Ch. 4, *Dvar Halacha* 28). However, Rav Shlomo Zalman personally was stringent with potato flour [starch] (ad loc. footnote 109). It is known that the *Badatz Eidah Hachareidis* of Yerushalayim were also stringent until the renowned *Minchas Yitzchak* became the *Ga'avad* and ruled that there was no reason to be *machmir*, even with potato starch. Other *Poskim* who explicitly permit potato starch on *Pesach* include the *Aryeh D'vei Ila'i* (*Shu"t, Kuntress Avnei Zikaron* 10, based on the *Pri Chodosh's hetter*—O.C. 461:2 regarding *matzah* meal), the *Levushei Mordechai* (*Shu"t* O.C. vol. 1:127) and *She'arim Metzuyanim B'Halacha* (117: end 7 s.v. *v'ugos*). See also *Shu"t Maharshag* (vol. 2, O.C. 119 s.v. *umetchilla*) who, as a side point to the main issue discussed, mentions as a *davar pashut* that there is no problem, even of *Maris Ayin*, regarding using potato flour on Pesach to bake. Thanks are due to R' Moshe Langer for pointing out this important source. On the other hand, although the *Arugas Habosem* (*Shu"t* vol. 2, O.C. 124) cites several *sevaros lehakel*, he nevertheless concludes that it is *assur*, based on the similarity of baking use of potato starch and *chometz*. Additionally, the *Chayei Adam's* stringent position on potatoes was based on the fact that "flour" can be made from it, and *leshittaso*, that is the biggest problem with *kitniyos*. See *Chayei Adam* (vol. 2, 127:1) and *Nishmas Adam* (*Hilchos Pesach*, Question 20).

considered peasant fare in many locales, including Ireland and Russia. This divergence of attitude actually has a *halachic* impact.

If a non-Jew cooks kosher food (from start to finish), it still might be prohibited for a Jew to consume it, based on the prohibition of *Bishul Akum*, literally, food cooked by a non-Jew.[30][31] This is a Rabbinic decree,

---

30 See Gemara *Avodah Zarah* (38a), *Rambam* (*Hilchos Maachalos Assuros* Ch. 17:14–22) and *Tur* and *Shulchan Aruch* (Y.D. 113) and relevant commentaries, for all related *halachos* of *Bishul Akum*. According to the *Yerushalmi* (*Shabbos* Ch. 1, *Halacha* 4; 12a in the Friedman edition and 9b in the *Me'orei Ohr* edition), the prohibition of *Bishul Akum* is one of the eighteen *Gezeiros* that Chazal established on that famous, fateful day when Beis Shamai overruled Beis Hillel. On the other hand, it is noticeably absent from the *Talmud Bavli's* list of these *Gezeiros* (see *Shabbos* 17b and *Avodah Zarah* 36a-b). Rabbeinu Tam (*Tosafos, Avodah Zarah* 37b s.v. *v'hashlakos*) opines that the prohibition of *Bishul Akum* actually predates those of Hillel and Shamai.

31 However, there is a practical distinction between Sefardic and Ashkenazic *psak* as to how much of the cooking process a Jew must perform in order to classify the food as *Bishul Yisrael*. Whereas the *Rema* (Y.D. 113:7) maintains that it is sufficient if a Jew lit the fire or stoked the coals (concluding "*v'chein nohagin*"), on the other hand, the *Shulchan Aruch* (ad loc. 6 and 7) rules that a Jew must take an active part in the cooking process, whether by placing the pot on the fire or stirring it on the stove. This is because he understands *Bishul Yisrael's* prerequisite to mean that a Jew's direct actions will cause the food to be cooked, at least to some degree. Rav Ovadiah Yosef (*Shu"t Yechaveh Daas* vol. 5:54 and *Shu"t Yabia Omer* vol. 9 Y.D. 6), discussing what Sefardim should do regarding eating in a restaurant that relies on this ruling of the *Rema*, where the only "cooking" the Jew does is light the fire, maintains that they may be lenient and eat there, due to a *sfek sfeika*: Perhaps the *halacha* follows the *Rema*, and perhaps *Bishul Akum* does not apply to non-Jewish workers in a Jewish home or establishment [this is the minority opinion of Rabbeinu Avraham ben Rav Dovid, which although the practical *halacha* does not actually follow [see *Tosafos* (*Avodah Zarah* 38a s.v. *ela*; citing Rabbeinu Tam) and *Tur* and *Beis Yosef* (Y.D. 113:1)], nonetheless, the *Rema* (ad loc. 4 and *Toras HaChatas* 75:17) still permits reliance on this *shittah b'dieved*]. However, Rav Ovadiah concludes that it is nonetheless preferable for Sefardim not to rely on this dispensation. Other contemporary Sefardic *Poskim*, including Rav Ben Tzion Abba-Shaul (*Shu"t Ohr L'Tzion* vol. 2, pg. 12:5) and Rav Mordechai

intended as a safeguard to combat the plagues of assimilation and intermarriage.[32] However, in order for food to be included in this prohibition, it must meet two requirements: be unable to be eaten raw, and it must be "*Oleh Al Shulchan Melachim*—Fit for a King's Table."[33] Any kosher food cooked by a non-Jew that does not meet these requirements (obviously with no other kashrus concerns) is permitted to be eaten.[34]

A common concern is figuring out which foods are considered "Fit for a King's Table." The *Chochmas Adam*, Rav Avraham Danzig, who lived in Vilna (located in modern-day Lithuania) in the early 1800s, ruled that

---

> Eliyahu (*Darchei Halacha* glosses to the *Kitzur Shulchan Aruch* 38:7), based on the *Ben Ish Chai* (Year 2, *Parashas Chukas* 18 and *Shu"t Rav Pe'alim* vol. 3, Y.D. 9), are more stringent, contending that there is no basis for such consideration, and assert that it is forbidden for Sefardim to eat in a restaurant that does not follow the *Shulchan Aruch's* strict definition of *Bishul Yisrael*.

32 There is an additional reason given for this restriction: that by eating even exclusively strictly kosher food cooked by a non-Jew, one may come to get too comfortable with non-Jews and their cooking and may come to eventually transgress eating *Maachalos Assuros*.

33 This rule is based on a difference of interpretation between the great Yeshivos of Sura and Pumbedisa on how they understood Rav Shmuel bar Rav Yitzchak's statement quoting Rav (*Avodah Zarah* 38a). The codified *halacha* follows both versions; see *Tur* and *Shulchan Aruch* (Y.D. 113:1).

34 There might also be an additional factor to take into account: When the Gemara teaches the requirements of *Bishul Yisrael*, after stating that any food that it is *Oleh Al Shulchan Melachim* is included, it adds "*lelafos bo es hapas*, to be eaten along with, or together with bread." There is a difference of understanding between the Rishonim whether the Gemara was simply stating a common method of serving or actually meant to qualify the rule, making a further stipulation in the *halacha's* application. When codifying the *halacha*, the *Rambam* (*Hilchos Maachalos Assuros* Ch. 17:15) and Rabbeinu Yerucham (*Sefer Ha'Adam*, *Nesiv* 17:7, pg. 160b, fourth column) use the same language of the Gemara, leading several notable Acharonim to rule that even if a food item is considered *Oleh Al Shulchan Melachim*, nonetheless, if it is not commonly served to be eaten with bread, it is exempt from the requirement of *Bishul Yisrael*. However, this issue is debated, and many Acharonim follow the *Rashba's* (*Toras Habayis*, *Bayis* 3, *Shaar* 7, 94a) understanding, ruling that

potatoes are considered an important food item, apropos for nobility.[35] As such, they are "Fit for a King's Table" and any cooked potato dish must be cooked by a Jew or else will be prohibited as *Bishul Akum*.

However, the *Aruch Hashulchan*, Rav Yechiel Michel Epstein, writing in the 1890s in Novardok (located in modern-day Belarus), vigorously disagreed, maintaining that potatoes are food for the common man, and nobles would only partake of them due to the land's overabundance of them and not due to any inherent importance.[36] Interestingly, and although written more than a century earlier, and in Germany, Rav Yaakov Emden similarly wrote that potatoes are exclusively "peasant fare."[37]

---

even if the food is not served with bread, as long as it is *Oleh Al Shulchan Melachim*, mandates *Bishul Yisrael*. To further complicate matters, the *Tur* and *Shulchan Aruch* (ibid.), though citing *"lelafos bo es hapas,"* still add *"parperes,"* generally understood to be dessert, to the list of foods needing *Bishul Yisrael*. Several Acharonim view this important addition as proof that *"lelafos bo es hapas"* was not meant be a qualification in the *halacha*, as who eats dessert with bread? Others understand the issue differently and maintain that any food that satiates and is served as part of a *seudah* is considered *"lelafos bo es hapas,"* even if said food item is not eaten with bread at all. There are also several authorities, who maintain that for a food item to be considered *Oleh Al Shulchan Melachim* it must have sufficient inherent importance that one would "invite his friend over to serve said food product." It does not seem too common to invite someone over simply to share french fries or potato chips! Practically, there is no clear-cut consensus on the matter, although Rav Shmuel *Halevi* Wosner (*Shu"t Shevet Halevi* vol. 2:43; see also vol. 9:23 and vol. 10:124) and Rav Dovid Feinstein (cited in *Shu"t Vidibarta Bam* vol. 2:255) advise to ensure that both desserts and *chashuv* food not eaten with bread be *Bishul Yisrael* (while allowing leniency *b'shaas hadchak*). On the other hand, and undoubtedly, following the lenient opinion would permit french fries without requiring *Bishul Yisrael*, as they are generally served as at most a side dish, and would certainly allow potato chips, which is merely a snack, and not any part of a *seudah*. This topic is discussed at length in the chapter titled "The Parameters of *Pas Palter*," regarding breakfast cereals.

35 *Chochmas Adam* (66:4).

36 *Aruch Hashulchan* (Y.D. 113:18).

37 *Shu"t Sheilas Yaavetz* (vol. 2:147, 4 s.v. *u'vhiyosi*).

The *Aruch Hashulchan* adds that it is entirely possible that in the time and place of the *Chochmas Adam* a potato dish might have been considered important, but by his time, the potato's widespread popularity ensured that it no longer could have been deemed "Fit for a King's Table," and consequentially is excluded from the *Bishul Akum* prohibition. It is interesting to note that nowadays potato's relevance is once again a matter of dispute among contemporary authorities regarding this important *halacha*:

- The Maharsham, Rav Shalom Mordechai Schwadron, maintained that in his time (1890s, Berezhan, modern-day Ukraine), a cooked potato was considered *Oleh Al Shulchan Melachim*, however, if it was roasted it was not, and would not fall under the *issur* of *Bishul Akum*.[38]
- The Debreciner Rav understands this to include potatoes roasting in oil (frying), and adds that nowadays any type of fried potato (french fries, anyone?) would definitely *not* be "Fit for a King's Table."[39]
- Other contemporary authorities are even more lenient, for example, Rav Yosef Eliyahu Henkin and Rav Ovadiah Hedaya (the *Yaskil Avdi*) seems to accept the *Aruch Hashulchan*'s position that standard potatoes are not *Oleh Al Shulchan Melachim*, even nowadays,[40] and therefore can be cooked by a non-Jew.
- On the other hand, Rav Shmuel *Halevi* Wosner and Rav Moshe Sternbuch are *machmir* for the *Chochmas Adam*'s opinion and maintain that nowadays potatoes can be considered *Oleh Al*

---

38 *Shu"t Maharsham* (vol. 2:262).

39 *Shu"t Ba'er Moshe* (vol. 4:49).

40 *Teshuvos Ibra* (Ch. 3:42; originally printed in Rav Nissan Telushkin's *Taharas Mayim* in a footnote on pg. 282 and more recently in *Shu"t Gevuros Eliyahu* vol. 2-Y.D. 26 and 28; however, he held that the reason is that they are not served as an accompaniment to bread, "*lelafos bo es hapas*," and therefore excluded from the requirement), and *Shu"t Yaskil Avdi* (vol. 7, Y.D. 6:4, 4).

Shulchan Melachim, and conclude that even concerning fried potatoes one should be *machmir*.[41]

- It should be noted that Rav Yaakov Kamenetsky and Rav Moshe Feinstein seem to rule that french fries and even potato chips are *Oleh Al Shulchan Melachim*, but for a different reason (they do seem to accept that nowadays potatoes are *chashuv*; Rav Moshe's *talmid*, Rav Aharon Felder, wrote that indeed Rav Moshe held that potatoes in modern times have the status of an important food and are subject to the strictures of *Bishul Akum*).[42]
- Rav Yosef Shalom Elyashiv is quoted as being *machmir* as well, but for an entirely novel reason.[43] Likewise, it is known that Rav Asher Zimmerman also deemed potato chips as requiring *Bishul Yisrael*.[44]

---

41 *Shu"t Shevet Halevi* (vol. 2:45; vol. 6:108, 4 s.v. *u'mikol makom*; vol. 9:23; see also vol. 10:124 where he is *machmir* even regarding potato chips) and *Shu"t Teshuvos V'Hanhagos* (vol. 1:438).

42 *Emes L'Yaakov* on *Tur* and *Shulchan Aruch* (Y.D. 113: footnote 42; he is quoted as holding that even though potato chips are not *chashuv*, nevertheless since potatoes are *chashuv*, all products stemming from the same basic *"min"* (species or variety etc.) would be included in the stricture; this *shittah* is first mentioned by the *Shu"t Chessed L'Avraham*, Y.D. 8, and cited by the *Darchei Teshuva*, ad loc. 9), *Shu"t Igros Moshe* (Y.D. vol. 4:48, 5; writing very briefly that the *"hetter"* for potato chips is unclear, but not to chastise those who are lenient), and *Rishumei Aharon* (vol. 1, pg. 35).

43 Rav Yosef Shalom Elyashiv is quoted (*Kerem Efraim* pg. 65 and *Ashrei Ha'Ish*, Y.D. vol. 1, 8:1; as cited in *Ohel Yaakov* on *Hilchos Maachalei Akum* pg. 93) as being *machmir* regarding potato chips, but for a different, albeit interesting and novel reason: chips can be eaten with soft cheese as an accompaniment to bread, *"lelafos bo es hapas,"* and are therefore considered *Oleh Al Shulchan Melachim*.

44 See *Hamodia's Inyan Magazine* (May 9, 2019, "Torah Greatness Amidst Simplicity," pg. 29–31). It is also reported there that Rav Zimmerman applied the same restrictions to peanut butter; that in his opinion it also requires *Bishul Yisrael*. This seems to be a quite novel approach as well.

- However, Rav Yisroel Belsky and Rav Dovid Feinstein disagree with this assessment,[45] asserting that fried and roasted potatoes are in no way nowadays considered *Oleh Al Shulchan Melachim*, and explain at length that what is commonly quoted in the names of Rav Moshe and Rav Yaakov is not precise, and maintain that they would certainly agree that potato chips are not considered *Oleh Al Shulchan Melachim*.
- Many other well-known *Poskim* expressly ruled leniently regarding potato chips. They include Rav Moshe Stern (the Debreciner Rav; as mentioned previously regarding fried potatoes), Rav Asher Weiss (the "*Minchas Asher*"), Rav Pesach Eliyahu Falk of Gateshead (the "*Machazeh Eliyahu*"), Rav Yisrael Pesach

---

45 *Shu"t Shulchan Halevi* (*Chelek Birurei Halacha* 25; see also the OU's *Kashrus Manual on Bishul Akum*, pp. 1–3) and *Shu"t Vidibarta Bam* (vol. 2:255, 2 s.v. *v'shamaati*). They also both strongly assert that *Oleh Al Shulchan Melachim* is not dependent on the "*min*," but rather the food item. One of the proofs to this is the case of rice bread, which after the *Shulchan Aruch* (Y.D. 112:1) rules is not a true "bread," the *Rema* (ad loc.) adds that it is not included in the category of *Bishul Akum* either, if it is not *Oleh Al Shulchan Melachim*. Other *Poskim* argue that there is no way that rice bread could possibly be considered "Fit for a King's Table." As rice's status of whether or not it is considered *Oleh Al Shulchan Melachim* is an earlier discussion [see *Teshuvos HaRosh* (19:21), *Tur* (Y.D. 112:1), *Bach* (ad loc. 4 s.v. *v'kasav*), *Shach* (ad loc. 5), and *Minchas Yaakov* (75:18)], why would the *Poskim* even entertain the notion that rice bread should be any different, unless this rule does not actually follow the "*min*," but rather the individual food item. See also *Shu"t Shevet Hakehasi* (vol. 6:274) who explains the distinction a bit differently, as follows: when a "*min*," such as meat, is intrinsically *Oleh Al Shulchan Melachim*, then not only steak, but even non-*chashuv* types of meat, such as innards, are included in this designation as well. Conversely, in a scenario where the "*min*" does not hold intrinsic importance, but can be cooked and prepared in a manner that makes it fit to be served on a "King's Table," then only when it is actually prepared in said manner is it considered *Oleh Al Shulchan Melachim*. Yet, when this "*min*" is prepared in a manner which is definitely not fit to be served on a "King's Table," it in no way is regarded as *Oleh Al Shulchan Melachim*. Although he does not apply this outright, this description seems quite apropos of potato chips and french fries vis-à-vis their parent "*min*," the potato.

Feinhandler (the "*Avnei Yashpei*"), and Rav Yochanon Wosner of Montreal (the "*Chayei Halevi*").[46]

- In fact, the OU's *Kashrus Manual on Bishul Akum* states simply that french fries and potato chips "don't require *Bishul Yisrael* because they aren't *olim al shulchan melachim*."[47] This assessment is shared by most other leading mainstream kashrus organizations, including the Star-K, OK, and COR (Toronto).[48] Similarly, the Swiss IRGZ (Zürich) Koscherliste, known for not relying on leniencies, dedicates a full listing of acceptable commercially produced Pommes Chips (potato chips/crisps) throughout Switzerland.
- Come what may, it is well known that the *Badatz Eidah Hachareidis* of Yerushalayim is stringent for the *machmir* opinion and makes sure that potato chips under their *hashgacha* are strictly *Bishul*

---

46 *Shu"t Ba'er Moshe* (vol. 4:49), *Minchas Asher* (*Parashas Devarim* 5:8), *Shu"t Machazeh Eliyahu* (vol. 2:40 and 41; originally published in *Kovetz Am HaTorah*, Mahadura 3, vol. 10 pg. 75–89; 5754), Rav Feinhandler's *teshuva* on potato chips is printed in *Ohel Yaakov* on *Hilchos Maachalei Akum* (pg. 95 and 634), and *Shu"t Chayei Halevi* (vol. 4, 50:10; however, he personally is *machmir* with french fries). They explain that as potato chips are eaten exclusively as a snack and generally not served as any part of a *seudah*, not as "*parperes*," and certainly not "*lelafos bo es hapas*," there is simply no reason to insist that they be *Bishul Yisrael*.

47 The OU *Kashrus Manual on Bishul Akum* (pg. 36).

48 See https://www.star-k.org/articles/articles/1182/food-fit-for-a-king-reviewing-the-laws-of-bishul-akum-bishul-yisroel/, http://www.ok.org/kosherspirit/winter-2016/consumer-questions-18, and http://cor.ca/view/210/the_technology_behind_a_cor_potato_chip.html. However, these agencies do not necessarily see eye-to-eye on every nuance of this *inyan*. The OK actually differentiates between french fries, which they mandate be *Bishul Yisrael*, and potato chips, which they do not, unless they are actually certifying the potato chip production. Rav Moshe Heinemann, Chief *Posek* for the Star-K, makes an interesting qualification in his ruling in the aforementioned article: "Obviously, in countries where potato chips reach a king's state dinner, potato chips would also be subject to the laws of *Bishul Akum*."

Yisrael, a much simpler proposition to ensure in Eretz Yisrael than in *Chutz La'aretz*.[49]

This Spud's for You!

It's amazing how not only our—but the entire world's—eating habits, have been changed by this simple vegetable. Can anyone even imagine Shabbos without *cholent* or *kugel*, or *Chanuka* without *latkes*, or Pesach without the potato? The common potato certainly has an uncommon and fascinating history, especially when viewed through the lens of *halacha*.

---

49 However, it should be noted that there currently are (comparably) small runs of *Bishul Yisrael* potato chips being manufactured under the *hashgachos* of smaller *Vaadei Kashrus*, such as Lieber's Potato Chips, produced under the supervision of Rav Menachem Meir Weissmandl of Nitra, that are easily obtainable in certain *"heimishe"* locales in America.

Chapter 18

The Odd Account of the Overnight Onion

THERE IS A FASCINATING GEMARA in *Maseches Nida* featuring an extremely strong yet puzzling statement by Rabbi Shimon Bar Yochai.[1] He states that one who eats a peeled onion, egg, or garlic that has been left sitting out overnight is literally endangering his life, and will be ultimately judged as a person who took his own life![2] The cause of this prohibition is a *"Ruach Ra'ah,"* a type of spirit of impurity or spiritual contamination that rests upon these three foods when peeled and left overnight.

Puzzling Phenomenon

The reason why this statement is considered intriguing is that although there does not seem to be a dissenting opinion, considering the severity of both the offense and the punishment stated, nevertheless, this prohibition is not codified by the classic *halachic* codifiers. Astoundingly, there is absolutely no mention of this proscription in any of the works of the greatest Jewish doctor, the *Rambam*,[3] and nothing in the *Rif*, *Tur*, or *Shulchan Aruch*!

---

1   *Nida* (17a). Also stated in *Derech Eretz Rabba* (Ch. 11).

2   *Rashi* (ad loc. s.v. *umischayav*), as explained by the *Aruch LaNer* (ad loc.). See also the *Maharsha's* explanation (ad loc.).

3   Although, as Rav Tzadok Hakohen M'Lublin (*Tiferes Tzvi* on Y.D. 116) points out in a related topic, the *Rambam's* omission of this *halacha* may not be a

Yet, many later authorities, including the *Pri Chodosh*, *Shulchan Aruch Harav*, Chida, *Ben Ish Chai*, and *Aruch Hashulchan*, **do** cite the Gemara's statement, and consequently rule that eating a peeled egg, onion, or garlic that sat overnight is strictly forbidden.[4] So how is it that it is not mentioned at all by the great *halachic* codifiers?

This question has baffled many for years and there is no clear-cut, one-size-fits-all solution. There are, however, several different perspectives that the *halachic* authorities take on this matter.

No More *Ruach Ra'ah*?

One way of understanding the codifiers' deafening silence on this issue is that they may have been of the opinion that *Ruach Ra'ah* is no longer applicable. This is not a new argument, but rather one that many Rishonim cite, including the Maharam M'Rothenburg, the *Mordechai* and *Tosafos*.[5] The Rashal as well famously declared that *Ruach Ra'ah* is

---

strong proof, as the *Rambam* himself did not hold of any sort of "*Ruach Ra'ah*," as proven in his *Shu"t Pe'er Hador* (146) and cited by the Maharam Elshakar (*Shu"t* 79) and *Kessef Mishneh* (*Hilchos Issurei Biyah* Ch. 21:1). See also *Shu"t Mishnah Halachos* (vol. 6:61) and the Forward (Ch. 7 and 8) to *Mori v'Rabi* Rav Yosef Yitzchok Lerner's excellent *Shemiras Haguf V'Hanefesh*.

4   *Pri Chodosh* (Y.D. 116:9), *Knesses Hagedolah* (ad loc. *Hagahos* on *Beis Yosef* 27 and on), *Shulchan Aruch Harav* (C.M. *Shemiras Guf V'Nefesh*, 7), *Menoras Hama'or* (*Ner* 6), Chida (*Birkei Yosef*, Y.D. 116:10), *Zivchei Tzedek* (ad loc. 61), *Ben Ish Chai* (Year 2, *Parashas Pinchas* 14), *Aruch Hashulchan* (Y.D. 116:22), and *Kaf Hachaim* (ad loc. 92). However, there are other later authorities, including the *Pischei Teshuva*, *Chochmas Adam*, and *Kitzur Shulchan Aruch*, whose exclusion of this issue remains quite conspicuous.

5   Maharam M'Rothenburg, cited by the *Mordechai* (*Shabbos*, Ch. 7, *Chiddushei Anshei Sheim* 3; *Hagahos Mordechai* Ch. 8 s.v. *u'mibeitza*), *Tosafos* (*Yoma* 77b s.v. *mishum*; *Chullin* 107b s.v. *hasam*), Rashal (*Yam Shel Shlomo*, *Chullin* Ch. 8:12). However, it should be noted that the prohibition is mentioned by several other Rishonim including *Tosafos* (*Shabbos* 141a s.v. *hani* and *Beitza* 14a s.v. *ika*), the *Rosh* (*Beitza* 14a:21), the *SMa"K* (*Mitzva* 171), and *Terumas Hadeshen* (cited in *Leket Yosher*, Y.D. pg. 6; see also *Terumas Hadeshen* 211, where he writes that we should still be *choshesh* for the *sakanos* mentioned by Chazal).

no longer prevalent among us. Several later authorities rule this way, maintaining that peeled overnight onions no longer give us any reason for worry, and may be eaten.[6] They maintain that this is the reason there is nary a mention of it by the great codifiers, and not due to any lacunae in their knowledge.

Ruach Ra'ah Still Abounds

Yet, as mentioned previously, many later authorities maintain that this prohibition still applies in full force, as once an issue is mentioned in the Gemara as a *halachic* problem, it cannot be discounted simply because many codifiers did not quote it. Also, several authorities suggest that the Maharam did not actually discount *Ruach Ra'ah* completely. On the contrary, they assert, he only entertained that leniency as a possible solution and not necessarily as a definitive ruling. Additionally, it can be argued that *Tosafos* and the Rashal were referring exclusively to a specific type of *Ruach Ra'ah* that no longer is applicable; the *Ruach Ra'ah* associated with overnight peeled eggs and onions may therefore still be pertinent. These *Poskim* therefore maintain that it is strictly prohibited to eat a peeled onion, egg, or garlic that was left out overnight.[7][8]

The Middle Road

A third approach to this issue is to synthesize the other approaches, taking all of the above into account. These authorities, including the *Chofetz Chaim*, Rav Moshe Feinstein, and the Steipler Gaon, maintain that if one wishes to be lenient, one definitely has what to rely upon. Yet, they recommend following the strict approach: not to partake of peeled overnight eggs, onions, and garlic.[9]

---

6 Including the *Aderes* (*Kuntress Over Orach*, 4), *Shu"t Pri Hasadeh* (vol. 3:61 and 62), *Shu"t Yad Meir* (19; cited in *Darchei Teshuva* 116:74), *Shu"t Kav Zahav* (14), and *Mishmeres Shalom* (Y.D. 116:4). The *Har Tzvi* (*Shu"t* Y.D. 74 s.v. *od*) seems to accept this as well. The *Rema* (O.C. 328:35) citing the *Shibolei Leket* (123), implies as well that *Ruach Ra'ah* is no longer a *sakana*.

7   Including those authorities mentioned previously, as well as *Shu"t Beis Shlomo* (vol. 1, Y.D. 189), the Maharsham (*Shu"t* vol. 4:148 and *Daas Torah*, O.C. 513:6), *Shlah* (*Shaar Ha'Osiyios* pg. 129), *Reishis Chochma* (Ch. *Derech Eretz*, *Shaar* 3, s.v. *v'garsinan*), *Yeish Nochlin* (15), *Shevet Mussar* (end Ch. 40), and *Shu"t Shem Aryeh* (from the *Arugas Habosem*; Y.D. end 56). The Maharsham proves from the fact that the Maharam prefaced his leniency with *"dilma,"* that it shows that he did not truly mean to rule leniently. However, the *Sdei Chemed* (*Maareches HaLamed* 141:31 s.v. *ha'oleh* and *Klalei HaPoskim* beg. 16; cited in *Shu"t Yabia Omer* vol. 2, Y.D. 7) maintains that the Maharam used *"dilma"* as a *"lashon anavah,"* but definitely did intend to rule leniently. The argument that *Tosafos* and Rashal were only lenient with a specific type of *Ruach Ra'ah* is made by the *Divrei Yatziv* (*Shu"t* Y.D. vol. 1:31, 4), *Chelkas Yaakov* (*Shu"t* vol. 3, Y.D. 39:3), and *Ba'er Moshe* (*Shu"t* vol. 3:115, 2, in the brackets).

8   Interestingly, overnight *peeled eggs* might actually be permitted according to several authorities, as *Rashi* (ad loc. s.v. *she'avar*), when explaining the prohibition, omits eggs from the criteria. Additionally, there is some debate among several later *Poskim* about what type of peeled eggs are intended for inclusion in the prohibition—cooked eggs or raw eggs. See at length *Shemiras Haguf V'Hanefesh* (vol. 1, Ch. 3:2 and 4, and relevant footnotes for explanation). Nevertheless, the common custom is that both raw and hardboiled peeled eggs are considered to be affected by *Ruach Ra'ah*. See *Shu"t Minchas Yitzchak* (vol. 4:108, 2) and *Shu"t Shulchan Halevi* (Ch. 23:3). Yet, as the *Tzitz Eliezer* (*Shu"t* vol. 18:46) notes, there will always be a *sfek sfeika* to permit it *b'dieved*, as whichever type of egg one peels that was left overnight, raw or cooked, it is always possible that *Ruach Ra'ah* is actually exclusive to the other type. That, coupled with the Maharam's *shittah*, plus the opinions who say eggs are excluded, should allow room for leniency.

9   Including the *Chofetz Chaim* (*Likutei Halachos*, *Nida* 17a, *Ein Mishpat* 7), Rav Yosef Chaim Sonnenfeld (*Shu"t Salmas Chaim*, old print vol. 4:4, 8), Rav Moshe Feinstein (*Shu"t Igros Moshe*, Y.D. vol. 3:20), the Steipler Gaon (cited in *Shemiras Haguf V'Hanefesh* vol. 1: Ch. 3, end footnote 1), the Debreciner Rav (*Shu"t Ba'er Moshe* vol. 3:115, 2), Rav Shlomo Zalman Auerbach (*Halichos Shlomo* on *Tefilla* Ch. 2, footnote 103), the *Minchas Yitzchak* (*Shu"t* vol. 2:68, 13), Rav Yisrael Yaakov Fischer (*Shu"t Even Yisrael* vol. 9:126, 3), the *Tzitz Eliezer* (*Shu"t* vol. 18:46), the *Az Nidberu* (*Shu"t* vol. 11:47), Rav Moshe Sternbuch (*Shu"t Teshuvos V'Hanhagos* vol. 3:256 s.v. *uv'ir hakodesh*), Rav

Eggsclusions…err…Exclusions

Even if one wishes to follow the recommended route of not eating overnight peeled onions, there are several important exclusions to the rule:

1. The Gemara itself cites an exception: If some (even a tiny amount) of the original outer layer, peel, shell, or root hairs remain, then one need not worry about *Ruach Ra'ah*, as it is not considered to be peeled.

2. Many *Poskim* rule that if the overnight onion was mixed together with another food item, such as part of a salad, then it would be permitted, as it lost its status of purely being an onion or an egg. Several contemporary authorities, including the *Ben Ish Chai*, *Chazon Ish*, Rav Shlomo Zalman Auerbach, and the *Minchas Yitzchak*, maintain that this holds true even if only a small amount of salt, sugar, flour, or oil was added to the onion or egg, that it no longer is considered a mere peeled egg or onion, but rather as part of a mixture, which *Ruach Ra'ah* cannot affect.[10]

Ovadiah Yosef (*Shu"t Yabia Omer* vol. 2, Y.D. 7), the *Shevet Hakehasi* (*Shu"t* vol. 2:247), and Rav Yisroel Belsky (*Shu"t Shulchan Halevi* Ch. 23:3). *Mori v'Rabi* Rav Yaakov Blau of the *Badatz Eidah Hachareidis* told this author that one should certainly be *choshesh* for *Ruach Ra'ah*, as in his opinion, we can not simply discount an issue that is explicitly mentioned in the Gemara.

10 Including the *SMa"K* (ibid.), *Zivchei Tzedek* (ibid.), *Ben Ish Chai* (ibid.), *Chazon Ish* (cited in *Shemiras Haguf V'Hanefesh* ibid. pg. 25, footnote and *Orchos Rabbeinu* vol. 1, top of pg. 210), *Tosefes Chaim* (cited in *Sefer Mataamim*, *Erech Yayin Seuda*, 18), *Kaf Hachaim* (ibid.), *Halichos Shlomo* (ibid.), *Shu"t Tzitz Eliezer* (ibid.), *Shu"t Yaskil Avdi* (ibid.), *Shu"t Yabia Omer* (ibid. 4 and vol. 10, Y.D. 9; adding that this certainly holds true regarding mayonnaise), *Shu"t Divrei Shalom* (vol. 6:pg. 293, *Piskei Teshuvos* 199), and *Taamei HaMinhagim* (*Likutim* 16). Rav Yisroel Belsky (*Shu"t Shulchan Halevi* ibid.) is lenient if the chemical balance (pH) is changed even slightly by adding the salt or sugar. The *Minchas Yitzchak* (*Shu"t* vol. 6:75) only allows salt and sugar if it is at least two percent of the mixture. [See *Shemiras Haguf V'Hanefesh* (vol. 2, *Miluim*, top of pg. 802 for an explanation from *Mori v'Rabi* Rav Yaakov Blau of the *Eidah Hacharedis*].

3. Some suggest a quite questionable leniency that if one wraps the peeled egg or garlic up well and then puts it in the fridge, it would consequentially be considered protected from *Ruach Ra'ah*.[11] The reason why many question, and ultimately reject, this proposition is that the Gemara explicitly states that even if the peeled onion is covered and wrapped up, it is still susceptible to *Ruach Ra'ah*. Therefore, most authorities do not abide by this leniency at all. Yet, others differentiate between how it was closed, for if it was hermetically sealed (which wasn't around at the time of the Gemara), some opine that it is as if it is still in its shell, and rule that it is permitted.[12]
4. Another opinion cited by many authorities is that *Ruach Ra'ah* does not affect dried onion powder, garlic powder, or powdered

---

Rav Moshe Sternbuch (*Shu"t Teshuvos V'Hanhagos* ibid.) is lenient *lechatchilla* only if the color is changed by the mixture. The Klausenberger Rebbe (*Shu"t Divrei Yatziv* ibid. 14 s.v. *u'lemaaseh* and Y.D. vol. 1:32, 3) maintains that one may only rely on this if the taste is actually changed by adding the salt or sugar; he further rules that one may not use eggs, garlic, or onions as the other ingredient in the mixture.

11 *Shu"t Rivevos Efraim* (vol. 3:495 and vol. 5:523) and *Shu"t Vayaan Dovid* (Y.D. 119). The *Tzitz Eliezer* (ibid.) rules that one may rely on this in cases of great loss, as there are many *sniffim lehakel*. The *Chazon Ish* (cited in *Orchos Rabbeinu* vol. 1, pg. 210:16) ruled similarly regarding a raw egg that was left out, that covering it was sufficient. [It is unclear, however, if he held that the same would apply to onions and garlic as well, as it is possible he was referring to the egg exclusion; additionally, perhaps he held that *Ruach Ra'ah* only affects cooked eggs.] Conversely, in *Shu"t Rivevos Efraim* (vol. 4:51 s.v. *b'siman*) a dissenting opinion is presented, that the Gemara (as well as the later authorities who rule this way, e.g., Shulchan Aruch Harav ibid. et al) explicitly rules that this leniency is not valid. Rav Ovadiah Yosef (*Shu"t Yabia Omer* vol. 10, Y.D. 9) rules similarly, based on a precedent of the *Ben Ish Chai's* (*Shu"t Rav Pe'alim* vol. 2, Y.D. 13). The same point is strongly made in *Shemiras Haguf V'Hanefesh* (vol. 1, pg. 23: footnote 5, s.v. *v'davar*).

12 *Shu"t Shulchan Halevi* (ibid.).

eggs, as not only are they not considered the original food item, but they are not even considered a food at all, rather a powder.[13]

Commercial Uses and Bakeries

A common question debated among contemporary authorities is what bakeries should do. Are they required to throw out trays of unused leftover eggs, and not use them the next day?

Several authorities, including the *Yad Meir* and Rav Shmuel *Halevi* Wosner, rule that nowadays the *Ruach Ra'ah* is non-applicable and therefore bakeries need not worry about this problem at all.[14] Others, including the *Minchas Yitzchak*, *Tzitz Eliezer*, and Rav Ovadiah Yosef,[15] maintain that although personally one should be stringent, nevertheless, in a commercial setting since there are many mitigating factors and rationales present (as sugar and/or salt often get added to the mix; in addition, the prohibited amount might have actually been nullified, etc.), it is permitted.

---

13 Including *Shu"t Degel Efraim* (28), *Darchei Teshuva* (ibid.; who cites the *Degel Efraim* with no dissenting opinion), *Shu"t Har Tzvi* (ibid.; albeit due to relying on the Maharam—see *Shemiras Haguf V'Hanefesh* vol. 1, pg. 28, end footnote 12), *Shu"t Chelkas Yaakov* (ibid.), *Shu"t Ba'er Moshe* (ibid.), *Shu"t Shevet Halevi* (ibid.), *Shu"t Yabia Omer* (ibid.), and *Shu"t Shulchan Halevi* (ibid.). Commercially sold onion and garlic powder would also be included in Rav Moshe's *hetter* mentioned later in this chapter. See also *Shulchan Aruch* (O.C. 202:16), that there is no *bracha* recited on dried-out *"Tavlin"* used to spice-up other foods, as at that point it is no longer *halachically* considered a "food" that is normally eaten by itself.

14 *Shu"t Yad Meir* (19; cited in *Darchei Teshuva* 116:74), *Shu"t Shevet Halevi* (vol. 3:169 and vol. 6:11:5, 7, and 9), *Shu"t Yaskil Avdi* (vol. 7, O.C. 44:4 and vol. 8, Y.D. 14). The *Har Tzvi* (*Shu"t* Y.D. 74 s.v. *od*) seems to accept this as well.

15 *Shu"t Minchas Yitzchak* (ibid.; however see *Shu"t Teshuvos V'Hanhagos* ibid. and *Shemiras Haguf V'Hanefesh* vol. 2, *Miluim*, top of pg. 802 for an explanation from *Mori v'Rabi* Rav Yaakov Blau of the *Eidah Hacharedis*), *Shu"t Tzitz Eliezer* (ibid), *Shu"t Yabia Omer* (ibid.; although he is hesitant to rely on this alone, he prefers that sugar be added with the eggs, as anyway they are usually meant

Rav Moshe Feinstein rules leniently as well, but from a different perspective. He posits that there is no *Ruach Ra'ah* when a company cracks eggs or peels garlic that will not be used for many weeks or months. He explains that *Ruach Ra'ah* only applies when someone is preparing food for the next day, as that would have been the standard scenario the Gemara was referring to, not for weeks later.[16] Accordingly, bakeries would be included in this exception.

Still, there are several contemporary authorities, chief among them the Klausenberger Rebbe, who did not allow any dispensation for industrially produced items, and exhorted extreme caution with all facets of this *halacha*, ruling that peeled overnight eggs, onions, or garlic are strictly prohibited in all cases, unless part of a mixture. He even once publicly asserted that negligence and lackadaisicalness with eating overnight peeled eggs and onions might be the cause for cancer, *Rachmana litzlan!*[17] This is why although many *Poskim* allow leniency when it comes to bakeries (due to the aforementioned rationales),

---

for cakes; see also *Yalkut Yosef, Kitzur Shulchan Aruch* Y.D. 113:18), and *Shu"t Az Nidberu* (ibid.).

16 *Shu"t Igros Moshe* (Y.D. vol. 3:20). See also *Mesores Moshe* (vol. 1, pg. 238:66). Although Rav Menashe Klein (*Shu"t Mishnah Halachos* vol. 12:21 s.v. *u'mah*) argues on this, maintaining that there should be no difference whether the onions and eggs are peeled many weeks in advance or the previous night, nevertheless, it is worthwhile to read Rav Yisroel Belsky's strongly worded defense of Rav Moshe's *shittah*. He writes (*Shu"t Shulchan Halevi* ibid. s.v. *u'lemaaseh*) that since the issue at hand is one of spiritual danger, once the universally recognized *Gadol Hador* rules that it does not apply, it is certain that no spiritual contamination will affect someone who relies on his ruling; see Gemara *Pesachim* (112b) that *mazikim* are subservient to the wishes of the *Gedolim*.

17 *Shu"t Divrei Yatziv* (Y.D. vol. 1:31; the quote about causes of cancer is found in a footnote in the responsum) at length. See also *Tuvcha Yabiu* (vol. 2, pg. 316) from Rav Yitzchak Zilberstein. Other contemporary *Poskim* who rule stringently include the *Chelkas Yaakov* (*Shu"t* vol. 3-Y.D. 39) and *Mishnah Halachos* (*Shu"t* vol. 12:20 and 21), following the rulings of the Maharsham and *Beis Shlomo* (ibid.) et al. Rav Moshe Yehuda Leib Landau of Bnei Brak was

nevertheless, bakeries run by Sanz and Klausenberg Chassidim are very stringent with this.

To sum up the matter, whether or not *Ruach Ra'ah* still exists today, it would seem that generally with a little bit of effort, we can minimize the possibility of it affecting our food. So, when next preparing an egg salad or garlic spread, it seems quite worthwhile whenever possible to strive to follow the guidelines that ensure "spiritual contamination" remains far from our food.

Postscript: *Davar Charif*

There is an additional aspect of *halacha* that onions and garlic (and other sharp foods including horseradish, radishes, and certain types of peppers, etc., but not eggs) strongly impact: that of "*davar charif*." This term refers to a food item that imparts extremely sharp taste, and it causes some of the most common and complicated kashrus questions. This is because in some ways, when added to an equation, a *davar charif* can be a "game-changer." Due to its strong *taam*, under certain conditions a *davar charif* has the unique ability to negate a *hetter* of Nat Bar Nat, and "re-awaken" absorbed taste long considered inert and irrelevant.[18] Moreover, when cooked in a dairy or meat pot, or sliced with a dairy or meat knife, even without meat or milk being present,

---

also known to be very *makpid* with bakeries under his *hashgacha* regarding this *halacha*.

18 Nat Bar Nat and its application is discussed at length in a chapter titled "The Great Dishwasher Debate."
Davar charif's ability to "re-awaken" imparted taste long considered "dead" denotes that it can cancel out a *hetter* of *aino ben yomo*. Meaning, in many instances, if the pot or cooking utensil in question has not been used with actual hot *milchigs* or *fleishig* for the last twenty-four hours, it can only impart a weak, *pagum* taste and usually can no longer affect a *sheilah*. Yet, when introducing a *davar charif* into the mix, it can "re-awaken" that taste, and the *hetter* of *aino ben yomo* may no longer be applicable to the case in question. See next footnote. *Davar charif* questions are among the most complicated kashrus questions a *halachic* authority is generally asked and every Rav "worth his salt" must be well versed in its intricacies.

a *davar charif* can revive the imparted *taam*, and in some ways make it as if one was actually cooking with or cutting meat or milk.[19] Many of the exact nuances of its status and application thereof are debated among authorities, and the *Tur*, *Shulchan Aruch*, and *Rema* and their main commentaries dedicate more than an entire *Siman* to *davar charif's* minutiae.[20] In other words, we should all be aware that *halachically* speaking, the onion gives quite a sharp "kick."

---

19 The *inyan* of *Davar Charif's* exceptional abilities is based on the Gemara's assessment in *Avodah Zarah* (39a) regarding "*kort shel chiltis*," that "*af al gav d'amar Mar nosein taam l'fgam muttar, agav churfeih d'chiltisa mei'chalia leih shamnunisa, v'haveih leih k'nosein taam l'shvach, v'assur.*"

20 *Yoreh Deah* 96 and other *se'ifim* scattered throughout *Hilchos Issur V'Hetter*, including 95:2, 103:6, 108:1, 121:7, and 122:3. There is even a recent *sefer* entirely dedicated to this topic, aptly titled "*Davar Charif.*"

Chapter 19

The Quinoa-*Kitniyos* Conundrum

GENERALLY, SPRINGTIME IS THE BUSIEST for *Rabbanim* the world over, as they field questions on every aspect of the myriad and complex *halachos* of Pesach observance. Yet, interestingly, the question that often seems to be utmost on people's minds is not about *chometz* or even cleaning properly. No, the biggest issue in recent years seems to be whether quinoa (pronounced keen-waah) is considered *kitniyos* and whether Ashkenazim can eat it on Pesach. Perhaps, it has something to do with the fact that the U.N. declared 2013 as the "International Year of the Quinoa." Whatever the reason, after receiving this question numerous times in one day, this author decided to thoroughly examine the issue.

Quinoa Questions

Quinoa has developed an international following. Packed with protein (essential amino acids) and fiber, as well as magnesium, phosphorus, calcium, and iron (and naturally cholesterol-free!), quinoa packs quite a dietary punch. Although billed as the "mother of all grains" and "the Super-Grain," this native of the Andes Mountains (think Bolivia and Peru) is actually a grain that isn't; it does not even contain gluten. It turns out that quinoa is really a member of the "goose-foot" family (*Chenopodium*), related to beets and spinach. However, while its health benefits sound terrific, it still may be problematic on Pesach.

Kitniyos Clash

It is well known that the actual prohibition of *chometz* on Pesach pertains exclusively to leavened products made from the five major grains: wheat, barley, oats, spelt, or rye.[1] Yet, as discussed in a previous chapter, already in place from the times of the Rishonim, there was an Ashkenazic prohibition against eating *kitniyos* (legumes; ostensibly based on its semi-literal translation: "little things") on Pesach, except in times of famine or grave need. Although referred to differently by the great authorities through the ages, and there was a minority opinion that opposed this prohibition, nonetheless, it is compulsory and binding on Ashkenazic Jewry in full force, even today.

As mentioned previously, the *Aruch Hashulchan* avers that "once our forefathers have accepted this prohibition upon themselves, it is considered a '*geder m'din Torah*' and one who is lenient is testifying about himself that he has no fear of Heaven." He adds, echoing Shlomo HaMelech's wise words in *Koheles* regarding a "*poretz geder*," that one who breaks this prohibition deserves to be bitten by a snake.

Several reasons are given for the actual prohibition including that *kitniyos* often grow in close proximity to grain; are commonly stored together with grain and actual *chometz* might actually end up mixed inside the *kitniyos* container; cooked dishes made from grain and *kitniyos* look similar; and that *kitniyos* can likewise be ground up into flour—a "bread" of sorts can actually be made from them. Since there are many who will not be able to differentiate between them and their Biblically forbidden *chometz* counterparts, *kitniyos* were likewise prohibited.

Potatoes, Peanuts, and Corn…Oh My!

So how does our quinoa measure up? Although it has been used in the Andes for millennia, it has only recently gained popularity around the world. Does quinoa fit the *kitniyos* criteria or not?

Perhaps we can glean some insight to quinoa's *kitniyos* status from *halachic* precedents of other now-common food staples that were

---

1   *Kitniyos* and potato-related issues are discussed at length in the chapter titled "The *Halachic* Adventures of the Potato."

introduced long after the *kitniyos* prohibition started, such as potatoes, peanuts, and corn.

It would seemingly be quite difficult for anyone to mix up potatoes with *chometz* grain, so that rationale to regard potatoes as *kitniyos* is out. Still, potatoes can be and are made into potato flour and potato starch, and there are those who do bake potato "bread." Yet, even so, we find that *lemaaseh*, potatoes are not considered *kitniyos*.

One of the main reasons for this is that at the time when the Ashkenazic Rishonim established the decree prohibiting *kitniyos*, potatoes were completely unknown. It is possible that had they been readily available they might have found themselves on the "forbidden list" as well. Yet, since they were never included, as well as do not fit most of the criteria, contemporary authorities could not add "new types" to the list.

However, it must be noted that there also are other important reasons why potatoes were excluded. Of the four criteria given for the *Gezeira* of *kitniyos*, potatoes only fit one—that they can be made into flour and a "bread" of sorts can be baked from them. No one would mix up a potato with a grain kernel. As Rav Shlomo Zalman Auerbach noted, Klal Yisrael never accepted the *kitniyos* prohibition to include potatoes.

We find that similar "New World" logic was used by several *Poskim*, including Rav Moshe Feinstein, to permit peanuts for Pesach for those who did not have an opposing *minhag*.[2] Yet, this was not as widely

---

2   Shu"t *Igros Moshe* (O.C. vol. 3:63; see also Rav Shmuel Kamenetzky's *Kovetz Halachos on Pesach*, Ch. 10:8 and footnote 9). Others who accept peanuts for Pesach include the *Seridei Aish* (Shu"t vol. 2, 37:2; new edition vol. 1, 5:2—through a combination of factors), the *Yeshuas Moshe* (Shu"t vol. 1:35; he opines that the *kitniyos* prohibition never applied to legumes that are eaten raw, but concludes similar to Rav Moshe, that if one has an existing *minhag* not to eat peanuts on Pesach he still should not do so), and the *Rivevos Efraim* (Shu"t vol. 7:257, only if it came still in its shell). [This logic is based on the *Shulchan Aruch Harav's* understanding (O.C. 453:5) that the prohibition of *kitniyos* only applies when it gets wet]. Other *Poskim* who ruled that way (that *kitniyos* cannot be more stringent than grain, which only can become *chometz* when wet) include the *Chayei Adam* (vol. 2, 128:1) and Maharsham (Shu"t vol. 1:183 and *Daas Torah* O.C. 453), who cites that Rav Shlomo Kluger (*Nidrei*

accepted[3] since peanuts are true legumes, and as opposed to potatoes,

---

Zerizin, 8) held this way as well. It is said (see Rav Ben Tzion Felman's *Kuntress Yemei Pesach* pg. 162) that the *minhag* in Russia and Lita was to eat peanuts on Pesach, and that Rav Yechezkel Abramsky would serve it to guests. The *Yesodei Yeshurun* (vol. 6, *Maareches Kitniyos*, pg. 421) cites an addendum to the *Minchas Pitim* that states that Rav Meir Arik (the renowned *Imrei Yosher*) also held this way. The recently published *Aliba D'Hilchasa* periodical (vol. 86, Kislev-Teves 5777, pg. 117:129) quotes Rav Avraham Rubin's *Shu"t Nachal Ayson* (vol. 1:9), citing Rav Osher Yaakov Westheim of Manchester and Rav Avraham Gurwicz of Gateshead, who aver the same regarding pre-war Vilna, as well as testimony from an elder that the *Aruch Hashulchan* permitted peanuts as well. Based on this, the Kedassia kashrus agency of London, and Rav Yaakov Landau, former Chief Rabbi of Bnei Brak, used to grant Pesach *hashgacha* on peanut oil. On the other hand, those who were stringent regarding peanuts include the *Shoel U'Meishiv* (*Shu"t Mahadura Kama* vol. 1:175), *Avnei Nezer* (*Shu"t* O.C. 373 and 533), *Maamar Mordechai* (*Shu"t* 32), *Sdei Chemed* (*Maareches Chometz U'Matzah* 6:1), *Lekutei Mahariach* (*Minhagei Leil Rishon* of Pesach, pg. 21), and *Pischa Zuta* (*Birkas HaPesach*, 2:8 and footnote 4). *Sefer Rebbi Chaim—M'Hilchosav V'Hangagosav* (pg. 8; as quoted in *Aliba D'Hilchasa* ibid.) cites an interesting story about Rav Chaim Kanievsky as a child who just came to Eretz Yisrael and the first time he ever saw a peanut, "not yet realizing that it was *kitniyos*." This issue was also one of the points of contention between Rav Kook and the *Badatz Hachassidim* of Yerushalayim regarding the permissibility of sesame oil for Pesach; this will be discussed in an upcoming footnote. See also *Shu"t Atzei Halevanon* (vol. 1:18) who also permits peanuts for Pesach, yet based on his description it seems he is referring to a pistachio (as per the *Yeshuas Moshe* ibid.).

3 There are several *Poskim* who technically agree that logically, the peanut should not be considered *kitniyos*; yet, still, since it can get mixed up with grain, they rule that only its oil or derivatives may be used. These include Rav Chaim Soloveitchik of Brisk (cited in *Mikra'ei Kodesh*, *Pesach* vol. 2, 60:2), the *Melamed L'Ho'eel* (*Shu"t* vol. 1:87 and 88, he mentions though that the *minhag* in Yerushalayim is to consider both the peanut and its oil *kitniyos*), the *Har Tzvi* (*Mikra'ei Kodesh* ad loc.), Rav Yosef Eliyahu Henkin (*Teshuvos Ibra* Ch. 2, 28:3; and in his posthumously published *Shu"t Gevuros Eliyahu* vol. 1-O.C. 141:3), and the *Chelkas Yaakov* (*Shu"t* new edition O.C. end 207). The issue of whether oil from *kitniyos* maintains *kitniyos* status is a complicated one and actually is huge *Machlokes HaPoskim* to this day. Additionally, some

authorities make a distinction if the *kitniyos* item in question is inedible in its natural form, such as cottonseed (which is also not true *kitniyos* but rather a seed). See *Terumas Hadeshen* (113), *Shu"t Maharil* (28), *Rema* (O.C. 453:1), *Shulchan Aruch Harav* (ad loc.), *Pri Chodosh* (O.C. 447, *se'if* 5), *Maaseh Rav* (184), *Nishmas Adam* (*Hilchos Pesach*, Questions 32 and 33), *Birkei Yosef* (O.C. 447:14 and 453:5), *Shu"t Shaarei Yeshua* (Shaar 6:4), *Shu"t Halachos Ketanos* (vol. 1:103), *Shu"t Beis Shlomo* (Y.D. 177), *Shu"t Beis She'arim* (O.C. 215), *Shu"t Ba'er Yitzchak* (11), *Shu"t Divrei Yissachar* (33), *Shu"t HaRadal* (6), *Shu"t Maharsham* (vol. 1:183), *Shu"t Avnei Nezer* (O.C. 373 and 533), *Shu"t Chavalim B'Ne'imim* (vol. 1:7), *Shu"t Marcheshes* (3), *Shu"t Lev Chaim* (vol. 2:92), *Sdei Chemed* (*Maareches Chometz U'Matzah* 1:2), *Shu"t Kol Gadol* (22), *Shu"t Minchas Elazar* (vol. 1:16 s.v. *ach hinei* and vol. 4:30), *Shu"t Yad Yitzchak* (vol. 3, 8:20), *Shu"t Darchei Noam* (10), *Shu"t Peulas Tzaddik* (vol. 2:116), *Shu"t Zichron Yehuda* (139), *Shu"t Maamar Mordechai* (32), *Shu"t Melamed L'Ho'eel* (vol. 1:87 and 88; he adds that Rav Samson Raphael Hirsch permitted sesame oil for Pesach), *Shu"t Seridei Aish* (vol. 2, 37:2; new edition vol. 1, 50:2), *Shu"t Orach Mishpat* (O.C. 111–113), *Shu"t Vayaan Yosef* (*Mishpatecha L'Yaakov* O.C. 41), *Mikra'ei Kodesh* (*Pesach* vol. 2, 60:2, and *Hararei Kodesh* ad loc.), *Shu"t Minchas Yitzchak* (vol. 3, 138:2 and vol. 4, 114:3), *Teshuvos Ibra* (Ch. 2, 28, 3), *Shu"t Gevuros Eliyahu* (vol. 1-O.C. 141:3; also printed in *Kovetz Am HaTorah* vol. 10, pg. 6; 1979), *Shu"t Cheishev Ha'Eifod* (vol. 2:18), *Shu"t Divrei Yatziv* (O.C. vol. 2:196), *Shu"t Chelkas Yaakov* (new edition O.C. end 207), *Shu"t Rivevos Efraim* (vol. 7:257), *Halichos Shlomo* (*Moadim* vol. 2, *Pesach* Ch. 4, *Dvar Halacha* 28), *She'arim Metzuyanim B'Halacha* (117: end 6), *Yesodei Yeshurun* (vol. 6, *Maareches Kitniyos*, pg. 421–425), *Kovetz Teshuvos* (vol. 3, 81:5), *Orchos Rabbeinu* (vol. 4, pg. 166:49), *Shmaatseh D'Moshe* (*Pesach*, *Shemuos Moshe* 453:2, pg. 368), *Mesores Moshe* (vol. 1, pg. 149:301), *Kuntress Yad Dodi* (pg. 119, *Hilchos Pesach*, Question 53), *Shu"t Yissa Yosef* (O.C. vol. 2, 111:4), *Aderes Shmuel* (*Hanhagos U'Psakim* of Rav Shmuel Salant; *Hilchos Pesach* 113, pg. 117–118), the *Badatz Eidah Hachareidis* of Yerushalayim's annual *Madrich HaKashrus* (e.g., 5772, pg. 47; 5773, pg. 163; 5774, pg. 172–173), Rav Avraham Blumenkrantz's annual *Kovetz Hilchos Pesach* (Ch. "Food Products on Pesach," par. Oil; 5766/2006, pg. 377–378), and *Kovetz Moriah* (vol. 388–390, Nissan 5774), in a posthumously published *teshuva* of Rav Akiva Yosef Schlesinger, author of *Lev Ha'Ivri*. Anecdotally, this author once heard from noted historian Rav Berel Wein that he was head of the OU's Kashrus department when the question arose whether or not to allow peanut oil for Pesach. Rabbi Wein related that he had remarked that

can get mixed up with grain. In fact, the *minhag* in Yerushalayim (dating back at least several centuries) is to consider both the peanut and its oil *kitniyos*.[4]

> "the great Kovno Rav, Rav Yitzchak Elchanan Spektor ruled that peanut oil is not *kitniyos*, and Berel Wein is not going to be the one to say it is."

4   See the Chida's *Birkei Yosef* (O.C. 447:14 and 453:5) who writes that in Eretz Yisrael, already in his time (late 1700s) they were *machmir* not to use sesame oil on Pesach. An early Acharon based in Yerushalayim, the Mahari Chagiz (*Shu"t Halachas Ketanos* vol. 1, O.C. 150) ruled similarly. This is also cited by the *Melamed L'Ho'eel* (*Shu"t* vol. 1:87 and 88) in the late 1800s, that the *minhag* in Yerushalayim (*Takkanas Yerushalayim*) dating back to at least 5602/1842 was not to use sesame oil, nor various nuts for Pesach. See also the recently published *Aderes Shmuel* (*Hanhagos U'Psakim* of Rav Shmuel Salant; *Hilchos Pesach* 113, pg. 117–118) that cites an article from Rav Yechiel Michel Tukachinsky published in the *Chavatzeles* in 5655/1885 that the *Gedolei* Yerushalayim of the time, Rav Shmuel Salant, the Maharil Diskin, and the Lubliner Gaon (author of *Shu"t Toras Chessed*), Rav Schneur Zalman Frodkin (Liader), all took a stand and publicized not to use sesame oil on Pesach (and not as erroneously publicized earlier in different periodicals that the Maharil Diskin permitted it). In fact, in 5669/1909 there was a huge *machlokes* between Rav Avraham Yitzchak *Hakohen* Kook (at the time Chief Rabbi of Yaffo) and members of the *Badatz Hachassidim* of Yerushalayim, Rav Dovid Lipman Shuvaks, Rav Yosef Yehuda *Halevi* Strasbourg, and Rav Avraham Hakohen, about the permissibility of using sesame oil for Pesach (as fascinatingly detailed at length, with the *teshuvos* of both sides printed in the plainly titled "*Kuntress*"). Although under his personal *hashgacha* for Pesach, Rav Kook was nevertheless informed not to let the manufacturers bring the sesame oil to Yerushalayim, as there it was always considered *kitniyos*. This is further attested to by Rav Yisrael Nissan Kuperstock in his *Shu"t Ani Ben Pachma* (26) in 5688/1928, that the leniency for sesame oil on Pesach was not accepted in Yerushalayim. An enlightening *teshuva* from that period, by Rav Akiva Yosef Schlesinger, detailing the above *machlokes*, as well as Rav Schlesinger's lenient ruling and logic, was recently printed in *Kovetz Moriah* (vol. 388–390, Nissan 5774). Many opine that this *minhag* Yerushalayim dates back to the *Talmidei HaGr"a*, as it is well known (see *Maaseh Rav* 184) that the Vilna Gaon was extremely *makpid* with even considering seeds, as well as their oils, as *kitniyos*. See *Shu"t Yissa Yosef* (O.C. vol. 2, 111:4) who writes that Rav Yosef Shalom Elyashiv's being *machmir* for cottonseed oil ["*Minhag Yerushalayim Shemen*

On the other hand, we find that another New World crop, corn, was seemingly unanimously included as part of the *kitniyos* prohibition.[5] Aside from the fact that the words "corn" and "grain" both stem from the same root, "corn" is actually only the name for the grain "maize" that is used in the United States, Canada, and Australia. In other parts of the English-speaking world and much of Europe, the term "corn" is a generic term for cereal crops, such as real *chometz*—wheat, barley, oats, or rye. In fact, the infamous British Corn Laws (1815–1846) were concerning wheat and other grains, not corn.[6]

Kutna Kitniyos B'Pesach"—see *Orchos Rabbeinu* (vol. 4, pg. 166:49], is based on the *Maaseh Rav*. The *Badatz Eidah Hachareidis* of Yerushalayim trace their *minhagim* regarding *kitniyos* back to the *Maaseh Rav* as well (see their *Madrich HaKashrus for Pesach*, 5773, pg. 163, and 5774, pg. 172–173). It is known that Rav Moshe Feinstein was personally *machmir* for the Vilna Gaon's *shittah* as well, and did not use cottonseed oil on Pesach. [See *Shmaatseh D'Moshe* (*Pesach, Shemuos Moshe* 453:2, pg. 368), *Mesores Moshe* (vol. 1, pg. 149:301), and *Kuntress Yad Dodi* (pg. 119, *Hilchos Pesach*, Question 53)]. This is opposed to the common American *minhag* to allow cottonseed oil for Pesach—based on the *Shulchan Aruch Harav's shittah* (ibid.) that the *kitniyos* prohibition does not include seeds, and especially as cottonseed is inedible in its natural form. Many authorities including the *Melamed L'Ho'eel* (ibid.), Tzehlemer Rav (as cited in Rav Avraham Blumenkrantz's annual *Kovetz Hilchos Pesach*, ibid.), Rav Yosef Eliyahu Henkin (ibid.), Rav Tzvi Pesach Frank (ibid.), the Klausenberger Rebbe (ibid.), and the *Chelkas Yaakov* (ibid.), permitted it for Pesach use outright. Additionally, the many Acharonim who permitted other types of questionable oils for Pesach (see previous footnote) would certainly allow cottonseed oil as well.

5   See *Chok Yaakov* (O.C. 453:1), *Elyah Rabba* (ad loc. end 2), *Pri Megadim* (ad loc. E.A. 1), *Ba'er Heitiv* (ad loc. 1), *Machatzis Hashekel* (ad loc. 1), *Aruch Hashulchan* (ad. loc. 3), *Mishnah Berurah* (ad loc. 4), *Shemiras Shabbos Kehilchasa* (new edition; vol. 1, Ch. 40:92), and *Mesores Moshe* (vol. 2, pg. 101:190). The *Chasam Sofer* (*Shu"t* O.C. 121) even feels that we should treat corn as a *"chashash dagan,"* suspected grain!

6   Thanks are due to Rabbi Arnie Wittenstein for pointing out this essential historical fact. This author recently found in Rav Yitzchak Isaac Krasilishtzikov's noteworthy *Toldos Yitzchak* commentary on the *Yerushalmi* [which quite

Additionally, corn exhibits many characteristics of real-deal *kitniyos*: it grows near other grains, has small kernels, is made into flour (that can be easily confused with grain flour), and corn bread is made from it. Therefore, since corn fits many of the criteria of *kitniyos*, as opposed to potatoes, it was included in the prohibition.

Contemporary Quinoa Controversy

All this said, which category should quinoa be a part of?

- Like the potato and be excluded from the prohibition?
- Or like corn and be considered *kitniyos*?

Actually, contemporary authorities and kashrus agencies have been debating just this very question.

It turns out that quinoa is *halachically* similar to the peanut, meaning that its status is debated.

View #1—Quinoa Is Not Kitniyos [Star-K, cRc, and Kof-K]

Several major American kashrus agencies, including the Star-K,[7] who follow the *psak* of Rav Moshe Heinemann, and the cRc (Chicago Rabbinical Council),[8] following the *psak* of Rav Gedalia Dov Schwartz,

---

incredibly, was written in secret over a period of thirteen years in Communist Russia and subsequently smuggled out] (*Challah* Ch. 1, Mishnah 1, 1b s.v. *v'hashifon*), that he translates *"shifon"* (rye; one of the five grains) as "corn *b'laaz*" (in the vernacular).

7   See *Kashrus Kurrents* article titled "Quinoa: The Grain That's Not" by Rabbi Tzvi Rosen of the Star-K, originally published in 1997, and the *Star-K 2013 Passover Directory* (pg. 52).

8   As per cRc alert dated February 23, 2012: "In 2007 HaRav Gedalia Dov Schwartz, *shlit"a*, the *Av Beis Din* of the *Chicago Rabbinical Council*, issued a *psak* that quinoa is not considered *kitniyos* and therefore may be used on Pesach. Most of the quinoa comes from Peru and Bolivia and has been grown in areas where other (problematic for Pesach) grains were generally not grown. However, as the popularity of quinoa has risen, this is no longer the absolute case. This was confirmed this year by a Star-K *mashgiach* who visited Bolivia and found that barley does indeed grow in those areas. It was also recently discovered that some farmers cover their quinoa with barley and/or oats to

as well as the Kof-K,[9] maintain that quinoa is essentially kosher for Pesach. Since it is not even remotely related to the five grains, (in fact, it is also not a legume and not botanically related to peas and beans, which are of the original species of *kitniyos* included in the decree) and was not around at the time of the *kitniyos* prohibition, it is not considered *kitniyos*. Additionally, the Star-K tested quinoa to see if it would rise, yet instead, it decayed, a sure sign that it is not a true grain. The only issue, according to them, is the fact that quinoa is processed in facilities that other grains are processed in. Therefore, they maintain,

---

keep the birds from eating the quinoa while it dries. Finally, there is a concern that the sacks used to transfer the quinoa may have been previously used to hold barley or oats. We have, therefore, determined that the only way to allow quinoa for use on Pesach is to track the quinoa from certain farms that are free from the above concern. The Star-K spearheaded this endeavor and sent a *mashgiach* to find such a farm. While they were successful in their search, it proved to be challenging from a practical point of view, as the company visited generally sells their products in large quantities. The Star-K has now worked with other companies to pack the usable quinoa into smaller packages, and several options have been approved for Pesach quinoa consumption."

[9] As per personal communication received from Rabbi Moishe Dovid Lebovits, Rabbinic Coordinator at the Kof-K in April, 2013. This author has heard similarly from Rabbi Michoel Scharf, Executive Kashrus Director of London's Kedassia kashrus agency (in April, 2019), that although they do not consider quinoa *kitniyos*, nonetheless, due to other Pesach concerns, a reliable *hashgacha* for Pesach is a necessity. The Kashrut Authority of Australia and New Zealand holds similarly, as in their *5777 Guide to Pesach* (pg. 45) they write: "Quinoa is subject to significant *halachic* debate. Some authorities opine that quinoa is not *kitniyot* at all. Others maintain that even if it is not *kitniyot* there is a common practice to cover harvested quinoa with barley that may be *chometz*. This is a serious concern and as such we can now only recommend quinoa that comes with a reliable kosher for Pesach certification such as an OU-P or Star-K P or any other reliable *hechsher* can be used. We do not consider quinoa *kitniyot* but it must come with reliable supervision." Kosher Australia's *Guide to Pesach 2017/5777* (pg. 25) states likewise, "There are various opinions re: the status of quinoa. Due to changes in the production of quinoa in recent years, only quinoa with reliable Kosher for Pesach approval should be used on Passover."

if quinoa is processed in facilities under special reliable Pesach supervision, there is no Pesach problem. In fact, every year since, the Star-K has given special kosher for Passover *hashgacha* on specific production runs of quinoa.[10]

View #2—Quinoa is Classified as Kitniyos

However, Rav Yisroel Belsky,[11] Rosh Yeshivas Torah Vodaath and chief *Posek* for the OU disagreed. He argued that since quinoa fits every criterion for *kitniyos*, it should be included in its prohibition. Quinoa is the staple grain in its country of origin. It is grown in proximity of and can be mixed up with the five grains. It is collected and processed the same way (and in the same facilities) as the five grains, and is cooked into porridge and breads the same as the five grains. He maintained that it should be compared to corn, which was, for similar reasons, included in the *kitniyos* prohibition. Although quinoa is a New World food item and was not included in the original prohibition, nevertheless, he explained that that line of reasoning applies exclusively to items that are not clearly *kitniyos*, to foods that may share only several characteristics with *kitniyos*. However, since quinoa and corn would certainly have been included in the *Gezeira* had they been discovered, as they share every criterion of *kitniyos*, they are consequently by definition considered *kitniyos*. This stringent view is shared by Rav Dovid Feinstein, Rav Osher Yaakov Westheim of the *Badatz Igud Rabbanim* of Manchester, and Rav Shlomo Miller of Toronto, among other well-known *Rabbanim*.[12]

---

10 As per the cRc and Kof-K, it is important to note that even the quinoa that is under Pesach supervision should be carefully checked before Pesach for any foreign matter (such as barley) before use. This can be done by spreading the quinoa out on a plate and carefully checking that there are no other grains or foreign matter mixed in. However, this author has been informed by Rabbi Zvi Goldberg of the Star-K that if one purchases the quinoa for Pesach that is under their *hashgacha*, checking is unnecessary.

11 *Sappirim* (vol. 25: *Ve'Kasher Hadavar*, July 2012, pg. 9).

12 As elucidated later on in this chapter. Rav Dovid Feinstein's opinion is stated in *Kuntress Yad Dodi* (pg. 119: *Hilchos Pesach*, Question 51). Rav Shlomo Miller's strongly-worded letter on topic dated 2 Nissan 5775, was first published in

The Approach of the OU and the OK

On the other hand, the OU's other main *Posek*, Rav Herschel Schachter, Rosh Yeshivas Rabbeinu Yitzchak Elchanan (YU), permits quinoa, concluding that if it is processed in a special facility with no other grains, it should be essentially permitted for Passover use. Due to the difference of opinions of their top *Poskim*, until fairly recently, the OU did not certify quinoa as kosher for Pesach.[13] However, in late 2013, the OU made a decision allowing quinoa for Pesach, provided that it is processed with special Passover supervision. In fact, the OU recommended quinoa for Pesach 2014 and actually started certifying special Pesach processing runs.[14] [15] [16] [17] This certification continued for

---

Kovetz Eitz Chaim (vol. 27; Nissan 5777, pg. 95). Rav Westheim's opinion was confirmed on March 5, 2018, by direct communication. He wrote, "Regarding quinoa for Pesach, it seems to me quite clear that quinoa is in fact *kitniyos* and therefore cannot be used by Ashkenazim who do not use *kitniyos* on Pesach (and probably also not by those Sefardim who don't eat all *kitniyos* for Pesach)." Thanks are due to R' Yaron Shulman for facilitation.

13 Although the OU's other main *posek*, Rav Herschel Schachter, permits quinoa, until recently the OU did not grant it Pesach approval out of deference to Rav Belsky's ruling. This is what the OU released about quinoa in the past: (http://oukosher.org/passover/guidelines/food-items/quinoa/): "There is a difference of opinion among Rabbinic decisors (*Machloket Ha-Poskim*) as to whether quinoa is considered *kitniyot*. Ask your Rabbi for his guidance. Additionally, while quinoa is not one of the five grains that can create *chometz* (wheat, oat, barley, spelt and rye), and quinoa is not grown in the same vicinity as the grains mentioned above, the processing of quinoa is sometimes done at the same location where they process wheat and wheat flour. It is highly doubtful that the mills are effectively cleaned between grains. The concern of wheat flour or particles finding their way into the quinoa flour would be a serious one." Indeed, in an OU Kosher Pre-Pesach webcast on March 12th, 2013 (available at: http://www.yutorah.org/lectures/lecture.cfm/791649/ Rabbi_Hershel_Schachter-Rabbi_Yisrael_Belsky/OU_Kosher_Pre-Pesach_ Webcast_5773_%282013%29), after Rav Belsky and Rav Schachter state their opinions on the matter, Rav Schachter notes that although he personally disagrees with Rav Belsky, the OU still follows Rav Belsky's opinion, and hotels under the OU will not use quinoa for Pesach.

14 This is what the OU released regarding quinoa on December 20, 2013: "Quinoa is Now Kosher for Passover with OU-P Certification" (http://www.ou.org/news/quinoa_kosher_for_passover_/). "Rabbi Menachem Genack, CEO of OU Kosher, announced today that quinoa, the grain-like seed grown in South America, is Kosher for Passover when processed with special OU Passover supervision and bearing the OU-P symbol. His statement is as follows: "It is only recently that quinoa has become popular outside of its high-altitude growing area in the Andean mountain region of South America. Known for its nutritional qualities, it has been referred to as a "superfood." In recognition of its unique properties and growing popularity with consumers, 2013 has been proclaimed by the UN "The International Year of Quinoa." Due to conflicting reports regarding growing conditions and final usage of this new world, gluten-free pseudo-cereal plant, OU Kosher was hesitant to conclusively declare it Kosher for Passover and non-*kitniyot*. (*Kitniyot* is a category of foods that were forbidden by Ashkenazic custom during Passover because 1) they bear similarities to and might become confused with forbidden grains and 2) can become intermingled with those grains. Included in this group are: beans (all), buckwheat/kasha, caraway, cardamom, chickpeas, corn, fennel, fenugreek, grains-of-paradise, lentils, millet, mustard, peas, poppy seeds, rapeseed/canola, rice, sesame seeds, snow peas, sorghum, sugar-snap peas, soybeans, sunflower seeds, and—according to some—include even cottonseed.) Following extensive research and on-site investigation of cross-contamination issues by OU Kosher personnel at all quinoa growing areas including: Puno, Cuzco, Arequipa, Ayacucho, Junin, and Chiclayo in Peru; and Alto la Paz and Chayapata in Bolivia; as well as the collection, washing and milling stations of quinoa, OU Kosher is pleased to announce that, for the first time, it is recommending quinoa for Passover, when processed with special OU Passover supervision and bearing the OU-P symbol. In addition to quinoa, OU Kosher has concluded that related canihua, kiwicha, and maca seeds processed under supervised conditions may also be approved for Passover (OU-P)."

15 This author has also communicated with Rabbi Shoshan Ghoori, then of *Aish HaTorah* Chile, who had the unique experience of performing the quinoa investigation in the Andes Mountains for the OU. He presented the following information and findings after studying various growing and processing regions of the Andes: Since quinoa is a prized product both for export and for local consumption it is generally grown in large fields that are focused on just quinoa. He added that as quinoa's popularity and prices rise, this point

Pesach 2015, and currently the OU continues to grant special Pesach supervision annually for quinoa.[18]

Similarly, although the OK considered quinoa *kitniyos* for many years, in 2018 they reversed their longstanding policy and no longer regard quinoa as *kitniyos*. As such, they presently allow it to be served at their Pesach programs, provided that it has a *hashgacha* for Pesach. However,

---

is even stronger. He has found that the traditional use of quinoa is not the same as the use of grains. It is not generally made into breads or other similar grain type foods by the Andean communities, but rather is an all around "superfood" used for soups and teas, etc., just like maca, canihua, and kiwicha. After visiting approximately fifteen quinoa processing plants, he has yet to find one (not a gathering nor a washing station) that produces or mixes problematic grains (that could be an issue for *chometz* or *kitniyos*) in the same plant as quinoa.

16 This does not mean that Rav Belsky had actually changed his position. In fact, this author has heard from several of his *talmidim*, as well as my father, renowned kashrus expert Rav Manish Spitz, who spoke with Rav Belsky directly shortly before his *petirah*, that he still personally did not recommend quinoa for Pesach use. This is also reported by his nephew, Rav Dovid Ribiat, in his recent *Kuntress Hilchos Pesach—Halachos of Pesach* (2015 edition, pg. 152) in a conversation on Pesach 5774, after the OU started Pesach supervision for quinoa. Indeed, the KM (Kosher Miami), whom one of their *Poskim* is Rav Yaacov Gross, Rosh Kollel of the Miami Beach (Lakewood) Community Kollel and son-in-law of Rav Belsky, does not allow quinoa in any of their Pesach programs due to Rav Belsky's *psak*.

17 This author was not entirely surprised by the OU's eventually permitting quinoa for Pesach use, as a contact at a Kashrus agency wrote to me in 2014 that "As far as U.S. *psak*, the Star-K, Kof-K, cRc Chicago, and half the OU (Rav Schachter) hold it's not *kitniyos*, so it's very strong and not likely to go away or become the *minhag* to *assur*. I think the OU will probably be *mattir* in future years based on Rav Schachter's *psak*, but I am only guessing."

18 As attested to in a recent article in the OU's 2019 pre-Pesach *Daf HaKashrus* (vol. 27, issue 3; March 2019) titled "OUP 2019:" "The OU continues to give certification to Passover Quinoa. Quinoa will be available with an OU-P from Goldbaum, Pereg, and La Bonne. La Bonne and Goldbaum's will also have OU-P chia seeds. Pereg will also be selling quinoa flour."

they currently do not actually grant certification to quinoa as "kosher for Passover."[19]

Other Agencies and *Poskim*

Although by 2019 all of the American "Big Five" kashrus agencies either permit or actually certify quinoa for Pesach, on the other hand, not every *hashgacha* in North America agrees with this permissive ruling. For example, the *Hisachdus HaRabbanim* (CRC) does not recommend quinoa for Pesach as they consider it *kitniyos*,[20] as does the COR of Toronto,[21] the MK of Montreal, and KM of Miami.[22] This also is the

---

19 As per personal communication received from a consumer liaison at the OK in March, 2014: "OK Kosher Certification considers quinoa as *Kitniyos*." The OK's new quinoa guidelines were confirmed by Rabbi Yakov Teichman, the OK's Food Service Operations Coordinator, in April 2019, via personal communication, and officially, in their Spring 2020 issue of *Kosher Spirit* magazine.

20 As per personal communication with a CRC Kashrus representative on Jan. 17, 2017. He added that those who are *meikil* with eating *kitniyos* on Pesach (Sefardim) should make sure to only use quinoa with a reliable Pesach *hashgacha*, as it otherwise is generally processed in the same plants as *chometz*. Not to get confused with the Chicago Rabbinical Council (cRc) mentioned earlier, the Central Rabbinical Congress of the U.S.A. and Canada (CRC) is commonly referred to as the "*Hisachdus HaRabbanim*" and is based out of Williamsburg, Brooklyn, New York.

21 As per an article on the COR website titled "Is Quinoa Quitniyos" (accessible at: http://cor.ca/view/159/is_quinoa_quitniyos.html); and in personal communication with Rabbi Tsvi Heber, Director of the COR. He wrote that while the COR will not change its *shittah* vis-à-vis its own certified establishments, it has decided to advise the *tzibbur* to consult with their own Rav regarding the status of quinoa.

22 Although in their *2019 Pesach Guide Book* the MK (Canada's Kosher Certifier) does not state an actual opinion on the matter, but rather that there are those that allow quinoa and others who do not recommend it, and each individual should ask their own Rav; nonetheless, in personal communication with a Kashrus representative (April, 2019), this author was informed that the MK does not approve nor recommend quinoa for Pesach use. In a similar vein, albeit "across the pond," according to Rabbi Hillel Royde, Kashrus Coordinator

Badatz Eidah Hachareidis of Yerushalayim's approach, as in their annual *Madrichei HaKashrus*,[23] they maintain that food items that are planted in the ground as seeds (*zironim*), harvested as seeds (*garinim*), and are edible are considered *kitniyos*. As mentioned previously, the Yerushalmi *mesorah* for this goes back centuries. They therefore quite definitively include quinoa as *kitniyos*.

---

for the Manchester Beis Din (also known as "MK") via personal communication (in April, 2019): "we are aware of the fact that there are various opinions. We have not been asked to give a *hechsher* for such products, but I presume that we would take a strict view and forbid quinoa." As mentioned previously, the KM of Miami does not allow quinoa in any of their Pesach programs.

23 *Badatz Eidah Hachareidis* of Yerushalayim's annual *Madrich HaKashrus* (Ch. 15:4; e.g., 5772, pg. 47; 5773, pg. 163; 5774, pg. 173). This can also be seen on pg. 38 of the 5773 Pesach *Madrich HaKashrus* regarding the listing of baby cereals which are permitted for Pesach use even though they contain *kitniyos*, such as rice, quinoa, and corn flour; and on pg. 133, quinoa is outright classified as *kitniyos* (pg. 143 in the 5774 edition). Thanks are due to Rabbi Tzvi Price for pointing this out. Although this author has heard differing accounts from various North American kashrus agencies as to what *Mori v'Rabi* Rav Yaakov Blau *zt"l*, head of the *Badatz's hashgacha*, held regarding quinoa, when I asked his son, Rav Chaim Yosef Blau (his father's successor and current Rav of Pagi/Sanhedria in Yerushalayim) about his father's position, he replied that he never heard his father discuss it, and that he would be quite surprised to hear that it would be different than the *Badatz's* official position. See also current Chief Rabbi of Israel Rav Dovid Lau's *Shu"t Maskil L'Dovid* (end 15, s.v. *quinoa*) who reports that after hearing differing accounts as to Rav Blau's *shittah* regarding quinoa, he asked him directly and Rav Blau replied that he never checked into the matter sufficiently to permit it for Pesach and when he was asked previously (over fifteen years prior) he simply replied that "he did not know (anything about the topic)." Thanks are due to Rabbi Naftali Zvi Frankel for providing this author with this important source. This author has heard similarly from Rav Gershon Bess of Los Angeles (in 2013), who informed this author that he also spoke with Rav Blau directly and Rav Blau told him that although it was said in his name that he was *mattir* quinoa, it is not accurate, and although he was asked this question, he did not tell them it is not *kitniyos* and was not *mattir*.

The View from Israel

Other *Poskim* who ruled similarly include Rav Yosef Shalom Elyashiv, who ruled that quinoa should be considered *kitniyos* after being shown it and hearing from representatives of various kashrus agencies,[24] and Rav Asher Weiss (the renowned *Minchas Asher*), who addressed this topic in his weekly *halacha shiur*, as well as in several responsa (including one to this author; appended at the conclusion of this chapter), and concluded that it is indeed *kitniyos*.[25] This is also the opinion of Rav Yehoshua Neuwirth, venerated author of *Shemiras Shabbos Kehilchasa*, Rav Yaakov Ariel of Ramat Gan, Rav Mordechai Najari of Maaleh Adumim, and insect-checking expert Rav Moshe Vaye.[26] Similarly, the current Ashkenazic Chief Rabbi of Israel, Rav Dovid Lau, wrote that quinoa is only permitted on Pesach for "*Ochlei Kitniyos.*"[27] This also appears to be the Israeli *Rabbanut's* position as well.[28]

---

24 As heard from Rav Elyashiv's noted *talmid*, Rav Nochum Eisenstein, *Mara D'Asra* of Maalot Dafna, Yerushalayim, and in personal communication with Rabbi Sholem Fishbane, Kashrus Administrator of the cRc. Rav Elyashiv's position and his meeting with members of American kashrus agencies regarding quinoa's status first appeared in the English Israeli *Yated Ne'eman* in 2006.

25 *Shiur* delivered on March 6, 2013, accessible at: https://www.box.com/shared/a1y5cl7vio1x34ziwh6h. Rav Weiss also has written several *teshuvos* on topic, including one to this author—see http://en.tvunah.org/2014/03/23/quinoa-on-pesach and *Kovetz Eitz Chaim* (vol. 27, Nissan 5777; pg. 92–95).

26 Rav Neuwirth's, Rav Ariel's, and Rav Najari's *shittos* are printed in a *maamar* by Rav Dovid Avraham Spektor of Beit Shemesh accessible at: http://www.ohelyonah.com/shutim/%D7%A7%D7%99%D7%A0%D7%95%D7%90 D7%94_%D7%91%D7%A4%D7%A1%D7%97.pdf. However, although Rav Spektor personally concludes that quinoa is indeed *kitniyos*, following the above mentioned *Rabbanim* as well as Rav Elyashiv, he also cites that Rav Avigdor Nebenzahl of the Old City of Yerushalayim and Rav Dov Lior of Kiryat Arba are of the opinion that it is not, and is permissible for Pesach. Rav Spektor adds that in his opinion, if one normally eats quinoa every day for health reasons, he may rely on the *mekilim* and do so on Pesach as well, even though this does not fit into the classic category of an actual *choleh*. Rav Vaye's *shittah* is printed in his recent *Pesach Kasher V'Samayach* (pg. 12:2).

The Quinoa-Kitniyos Conundrum

Additionally, the largest Sefardic kashrus agencies in Israel, the *Beit Yosef* and Rav Shlomo Machpud's *Yoreh Deah*, although giving *hashgacha* on quinoa for Pesach, both qualify that it is reserved exclusively for "*Ochlei Kitniyos*," squarely calling quinoa *kitniyos*. In light of all this, in addition to the *Badatz Eidah Hachareidis*' prevailing approach of following the Yerushalmi *mesorah* based on the *talmidim* of the Vilna Gaon, it seems much less likely to see quinoa gracing Pesach tables in Eretz Yisrael.[29]

In Israel, even the Sefardic hechsherim classify quinoa as kitniyos.

A Balanced Approach

Rav Avraham Blumenkrantz, in his annual *Kovetz Hilchos Pesach*, took a middle road approach, acknowledging both sides to this quinoa quarrel. He did not give carte blanche for everyone to use it for Pesach, but concluded that anyone who suffers from gluten or any Pesach-related allergies or conditions (e.g., celiac) may comfortably use quinoa on Pesach without hesitation. This is also the opinion of Rav Dovid Ribiat, author of *The Thirty-Nine Melachos*, as well as the view of the London Beis Din (KLBD).[30]

---

27 *Shu"t Maskil L'Dovid* (end 15, s.v. *quinoa*). He concludes that although quinoa is commonly referred to as "the mother of all grains," nonetheless, since it is not an actual grain, it is still permitted **for Sefardim** to eat on Pesach.

28 Rav Lau's *teshuva* on *kitniyos* and quinoa is reprinted in the *Rabbanut's Madrich HaKashrus* (Pesach 5774, pg. 47) as their official position on quinoa.

29 Indeed, while researching this topic, I came upon this amusing anecdote from a website titled "*Galus Australis*" (dated March 31st, 2013): "While shopping in a local Jerusalem supermarket during *Hol Hamoed* I asked a worker (who happened to be Arab) where I might find quinoa. This gentleman looked at me aghast and, with a tone filled with rebuke, informed me that quinoa was not kosher for Passover...."

30 *Kovetz Hilchos Pesach* (2006, pg. 141–143). This is also the position taken by Rav Dovid Ribiat, author of *The Thirty-Nine Melachos*, in his recent *Kuntress*

Rav Mordechai Tendler, grandson of Rav Moshe Feinstein and author of *Mesores Moshe*, told this author that this is the approach that he felt his venerated grandfather would have taken and not (as many mistakenly opine) that Rav Moshe would have permitted it outright, had quinoa been introduced while he was still alive.

In this author's estimation, the point Rav Tendler was making is that there seems to be a common misconception that Rav Moshe Feinstein, in his oft-cited *teshuva* defining peanuts' *kitniyos* status, gave a blanket *hetter* for any "New World" food item. In this author's opinion, this is not entirely correct, as was mentioned previously that everyone considers corn as *kitniyos*, even though it was introduced long after the *kitniyos* restriction. Rather, Rav Moshe used that as a *sevara* (and he was neither the first nor the only *Posek* to do so) to explain why potatoes were not included in the restriction, as well as peanuts for those who did not have an existing *minhag*.

Meaning, Rav Moshe held that *minhag* and similarity to all *kitniyos* factors also play an important role in classifying *kitniyos*; ergo, he did not intend to give a carte blanche *hetter* for every "new food." As such, Rav Tendler was relating, it would seem tenuous at best to apply that *teshuva* as the exclusive basis to a *hetter* permitting quinoa for Pesach.

This is also the understanding of his uncle, Rav Moshe's son, Rav Dovid Feinstein, as well as his father and Rav Moshe's son-in-law, Rav Moshe Dovid Tendler; both of whom do not recommend Ashkenazim eating quinoa on Pesach. In fact, this is explicitly written as Rav Moshe's *shittah* in the recently published *Mesores Moshe* vol. 2, that Rav Moshe

---

Hilchos Pesach-Halachos of Pesach (2015 edition; pg. 153:3, par. "*Halachic* conclusion*"*): "In practice, persons with limited diets, or who are otherwise sensitive to gluten and ordinary grain products may rely on the lenient opinions regarding quinoa. This applies even to those whom grain products are not dangerous, but merely a cause of significant discomfort." The KLBD recently released this statement (United Synagogue's *Daf Hashavua*, *Parashas Tzav* 5775, pg. 4): "Given its *kitniyot* qualities, KLBD does not permit eating quinoa on Pesach unless you have specific health-based dietary requirements. If you have such requirements, please contact both your rabbi and doctor for advice before Pesach."

related that although corn is also a New World food item, it was nonetheless added to the restriction as it fits many of the same criteria of the prohibited *kitniyos*, as opposed to potatoes and peanuts.[31]

Quinoa Conclusion?

It seems that there truly is no quiet, clear-cut conclusion to this contemporary kashrus controversy. Can one eat it on Pesach? One must

---

31 *Shu"t Igros Moshe* (O.C. vol. 3:63), see *Kuntress Yad Dodi* (pg. 119: *Hilchos Pesach*, Question 51), and *Mesores Moshe* (vol. 2, pg. 101, O.C. 190). In a recent *teshuva* to this author (first printed in *Kovetz Eitz Chaim* vol. 27, Nissan 5777, pg. 94–95, and later in this author's *M'Shulchan Yehuda* pg. 33), Rav Asher Weiss concurred with this understanding of Rav Moshe's *psak*. Although there are those who claim that Rav Dovid Feinstein has recently changed his mind, and this author was even shown a video attesting to this [where after Rav Dovid was first informed that quinoa is a type of spinach and that Rav Moshe Heinemann of the Star-K ruled that it was not *kitniyos* as it is a New World food item, and that although Rav Dovid himself would not eat it on Pesach, he was then asked if could others rely on the opinion that it was not *kitniyos*, and Rav Dovid responded in the affirmative], nonetheless this claim seems to be not fully accurate. In the words of Rav Yitzchok Dovid Frankel, long-time *talmid*, author of the aforementioned *Kuntress Yad Dodi* (a compendium of Rav Dovid's *psakim*), and Rav of Agudath Israel of the Five Towns, via personal communication in April, 2019: "This is a complicated issue based on seemingly contradictory approaches. Reb Dovid has not changed his mind and personally will not eat or permit quinoa irrespective of any videos to the contrary. How the question is framed makes all of the difference. Reb Dovid will never tell anyone that he can't be *somech* on a reliable opinion even if he disagrees (see *Yad Dodi* page 143, #37). The *Rosh HaYeshiva ztzvk"l* (meaning Rav Moshe) held very strongly about *aid echad ne'eman*. So if someone asks "May I be *somech* on the OU *hashgacha* of Quinoa (on Pesach)?" He will say yes! They don't ask "Does the *Rosh HaYeshiva* hold that quinoa is *muttar*?" This is quite reminiscent of the cottonseed oil disagreement (see *Yad Dodi* page 145, #46)." Regarding cottonseed oil, Rav Frankel is referring to Rav Moshe's known adverseness to it as he held it was truly *kitniyos*, but nevertheless, since it was already *mekubal* when he came to America (as most *Poskim* in America had *paskened* like the *Shulchan Aruch Harav* over the Vilna Gaon's opinion on this topic), he never told anyone that they should not use it for Pesach. This was discussed at length in a previous footnote.

ask his own personal local *halachic* authority for guidance to clear up any quinoa/*kitniyos* kashrus confusion or questions.[32]

All else equal, in this author's mind, one thing is certain regarding a holiday that is all about *mesorah* and tradition: quinoa was not served at Bubby's *Seder*!

---

32 This author was recently interviewed on the "Kashrus on the Air" radio show, discussing both sides of the debate regarding whether quinoa should be considered *kitniyos*. A recording of this show may be accessed at: https://soundcloud.com/jroot-radio/yosef-wikler-apr-07?in=jroot-radio/sets/kashrus-on-the-air.

The Quinoa-Kitniyos Conundrum   255

אשר זעליג וייס
כגן 8
פעיה"ק ירושלם ת"ו

בס"ד

כבוד ידי"נ ויקיר לבבי
חכם וסופר, מורה הוראה ומרביץ תורה
הרה"ג ר' יהודה בצלאל שפיץ שליט"א

הנני במענה קצר למכתבו היקר, ובהתנצלות מרובה על איחור תשובתי.

בדבר גדר קטניות שכתבתי (לעיל סימן ???) שאין דעתי נוחה ממה שכתב מרן האגרות משה (או"ח ח"ג סימן ס"ג) דאין איסור קטניות בבוטנים משום שמין זה לא היה מצוי באירופה בדור שבו אסרו את הקטניות, ולענ"ד אין הלכה זו תלויה כלל במין המסויים והמוגדר אם היה בכלל הגזירה ולא מצינו בדברי הראשונים רשימה של המינים שנאסרו, אלא אמרו איסור כללי למיני הקטניות והפוסקים שבכל דור ודור פלפלו ודנו מה בכלל ומה יוצא מן הכלל, ואבן הבוחן היה מאז ומעולם הטעם שאסרו את קטניות, וכל שלפי הטעם והסברא יש לחשוש בו בכלל האיסור וכל שלפי הטעמים לאסור קטניות אין לחשוש בו מותר.

ואחד הטעמים שדחיתי סברת האג"מ, מה שנקטו כל הפוסקים שתירס בכלל איסור קטניות הוא אף שגם התירס לא היה מצוי באירופה בימי הראשונים והגיע מאמריקה לאירופה לפני כחמש מאות שנה.

ומעיקר"ד טעם מאז שגם הגרמ"פ לא היה נחרץ בסברא זו ועיקר טעמו בהיתר הבוטנים לא היה משום המנהג והמסורה, ובמדינת ליטא לא נהגו איסור בבוטנים.

ובמכתבו ציין לספר "מסורת משה" שזה עתה יצא לאור, ורואח ק"ץ (ועמוד קי"א) מובא שכן שאלו את פי הגאון מה בין בוטנים לתירס, והשיב "כנראה חכמי הדור שבהם בא התירס כן אסרו אותו, ומסתמא שייך עליו הטעמים שיש בשאר קטניות, שעושים ממנו לחם וכו' מה שאינו בבוטנים".

ושמחתי לראות את הדברים כי יש בזה חיזוק למה שדרשתי וכתבתי מאז ומקדם, שאין הדבר תלוי אלא בטעם האיסור, והעיקר כיון שאין לאיסור זה כל מקור בדברי חז"ל אלא מסורת מדורות הראשונים אין הדבר תלוי אלא מנהג אבותינו שבידינו, ובמקום שאין מנהג, ובמינים החדשים שאין לגביהם מנהג יש לדון לפי טעמי האיסור ביושר הסברא.

בְּאַהֲבָה יְתֵירָה
וּבְהוֹקָרָה מְרוּבָּה
אשר וייס

A Teshuva that this author received from Rav Asher Weiss regarding quinoa and kitniyos.

Chapter 20

The Coca-Cola Kashrus Controversy

Ice-Cold Sunshine

Aah! The cool refreshing taste of "The Real Thing"! Is there anything (besides maybe baseball and apple pie) that is considered more American? Everyone also knows that around the world (pretty much) there is almost nothing more kosher than good, old-fashioned Coke. Why, you can even ask Grandma, who'll tell you that back in the day, before iPods, mp3s, microwaves, dishwashers, and even World War II, it was "Always Coca-Cola." Indeed, "Dr. Pemberton's Pick-Me-Up," later regarded as "the great national temperance beverage," was THE drink of choice for all, even the strict kosher consumer.

However, it wasn't always that way. We all have a certain person to thank for that—Rav Tuvia (Tobias) Geffen (1870–1970), Chief Rabbi of Atlanta, Georgia, for many decades. He was one of the select few who actually knew the closely guarded secret ingredient in Coke.

Coke cap from the 1930s featuring Rav Geffen's hashgacha.

How did this come about?

Back in the 1920s and 30s, Coke was (and I'm sure still is) looking to expand their market share. It came to their attention that if they received a *hashgacha*, many more Jews (and others who look specifically for kosher products) would drink freely of the "pause that refreshes."

So, the directors approached the most likely candidate to grant rabbinic supervision, Rabbi Geffen. Coke was, after all, invented and headquartered in Atlanta. He was more than willing to check it out, as many of his congregants were asking him about the kashrus status of Coke.

Kosher Coke?

His findings were mixed for, although technically the drink was kosher and was permitted to be drunk, it was questionable whether he could give it his seal of approval to allow observant Jews to purchase it. The reason was that although they claimed it to be "as pure as sunlight," it turned out that there was a non-kosher ingredient, later revealed to be animal-based glycerin,[1] in the makeup of Coke, but it was only present in minute quantities. Therefore, it would technically be permitted to drink, for the non-kosher ingredient was *battel b'shishim*, and therefore considered nullified.[2]

However, for Rav Geffen to grant Coke *hashgacha* posed a potential problem in a different category, that of *"Ain Mevattlin Issur Lechatchilla."*[3] This means that although if a non-kosher substance would accidentally

---

[1] Animal-based glycerin is generally considered non-kosher, following the Mishnah's (*Bechoros* 5b) dictum *"hayotzei min hatamei, tamei*—anything that comes out from (or its basis is from) a non-kosher animal is deemed non-kosher." As such, even though animal-based glycerin is technically an industrial by-product that includes other ingredients in its makeup and is formed after a strong chemical reaction, nevertheless, a food's kashrus status depends on the source material from which it was drawn, and hence such glycerin is commonly considered non-kosher. [See for example, Rav Moshe Sternbuch's *Shu"t Teshuvos V'Hanhagos* (vol. 3:255) and Rav Yisroel Belsky's *Shu"t Shulchan Halevi* (Ch. 20:1 and *Chelek Birurei Halacha* 18) for a discussion as to the kashrus issues inherent in glycerin.] However, see the postscript of this chapter for an alternate, minority view of glycerin when it is but a small part of a mixture and not added for taste, allowing room for leniency in a final food product based on a combination of various *halachic* rationales.

[2] Although there are exceptions, this is the standard rule of nullification in *halacha*. If there is present sixty times the amount of non-kosher, then the non-kosher substance is considered nullified, and the mixture permitted *ex post facto*. See *Tur*, *Shulchan Aruch*, and main commentaries to *Yoreh Deah* (98).

fall into kosher food (as long as there was the prerequisite sixty times the amount of non-kosher that fell in), it would be permitted to drink, nonetheless, if one would add it on purpose with the express intention of nullifying it, the entire mixture becomes forbidden for the person who transgressed and for whomever he intended to benefit.[4]

Can I Buy the World a Coke?

The issue at stake here was that the Coca-Cola Company was obviously putting this non-kosher ingredient in the batch purposefully, as it was part and parcel of the Coke everyone knew and loved.

On the other hand, it was not just a simple open-and-shut question, for the Coca-Cola Company was not owned or run by Jews, and quite obviously was not marketing Coke exclusively for Jews.

Therefore, Rav Geffen was in a bit of a dilemma: Did this situation fall under the category of *"Ain Mevattlin Issur Lechatchilla"* and therefore Coke would be unacceptable for purchase by the kosher consumer? And,

---

3   See *Shulchan Aruch* (Y.D. 99:5) and main commentaries ad loc.

4   There is an interesting *machlokes* Acharonim as to how to properly define the prohibition as it relates to others. The *Taz* (Y.D. 99:4), citing precedent from the Rashal (*Yam Shel Shlomo*, *Chullin* Ch. 7:59), maintains that the prohibition only applies to the nullifier's family and/or if the person whom the nullification was performed on his behalf knows about it and wanted it done. On the other hand, Rav Akiva Eiger (ad loc. 4), citing precedent from the *Rivash* (*Shu"t* 498 s.v. *v'af al pi*), argues, asserting that the prohibition applies even in a commercial setting. He rules that if one nullifies *issur* with no one specific in mind, it becomes prohibited for all to benefit from it, as it is considered as if it was nullified expressly for their purchase. Accordingly, although the customer is entirely ignorant of what has transpired, he may not partake of the product. Although other Acharonim are divided as to whom the *halacha* follows with no clear-cut consensus, and some argue that the precedents are not entirely accurate, nevertheless, many later authorities exhort caution with purchasing such products, following the ruling of Rav Eiger. See *Shu"t Atzei Halevanon* (Y.D. 43), *Chazon Ish* (Y.D. 37:13 s.v. *ulefi zeh*), *Shu"t Seridei Aish* (vol. 2:69; new edition vol. 2:21 s.v. *bram*), *Shu"t Minchas Yitzchak* (vol. 2:28, 20), and *Shu"t Igros Moshe* (Y.D. vol. 2:32).

even if it did not, and was permissible for purchase, was he allowed to give his *hashgacha* on a product that contained a non-kosher ingredient? Before we get to the punch line, let us "go through the *inyan*."

Non-Jewish Nullification

Already in the 1500s, the *Radbaz* made a distinction between a scenario where a non-Jew nullifies a non-kosher ingredient in a kosher product, where he permits a Jew to partake of the mixture, as opposed to where a non-Jew is selling such a product, where he rules that it is forbidden for a Jew to purchase. He maintains that when a Jew is purchasing the item, it is as if he himself nullified it, and therefore it becomes prohibited for him to eat.[5]

Many *halachic* authorities concurred with his reasoning and likewise forbade a Jew from purchasing items that had non-kosher nullified inside of it.[6]

However, the majority of *Poskim* disagreed with this rationale, concluding that it is improbable to make such a distinction,[7] as the *Rambam*

---

5   *Shu"t HaRadbaz* (vol. 3:978; old print 547).

6   See Chida (*Shiyurei Bracha* Y.D. 99:5), *Levushei Srad* (*Chiddushei Dinim, Hilchos Nosein Taam Lifgam* 58:153), *Zechor L'Avraham* (vol. 3, Y.D. s.v. "*Bitul*"), *Beis Avraham* (Y.D. vol. 2:108, 13), *Beis Yehuda* (*Shu"t Minhagei Ar'jil* [Algiers] pg. 115, third column:68), *Shu"t HaMaharshdam* (Y.D. 53), and *Shu"t HaRashbash* (560). The *Bach* (*Shu"t* 123) implies this way as well, that purchasing from a non-Jew is considered "*lechatchilla*," and is therefore prohibited as *bitul issur* is only permitted *b'dieved*. The *Minchas Yitzchak* (*Shu"t* vol. 2:28, 20) seems to be *choshesh* for this opinion as well.

7   *Shu"t Maharam M'Lublin* (104), *Minchas Yaakov* (35:2), *Shu"t Noda B'Yehuda* (*Tinyana* Y.D. 56 and 57), *Shu"t Beis Yitzchak* (Y.D. vol. 1:142, 8 and *Kuntress Acharon* 31), *Shu"t Chasam Sofer* (Y.D. 82), *Shu"t Ksav Sofer* (O.C. 87), *Pischei Teshuva* (Y.D. 134: end 8), *Shu"t Imrei Binah* (*Dinei Bassar B'chalav V'Taaruvos* 14; although he concludes that it is preferential to be *machmir* in both instances), *Erech Hashulchan* (Y.D. 99:8), *Zivchei Tzedek* (ad loc. 36), and *Shu"t Beis Shlomo* (O.C. 97), that whatever was produced by a non-Jew is already considered "*b'dieved*" and therefore permissible for purchase. Many contemporary authorities concur with this assessment, including Rav Eliyahu

himself held that it is acceptable to procure such items as long as the prohibited act of nullification was performed by a non-Jew, as for him, it was never forbidden. They therefore maintain that such a product is still suitable for purchase by a Jew. [8]

Still, to further complicate our case, the *Tashbetz* made a further qualification to this permissible ruling, following the precedent of the *Rashba* and *Raavad*.[9] They explain that although one may rely upon a non-Jew's nullification for purchase in infrequent circumstances, conversely, if the non-Jew is doing it for his job, or on a frequent basis, then certainly it is considered as if the Jew himself nullified it. Several *Poskim* agreed with this decision as well.[10] Following this ruling would seem to

---

    Gutmacher (*Shu"t Mahar"a Gutmacher* Y.D. 32), Rav Henoch Padwa (*Shu"t Cheishev Ha'Eifod* vol. 2: end 104, s.v. *v'ata*), Rav Moshe Feinstein (*Shu"t Igros Moshe* Y.D. vol. 1:62 s.v. *u'mdin*, and 63; Y.D. vol. 2:32 and 41), Rav Betzalel Stern (*Shu"t B'tzeil Hachochma* vol. 4:89, 13 and 14; and 104:18), his brother, the Debreciner Rav (*Shu"t Ba'er Moshe* vol. 3:109, 21), and Rav Ovadiah Yosef (*Shu"t Yabia Omer* vol. 7, Y.D. 7).

8   *Rambam* (*Hilchos Maachalos Assuros* Ch. 3:13). This is also the ruling of his *rebbi*, the *Ri Migash* (cited by the *Ran* in *Avodah Zarah*, 13b in the *Rif's* pagination, s.v. *v'hisi'u ledavar achar*).

9   *Shu"t Tashbetz* (vol. 3:10), *Shu"t HaRashba* (vol. 3:214; cited by the *Beis Yosef*, Y.D. end 134 s.v. *chometz*, and by the *Magen Avraham* O.C. 442: end 1), and *Raavad* (cited by the *Ran* and *Beis Yosef* ibid). A case can be made for positing that this is also the *Ran's* opinion, as he concludes his passage with the words of the *Raavad*.

10 *Shulchan Aruch Harav* (O.C. 442:6, and *Kuntress Acharon* 5; who adds that "...*b'Yoreh Deah hiskimu hakol l'divrei HaRashba*"), *Chida* (*Birkei Yosef, Shiyurei Bracha* Y.D. 134:4, Din 14 s.v. *kol hamashkim*), *Shu"t Divrei Chaim* (vol. 2, Y.D. 53), *Shu"t Maharam Schick* (O.C. 9), *Shu"t Imrei Aish* (vol. 1, Y.D. 42), *Shu"t Avnei Tzedek* (O.C. 51), *Sdei Chemed* (vol. 1, *Klalim, Maareches Ha'Alef*, 360, and in *Pe'as Hasadeh* 10), *Arugas Habosem* (*Kuntress HaTeshuvos* 15), *Shu"t Atzei Halevanon* (Y.D. 43 s.v. *ach da*), and *Shu"t Tiferes Shmuel* (17). Conversely, the *Pischei Teshuva* (Y.D. 134: end 8) and *Gilyon Maharsha* (ad loc. s.v. *kol*; however and quite interestingly, in the beginning of *Hilchos Taaruvos*, Y.D. 98 s.v. *issur* he implies that one needs to be *machmir* for a non-Jew mixing in *issur* frequently) conclude that the *ikar* follows the *Noda B'Yehuda* (ibid. s.v.

imply that Coke would have to be prohibited to the kosher consumer, as it is definitely mass produced.

How About a Coke?

So, with our being the wiser, having a basic understanding of the issues involved, what did Rav Geffen decide to do? Feeling uncomfortable by having to make such a difficult decision, where *Gedolim* through the ages have taken stands on both sides of the matter, he did the only thing he felt he could do—try to make *shalom*! He went to Coca-Cola and actually asked them to change their formula. Surprisingly, out of respect for him, the executives listened and the company removed the problematic ingredients and replaced them with kosher alternatives (vegetable-based glycerin), making the soft drink kosher *lechatchilla* for everyone, proving the adage that "things," including kashrus, "go better with Coca-Cola."

---

v'amnam) who rules leniently based on the *Rambam* and *Ri Migash* over the *Rashba* and *Raavad*. The *Noda B'Yehuda* adds that the *Shulchan Aruch* himself implied this way [however, the *Minchas Yitzchak* (*Shu"t* vol. 2:28, 9–18) questions this assessment, citing that the *Shulchan Aruch* in Y.D. 134:13 expressly rules like the *Rashba*; see how he deals with this difficulty at length, concluding that the *Noda B'Yehuda* was drawing a distinction between *taam* that was *nirgash* or not]. A similar assessment is given by the *Seridei Aish* (*Shu"t* old print, vol. 2:69; new edition vol. 2-Y.D. 21 s.v *ulam* and *v'hinei*). On the other hand, although there is undeniably what to rely upon, other contemporary authorities nonetheless advise caution, and especially *lechatchilla*. In fact, the *Melamed L'Ho'eel* (*Shu"t* vol. 2, Y.D. 29) only allows one to rely on this *b'shaas hadchak*. Others, including the Mahari Assad (*Shu"t Yehuda Yaaleh* vol. 2:122), maintain that one who can be *machmir* "*tavo alav bracha*." Rav Yosef Eliyahu Henkin (*Eidus L'Yisrael* pg. 177; and in his recent posthumously published *Shu"t Gevuros Eliyahu* vol. 2-Y.D. end 16 s.v. *u'bvaday* and 25) advised to be *choshesh* for this as well. See also Rav Shmuel Chaim Yaakov Gruber's *maamar* in *Kovetz Ohr Yisroel* (vol. 30, pg. 123; who quite interestingly cites only the *lomdus* of Rav Geffen's *teshuva*, with no mention of the practical outcome) and Rav Yisroel Belsky's *Shu"t Shulchan Halevi* (Ch. 25:1) who concludes that although there is what to rely upon, nevertheless, "*mikol makom nireh pashut shebaal nefesh yisrachek mizeh*."

Rav Geffen later published the whole account, as well as the *halachic* reasoning behind his actions, in his responsa.[11] Later *halachic* authorities as well ruled similarly to Rav Geffen's sound logic and reasoning, averring that although there is what to rely upon regarding purchasing, nevertheless, when it comes to granting *hashgacha*, a rabbinic authority should not give a seal of approval to an item that contains nullified *issur*.[12] In fact, as mentioned in a previous chapter, Rav Moshe Feinstein classified doing so, if nullification is the only justification they are relying upon to proclaim the product kosher, as *"mechuar hadavar*, utterly disgraceful or disgusting."

Knowing all this, the next time you partake in a nice, cool, refreshing glass of Coke, you should think of Rabbi Geffen, as well as all the behind-the-scenes kashrus issues that went into making sure that even the kosher consumer can enjoy "the cold, crisp taste of Coke." [13]

---

11 *Shu"t Karnei HaHod*, vol. 2, last responsum in the *sefer*, titled *"B'dvar Hamashkeh HaCoca-Cola."* This *teshuva*, perhaps the most famous in the annals of American history, has also been translated to English and can be found on the HebrewBooks website—http://www.hebrewbooks.org/pdfpager.aspx?req=2379andst=andpgnum=122andhilite=.

12 See Rav Moshe Feinstein's *Shu"t Igros Moshe* (Y.D. vol. 2:41 s.v. *v'im*), Rav Moshe Sternbuch's *Shu"t Teshuvos V'hanhagos* (vol. 1:440), Rav Menashe Klein's *Shu"t Mishnah Halachos* (vol. 7:113, 2), and Rav Shmuel Halevi Wosner's *Shu"t Shevet Halevi* (vol. 9:165).

13 However, this was not the last time Coke's kashrus status was challenged. In 1957, Cincinnati based Proctor and Gamble (P&G), the source of Coke's vegetable-based glycerin, changed their glycerin production lines from the batch processing method to a continuous flow system, making the kosher glycerin processed on the same lines as the non-kosher animal equivalent, and thus, due to the issue of *bliyos*, absorption, rendering its technically kosher vegetable glycerin non-kosher. Rav Eliezer Silver, Rav of Cincinnati and *Rosh Agudas HaRabbanim* of the United States and Canada, intervened, and at his behest, P&G constructed a parallel production line exclusive to vegetable-based glycerin, and thus ensuring Coke's kashrus. According to historian Roger Horowitz, in his recent book *Kosher USA: How Coke Became Kosher and Other Tales of Modern Food* (pg. 43), this modification came at a cost of thirty thousand dollars, quite a large sum for the time. More recently,

Passover Passport to Refreshment

There is actually more to the story. It turns out that another ingredient inside Coke (later revealed to be grain alcohol) was *chometz*, and as the laws of *bittul* do not apply to *chometz* on *Pesach,* Coke was therefore technically not kosher for Passover. At Rav Geffen's behest, this ingredient was also replaced by a kosher *l'Pesach* alternative (alcohol from fermented molasses). In fact, Coca-Cola was considered kosher for Pesach all year long until the "New Coke" debacle in the mid-1980s. When the general public rejected the new flavor and the company reinstated the "Original Coca-Cola Classic," there was one minor change in the formula. Cane sugar was replaced with a cheaper alternative: high-fructose corn syrup. The one kashrus concern with this is that it is *kitniyos,* which Ashkenazim do not consume on Pesach.[14] That is why Coca-Cola and other soft drinks require specific Passover supervision. There are numerous die-hard Original Coke aficionados who drive many miles during the Passover shopping season to major metropolitan areas with a large Jewish concentration, just to purchase "the Coke with the yellow bottle cap." For these fans, if it's not the Passover Coke, it's just not the "Real Thing."

Postscript: Coca-Cola: The First *Hashgacha*

Interestingly, it is known that, historically, Rav Geffen was not actually the first to grant *hashgacha* on Coca-Cola. In certain regional

---

in January 2014, an anonymous writer in the controversial *HaPeles* newspaper in Jerusalem made an astonishing and entirely unsubstantiated claim that all Coca-Cola in the world nowadays, including that under strict *hashgacha*, is actually non-kosher. His misleading "findings" were based on "an anonymous kashrus expert" and the *first half* of Rav Geffen's *teshuva* from 1935, with absolutely no mention of the responsum's conclusion—how Rav Geffen persuaded Coke to change their formula and that it was subsequently rendered kosher *l'divrei hakol*! In response, this author submitted the full text of Rav Geffen's *teshuva*, as well as a sharply written rejoinder *"lehaamid davar al boryo,"* which was consequently published to correct misconceptions.

14   This issue is discussed at length in the chapter titled "The *Halachic* Adventures of the Potato."

markets, several *Rabbanim* had given *hashgacha* in the late 1920s and early 1930s, and the *Vaadei HaKashrus* of Buffalo, Chicago, Montreal, and Rochester likewise followed. In fact, there were ads for kosher Coke published in the famed *HaPardes* Torah Journal. These ads contained a small letter from Rav Shmuel Aharon Halevi Pardes, the journal's editor, that he visited the Coca-Cola factory in Atlanta, and that they "revealed to him all of their secrets, including their secret formula," and he found "*hamashkeh Coca-Cola kosher lishtoso al pi hadin*"[15] (based on an original letter Rav Pardes wrote, dated March 9, 1931).

Long-running ad for kosher Coke in HaPardes, featuring a brief letter from Rav Shmuel Pardes attesting to its kashrus status.

Ad for kosher Coke from 1931, featuring the hashgacha of Rav Yaakov "JB" Bienenfeld and several Vaadei HaKashrus. (Picture courtesy of his descendant, Rabbi Yaakov Bienenfeld)

These *Rabbanim* included Rav Yaakov "JB" Bienenfeld of New York, Rav Avraham Meir Franklin of Buffalo, and Rav Shmuel Aharon Pardes of Chicago himself, who, aside from being well-known *talmidei chachamim*, were not exclusively relying on the lenient precedent of many *Poskim*

---

15 In this author's estimation, Rav Pardes seems to have purposely worded his letter in an exacting manner. He wrote that Coke was permitted to be drunk "*al pi hadin*." This phraseology is usually reserved for stating that an item is technically permitted on a basic level, but not necessarily in the most optimal manner or for those who were more scrupulous to adhere to a more stringent level of kashrus. [Although it is interesting that the ad itself that printed his words on the bottom, claimed that Coke was kosher "*b'tachlis hakashrus*."] Contrast Rav Pardes' succinct wording with that of Rav Geffen's *teshuva* after

[including the *Noda B'Yehuda*, *Pischei Teshuva* and *Gilyon Maharsha*, who followed the *Ri Migash* and *Rambam's* permissive positions over that of the *Rashba*, *Raavad*, *Tashbetz*, and *Shulchan Aruch Harav* et al.] regarding the nullification of *issur* performed by non-Jews, even on a steady basis. They also maintained that since in this case the potential non-kosher ingredients were added in such a minuscule amount that they were not being used for actual taste, and originated in a laboratory that put them through a chemical change, they were no longer considered food and therefore permitted. Not only is this *shittah* supported by several Rishonim,[16] but Rav Pardes wrote extensively on this topic, including a

---

Coke's formula was later changed at his behest with all problematic ingredients removed: "*attah yuchlu le'henos u'lishtos me'hamashkeh Coca-Cola af HaMehadrin b'yoseir*, now even those who are the most exacting with kashrus can drink and enjoy Coca-Cola."

16 Including Rabbeinu Yonah (cited by the *Rosh* in *Brachos* Ch. 6:38; regarding musk), as well as the *Ran* to *Avodah Zarah* 39a (17b s.v. *misrach* in the *Rif's* pagination) regarding honey manufactured by non-Jews; see also *Magen Avraham* (O.C. 216:3), as well as the *Machatzis Hashekel* (O.C. 427: end 45) who posits that the *shittas hamachmirim* is only applicable when the nullified product is explicitly added for taste or *maamid* purposes, which is seemingly not the case with Coca-Cola, as the glycerin was chemically altered and added in such minute quantities (.09%). Additionally, scientifically speaking, glycerin is essentially an industrial by-product that assumes independent existence during the processing of fatty oils for soap. Although sweet, it is the predominant chemical left in after the soap is extracted, and as it is generally used to keep foods "moist and fresh," was likely used in Coke simply to aid the taste of the main ingredients diffusing evenly. As such, according to Rabbi Yaakov Bienenfeld, descendant of Rav Yaakov "JB" Bienenfeld who gave the first *hashgacha* on Coke [this *sevara* is also cited and applied to glycerin by Rav Pardes in his posthumously published *Avnei Shmuel* (*Birurei Halacha*, end 20)], the animal fat is certainly not the sum total of the glycerin process, as in order to make glycerin, many other ingredients are involved. Hence, even if we would hold *lechatchilla lo batul*, nevertheless, when it is placed in minute quantities in the original Coke there is arguably another strong factor to allow it: since it is essentially the second *taaruvos* that the non-kosher ingredient was placed inside, it should qualify as "*trei mashehu lo amrinan*" [see *Taz* (Y.D. 92:16) regarding a double *taaruvos* including *chometz*, based on the *shittah* of

letter to the *Gadol Hador*, Rav Chaim Ozer Grodzenski, who agreed that it is indeed *muttar*.¹⁷

Certainly, combining these factors, there was ample support for these renowned *Rabbanim* to grant *hashgachah* to Coke,¹⁸ even without its

---

Rabbeinu Tam (*Tosafos, Chullin* 100a s.v. *b'shekadam*; as cited by the *Tur*, Y.D. 92:4); however, it must be noted that the *Shach* (*Nekudos Hakesef* ad loc. 4) strongly disagrees with the *Taz's* understanding and application of Rabbeinu Tam's *klal*)] and by the second time (meaning the actual drink itself) it should be considered nullified and the drink permitted.

17 See, for example, *Shu"t Tzemach Tzedek* (*Hachadoshos*; Y.D. 67), *Yeshuos Yaakov* (end Y.D. 105), *Shu"t Maharsham* (vol. 3:234), *Shu"t Achiezer* (vol. 2-Y.D. 11:5), *Shu"t Seridei Aish* (old print, vol. 2:69; new edition vol. 2-Y.D. 21), *Avnei Shmuel* (*Birurei Halacha* 20), *Shu"t Chavalim B'Ne'imim* (vol. 5:17), *Shu"t Tzitz Eliezer* (vol. 6:16, 9–11), and *She'arim Metzuyanim B'Halacha* (47:5), who discuss the practicality of utilizing this *shittah* of the Rishonim *lemaaseh*; several of these *Poskim* actually discuss non-kosher glycerin used in small quantities as part of *taaruvos*. There is also a novel approach raised by Rav Chaim Halpern in his *maamar* (from 5742) printed in *Zecher Shlomo* (*Sefer Zikaron* for Rav Shlomo Zalman Goldshtoff, pg. 547–557), that perhaps the *Rashba* and *Raavad* were only referring to the *issurim* of non-Jews mass-nullifying their wine and vinegar, and not necessarily other food items. However, it must be noted that the vast majority of Acharonim throughout the centuries did not understand their opinions this way and this *havanna* in their *shittos* seemingly remains a *chiddush*.

18 It is important to point out that Rav Moshe Feinstein's later classification of granting *hashgacha* exclusively based on nullification as "*mechuar hadavar*," utterly disgusting, certainly was not at all analogous to and did not apply to the kashrus supervision of Coca-Cola of the 1920s and 30s. In Rav Moshe's case, the non-Jew initiated the desire to sell to Jews and requested rabbinical supervision in order to be granted certification to this end. However, in the 1920s, Coca-Cola was already around for several decades and everyone, many Jews included, was already drinking it assuming it was kosher, and the Coca-Cola Company itself in 1929 had no pressing reason to capture a minuscule "kosher market." Additionally, and as an interesting side point, it is unclear whether Rav Moshe personally would have ruled stringently in this specific case, as said non-kosher ingredient was later revealed as glycerin. This is because he was of the opinion (see *Shu"t Igros Moshe* Y.D. vol. 1:62 s.v. *u'mitzad*

later change of formula. As an aside and quite interestingly, as revealed by historian Roger Horowitz, Rav Geffen and Rav Pardes and other leading *Rabbanim* of that era actually exchanged *halachic responsa* on whether or not to rely on such rationales,[19] preceding and somewhat

---

chashash and Y.D. vol. 2:24 s.v. *ach af*) that glycerin as an ingredient does not give off a pleasant taste and is generally placed in products simply to make them easier to swallow; as such he held that it is not considered a food item and is therefore *battel b'rov* and not *b'shishim*. [Rav Yaakov Kamenetsky (*Emes L'Yaakov* on *Tur* and *Shulchan Aruch* (Y.D. 103, footnote 40) ruled similarly regarding toothpaste containing glycerin. On the other hand, their *talmid*, Rav Yisroel Belsky (*Shu"t Shulchan Halevi, Chelek Birurei Halacha* 18 s.v. *glycerin*), as well as Rav Moshe Sternbuch (*Shu"t Teshuvos V'Hanhagos* vol. 3:255), took an opposing viewpoint, explaining that although it goes through a chemical process, nonetheless, refined glycerin is essentially sweet, maintaining that it is commonly used by manufacturers as a sweetener as well. Rav Belsky adds that the word "glycerin" actually comes from the Greek *"glykeros,"* meaning "sweet." He relates an amusing anecdote about the Yeshiva janitor drinking diluted glycerin and commenting on how sweet and tasty it was. They draw a parallel and precedent from the *Chavas Daas* (Y.D. 103, *Biurim* 1), who holds that when a non-kosher item becomes *pagum*, if the *"davar mar,"* bitter ingredient, is later removed, and the item becomes sweet, it reverts to its original *assur* status. Rabbi Eli Gersten, in the OU's *Daf HaKashrus* (Tamuz 5778/June 2018, "Glycerin") writes that "while it is certainly possible that in former times the lye and salt were not completely separated from the glycerin and it remained with a foul taste (crude glycerin), today food-grade glycerin is very pure, and has a sweet pleasant taste."] Although it's technically true that Rav Moshe's *teshuvos* cited above were not discussing this exact *inyan* and nuance, nonetheless, it is still what Rav Moshe personally held, as this author personally confirmed with his son, Rav Reuven Feinstein, several years ago, as well as previously with his grandson, Rav Mordechai Tendler, both of whom informed me that this was indeed Rav Moshe's *shittah*. This is further corroborated by Rav Moshe's older son, Rav Dovid Feinstein, in the recently published *Shu"t Vidibarta Bam* (vol. 2:246 s.v. *v'shamaati*). Hence, as the glycerin was placed in minute quantities in the Coke, but was not added for taste, and with the additional various *halachic* rationales extant allowing leniency in this specific case, it is fairly certain that Rav Moshe would not have considered granting *hashgacha* to Coke in the 1920s and 30s as *"mechuar hadavar."*

paralleling the later *halachic* debate regarding the permissibility of animal-based gelatin.[20]

Still, Rav Tuvia Geffen's actions, unheard of for the time—persuading the Coca-Cola Company to actually change their formula, which was a monumental contribution in upgrading the ingredients and ensuring that Coke had zero potential kashrus concerns, and was permitted unequivocally—set a public precedent for later *Vaadei Kashrus* to follow as well: Even if an item is deemed *halachically* kosher, to try to go above and beyond the letter of the law, making certain that there is no *sheilah* on the product in question. This encapsulated Rav Geffen's greatness and is perhaps the reason that he is the one most commonly and closely associated with ensuring that "Coke is it" for the kosher consumer.[21]

---

19 *Kosher USA: How Coke Became Kosher and Other Tales of Modern Food* (pg. 34–36). This author wishes to thank Roger Horowitz for making available several of the original handwritten *teshuvos*. Although there are several responsa by Rav Pardes, as well as from Rav Avraham Nachman Schwartz of Baltimore and Rav Hersch Kohn of New York (perhaps best known as the rabbi who originally certified Maxwell House coffee as *Kosher L'Pesach*, and consequently the impetus for the ubiquitous *Maxwell House Haggadah* that "America grew up with"; quite the best-seller, this long-running "ad campaign" has seen more than fifty million copies published since 1934!), unfortunately, it seems that Rav Geffen's actual letters in response to them seems to have been lost to history.

20 This debate was addressed at length in the chapter titled "Genetically Engineered Meat," as well as extensively in the appendix.

21 This chapter was written in honor of my brother-in-law, Rabbi Ezra Carter, who, as a native Atlantean, was the impetus for my interest and research on this subject.

Chapter 21

Of Bull's-Eyes, the *Korban* Cheesecake, and Dairy Bread

THE HOLIDAY OF SHAVUOS, ASIDE from its most common name, has several others: *Chag HaKatzir* (The Holiday of the Harvest), *Atzeres* (Assembly), *Yom HaBikkurim* (Day of the offering of the first fruits), and *Zman Mattan Toraseinu* (The Time of the Giving of the Torah).

Yet, in Israel, it has gained a new moniker: *Chag HaGevinah*—The Holiday of the Cheese! It is amazing to find a Jewish custom that has become so commercialized.

Although no one really minds paying a lot less for all the various cheeses on sale during the weeks leading up to Shavuos, still, the idea that a "holiday" can be commercially sponsored (by the cheese companies, no less) should give us pause.

Interestingly, having cheesecake on Shavuos is one *minhag* with which many non-practicing Jews are stringent! Have you ever met someone who turned down a piece of cheesecake? Where does this time-honored traditional custom of consuming cheesecake on *Shavuos* come from?

Korban Cheesecake?!

It seems that one of the earliest mentions of such a *minhag* is by the great *Rema*, Rav Moshe Isserles, the authoritative decisor for all Ashkenazic Jewry, who cites the "prevailing custom" of eating dairy items specifically on Shavuos. Although there are many rationales and reasons opined through the ages to explain this custom,[1] the *Rema* himself provides an enigmatic one: to be a commemoration of a special *Korban*, the *Shtei Halechem* (Two Loaves of Bread) offered exclusively on Shavuos during the times of the *Beis Hamikdash*.[2]

However, since the connection between dairy food and the Two Loaves of Bread offering seems tenuous, the *Machatzis Hashekel* offers a remarkable glimpse as to the *Rema's* intent:

The *halacha* states that one may not use the same loaf of bread at both a dairy meal and a meat meal. The reason for this is that there may be some (possibly unnoticed) residue on the bread, and thus one might come to eat a forbidden mixture of milk and meat.[3]

---

1 This topic has been addressed by many—see the relevant commentaries to the *Rema's* (O.C. 494:3) comment, as well as Rav Yaakov Kamenetsky's *Emes L'Yaakov* on *Tur* and *Shulchan Aruch* (ad loc. s.v. *v'nohagin*) and Rav Shlomo Zalman Auerbach's *Halichos Shlomo* (*Moadim* vol. 2, Ch. 12, *Orchos Halacha* 1 and 35, and *Dvar Halacha* 10). There is even a recent *sefer*, *Metaamei Moshe*, who lists 149 (!) different reasons for this *minhag*. Actually, several Rishonim, including the *Kol Bo* (72 and in *Orchos Chaim, Tefillas HaMoadim* 13) and the *Melamed HaTalmidim* (pg. 121b) predate the *Rema* on this by several centuries, yet their mention is that of eating "milk and honey" together in order to be *yotzei* the *pasuk* in *Shir HaShirim* (Ch. 4:11), "*devash v'chalav tachas leshonecha*," that the Torah is compared to milk and honey. Interestingly, other Rishonim, including Rav Avigdor HaTzarfati (pg. 478) and the *Hagahos* to Rav Yitzchak Isaac Tirnau's *Sefer HaMinhagim* (*Hilchos Shavuos* 49), write a different reason to eat *milchigs* on Shavuos. The *pasuk*, when describing the holiday of Shavuos (*Bamidbar, Parashas Pinchas* Ch. 28:26) states that one should bring a "*mincha chodosha la'Hashem Bashavuoseichem*" of which the first letters spell "*meichalav*, with milk," implying that milk products should be eaten on Shavuos. This *minhag* is also mentioned by the *Terumas Hadeshen* (cited in *Leket Yosher* pg. 103) and Maharil (*Minhagim* pg. 85), yet, it was not until the *Rema* actually codified this *minhag* in *halacha* that it became widespread. See also Rabbi Dr. Eliezer Brodt's excellent recent related article "The Mysteries of *Milchigs*" (*Ami Magazine*, May 12, 2013, pg. 88–93).

2 See *Shemos* (*Parashas Ki Sisa*, Ch. 34:32), *Vayikra* (*Parashas Emor* Ch. 23:15–22); *Bamidbar* (*Parashas Pinchas* Ch. 28:26). This is the first Temple offering from the new wheat crop.

Therefore, in order to properly commemorate this unique *Korban* which had two loaves of bread, one should have a separate dairy meal, aside from the traditional meat meal one has on Yom Tov. This way, he will be mandated to have separate breads for each of these meals, as the *challah* meant for the dairy meal cannot be used for the meat meal, and vice versa.[4]

It is well known that our tables are compared to the *Mizbe'ach* and our food to *Korbanos*.[5] Therefore, serving a food item at a meal is considered an appropriate commemoration for a *Korban*. Consequently, by having an additional dairy meal, the outcome is a suitable commemoration for this unique *Korban*, as now on Shavuos, two separate distinct breads are being served. In fact, the venerated Rav Moshe Feinstein cites this explanation as the proper one for maintaining two separate types of meals on Shavuos, one milky and one meaty.[6]

Terrific! So now we can appreciate that by eating cheesecake on Shavuos, we are actually commemorating a special *Korban*! However, before we sink our teeth into a luscious calorie-laden (it can't be sinful—it's commemorating a *Korban*!) cheesecake, we should realize that

---

3   *Shulchan Aruch* (Y.D. 89:4) and relevant commentaries. See also Rav Chaim Palaji's *Kaf Hachaim* (Ch. 24:20), *Yalkut Me'am Loez* (*Parashas Mishpatim* pg. 890 s.v. *bassar achar gevina*), and *Shu"t Igros Moshe* (Y.D. vol. 1:38) for the parameters of this *halacha*.

4   *Machatzis Hashekel* (O.C. 494:7 s.v. *hu hadin b'Shavuos*). This explanation is also later cited by the *Mishnah Berurah* (ad loc. 14 and 15) and *Kaf Hachaim* (ad loc. 63). As mentioned in a previous chapter, he maintains that optimally, both should be part of the same meal.

5   See Gemara *Brachos* (55a), *Beis Yosef* (O.C. 167; quoting the *Shibolei Leket* 141), *Rema* (ad loc.), *Mishnah Berurah* (ad loc. 30) and *Shlah* (*Shaar Ha'Osiyos*, *Eimek Bracha* 66). This was addressed at length in the chapter titled "Salting with Sugar?!"

6   *Shu"t Igros Moshe* (O.C. vol. 1:160). See also *Darchei Teshuva* (89:19) who discusses the topic of *milchigs* on Shavuos at length, concluding similarly that it is proper to have a *milchig Kiddush* right after davening and later a *fleishig seudah*. This way, "*yotzin b'zeh l'kuli alma…v'zehu haminhag hamuvchar.*"

potentially, there might be another *halachic* issue involved: the prohibition against baking dairy bread.

Dairy Dilemma

Bread has been mankind's basic staple since time immemorial.[7] Therefore, Chazal were concerned that an unsuspecting person might mistake dairy bread for plain pareve bread and eat it together with meat. He would thus inadvertently violate the prohibition of eating a forbidden mixture of milk and meat. They thereby decreed that one may not bake dairy bread unless certain criteria are met:[8] either changing the shape of the dough prior to baking[9] (known as making a *shinui*), thereby making it instantly recognizable to all[10] as milky,[11] or baking dairy bread exclusively in small quantities.[12] The same prohibition and exclusions apply to meaty bread as well, due to bread's propensity to be eaten with a dairy meal.

---

7   *Devarim* (*Parashas Eikev* Ch. 8:3):"*Ki lo al halechem levado yichyeh ha'adam.*"

8   *Gemara* (*Pesachim* 30a and 36a).

9   According to the vast majority of *Poskim* this leniency only applies if the change was made prior to the baking. See *Pri Megadim* (Y.D. 97, S.D. 1 s.v. *v'im*), *Pischei Teshuva* (ad loc. 3), *Gilyon Maharsha* (ad loc. 2), *Chavas Daas* (ad loc. *Chiddushim* 5 and *Biurim* 3), *Arugas Habosem* (ad loc.), Maharsham (*Daas Torah* ad loc. 1), *Ben Ish Chai* (Year 2, *Parashas Shlach* 17 and *Shu"t Rav Pe'alim* vol. 2, Y.D. 11), *Yad Yehuda* (ad loc. *Peirush Ha'aruch* 3), *Zer Zahav* (on the *Issur V'Hetter* 40:4), *Levushei Srad* (*Chiddushei Dinim* Y.D. 139), *Ksav Sofer* (*Shu"t* Y.D. end 61), and *Aruch Hashulchan* (Y.D. 97:9). An interesting story is related about the *Chazon Ish* (cited in *Orchos Rabbeinu*, new edition, vol. 4, 26:6) that someone sent a dairy bread to a Yeshiva for the resident *bochurim* to enjoy; however, there was a note attached denoting that it was *milchig*. The *bochurim*, knowing the *halachos* of dairy bread, poured water on the bread in order to ruin it, as since there was no *shinui* baked into it, just an *ex post facto* note, which is *halachically* considered insufficient in this case, the bread would have been prohibited to be consumed. The *Chazon Ish* later concurred that they acted correctly, and did not have to worry that they might have violated the prohibition of *Bal Tashchis*, wasting edible food [see *Parashas Shoftim* (*Devarim* Ch. 20:19) and *Sefer Hachinuch* (ad loc. Mitzva 529)]. See following footnotes.

10 Shu"t Maharit (vol. 2:18), Pischei Teshuva (Y.D. 97:3), Pri Chodosh (ad loc. 1), Pri Toar (ad loc. 2; he adds that this is an issue only *lechatchilla*), Chochmas Adam (50:3), Aruch Hashulchan (Y.D. 97:7), and Kaf Hachaim (ad loc. 12). They all maintain that the *shinui* made to allow dairy bread must be known to all, and not just the local townspeople. A dissenting opinion is that of the Yad Yehuda (ad loc. Peirush Hakatzer 7), who argues that we need not concern ourselves with visiting guests for this *halacha*. The Kreisi U'Pleisi (ad loc. Kreisi 2) mentions similarly (although he notes that he protested), that since in his town every bakery baked with milk and everyone knew about it, it was considered a *hekker*. He concludes, however, that it would be preferable not to rely on this.

11 There is an interesting debate regarding "*biskugies*," apparently a type of bread that was commonly sold as pareve, with the Mahari Chagiz (Shu"t Halachos Ketanos vol. 1:56) writing briefly that since they are a type of bread and everyone assumes they are pareve, they also fall in the category of the dairy bread prohibition. This is according to the understanding of Rav Yaakov Emden (Shu"t Sheilas Yaavetz vol. 1:62), the Chida (Shiyurei Bracha Y.D. 97:1), and Zivchei Tzedek (ad loc. 8), and not like the Mahari's own son, who wrote, by amending and adding a few words to his father's responsum, that his father truly meant to permit them. The Yaavetz himself concludes that he does not know what "*biskugies*" actually are, but if they are, as he suspects, biscuits or cookies, then they are permitted to be baked dairy as they are not actual "bread." See also following footnotes.

12 Although most authorities are stringent even if someone violated the prohibition accidentally (as mentioned in a previous footnote), there are those, however, who are lenient if a tiny amount of milk *accidentally* spilled on bread—see Shu"t Aish Das (end 12), Shu"t Shoel U'Meishiv (Tinyana vol. 4: end 189), Nachlas Tzvi (Y.D. 97:1), Shu"t Nefesh Chaya (36), and Imrei Binah (Hilchos Bassar B'chalav 13). The Kreisi U'Pleisi (97, Pleisi 1, s.v. shamaati and Kreisi 3) quotes his grandfather as allowing one who made a large batch of dairy bread without a *shinui* to divide it up into small quantities and give it out to various households. Although the Chamudei Daniel (Taaruvos vol. 2:18) agrees with this, nevertheless most authorities do not, and rule that it is prohibited. The Kreisi U'Pleisi himself concludes that it is *tzarich iyun* to be lenient with this, and only allows its use as a *snif lehakel*. Yet, the Yad Yehuda (97, Peirush Ha'aruch 3), Chochmas Adam (50:5 and Binas Adam 51; in some editions 70), Zivchei Tzedek (97:6), Atzei Ha'Olah (Hilchos Bassar B'chalav

Bull's-Eye!

The *hetter* of baking dairy bread at all (according to the conditions above) is called by Chazal *"k'eyn tura"* (literally, like the eye of an ox; possibly the source for the expression "bull's-eye").[13] Although this expression is debated by the Rishonim, with *Rashi* explaining that it means a small amount (seemingly taking the bull's-eye idiom literally), while the *Rif*, *Rashba*, and *Rambam* maintain that it is referring to a changed shape so it may be obvious to all that it is dairy or meaty, nonetheless, the *Shulchan Aruch* rules that either one is an acceptable technique to ensure that the dairy bread will not be mixed up.[14]

Yet, even so, there is a practical difference between Sefardic and Ashkenazic *psak*:

- According to the *Shulchan Aruch*, the small amount of *milchig* bread that is permissible to make is only enough for **one meal**. This view is duly followed by Sefardic authorities.[15]
- The *Rema*, however, is a bit more lenient, allowing an amount necessary for **one day**, meaning a twenty-four hour period. This is the common Ashkenazic custom.[16]

12:3), *Aruch Hashulchan* (Y.D. 97:9), and *Kaf Hachaim* (ad loc. 9 and 11), rule that in case of great loss and it was done accidentally, one may indeed rely on this. This is also the ruling of the *B'tzeil Hachochma* (Shu"t vol. 6:84, 3 and 4) and the *Maadanei Hashulchan* (Y.D. 97:3 and in his Shu"t *Maadanei Melachim* 123). The *Ksav Sofer* (Shu"t Y.D. end 61) maintains that a baker is allowed to mass produce dairy bread on condition to exclusively sell a small amount to each family, as that is the normal method of selling. See also Shu"t *Even Yisrael* (vol. 9:67) and Shu"t *Shevet Hakehasi* (vol. 5:128).

13 Gemara *Pesachim* (36a).

14 *Rashi* (ad loc. s.v. *k'eyn tura*), *Rif* (Chullin 38a), *Rashba* (Toras Habayis Hakatzer Bayis 3, Shaar 4, 86a), *Rambam* (Hilchos Maachalos Assuros Ch. 9:22), and *Shulchan Aruch* (Y.D. 97:1).

15 *Shulchan Aruch* (ibid.). See *Ben Ish Chai* (Year 2, Parashas Shlach 17), *Kaf Hachaim* (Y.D. 97:7), and *Yalkut Yosef* (Kitzur Shulchan Aruch, Od M'Hilchos Bassar B'chalav 15).

16 *Rema* (ad loc. and *Toras HaChatas* 36:9). See *Pri Megadim* (ad loc. S.D. 1, s.v.

Let Them Eat (Cheese)Cake!

Although several authorities extend this prohibition to include other baked goods, such as cookies and bourekas,[17] which, if baked milky, might be mistakenly eaten with meat, nevertheless, the prevailing ruling is that the prohibition only applies to bread.[18] Even so, aside from the signs in bakeries proclaiming which items are dairy and which are pareve, it is nonetheless a widespread practice throughout Israel that bakeries form dairy baked goods (cheese bourekas, anyone?) in a triangular shape and pareve ones in a rectangular shape as an extra safeguard against mix-ups. Since at busy bakeries the potential for mistakes is quite high, this is done as an added precaution, even though *me'ikar hadin* it is deemed unnecessary by most authorities.[19]

So…does this ruling affect our beloved cheesecake in any way?

Actually, not much. In a typical cheesecake, since the cheese aspect of it is quite conspicuous,[20] it would be considered as if produced with a changed shape from standard dough. Additionally, cheesecake is universally recognized as…containing cheese (!) and thus known worldwide

---

v'im), *Chavas Daas* (ad loc. *Biurim* 3), *Yad Yehuda* (ad loc. *Peirush Hakatzer* 6), *Aruch Hashulchan* (ad loc. 4), *Atzei Ha'Olah* (*Hilchos Bassar B'chalav* 12:1), and *Darchei Teshuva* (ad loc. 17).

17 Including the *Taz* (Y.D. 97:1), *Pri Toar* (ad loc. 2), *Erech Hashulchan* (ad loc. 2), *Zivchei Tzedek* (ibid.), and *Ben Ish Chai* (ibid.).

18 Including the *Maharit* (*Shu"t* ibid.), *Pri Chodosh* (Y.D. 97:1), *Minchas Yaakov* (60:3), *Chavas Daas* (Y.D. 97:1), *Chida* (*Shiyurei Bracha* Y.D. 97:3), *Pischei Teshuva* (ad loc. end 3), *Yeshuos Yaakov* (ad loc. 1), *Yaavetz* (*Shu"t* ibid.), *Machatzis Hashekel* (Y.D. 97 s.v. *ayin*), *Chochmas Adam* (50:3 and 7), *Atzei Ha'Olah* (ibid. 4), and *Aruch Hashulchan* (Y.D. 97:2). See also Rav Yisroel Belsky's *Shu"t Shulchan Halevi* (Ch. 22:7 and 8) and *Yalkut Yosef* (*Kitzur Shulchan Aruch, Od M'Hilchos Bassar B'chalav* 13).

19 See, for example *Ben Ish Chai* (ibid. mentioned as *minhag Baghdad*, and proper to do when selling *Mezonos* commercially), *Yalkut Yosef* (ibid. 12), and the *Badatz Eidah Hachareidis'* annual *Madrich HaKashrus* (e.g., 5778, vol. 2—*L'yemos Hashana*, pg. 121).

20 The *Be'er Sheva* (*Shu"t* 32) maintains that as long as some cheese is noticeable,

as being dairy.[21] No one would make a mistake confusing cheesecake with pareve bread. Therefore, even according to the opinions of those authorities who maintain that the prohibition of dairy bread extends to cakes, even so, they all agree it would be permissible to make plenty of cheesecake for Shavuos, even in large quantities.

Thankfully, when it comes time to indulge in a piece of traditional cheesecake on the holiday of Shavuos, we can "have our cake and eat it too," both in the literal sense as well as in the spiritual sense; knowing we have fulfilled the *halachic* requirements and are even commemorating a unique *Korban*.[22]

Postscript: Two *Brachos* for One (Cheese) Cake?

Another common question related to cheesecake concerns the proper *bracha* to recite, whether *Mezonos* or *Shehakol*. It seems that the consensus of contemporary authorities is that the correct *bracha* is subjective, depending on the makeup of each individual cheesecake and its crust,

---

it is considered an adequate *shinui* to allow it to be made. This is also cited by the *Pri Chodosh* (Y.D. 97: end 3), *Pri Megadim* (ad loc. S.D. 1), *Zivchei Tzedek* (ad loc. 10), *Ben Ish Chai* (ibid.), *Aruch Hashulchan* (ad loc. 5; who calls it *"Minhag Yisrael Torah"*), and *Kaf Hachaim* (ad loc. 1). Although the *Atzei Ha'Olah* (*Bassar B'chalav* 12, *Chukei Chaim* 1) is uneasy about a small amount of cheese being noticed, and others, including the *Gilyon Maharsha* (ibid.) and *Chamudei Daniel* (ibid.) maintain that said *shinui* must affect the entire dairy bread, nevertheless, where it would be recognizable throughout, as a cheesecake is, it would definitely be permitted. See also Rav Mordechai Eliyahu's *Darchei Halacha* glosses to the *Kitzur Shulchan Aruch* (46:13) and *Yalkut Yosef* (*Kitzur Shulchan Aruch, Od M'Hilchos Bassar B'chalav* 12).

21 *Maharit* (*Shu"t* ibid.), *Pri Chodosh* (Y.D. 97:1), *Ben Ish Chai* (ibid.), *Yad Yehuda* (ad loc. *Peirush Hakatzer* 7), *Aruch Hashulchan* (ad loc. 8), *Kaf Hachaim* (ad loc. 12, s.v. *u'va'ir*). As mentioned in a previous footnote, if it is recognizable to all, it is considered a proper *shinui*.

22 The author wishes to thank friend and colleague Rabbi Elie Schoemann, Rabbinic Coordinator of the *London Beis Din* Kashrus Division (KLBD), as his relevant article served as the impetus for my interest and research on this topic.

based on the laws of *Ikar* and *Tafel*—primary and secondary food.[23] If the crust is indeed deemed significant and adds necessary taste and crunch to the cheesecake, many *Poskim* maintain that making two separate *brachos* is the preferred option.[24] One should ascertain a final ruling on the matter from his or her own local *halachic* authority.

---

23 See *Orach Chaim* (212), based on Gemara *Brachos* (44a).

24 For example, see *Shu"t Igros Moshe* (O.C. vol. 4:43), *Shu"t Shevet Halevi* (vol. 4:23, 1), *Shu"t Rivevos Efraim* (vol. 2:77, end s.v. *nishalti*), *Shu"t Minchas Shlomo* (*Kama* vol. 2, 91:4), and *Shu"t Vidibarta Bam* (vol. 2:43; also citing Rav Dovid Feinstein's view). For more on the topic of *Ikar* and *Tafel*, see Rav Nissan Kaplan's *Shalmei Nissan* (*Perek Keitzad Mevorchin*, 80–84), Rabbi Mordechai Zev Trenk's *Brachos Basics* (Ch. 4), and Rabbi Avi Wiesenfeld's discussion on the *DinOnline.org* website: http://www.dinonline.org/2011/04/05/q-a-guide-to-the-halachos-of-brachos-ikar-tafel/#identifier_72_10407-Par. Cheesecake. The topic of the proper *bracha* of cheesecake is discussed at length in several recent *sefarim* devoted to the subject of *brachos*, including *V'zos Habracha*, *V'sein Bracha*, Rav Binyomin Forst's *Pischei Halacha: The Laws of Brachos*, and Rabbi Avi Wiesenfeld's *Pocket Halacha Series: The Halachos of Berachos: Ikar V'Tafel*.

Part 4

WASHING AND *PAS*

Chapter 22

The Colored Water Caper

IN NOVEMBER 2012, PLEASURE SEEKERS at Australia's famous Bondi Beach were left high and dry when a "Crimson Tide" rolled in, effectively transforming its normally tranquil waters into the "Red Sea." This rare natural phenomenon, more commonly known as an algal bloom, occurs when there is a rapid increase or accumulation in the production of microscopic algae (dinoflagellates, usually toxic phytoplankton) in an aquatic system. This results in a visible coloration of the water, typically taking on a reddish hue. Apparently, all was not "fair dinkum" in the Land Down Under. Not that it's any consolation for those robbed of a pleasure swim, nonetheless, this occurrence at least gives us an inkling of what *Makkas Dam* (Plague of Blood) might have seemed like, and also helps us understand an interesting *halacha*.

Colored Water?

The *Shulchan Aruch* rules, as the *Tur* did before him, and based on a Mishnah in *Maseches Yadayim*,[1] that regarding *Netillas Yadayim*[2] for

---

1 *Tur* and *Shulchan Aruch* (O.C. 160:1), *Maseches Yadayim* (Ch. 1, Mishnah 3).

2 The *Mishnah Berurah* (158:1; see also *Shaar Hatziyun* ad loc. 1 and 2) gives an excellent summary of the sources and reasons why *Netillas Yadayim* is mandated before eating bread, one of them being that it is alluded to by the *pasuk* in *Parashas Kedoshim* (*Vayikra* Ch. 20:7): "*V'hiskadeeshtem, V'heyisem Kedoshim*—And you shall sanctify yourselves, and be holy." The Gemara (*Brachos* 53b) clarifies that "And you shall sanctify yourselves" refers to washing the hands before the meal, *Mayim Rishonim*, and "and be holy" refers

eating bread,[3] if the water's appearance has changed, whether by itself or due to something else falling inside it or due to its location, that

---

to washing the hands after the meal, *Mayim Acharonim*. In other words, by washing our hands before making a *bracha* (in this case before eating bread), we are properly sanctifying ourselves. Another reason why we wash is to be akin to the *Kohanim* eating *Terumah*, who had to eat their food in purity. One should not make light of this obligation, as the *Shulchan Aruch* writes (O.C. 158:9) extremely strong ramifications for one who does, based on three separate *maamarei* Chazal (*Eiduyos* Ch. 5, Mishnah 6; *Shabbos* 62b; and *Sotah* 4b). For a thorough explanation of why Chazal were so *makpid* about this, see my ancestor and namesake the Maharal M'Prague's *Nesivos Olam* (*Nesiv Ha'Avodah* Ch. 16) at length. See also *Shemiras Haguf V'Hanefesh* (vol. 1, Ch. 55 at length).

3 Although this discussion actually pertains to washing before eating bread, and technically speaking, washing for *Hamotzi* and washing for morning *Netillas Yadayim* are each done for entirely different reasons (morning *Netillas Yadayim* is for *Nekiyus* and getting rid of *Ruach Ra'ah*) and should not share the same *halachos*, nevertheless practically, this whole discussion might actually apply to morning *Netillas Yadayim* as well. Although the *Shulchan Aruch* writes in *Orach Chaim* (4: end 1) concerning water whose appearance has changed or water "that work was done with," that it is unfit only regarding *Netillas Yadayim* for *Hamotzi*, yet, he adds in *se'if* 7 that one should be *makpid lechatchilla* even regarding water for *Netillas Yadayim* in the morning for the same issues as one does by washing for *Hamotzi* (see *Magen Avraham* and *Levushei Srad* on *se'if* 7). [If not, one might need to make a different *bracha* of "al nekiyus yadayim," see *Shulchan Aruch* (ad loc. 4: end 1) and *Levush* (ad loc.), but others disagree.] The *Abudraham* (*Hilchos Birchos Hashachar*), *Magen Avraham* (ad loc. 6), Vilna Gaon (*Biur HaGr"a* ad loc. s.v. *mihu*), *Pri Megadim* (E.A. ad loc. 3 and 4), *Chayei Adam* (vol. 1:2, 3) and *Mishnah Berurah* (4:16) all conclude that *me'ikar hadin* one does not need to be *makpid* on water "that work was done with" for morning *Netillas Yadayim*, but even so, *lechatchilla* one should strive to, if at all possible. However, Rav Yaakov Emden (*Mor U'Ketziah*, beg. 4) and the *Aruch Hashulchan* (O.C. 4:8 and 9) cite proof from the *Zohar* (*Parashas Vayeishev*, vol. 1, 184b), *Rambam* (*Hilchos Brachos* Ch. 6), and *Rashba* (*Shu"t* vol. 1:191), who do not seem to distinguish between the different types of washing (not that they necessarily agree with every varied nuance of *Hilchos Netillas Yadayim*), and rule that even regarding morning *Netillas Yadayim*, one is obligated *m'din* to make sure that the water was not

water is *pasul*, disqualified for being used for washing purposes. This *halacha* is gleaned from the water in the *Kiyor* (multi-fauceted laver) in the *Beis Hamikdash*, used to wash the *Kohanim*'s hands and feet. Just as if that water's appearance was changed it would be rendered unfit for use, so too our *Netillas Yadayim* water would as well.[4] This would mean that it should be prohibited to use sea water during a "red tide" to wash for *Hamotzi*.

Yet, we find that many authorities argue on part of the *Shulchan Aruch*'s statement. They point out that the Mishnah does not actually mention the water color being changed "by itself" with no outside stimulus, as making the water *assur*. The Mishnah only mentions the other criteria, namely different types of inks and dyes falling in, for prohibiting colored water.

Additionally, regarding such dyed water for use as a *mikva*, only when the color has changed due to something else falling in would such a *mikva* be invalidated, and not when the color has changed by itself.[5] It stands to reason that the rules of *Netillas Yadayim*, which are a *Takkanas Chachamim*, cannot be any stricter than those regarding the Biblical *mikva*!

A further proof cited is that the *Rambam*,[6] when codifying this *halacha*, omitted any mention of water whose color has been changed by itself being prohibited. Therefore, many *halachic* authorities, including the *Taz, Magen Avraham, Gr"a, Pri Megadim, Shulchan Aruch Harav, Chayei Adam, Kitzur Shulchan Aruch, and Mishnah Berurah*,[7] rule that water whose color has been changed by itself is perfectly permissible to be

---

"worked with," etc., and conclude *tzarich iyun* on the *meikilim*. To sum it up, one should indeed strive to ensure that the water used for morning *Netillas Yadayim* should meet the same strict requirements as washing for *Hamotzi*, even if not mandated *me'ikar hadin*.

4   See *Ra'ah* (*Brachos* 53b s.v. *chamei*), cited by the *Beis Yosef* (O.C. 161:1 s.v. *tzarich*) and *Mishnah Berurah* (ad loc. 1).

5   *Mikvaos* (Ch. 7, Mishnah 3), *Rambam* (*Hilchos Mikvaos* Ch. 7:12), *Beis Yosef* and *Shulchan Aruch* (Y.D. 201:25-27).

6   *Rambam* (*Hilchos Brachos* Ch. 6:7).

used for *Netillas Yadayim*. Accordingly, this would mean that "red tide" water caused by an algal bloom would, in fact, be permitted for *Netillas Yadayim*, as no one added anything and it is a natural phenomenon that is actually occurring on a microscopic level.

Color Coded

However, other authorities disagree, concurring with the *Tur* and *Shulchan Aruch*'s stringent ruling. They explain that there truly is no such thing as water changing color "by itself." It actually occurs when the water is sitting exposed to the elements, that it gets contaminated, possibly by (microscopic) organisms in the air, which change its color. It is only referred to as changing by itself because nothing was purposely added to the water that might change its color. Proof is that if someone would place water in an airtight sealed clear container, its appearance would remain unchanged.

These authorities argue that the *Rema*, who does not comment on the *Shulchan Aruch*'s ruling, and perhaps even the *Rambam*, would actually agree to this. Although the *Rambam* did not mention water whose appearance changed "by itself," he nonetheless added that water whose color was changed "by the ground" is *passul* for use for *Netillas Yadayim*. These authorities suggest that it is possible that this was his intent, referring to water sitting exposed on the ground whose appearance was changed naturally.

Additionally, they point out that Chazal, and later the *Shulchan Aruch*, use extremely strong terms for the punishments awaiting those negligent with washing *Netillas Yadayim* properly.[8] Therefore, they maintain that one may not compare it to a *mikva*, which would not become invalidated with this type of water. In fact, many *halachic* authorities, including the *Prishah*, Chida, *Maamar Mordechai*, Shulchan HaTahor, Ben Ish Chai, Aruch Hashulchan, Kaf Hachaim, and Chazon Ish

---

7   Taz (O.C. 160:1), *Magen Avraham* (ad loc. 2), *Biur HaGr"a* (ad loc. 1), *Pri Megadim* (M.Z. ad loc. end 1), *Shulchan Aruch Harav* (ad loc. 1), *Chayei Adam* (vol. 1:39, 1), *Kitzur Shulchan Aruch* (40:8), and *Mishnah Berurah* (160:2).

8   As discussed in previous footnotes.

rule that water whose color has been changed by itself is prohibited to be used for *Netillas Yadayim*.⁹ This would also seemingly include our "Crimson Tide."

Breaking Out the Bubbly?

This whole background discussion will help us understand a more common case. Have you ever filled up your cup to wash for *Hamotzi* and found the water a bit whitish, cloudy, or bubbly? Usually, the water settles down and returns to its normal appearance after a few seconds. A quite common question is whether one needs to wait for the water to settle down in order to wash, as perhaps it would maintain the status of water that's appearance changed "by itself," or whether this case is somehow different and the water can be used immediately.

Many contemporary *Poskim*, including Rav Yosef Shalom Elyashiv, Rav Yisrael Yaakov Fischer, Rav Ben Tzion Abba-Shaul, Rav Nosson Gestetner, and the *Yalkut Yosef*, rule that there is no reason to wait for

---

9   *Prishah* (O.C. 160:2), Chida (*Birkei Yosef* ad loc. 2), *Maamar Mordechai* (ad loc. 1), *Shulchan HaTahor* (ad loc. 1), *Ben Ish Chai* (Year 1, *Parashas Kedoshim* 1), *Aruch Hashulchan* (O.C. 160:3; who writes that the appearance change is due to maggots and flies), *Kaf HaChaim* (ad loc. 5) and *Chazon Ish* (O.C. 22:7 and 13). Additionally, the *Bach* (O.C. 160: end 1) who argues on this rule, nevertheless concludes that if at all possible it is nonetheless preferable to be stringent. Similarly, the *Machatzis Hashekel* (ad loc. end 2) who likewise refutes this rule, still concludes that if after washing with the colored water one finds water that's appearance has not changed, it would be prudent to wash again without a *bracha*. See also Rav Yosef Eliyahu Henkin's posthumously published *Shu"t Gevuros Eliyahu* (vol. 1-O.C. 52:3, and in his *Ezras Torah Luach, Minhagei Beis Haknesses*) where he rules that "*Mayim shenishtanu maraihen...pesulim l'Netillas Yadayim*," with no differentiation between how the water's appearance actually changed; heavily implying that even if it was changed "by itself," it would still be unfit for use. See also *Shu"t Igros Moshe* (Y.D. vol. 1, end 120:8) for a scholarly analysis as to the sources of this dispute regarding whether or not water that has changed color is permissible for *Netillas Yadayim*, the potential distinctions inherent regarding a *mikva*, and a possible approach in understanding the *machlokes* between the *Ra'ah* and *Rambam* (ibid.) concerning water whose appearance "changed by itself."

the water to settle.[10] They explain that the reason the water looks this way at first is simply due to air pressure in the pipes. Therefore, they maintain that this is not the same case as *"shinui mareh machmas atzmo,"* as the water's appearance did not truly change. They bring proof from the *Shulchan Aruch* himself, who rules that if the water's appearance changed due to rocks and dirt getting mixed in, then it is still kosher for *Netillas Yadayim*.[11] Therefore, a temporary whitish tinge or bubbles in the water cannot be considered any worse for *Netillas Yadayim*.

Yet, several other authorities, including the *Minchas Yitzchak*, *Mori v'Rabi* Rav Yaakov Blau, and the *Nitei Gavriel*,[12] still maintain that even though washing with such water would be permissible, it is *lechatchilla* preferable to wait until the water clears before washing.

---

10   *Shu"t Rivevos Efraim* (vol. 6:410; citing Rav Elyashiv's opinion), *Shu"t Even Yisrael* (vol. 7:11), *Shu"t Ohr L'Tzion* (vol. 2, Ch. 11:7), *Shu"t Lehoros Nosson* (vol. 4, O.C. 8), and *Yalkut Yosef* (*Kitzur Shulchan Aruch* O.C. 160:2). The *Chazon Ish* (O.C. 22:9 s.v. *sham*) implies this way as well, regarding permitting water that got "dirty" due to something small falling in that does not intrinsically change the water's actual color.

11   *Shulchan Aruch* (O.C. 160:9). However, it still must be water that a dog would drink. Although there are two different explanations why the *Shulchan Aruch*'s ruling holds true, it is possible that both would apply here. The *Pri Megadim* (ad loc. M.Z. 1) explains that since in the end the water itself remains truly clear, as the dirt and mud do not actually change the color of the water itself, it is not deemed a problem. The *Shulchan Aruch Harav* (ibid.), however, maintains that since it is the *derech* of the "*gidul*" of water (meaning its natural state is) to have dirt and mud mixed in, it won't affect the water's status. See also *Mishnah Berurah* (ad loc. 3).

12   *Shu"t Minchas Yitzchak* (vol. 9:13), *Nitei Gavriel* (*Hilchos Yom Tov* vol. 2, Ch. 66:7, pg. 441; citing the *Pischei Olam*, 160:1, maintaining that the whitish appearance is due to "*taaruvos chomarim hanitan besocham*"). This author personally heard this *psak* of Rav Blau's, to be *choshesh lechatchilla* for the *Minchas Yitzchak*'s position, approximately a week before he was *niftar*. The *Minchas Yitzchak* maintained that the *hetter* of rocks and dirt mixing into the water was not a comparable case according to several opinions and it therefore would be preferable to wait until the water settled down. The *Nitei Gavriel* concludes "*ulam, m'dina ain kepeida.*"

When one views the world through the lens of *halacha*, current events, Crimson Tides, and even simple tasks like handwashing, take on a whole new dimension.[13]

Postscript: Seltzer Status

There is another interesting related topic about whether water with bubbles has the *halachic* status of water: drinking seltzer during *Shalosh Seudos* (*Seudas Shlishis*). There is a seemingly obscure custom of not drinking water during *Bein Hashmashos* on Shabbos. This is loosely based on the *Rema's* comment about the dangers of drinking well water during this time period.[14] The Steipler Gaon, as well as his son Rav Chaim Kanievsky, maintain that this includes seltzer, which

---

13   The author wishes to thank his friend and *talmid*, renowned business consultant and marketing specialist Rabbi Issamar Ginzberg, whose *sheilah* was the impetus for this author's interest and research in this topic.

14   *Rema* (O.C. 291:2). See *Shulchan Aruch Harav* (O.C. 291:2) and *Aruch Hashulchan* (ad loc. 5) for an explanation. This *minhag* is based on a Midrash (*Shochar Tov* on *Tehillim* Ch. 11) and is cited by several Rishonim including *Tosafos* (*Pesachim* 105a s.v. *v'hachi nami*), *Rosh* (ad loc. Ch. 10:13), *Mordechai* (ad loc. 36b, end second column), *Agudah* (ad loc. 81) and *Tur* (O.C. 291). As the *Rema* himself mentions *shittas* Rabbeinu Meshulem, there is also some debate whether this is really referring to *Bein Hashmashos* of Shabbos turning into Motzai Shabbos or actually on Erev Shabbos turning into Shabbos. See *Hagahos Maimoniyos* (*Hilchos Shabbos* Ch. 30, 10:2), *Beis Yosef* (O.C. 291 s.v. *v'Rabbeinu Taam*) and *Bach* (ad loc. s.v. *v'Rabbeinu Taam*). See also *Shemiras Haguf V'Hanefesh* (vol. 2, Ch. 130) and *Shu"t Divrei Moshe* (O.C. 13) at length, elucidating how this custom of not drinking water at all during this time period can be sourced in the *Rema's* enigmatic and seemingly unrelated ruling regarding drinking well water. The Debreciner Rav (*Shu"t Ba'er Moshe* vol. 4:34) maintains that as this Midrash-based *minhag* is not cited *lemaaseh* by the *Shulchan Aruch*, and the *Rambam* (*Hilchos Shabbos* Ch. 30:10) seemingly directly argues on it, and there are opinions that it only applies on Erev Shabbos, rules that certainly one need not be concerned regarding water that was already in the house. He adds that one who wishes to be stringent may simply add some "orange soda" or something else that will change the water's taste, as then it would be considered "*shaar mashkim*."

is intrinsically water with carbon dioxide added in, as the bubbles do not detract from the water's status.[15] However, Rav Moshe Halberstam, citing many earlier authorities including the Maharsham, argues that seltzer is not included in the water category in respect to this *minhag*.[16] Accordingly, from a *halachic* perspective, it seems that a little fizz goes a long way.[17]

---

15 The Steipler Gaon's *minhag* being of *machmir* is found in *Orchos Rabbeinu* (new edition; vol. 1, pg. 238–239:13 and 14). Rav Chaim Kanievsky's short responsa on the topic, defending his father's *shittah*, is printed in *Shu"t Divrei Moshe* (O.C. end 14). He concludes that it is *"kasheh lehakel b'makom sakana."*

16 *Shu"t Divrei Moshe* (O.C. 14) at length, Maharsham (*Shu"t* vol. 3:375; *Daas Torah*, O.C. 158 and Y.D. 339:5).

17 Thanks are due to Rabbi Yaakov Nissan for pointing out this related interesting *machlokes*.

Chapter 23

The Parameters of *Pas Palter*

Pas (Akum) Nisht

IN THE TIMES OF THE Mishnah, Chazal forbade us from eating *Pas Akum*, bread and bread-like items that were baked by non-Jews,[1] even if said bread does not have any kashrus concerns,[2] in order to dissuade us from assimilation and intermarriage.[3] This prohibition pertains exclusively to bread products containing one or more of the five major grains: wheat, barley, oats, spelt, or rye,[4] and generally includes baked goods that have the form of bread (*tzuras hapas*).[5]

---

1   See Mishnah in *Avodah Zarah* (35b) and accompanying Gemara (36a-b). The prohibition of *Pas Akum* is one of the eighteen *Gezeiros* that Chazal established on that famous, fateful day when Beis Shamai overruled Beis Hillel. See aforementioned Gemara, Mishnah in *Shabbos* (13b) and accompanying Gemara (17b), as well as *Yerushalmi* (*Shabbos* Ch. 1, *Halacha* 4; 12a in the Friedman edition and 9b in the *Me'orei Ohr* edition).

2   See *Pischei Teshuva* (Y.D. 112:2), and on more of a contemporary note *Kovetz M'Beis Levi on Yoreh Deah* (pg. 47; citing Rav Shmuel *Halevi* Wosner).

3   *Tur* and *Shulchan Aruch* (Y.D. 112:1). This prohibition applies even when intermarriage does not, i.e. eating with a non-Jewish priest who has no children. See *Rashba* (*Shu"t* vol. 1:148), *Rema* (Y.D. 112:1), *Shach* (ad loc. 4), *Taz* (ad loc. 1), *Chochmas Adam* (65:1), *Pri Megadim* (Y.D. 112, M.Z. 1), and *Kaf Hachaim* (Y.D. 112:9). The *Ramban* (*Chiddushim* to *Avodah Zarah* 35b s.v. *od ra'isi*) declares that anyone who thinks that the *Gezeira* of *chasnus* no longer applies, is making a *"ta'us gedolah, u'mi shehorah kach, ain lismoch alav."*

4   *Tur* (Y.D. 112; quoting his father, the *Rosh*), *Shulchan Aruch* (ad loc. 1), and *Taz*

If, however, a Jew participated by lighting the fire, stoking the coals under the bread being baked, or by putting the bread on the fire, and thereby taking an active part in the actual baking process, or even in some small way such as throwing a small sliver of wood into the fire (*hashlachas kiseim*),[6] the bread becomes permitted, and is known as *Pas Yisrael*.

Palter-geist

In later years, due to the fact that many baking ovens were owned or operated by non-Jews, making it difficult to procure *Pas Yisrael* products, Chazal qualified this prohibition, and created a new class of bread products known as *Pas Palter*, literally "Baker's Bread." This refers to

---

(ad loc. 2). The *Pri Chodosh* (ad loc. 5), however, advances the notion that in far-off islands where all bread is made out of a *halachically* inferior grain (e.g., rice), then this prohibition might possibly apply to it as well.

5 See *Tur*, *Shulchan Aruch*, and main commentaries to *Yoreh Deah* 112 at length. The different types of foods to which this applies will be addressed later in the chapter.

6 According to the *Shulchan Aruch* and *Rema* (ad loc. 9 and Y.D. 113:7), this includes increasing the heat level even minutely, by throwing a toothpick into the fire or blowing on it. Most Acharonim agree as well [see for example the Chida's *Shiyurei Bracha* (Y.D. 112:18) and *Ben Ish Chai* (Year 2, *Parashas Chukas* 5)]. However, the *Aruch Hashulchan* (Y.D. 112:27) and *Kaf Hachaim* (ad loc. 60) maintain that one should only rely on these leniencies under extenuating circumstances; rather, one should strive to perform the actions listed above, as they are actually mentioned by the Gemara. Additionally, several Rishonim, including the *Ramban* (cited in the *Ran* 15b s.v. *v'assa* and *v'af*) and *Rosh* (*Avodah Zarah* Ch. 2:33) disapproved of relying on said leniencies, as throwing a toothpick into a fire does not really add much to the baking process. [This argument is partially based on how these Rishonim understood the *hetter* of the Gemara. The *Rambam* (*Hilchos Maachalos Assuros* Ch. 17: end 13; see also *Teshuvos HaRashba* vol. 1:228) understood that the act of throwing a toothpick into the fire makes it recognizable that a Jew added something, albeit small, to the baking process, and that is sufficient. The *Ramban* and *Rosh*, however, maintained that the thrust of the Gemara's *hetter* was that a Jew needed to be an active part of the actual baking process, and a toothpick's

bread products baked in a bakery or commercial setting, where there is no personal or intimate contact between the baker and customer, thereby drastically reducing the chance of intermarriage. Such bread is therefore permitted.[7]

Some authorities, including the *Rema*, maintain that Chazal's *hetter* of *Pas Palter* applies in all cases, even when *Pas Yisrael* is readily available.[8] However, many authorities, including the *Shulchan Aruch* and the *Shach*, argue that this *hetter* is only applicable if one cannot purchase *Pas Yisrael* of similar type, quality, or price (any of the three is sufficient cause for dispensation),[9] and they stress that one should otherwise strive to obtain *Pas Yisrael* exclusively.[10]

---

overall contribution is quite negligible.] This is also the *Minchas Yitzchak's* (*Shu"t* vol. 4:28, 4) conclusion *lemaaseh*.

7   *Yerushalmi* (*Shabbos* Ch.1, *Halacha* 4; 9b-10a in the *Me'orei Ohr* edition), *Rif* (*Avodah Zarah* 14b in his pagination), *Tosafos* (*Avodah Zarah* 35b s.v. *michlal*), *Tur* and *Shulchan Aruch* (Y.D. 112:2). Rav Moshe Feinstein (*Shu"t Igros Moshe*, Y.D. vol. 1:48) ruled that if a Jewish-owned large commercial bakery needed to hire non-Jewish workers, even though the bread might actually have been baked by those non-Jewish workers, the bread does not have the status of *Pas Akum*, and is fully permitted to be eaten.

8   Including the *Rema* (Y.D. 112:2), *Biur HaGr"a* (ad loc. 4), *Levush* (ad loc. 3), *Kitzur Shulchan Aruch* (38:1), and *Ben Ish Chai* (Year 2, *Parashas Chukas* 2).

9   Although the *hetter* of price difference is not clearly mentioned by the *Shulchan Aruch*, it is nonetheless mentioned by several Acharonim, including the *Pri Toar* (112:6; who explains that "nicer bread" is actually referring to saving money on it), the *Zivchei Tzedek* (ad loc. 14), and the *Kaf Hachaim* (ad loc. end 30). This author also seen this *hetter* quoted in the name of Rav Yosef Shalom Elyashiv. However, Rav Shmuel *Halevi* Wosner is cited (*Kovetz M'Beis Levi* on *Yoreh Deah*, pg. 47, end footnote 8) as not relying on this leniency. Rav Moshe Feinstein is quoted (*Mesores Moshe* vol. 1, pg. 238:61) as explaining the *shittah* of the *Shulchan Aruch* and *Shach* as that it is preferable not to rely on the *hetter* of price difference unless one is an *"ani"* and therefore cannot afford the more expensive *Pas Yisrael* bread, or if one does not (at the time of purchase) have the money on him to pay for the more expensive *Pas Yisrael* bread. See Rav Yaakov Skoczylas' recent *Ohel Yaakov* on *Hilchos Maachalei Akum* (pg. 22) who cites both sides to this debate, including the opinions of

many contemporary *Poskim* who ruled leniently. See also *Chelkas Binyomin* (112:51) who posits to be stringent, without citing any sources, simply stating that this is the *mashmaos* of the *Shulchan Aruch*. This position has struck this author as odd, as several earlier authorities explicitly ruled to be lenient with this exact issue.

10   Including the *Shulchan Aruch* (Y.D. 112:2 and 5), *Shach* (ad loc. 9), Arizal (cited by the *Ben Ish Chai* ibid.), *Chochmas Adam* (65:2), *Aruch Hashulchan* (Y.D. 112:9), and *Kaf Hachaim* (ad loc. 23). According to this opinion, the distance given that one should travel to obtain *Pas Yisrael* products (instead of being lenient and eating *Pas Palter*) is four *mil* [see *Shulchan Aruch* (ibid. 16)], generally assumed to be seventy-two minutes (but there are opinions of up to ninety-six minutes). The *Pri Chodosh* (ad loc. 28) points out that this is only if one was already traveling in that direction; however, if one is not traveling, then he does not have to travel that length of time, but rather only eighteen (or twenty-four) minutes [as per the *Chochmas Adam*'s (65:4) understanding of the *Pri Chodosh*'s opinion]. The *Pischei Teshuva* (ad loc. 6) cites the *Shu"t Beis Yaakov* (35) that there is no difference if one is walking or riding on a horse, that one must traverse the same distance. The *Aruch Hashulchan* (ibid. end 18) echoes this as well, that the "*Chachamim hishvu midoseihem*," or made a one-size-fits-all edict. However, the *Mishnah Berurah* (163, *Biur Halacha* s.v. *b'richuk*) writing on a similar topic where Chazal (*Pesachim* 46a) and later, the *Shulchan Aruch* (O.C. 163:1) give a distance of four *mil* (*Netillas Yadayim* prior to "breaking bread"), comments that it is improbable to differentiate between someone walking or riding on a "flying camel," and understands that the *Gezeira* was referring to an amount of time, which is one-size-fits-all, that one must travel the amount of time it takes to walk such a distance, meaning seventy-two minutes and not an actual distance. On this topic, see *Chelkas Binyomin* (pg. 59, *Biurim* s.v. *ad dalet milin*). [Yet, in this author's estimation, it seems possible to say that "*Chachamim hishvu midoseihem*" on this topic that "there is no difference between walking or riding on a horse" cited by the *Aruch Hashulchan*, might actually be referring to time, like the *Mishnah Berurah*'s opinion, and they may not actually be disagreeing; *v'tzarich l'ayen b'zeh*]. This discussion affects another contemporary debate upon the distance one in the city must travel to *daven* with a *minyan* (*Tefilla B'Tzibbur*), *shiur mil*. [See *Shulchan Aruch* (O.C. 90:16; based on Gemara *Pesachim* 46a), *Chayei Adam* (vol. 1, 40:11), *Shulchan Aruch Harav* (O.C. 90:17), *Mishnah Berurah* (ad loc. 52), and *Aruch Hashulchan* (ad loc. 20; adding that this is the distance of a "Russian *Parsa*").] Rav Shmuel *Halevi* Wosner (*Shu"t Shevet Halevi* vol. 8:19

Don't Let It *Pas* You By

Although the leniency of *Pas Palter* remains in effect year round, the *Shulchan Aruch* and *Rema*, in *Hilchos Rosh Hashanah* qualify it, writing that during the *Aseres Yemei Teshuva*, the Ten Days of Repentance between *Rosh Hashanah* and *Yom Kippur*,[11] as well as on *Shabbos* and *Yom Tov*,[12] one should ensure that all one's bread products are *Pas Yisrael*.

---

and vol. 9:37) asserts that regarding *Tefilla B'Tzibbur* (as opposed to *Netillas Yadayim*), even the *Mishnah Berurah* would agree that the *halacha* is referring to distance and not time, citing precedent from the *Shoel U'Meishiv* (*Shu"t Mahadura Kama* vol. 3: end 103), who maintains that *halachic shiurim* are set "*lefi derech hateva*," and do not take innovations into account. On the other hand, Rav Moshe Sternbuch (*Shu"t Teshuvos V'Hanhagos* vol. 1:97 and 98), in a discussion on the importance of *Tefilla B'Tzibbur*, opines that even regarding *Tefilla B'Tzibbur*, the *shiur mil* is referring to time and not distance, adding that Hashem will surely repay expenses incurred while ensuring to daven *Tefilla B'Tzibbur*. [Regarding the significance of *Tefilla B'Tzibbur*, see also *Shu"t Igros Moshe* (O.C. vol. 2:27).] Also regarding the *din* of *Pas Palter*, the *Be'er Sarim* (*Shu"t* vol. 4:49; see *Shach* ibid. 13, et al.) maintains that even according to the *machmir* opinion if one did not have access to *Pas Yisrael* and relied on eating *Pas Palter*, and *Pas Yisrael* later became available, the *Pas Palter* bread already in his possession still remains permitted to be eaten, "*l'kol hadei'os*."

11   *Shulchan Aruch* (O.C. 603:1), based on the *Tur* (ad loc.) quoting the *Yerushalmi* (*Shabbos* Ch. 1, *Halacha* 3). Also ruled by the *Rosh* (end *Maseches Rosh Hashanah*), *Ravyah* (cited by the *Mordechai* ad loc. end 559), *Ran* (ad loc. s.v. *garsinan b'Yerushalmi*), *Rema* (*Toras HaChatas* 75:1), *Levush* (ad loc. 1), *Shach* (Y.D. 112:9), *Beis Hillel* (ad loc. 2), *Chayei Adam* (vol. 2, 143:1), *Kitzur Shulchan Aruch* (130:2), *Matteh Efraim* (603:1), *Aruch Hashulchan* (O.C. 603:1 and Y.D. 112:17), *Mishnah Berurah* (603:1), and *Kaf Hachaim* (ad loc. 1 and Y.D. 112:23).

12   Including the *Magen Avraham* (O.C. 242:4), *Matteh Yehuda* (ad loc. 5), *Shulchan Aruch Harav* (ad loc. 13), *Chayei Adam* (vol. 2, 1:4), *Kitzur Shulchan Aruch* (72:6), *Aruch Hashulchan* (O.C. 242:45), and the *Mishnah Berurah* (ad loc. 6). The *Rema* himself (*Darchei Moshe* O.C. 603:1) writes that it is proper to follow this *minhag*, as well. There is however, the notable minority opinion of the *Elyah Rabba* (O.C. 242:10; and in *Elyah Zuta* ad loc. 8) who maintains that regarding *Shabbos*, while it is nevertheless proper to be *makpid* on *Pas Yisrael* on Shabbos and Yom Tov due to *Kavod Shabbos V'Yom Tov*, it is not an actual *halacha* to do so, as he holds that is not comparable to the requirement during

Nevertheless, if one is unable to obtain *Pas Yisrael* products during these special times, one may rely on *Pas Palter*.[13]

---

the *Aseres Yemei Teshuva*. The *Yad Efraim* (ad loc. s.v. *u'meivi*) implies this way as well, and the *Levushei Srad* (ad loc. s.v. *u'mikol makom*) cites both sides of the *machlokes* with no clear ruling. Yet, both the *Machatzis Hashekel* (ad loc. 4 s.v. *shehataam*) and *Pri Megadim* (E.A. ad loc. 4 s.v. *b'Darchei Moshe*) resolve the *Elyah Rabba*'s *taynos*, and maintain that one must indeed be stringent on *Shabbos* with *Pas Yisrael* products as well. The *Mishnah Berurah* (ad loc. *Shaar Hatziyun* 18) adds that *"afilu b'soch haseudah nachon lizaher,"* and concludes (ad loc. 6) that if one is *"anus"* and the only possible bread he has to make *Kiddush* on is not *Pas Yisrael*, he may then nevertheless use it for *Kiddush* (*Hamotzi*). This topic was addressed at length in an article titled "Pie Crusts, *Pas Palter*, and the *Aseres Yemei Teshuva*" (*Yated Ne'eman*, 24 Elul 5774/September 19, 2014 and online at: http://ohr.edu/this_week/insights_into_halacha/4893). The importance of exclusively eating *Pas Yisrael* products on Shabbos was emphasized in an amusing anecdotal exchange that I recently heard from my father, renowned kashrus expert Rav Manish Spitz. Approximately thirty-five years ago, he met Rav Berel Wein, who was head of the OU's Kashrus department at that time, and asked him why the OU granted *hashgacha* on Stella D'oro (Swiss Fudge) cookies (a.k.a. "Shtreimel Cookies"), as they were merely *Pas Palter*. [Meaning, he wanted to know why the OU did not ensure that their *Pas* products were *Pas Yisrael*.] Rav Wein's adroit retort was succinct: "So don't eat them on Shabbos!"

Interestingly, according to a New York Times article in 2003 (accessible at: https://www.nytimes.com/2003/01/12/nyregion/of-milk-and-cookies-or-how-orthodox-jews-saved-an-italian-recipe.html), Orthodox Jews are so widely associated with the Italian Stella D'oro "Shtreimel Cookies," that just the idea that these cookies were being reformulated as dairy caused such an outcry and sales to plummet, that parent company Kraft Foods ultimately rescinded their plan, keeping the beloved cookies pareve.

13 *Tur* (Y.D. 112:2), citing the Gaonim. Also cited by the *Ramban* (*Chiddushim* to *Avodah Zarah* 35b s.v. *mah*), *Ran* (ad loc. 14a in the *Rif's* pagination), *Rashba* (*Toras Habayis*, *Bayis* 3, *Shaar* 7), and *Beis Yosef* (ad loc.), and practically by the *Mishnah Berurah* (ad loc. 1) as well. In his *Shaar Hatziyun* (ad loc. 4), the *Mishnah Berurah* cites the *Nachlas Shivah* (*Shu"t* 72), who maintains that in years of famine, even during the *Aseres Yemei Teshuva*, it is fully permitted to purchase rolls from a non-Jewish baker, and then re-cook them

What is Considered "Bread"?

This *din* of "*Pas*" (bread) is not exclusive to what we refer to as "bread," but rather includes various baked goods that have the form of bread (*tzuras hapas*).[14] Following are various types of common foods and their status vis-à-vis this important *halacha*:

Cake and cookies:[15] Several authorities are of the opinion that for a piece of cake, a cookie, or other similar baked delicacy to be included in the "bread" category, not only must it be of a type that if one eats enough and is *koveya seudah* (bases an actual meal) on it, he must wash and make *Hamotzi*,[16] but it must also have been formulated from a

---

afterward (even though this generally would not be sufficient to be considered *Pas Yisrael*).

14 See *Tur* and *Shulchan Aruch* (Y.D. 112 ad loc.). The Gemara (*Brachos* 37b) refers to this as "*Turisa D'Nahama*."

15 See *Tur, Shulchan Aruch* and *Rema* (ad loc. 6), *Toras HaChatas* (75:12), *Toras Ha'Asham* (ad loc. s.v. *aval*), and *Shiyurei Bracha* (Y.D. 112:1). There is also an interesting dissenting minority opinion of Rav Shimon Shapiro, *Av Beis Din* of Prague, cited by the *Minchas Yaakov* (75:21), that since cake is not actually referred to as bread and bakery bread is anyway technically *muttar* but rather many are nevertheless stringent, that abstaining from it is akin to a personal *neder* (vow). Therefore, since *nedarim's* intent follows the colloquial language, cake (and other bread-like items) would not be included in the prohibition. However, the *Minchas Yaakov* (ibid and ad loc. 2) argues that since *Pas Akum* is a *Gezeira Derabbanan*, the laws of *nedarim* are not applicable. In fact, across the board, the vast majority of *Poskim* consider cake to have *tzuras hapas*. See also *Teshuva Mei'ahava* (Y.D. 112:6) who defends his ancestor's *shittah*, arguing that Rav Shapiro was referring to someone who made an actual *neder* to exclusively eat *Pas Yisrael*, who may be lenient with cake, and even during the *Aseres Yemei Teshuva*, even though everyone else lenient year-round is then vigilant. The *Chasam Sofer* (*Chiddushim* to Y.D. 112:11; cited in *Shu"t Zichron Betzalel* vol. 3:53, 20) answers similarly, that perhaps Rav Shapiro was referring to far-off places where they were unaware of the *Takkanas Chachamim* against *Pas Akum*, but the *Perushim* made personal vows to abstain; they may rely on *lashon bnei adam* to permit cake. However, all would seem to agree that such a *hetter* is no longer applicable.

16 See Gemara *Brachos* (42a). Although there is much debate among the

"thick batter" and have *tzuras hapas*.[17] However, most authorities contend that as long as the cake's status is that if one eats enough and is *koveya seudah* on it, he is mandated to wash and make *Hamotzi*, this is sufficient indication that it possesses *tzuras hapas*, regardless of the type of batter.[18] Contemporary practice is to assume all cake and cookies

---

Acharonim as to their understanding of the exact *shiur* necessary to warrant this, whether it depends on personal level of satiation (*shiur seviah*) or a general estimate, and if it depends on the food item alone or the whole meal one is eating it with (e.g., meat or fish) [see *Magen Avraham* (O.C. 168:13), *Pri Megadim* (ad loc. E.A. 13), *Elyah Rabba* (ad loc. 17), *Chayei Adam* (vol. 1, 54:3 and 4 and *Nishmas Adam* ad loc. 1; also citing the *Gr"a*), *Shulchan Aruch Harav* (ad loc. 8), *Kitzur Shulchan Aruch* (48:3), *Ben Ish Chai* (Year 1, *Parashas Pinchas* 19), *Aruch Hashulchan* (O.C. 168:15–18), and *Kaf Hachaim* (ad loc. 45)], nonetheless, as the *Mishnah Berurah* (168:24) concludes, *lechatchilla* we should be *machmir* that when eating the amount of *Arba'ah Beitzim*, four eggs-worth of the *Mezonos* bread-like item, that this is already considered *keviyus haseudah*.

17   *Shach* (ad loc. 18), *Ba'er Heitiv* (ad loc. 9), and *Chochmas Adam* (65:1). This *shittah* is based on the *Rema* in his *Toras HaChatas* (75:12; see also *Toras Ha'Asham* ad loc. s.v. *u'blilasan avah*), explaining the ruling of the *Tashbetz* (*Shu"t* vol. 1:89) that "*minei mesika sheblilasan raka*" do not have the status of "*Pas*," but rather "*Shlakos*," considered cooked, and possibly in the more stringent *Bishul Akum* category. However, this understanding of the *Rema's* ruling is not so simple. See next footnote.

18   *Taz* (Y.D. 112:6), *Biur HaGr"a* (ad loc.15), *Pri Chodosh* (ad loc. 17), *Shiyurei Bracha* (ad loc. 9), and *Beis Meir* (ad loc. se'if 6). This would also seemingly fit well with the *shittos* of the *Rivash* (*Shu"t* 28) and *Aruch Hashulchan* (Y.D. 112:31; see below). This issue is essentially a *machlokes* Acharonim how to understand the *Rema's psak* in *Yoreh Deah* 112:6, regarding cakes and "*minei mesika*" that are considered "*Pas*." Several of these authorities counter the *Shach's* assertion (see previous footnote) that the *Rema's* opinion follows his own explanation that he wrote earlier in his *Toras HaChatas* (75:12), with the fact that several chapters prior (*Toras HaChatas* 69:4), the *Rema* himself seemingly qualified this assessment, citing that Rabbi Yechiel M'Paris (see *Tosafos*, *Beitza* 16b, end s.v. *ka mashma lan*) ruled that this *inyan* depends on whether or not one can be *koveya seudah* on it, and not necessarily dependent on the type of batter. Indeed, in the source parenthesis in the *Shulchan Aruch* (ad loc. end 6), it sources Rabbi Yechiel M'Paris as the precedent for the

are included in the category of "bread" and would thereby be subject to the *halachos* of *Pas Yisrael* and *Pas Palter*.[19]

Bagels: Even though true bagels are first boiled, nevertheless, since at that stage they are not fit to be eaten until actually baked, they are still included in the category of "*Pas.*"[20]

Pancakes: Although pancakes are "fried" in a frying pan, if the only oil used is there to make sure the pancakes do not stick to the pan, then they would still be considered "baked," not fried,[21] as they still share enough similarities with bread to be considered "*Pas.*" However, this would technically depend on the actual recipes used for making

---

Rema's ruling, strongly implying that the *Rema's* actual *psak lemaaseh* follows this *shittah* and not as the *Shach* understood. Moreover, in his *Darchei Moshe* (Y.D. 113:9), after the *Beis Yosef* (ad loc. s.v. *kasav Harav Shimon bar Tzemach*) cited the *shittah* of the *Tashbetz* (see previous footnote), the *Rema* remarked "*u'miyamai lo ra'isi shum adam choshesh l'divrei teshuva zu*," that he never saw anyone rule following the words of this responsum of the *Tashbetz*.

19 See *Kovetz M'Beis Levi* (vol. 8, pg. 24:40), Rav Yisroel Belsky's ruling in the OU's *Kashrus Manual on Bishul Akum* (pg. 40), and *Chelkas Binyomin* (112:64), who maintain that the *halacha* here follows the *Taz* and *Beis Meir* et al. However, Rav Moshe Sternbuch (*Shu"t Teshuvos V'Hanhagos* vol. 3:248 s.v. *sof*) qualifies that regarding cake or cookies made from thin, runny batter that a non-Jew baked, then *me'ikar hadin* one may rely on the *Shach's hetter*, that it is not included in the prohibition.

20 See *Aruch Hashulchan* (ad loc. 31), *Shu"t Igros Moshe* (Y.D. vol. 2:33 and Y.D. vol. 4:4), *Chazon Ish* (O.C. 26:9), *Shu"t Beis Avi* (vol. 5:7, 7), and *Shu"t Vidibarta Bam* (vol. 2:256). A similar *sevara* is given by the *Soles L'Mincha* (61:11 s.v. *u'kruv*) and the *Chasam Sofer* (*Chiddushim* to Y.D. 112:12 s.v. *v'hinei*) regarding "pretzels" that are first shortly boiled prior to baking. The *Kitzur Shulchan Aruch* (48:6; albeit regarding its *bracha*) as well, classifies bagels as "*lechem gamur.*"

21 *Shu"t Rivash* (28). See also *Rema* (O.C. 168:14; citing many Rishonim), *Chayei Adam* (vol. 1, 54:7), *Kitzur Shulchan Aruch* (48:5), *Kaf Hachaim* (O.C. 168:128; regarding Arab Bread, a.k.a. *laffa* and pita), and *Shu"t Ohr L'Tzion* (vol. 2, Ch. 46:9), all of whom rule similarly regarding *brachos* and *keviyus haseudah*, that a small amount of oil used to ensure that the batter does not stick to the pan or oven, does not change a bread's *tzuras hapas* status.

pancakes. If one would make them with thin, runny batter, or deep-fry them, then they would likely not be deemed as having *tzuras hapas*.[22]

Wafers: Wafers are crafted from a liquidy batter that is poured onto/into hot griddle-like machinery with a criss-cross pattern, thus resulting

---

22   As mentioned previously, many *Poskim* are of the opinion that a food item can only be considered *"Pas"* if one eats enough and is *koveya seudah* (bases an actual meal) on it, that *halachically* speaking, he must wash and make *Hamotzi*. Yet, regarding *Terisa*, which the *Shulchan Aruch* (O.C. 168:15; following the first understanding of the Gemara *Brachos* 37b; see *Rashi* ad loc. s.v. *gvil*) describes as a liquidy mixture of flour and water that is poured onto a stovetop, where it spreads out (expands) and is baked that way, which sounds remarkably like our common pancakes, that its *bracha* is always *Mezonos*, even if one would be *koveya seudah* on it, as it does not have *tzuras hapas*. Yet, the *Tur* (ad loc. according to the *pashtus b'lashono*; see *Bach* ad loc. and not following the *Beis Yosef's* amendment ad loc. s.v. *u'lefikach*) holds that if one is *koveya seudah* on *Terisa*, he would make *Hamotzi*. This *psak* is seconded by the *Magen Avraham* (ad loc. 41), who maintains that the Gemara was only referring to *Hilchos Challah* that *Terisa* is exempt from [see *Tur* and *Shulchan Aruch* (Y.D. 329:5) that this is indeed the *halacha*], and not *Hilchos Seudah*. The *Aruch Hashulchan* (ad loc. 48) writes that the *Talmud Bavli* is *mashma* like the *Shulchan Aruch* while the *Yerushalmi* is *mashma* like the *Tur*. He concludes *"ain lehaarich bazeh, ki etzleinu leika klal minim eilu,"* that he personally held that this debate is academic, as this type of food was not extant in his locale (1890s Volozhin). Other *Poskim*, including the *Shulchan Aruch Harav* (O.C. 168:13 and *Seder Birkas Hanehenin* Ch. 2:6) and *Mishnah Berurah* (ad loc. 90; also citing the *Elyah Rabba* ad loc. 31) leave this disagreement unresolved, asserting that it is proper to only eat *Terisa* after making *Hamotzi* on a different type of bread. The *Kaf Hachaim* (ad loc. 34) writes that one can make a *Mezonos* on *Terisa*, provided that he makes sure not to eat a large amount, thus avoiding entering into the question of *keviyus haseudah*. Due to all of the above, pancakes' final status regarding *tzuras hapas* and *keviyus haseudah* is not so clear-cut. *Lemaaseh*, both Rav Shlomo Zalman Auerbach and Rav Yosef Shalom Elyashiv (cited in *V'zos Habracha*, Ch. 4, footnote 4) maintain that as long as they are "fried" in minimal oil just so they will not stick to the pan or burn, pancakes are considered to have *tzuras hapas*, and if one is *koveya seudah* on them, they will need to make *Hamotzi*.

in "paper-thin" wafers with a flaky consistency. They are therefore not considered possessing *tzuras hapas*.²³

---

23   The *Magen Avraham* (O.C. 168:40), citing the *Shlah* (*Shaar Ha'Osiyos, Eimek Bracha* 2:3; 254 in the recent *Yad Ramah* edition, s.v. *v'ein lomar* and *Hagahah*), writes that he agrees regarding "*Volaplatkes*," which are defined as being manufactured utilizing wafer-thin batter that is poured onto a hot griddle with a criss-cross pattern, that they certainly do not have the consistency of bread at all, as they are "*dakim u'klushim b'yoseir*" (ultra-thin and weak, i.e. flaky or fall apart easily), and are always *Mezonos*. The *Shlah* adds that this *shittah* dates back to the Rishonim, as it was the opinion of Rabbeinu Yitzchak Hazaken, as cited by Rabbeinu Yonah (*Brachos* 27a in the *Rif's* pagination, s.v. *v'ee*). Although the *Taz* (ad loc. 9) seems to disagree *lemaaseh* [see *Pri Megadim* (ad loc. M.Z. 9; who concludes *tzarich iyun*)], the *Ba'er Heitiv* (ad loc. 34), *Kitzur Shulchan Aruch* (48:5), and *Mishnah Berurah* (ad loc. 38 and *Shaar Hatziyun* ad loc. 35 and 36) practically rule like the *Magen Avraham* and *Shlah*. [Interestingly, the *Mishnah Berurah* concludes with the *Shlah's* assessment that these wafers are *halachically* similar to *Terisa*, even though he personally did *not* practically conclude that they share the same *din* (see previous footnote).] This seems to be the contemporary consensus as well, as this defines our common wafers to a "T." See *Shu"t Minchas Yitzchak* (vol. 1:71, 6; who applies this logic to [the famous British] Ryvita crispbreads, even though they start out "*blilasan avah*" and are flattened by mechanical rollers to extremely thin, but airy crackers), Rav Mordechai Eliyahu's *Darchei Halacha* glosses to the *Kitzur Shulchan Aruch* (48:7), *V'zos Habracha* (Ch. 4:3, and footnote 3; citing Rav Chaim Pinchas Scheinberg), Rav Binyomin Forst's *Pischei Halacha* on *Hilchos Brachos* (Ch. 8:33), and Rav Yisrael Pinchos Bodner's *V'sein Bracha* (Ch. 27) and *Sefer K'zayis Hashalem* (pg. 191; English edition pg. 124). On the other hand, there is a novel dissenting minority opinion of the *Olas Yitzchak* (Ratzabi; *Shu"t* 36), who maintains that nowadays as the common wafer is made up of many wafer-thin layers pressed together with a filling-all in one wafer, it now has a *din* of "*Pas*," and if one is *koveya seudah* on it he would need to make *Hamotzi*. Although he writes that Rav Chaim Kanievsky agreed with his estimation, this approach does not seem to be taken into account by most contemporary authorities. Perhaps it is due to the rationale that if one thin, flaky, wafer layer does not possess a bread-like consistency, it stands to reason that several of them pressed together do not either.

Pretzels: Since pretzels are essentially fashioned from dough and baked, they are considered to have *tzuras hapas* even though they are twisted into a unique, non-bread-like shape.[24]

Doughnuts: Their inclusion in this category is a matter of *halachic* debate i.e., whether anything fried can be considered to have a "form of bread," or if it depends on the thickness of batter.[25] Several *Poskim* maintain that it depends on the batter—that a thick batter, even when deep-fried, maintains its status as *tzuras hapas*.[26] Others are of the opinion that once it's fried, it loses its status of "bread" and is therefore subject to the more stringent parameters of "*Bishul Akum*," as it is considered "cooked," and not "baked," by the deep-frying.[27] The *Shulchan Aruch* himself cites both opinions as valid and does not rule conclusively regarding its proper *bracha*.[28] All would agree that a thin, runny batter that is deep-fried would not be considered to have *tzuras hapas*.[29] Rav Ovadiah Yosef, addressing the issue of buying kosher doughnuts in a

---

24 See *Soles L'Mincha* (61:11 s.v. *u'kruv*), *Chiddushei Chasam Sofer* (Y.D. 112:12 s.v. *v'hinei*), *Darchei Teshuva* (112:49–50), *Aruch Hashulchan* (ad loc. 31), *Shu"t Zichron Betzalel* (vol. 3:92, 21), and *Kuntress Yad Dodi* (*Rosh Hashanah* and *Aseres Yemei Teshuva*, Question 11).

25 This issue is debated between Rabbeinu Tam (see *Tosafos* in *Pesachim* 37b s.v. *d'kuli alma* and *lechem* and *Brachos* 37b s.v. *lechem*) and Rabbeinu Shimshon (the *Rash M'Shantz*; in his commentary to *Maseches Challah* Ch. 1, Mishnah 5; also cited by Rabbeinu Yonah, *Brachos* 27a in the *Rif's* pagination, s.v. *u'mizeh*).

26 Including the *Rivash* (*Shu"t* 28), *Pri Chodosh* (Y.D. 112:17), and *Aruch Hashulchan* (ad loc. 31).

27 Including the *Tashbetz* (*Shu"t* vol. 3:11) and the *Yad Efraim* (Y.D. 112:6).

28 *Shulchan Aruch* (O.C. 168:13). He adds that due to this *safek*, a "*Yarei Shamayim*" will only eat a doughnut as part of a bread meal, having made a *Hamotzi* on actual bread.

29 See, for example, *Toras HaChatas* (75:12), *Pri Chodosh* (Y.D. 112:17), *Beis Meir* (ad loc. s.v. *v'osan*), *Chochmas Adam* (65: end 7), and *Ben Ish Chai* (Year 2, *Parashas Chukas* 15). This is because one would not be able to make *Hamotzi* even if one would be *koveya seudah* on such an item. On the other

restaurant, maintains that one may rely on the opinions that they are considered having *tzuras hapas* and are therefore *Pas Palter* and thereby essentially permitted.[30]

---

hand, this potentially would put the food item in the more stringent *Bishul Akum* category.

30 *Shu"t Yechaveh Daas* (vol. 5:53). Although Rav Ovadiah was ruling for Sefardim as well, that they can consider doughnuts a bread and therefore not included in the more stringent category of *Bishul Akum*, on the other hand, it should be noted that several other contemporary Sefardic *Poskim*, including Rav Ben Tzion Abba-Shaul (*Shu"t Ohr L'Tzion* vol. 2, pg. 98), Rav Shalom Messas (Meshash) (*Shu"t Shemesh U'Magen* vol. 2, Y.D. 12 and *Shu"t Tevuos Shamesh*, Y.D. 70), and Rav Mordechai Eliyahu (*Darchei Halacha* glosses to the *Kitzur Shulchan Aruch* 38:4), maintain that a Sefardi should be stringent and not rely upon this. They base this on the *Shulchan Aruch*'s ruling (Y.D. 329:1 and 3) that doughnuts are exempt from the obligation of *hafrashas challah* [however, the *Shach* (ad loc. 4) argues, citing "*harbei Poskim cholkim*," and contends that if the amount of dough used in the batter is a *shiur challah*, then *challah* should be taken without a *bracha*]. Since only baked "bread" items are obligated in *hafrashas challah* as opposed to cooked items, this implies that the *Shulchan Aruch* meant for doughnuts, although fried, to be included in the *Bishul* category. Additionally, the *Rambam* (*Hilchos Maachalos Assuros* Ch. 17:18) squarely places "*sufganin* that are deep fried in oil by a non-Jew" in the prohibited category of *Giyulei Akum* [however, this brief statement of the *Rambam* does not necessarily encompass every item that we would nowadays call a "doughnut"; see the Chida's *Shiyurei Bracha* (Y.D. 112:11)]. If so, they conclude, a Sefardi should not rely that they are merely *Pas Palter*, but potentially subject to the more stringent *Bishul Akum*. Rav Dovid Feinstein is also quoted as holding this way, that doughnuts are not considered *pas*, but rather a *tavshil* (*Kuntress Yad Dodi*, *Rosh Hashanah* and *Aseres Yemei Teshuva*, Question 12b). However, he (cited in *Shu"t Vidibarta Bam* vol. 2:256 s.v. *v'shamaati*), as well as Rav Yisroel Belsky and Rav Herschel Schachter (see the OU's *Kashrus Manual on Bishul Akum* pg. 11-12), maintain that generally speaking, most doughnuts, although considered a "*tavshil*," would nonetheless still be permitted, as they are not considered "*Oleh Al Shulchan Melachim*, Fit for a King's Table." This topic is discussed further in this chapter and in the chapter titled "The *Halachic* Adventures of the Potato."

Crackers: Since crackers are made from flour and water and simply baked, they are considered bread-like even though they are much thinner.[31] Although several authorities argue that snacks which are not "*Oleh Al Shulchan Melachim,* Fit for a King's Table," would not be included in the *Pas Akum* prohibition, similar to the parameters of *Bishul Akum,*[32] conversely, the majority consensus is to include them, as the *Tur, Shulchan Aruch,* and their main commentaries do not seem to make such a distinction regarding *Pas* products.[33]

Noodles, couscous, and farfel: These would be excluded from this rule entirely, as they do not have a form of bread at all.[34]

Cereal: Many kashrus agencies in America, including the OU and cRc (Chicago), maintain that Cheerios and other cereals do not have a true *tzuras hapas* and are therefore exempt from needing *Pas Yisrael* status.[35] The reason for this is that breakfast cereals, including Cheerios, are

---

31 See *Shulchan Aruch* (O.C. 168:8), *Mishnah Berurah* (ad loc. 36), and *Shu"t Shevet Halevi* (vol. 8:33). On the other hand, if they are ultra-thin (i.e. "paper-thin"), they would have a *din* akin to wafers and not be considered to have *tzuras hapas*. See *Shu"t Minchas Yitzchak* (vol. 1:71, 6) regarding Ryvita crispbreads, who explains that even though they start out "*blilasan avah,*" since they are flattened by mechanical rollers to extremely thin but airy crackers, they do not have *tzuras hapas*. Rav Shlomo Zalman Auerbach is quoted as holding similarly (*Sefer K'zayis Hashalem*, pg. 191, footnote 12).

32 Including the *Matteh Yonason* (Y.D. 112:1) and *Avnei Nezer* (*Shu"t* Y.D. 92:7). *Lechorah*, Rav Shimon Shapiro, *Av Beis Din* of Prague (as discussed in a previous footnote) would concur with this *lemaaseh*, as these snacks are not truly referred to as an actual "bread" by the general populace.

33 See *Pri Megadim* (Y.D. 112, M.Z. 3), *Tiferes L'Moshe* (ad loc. 2), *Aruch Hashulchan* (ad loc. 13, 14, and 31), and *Kaf Hachaim* (ad loc. 19), who assert this outright. Additionally, the *Rema* (*Toras HaChatas* ibid.) explicitly puts all bread-based products (with thick batter) where the flour content is the main ingredient, in the category of having *tzuras hapas*.

34 See *Rema* (O.C. 168:13), *Kovetz M'Beis Levi* (vol. 8, pg 24:4), and *Shu"t Yabia Omer* (vol. 8, O.C. 21:13).

35 See https://oukosher.org/blog/kosher-professionals/creating-pas-yisroel and http://www.crcweb.org/kosher_articles/pas_yisroel_during_aseres.php.

actually manufactured by first thoroughly cooking the grains. Although afterward they do undergo a drying process, nevertheless since this drying does not cause *krimas panim* (forming of a crust/caramelization) but rather just dries out the cereal to give them crunch, they are more similar to bread that is baked by leaving it out in the sun. Accordingly, breakfast cereal would be considered a *"tavshil"* and not *"pas"* and therefore is not subject to the laws of *Pas Yisrael*.[36] [37] [38]

---

36 Rav Yisroel Belsky (in the OU's *Kashrus Manual on Bishul Akum* pg. 14–16 and in *Sappirim* vol. 25; *V'Kasher Hadavar* pg. 2–3) cites a precedent to this ruling from the *Beis Meir* (Y.D. beg. 113, end s.v. *HaPri Chodosh*), who states that in order for a food item to be considered in the '*Bishul*' category, it must undergo a process that changes its appearance, such as cooking or roasting. Drying out, on the other hand, is not considered as such. Accordingly, as cereal is first cooked thoroughly and then only dried out, Rav Belsky asserts that it is still considered a *"tavshil"* and not *"pas."* Although this would seemingly place the breakfast cereal in the stricter *Bishul Akum* category, and there are those who mandated *Bishul Yisrael* for cereal [including Rav Asher Zimmerman (see *Hamodia's Inyan Magazine*, May 9, 2019, "Torah Greatness Amidst Simplicity"; pg. 29; see also following footnotes)], nonetheless, most *Poskim* hold that it would be exempt from this classification as well, as they do not deem cereal as *"Oleh Al Shulchan Melachim*, Fit for a King's Table." See, for example Rav Yosef Eliyahu Henkin's responsum (originally published in a footnote in Rav Nissan Telushkin's *Taharas Mayim*, Ch. 60; pg. 252 and later in *Teshuvos Ibra* Ch. 3:42, and most recently in *Shu"t Gevuros Eliyahu* vol. 2-Y.D. 26), *She'arim Metzuyanim B'Halacha* (vol. 1, 38:6), *Shu"t Chayei Halevi* (vol. 4, 50:10; citing the Debreciner Rav), *Kuntress Yad Dodi* (*Rosh Hashanah* and *Aseres Yemei Teshuva*, Question 11 and *Yoreh Deah*, *Bishulei Akum*, Question 2; *Psakim* of Rav Dovid Feinstein), *Minchas Asher* (*Parashas Devarim* 5:8; and in a responsum to this author; cited in Rav Yaakov Skoczylas' recent *Ohel Yaakov* on *Hilchos Maachalei Akum* pg. 109), Rav Shmuel Kamenetsky's *Kovetz Halachos* (*Hilchos Yomim Noraim* Ch. 22:2), Rav Pesach Eliyahu Falk's *Shu"t Machazeh Eliyahu* (vol. 2:40 and 41; originally published in *Kovetz Am HaTorah*, Mahadura 3, vol. 10 pg. 75–89; 5754), the OU's *Kashrus Manual on Bishul Akum* (pg. 14–16), and *Ohel Yaakov* on *Hilchos Maachalei Akum* (pg. 107–110; at length). [Although there seems to be an opposing opinion of Rav Shlomo Zalman Auerbach and Rav Yosef Shalom Elyashiv, cited in *V'zos Habracha* (new edition, pg. 232; arguing on the lenient opinion of Rav Chaim Pinchas Scheinberg), that they held that

Cheerios has *tzuras hapas*, implying that these *Gedolim* considered Cheerios to be *"pas"* and not *"tavshil"*; it is important to note that their statements were exclusively regarding the *inyan* of *keviyus haseudah*, that they were stringent concerning one eating a large amount of Cheerios—that he would need to wash and make *Hamotzi*. There is no mention of whether they were of the opinion that one must therefore also refrain from eating them on Shabbos, *Yom Tov*, and the *Aseres Yemei Teshuva*. This author pointed out these important details to the *sefer's* author, Rabbi Alexander Mandelbaum, but has yet to receive a full response. Perhaps this issue will be addressed in the next edition of *V'zos Habracha*.] Interestingly, Rav Telushkin himself (*Taharas Mayim* ibid., Ch. 60:2) held that since cereal is dried out after the cooking, it is akin to bagels and therefore should be considered *Pas Palter* (seemingly not like the *Beis Meir* and the contemporary *Poskim* mentioned above). Accordingly, and although not explicitly mentioned, he should hold that eating a grain-based cereal would be an issue on Shabbos, *Yom Tov*, and the *Aseres Yemei Teshuva*. However, he does write that cereal in no way should be considered *Oleh Al Shulchan Melachim*. The topic of *Oleh Al Shulchan Melachim* is addressed in the following footnotes and in the chapter titled "The *Halachic* Adventures of the Potato."

37   Although the exact *geder* of *Oleh Al Shulchan Melachim* is defined differently by different *Poskim*, and it seems that some might consider cereal as such [the *Chazon Ish* is widely rumored to have held similarly, maintaining a novel approach that any food a king or queen might eat during the day, including snacks, are considered *Oleh Al Shulchan Melachim*], nonetheless, there are several additional rationales in this case explaining why the majority of contemporary authorities do not classify cereal in that category. When the Gemara (*Avodah Zarah* 38a) teaches the requirements of *Bishul Yisrael*, after stating that any food that it is *Oleh Al Shulchan Melachim* is included, it adds *"lelafos bo es hapas*, to be eaten along with, or together with bread." There is a difference of understanding between the Rishonim [see *Rashba* (*Toras Habayis*, Bayis 3, Shaar 7, 94a), *Ritva* (*Avodah Zarah* ad loc. s.v. *ika*, and *Meiri* (ad loc.)] whether the Gemara was simply stating a common method of serving or actually meant to qualify the rule, making a further stipulation in the *halacha's* application. The *Rambam* (*Hilchos Maachalos Assuros* Ch. 17:15) and Rabbeinu Yerucham (*Sefer Ha'Adam*, Nesiv 17:7, pg. 160b, fourth column) when codifying the *halacha*, use the same language of the Gemara, leading several notable Acharonim including the *Pri Chodosh* (Y.D. 113:3), *Maharit Tzahalon* (*Shu"t* end 60), *Chasam Sofer* (Y.D. 113:1), *Toras Chaim* (*Avodah Zarah* ad loc.), and

Toras Yekusiel (113 ad loc.; see *Darchei Teshuva* ad loc. 12), to rule that even if a food item is considered *Oleh Al Shulchan Melachim*, nonetheless, if it is not commonly served to be eaten with bread, it is exempt from the requirement of *Bishul Yisrael*. However, this issue is debated, and many Acharonim, including the *Pri Toar* (ad loc. 3), *Beis Meir* (ad loc. s.v. *sham*), *Chochmas Adam* (61:1), *Aruch Hashulchan* (Y.D. 113:6 and 7), and *Kaf Hachaim* (ad loc. 7), follow the *Rashba's* understanding, ruling that even if the food is not served with bread, as long as it is *Oleh Al Shulchan Melachim*, mandates *Bishul Yisrael*. To further complicate matters, the *Tur* and *Shulchan Aruch* (Y.D. 113:1), though citing *"lelafos bo es hapas"* still add *"parperes,"* generally understood to be dessert, to the list of foods needing *Bishul Yisrael*. Several of the aforementioned Acharonim view this important addition as proof that *"lelafos bo es hapas"* was not meant be a qualification in the *halacha*, as who eats dessert with bread? [Interestingly, regarding *Hilchos Seudah*, the *Mishnah Berurah* (177:1 and *Biur Halacha* ad loc.); citing the *Rosh* (*Brachos* Ch. 6:26), *Talmidei Rabbeinu Yonah* (ad loc. 29b in the *Rif's* pagination, s.v. *v'Rabbeinu Yitzchak Hazakein*), and *Tosafos* (41b s.v. *hilchasa*), writes that any food that satiates and is served as part of a *seudah* is considered *"lelafos bo es hapas,"* with no mention of our *machlokes* regarding *Bishul Yisrael*. However, Rav Moshe Feinstein is quoted (*Mesores Moshe* vol. 2, pg. 185:44) as understanding it this way regarding *Bishul Yisrael* as well.] There is also the *shittah* of the *Toras Chaim* (ibid.), and also implied by the *Chasam Sofer* (ibid.), that these are two distinct rules. Accordingly, an interesting dichotomy arises, as they would maintain that any food that is served by itself as a dessert, even if not deemed *chashuv*, would necessitate *Bishul Yisrael*, whereas a food item that inherently would be *Oleh Al Shulchan Melachim*, but is generally served as part of a meal but not eaten with bread, would not. Moreover, there are several authorities, including the *Levush* (Y.D. 113:3), *Taz* (ad loc. 1) and *Chochmas Adam* (66:1), who maintain that for a food item to be considered *Oleh Al Shulchan Melachim* it must have sufficient inherent importance that one would "invite his friend over to serve said food product." This author has never heard of anyone inviting someone over for a bowl of cereal! There seems to be no clear-cut consensus on the exact parameters of this complicated topic [although the *Shevet Halevi* (*Shu"t* vol. 2:43) and Rav Dovid Feinstein (cited in *Shu"t Vidibarta Bam* vol. 2:255; although lenient *b'shaas hadchak*) advise to ensure that both desserts and *chashuv* food not eaten with bread be *Bishul Yisrael*], nevertheless, as Rav Henkin notes, following the lenient opinion would certainly permit breakfast cereal without requiring *Bishul Yisrael*.

In conclusion, although the idea of buying bread possibly leading to intermarriage may seem far-fetched to some, we can clearly see and appreciate to what extent Chazal were concerned about mingling with non-Jews.

---

38 Additionally, it is quoted in the name of Rav Moshe Feinstein by Rav Nota Greenblatt (responsum published in *Kovetz Mesorah* vol. 1, pg. 94; who wrote that Rav Moshe agreed to this *psak*) concerning food that is cooked in a factory using equipment that one would not have at home (meaning the factory uses specialized equipment to make said food products), with absolutely no contact between the non-Jewish workers and the customer, is not included in the prohibition. This *psak* is also quoted in *Shu"t Rivevos Efraim* (vol. 5:596), where he adds that Rav Reuven Feinstein confirmed that this indeed was his father's opinion, as well as the OU's *Kashrus Manual on Bishul Akum* (pg. 16), where it was confirmed by Rav Yisroel Belsky, that he personally asked Rav Moshe as well. See also *Shu"t Igros Moshe* (Y.D. 4:48, end 5) where he rules similarly. This is an analogous *shittah* to the Maharit Tzahalon (*Shu"t* 161; cited by the Chida in his *Shiyurei Bracha*, Y.D. 112:9 s.v. *v'all*). Although the Chida (ibid. s.v. *v'ani*) and later, the *Chazon Ish* (brief *teshuva* printed in *Orchos Rabbeinu*, new edition vol. 2, pg. 296, and vol. 4, top of pg. 30; cited *lemaaseh* in *Shu"t Shevet Halevi* vol. 6:108, 6 and vol. 9:23 and *Shu"t Teshuvos V'Hanhagos* vol. 3:247) was unconvinced and maintained that a factory setting would not be considered any different than any other type of store, even so, common custom (based on the opinions of several contemporary authorities) is to accept this leniency as a *tziruf*, when it is combined with other mitigating factors allowing dispensation. See *Shu"t Minchas Yitzchak* (vol. 3:26, 6 and vol. 7:62), *Shu"t Yabia Omer* (vol. 5, Y.D. 9:5), *Teshuvos* of the *Ba'er Moshe* (printed in *Pischei Halacha* on *Hilchos Kashrus*, pg. 117), *Shu"t Shulchan Halevi* (*Chelek Birurei Halacha* 25:2), *Shu"t Minchas Asher* (vol. 3: end 54), Responsum of Rav Herschel Schachter (dated 24 Cheshvan 5756), and the OU's *Kashrus Manual on Bishul Akum* (pg. 14–16). This certainly seemingly holds true following the *Shulchan Aruch's* dictum regarding *Bishul Akum* (*Shu"t Avkas Rochel* 30): "*ain lehachmir, ela lehakel b'd'efshar.*" Accordingly, one may eat Cheerios, et al, during the *Aseres Yemei Teshuva*. Indeed, Rav Dovid Feinstein, Rav Asher Weiss, and Rav Yisroel Belsky (ibid. previous footnotes) state this outright. On the other hand, see Rav Moshe Sternbuch's *Shu"t Teshuvos V'Hanhagos* (vol. 5:249; this author has heard that this was also the opinion of *Mori v'Rabi* Rav Yaakov Blau) who explains that although *me'ikar hadin* this is correct, nevertheless, based on the above *sefeikos* and *sheilos*, the *Badatz Eidah Hachareidis* of

The message is clear: When one's goal is preserving the sanctity of the Jewish nation, we take no shortcuts. Just something to think about the next time you run out for some bagels or cookies.

Yerushalayim is *"mehadar"* to ensure that cereals under their *hashgachah* are *Bishul Yisrael* as well; meaning that if at all possible, it is proper to be *choshesh* for the more stringent opinion. Practically, this is a far easier prospect to ensure in Eretz Yisrael than in other countries. However, it should be noted that there currently are (comparably) small runs of *Bishul Yisrael* cereal being manufactured under the *hashgachos* of smaller *Vaadei Kashrus* that are easily obtainable in certain *"heimishe"* locales in America. These include Unger's brand, under the supervision of New Square Kashrus, and Kemach brand, under the supervision of Rav Nosson Naftali Horowitz of Ohr Yechezkel in Boro Park.

Chapter 24

Mayim Acharonim, Chova?

IN *PARASHAS LECH LECHA*, we are introduced to an interesting personality named Bera, *Melech S'dom*, the King of S'dom. While he was certainly not known for his morality and impeccable character, nonetheless, his title, as well as the destruction of his hometown using salt, described in *Parashas Vayera*,[1] seemingly references a catalyst to a Mitzva that many are wholly unfamiliar with: its homonym, "*Melech S'domis*" or S'dom Salt. The Mitzva I am referring to is *Mayim Acharonim*, the handwashing before *Birkas Hamazon*.[2]

---

1 See *Parashas Vayera* (*Bereishis* Ch. 19:24 and 25) and *Parashas Nitzavim* (*Devarim* Ch. 29:22), which, as part of the *tochacha* (rebuke) Moshe Rabbeinu gives Bnei Yisrael, warning them of the dire consequences of not listening to the word of Hashem, states "*gafris v'melach sereifah kol artzah...k'mahpeichas S'dom*—Sulfur and salt will burn your whole land...just as (it did) in the turning over (destruction) of S'dom." According to the author of the *Zera Gad* on the *Haggadah*, Rav Tzvi Hirsch of Horodna, in his glosses to *Targum Rav Yosef* on *Divrei Hayamim* (II, Ch. 13:5; as cited by the *Mareh Yehoshua* on the *Maaseh Rav*, 84), who explains *Dovid HaMelech's* eternal *Bris Melach* with Hashem as parallel to the salty seas never becoming sweet, this is the true source of *Melach S'domis*. Rav Tzvi Hirsch explains that the current *Yam Hamelach* (Dead Sea) sits upon the former site of S'dom and its sister cities. Since all of the seas and oceans are connected, the salty destruction of S'dom is what turned them all salty. Accordingly, "*Melach S'domis*" is still extant, if highly diluted. He therefore maintains that washing *Mayim Acharonim* is still actually obligatory nowadays, akin to the opinion of the Vilna Gaon (as will be cited later in this chapter). The wording of the *Aruch Hashulchan* (O.C. 181:5) implies that he concurs with this understanding as well.

Mitzva?!

I am sure that many readers are shaking their heads in disbelief, wondering how I can call this known *chumrah* a Mitzva. This common, but slightly mistaken belief was made evident to this author when a neighborhood housewife asked an interesting *sheilah*. Apparently, after hosting several friends and relatives for a *Shabbos seudah*,³ she washed *Mayim Acharonim* along with the men, earning her much scorn and ridicule. The incredulous men commented that their washing *Mayim Acharonim* was only a *chumrah*, and there obviously was no basis for a woman to do it. Our distraught domestic denizen wanted to know who acted correctly, and was astounded when I replied that, technically speaking, they both were.

A Bit of Background

Mayim Acharonim has an interesting background, as it actually has two entirely different sources and rationales mandating it:

---

2   While Bera's personal connection to the Mitzva of *Mayim Acharonim* is tenuous at best, relying on homonyms and clever wordplay, on the other hand and quite remarkably, due to Avraham Avinu's famous "thread and shoelace" rebuttal to his "largesse," Bera unwittingly became the catalyst for the Mitzvos of *Tzitzis* and *Tefillin*. See Gemara *Sota* (17a) and *Chullin* (89a). Interestingly, a related anecdote is told of Rav Yonason Eibeshutz (1690–1764), one of the greatest Torah giants of his period and famed author of the renowned *Yaaros Devash*, *Urim V'Tumim*, and *Kreisi U'Pleisi*. When he was a child, his *melamed*, wishing to test the child prodigy's mental acumen, asked him what the King of S'dom's real name was, as in the *Pitum HaKetores Tefilla*, (based on Gemara *Kerisos* 6a; referring to the amount of S'dom Salt used as part of the *Ketores*) it states "*Melach S'domis Rova*." So was his name really Bera or Rova? The young genius wryly replied that in his opinion, at first his name was Bera, but after the *Malachim* overturned S'dom, his name was also turned over and became Rova (as both names share the same Hebrew letters ב-ר-ע). Thanks are due to Rabbi Reuven Chaim Klein for pointing out this amusing anecdote from several biographical *sefarim*.

3   There is a common misconception that washing *Mayim Acharonim* is only applicable on Shabbos. This idea perhaps stems from the *Shabbos seudos*, as the whole family sits down together for a "bread meal" and therefore also washes

- The first, the Gemara in *Brachos*, discussing the source for ritual handwashing, explains that one can not make a *bracha* with dirty hands, and cites the *pasuk* in *Parashas Kedoshim* "*V'Hiskadeeshtem, V'Heyisem Kedoshim*, And you shall sanctify yourselves, and be holy."[4] The Gemara clarifies that "and you shall sanctify yourselves" refers to washing the hands before the meal, *Mayim Rishonim*, and "and be holy" refers to washing the hands after the meal, *Mayim Acharonim*.[5] In other words, by washing our hands before making a *bracha* (in this case before *bentching*), we are properly sanctifying ourselves.
- The second source, Gemara *Chullin*, on the other hand, refers to *Mayim Acharonim* as a "*Chova*," an outright obligation. The Gemara elucidates that there is a certain type of salt in the world, called "*Melach S'domis*," (actually one of the ingredients needed to make the *Ketores* properly)[6] that is so caustic, that if it gets into a person's eyes, it can *chas v'shalom* cause blindness. Since one is supposed to have salt at his table at every meal,[7] *Chazal*

---

and *bentches* together. Although making sure to wash *Mayim Acharonim* on Shabbos is certainly commendable, nevertheless, *halachic* literature does not make such a distinction, and *Mayim Acharonim* applies (or doesn't apply anymore, depending on the views we will see below) during the week as well. On the other hand, it is important to note that the *Matteh Efraim* (583:4 and 619:1), who is considered the leading authority on issues relating to the *Yomim Nora'im*, writes that one who is lenient regarding *Mayim Acharonim* year-round should nonetheless be vigilant with ensuring to wash *Mayim Acharonim* on *Rosh Hashanah*, as well as at the *Seudah Hamafsekes* on *Erev Yom Kippur*.

4   *Vayikra* (Ch. 20:7).

5   *Brachos* (53b).

6   See Gemara *Kerisos* (6a) and *Rambam* (*Hilchos Klei HaMikdash* Ch. 2:3).

7   There is a Mitzva to have salt on the table when having a meal, which is directly based on the requirement to have salt on every *Korban* (*Vayikra* Ch. 2:13), as our tables are compared to the *Mizbe'ach* (Altar) and our food to a sacrifice. See Gemara *Brachos* (55a), *Tosafos* (ad loc. s.v. *haba*), *Beis Yosef* (O.C.

were concerned that this specific type of salt may have found its way onto our tables and consequently could cause someone to become blind if he rubs his eyes after eating. Therefore, as a way to mitigate this salt's potentially devastating effects, they mandated handwashing after eating, the act of which has become known colloquially as *Mayim Acharonim*.[8]

In fact, the Gemara's words are codified as *halacha* by the *Tur* and *Shulchan Aruch*, stating simply "*Mayim Acharonim Chova*."[9] The *Rambam* as well, writes that it is an obligation due to the potential *Sakana* involved.[10] As an aside, the *Ben Ish Chai* advises that when eating, one should say this three word formula ("*Mayim Acharonim Chova*") and that way fulfill the *halacha* of speaking *Divrei Torah* at a meal.[11]

167, quoting the *Shibolei Leket* 141), *Shulchan Aruch* and *Rema* (O.C. 167:5), *Magen Avraham* (ad loc. 15), *Machatzis Hashekel* (ad loc. 15), *Ba'er Heitiv* (ad loc. 7; citing the Arizal), *Aruch Hashulchan* (ad loc. 12), *Mishnah Berurah* (ad loc. 30), and *Kaf Hachaim* (ad loc. 40). See also *Shlah* (*Shaar Ha'Osiyos*, *Eimek Bracha* 66), *Kiryas Chana Dovid* (49), and *Halachic World* (vol. 2, pg. 151, "Table Salt"). *Lemaaseh*, although nowadays our bread is considered *"nekiya"* and we would not have a requirement to dip it into salt *me'ikar hadin*, nevertheless, due to Chazal's comparison of our tables to the *Mizbe'ach*, one should still have salt on the table while eating. Additionally, Kabbalistically speaking, one should still dip his bread into salt three times. See also R' Zvi Ryzman's recent *Ratz KaTzvi* on *Maagalei Hashana* (vol. 1, 3, Ch. 2:10) who adds a potential reason based on the *Baal HaTurim* (*Vayikra* Ch. 2:13) regarding the three times that salt is mentioned in said *pasuk*. This topic is discussed further in the chapter titled "Salting with Sugar?!"

8   *Chullin* (105a-b) and *Eruvin* (17b).

9   *Shulchan Aruch* (O.C. 181:1), based on the opinions of many Rishonim, including the *Rif* (*Chullin* 37b), *Sefer Hachinuch* (*Parashas Eikev*, Mitzva 430 s.v. *mayim*), and *Tur* (O.C. 181).

10 *Rambam* (*Hilchos Brachos* Ch. 6:3). The *Rambam* implies that he holds that "*Melach S'domis*" is still extant.

11 *Ben Ish Chai* (Year 1, *Parashas Shlach* 7), quoting his esteemed father and grandfather. See *Pirkei Avos* (Ch. 3, Mishnah 3).

Chova?

Well, if the Gemara and even the *Shulchan Aruch* consider washing *Mayim Acharonim* an actual obligation, then why do many treat it as a mere stringency? Furthermore, there are those (many of Germanic origin) who claim that their custom is to specifically **not** wash *Mayim Acharonim*! Additionally, if it is a binding *halacha*, why don't women generally observe this washing?

The answer lies in the commentary of the *Baalei Tosafos* to both aforementioned Gemaros.[12] *Tosafos* comments that "nowadays, as "*Melach S'domis*" is no longer found among us, we are no longer accustomed to washing *Mayim Acharonim*, and one may *bentch* without first washing his hands." In other words, *Tosafos* maintains that although washing *Mayim Acharonim* used to be an obligation, since the problematic S'dom Salt was no longer prevalent already in their days, one is no longer required to wash *Mayim Acharonim*. In fact, not washing for *Mayim Acharonim* is cited as the common *minhag* by several Ashkenazic Rishonim, as well as the *Rema* and the *Levush*.[13]

An additional rationale for leniency is put forward by the famed Rav Yaakov Emden: He points out that ever since the advent of cutlery, most civilized people (hopefully) do not do the bulk of their eating with their hands, rather with a fork and spoon. Therefore, he explains, one who eats with silverware (or even plasticware) and did not actually touch his food, has no need to wash *Mayim Acharonim*.[14]

---

12 *Tosafos* (*Brachos* 53b s.v. *v'heyisem*; *Chullin* 105a s.v. *mayim*; *Eruvin* 17b s.v. *Mayim Acharonim*).

13 Including the *Rosh* (*Brachos* Ch. 8:6), *Ohr Zarua* (vol. 1:72), *Agur* (235), *SMa"G* (*Mitzvos Asei* 27), *Rema* in his *Darchei Moshe* glosses to the *Tur* (ad loc. 2), and the *Levush* (O.C. 181:9). See also *Shu"t Hisorerus Teshuva* (vol. 1:63), who defends the "common custom" of *not* washing *Mayim Acharonim*.

14 *Mor U'Ketziah* (end 181 s.v. *daf*). This is *leshittaso*, as the Yaavetz rules similarly by the handwashing requirements of a *davar hateebulo b'mashkeh*. However, the *Kaf Hachaim* (ad loc. 27) cites several authorities who do not agree with the Yaavetz's leniency. He concludes that even if one ate exclusively with utensils, he must still wash *Mayim Acharonim*. Similarly, regarding different

Interestingly, at the end of the very same *siman* where he rules that "*Mayim Acharonim Chova,*" the *Shulchan Aruch* cites *Tosafos'* lenient view that *Mayim Acharonim* is not actually required.[15] Several authorities explain his seemingly contradictory intent that indeed nowadays one is **no longer mandated** to wash *Mayim Acharonim*. Yet, the *Shulchan Aruch* is telling us that nevertheless, we still should strive to do this important Mitzva.[16]

This view is cited by many *halachic* authorities, including the *Chayei Adam, Shulchan Aruch Harav, Kitzur Shulchan Aruch, Aruch Hashulchan,* and *Mishnah Berurah,* who relate that although *Mayim Acharonim* may no longer be obligated by the strict letter of the law, but rather as *minhag,* nonetheless, one still should be very stringent with its adherence.[17] Other authorities cite Kabbalistic reasons to be strict with

---

halachos related to handwashing, we find that although according to the letter of the law it need not be required, nevertheless, many authorities rule that one should still wash his hands, as handwashing does not usually entail much effort. This topic was addressed in the first chapter, "The Importance of a *Diyuk.*"

15 *Shulchan Aruch* (O.C. 181:10).

16 *Shu"t Nechpeh B'Kessef* (vol. 1, pg. 154, fourth column), *Yalkut Yosef* (vol. 3, *Dinei Birkas Hamazon U'Brachos*, 181, footnotes 1 and 2; and *Kitzur Shulchan Aruch*, O.C. 181:1), *Halichos Olam* (*Parashas Shlach* 1), *Halacha Berurah* (vol. 8, O.C. 181, *Birur Halacha* 1 s.v. *v'hinei*).

17 *Chayei Adam* (vol. 1, 46:1), *Shulchan Aruch Harav* (O.C. 181:9), *Kitzur Shulchan Aruch* (44:1), *Aruch Hashulchan* (O.C. 181:5), and *Mishnah Berurah* (ad loc. 22). Other *Poskim* who rule this way include the Rashal (*Yam Shel Shlomo, Chullin* Ch. 8:10), *Magen Avraham* (O.C. 181:10), *Elyah Rabba* (ad loc. 9), *Pri Megadim* (ad loc. M.Z. 1; citing several reasons for stringency), Maharsham (*Daas Torah*, ad loc. 10; quoting the *Toras Chaim*), *Ben Ish Chai* (Year 1, *Parashas Shlach* 6), *Shoneh Halachos* (vol. 1, 181:1), *Shu"t Ohr L'Tzion* (vol. 2, pg. 303), *Yalkut Yosef* (ibid.) and *Halacha Berurah* (ibid.). Many of these authorities suspect that even though actual "*Melach S'domis*" might no longer be prevalent, still, there are other types of common salt that would be harmful if rubbed into eyes. [This *chashash* was first mentioned by *Talmidei Rabbeinu Yonah* (*Brachos* 40b in the *Rif's* pagination) in the name of the *Rambam* (ibid.), "*shema yeish bo*

its observance.[18] The Vilna Gaon was known to be extremely *makpid* on this *halacha*, referring to it as both a "*Chova*" and a "*Mitzva*," even nowadays.[19]

Wash This Way!

Interestingly, authorities debate the proper way to perform washing *Mayim Acharonim*. One *machlokes* involves how much water to use. The basic *halacha* is that this handwashing has no set limit or minimum,

---

Melach S'domis **oh melach sheteva k'Melach S'domis**."] Additionally, even if salt was no longer an issue, still, one fulfills the Mitzva of "*V'heyisem Kedoshim*" by washing *Mayim Acharonim*.

18   The *Kaf Hachaim* (O.C. 181:1) states that the words of Chazal are really "*Sod*" wrapped in "*Pshat*." Therefore, even if the "*Peshat*" is no longer relevant, the hidden meanings still are. He then cites that the *Zohar* (*Parashas Terumah* pg. 154b and *Parashas Pinchas* pg. 246a) and the Arizal (*Shaar HaMitzvos, Parashas Eikev*) write that one should be extremely vigilant with *Mayim Acharonim* due to Kabbalistic reasons. This *zehirus* with *Mayim Acharonim* based on Kabbalistic reasons is also cited by the *Shlah* (*Shaar Ha'Osiyos, Os Kuf* s.v. u'ksheim), the *Magen Avraham* (ibid.), the Chida (*Birkei Yosef*, O.C. 181:7), the *Pele Yo'etz* (*Os Nun, Netillas Yadayim* s.v. v'yeish), *Shulchan HaTahor* (181:1 and footnote; who calls it a "*Chova Gamur*"), Rav Chaim Palaji (*Kaf Hachaim* 25:2, 8 and 9, quoting the *Yalkut Reuveini* on *Vayikra*), the *Matteh Moshe* (vol. 2:306), *Ben Ish Chai* (ibid.), and in *Shu"t Min Hashamayim* (57). See *Mori v'Rabi* Rav Yosef Yitzchok Lerner's classic *Shemiras Haguf V'Hanefesh* (vol. 1, Ch. 56) at length.

19   See *Biur HaGr"a* (O.C. 181:12) who was extremely stringent with this *halacha*, as he rejects the common leniencies offered by *Tosafos* and the *Rosh*. Additionally, *Maaseh Rav* (84) and *Piskei HaGr"a* (O.C. 181:10), mutually in the *Gr"a's* name, refer to *Mayim Acharonim* as both a "*Chova*" and a "*Mitzva*," even nowadays. This is also how it is cited in *Kesser Rosh* (82:1), that the Vilna Gaon's prime *talmid*, Rav Chaim Volozhiner, held as well. See also *Mishnah Berurah* (181:22) who explains that according to the *Gr"a*, the *sakana* of "*Melach S'domis*" still applies nowadays. This also seems to be the *Rambam's* understanding (*Hilchos Brachos* Ch. 6:3), and is cited by the *Aruch Hashulchan* (O.C. 181:5) as well, that those who use sea salt should still be wary of "*Melach S'domis*," which would fit in with the explanation of the *Zera Gad* (as elucidated in the first footnote in this chapter).

rather even a small amount of water is sufficient.[20] Indeed, the Kabbalistic approach mandates specifically using only a small amount of water.[21] Conversely, the Vilna Gaon was *makpid* to use a full *Reviis* of water, as he considered *Mayim Acharonim* a full washing, akin to the *Netillas Yadayim* required before eating bread (*Mayim Rishonim*).[22]

---

20 The *Kol Bo* (23), quoting the *Raavad*, as well as the *Beis Yosef* (O.C. 181 s.v. *mashma*) citing the opinion of Rabbeinu Bachya (*Shulchan Shel Arba*, Shaar 1 s.v. *v'yeish hefresh*), ruled that there is no *shiur* for the amount of water needed for *Mayim Acharonim*, and even a small amount will do. The *Elyah Rabba* (ad loc. 3) and *Aruch Hashulchan* (ad loc. 8) wrote that this is indeed the *halacha*. This seems to be the common custom; see *Mishnah Berurah* (ad loc. 19). Similarly, several contemporary authorities, including the *Chazon Ish* (cited in *Orchos Rabbeinu* vol. 1:70), Rav Yosef Eliyahu Henkin (*Shu"t Gevuros Eliyahu* vol. 1-O.C. 53:4), and Rav Shmuel *Halevi* Wosner (*Kovetz M'Beis Levi* vol. 17, pg. 22:3) wrote that the prevalent *minhag* is that one only needs to use a small amount of water.

21 See *Ben Ish Chai* (Year 1, *Parashas Shlach* 8), *Kaf Hachaim* (Palaji; 25:2), and *Kaf Hachaim* (Sofer; O.C. 181:6). See next footnote.

22 *Maaseh Rav* (84), cited by the *Mishnah Berurah* (181:19). The Gr"a's prime *talmid*, Rav Chaim Volozhiner, is cited (*Kesser Rosh* 82:1) as holding this way as well. The *Aruch Hashulchan* (ad loc. 8) notes that many *Gedolim* washed with a full *Reviis*, and he personally does not see any reason to be *makpid* on only using a small amount of water. As pointed out by Rabbi Dr. Seth Mandel, Rav Yosef Dov Soloveitchik, Rosh Yeshivas Rabbeinu Yitzchak Elchanan (YU), citing family *minhag* dating back to Rav Chaim Volozhiner and the Vilna Gaon, was *makpid* on washing his entire hands with a *Reviis* of water. However, the *Chazon Ish* is quoted (*Orchos Rabbeinu* vol. 1:70; citing the Steipler Gaon; and in the recent Weinreb edition of *Maaseh Rav*, Miluim pg. 320, s.v. *u'l'inyan*; quoting Rav Chaim Kanievsky) as not believing that the Gr"a was actually *makpid* on a *shiur Reviis* for *Mayim Acharonim*. However, see *Shu"t Teshuvos V'Hanhagos* (vol. 1:173 s.v. *v'achshav*) who writes that "this *shemua* is *tzarich iyun gadol*," as why should this ruling in *Maaseh Rav* be any less reliable as to the Gr"a's personal *hanhaga* than any other one in the *sefer*, especially as his *talmidim* were known to be stringent for washing this way. He attempts to answer that perhaps the *Chazon Ish* was referring to washing only to the second knuckle (as opposed to the whole hand) with a *Reviis*, that he did not believe

Another *machlokes* revolves around how much of the hand must be washed by *Mayim Acharonim*. Although the basic *halacha* only requires from the fingertips to the second knuckle,[23] nevertheless, Kabbalistically speaking, one should wash one's entire fingers.[24] A third opinion, that of the Vilna Gaon, is that the whole hand should be washed, as he considered *Mayim Acharonim* a full *Netillas Yadayim*, as stated previously.[25]

---

was the *Gr"a's* true *shittah*. However, he reiterates, washing the whole hand with a *Reviis* (meaning a full *Netillas Yadayim*) was indeed the *Gr"a's* opinion.

23 *Shulchan Aruch* (O.C. 181:4), quoting the *Tur* (ad loc.) and *Rashba* (*Toras Habayis*, *Bayis* 6, *Shaar* 1, Ch. 9), *Levush* (ad loc.), *Magen Avraham* (ad loc. 4), *Pri Megadim* (ad loc. E.A. 4), *Chayei Adam* (vol. 1, 46:1), *Kitzur Shulchan Aruch* (44:1), and *Aruch Hashulchan* (ad loc. 7). Indeed, in his *Beis Yosef* commentary (ad loc. 4), the *Shulchan Aruch* explicitly rules against Rabbeinu Bachya's opinion (*Shulchan Shel Arba* pg. 466) of mandating washing the whole finger. Several contemporary authorities, including Rav Yosef Eliyahu Henkin (*Shu"t Gevuros Eliyahu* vol. 1-O.C. 53:4), and Rav Shmuel *Halevi* Wosner (*Kovetz M'Beis Levi* vol. 17, pg. 22:3) wrote that the prevalent *minhag* is that one only needs to wash until the second knuckle. The *Mishnah Berurah* (ibid. end 10) writes that he sees people who are scrupulous with washing *Mayim Acharonim*, yet only wash the tips of their fingers, not realizing that they must wash until the second knuckle to fulfill the Mitzva. He calls this minute washing a "*Maaseh Ra*," and exhorts everyone to wash at least until the second knuckle.

24 The *Arizal* (*Shaar HaKavannos* pg. 72b) and the *Siddur HaRashash* maintain that Kabbalistically, the entire fingers must be washed during *Mayim Acharonim*. The *Kaf Hachaim* (O.C. 181:17) rules this way as well. [In his commentary to *Orach Chaim* 157 (22), the *Kaf Hachaim* explains the Arizal's reasoning for this.] He adds a rule that anytime a *halacha* is not specifically mentioned in the Gemara, but its practical application is debated by *Poskim*, we should follow the practice of the Kabbalists. He adds that certainly, if the *Shulchan Aruch* would have seen the ruling of the Arizal he would have mandated whole finger washing as well. As mentioned in a previous footnote, requiring the whole fingers to be washed was also the opinion of Rabbeinu Bachya (*Shulchan Shel Arba* pg. 466). The *Mishnah Berurah* (181:4, *Biur Halacha* s.v. *ad*) concludes that *lechatchilla* one should try to be *machmir* for this opinion. [Interestingly, he refers to it as the *Gr"a's shittah*. On this, see *Shu"t Teshuvos V'Hanhagos* (vol. 1:173) who explains that the *Gr"a's* true *shittah* was washing the full hand. See next footnote.]

The unifying thread of these disparate *shittos* is their mandating adherence to the strict performance of *Mayim Acharonim*.

Women's Role

Yet, so far, none of this explains why women commonly do not wash *Mayim Acharonim*. This "custom" seems to be an anomaly, as technically, women and men share the same obligation in this Mitzva, and we do not find a *halachic* codifier making such a distinction.

Several contemporary authorities, including Rav Shmuel *Halevi* Wosner and Rav Moshe Sternbuch, offer a possible justification.[26] They explain that although women and men were both equally obligated in this Mitzva, nevertheless, since it is no longer mandated as a strict requirement due to the dearth of "*Melach S'domis*," but rather as a proper "*minhag*," it is entirely possible that women collectively never accepted this stringency upon themselves. Therefore, nowadays they are not required to wash *Mayim Acharonim*.[27] Indeed, Rav Yonah Merzbach (M'Roshei Yeshivas Kol Torah and formerly Rav of Darmstadt,

---

25 See *Biur HaGr"a* (O.C. 181:12, s.v. *yeish*), *Chidushei HaGr"a Imrei Noam* (on *Brachos* 15a and 53b), *Maaseh Rav* (84), and in many glosses to the *Maaseh Rav*, including *Damesek Eliezer*, *Ohr Chodosh*, and *Biurei Rav Naftali Hertz Halevi* (ad loc.). This was also attested to by the *Gr"a's talmid*, Rav Zundel Salant (*HaTzaddik Ri"Z M'Salant* pg. 115), and was the personal *hanhaga* of the Brisker Rav [see *Shu"t Teshuvos V'Hanhagos* (vol. 1:173) at length on the *Gr"a's shittah* of *Mayim Acharonim*].

26 *Shu"t Shevet Halevi* (vol. 3, 23:3 s.v. *l'inyan*) and *Shu"t Teshuvos V'Hanhagos* (vol. 1:174). However, Rav Sternbuch concludes that nevertheless women still should wash *Mayim Acharonim*. He notes that certainly according to the *Gr"a* and others who maintain that even nowadays *Mayim Acharonim* is obligatory, there would be no difference between men and women in this respect.

27 There are several other possible justifications for women's general lackadaisicalness with *Mayim Acharonim*: The Yaavetz (*Mor U'Ketziah* ibid.) posits that since women are generally more rigorous regarding hygiene and cleanliness, they certainly would make sure not to eat with their hands, and *leshittaso* not be required in *Mayim Acharonim* [however, he concludes that barring that, women and men have equal obligation in this Mitzva]. Others [see *Shu"t*

Germany) was quoted as stating that the common *minhag* for women in Ashkenaz, even among "*Chareidim L'Dvar Hashem*," was **not** to wash *Mayim Acharonim*.[28]

On the other hand, many other contemporary *halachic* authorities, including Rav Yosef Chaim Sonnenfeld, Rav Shlomo Zalman Auerbach, Rav Yosef Shalom Elyashiv, Rav Chaim Pinchas Scheinberg, Rav Ovadiah Yosef, Rav Mordechai Eliyahu, and the *Rivevos Efraim*, as well as Rav Moshe Sternbuch and the *Shevet Hakehasi*, all rule that regardless of the rationale, women still should be vigilant with washing *Mayim Acharonim*.[29] Some conclude that even so, it is preferable that they should wash unobtrusively, not to fall into the category of "giving an impression of showing off" (*mechzei k'yuhara*), as women might not be obligated to do so according to the strict letter of the law.[30]

Vayevarech Dovid (vol. 1, O.C. 30) and *Yalkut Yosef* (ibid.)] opine that since men are only *makpid* due to Kabbalistic reasons and not because of actual *halachic* concerns, women are not beholden to keep it.

28 Cited in *Halichos Bas Yisrael* (pg. 58, end of footnote 11).

29 Rav Yosef Chaim Sonnenfeld (*Shu"t Salmas Chaim*, new edition, O.C. 174), Rav Shlomo Zalman Auerbach (cited in *Halichos Bas Yisrael* Ch. 3, footnote 11), Rav Yosef Shalom Elyashiv (*He'aros B'Maseches Chullin* 105b), Rav Chaim Pinchas Scheinberg (cited in *Orchos Harav V'Rosh HaYeshiva*, end Ch. 8, pg. 61, as well as in the ArtScroll *Ohel Sarah Women's Siddur*, endnote 105), Rav Ovadiah Yosef (*Halichos Olam* vol. 2, *Parashas Shlach* 1; pg. 44), Rav Mordechai Eliyahu (*Darchei Halacha* glosses to *Kitzur Shulchan Aruch* 44:1), the *Rivevos Efraim* (*Shu"t* vol. 1:140, 3), Rav Moshe Sternbuch (*Shu"t Teshuvos V'Hanhagos* vol. 1:174), and the *Shevet Hakehasi* (*Shu"t* vol. 1:94). Other contemporary *sefarim* who rule that women should wash *Mayim Acharonim* include *Halichos Baysa* (Ch. 12:2), *Yalkut Yosef* (ibid. and his *Kitzur Shulchan Aruch*, O.C. 181:2), and *Halacha Berurah* (ibid.). In fact, the *Aruch Hashulchan* (O.C. 181: end 5) already mentioned that one should make sure that "*kol bnei beiso*" wash *Mayim Acharonim*. Anecdotally, it is told that Rebbetzin Feiga Chaya Zaks, daughter of the *Chofetz Chaim* (she was born when he was sixty-four), was particular to wash *Mayim Acharonim*, saying that her saintly father instructed her to wash with a *Reviis* of water before *bentching*.

To Wash or Not to Wash?

Back to our dilemma. Now it is clear why I informed that harried housewife that technically speaking both she and her relatives were correct. She undeniably had what to rely upon *not* to wash *Mayim Acharonim*. Yet, she was definitely correct in making sure to do so anyway. As the *Pele Yo'etz* explains, even if there no longer is a danger posed from salt that blinds our eyes, nevertheless, we still have an obligation to listen to the words of our *Chachamim*, and not "blind ourselves" to their wisdom.[31]

Postscript: Talking After Washing

Although the Vilna Gaon is the *machmir shittah* in the three separate *Mayim Acharonim*-related *machlokasim* cited above, there is one dispute regarding *Mayim Acharonim* where he is quoted as being the lenient opinion: talking between *Mayim Acharonim* and *bentching*. This issue of talking before *bentching* is a large topic in its own right. The Gemara in *Brachos* writes that one may not be *mafsik* (make a separation) between washing and *Birkas Hamazon*. There is a *machlokes* Rishonim how to understand the Gemara. *Rashi*, as well as the *Rambam*, understand that this means that one may not eat (there is a whole separate *machlokes* Rishonim whether or not this includes drinking) and this is how the *Tur* and *Shulchan Aruch* cite the *halacha* as well. According to Rav Yosef Karo,

---

30   Shu"t Teshuvos V'Hanhagos (ibid.). He adds that he has seen many "*Chassidim V'Anshei Maaseh*" whose wives were particular to wash *Mayim Acharonim*.

31   *Pele Yo'etz* (*Os Nun, Netillas Yadayim* s.v. *v'yeish*). There are several additional reasons to be vigilant with *Mayim Acharonim*. In *Shu"t Min Hashamayim* (ibid.; cited by the *Aruch Hashulchan* ibid.) he explains that "*kol hameikil b'Mayim Acharonim mekilim lo mezonosav min HaShmayim.*" Additionally, the Chida (*Birkei Yosef* idid.) cites that his saintly grandfather was told in a *She'eilas Chalom* that "*hameikil b'Mayim Acharonim mekilin lo yamav u'shnosav!*" Definitely excellent reasons to observe this washing. For more on the topic of *She'eilos Chalomos* in general, see Rabbi Dr. Eliezer Brodt's *Lekutei Eliezer* (pg. 59–63) and Rabbi Mordechai Zev Trenk's recent *Magic, Mysteries, and Mysticism: Illuminating Insights on Esoteric Torah Topics* (pg. 76–78 and 235–239).

in his *Kessef Mishneh* commentary on the *Rambam*, this understanding excludes talking, meaning the only problematic *hefsek* is eating and/or drinking; ergo, talking would be permitted.[32]

Yet, the *Rosh* understands the Gemara's rule as meaning that once one performs *Mayim Acharonim*, it is as if he answered the *zimun* (i.e., akin to have started *bentching*).[33] If so, talking would be proscribed as well. Other Rishonim seem to accept the *Rosh's* position on this.

What is interesting is that in his later *Beis Yosef* commentary, Rav Karo retracted his lenient position, ruling akin to the *Rosh*, that even speaking between *Mayim Acharonim* and *bentching* is prohibited.[34]

On that, the *Magen Avraham* takes him to task for his retraction, and seemingly ruling following Rav Karo's opinion in his *Kessef Mishneh* that talking between *Mayim Acharonim* and *bentching* is permitted. In fact, that is how the *Ba'er Heitiv* cites the *Magen Avraham's* intent—as practically ruling leniently. Yet, there is some confusion as to whether or not this was his actual conclusion *lemaaseh*.[35]

The *Mishnah Berurah* disagrees with this understanding, maintaining that the *Magen Avraham's* conclusion was truly to be *machmir* following the *Rosh's shittah*, corresponding to what Rav Karo wrote in his *Beis Yosef*, and not like what he wrote in his *Kessef Mishneh* as per the *Rambam*.[36]

Most *Poskim* rule this way, prohibiting talking between *Mayim Acharonim* and *bentching*. These authorities include the *Bach*, *Elyah Rabba*, *Chayei Adam*, *Ben Ish Chai*, *Mishnah Berurah*, and *Kaf Hachaim*. In fact, the *Mishnah Berurah* implies that talking might be considered a bigger problem than eating; if one eats, we seem to follow the opinion of the *Pri Megadim* that it cancelled out the first *Mayim Acharonim*, so

---

32 Gemara *Brachos* (42a), *Rashi* (ad loc.), *Rambam* (*Hilchos Brachos* Ch. 6:20), *Kessef Mishneh* (ad loc.), and *Tur* and *Shulchan Aruch* (O.C. 179:1).

33 *Rosh* (*Brachos* Ch. 6:31).

34 *Beis Yosef* (O.C. 179 s.v. *yeish l'dakdek*).

35 *Magen Avraham* (O.C. 181:1) and *Ba'er Heitiv* (O.C. 179:1).

36 *Shaar Hatziyun* (179:1).

we may simply wash again before *bentching*. Whereas since it is not so clear-cut that talking is considered a *hefsek*, it is unclear if one is allowed to wash again to *bentch*; he might now not be allowed to *bentch*! [Although it is important to note that this is not the normative *halacha*.] The *Mishnah Berurah* also seems to hold that talking after *Mayim Acharonim* is more problematic than talking after *Mayim Rishonim* (for *Hamotzi*).[37]

An additional factor is that the Arizal was *machmir* with this issue, and drove the point home with an interesting tale about one who had unexplained shoulder pain. The Arizal instructed him not to talk between *Mayim Acharonim* and *bentching*…and the pain subsequently subsided. He explained that "*Netilla* **Teikef** *L'Bracha*" (washing immediately prior to *bentching*), is connected to **Katef** (shoulder) and therefore one should be stringent. The Chida, quoting his ancestor, Rav Avraham Azulai, citing the *Yeushalmi*, avers that if one is particular about reciting *bentching* immediately after *Mayim Acharonim*, the Satan will not have the ability to level accusations against him during that meal.[38]

A middle-ground opinion is found in the *Shulchan Aruch Harav*, who writes that a few necessary words are permitted, as "*hefsek*" is only referring to *Divrei Torah* or an actual conversation.[39]

So where does the *Gr"a* fit in? In his *Biur HaGr"a* he cites the whole background to the *machlokes*, citing the many Rishonim and the *shakla v'tarya*. Yet, he concludes simply that in the *Rosh's* commentary on *Chullin* he seems to have retracted his stringent position, asserting that "*v'chein daas kol haPoskim.*" In other words, the Vilna Gaon held that since there is a seeming contradiction in the *Rosh*, and all of the

---

37 Bach (O.C. 181:4), *Elyah Rabba* (ad loc. 9), *Chuyei Adam* (vol. 1, 44:1), *Ben Ish Chai* (Year 1, *Parashas Shlach* 15), *Mishnah Berurah* (179:1 and 181:24, and *Shaar Hatziyun* 179:7), *Kaf Hachaim* (O.C. 179:1 and 181:20), and *Pri Megadim* (O.C. 179, E.A. 1).

38 *Shaar HaMitzvos* (*Parashas Eikev*) and *Birkei Yosef* (O.C. 181:3).

39 *Shulchan Aruch Harav* (O.C. 181:6).

stringent opinions are intrinsically based on his *shittah*, one need not be *machmir* with the no-talking-before-*bentching* rule.⁴⁰

However, although the *Aruch Hashulchan* seems to rule this way and declares that talking is not the *hefsek* that the Rishonim were debating, he concludes that nevertheless, "*lechatchilla aino kedai lehafsik*" as the Gemara taught "*Teikif L'Netillas Yadayim Bracha*" and therefore "*m'kol makom aino kedai laasos kein*," it is not worthwhile to talk between washing *Mayim Acharonim* and *bentching*.⁴¹

---

40 *Biur HaGr"a* (O.C. 179:2), *Rosh* (*Chullin* Ch. 6:2 s.v. *d'amar*).

41 *Aruch Hashulchan* (O.C. 181:1 and 9).

Part 5

KEY CONCEPTS

Chapter 25

Chodosh in *Chutz La'aretz*

Part I—Earlier Sources

DURING THE FALL, ONE MIGHT notice religious Jews in the local supermarkets checking labels on products and looking at the packing dates printed on the packaging, even on products that are known to be reliable. No, they aren't worried that the product has expired. Rather they are checking as to its *chodosh* or *yoshon* (literally, new or old) status.

Contrary to popular belief, these terms do not mean ascertaining how old and possibly rotten a product is, but rather are referring to which crop the grain used in the product comes from (i.e., winter wheat or spring wheat). Before we ask why one should care how old his grain is, some explanation is in order.

The Torah states: "*V'lechem, V'kali, V'karmel*—bread, sweet flour made from toasted kernels, or the toasted kernels themselves—may not be eaten until that very day, until you bring the offering to your G-d. This is a law that you must always observe throughout your generations in all your dwelling places."[1] "That very day" refers to the second day of Pesach, the day that the *Korban Omer*, the "offering" mentioned in the *pasuk*, is brought. (This is the same day that we begin counting the *Omer*, a practice we continue until Shavuos.) The Torah is teaching that available grain that grew after the second day of Pesach the previous year is prohibited to be eaten until the second day of Pesach of the

---

1 *Vayikra (Parashas Emor* Ch. 23:14).

current year, when it becomes permitted. Meaning, we need to wait a whole year (pass a Pesach) to eat the new crop of grain. This law applies to the same varieties of grain that can become *chometz*: wheat, barley, oats, spelt, and rye.[2]

"New" Grain versus "Old" Grain

Once Pesach passes, all grain that took root prior is now called *yoshon*, old, even though it may have been planted only a short time before,[3] and is one hundred percent permissible to be eaten. On the other hand, grain that took root *after* the second day of Pesach is categorized as "new" grain that may not be eaten until the second day of the next Pesach. Nowadays, as we do not have the *Korban Omer*, the promotion from *chodosh* to *yoshon* transpires automatically on the second day of Pesach; all the existing *chodosh* becomes *yoshon* grain on that day, even that which is still growing. The only requirement is that by then the grain has taken root. Thus, designating the grain as "old" does not mean that it is either wizened or rancid. Grain planted in the late winter or early spring often becomes permitted well before it even completed growing.[4]

---

2 See Mishnah in *Menachos* (70a) and accompanying Gemara (70b), *Maseches Challah* (beg.), *Rambam* (Hilchos Maachalos Assuros Ch. 10:1), *SMa"G* (*Mitzvos Lo Sa'aseh* 142–144), *SMa"K* (Mitzva 217), *Sefer Hachinuch* (*Parashas Emor*, Mitzva 303), and *Tur* and *Shulchan Aruch* (Y.D. 293:1). These grains are also those to which the prohibition of *Pas Akum* applies. This topic is addressed at length in the chapter titled "The Parameters of *Pas Palter*."

3 The exact amount of time needed to be considered "old" grain is a *Machlokes HaPoskim* with no clear consensus as to whether it takes three days or fourteen days after planting to have taken root. See *Terumas Hadeshen* (191), *Shach* (Y.D. 293:2, and *Nekudos Hakessef* ad loc. 1), *Pischei Teshuva* (ad loc. 4 and 5), *Noda B'Yehuda* (*Dagul Mervavah* ad loc. 1 and *Shu"t Noda B'Yehuda, Tinyana* O.C. 84), Rav Akiva Eiger (ad loc. 1), *Biur HaGr"a* (ad loc. 2), *Chochmas Adam* (*Shaarei Tzedek, Shaar Mishpetei Ha'aretz* Ch. 7:1, *Binas Adam* 1), *Shu"t Chasam Sofer* (Y.D. 284 and 286), *Shu"t Maharam Schick* (Y.D. 292), *Shu"t Mishkenos Yaakov* (end 64), *Birkei Yosef* (Y.D. 293:4), *Shu"t Shaagas Aryeh* (*Hachadoshos, Dinei Chodosh* Ch. 1–2), *Aruch Hashulchan* (Y.D. 293:7–9), *Shu"t Minchas Yitzchak* (vol. 6:43), and *Shu"t Ba'er Moshe* (vol. 8:255).

Which Crop Is Which?

There are two types of crops—winter crops and spring crops:

- In the Northern Hemisphere (e.g,. America), winter crops are generally planted in the fall, remain in the ground throughout the winter (including Pesach) and are harvested in early summer. Therefore, by the time this crop is harvested, all of it is already *yoshon*.
- Spring crops, however, are usually planted *after* Pesach and are harvested at the end of the summer. Consequently, from the time of their harvest until the following Pesach, they are considered *chodosh*.[5]

Note that it generally takes a few months until the most recent grain "hits the stores." That is why fall is usually when the "*chodosh* season" starts in earnest, as the spring crop starts being used commercially, and the particular kosher consumer needs to be aware of what grain is being used as an ingredient in his favorite products. As mentioned above, this lasts until Pesach, when all existing grain becomes *yoshon*. And then the yearly cycle starts anew. This is what checking the packing code is for, as through it one can ascertain which crop the product came from, and accordingly, its *chodosh/yoshon* status.[6]

Although there is a general rule that agricultural Mitzvos, *Mitzvos Hateluyos Ba'aretz*, apply only in Eretz Yisrael, nonetheless, the fact that the Torah concluded the Mitzva with "in all your dwelling places" teaches

---

[4] This elucidating explanation is excerpted from Rav Yirmiyohu Kaganoff's enlightening relevant article "The Laws of *Yoshon*," http://rabbikaganoff.com/the-laws-of-yoshon/.

[5] As explained in Rabbi Yoseph Herman's essential authoritative annual *Guide to Chodosh* (sec. 1.1).

[6] There are certain products that are generally made from spring crop, such as many breads, pizza dough, pasta, high gluten flour, and cakes (such as babka and danishes). On these products, checking the dating code would ascertain if flour from the new spring crop (*chodosh*) or the previous year's spring crop (*yoshon*) is being used. Other products such regular hard pretzels, crackers, matzah, and licorice generally use winter wheat.

that this prohibition of *chodosh* applies to *all your dwelling places*—even those outside Eretz Yisrael as well! Although there is some debate to this among the Tannaim,[7] the conclusion of the Mishnah is "*Hachodosh assur min HaTorah b'chol makom*," *chodosh* grain is Biblically prohibited to be eaten in all places,[8] meaning even in *Chutz La'aretz*. The Gemara follows this as well, as we see that the *chodosh* prohibition was practiced in Bavel, even though it is outside Eretz Yisrael.[9] This is also how the vast majority of *halachic* authorities throughout our chain of *mesorah* rule, including the *Rif*, *Rosh*, *Rambam*, *Tur*, and *Shulchan Aruch*.[10]

---

7   *Kiddushin* (37a-39a). This prevailing opinion is the *shittah* of Rabbi Eliezer. However, Rabbi Yishmael (a.k.a. the *Tanna Kama* or *Chachamim* of Rabbi Eliezer in this instance) contends that *chodosh* indeed follows the general rule of agricultural Mitzvos and applies only in Eretz Yisrael.

8   *Orlah* (Ch. 3, Mishnah 9). See the commentaries of the *Rash* and *Tosafos Yom Tov* (ad loc.), who cite proof to this from the *Yerushalmi* (ad loc. Halacha 7) that the Mishnah at the end of the first chapter of *Kiddushin* indeed follows Rabbi Eliezer's opinion. Conversely, and contrary to the rulings of the vast majority of the Rishonim, the *Tosafos Yom Tov* himself writes several times (for example, see his commentary on *Kiddushin* Ch. 1, Mishnah 9; *Sota* Ch. 9, Mishnah 1; and *Temura* Ch. 7, Mishnah 5) that he is of the opinion that one may not bring proof from *Mishnayos* in a different *Masechta* to glean a practical *halacha* from a *Stam Mishnah*. Interestingly, in his commentary on *Temura* (ibid.) he enigmatically adds that to see his conclusion regarding *chodosh* see his *Toras Ha'Asham* (end 74). However, this author checked up this source, but this passage unfortunately seems to be one of those missing from the *sefer*, as the full manuscript is not extant. On a historical note, the *Chasam Sofer* famously used this line ("*Hachodosh assur min HaTorah b'chol makom*") to combat Reform's inroads against authentic Torah Judaism. For example, see *Shu"t Chasam Sofer* (O.C. 28 and 148) and *Kovetz Teshuvos Chasam Sofer* (beg. 58; where he explains his intent to the *Maharatz Chiyus*).

9   *Menachos* (68b).

10 *Rif* (*Kiddushin* 15a and *Pesachim* 28a in his pagination), *Shu"t HaRosh* (*Klal* 2:1), *Rosh*'s commentary to *Kiddushin* 37a (62 and *Pesachim* 121a, Ch. 10:42), *Rambam* (Hilchos Maachalos Assuros Ch. 10:2 and *Hilchos Tamidin U'Mussafin* Ch. 7:11), and *Tur* and *Shulchan Aruch* (Y.D. 293:2). This ruling is also cited by the *Ramban* (*Parashas Emor* Ch. 23, 16 s.v. *v'taam*), *Rashba*, *Ritva*, *Meiri*,

If so, a question remains. If all these great luminaries ruled that there is a Biblical prohibition against eating *chodosh* products in *Chutz La'aretz*, why is *chodosh* observance not more widespread—or even known about? In fact, it seems that the traditional approach was to

---

and *Piskei Ri"d* (Kiddushin 37a-38a), *Mordechai* (Kiddushin Ch. 1:501), *Baal Ha'Itur* (vol. 2, pg. 137a), *Ravyah* (vol. 2, Pesachim 527), *SMa"G* (*Mitzvos Lo Sa'aseh* 142-144), *SMa"K* (Mitzva 217), *Orchos Chaim* (Lunil; *Hilchos Sefiras Ha'Omer*), *Rokeach* (294), *Agudah* (Kiddushin 34), Rabbeinu Yerucham (*Sefer Ha'Adam*, *Nesiv* 5:4), *Tashbetz* (*Zohar HaRakia*, *Mitzvos Lo Sa'aseh* 90), *Sefer Hachinuch* (*Parashas Emor*, Mitzva 303), *Bartenura* (Kiddushin Ch. 1, Mishnah 9), Rabbeinu Yonah (*Shaarei Teshuva, Shaar Shlishi* 105), and *Kaftor Vaferach* (Ch. 56), as well as the *Noda B'Yehuda* (*Shu"t Tinyana* O.C. 87 s.v. *b'parashas*) as a *davar pashut*, based on the additional words the Torah states by this Mitzva, "*chukas olam l'dorosaichem b'chol moshvoseichem*." The *Chasam Sofer* (*Chiddushim* to Kiddushin 37a; cited in Rabbi Yonason Rosman's *Kuntress Chodosh Mipnei Yoshon Totzi'u*, pg. 7 s.v. *uv'Pesachim*) asserts that this is also the opinions of *Rashi* and the *Rashbam* in their commentaries to Pesachim 109a. The *Rambam* (*Hilchos Maachalos Assuros* Ch. 15:10) even classifies *chodosh* grain as "*Davar Sheyeish Lo Mattirin*" (see also next footnote) and therefore has no nullification when mixed in with similar *yoshon* grain. Interestingly, the *Matteh Efraim* (625:56), who is considered the leading authority on issues relating to the *Yomim Nora'im*, when elucidating the rule that one is not *yotzei* the Mitzva of eating in the Sukkah on the first night of *Sukkos* with "*Pas shel Issur*," uses bread made with *chodosh* grain as a prime example. On the other hand, there were several Rishonim, including Rabbeinu Baruch (whose opinion will be later addressed at length), the *Ohr Zarua* (vol. 1:328), *Maharil* (*Likutim* 26), and *Terumas Hadeshen* (191) [and some include the *Raavan* (Kiddushin ad loc.), as he copies the language of said Mishnah in Kiddushin minus the prevailing opinion of Rabbi Eliezer] who were more lenient, relying on opinions that *chodosh* in *Chutz La'aretz* is essentially a Rabbinic prohibition, and/or other rationale to allow leniency. As such, since the exact time when the grain took root is uncertain, they rule that one may eat such grain as *Safek Derabbanan L'kula*. However, even so, they did not rule entirely leniently with all *chodosh* grain in *Chutz La'aretz*. As the *Terumas Hadeshen* (ad loc.) himself averred at a time when the ground was frozen almost up until Pesach one year, "*kol Yarei Shamayim yachush l'atzmo*," although ultimately concluding "*aval limchos b'hamon am lav shaper dami*."

permit the use of new grain. What is the basis to be lenient when most authorities rule that *chodosh* is prohibited even outside Eretz Yisrael?

There are several different approaches and leniencies that many authorities through the ages used in order to answer this longstanding question, and especially in light of the difficulties that many had in procuring *yoshon* flour.

Part II—*Sevaros Lehakel*

Compounded Doubt

The *Tur* and *Rema* permitted the new grain because the new crop *may* have been planted early enough to be permitted, and, in addition, the possibility exists that the available grain is from a previous crop year, which is certainly permitted.[11] This approach accepts that (theoretically) *chodosh* applies equally in *Chutz La'aretz* as it does in Eretz Yisrael, but contends that when one is uncertain whether the grain available is *chodosh* or *yoshon*, one can rely that it is *yoshon* and consume it. Because

---

11   *Tur* and *Rema* (Y.D. 293:3). This approach was first introduced by the Maharam M'Rothenburg (*Shu"t, Mahadura Cahana*, vol. 2, *Psakim* 95), and cited *lemaaseh* by the *Rosh* (*Shu"t HaRosh*, *Klal* 2:1; although he disagrees with some of the *limudim*, stating that what was written in the Maharam's name was not exact) and brought by the *Mordechai* (*Kiddushin* 501), and later the *Tur* (ibid.). *Tosafos* (*Kiddushin* 36b s.v. *kol*) implies this way as well. As the *Chayei Adam* notes (*Shaarei Tzedek, Shaar Mishpetei Ha'aretz* Ch. 7:3), this was the basis for the widespread *hetter* in Ashkenazic countries, as there the new grain was planted before Pesach. Interestingly, in his *responsa* (*Shu"t HaRema* 132:15) the *Rema* does not mention the *hetter* of *sfek sfeika* but rather that *M'Deoraysa* the *chodosh* grain is *battel b'rov* and all that is remaining is a *safek Derabbanan*, and therefore one does not have to be too concerned with the prohibition. The *Aderes* (*Kuntress Over Orach*, 489:10, printed at the end of *Orchos Chaim-Spinka* vol. 2) adds that certainly *chodosh* in *Chutz La'aretz* would be *battel b'rov*, and is not considered a *Davar Sheyeish Lo Mattirin*, because "*bal tashchis d'guf adif.*" Accordingly, similar to pots that need to be *kashered* being excluded from this prohibitive rule (see *Tur* and *Shulchan Aruch* and main commentaries to *Yoreh Deah* 102:3), so would *chodosh* grain, and it would therefore at least be able to be nullified easily, especially as otherwise, people would simply not have what to eat for half of the year.

of this double doubt, called a *sfek sfeika,* several major authorities permitted people to consume the available grain.

However, Rav Akiva Eiger questions the validity of this approach, and maintains that there really is no compounded doubt. He explains that the *sfeikos* of when the grain rooted are all really one *safek,* since planting before the cutoff date is considered the previous year! Therefore, since the *halacha* states that *chodosh* is Biblical, the rule should be *Safek Deoraysa Lechumrah,* and a single case of doubt should not be sufficient to allow it to be eaten. Additionally, even if one would rely on this leniency, it must be noted that this *hetter* is dependent on available information: If one knows that the grain being used is actually *chodosh* (which, sometimes, we do), one may not consume the grain. Moreover, the *Rema* himself concludes that in this instance, regarding grain that is possibly *chodosh,* it is preferable that the masses transgress unwittingly (*shogegin*) than purposely (*mazidin*), implying that relying on this rationale is not ideal.[12]

---

12   Rav Akiva Eiger (Glosses to Y.D. 293:3), quoting the *Shu"t Mutzal Mei'aish* (50). This question is also asked by the *Kreisi U'Pleisi* and *Chavaas Daas* (Y.D. 110, *Klalei Sfek Sfeika* 10 s.v. *umashekasav,* cited in *Shu"t Beis Avi* vol. 4:138, 7). Although the *Aruch Hashulchan* (Y.D. 293:16) attempts to address this difficulty (*dochek terutz*) and explain how our case might still be a *sfek sfeika,* still Rav Akiva Eiger's *kushyos* are not to be taken lightly. However, see *Yad Yehuda* (110, *Klalei Sfek Sfeika* 18 and 19) for a different approach as to how *sfek sfeika* here might still be applicable. See also *Tiferes Yisrael* to *Kiddushin* (Ch. 1, Mishnah 9, *Yachin* 74) who writes simply that *"kayma lan d'chodosh muttar b'Chutz La'aretz,"* referencing his commentary to *Maseches Challah* (Ch. 1, Mishnah 1:7). There he writes that as *"Chayei Nefesh"* is dependent on food, the *Rabbanim* ruled leniently with *chodosh* due to the aforementioned *sfek sfeika.* He adds that although it is not a true *sfek sfeika* (as the *Terumas Hadeshen* ibid. earlier noted), nevertheless, the *Rabbanim* were *metztaref* the minority *shittah* of Rabbi Yishmael in the Mishnah, that *chodosh* does not apply at all in *Chutz La'aretz,* as the Gemara does not explicitly rule against him, rather a *Stam Mishnah* in *Orlah,* and it is possible that *Orlah* was taught first, resulting in a *"Stam V'Achar Kach Machlokes."* [The *Magen Avraham* (O.C. 489:17) later cites this rationale as well.] Although this is not the normative *halacha,* nonetheless, as mentioned in a previous footnote, the *Tosafos Yom*

Taz's Take—Rely on Minority

The *Taz* offers an alternate rationale: He permitted the *Chutz La'aretz* grain, relying on the minority opinion that *chodosh* is a Mitzva that applies only in Eretz Yisrael. This is based on a Gemara that states that when something has not been ruled definitively (and regarding *chodosh*, the Gemara itself does not outright rule), one may rely on a minority opinion under extenuating circumstances. The *Taz* wrote that in his time, due to lack of availability of *yoshon* flour, it was considered *Shaas Hadchak* (extenuating circumstances), as apparently "let them eat cake" would not be a sufficient response to address the needs of the hungry masses with no bread to eat, and he therefore maintained that one may rely on the minority opinion that the *chodosh* proscription does not apply in *Chutz La'aretz*.[13]

However, the *Shach* emphatically rejects this approach and concludes that one must be stringent when one knows that the grain is *chodosh*. The *Ba'er Heitiv*, as well as the *Beis Hillel*, likewise voice their rejection of this *hetter*, in the strongest of terms—emphatically declaring that there are "clear proofs" against this logic, and that all major *Poskim* (including the *Rif*, *Rambam*, *Rosh*, *Tur*, and *Shulchan Aruch*) effectively ruled against it—that *chodosh* in *Chutz La'aretz* is prohibited Biblically, period.[14]

Near, Not Far

The *Magen Avraham* puts forward a different approach: It is not so clear-cut that the *halacha* follows Rabbi Eliezer in the Mishnah (that eating *chodosh* is a Biblical prohibition), and therefore, "in order to reconcile the *minhag* of the world, we must say that we follow the *shittah* of Rabbeinu Baruch (a Rishon), who was of the opinion that the prohibition of *chodosh* in *Chutz La'aretz* is a *Gezeira Derabbanan* (Rabbinic enactment), and Chazal only prohibited *chodosh* products in countries

---

Tov averred similarly. As an aside, recently, a brilliant potential solution to Rav Akiva Eiger's *kushya* was posited by Rav Aharon Yehuda Leib Shteinman (printed in *Kovetz Moriah* 388–390, Nissan 5774).

13   *Taz* (Y.D. 293:4), based on Gemara *Nida* (9b).

14   *Nekudos Hakessef* (Y.D. 293:1), *Ba'er Heitiv* (ad loc. 4), *Beis Hillel* (ad loc. 1).

nearby to Eretz Yisrael."[15] Accordingly, the prohibition would not apply to countries further away. However, the *Magen Avraham* concludes that nonetheless, a *"baal nefesh"* should still be stringent as much as possible.[16]

The *Aruch Hashulchan* ruled this way as well, explaining that in Russia where (he lived and) the land was frozen until past Pesach, there is no *hetter* of *safek* or *sfek sfeika* (compounded doubt) to rely upon, for they knew that the farmers were unable to plant until after Pesach—in other words, the grain was unquestionably *chodosh* until the next Pesach. Rather, he wrote that the *issur* of *chodosh* is interrelated to the *Korban Omer*, and therefore only applies to places from where the *Korban* could possibly be brought. Therefore, Chazal were not *gozer* on lands far away from Eretz Yisrael, for there would be no reason to do so, as those grains will never even reach Eretz Yisrael.[17] He adds that since if

---

15 Although this author has seen *sefarim* referring to him as "Rabbeinu Baruch Baal HaTerumos," ostensibly the renowned Rabbeinu Baruch ben Rav Yitzchak of Magentza, one of the *Baalei Tosafos* and author of *Sefer HaTerumah*, it appears that this is a misnomer. The original *teshuva* printed in the Lvov (Lemberg) edition of *Shu"t Maharam M'Rothenburg*, is signed "Baruch ben Rav Shmuel" and not "ben Rav Yitzchak." So it appears that this Rabbeinu Baruch is not the same one, but rather a different Rishon.

16 *Magen Avraham* (O.C. 489:17), quoting Rabbeinu Baruch, as mentioned in *Shu"t HaRosh* (*Klal* 2:1; who quite interestingly outright rejects this approach). This *teshuva* of Rabbeinu Baruch's was originally printed in *Shu"t Maharam M'Rothenburg* (Lvov [Lemberg] edition; 199). The *Magen Avraham* adds that in his opinion, this was the true intent of the Maharil, *Terumas Hadeshen*, and *Tosafos Yom Tov* (ibid.) who maintained that *chodosh* in *Chutz La'aretz* was only prohibited *M'Derabbanan*. He adds that it stands to reason that they held like Rabbeinu Baruch, that even the *Tanna Kama* (Rabbi Yishmael) was really of the opinion that *chodosh* was prohibited Rabbinically in *Chutz La'aretz*—but exclusively pertaining to lands surrounding Eretz Yisrael. There is somewhat of a precedent to a similar rationale given by *Tosafos* (*Avodah Zarah* 58b-59a s.v. *batzar*) regarding *Terumos* and *Maasaros*. The *Magen Avraham* concludes *"kach nireh li l'daas Rabbeinu Baruch u'l'yashev minhag ha'olam."*

17 It can be debated that the *Aruch Hashulchan's hetter* would no longer apply nowadays, when *chodosh* products from America, such as Cheerios, are easily

one would not partake of the *chodosh* grains, he would be unable to eat *any* grain product for at least six months of the year, Chazal would not have made a *Gezeira* that the *tzibbur* would not be able to withstand, and especially regarding grain which is man's main sustenance ("*chayei nefesh mamash*").[18]

---

purchasable in Israel. For more on this topic of *chodosh* grain from *Chutz La'aretz* imported in and used in Eretz Yisrael, see *Minchas Chinuch* (*Parashas Emor*, Mitzva 301:19 and Mitzva 303:1), *Shu"t Chelkas Yoav* (Y.D. 33), *Shu"t Maharsham* (vol. 1:72), *Shu"t Tzitz Hakodesh* (vol. 1:17), *Shu"t Beis Halevi* (vol. 3:52), *Shu"t Achiezer* (vol. 2:39), *Chazon Ish* (*Demai* 5:3 and 15:4), *Shu"t Har Tzvi* (Y.D. 239–240 and *Har Tzvi al HaTorah*, *Parashas Emor*; also citing Rav Moshe Mordechai Epstein and Rav Isser Zalman Meltzer), *Shu"t Tzitz Eliezer* (vol. 20:40, 1; in the name of Rav Shmuel Salant, originally printed in *Kovetz Knesses Chachmei Yisrael* vol. 7:126, 1), *sefer Mizbe'ach Chodosh* (on *Inyanei Challah*, vol. 3, Ch. 3, pg. 54a), *Shu"t Kerem Avraham* (25), *Shu"t Gevuros Eliyahu* (vol. 2-Y.D. 151), *Shu"t Chelkas Yaakov* (Y.D. 182 and 183), *Orchos Rabbeinu* (vol. 4, pg. 30:70; and in the new edition vol. 3, pg. 200:1; quoting the *Chazon Ish* and the Steipler Gaon), *Toras Rabbeinu Shmuel Salant* (vol. 1:37, pg. 204–212), and *Aderes Shmuel* (*Hanhagos U'Psakim* of Rav Shmuel Salant; pg. 295:288 and footnote 336). Many of these *Poskim* cite precedent from the *Rambam* (*Hilchos Terumos* Ch. 1:22) who writes that fruits from *Chutz La'aretz* that are brought into Eretz Yisrael are still obligated in *Terumos* and *Maasros*, with the *Kessef Mishneh* (ad loc.) adding that the same applies with separating *Challah*—which is only Rabbinically mandated nowadays. *Mori v'Rabi* Rav Yaakov Blau, in his classic *Leket Ha'Omer* (Ch. 1:4 and footnote 13) cites the *Kessef Mishneh's* opinion regarding *Challah* and concludes "*kein nireh Haskamas HaPoskim*." Several of the aforementioned authorities maintain that the same should certainly apply regarding *chodosh*, as it is intrinsically *M'Deoraysa*, while others remain uncertain of this application. An additional concern regarding imported *chodosh* goods in Eretz Yisrael is that since the various rationales for leniency with the *chodosh* proscription do not apply in Eretz Yisrael where all agree that it is considered a full Biblical prohibition, Rav Yosef Shalom Elyashiv (as recorded by his *talmid*, Rav Nochum Eisenstein, in his *Gilyon Dvar Halacha* #71, *Parashas Beshalach* 5779) ruled that it is prohibited to consume such products in Eretz Yisrael due to the dictum of "*nosnin alav chumrei makom shehalach lesham*" (Mishnah *Pesachim* 50a), that one must accept upon himself the established strictures of the locale. [See *Mishnah Berurah* (468:14) for the practical parameters of this rule.]

However, the vast majority of *halachic* authorities through the ages effectively ruled against this, stating that *"Hachodosh assur min HaTorah b'chol makom,"* including *Chutz La'aretz*.

The Beer Necessities of Life

Another *hetter* is that of the *Lechem Mishneh* (cited by the *Shach*) and *Pnei Yehoshua* that drinks that are made utilizing *chodosh* grain, such as beer—which seems to have been the mainstay drink in those days—should be permitted, as these drinks are not the actual grain itself, but rather a derivative. Moreover, they are not actual food products, but drinks.[19] These *Poskim* assert that whichever leniency might

---

18   *Aruch Hashulchan* (Y.D. 293:19). He actually disagreed with the *Magen Avraham's* proof (similar to the *Machatzis Hashekel* ad loc. end 2), but still *paskened lemaaseh* like him. The *Panim Meiros* (*Shu"t* vol. 3:34) writes similarly, that although not the *pashut pshat* and acknowledging that most authorities do not accept this logic, nonetheless concludes that those who are lenient may rely upon the fact that the *Korban Omer* could not be brought from barley from *Chutz La'aretz*. Interestingly, as pointed out to this author by R' Dovy Lebowitz, the *Aruch Hashulchan* himself, in *Hilchos Rosh Hashanah* (O.C. 603:2) considers the common *hetter* of eating *chodosh* in *Chutz La'aretz* a *davar* "*sheyeish poskim l'assur min hadin ela shenohagim al daas hamatirim,*" and therefore maintains that one who is lenient should **not** take on keeping *yoshon* for the *Aseres Yemei Teshuva* (as a *chumrah* or *hiddur* for those special days), as then one will not be able to go back to relying on eating *chodosh* afterward.

19   *Lechem Mishneh* (end of *Mishnayos Terumos*; cited by the *Shach* Y.D. 293:6) and *Pnei Yehoshua* (end of *Kiddushin*, *Kuntress Acharon* 51, s.v. *din hashlishi*). See also *Shu"t Panim Me'iros* (vol. 1:107) who maintains a similar *hetter* regarding mead that contains *chodosh* residue in its makeup. Interestingly, earlier in the passage, the *Pnei Yehoshua* recounts (ibid. s.v. *lachein chal*) that one year it was almost certain that the grain used in making beer in his locale was indeed *chodosh*. He writes that refraining from drinking beer that year was *"kashah alei ad me'od,"* so he decided to track down an original copy of the *Lechem Mishneh*, in order to personally perceive and explore his "beer *hetter*." He relates that it took him three years to find a *Mishnayos* with the *Lechem Mishneh*'s commentary, and was then able to expound upon and clarify the issue, until *"lefi aniyas daati hadavar barur k'shemesh sheyeish yesod v'ikar l'hetter zeh."* Thanks are due

apply by food would certainly apply by drinks. Several authorities qualify this by saying that one may only be lenient in a case of whiskey or beer that was derived from a mixture (*taaruvos*) of different grains, including *chodosh* grains, but not if the drink was made exclusively from *chodosh* grain.[20]

However, the *Shach* himself seems uneasy about using this leniency, as the *Rosh* implied that it should also be prohibited. The *Chacham Tzvi*, as well as the *Minchas Yaakov*, *Chayei Adam*, and *Aruch Hashulchan* rule that one may not rely on this *lemaaseh*.[21] The Vilna Gaon is reported as being so stringent with this that he called someone who buys beer made from *chodosh* grain for someone else as transgressing on *Lifnei Iver*.[22]

---

to Rabbi Moshe Wachsman for pointing out this fascinating anecdote of the *Pnei Yehoshua's*.

20 *Shulchan Aruch Harav* (*Shu"t* 20 and O.C. 489: end 30) and *Beis Lechem Yehuda* (Y.D. end 293). On the other hand, the *Chochmas Adam* (*Binas Adam* 54 [73]) maintains that even regarding a *taaruvos*, in order for this leniency to apply, there would need to be present at least 60 times the *yoshon* grain against the amount of *chodosh* grain.

21 *Shu"t Chacham Tzvi* (80), *Minchas Yaakov* (*Chok Yaakov* O.C. 489:22 s.v. *le'echol*), *Chayei Adam* (vol. 2, 131:12; see also previous footnote), *Aruch Hashulchan* (Y.D. 293:23), and *Shu"t Knesses Yechezkel* (51). Interestingly, in his *Shaarei Tzedek* (*Shaar Mishpetei Ha'aretz* Ch. 7:2), the *Chayei Adam* seems to backtrack somewhat, writing that it is impossible to argue on those who are lenient with drinking beer and whiskey made from *chodosh* grain, as they hold that a drink made from the grain is not the actual "*guf shel issur*"; even so, he still concludes that "*kol baal nefesh yachmir al atzmo.*"

22 *Maaseh Rav* (89). Similarly, Rav Chaim Kanievsky is quoted (*Shu"t Rivevos Efraim* vol 8:599) as ruling that if one is stringent on *chodosh*, it is prohibited for him to feed *chodosh* food to someone who is not *machmir*. The *Minchas Yitzchak* (*Shu"t* vol 8:113) proves that the *Chasam Sofer* agreed with the *Chacham Tzvi* on this, that any derivative of *chodosh* still maintains the same status and is *assur M'Deoraysa*. His own conclusion is that only one who relies on a *hetter* of *chodosh* in *Chutz La'aretz* being *Derabbanan* may rely on the *hetter* of beer, as it is improbable to make such a distinction. However, other contemporary *Poskim* including the *Beis Avi* (*Shu"t* vol. 4:138, 19), hold that nonetheless one should be stringent regarding beer. See also *Emes L'Yaakov*

There are those who took a middle of the road stance on beer, including the *Mishkenos Yaakov*, who although disagreeing with the *Chacham Tzvi*, nevertheless ruled that only for a *tzorech gadol* and *shaas hadchak* (extremely extenuating circumstances) may one rely on beer and other drinks derived from *chodosh* grain.[23] Similarly, the *Beis Hillel* also disagrees with this *hetter*, but adds that if someone is weak and sickly, and it would be a danger for him not to drink it, he may rely on this *hetter*, as the Torah says "*V'Chai Bahem*," *v'lo sheyamus bahem*.[24]

The Bach's Hetter—Non-Jewish Owned Grain

The *Bach* advances a different *halachic* basis to permit use of the new grain. He suggests that *chodosh* applies only to grain that grows in a field owned by a Jew, and not to grain grown in a field owned by a non-Jew. Since most fields are owned by gentiles, one can be lenient when one does not know the origin of the grain and assume that it was grown in a gentile's field, and it is therefore exempt from *chodosh* laws. The *Bach* notes that many of the greatest luminaries of early Ashkenazic Jewry, including Rav Shachna (*Rebbi* of the *Rema*) and the Maharshal, were lenient regarding *chodosh* use in their native Europe. He shares that as a young man he advanced his theory that *chodosh* does not exist in a field owned by a gentile to the greatest scholars of that generation, including the Maharal M'Prague, all of whom accepted it.[25]

---

    on *Tur* and *Shulchan Aruch* (O.C. 489, footnote 461) who writes that even those who are lenient with the *chodosh* proscription regarding wheat due to various rationales, should nevertheless be stringent with barley, implying that he would be of the opinion that beer, whose primary ingredient is barley, should be avoided as well.

23 *Shu"t Mishkenos Yaakov* (Y.D. end 68) and *Beis Hillel* (ibid.). See also *Yeshuos Yaakov* (O.C. end 489) who cites both sides of the beer debate, and concludes that "I personally am stringent with beer, and regarding actual *chodosh* grain, it is worthwhile for everyone to be stringent."

24 *Vayikra* (*Parashas Acharei Mos* Ch. 18:5). See Gemara *Yoma* (85b), *Sanhedrin* (74a), and *Avodah Zarah* (27b and 54a).

25 *Bach* (Y.D. 293, s.v. *umashekasav bein* and further). See also *Shu"t HaBach* (*Hachadoshos*, 42). The *Bach*, himself, further (ad loc. s.v. *ulfa"d*) contends

In fact, the *Baal Shem Tov* is quoted as having a dream revealing that when the *Bach* died, *Gehinnom* was cooled down for forty days in his honor; when the *Baal Shem Tov* woke up he exclaimed that he did not realize the greatness of the *Bach*, and thereupon ruled that his opinion regarding *chodosh* is worthy of being relied upon.[26] Possibly based on the above, it is well known that most Chassidim worldwide are lenient with eating *chodosh* in *Chutz La'aretz*.[27]

> that although the *Rosh* in his responsum (*Shu"t HaRosh* ibid.) rejected this approach, he is of the opinion that the *Rosh* subsequently changed his mind, as in his *halachic* code (*Kiddushin* ibid.), which was written after his responsa [see *Tur* (C.M. end 72)], while listing other *issurim* that apply when grown by a gentile, like *Orlah* and *Kilayim*, the *Rosh* omits mention that the prohibition of *chodosh* applies to gentile-grown grain.

26 *Baal Shem Tov al HaTorah* (*Parashas Emor* 6, based on *Zichron Tov* pg. 12a, 11). Also cited in *Pardes Yosef* (*Vayikra*, pg. 274 s.v. *chukas*) and Rabbi Dr. Eliezer Brodt's *Lekutei Eliezer* (pg. 63 s.v. *yeish* and footnote 116).

27 There are potentially other reasons why this is so. See *Shu"t Tzitz Eliezer* (vol. 20:40) who states that the *Bach* used to be the Rav of both Medzhibuzh and Belz, and posits that this is possibly why many Chassidim are lenient when it comes to eating *chodosh* products. However, the *Shu"t Beis Avi* (ibid. 2) quotes that the *Sar Shalom* of Belz was very stringent with the *issur* of *chodosh*, so it seems unlikely that Belzer Chassidim would be *meikil* exclusively based on the *Bach*'s *shittah*. He also cites (ibid. 19) a different precedent—that the *Darchei Teshuva* (of Munkacs) quoted that the *Divrei Chaim* (of Sanz) ruled leniently regarding *chodosh* in *Chutz La'aretz*. This is also cited in *Darchei Chaim V'Shalom* (of Munkacs; 873, *Likutei Dinim M'Yoreh Deah*) writing about the famed *Minchas Elazar*, that he was of the opinion that "nowadays one need not be stringent with the prohibition of *chodosh* in *Chutz La'aretz*, as he wrote in his *Nimukei Yoreh Deah* (293)," citing his father, the *Darchei Teshuva*, who heard from the *Divrei Chaim* to rule leniently. Another possibility is that Chassidim relied on the tremendous *drush* of the *Chiddushei HaRim* (of Gur; *Shu"t HaRim* Y.D. 19) who writes extensively to "turn the *sugya* around," maintaining that really R' Eliezer's opinion is the minority one and the majority opinion is that *chodosh* in *Chutz La'aretz* is truly *Derabbanan*. See also *Shu"t Avnei Nezer* (of Sokatchov; vol. 4, C.M. 115) who, in a discussion regarding the permissibility of using Corfu *esrogim*, adds that the reason "Chassidim in Poland" relied on the *Bach*'s *hetter* regarding *chodosh*, is due to the great

However, even though there are several *Poskim* who rule like the *Bach*,[28] nevertheless, the vast majority of authorities categorically reject this logic and rule explicitly that the *chodosh* prohibition does apply to grain grown in a gentile's field, including the *Rosh*, *Rambam*, *Rashba*,

---

Chozeh M'Lublin publicly stating that once his ancestor, the *Bach*, permitted it, there was no need to be concerned further. [This author wishes to thank Rabbi Yaakov Nissan for pointing out this source.] The renowned Kamarna Rebbe (*Otzar Hachaim*, Mitzva 306, *Vayikra*, pg. 220–225a) wrote extensively on topic, strongly defending the *Bach's shittah*, averring that this certainly was the accepted ruling by the "*Mesivta D'Rakia*" as was transmitted from great *Tzaddikim* who merited "*Giluy Eliyahu*," concluding "*v'zeh barur v'ein od*."

28 Including the *Drishah* (Y.D. 293:1; citing precedent from Rabbeinu Avigdor Kohen-Tzedek and the Maharam Metz), *Ba'er Hagolah* (Y.D. 293:7), *Knesses Yechezkel* (*Shu"t* 41; although contending that the *chodosh* prohibition exclusively does not apply when it is in both in *Chutz La'aretz* and a gentile's grain, but would apply to each factor individually), *Shev Yaakov* (*Shu"t* 61), *Chelkas Yoav* (*Shu"t* Y.D. 33; maintaining that the *meikilim* actually rely on a *tziruf* of *sevaros*), and the *Makneh* (*Kiddushin* 38; who qualifies his *hetter* that in Eretz Yisrael the prohibition would apply by grain owned by a non-Jew). *Moshav Zekeinim al HaTorah* (*Vayikra* Ch. 23:14) writes that the *Ritzba* held this way as well, that *chodosh* does not apply in *Chutz La'aretz* to grain owned by non-Jews. There are others who try to answer up for the common *minhag* of being lenient through *sevara*, and not *psak lemaaseh*, including the *Avnei Nezer* (*Shu"t* Y.D. 386; who wrote a *teshuva* on this topic when he was sixteen (!) where, although not writing for *psak lemaaseh*, he still brings *sevaros* to be *meikil* like Rabbeinu Baruch; but he does note that the *Rambam leshittaso* would not hold of them), Rav Meshulam Igra (*Shu"t* vol. 1, O.C. 40; while not *paskening*, similarly answers up for the *sevara* of Rabbeinu Baruch to say *chodosh* in *Chutz La'aretz* could be *Derabbanan*, but also disproves that it is dependent on the *Korban Omer*), and Rav Zalman of Volozhin (cited in the appendix to the recent Weinreb edition of Rav Chaim of Volozhin's *Kesser Rosh*; *Miluim* to 149; who nonetheless concludes that he did not want his *sevara lehakel* publicized, to ensure that people should not come to be *meikil* with the "*Issur of Chodosh*"). The *Minchas Chinuch* (*Parashas Emor*, Mitzva 303:1) implies that he was *notteh* to the *Bach's hetter*. The *Aderes* (*Oznei Yerushalayim* 26) and Rav Shmuel Salant (*Aderes Shmuel*; *Hanhagos U'Psakim* of Rav Shmuel Salant; pg. 297:289 and footnote 337) imply this way as well.

Ran, *Tosafos*, *Mordechai*, *Tur*, and *Shulchan Aruch*,[29] as did many later *Poskim*, including the *Shach*, *Taz*, Vilna Gaon, Chida, *Pnei Yehoshua*, *Shaagas Aryeh*, and the *Aruch Hashulchan*.[30] Additionally, although seemingly not widely known, the fact is that later on in his life, the

---

29   Most authorities cited previously. *Tosafos* (*Kiddushin* 36b end s.v. *kol*; citing the *Yerushalmi*). See also *Leket Yosher* (vol. 1:96). This author finds it noteworthy that other Rishonim who are considered lenient regarding *chodosh* in *Chutz La'aretz*, including the *Ohr Zarua* (vol. 1:328) and the Maharam M'Rothenburg/Rabbeinu Baruch (*Shu"t Maharam M'Rothenburg*, Lvov [Lemberg] edition; 199), outright rejected the notion that there should be a difference between Jewish and non-Jewish owned grain. On the other hand, it is worthwhile to see the *Pnei Yehoshua's* (*Kiddushin*, *Kuntress Acharon* 51, *Psak B'Inyan Chodosh* s.v. *din hasheini*) related comment that in his opinion, those who hold that *chodosh* in *Chutz La'aretz* is *Deoraysa*, there should be no more of a *"tzad kula klal"* to be more lenient with a non-Jew's grain; but rather this rationale is only applicable to those who maintain that *chodosh* in *Chutz La'aretz* is *Derabbanan*.

30   *Shach* (Y.D. 293:6), *Taz* (ad loc. 2), Vilna Gaon (*Biur HaGr"a* ad loc. 2; who writes in very strong fashion that the *Ba'er Hagolah* made such a mistake by *paskening* like the *Bach*, that it's not worth even addressing the issue, adding that it would have been preferable had he remained silent; see also *Maaseh Rav* (89–90), *Sheiltos* (82), *Chayei Adam* (vol. 2:131, 12), and Rav Chaim Volozhiner's *Kesser Rosh* (151) on how strict the *Gr"a* was with this *halacha*, including being stringent with *chodosh bliyos*; see below), Chida (*Birkei Yosef* ad loc. 1), the *Pnei Yehoshua* (*Shu"t* Y.D. 34; also known as the *Maginei Shlomo*, he was the grandfather of the *Pnei Yehoshua* on *Shas* who was more lenient regarding this prohibition; he writes extremely strongly against the *Bach*, even calling his *hetter* "worthless"), the *Shaagas Ayreh* (*Shu"t Hachadoshos*, *Dinei Chodosh* Ch. 1–2; who was even *makpid* on all the *dinim* of *Taam K'Ikar* (*keilim*) for *chodosh* grain [akin to the *shittas HaGr"a* and *Chayei Adam* (ibid. and in *Shaarei Tzedek* ibid.; *l'daas hamachmirim* "ul'rov haposkim") and not like the *shittah* of the *Rema* (*Shu"t HaRema* 132:15), *Magen Avraham* (ibid.), *Shulchan Aruch Harav* (ad loc. 30), and *Mishnah Berurah* (489:48), who maintain that even if one is *machmir* with eating *chodosh*, he need not be concerned with its *bliyos*; however, it is important to note that all would agree that when the prohibition of *chodosh* becomes lifted annually at the end of the 16th of Nissan, all *bliyos* inside of *keilim* become permitted as well, and there is no

Baal Shem Tov retracted his opinion and he himself became stringent after he found out that a certain *Gadol* in his time, Rabbeinu Yechiel of Horodna, ruled stringently on this matter.[31] It is also worthwhile to note that the *Chazon Ish* quoted the *Chofetz Chaim* as saying that after someone passes on to the World of Truth, he will be asked why he ate *chodosh*. If he replies that he relied on the *hetter* of the *Bach*, then he will be asked why he spoke *lashon hara*, as the *Bach* did not allow that—implying that in Heaven he will be labeled a hypocrite.[32]

Let Them Eat Bread

It should be further noted that even among those authorities who allowed consumption of *chodosh* based on the *Bach's hetter*, it is crucial to note that the vast majority gave that ruling only since it was *shaas hadchak* (extenuating circumstances), as otherwise there would be no

---

reason to *kasher* those *keilim*—see *Shu"t Shevet Halevi* (vol. 10:183, 2) and *Ashrei Ha'Ish* (O.C. vol. 3, Ch. 69:8)] and the *Aruch Hashulchan* (ibid. 12). See also *Shu"t Shoel U'Meishiv* (vol. 6:38), who wrote a *pilpul* (only *sevarah* and not *psak*) proving that *chodosh* should apply by grain owned by a non-Jew. Rav Akiva Eiger (*Drush V'Chiddush Rabbi Akiva Eiger, Maracha* 9) brings proofs to both sides of this *machlokes*, but concludes that the proper *halacha* follows the opinion of the *Rambam*, that the prohibition of *chodosh* applies to non-Jewish owned grain as well. See also *Orchos Rabbeinu* (new edition; vol. 3, pg. 200:1–2) and *Pe'er Hador* (vol. 1, pg. 168) who describe how *machmir* both the *Chazon Ish* and Steipler Gaon were with this prohibition, even with gentile *chodosh* grain. They relate that the *Chazon Ish* used to credit vigilance with keeping the *chodosh* prohibition as what saved him from the *Haskalah*. In his youth, the *Chazon Ish* traveled to learn in the legendary Volozhin Yeshiva. However, at that time, there was no *yoshon* food available, and after three days, the young *Chazon Ish* returned home. It was during that same period when the *Haskalah* had gained a strong foothold in the Yeshiva and many of Volozhin's finest were swayed and eventually lost to its wiles in the name of "enlightenment." The *Chazon Ish* surmised that he would have been susceptible to its influence, and that is why he asserted that vigilance with *chodosh* saved him.

31 *Baal Shem Tov al HaTorah* (*Parashas Emor*, 7), based on *Imrei Pinchas* (*Shaar* 3:201).

32 Cited in *Orchos Rabbeinu* (ibid).

grain products allowed to be eaten. Barring that essential detail, they were clear that one should not rely on this leniency. This includes such renowned authorities as the *Pri Megadim, Chayei Adam, Shulchan Aruch Harav, Kitzur Shulchan Aruch, Mishnah Berurah*, and the *Kaf Hachaim*.[33] This is similar to the *Magen Avraham* and *Aruch Hashulchan's* approach (detailed previously) of finding a *hetter*, in order that Klal Yisrael will be "clean of sin" for their actions.

---

33   *Chayei Adam* (vol. 2, 131:12) writes that since it is difficult for everyone to keep, one may rely on the minority opinion, however anyone who is an *"ohev nafsho"* would distance himself from relying on this; *Shulchan Aruch Harav* (O.C. 489:30) who calls it a *"melamed zechus"* and that every *baal nefesh* should be as *machmir* as possible—since that is the proper *halacha*, all the while acknowledging that the common custom is that most are *meikil*; *Kitzur Shulchan Aruch* (172:3) who maintains that many rely on the *Bach's hetter b'shaas hadchak*, however since the majority argue on this opinion, one who is stringent—"*tavo alav bracha*"; *Pri Megadim* (O.C. 489, E.A. end 17)—"*B'avonoseinu harabbim hadoros chalushim, v'ee efshar lizaher kol kach b'zeh*"; *Mishnah Berurah* (ad loc. 45, *Biur Halacha* s.v. *v'af*) although writing that one may not object against someone who is lenient, nonetheless uses very strong words against it and also calls the *hetter* a *"melamed zechus,"* since it's a *"davar kasha"* to be vigilant about eating *chodosh*, and maintains that everyone should try to keep it as much as they possibly can; in his *Shaar Hatziyun* (ad loc. 54), he adds that the Vilna Gaon treated the *chodosh* prohibition like any other Biblical prohibition; he furthermore comments that with the advent of the train (*mesilas habarzel*), the grain might be coming from faraway lands such as Russia, where it's *vaday chodosh* (like the *Aruch Hashulchan* observed); and the *Kaf Hachaim* (end O.C. 489:110 and 11) who tries to find *hetterim* for why the *"olam* is *meikil."* Even the *Ohr Zarua* himself (vol. 1:328), upon whom the Maharil (ibid.) and *Terumas Hadeshen* (191) base their similar lenient *psak*, one of the early proponents of ruling that *chodosh* in *Chutz La'aretz* is only a Rabbinic enactment, qualifies his *psak*, stating that his lenient ruling only applies in a case of *safek* when the grain was planted (and therefore *Safek Derabbanan L'kula*), and only since it's *shaas hadchak*, for it is impossible not to buy grain and bread, therefore *"kedai lismoch b'shaas hadchak."*

Part III—*Ain Kol Chodosh Tachas Hashemesh*[34]

Five separate rationales for allowing leniency when eating *chodosh* grain in *Chutz La'aretz* have been presented, as well as the issues and difficulties involved with relying on each of them. But we haven't yet really been able to clearly explain why the common custom seems to be lenient when most authorities rule that *chodosh* is prohibited, even outside Eretz Yisrael.

Justification to Feed the Masses

The most important factor to note is that many *Gedolim* through the ages worked tirelessly to find *any* sort of justification to allow the masses to partake of *chodosh* products. The reason was (as was previously mentioned) that in many parts of the world where Jewry was located, if one would not eat the *chodosh* grain, he would be unable to eat any grain product for at least six months of the year, leading to possible starvation.

A prime example of one of these authorities is the *Mishkenos Yaakov*, who upon hearing from Rav Chaim Volozhiner that it is proper to be *melamed zechus* (seek merit) for Klal Yisrael for eating *chodosh*, wrote a twenty-five page responsum (!), point by point, logical proof by logical proof, all in order to reconcile the general practice of allowing leniency regarding *chodosh* in *Chutz La'aretz* and consequently "so Hashem should judge them meritoriously, and not *chas v'shalom* causing them to inadvertently sin."[35] However, he explains many times throughout this monumental *teshuva* that the *hetterim* are all exclusively regarding extenuating circumstances, as in many countries it was extremely difficult to obtain *yoshon* grain.

Several other authorities, including the *Pnei Yehoshua*[36] and *Tzemach Tzedek*[37] wrote similarly, that after toiling to find sources for *hetterim* to be lenient and rely that *chodosh* in *Chutz La'aretz* is only a Rabbinic enactment, that *chas v'shalom* that they would argue on all the *Poskim* who hold it is a Biblical prohibition, rather, they stress that they are

---

34 *Koheles* (Ch. 1:9).

35 *Shu"t Mishkenos Yaakov* (Y.D. 67).

trying to find a *hetter* for those who are lenient, since not being able to eat *chodosh* products is considered an extenuating circumstance. The *Magen Ha'Elef* similarly writes extensively, citing Talmudic theories and hypotheses to be "*melamed zechus* on the Nation of Hashem," but even so, concludes that a "*baal nefesh*" should be stringent.[38]

36 *Pnei Yehoshua* (*Kuntress Acharon* on *Kiddushin*, 51). As mentioned previously, he is the grandson of the other renowned *Pnei Yehoshua* (also known as the *Maginei Shlomo*) who ruled very stringently in regard to eating *chodosh*. He utilizes a combined leniency approach: only grain from a non-Jew in *Chutz Laaretz* that is not near Eretz Yisrael, and only combined with another *safek*, concluding "*kol divarei bazeh aino ela lelamed zechus al minhagan shel Yisrael d'dashu bah rabbim leheteira delo mikru avaryana....*" The *Minchas Chinuch* (*Parashas Emor*, Mitzva 303:1) implies that he is *notteh* to the *Pnei Yehoshua's shittah*.

37 *Tzemach Tzedek* (*Hachadoshos*; *Shu"t* Y.D. 218). After bringing sources and proofs to hold like the *Bach* and *Pnei Yehoshua* (see previous footnote), he writes that "anyone with fear of Heaven should be stringent—like the *Rif*, *Rambam*, *Tur*, and *Shulchan Aruch* that *chodosh* in *Chutz La'aretz* is *Deoraysa*, and that the *ikar* is that there is no difference whether the grain was owned by a Jew or non-Jew."

38 *Magen Ha'Elef* (O.C. 489, *Kuntress Sheim Chodosh*). See also *Shu"t Meshivas Nafesh* (vol. 1: end 16, s.v. *v'yadaati*) by the same author, who—while addressing the issue about a son who eats *chodosh* grain in *Chutz La'aretz*, whether he is required to keep *yoshon* because of "*kibbud av v'aim*"—writes in an interesting footnote that even though no one is as great as the *Gr"a* (who, as mentioned previously, was extremely stringent regarding *chodosh* produce), still, *chalila* to turn the whole world into *Reshaim* by claiming they are transgressing an *aveira Deoraysa*; and we therefore cannot bring proof based on the Vilna Gaon's greatness, similar to Rabbi Shimon Bar Yochai, whom the *halacha* does not always follow, despite his greatness that he was the one to reveal the *Zohar*. Interestingly, the *Yalkut Yosef* (*Kitzur Shulchan Aruch* Y.D. 293:35) writes that the opposite scenario holds true as well: If a son is *makpid* on *yoshon* grain in *Chutz La'aretz* and his father wants him to eat *chodosh* grain due to "*kibbud av v'aim*," the son is nevertheless not required to listen.

Universal Minhag?

There are also *Gedolim* who took the *melamed zechus* (merit-seeking) a step further. The *Sdei Chemed*,[39] after citing many *Poskim* and much logic on both sides of the issue, concludes with the words of the *Teshuos Chein*: "Since Klal Yisrael generally has been lenient in the issue of *chodosh* in *Chutz La'aretz* for many generations due to the various *hetterim* and extenuating circumstances, it has developed into a '*minhag hakadmonim*' (long-standing custom), and even though it is against the standard *halacha*, one may not question those who keep it, for they have what to rely upon."[40] Rav Yitzchak Shlomo Yoel Sherman, the *Av Beis Din* of Rovno, wrote extensively in this vein, "For it is a Mitzva to be *melamed zechus* where the majority of the population will be unable to eat grain for three quarters of the year. And if we would rule stringently, then we will have effectively disqualified every divorce documentation from *Chutz La'aretz*, (for all the witnesses would be considered ineligible if they publicly transgressed a Biblical Commandment)."[41]

The *Chelkas Yoav* writes similarly, that even according to those who rule leniently, *chodosh* in *Chutz La'aretz* should still be a Rabbinic prohibition. However, he explains that everyone relies on a combination of the lenient opinions. Namely, that *chodosh* in *Chutz La'aretz* is possibly only Rabbinic in origin, and furthermore may only apply to countries next to Eretz Yisrael.[42] Additionally, most grain worldwide is grown by non-Jews. Therefore, taking all these opinions into account renders it

---

39 *Sdei Chemed* (vol. 8, *Kuntress Haklalim, Asifas Dinim, Maareches Chodosh B'zman Hazeh*).

40 *Shu"t Teshuos Chein* (25).

41 He wrote the second half of *Sdei Chemed's* extensive *kuntress* on *chodosh*.

42 *Shu"t Chelkas Yoav* (Y.D. 33 s.v. *v'af*). See also *Chok Yaakov* (O.C. 489:22 and 24) who cites several of the *sevaros* to rule leniently, acknowledges that each of them is against the majority rule and although consequently *chodosh* should technically be prohibited, nevertheless concludes that "we add that it is *shaas hadchak, l'chein nohagin lehakel*." He concludes "*lo ratziti lehaarich lefi she'ein nohagin achshav issur chodosh*." Likewise, the *Korban Nesanel* (end *Pesachim*, 5) writes that in their countries, "*nohagin hetter, v'yeish lahem al mi*

muttar to be eaten. The Butchatcher Rav likewise defends the "*minhag* to be *meikel*," stating that since all of world Jewry was lenient, it became a "*minhag l'halacha amitis*," a *halachically* viable *minhag*, even though it's against the standard *halacha*![43]

Relying on this, however, is not so clear-cut, as historically this would not seem quite accurate; there never was any prevalent "universal *minhag*." The reason why people in Russia were lenient is not the same reason why others were lenient in Poland. For example, the *Aruch Hashulchan* and *Mishnah Berurah* (ibid.) both stated that there is no

---

sheyismachu," concluding that when the *Beis Hamikdash* will be rebuilt, "*nihi-yeh Mitzvas Chodosh*."

43 *Eishel Avraham* (O.C. 489. s.v. *od matzasi*). On a more contemporary note, see also *She'arim Metzuyanim B'Halacha* (172:3) who likewise cites different *sevaros* and *shittos* to be lenient. The Debreciner Rav (*Shu"t Ba'er Moshe* vol. 7:pg. 245) as well, writes simply that in *Chutz La'aretz* the *minhag* is to be lenient like the Acharonim who ruled leniently, and it's almost a forgotten matter (that there is even an issue at all). On the other hand, it is known that several *Gedolim* were extremely *makpid* with even a *chashash* of *chodosh*, including the Maharam Ash (*Zichron Yehuda* pg. 23) and Rav Yisrael Salanter (*Tenu'as HaMussar* vol. 1:343). It is told that the Rogatchover Gaon (who lived in Dvinsk) did not eat bread most of the year due to *chashash* of *chodosh* (as per *Mishpacha Magazine* issue 500, March 05, 2014, "At the Rogatchover's Knee," quoting Rav Yehuda Tzivyon, *mechutan* of Rav Chaim Kanievsky). Similarly, it is known that the world-renowned *Gaon* and *Rosh Agudas HaRabbanim*, Rav Eliezer Silver of Cincinnati, Ohio, who was *niftar* in 1966, would never eat out, and instead carried a sandwich in his top hat. One of the reasons he did so was because he was *makpid* on *yoshon* in *Chutz La'aretz* (as heard from my father, native Cincinnatian and renowned kashrus expert Rav Manish Spitz). As a historical aside, this author has heard *b'sheim* Rav Moshe Heinemann of the Star-K, that it is known that in the *shul* of the *Chasam Sofer* [who was meticulous with the *issur* of *chodosh*—see *Shu"t Chasam Sofer* (O.C. 15; *hanhaga* of his Rebbi, Rav Nosson Adler; and Y.D. 19) and *Shu"t Levushei Mordechai* (vol. 2, O.C. 170)], only a person meticulous in the fulfillment of this Mitzva was eligible to be called up to the Torah when the *pesukim* relating to *chodosh* were read. [Indeed, the *Yalkut Yosef* (*Kitzur Shulchan Aruch* Y.D. 293:34) rules this way *lemaaseh*, that one who is not *makpid* on *chodosh* should not receive the "*Levi*" Aliyah on the first day of *Sukkos*, unless it will cause *machlokes* in

sfek sfeika (compounded doubt, a.k.a. the *Rema's hetter*) to rely upon in Russia where the farmers were unable to plant grain before Pesach due to the frozen ground, and had to rely on an alternative *hetter*; whereas *Poskim* from Eastern Europe felt that in their environs there was always a *safek* as to the grain's status (not clearly *chodosh* or *yoshon*). Some places held of the *Bach's hetter*, others relied on the *Taz's,* and others on the *Magen Avraham's*. So even though the end result may have been that many (if not most) throughout Europe and Russia were indeed lenient in this manner, it does not seem compelling to attribute this to the same source, claiming that everyone relied on the same "*minhag*" or *psak*. Indeed, even the *Sdei Chemed* himself, a prime proponent of classifying eating *chodosh* in *Chutz La'aretz* as a "*minhag hakadmonim*," nonetheless concludes that "anyone who fears Hashem should be stringent like the *Rif, Rambam, Rosh*, and the *Baalei Tosafos*."[44]

Rav Moshe Sternbuch addresses the issue and writes that "in our times, in places where there is no great difficulty to obtain *yoshon* flour, it is a strong *issur* to be *mezalzel* in the *psak* of the *Shulchan Aruch* and *Gedolei HaPoskim* who maintain that *chodosh* produce is prohibited." He continues that if it is easily obtainable, how can one rely on the *Poskim* who were *moser nefesh* to be *melamed zechus* on Klal Yisrael in times of extenuating circumstances? He contends that if at all possible, it

---

the *shul*.] This author has also recently seen a letter of *Hashgacha* that Rav Avraham Yitzchak *Hakohen* Kook gave the flour used by the Manischewitz Matzah factory in America in 5683/1923, certifying that the flour used was indeed *yoshon*.

44 Not to mention the *Tur* and *Shulchan Aruch*, as well as later authorities including the *Shach, Taz*, and *Gr"a*, etc. Similarly, the *Shlah* (*Shaar Ha'Osiyos, Kedushas Ha'achilah* 107; cited briefly by the *Chok Yaakov* ibid.) bemoaned that many do not keep the prohibition of *chodosh* in *Chutz La'aretz* and commanded his children to be extremely vigilant with this Mitzva. Likewise, Rav Yaakov of Lisa (a.k.a. the *Nesivos Hamishpat* and *Chavas Daas*) in his *tzava'ah* (ethical will) printed at the end of his *Derech Hachaim*, did the same, exhorting his children not to simply rely upon the *kulos* of the Acharonim, that were only given "*leyashev haminhag.*"

is axiomatic that one should not eat *chodosh* products, and thus avoid entertaining the possibility of eating something that is prohibited.[45]

Sof Davar Hakol Nishma…[46]

In the final analysis, between the many rationales and differing authorities, there most definitely seems to be what to rely upon to partake of *chodosh* products, and especially in places where *yoshon* flour is not readily available. However, what remains to be seen is the reason for the widespread use of eating *chodosh* products in *Chutz La'aretz*

---

45   *Shu"t Teshuvos V'Hanhagos* (vol. 1:655). This concern is also echoed by other *Rabbanim*; for example, see *Gidulei Chodosh* by Rav Shmuel Eliezer Stern (*Shevivei Aish* 1:29). This author has heard similar declarations in the name of Rav Yisroel Belsky and the Karlsburger Rav, Rav Yechezkel Roth. See also Rav Mordechai Eliyahu's *Darchei Halacha* glosses to the *Kitzur Shulchan Aruch* (172:1) who simply states that "we hold that *chodosh* is prohibited from the Torah, both in Eretz Yisrael and *Chutz La'aretz*, whether the grain is from a Jew or non-Jew." In a similar vein, Rav Yitzchak Yosef (*Yalkut Yosef, Kitzur Shulchan Aruch* Y.D. 293:10), although acknowledging that it is hard to be *makpid* exclusively on *yoshon* products in *Chutz La'aretz* and that many therefore rely on the *Poskim* who ruled leniently, nonetheless exhorts Sefardim, who follow the *psakim* of the *Shulchan Aruch*, to be *makpid* with this issue, as he ruled that the *chodosh* prohibition still applies nowadays, even in *Chutz La'aretz*, and did not distinguish between Jew or gentile-owned grain. My father, renowned kashrus expert Rav Manish Spitz, a *talmid* of Rav Aharon Soloveitchik (who was extremely *makpid* with *yoshon*, and certified the first *yoshon* bakery in Chicago, and possibly America, Tel Aviv Bakery, which at the time was known as Taam Tov Bakery), related to me that the real starting point in America for *chodosh* issues was the Russian Wheat Deal of 1972. Until then, the United States had a major surplus of wheat, and therefore all flour used was older flour and thereby *yoshon*. But with the commencement of the wheat act (a.k.a "The Great Grain Robbery;" as U.S. grain prices shot up) the U.S. sent the surplus (*yoshon*) wheat to the U.S.S.R., and used the more recent wheat (*chodosh*) for themselves. That's when *chodosh* became a real *sheilah* in America. It has been surmised that perhaps this somewhat recent application of this issue in America has resulted in the public's general lack of awareness.

46   *Koheles* (Ch. 12:13).

lechatchilla nowadays in places where *yoshon* flour is easily obtainable.[47] Even with the many reasons and logic given to be *melamud zechus*, it must be stressed that the majority of *Poskim* disagreed with each and every one of them.

Nevertheless, although he wrote extensively exhorting all to try to be stringent in this matter to the fullest of their abilities, the *Mishnah Berurah* declared that one may not object to someone who is lenient, as that fellow does have what to rely upon;[48] a *hetter* which some label a "universal *minhag*."

---

47 Although this author has long wondered why so many more people (especially Chassidim) are *makpid* with *Chalav Yisrael* than are with *chodosh* in *Chutz La'aretz*, when *Chalav Yisrael* is a *Gezeira Derabbanan* and *chodosh* is at least a *safek Deoraysa* (and in this author's estimation the question is certainly stronger than any answer), nonetheless, it seems that this status quo is more a matter of tradition than *halacha*. This is because to most of European Ashkenazic Jewry, for whatever the reason, and perhaps even due to *shaas hadchak*, the prohibition of *chodosh* was not widely adhered to, and possibly not even known about. Yet, there they were traditionally *makpid* on *Chalav Yisrael*. [This is discussed in detail in the chapter titled "*Chalav Yisrael*: A *Halachic* History."] As the *hetterim* regarding *Chalav Stam* only came about later in the 1950s America, it was generally considered a breach of tradition by this segment of society. Hence, as in Europe they traditionally were very *makpid* on *Chalav Yisrael* but not *chodosh*, their observances and customs carried over to American shores, even if the set of *halachic* circumstances are not exactly analogous. On a somewhat different note, this author has heard from a certain esteemed Rabbinic personality who requested not to be named, that there are those who posit that since *yoshon* flour is older, it likely has a higher infestation rate than *chodosh* flour, especially if it is not stored properly. Therefore, some maintain that it is preferable to eat *chodosh* products, which with all the *hetterim* involved is at worst a *safek issur*, as opposed to eating *yoshon* which has a greater chance of unwittingly eating an insect and thereby transgressing several definite *Issurei Deoraysa*.

48 *Mishnah Berurah* (489:45, and *Biur Halacha* s.v. *v'af*). Even so, as related in *Dugma M'Darchei Avi* (pg. 29), it is known that the *Chofetz Chaim* himself did not rely on any of the *hetterim* and did not partake of *chodosh* grain nor *chodosh* beer. Likewise, it is said that Rav Moshe Feinstein, in line with the reasoning of the *Mishnah Berurah*, was very scrupulous about this and made sure to have

Postscript: Life in Israel

In Eretz Yisrael, especially nowadays (and perhaps somewhat counterintuitively), it actually is much easier than in *Chutz La'aretz* to be particular with exclusively eating *yoshon* products. As the various rationales for leniency with the *chodosh* proscription do not apply in Eretz Yisrael, where all agree that it is considered a full Biblical prohibition, the *hashgachos* ensure that all grain-based food products manufactured in Israel are made with *yoshon* ingredients. As noted by Chief Rabbi of Israel Rav Yitzchak Yosef, there is no spring wheat grown in Israel,[49] and all imported grain used in local commercial food production is certified *yoshon*. In fact, many in Eretz Yisrael do not even realize that this topic is an issue at all.[50] This is why in his annual authoritative *Guide to Chodosh*, Rabbi Yoseph Herman asserts that all packaged products made in Israel under reliable kashrus *hashgachos* are always *yoshon*.[51] Perhaps another great reason to live in Eretz Yisrael.[52]

---

at least *yoshon* oats and barley, since it was much easier to observe *yoshon* with them than with wheat. Rav Yaakov Kamenetsky (*Emes L'Yaakov* on *Tur* and *Shulchan Aruch* O.C. 489, footnote 461) ruled similarly, that nonetheless one should be stringent with barley. See also *Shu"t Igros Moshe* (Y.D. vol. 4: end 46) where although he maintains there is what to rely upon *lemaaseh*, maintains that still one should try to ascertain where he can purchase *yoshon* flour, as it is still indeed preferable.

49 *Yalkut Yosef* (*Kitzur Shulchan Aruch* Y.D. 293:2 and 11).

50 However, they should, as although the grain used for Israeli commercial manufacture may nowadays always be *yoshon*, nevertheless, imported food products such as cookies and cereals from *Chutz La'aretz* may still indeed be *chodosh*. This issue and its *halachic* ramifications were discussed in a previous footnote.

51 This is also why many who are *makpid* on *chodosh* in *Chutz La'aretz* try to locally find food products that were produced in Eretz Yisrael under a reliable *hashgacha*.

52 The author wishes to thank his father, prominent kashrus expert Rav Manish Spitz, for his assistance with all matters *Yoshon*. Thanks are also due to Rabbi Yoseph Herman, for being on the forefront of spreading *Yoshon* awareness in his annual *Guide to Chodosh*, and to renowned *Posek* and author Rav Yirmiyohu Kaganoff, as his relevant article was the impetus for my interest and research on this topic.

Chapter 26

Chatichah Hareuyah L'Hischabed: All about Honor

THE *RAMBAN* EXPRESSES GREAT INTEREST in every detail related by the Torah, and introduces us to the fundamental concept of "*Maaseh Avos Siman L'Banim*."[1] This refers to the idea that the actions of our forefathers created a spiritual reality which was symbolic for their descendants. In other words, the challenges met by our great patriarchs transmitted to their children a unique form of spiritual DNA, whereby the potential was created for their descendants to emulate their deeds. Thus, it is incumbent upon us to explore the deeper concepts found in the familiar stories of the Avos and comprehend their relevance today.

In the footsteps of Avraham Avinu, we find that one of the hallmarks of the Jewish nation is *chessed*.[2] Aside from emulating his kindness, the

---

1   See the *Ramban's* famous explanation (*Parashas Lech Lecha* Ch. 12:6; and in his introduction to *Sefer Shemos*), based on the *Midrash Tanchuma* (*Parashas Lech Lecha* 9) and cited by many later authorities [see, for example, *Kli Yakar* (*Parashas Toldos* Ch. 26:19 and *Parashas Vayeishev* Ch. 38:18), *Maharsha* (*Chagiga* 5b and *Avodah Zarah* 8b), and *Shu"t Sheilas Yaavetz* (vol. 1:75)], that the purpose of showcasing the actions of the Avos is to demonstrate that a physical action, small as it may be, serves as a conduit to actualize and channel a Divine decree; in this case creating and enabling abilities in future generations.

2   See Gemara *Yevamos* (79a) and *Kesuvos* (8b), based on *Parashas Vayera* (Ch. 18:19); *Yerushalmi Kiddushin* (Ch. 1, *Halacha* 1), based on *Parashas Eikev* (*Devarim* Ch. 7:12), and the *Torah Temima's* explanation (*Parashas Eikev* ad loc. 19).

refined manner in which he served his guests turns out to be of *halachic* interest to us.

Who's Coming to Dinner?

For example, in a complicated kashrus question, there are times when *halacha* may dictate that only in extenuating circumstances may one be lenient. These dispensations include *hefsed merubah* (great financial loss), *l'tzorech* Shabbos, or if guests are coming.[3] There is debate among the Acharonim which type of guests would allow one to qualify for this last *halachic* dispensation:

- The *Tosafos Yom Tov* rules that only important guests that one would want to impress would qualify; conversely, poor charity cases would not make the grade.
- However, the *Minchas Yaakov* argues that we see that Avraham Avinu welcomed guests whom he thought were "three simple wandering pauper Arabs" and accorded them highest honors. Certainly, he maintains, leniencies involving *Hachnassas Orchim* would apply to downtrodden Jews as well.[4]
- Most authorities, including the *Chofetz Chaim*, actually conclude that one who invites in such *Yidden* not only fulfills the Mitzva of *Tzadaka*, but *Hachnassas Orchim* as well.[5]

---

3 For a good example, see the *Rema's* preface to his *Toras HaChatas*, as well as his glosses to *Yoreh Deah* (69:6).

4 *Soles L'Mincha* (on the *Toras HaChatas*, 15:3), arguing on the premise of the *Tosafos Yom Tov* (*Toras Ha'Asham* ad loc.); cited briefly in *Pischei Teshuva* (Y.D. 69:13).

5 Although there are different *mehalchim* in understanding this *machlokes*, nonetheless Rav Moshe Halberstam (*Shu"t Divrei Moshe* 42:2) posits that it is based on how these authorities understood the Maharil (end *Lekutei Maharil*), who is the source of the dispensation given *L'chvod Orchim*. Apparently, the Maharil did not discuss "*Orchim Aniyim*." Therefore, the *Tosafos Yom Tov* understood them to be only included in the category of *Tzedaka*, and not *Kavod Orchim*, as he maintained that that Mitzva was reserved for guests whom the *baal habayis* would want to honor. However, the *Minchas Yaakov* understood

Chatichah Hareuyah L'Hischabed

Yet, the flip side of the Mitzva of Honoring Guests is not a dispensation, but rather a *halachic* stringency: Generally, if a piece of non-kosher food gets mixed up with two or more identical pieces of kosher food, it is *battel b'rov*—it becomes nullified within the majority. However, if the non-kosher food is a *Chatichah Hareuyah L'Hischabed*, an honorable piece that is fit to be served to an important guest,[6] it is not *battel* (nullified). Regardless of how many pieces are involved, whether three or three thousand, the entire mixture is forbidden, and none of the pieces may be eaten.[7]

Size Matters

Still, the exact parameters of this designation are debated. For example:

- The *Shulchan Aruch* maintains that a *Chatichah Hareuyah L'Hischabed* refers exclusively to a respectable portion that is cooked and ready to be served. All others, even a desirable and

---

it to be an inclusive *hetter*, for anyone invited, no matter how worthy they are of the honor. He then concludes that most authorities count serving poor guests as fulfilling both Mitzvos: *Hachnassas Orchim* and *Tzedaka*. These include the *Maharsha* (*Brachos* 10b s.v. *harotzeh*), *Shelah* (*Pesachim*, end *Ner Mitzva*, s.v. *u'schar gadol*), *Pele Yo'etz* (*Os Aleph, Orchim*), and *Chofetz Chaim* (*Ahavas Chessed* vol. 3: Ch. 1, s.v. *v'da*). See also *Mori v'Rabi* Rav Yosef Yitzchok Lerner's *Sefer HaBayis* (Ch. 33:9 and footnote 13) at length, who explains that these *Poskim* are not arguing on the Maharil, rather explaining that this was his intent, to include serving the destitute in the Mitzva of *Tzedaka*, but not to exclude them from *Hachnassas Orchim*.

6 Although the *Shulchan Gavoah* (Y.D. 101:1) implies that a portion served that any guest would find *b'kavodik* would qualify for this designation, however, most authorities including the *Terumas Hadeshen* (78), Rashal (*Yam Shel Shlomo, Chullin* Ch. 7:53), *Knesses Hagedolah* (Y.D. 101, *Hagahos* on *Tur* 9), and *Pri Megadim* (ad loc. M.Z. and S.D. 1; Y.D. 72:7; and *Klalei Horaah* 7) maintain that in order to be considered a *Chatichah Hareuyah L'Hischabed* it must be fit to be served to an important guest such as a dignitary or *Baal Torah*.

7 See *Yoreh Deah* 101 at length for the full parameters of this *halacha*.

expensive cut of meat, would not meet this criterion, as one would presumably not honor a distinguished guest with a raw steak; it therefore can be nullified.
- However, according to the *Rema*, whom Ashkenazic practice follows, even large pieces of raw meat (e.g., steak, cutlets, brisket, etc.) would fall into the category of *Chatichah Hareuyah L'Hischabed*. He understands that once the meat is of a respectable size, which then can potentially be carved up, cooked, and served to an important guest, it is still considered fit for honoring a guest.

Based on the above, if a non-kosher raw steak is accidentally mixed up with five hundred similar kosher steaks, the basic *halacha* would depend on this dispute:
- According to the *Shulchan Aruch*, since the steak is raw, it is not fit for guests, and can be nullified, allowing the steaks to be eaten.
- However, according to the *Rema*, generally speaking they would all be prohibited.

Although there are Ashkenazic authorities who maintain that in a case of extenuating circumstances or great loss one may rely on the *Shulchan Aruch*'s opinion, while others only allow use of this rationale as one of several factors (*snif*) to permit leniency, but not on this basis alone, many other authorities disagree entirely and are stringent in all cases.[8] As with all *halachic* issues, if such a situation arises the question should be referred to a knowledgeable *halachic* authority.

---

8   The *Chasam Sofer* (*Shu"t* Y.D. 91; cited in *Pischei Teshuva* Y.D. 101:4) maintains that since many Rishonim, including the *Rashba* (*Toras Habayis Ha'aruch*, *Bayis* 4, *Shaar* 1, pg. 13b), *Ran* (*Chullin* 36b s.v. *v'garsinan*), *Ra'ah* (*Bedek Habayis*, *Bayis* 4, *Shaar* 1, pg. 17a), and *Rambam* (*Hilchos Maachalos Assuros* Ch. 16:5), whom the *Shulchan Aruch* bases his *psak* on, and other *Poskim* including the *Pri Chodosh* (Y.D. 101:12) rule like the *Shulchan Aruch's shittah*, one may therefore definitely rely on the lenient opinion *b'makom hefsed merubah*, if there is any sort of additional *safek* involved. Other Ashkenazic authorities who rule similarly include the *Shvus Yaakov* (*Shu"t* vol. 3:68), the *Maharsham* (*Daas Torah*, Y.D. 49:19), *Yaavetz* (*Shu"t Sheilas Yaavetz* vol. 1: end 58, s.v. *od*), and the *Aruch Hashulchan* (Y.D. 101:15). However, the *Pri Megadim* (Y.D. 101, S.D. end

Non-Deplumed

One situation all agree on is that a raw chicken still in feathers cannot qualify as a *Chatichah Hareuyah L'Hischabed* and can be nullified. The same would apply to a side of beef that has not yet been skinned. At that stage it would be too much of a jump in logic to consider honoring someone with it. Even though nowadays, with the advent of modern technology, de-feathering chickens is no longer a time-consuming and arduous task, *halachically* speaking, it still would not change that chicken's inability to be considered honorable in its present state.[9] [10]

Shawarma Surprise

Another interesting issue that arises is whether a portion of food, rather than one large piece, can claim to be a *Chatichah Hareuyah L'Hischabed*. For example, can a plate of shawarma be nullified? It itself would be considered an honorable meal, especially in the Middle East, but it is not one *chatichah*. If someone accidentally mixed several strips of non-*kosher* shawarma amid many other *kosher* ones, what is the shawarma's status?

The answer to this question is based on a comment of the *Rema* regarding *or shuman avaz*, fried goose skin. Apparently, back in the day this was quite a popular delicacy, and the *Rema* ruled that it is considered a *Chatichah Hareuyah L'Hischabed*.[11] Yet, the *Taz* points out that the most respectable method of preparing this delectable dish is by cutting it into small strips and frying it. Therefore, he posits, since a plate of small strips of fried goose skin would be served to a guest, a single piece of it could also be considered a *Chatichah Hareuyah L'Hischabed*, even though no one would think to serve a single small strip! Based on this

---

8 and *Klalei Horaah* 6) is uneasy to accept this leniency and concludes *tzarich iyun*. Other authorities, including the *Pri Toar* (101:6), *Yeshuos Yaakov* (ad loc. 7), and *Chochmas Adam* (53:9), rule exclusively like the *Rema*. Additionally, the *Beis Shlomo* (*Shu"t* Y.D. vol. 1:122), Rav Shlomo Kluger (*Hagahos Chochmas Shlomo* to Y.D. 102), and the *Yad Yehuda* (101, *Peirush Ha'aruch* 9 and *Peirush Hakatzer* 16) all maintain that an Ashkenazi may not rely on the *Shulchan Aruch's shittah* regarding this *halacha*, even *b'makom hefsed merubah*. See more on this in the chapter titled "The Erev Pesach Meat Scandal."

9   The *Shulchan Aruch* and *Rema* (Y.D. 101:3) both agree on this, as at that stage it is simply *"mechusar maaseh gadol"* to actually honor someone with it. Although the *Badei Hashulchan* (Y.D. 101:32 and 36) opines that nowadays with modern technology chickens in their feathers might still potentially be considered *Chatichah Hareuyah L'Hischabed* as they can be deplumed in seconds, he nevertheless concludes (the second time he mentions it) that his *sevara* is *tzarich iyun*. Yet, many other contemporary *Poskim*, including Rav Chaim Kanievsky (in an as-yet unprinted responsa to Rabbi Yitzchak Winkler), *Mori v'Rabi* Rav Yaakov Blau (personally told to this author), Rav Moshe Sternbuch, Rav Ezriel Auerbach (both *psakim* told to this author by Rabbi Daniel Yaakov Travis, Rosh Kollel Toras Chaim), the *Megillas Sefer* (on *Bassar B'chalav* and *Taaruvos* 101:9 and 10), the *Kinyan Deah* (Y.D. 101), and the *Dam Anavim* (ad loc.), unequivocally reject his *sevara* and rule that even nowadays we would not consider it a *Chatichah Hareuyah L'Hischabed* due to a variety of reasons, including: **1)** The whole *din* of *Chatichah Hareuyah L'Hischabed* is *Derabbanan* and even if we would forward the notion that this case might be considered as such, we still *pasken l'kula* in a case of *safek* whether something is a *Chatichah Hareuyah L'Hischabed*, and it is still *battel bshishim*. (See *Shach* Y.D. 101:2 and *Taz* 101:1.) This is especially true according to the rule set down by the great Rav Chaim Ozer Grodzenski (*Shu"t Achiezer* vol. 2:15, 6) that *Chatichah Hareuyah L'Hischabed* needs to be definitively defined as such, but anything that is in doubt by anyone if such an item can be used to honor someone, is definitely *not* considered *Chatichah Hareuyah L'Hischabed*. **2)** The *Shach* (ad loc. 7) quotes the Rashal and *Bach* that chickens still feathered are also not considered *Davar Sheb'minyan*, and anything that is *battel* from *Davar Sheb'minyan* is also not considered a *Chatichah Hareuyah L'Hischabed*. The *Pri Megadim* (ad loc. S.D. 7) explains their reasoning that it is still considered *"ma'us*—disgusting" and therefore cannot be considered *chashuv*, and consequently is neither *Davar Sheb'minyan* nor *Chatichah Hareuyah L'Hischabed*. So, even if we would opine that nowadays it should be considered a *Chatichah Hareuyah L'Hischabed* based on *"tircha,"* it would still not be considered as such due to this reason. **3)** The entire set of rules concerning *Chatichah Hareuyah L'Hischabed* was made regarding respectable pieces of meat that one would serve a guest in his home. Unless referring to those who live in a chicken processing plant, it is quite incongruous to suggest that the fact that chickens in a factory setting are more easily defeathered than they were in the past, applies to one trying to serve a guest a portion of chicken in his home, with no access to such industrial equipment. **4)** There is a well-known

understanding, the same should apply to our shawarma. Accordingly, if even a single non-kosher shawarma strip would get mixed in with a plate of kosher shawarma, the entire mixture would be prohibited.

Yet, there still is hope for shawarma lovers. The vast majority of authorities strongly disagree with the *Taz's* logic and maintain that in order to designate an item as a *Chatichah Hareuyah L'Hischabed*, it primarily must be a solitary *chatichah* that one would want to use to honor a guest. Since no one would be skimpy enough to serve a guest a solitary piece of this fried skin, but rather would exclusively serve this dish with many strips together, it cannot be considered a true *Chatichah Hareuyah L'Hischabed*.[12] The same would apply to our shawarma. Delicious as it

---

halachic dictum, quoted by authorities throughout the ages and spectrum: "*Ain lanu l'hosif al mah shelo nizkar b'Chazal*—we should not add to *Gezeiros* not mentioned by Chazal." This would certainly apply here as well, when the *machmir* by *Chatichah Hareuyah L'Hischabed*, the *Rema*, explicitly writes that feathered chickens cannot be considered as such; how then can we add a new *Gezeira* to *assur*?! Due to the above, the consensus of *Poskim* is that even nowadays a chicken still "feathered" cannot be considered a *Chatichah Hareuyah L'Hischabed*. [There are several other compelling reasons for this ruling. Although beyond the scope of this work, this issue was discussed at length in this author's *M'Shulchan Yehuda*, in the *Nispach* to "*Parashas Habassar 5773*."]

10 Another interesting dispute between later authorities who follow the Ashkenazic practice is whether the need to carve it down to a serving size is enough to consider it a non-*Chatichah Hareuyah L'Hischabed*. The *Shvus Yaakov (Shu"t* vol. 3:68) rules that a large bovine that still needs to be carved up into quarters and pieces, etc., would not be considered a *Chatichah Hareuyah L'Hischabed*, as there would be too much *tircha* to carve it down to a serving size, even according to the *Rema's shittah*. However, the *Yad Yehuda* (101, *Peirush Ha'aruch* 10, and *Peirush Hakatzer* 19) disagrees, maintaining that cutting down to size is not a true *tircha*; therefore, if that is all that is missing, it still would be designated a *Chatichah Hareuyah L'Hischabed*.

11 *Rema* (Y.D. 101:4), *Taz* (ad loc. 10).

12 The *Taz* is a *daas yachid* on this and the *halacha pesuka* follows the *Shach* (*Nekudos Hakessef*, Y.D. 101:1) who argues on his *shittah*, as virtually all *Poskim* including the *Issur V'Hetter* (25:23; quoting the Maharil—*Shu"t Hachadoshos* 72), the *Rema* himself (*Toras HaChatas* 40:4), the *Rashal* (*Yam Shel*

might be, one small strip just would not cut it, and the rules of nullification are still in play.[13]

It would certainly behoove us to emulate our esteemed forefathers and the lessons they have imparted to us. As my ancestor and namesake, the renowned Maharal M'Prague explains, the three pillars holding up the world, "*Torah, Avodah,* and *Gemillus Chassadim,*"[14] are exemplified by our esteemed *Avos* and their unique *middos*.[15] Our *Avos* teach us so much, both by their actions which we aspire to emulate, and by the

---

Shlomo, Chullin Ch.7:53), *Lechem Chamudos* (ad loc. 164; quoting Rav Shlomo Luria), *Pri Chodosh* (Y.D. 101:17), *Minchas Yaakov* (40:9), *Beis Lechem Yehuda* (ad loc. 14), *Shulchan Gavoah* (ad loc.), *Kreisi U'Pleisi* (ad loc. 11), *Chavas Daas* (ad loc. *Biurim* 6 and *Chiddushim* 12), *Pri Megadim* (ad loc. M.Z. 10), *Chochmas Adam* (53:11), *Hisorerus Teshuva* (Shu"t vol. 4, *Hashmatos* pg. 127 s.v. *Rema*), *Yad Yehuda* (101, *Peirush Ha'aruch* 12 and *Peirush Hakatzer* 27), *Beis Yitzchak* (vol. 1, *Amudei Zahav* 33), *Zivchei Tzedek* (101:26), *Ben Ish Chai* (Shu"t Rav Pe'alim vol. 1, Y.D. 23), *Aruch Hashulchan* (Y.D. 101:19), and *Kaf Hachaim* (ad loc. 43) *pasken* like the *shittah* of the *Shach*, that each individual piece has to be considered a *Chatichah Hareuyah L'Hischabed*, and not the serving dish. Due to the strength of their arguments, several of these *Poskim* actually reject the *Rema's* notion that *or shuman avaz* can ever be considered *Raui L'Hischabed*. Others, such as the *Pri Megadim* (ibid.), posit that the *Rema* must have been referring to large pieces of *or shuman avaz*, that each one individually would be considered a *Chatichah Hareuyah L'Hischabed*. Either way, to sum it up, as the *Vayizrach Yitzchak* (on *Hilchos Taaruvos* pg. 114) concludes, "*Ha'ikar k'rov minyan u'rov binyan hacholkim al HaTaz.*"

13   Although consideration of whether a food item is deemed honorable is dependent on "*Hakol lefi HaMakom V'Hazman*," however, and as opposed to shawarma which has the potential to be considered a respectable food, it should be noted that this *sheilah* would not arise when referring to lower class food such as french fries. Aside from the famous debate between the *Chochmas Adam* (66:4) and *Aruch Hashulchan* (Y.D. 113:18) whether a potato can ever be considered a *chashuv* food, the vast majority of *Poskim* would certainly agree that when it is fried and turned into cheap, plebian, common fare, it certainly cannot be considered a *Chatichah Hareuyah L'Hischabed*. This issue, as related to the *halachos* of *Bishul Akum*, is addressed at length in the chapter titled "The *Halachic* Adventures of the Potato."

14   *Avos* (Ch. 1, Mishnah 2).

details of their conduct, which reverberate and result in the nuances of *psak halacha*, from ancient tomes to modern times.

---

15 See the Maharal's *Derech Hachaim* commentary to *Avos* (vol. 1, Ch. 1:2, pg. 28–30).

Chapter 27

Margarine, Misconceptions, and *Maris Ayin*

THE ORIGIN OF GOOD OLD-FASHIONED (or bad old, depending if one is health conscious) ordinary margarine is surprisingly fascinating. In France, in the 1860s, with the rising popularity and cost of butter (due to the universal constant known as the law of supply and demand), Emperor (Louis) Napoleon III made a contest offering a considerable prize to anyone who could create a satisfactory substitute for butter. Additionally, the contest rules stipulated that this substitute must be inexpensive enough for the common man (apparently this French leader wanted to keep his head), as well as be able to be mass produced for their Armed Forces. In 1869, chemist Hippolyte Mège-Mouriès invented a substance he called "oleomargarine," now known worldwide as margarine, and won the substantial prize. Unfortunately for him, margarine never really took off in his lifetime, and after selling the patent in 1871, he died a pauper in 1880. Over time, the product became very popular.

However, as big a role as it plays in our daily lives, it interestingly plays a *halachic* role as well.

First Impressions…

There is a remarkable Rabbinic enactment known as "*Maris Ayin*." The most basic definition of this law is the prohibition of taking actions which, strictly speaking, are actually permitted according to *halacha*, but nevertheless give onlookers the *impression* that we are doing something *halachically* forbidden. In other words, although an observer has an obligation to judge others favorably (*dan l'kaf zechus*),[1] nevertheless we still have an obligation not to perform actions that might raise an observer's suspicions by engaging in questionable-looking activities.[2]

The Mishnah in *Shekalim* regarding the emptying of the *Kupos* in the *Beis Hamikdash* treasury,[3] bases the prohibition of *Maris Ayin* on the *pasuk* in *Parashas Mattos*: "*V'hiyisem Nekiyim MeiHashem U'meiYisrael*—And you shall appear clean (sinless) before G-d and before the people of Israel."[4] This prohibition is cited several times throughout *Shas*.[5] The *Chasam Sofer* stressed the importance of this *pasuk*, and lamented that he is not sure if anyone could possibly fulfill it properly![6]

Although some commentaries describe this prohibition using the terms "*Chashad*" and "*Maris Ayin*" interchangeably, Rav Moshe Feinstein explains that *Chashad* is a Biblical prohibition while *Maris Ayin* is Rabbinic in nature,[7] and explains the subtle differences between them.[8]

---

1 See Gemara *Shabbos* (127b), Gemara *Shavuos* (30a), and Rabbeinu Yonah's *Shaarei Teshuva* (Shaar 3, 218 s.v. *v'hinei*).

2 See *Shu"t Igros Moshe* (O.C. vol. 1:96) and *Shu"t Minchas Shlomo* (vol. 2:58, 29; *Tinyana* 53:3) how the *Gedolim* actually define the *issur*. *Maris Ayin* does not include worrying that someone might mistakenly think something permitted is prohibited (the example Rav Moshe gives is driving in a car on Friday afternoon after candlelighting time, that it is not *Maris Ayin*, even though some people mistakenly think that it is already considered *Shabbos* and might further assume that one would drive on *Shabbos* as well); one need not concern himself with others' mistaken notions of what is prohibited or allowed, only actual *halachic* concerns.

3 *Shekalim* (8a; Ch. 3, *Halacha* 2).

4 *Bamidbar* (Ch. 32:22).

5 Including *Shabbos* (61b, 64b, and 146b), *Bava Basra* (8b), *Avodah Zarah* (12a), *Kerisos* (21b), and *Bechoros* (43b-44a).

6 *Shu"t Chasam Sofer* (vol. 6:59).

7 *Shu"t Igros Moshe* (O.C. vol. 4:82).

8 See also *Shu"t Minchas Asher* (vol. 1:65 and 66), who defines the terms a bit differently. The *Divrei Malkiel* (*Shu"t* vol. 4:61), however, explains at length

Of Almonds and Fish Blood

One of the more famous applications of this rule applies to cooking (and/or eating)[9] meat in/with (pareve) almond milk, as cited by the *Rema*.[10] Since this action appears to an onlooker as cooking *Bassar B'chalav*, the forbidden mixture of meat and milk, it is therefore Rabbinically forbidden due to *Maris Ayin*.[11] [12]

There is a solution, though, to place almonds down next to where the cooking/eating is being done, to show to all that there is no actual prohibition occurring. This is similar to the Gemara's allowance of

---

that *Maris Ayin* actually contains six different classifications. For further treatment on the *klalim* of the *issur(im)*, see the commentary of the *Talmidei Rabbeinu Yonah* (*Brachos* 3b in the *Rif's* pagination), and *Encyclopedia Talmudis* (*Erech Chashad-Maris Ayin*).

9 See *Shach* (Y.D. 87:7 and 11) who argues, maintaining that the prohibition only applies to eating them together but not cooking them together. See also *Pri Megadim* (*Sifsei Daas* ad loc. 7 and 11).

10 *Rema* (Y.D. 87:3).

11 See major commentaries ad loc., as well as *Shulchan Aruch* and *Rema* and commentaries to *Yoreh Deah* (87:4). Although this case is generally accepted by most authorities as *Maris Ayin*, there is also the minority opinion of the *Pri Chodosh* (Y.D. 87:7; O.C. 461:2) who only begrudgingly accepts this scenario as a case of the *issur* of *Maris Ayin* and states that the prohibition of *Maris Ayin* does not extend beyond what is explicitly prohibited in the Gemara. The *Gilyon Maharsha* (Y.D. 298:1) echoes this as well. Although most authorities do not seem to agree with this assessment, Rav Yaakov Kamenetsky is quoted as being inclined to accept it as a *tziruf b'shaas hadchak* (*Emes L'Yaakov* on *Tur* and *Shulchan Aruch*, *Orach Chaim* 266, footnote 279). However, other authorities, including the *Kreisi U'Pleisi* (ad loc. 7) and *Yeshuos Yaakov* (ad loc. 5) do not accept this scenario of almond milk as *Maris Ayin* for a different reason. They explain that almond milk is not really any sort of milk; they maintain that in order to be concerned for *Maris Ayin*, the items have to be of the same type. Meaning, cooking in mother's milk would be *Maris Ayin*, as it's an actual milk, just not a dairy one; while coconut or almond milk would not be included as they are not intrinsically milk.

12 There is also a separate question whether it is possible to have a prohibition of *Maris Ayin* when the questionable act appears to be a Rabbinic prohibition.

drinking fish blood (yum!) provided that the fish's scales are noticeable.[13] Although fish blood is technically permitted, still, due to *Maris Ayin*, some might mistake the fish blood for prohibited blood. Hence, the need for the scales. Here too, the presence of the almonds would allay any *Maris Ayin* concerns.

Employing this logic, updated for modern times, would seem to imply that having a cold-cut sandwich lathered with margarine might just be

---

This is actually a four-way dispute with no clear-cut final *halachic* ruling. The basic opinions are of the *Rema* (ibid.), who rules that the *Maris Ayin* prohibition does not apply with *Issurei Derabbanan*; the *Taz* (ad loc. 4), who asserts that *lechatchilla* one should not do so, but *b'dieved* it's permissible; the *Shach* (ad loc. 6; also citing the *Shu"t Be'er Sheva*, 17; the Rashal, *Yam Shel Shlomo*, *Chullin*, Ch. 8:52 implies this way as well) who holds that it is *assur*, even *b'dieved*; and the *Ba'er Heitiv* (ad loc. 7) and *Pri Megadim* (ad loc. M.Z. 4), who maintain that the *Rema* only intended to rule leniently when it's a double *Derabbanan* (or *"tarti l'teivusa"*), i.e. the actual case the *Rema* cites as non-problematic: cooking *chicken* in *almond milk*. Since cooking chicken, as opposed to meat, in real milk would only be an *Issur Derabbanan*, in this instance, when coupled with cooking in almond milk, which is not an actual milk, would it be *muttar* and not a concern of *Maris Ayin*, as this scenario has two degrees of separation from the actual *Issur Deoraysa* of *Bassar B'chalav*, cooking real meat in real milk. There is also the opinion of the *Pischei Teshuva* (ad loc. 10 and *Nachlas Tzvi* ad loc. 3) who contends that only in someone's private home would the *halacha* be relaxed by an *Issur Derabbanan*. [This is because regarding *Maris Ayin* that appears to be an *Issur Deoraysa*, Chazal ruled (see *Shabbos* 64b and 146b, *Beitza* 9a, and *Avodah Zarah* 12a) that "*afilu b'chadrei chadarim assur.*"] Many later authorities are divided as to the proper *halacha* and several rule like each of these opinions with no clear consensus.

13 *Kerisos* (21b), and *paskened lemaaseh* in *Shulchan Aruch* (Y.D. 66:9). There is an interesting difference among the Acharonim's understanding of the Gemara as to whether the scales need to be placed near where one is drinking the fish blood, or whether they need to actually be inside the cup of fish blood. The same debate should apply regarding the almonds and the chicken cooked in almond milk. See *Yam Shel Shlomo* (*Chullin* Ch. 8:52), Rav Akiva Eiger (Y.D. 66:6), *Chochmas Adam* (40:3), *Badei Hashulchan* (87:46 and *Tziyunim* 92), and *Shu"t Maadanei Melachim* (68:1 and 2).

forbidden, due to *Maris Ayin*, as the margarine can easily be mistaken for butter! If so, why is this not more widely known?

Silky Situation?

The answer lies with a silky situation. The Mishnah rules that combining wool and silk does not violate the Biblical prohibition of *shatnez* (wearing a mixture of wool and linen),[14] yet is nonetheless forbidden Rabbinically due to *Maris Ayin*, as such garments could easily be mistaken for *shatnez*.[15] Still, centuries later, the *Rosh*, and even later, the *Shulchan Aruch*, ruled that in their times this was no longer an issue, as silk had become so common that it was easily recognizable, and no one would suspect a silk-blend garment of being *shatnez*. The *Rema* takes this ruling a step further and maintains that even a *kanvas* (cannabis?) blend garment, if it is commonplace, is also considered above suspicion; the *Shach* affirms that in his locale *kanvas* was common and therefore not applicable to the law of *Maris Ayin*.[16]

Common Criteria

The renowned *Kreisi U'Pleisi*, Rav Yonason Eibeshutz, extrapolates and expands on this concept even further, applying it as a general *halachic* rule across the board: Any time that the questionable object (or action) becomes commonplace, *Maris Ayin* no longer applies, as it will no longer arouse suspicion. The example he gives is if in a locale where cooking with almond milk is the norm, then accordingly it would not be necessary to place almonds next to the pot, as the average onlooker would simply assume that one is cooking in pareve almond milk, and not real milk.[17] Other later authorities, including the Maharsham and *Yad Yehuda*, have echoed Rav Eibeshutz's ruling.[18]

---

14 *Devarim* (*Parashas Ki Seitzei* Ch. 22:11).

15 *Kilayim* (Ch. 2, Mishnah 9).

16 *Rosh* (commentary to *Nida* Ch. 9:7), *Tur, Shulchan Aruch*, and *Rema* (Y.D. 298:1 and 2). Later authorities ruled similarly as well in their times, including the *Bach* (ad loc. 5), *Prishah* (ad loc. 4), *Shach* (ad loc. 2), and *Aruch Hashulchan* (ad loc. 4 and 5).

In fact, this basis for being lenient in cases of *Maris Ayin* has been widely accepted by contemporary authorities as well; the only issue being how common that item has to be in order to be entitled to this exemption. There was a famous dispute recorded approximately a hundred years ago between the *Pe'as Hasadeh* and the *Yagel Yaakov* regarding some novel egg-based desserts served at a wedding that looked remarkably dairy-like. Although both agreed with the *Kreisi's* approach, they disagreed as to its application: whether such desserts were considered common enough in their day to negate the rule of *Maris Ayin*.[19]

Above Suspicion?

However, nowadays, with popular and familiar daily staples such as margarine, soy schnitzel, burgers, and hot dogs, non-dairy creamers, pareve ice creams, and whipped desserts so commonplace, the vast majority of contemporary authorities assert that *me'ikar hadin* there no longer is a *Maris Ayin* issue with these products at all.[20] Who would

---

17 *Kreisi U'Pleisi* (87:8).

18 Maharsham (*Daas Torah* on Y.D. 87:3) and *Yad Yehuda* (ad loc. *Peirush Ha'aruch* end 5). Other *Poskim* who ruled accordingly include the *Arugas Habosem* (Belchover; *Kuntress HaTeshuvos* 13), the *Harei Besamim* (*Shu"t Mahadura Chamisha'ah* vol. 4:33), and the *Eimek Halacha* (*Shu"t* O.C. 134 s.v. *od*).

19 *Shu"t Pe'as Hasadeh* (vol. 1:36) and *Shu"t Yagel Yaakov* (Y.D. 23). Other *Poskim* of the time who permitted their dairy-looking pareve spreads based on this *klal* include the Maharash Engel (*Shu"t* vol. 6:40) and the *Divrei Malkiel* (*Shu"t* vol. 5:85). Regarding *Maris Ayin* at Jewish weddings and *Seudos Mitzva*, see also *Knesses Hagedolah* (Y.D. 87, *Hagahos* on *Beis Yosef* 8), Chida (*Machzik Bracha* ad loc. 6), *Yad Efraim* (ad loc. s.v. *v'nahagu*), *Zivchei Tzedek* (ad loc. 21–23), and *Kaf Hachaim* (ad loc. 26–27).

20 Including Rav Henoch Padwa (*Shu"t Cheishev Ha'Eifod* vol. 1:20), the Debreciner Rav (*teshuva* printed in *Pischei Halacha* on *Hilchos Kashrus*, pg. 113:7), Rav Yosef Shalom Elyashiv (cited in Rabbi Yaakov Skoczylas' *Ohel Yaakov* on *Issur V'Hetter*, revised edition, 87, footnotes 42–44), Rav Shmuel Halevi Wosner (*Shu"t Shevet Halevi* vol. 9:157), Rav Ovadiah Yosef (*Shu"t Yabia Omer* vol. 6, Y.D. 8:4 and *Shu"t Yechaveh Daas* vol. 3:59), Rav Mordechai Eliyahu (cited in *Kol Tzofayich* vol. 100), Rav Menashe Klein (*Shu"t Mishnah*

suspect a religious Jew of using dairy butter, milk, or ice cream after eating meat, instead of assuming that the pareve alternative is being used?

Although some authorities maintain that it is still preferable to exercise caution since the dairy versions are presently still more common, and maintain that one should optimally keep the container or wrapper on the table at the time of eating, nevertheless they agree to this *halachic* principle. That is why nowadays many do not even think twice

---

Halachos vol. 5:96), Rav Levi Rabinowitz (*Shu"t Maadanei Melachim* 63:3; 64; 65; 67:2 and *Maadanei Hashulchan* Y.D. 87:20), Rav Yisroel Belsky (*Shu"t Shulchan Halevi* Ch. 22:9), the *Avnei Yashpei* (*Shu"t* vol. 6:64, 4), as well as Rav Avigdor Nebenzahl (*Shu"t M'Tzion Teitzei Torah* 170, pg. 136–137), Rav Yochanon Wosner (*Shu"t Chayei Halevi* vol. 4:47, 14 and 15), the *Minchas Pri* (*Shu"t* vol. 3:57), the *Megillas Sefer* (on *Bassar B'chalav* 87:7 s.v. *v'hinei*), the *Ohr Yitzchak* (*Shu"t* vol. 2, Y.D. 3), the *Divrei Binayahu* (15 and 16), and the *Vayizra Yitzchak* (*Shiurei Issur V'Hetter* pg. 116). Several of these authorities are referring to margarine, others to soy schnitzel, and others pareve creamer; and although some maintain that it is preferable to keep the container or wrapper on the table at the time of eating, or in a public setting it should state its pareve status on the menu, nevertheless, they all follow the *Kreisi's* principle. See also *Shu"t Minchas Asher* (vol. 1:66), who although agreeing in principle, nevertheless maintains that one should preferably not rely upon this dispensation *lechatchilla*, since the dairy versions are still far more common. A lone dissenting opinion, who apparently argues on all aforementioned authorities, is that of the *Badei Hashulchan* (Y.D. 87:48 and *Biurim* pg. 11–12 s.v. *mishum*) who does not seem to accept the *Kreisi's* logic et al. to permit these items nowadays. He argues that the original case cited by the *Rema* in *Yoreh Deah* 87, cooking meat in almond milk, was apparently prevalent in those days, and yet we still find that the *Rema* considered it *Maris Ayin* and mandated placing almonds nearby. Hence, he feels that "common consumption" is not enough to permit these items. However, in this author's estimation, this concern can be resolved by a careful reading of the *Shach* (ibid.), citing the Rashal (ibid.), that this dish was a popular delicacy specifically *on Purim* (as a type of "*Vinehafoch Hu*"), implying that otherwise it was not commonly cooked in almond milk the rest of the year. Therefore, it seems entirely plausible that this delectable dish was not considered widespread enough to give it a dispensation from *Maris Ayin* year-round.

about "buttering" their sandwich with margarine or having pareve "ice-cream," or coffee with non-dairy "milk," even at a *fleishig* meal.

This is an excellent example of *halacha's* adaptability to a changing world. The rule remains the constant, but its practical application is dependent on our great authorities' interpretation. So, to sum it up, although the creator of margarine never got to enjoy its questionable benefits, we at least can, both in the physical sense and the *halachic* sense.[21]

---

21 Regarding the permissibility of taking a drink, using the restroom, or taking part in a business meeting in a non-kosher restaurant nowadays, see *Shu"t Igros Moshe* (O.C. vol. 2: end 40 s.v. *u'vadavar*), *Emes L'Yaakov* (on *Tur* and *Shulchan Aruch*, C.M. 425, footnote 27 s.v. *v'nirah she'im*), *Shu"t Minchas Asher* (vol. 1:67), and *Shu"t M'Tzion Teitzei Torah* (168–169, pg. 135–136).

Chapter 28

Leeuwenhoek's *Halachic* Legacy: Microscopes and Magnifying Glasses

ANTONIE VAN LEEUWENHOEK (1632-1723), although not the developer of the first rudimentary microscope, nonetheless is the figure most closely associated with the microscope's mystique. He is credited for discovering microorganisms, and is considered the greatest contributor toward making the microscope the essential research and diagnostic tool that it is known as, even today. In fact, his designs for improving the microscope were not successfully replicated until 1957, over two hundred years after his death!

Although the scientific, research, and medical significance and benefits of Leeuwenhoek's work are obvious, this chapter sets out to explore what *halachic* relevance his innovations have.

Mitzva Magnifyer?

This issue actually affects many different aspects of *halacha*, the foremost being what status something that can only be seen with a microscope has in Judaism. For example, Sukkos time everyone checks their *esrogim* for blemishes. What is the status of an *esrog* that has no noticeable blemish, but when viewed under magnification glass, loupe, or microscope, one can perceive imperfections? Similarly, if one can ascertain a problem in the script of a *Sefer Torah* only via a magnifier, would that invalidate the *Sefer Torah*?

The most common question, though, arises when checking produce for insects, which we are forbidden to eat.[1] This is a very important

---

[1] *Halachically* speaking, there are several categories of insect infestation that may or may not require produce checking: **1)** A standard fruit or vegetable that has no known insect issues does not need to be checked before consumption. However, even so, several Acharonim, including the *Chochmas Adam* (38:20) and *Maaseh Rav* (94), advise to always "keep your eyes open" when eating. The *Chochmas Adam* writes that anecdotally, this awareness saved him from transgressions of unwittingly ingesting insects many times over the years. The *Ohr Hachaim* (*Parashas Shemini* Ch. 11:44) and *Kaf Hachaim* (Y.D. 84:120) add that if one does his utmost to be vigilant in this area, he will be aided *Min Hashamayim* in ensuring that he does not eat insects. **2)** If one finds three insects inside a dish of food, e.g., soup (although there are those who are stringent after finding two), said dish becomes prohibited to eat from unless it checked and strained and thus ascertained that there are no more insects lurking within (see *Shulchan Aruch* and main commentaries to *Yoreh Deah* 100:4). **3)** If a majority (over fifty percent) of a type of produce is known to be infested (*muchzak b'tolaim*), then that type of produce is prohibited to be eaten unless it can be ascertained that said produce is completely clear of insects (see *Shulchan Aruch* and main commentaries to *Yoreh Deah* 84:8 and 9). **4)** A fourth category is when a type of produce is known to have a *miut hamatzui*, or a small but steady percentage of insect issues, then it may not be eaten before it is properly checked; in layman's terms, "it is *chayav* a *bedikah*." [See *Rema* (Y.D. 84:8), based on the *Rashba* (*Toras Habayis Ha'aruch*, *Bayis* 3, *Shaar* 3 and *Shu"t* vol. 1:274); as well as *Darchei Teshuva* (39:3). There is however, some debate whether this obligation is *M'Deoraysa*, *M'Derabbanan*, or simply a *chumrah*. See *Shach* (Y.D. 39:8), *Pri Megadim* (S.D. ad loc. 3, and 84:28), *Shu"t Mishkenos Yaakov* (Y.D. 17), *Shu"t Beis Efraim* (Y.D. 6), *Pnei Yehoshua* (*Pesachim* 9b s.v. *uv'Tosafos*, old print pg. 111b, bottom of right-hand column), and *Meshech Chochma* (*Parashas Bo*, Ch. 13:3 s.v. *m'yamim yamimah*).] Although there are several different opinions how to properly define this *miut hamatzui* that obligates a *bedikah* before consumption [including the *Rivash's* (*Shu"t* 191) *shittah* that it is "*karov l'mechtzah*," and at the other end of the spectrum, that its application would depend on each individual situation—how *consistently* insects are found in that specific type of produce, meaning a far smaller percentage—see *Shu"t Shevet Halevi* (vol. 4:81), Rav Pesach Eliyahu Falk's *Madrich L'Bedikas Tolaim* (pg. 10:30 s.v. *v'tamuah*), and *Minchas Asher* (*Vayikra*, *Parashas Shemini* 16:3; he understands this to be the

issue,[2] as if one would accidentally consume an insect, depending on whether it is a land, sea, or air bug, one might unwittingly transgress up to six separate *Issurei Deoraysa*![3]

---

true *shittah* of the *Mishkenos Yaakov* and not that he intended to "set in stone" an actual percentage)], nonetheless, the *Mishkenos Yaakov's shittah* (ibid.) of ten percent is widely accepted. [See for example, the Maharsham's *Daas Torah* (Y.D. 39:3), *Shu"t Minchas Shlomo* (Tinyana 63:1), *Kovetz Teshuvos* (vol. 3:113), *Even Yisrael* (vol. 2, on the *Rambam*, *Hilchos Shechita* Ch. 7:2), *Shu"t Mishnah Halachos* (vol. 7:99 s.v. *uv'Shu"t*; who writes that we certainly would not need to be *machmir* more than this *shittah*), Rav Yisroel Belsky's *Reshimos B'Inyanei Hilchos Tolaim* (available on the OU's website, www.oukosher.org; he is cited as understanding this application similar to the aforementioned opinion of the *Minchas Asher*), and the "*Halachic* Introduction" to *The OU Guide to Preparing Fruits and Vegetables*.] This means that practically speaking, we are obligated to properly check fruits or vegetables that are known to have infestation levels of at least ten percent, in order to ensure that said produce is actually insect-free. See next footnote. For more on the topic of defining *miut hamatzui*, see Rabbi Dovid Cohen of the cRc Chicago's recent *The Halachos of Insects* (Ch. 28).

2   Many applications of contemporary Rabbinic directives regarding specific fruits and vegetables, i.e. soaking in vinegar, rinsing under a heavy stream of water, triple-wash cycle, only acceptable when frozen, et al., are related to *miut hamatzui*, and those specific actions mandated are ways of lessening the odds and percentages of said produce's probable infestation levels, and thus making them acceptable for consumption. Sometimes even grinding up the food and making a "smoothie" is recommended [but exclusively when it is only a *safek sheyeish tolaim* and not *muchzak b'tolaim*, and the *kavanna* was to be *metaken* the food item and not to eat the insect, and usually when there are other *sfeikos* and *sniffim* present, etc.; otherwise it may be a violation of *Ain Mevattlin Issur*]. See *Shu"t Maharsham* (vol. 1:174), *Kovetz Teshuvos* (vol. 1:74), *Shu"t Minchas Shlomo* (Tinyana 63:2), *Shu"t Igros Moshe* (Y.D. vol. 1:35 and O.C. 4:91, 3), *Shu"t Minchas Yitzchak* (vol. 3:72), *Shu"t Shulchan Halevi* (Ch. 21:1–3), *Yalkut Yosef* (*Issur V'Hetter* vol. 2, pg. 195–199 and 240–247), *Bedikas Hamazon K'Halacha* (Ch. 7: note 12; citing Rav Yosef Shalom Elyashiv, Rav Shmuel *Halevi* Wosner, Rav Ben Tzion Abba-Shaul, and Rav Nissim Karelitz), and this author's *maamar* in *Techumin* (vol. 35; 5775, pg. 194, footnote 1) citing *Mori v'Rabi* Rav Yaakov Blau of the *Eidah Hachareidis*.

If one cannot detect any sign of bugs in the produce, but they may perhaps be visible through magnification, is one allowed to eat the produce? And if not, is one required to use such a magnifying device to check to ensure that there are no lurking insects?

This issue, although a recurring theme in Judaism, is not a new one; it has already been addressed hundreds of years ago. There is a minority opinion that if a magnifying glass can help better find insects, one would be required to use it to do a proper thorough inspection.[4] However, the vast majority of Acharonim, including such luminaries as Rav Shlomo Kluger,[5] the *Chochmas Adam*,[6] *Tiferes Yisrael*,[7] and *Aruch Hashulchan*,[8] emphatically state that the Torah would not require something that could not have been kept at all times. As such, a magnifying glass or microscope could not possibly have been mandated for a *halachic* inspection, as it has only been around for several hundred years. Additionally, when the Torah commands an inspection, it must

---

3 Prohibitions are stated in *Parashas Shemini* (*Vayikra* Ch. 11; see also *Parashas Re'eh*, *Devarim* Ch. 14:19). See Abaye's statement in Gemara *Makkos* (16b), *Pesachim* (24a), and *Eruvin* (28a), as well as *Rambam* (*Hilchos Maachalos Assuros* Ch. 2:14 and 23), *Tur* and *Shulchan Aruch* (Y.D. 84:6 and Y.D. 100), and *Kitzur Shulchan Aruch* (46:45).

4 Rav Yaakov Emden (*Shu"t Sheilas Yaavetz* vol. 2:124), *Sefer HaBris* (cited in *Binas Adam* 38), and *Shu"t Pri Hasadeh* (vol. 3:80) seem to hold this way. Rav Menachem Meir Weissmandl, in a *maamar* in *Kovetz Ohr Yisroel* (vol. 20), opines that there is no real argument and differentiates between a magnifying glass and microscope. However, in this author's estimation, it must be noted that from the actual words of the authorities, it seems tenuous to make this distinction and it appears they would maintain that neither makes a *halachic* difference if one cannot discern an insect without its aid. This is addressed further on in this chapter.

5 *Shu"t Tuv Taam V'Daas* (*Tinyana*, *Kuntress Acharon*, 53), who strongly objects to the Yaavetz's contention.

6 *Binas Adam* (34; to *Klal* 38), who completely rejects the opinion of the *Sefer HaBris*.

7 *Tiferes Yisrael* (*Avodah Zarah* Ch. 2, Mishnah 6, *Boaz* 3).

8 *Aruch Hashulchan* (Y.D. 84:36).

be something that the average Joe can personally perform,[9] without the aid of specialized instruments.

Seeing Is Believing

These authorities cite several proofs to this from diverse Biblical passages, such as the *parashah* dealing with the laws of the *Nazir* (Nazirite),[10] to whom all wine and wine by-products (including wine vinegar) are prohibited, and the verse in which Rus HaMoaviah was instructed by the greatest authority of the time to dip her bread in vinegar.[11] Yet, nowhere do we find that they pulled out a magnifying glass to check the vinegar (which was one product that over the millennia has been shown to have a high insect infestation rate) to ascertain that no microscopic insect might have been inside. Furthermore, if minuscule mites would be prohibited due to the ability to see them under a microscope, how can anyone breathe? Every time we inhale we would be ingesting thousands of infinitesimal insects! The Torah was given to people, not angels.[12]

The vast majority of contemporary authorities, almost without exception, rule this way as well, that *re'iyah*—seeing—can only be referring to natural G-d-given eyesight, and any magnifying tool will not change the *halachic* status of whatever needs to be checked, whether an *esrog*, *tefillin*, *Sefer Torah*, or flour.[13]

---

9   Several authorities stress that the *halacha* is referring to people with strong eyesight (20/20 vision) to be able to check properly. See *Shu"t Chasam Sofer* (O.C. 132 s.v. *v'odos*), *Divrei Shaul V'Yosef Daas* (beg. Y.D. 84), *Shu"t Dvar Moshe* (*Tinyana* 98:60), *Darchei Teshuva* (84:15), and *Mishnah Berurah* (473:42). Rav Asher Weiss (*Minchas Asher, Vayikra, Parashas Shemini* 16:2 and *Shu"t Minchas Asher* vol. 1:41) explains at length that this does not mean that only people with "super-human eyesight" can check properly; rather, one who has strong eyesight and the know-how to check properly is perfectly reliable. We should not and do not assume that there might be someone in the world who has stronger vision and might be able to see potential possible insects better.

10 *Bamidbar* (*Parashas Nasso* Ch. 6:3).

11 *Rus* (Ch. 2:14).

12 *Brachos* 25b, *Yoma* 30a, *Kiddushin* 54a, *Meilah* 14b.

Seeing Spots

However, there are those who maintain that it might be worthwhile to use a magnifier to help check better, if one can already ascertain something, but is unsure what he is seeing. For example, if one can see a black dot, many authorities rule that one needs to use a magnifying

---

13 Including Rav Chaim Soloveitchik of Brisk (cited in *Shu"t Igros Moshe* Y.D. vol. 2:146 s.v. *u'mah*), the Butchatcher Rav (*Daas Kedoshim* O.C. 32:50), the Kozoglover Gaon (*Shu"t Eretz Tzvi* 12:13), the *Even Yikara* (*Shu"t* vol. 2:33), the *Mayim Chaim* (*Shu"t* O.C. 259), the *Melamed L'Ho'eel* (*Shu"t* vol. 2-Y.D. 27), the *Chazon Ish* (cited in many *sefarim* including *Orchos Rabbeinu* vol. 3, *Hagahos* to *Orach Chaim, Hilchos Tefillin* 12; *Maaseh Ish* vol. 1:pg. 20; and *Nezer Chaim* pg. 375, *Klalim Nifradim* 1), the Steipler Gaon (*Kraina D'Igresa* vol. 2:77), Rav Yosef Eliyahu Henkin (*Shu"t Gevuros Eliyahu* vol. 1-O.C. 99: end 1), Rav Moshe Feinstein (ibid. and *Shu"t Igros Moshe*, E.H. vol. 3:33 s.v. *aval* and Y.D. vol. 4:2), the Tchebiner Rav (*Shu"t Dovev Meisharim* vol. 1:1), Rav Shlomo Zalman Auerbach (*Shu"t Minchas Shlomo, Tinyana* 63:2 s.v. *ume'attah*; *Halichos Shlomo* on *Tefilla* Ch. 4: footnote 78 and *Halichos Shlomo* on *Moadim* vol. 2, *Pesach* Ch. 7:25), the Debreciner Rav (*Shu"t Ba'er Moshe* vol. 5:16), Rav Yosef Shalom Elyashiv (cited in *Ashrei Ha'Ish* O.C. vol. 3:pg. 211, end 13), Rav Shmuel Halevi Wosner (*Shu"t Shevet Halevi* vol. 7:2, 10), Rav Moshe Sternbuch (*Shu"t Teshuvos V'Hanhagos* vol. 1:628 and vol. 3:323), Rav Ovadiah Yosef (*Shu"t Yabia Omer* vol. 4, Y.D. 21:7 and *Shu"t Yechaveh Daas* vol. 6:47), Rav Ben Tzion Abba-Shaul (*Shu"t Ohr L'Tzion* vol. 1:4), Rav Menashe Klein (*Shu"t Mishnah Halachos* vol. 4:128 and 129 and vol. 5:157), Rav Asher Weiss (*Shu"t Minchas Asher* vol. 1:41 at length), the *Pri Chaim* (*Shu"t* Y.D. 43), *Beis Avi* (*Shu"t* vol. 1, O.C. 64), *She'arim Metzuyanim B'Halacha* (46:16 and 20), and *Yalkut Yosef* (*Issur V'Hetter* vol. 2:84, 6). See also *Shu"t Vidibarta Bam* (vol. 1:208 and vol. 2:238, 8) and Rav Yisroel Belsky's *Reshimos B'Inyanei Hilchos Tolaim* (available on the OU's website, www.oukosher.org). Although the *She'aris Yisrael* (*Shu"t* vol. 1, O.C. 11 and 12) argues on the *Dovev Meisharim* and *Chazon Ish* by a certain specific case, see *Shu"t Lehoros Nosson* (vol. 5:2, 2) who explains that he only disagrees by that specific case but the rule nevertheless holds true. Similarly, although Rav Dovid Baharan (brought in the *Kuntress Bein Hashmashos* of the *Even Ha'Azel*) cites a proof from the Gemara in *Bechoros* 52b that the Torah can be referring to supernatural eyesight, the *Even Ha'Azel* himself (vol. 8, *Hilchos Kriyas Shma* Ch. 1:3 s.v. *v'hinei harav*) dispels his proof, and maintains that this ruling indeed holds true.

glass to ascertain whether it is an actual insect or merely dirt before partaking of the produce.[14]

However, not everyone agrees with this course of action, and there is a minority opinion that classifies it instead as not considered true "seeing." According to this understanding, one need not be concerned with such minuscule dots, since all anyone is physically capable of seeing is a black dot, it therefore cannot be considered a prohibited insect that is discernable to the naked eye.[15]

Another application of this concept is checking lettuce, etc., by using the magnifier in order to familiarize yourself with what you are seeing. This is because it is entirely possible that you are really seeing an insect (with your plain eyes), but simply don't realize it as it might be camouflaged. Once one checks with magnification, one will be able to recognize what the bugs actually look like and will be able to properly see them thereafter without visual aid.[16]

---

14 This is essentially a difference of understanding between *Rashi* (*Eiruvin* 28a s.v. *tzirah* and *Chullin* 67b s.v. *b'aviha*) and the *Rashba* (*Shu"t* vol. 1:275) whether one needs to ascertain actual movement of the dot to identify it as an insect (as the prohibition is "*sheretz hashoreitz*"), or one has to assume that it is a bug even without. On this topic, see *Shulchan Aruch* and *Rema* (Y.D. 84:6), *Shach* (ad loc. 20), *Minchas Yaakov* (46:7), *Pri Megadim* (Y.D. 84, S.D. 20), *Chochmas Adam* (38:9), *Shu"t Beis Efraim* (*Hachadoshos* pg. 8), *Shu"t Tzemach Tzedek* (*Hachadoshos* Y.D. 92, in the brackets), *Mishmeres Shalom* (84 S.D. 8:2, citing the Maharsham), *Darchei Teshuva* (84:28 s.v. *ayin sham*), *Kitzur Shulchan Aruch* (46:34), and *Ben Ish Chai* (Year 2, *Parashas Nasso* 6). The *Chazon Ish* (cited above) was known to have ruled stringently with this.

15 See for example, *Shu"t Shevet Halevi* (vol. 7:122; and not as quoted in *Bedikas Hamazon Kehalacha*, beg. Ch. 3), *Shemiras Shabbos Kehilchasa* (Ch. 3:37, footnote 105; and in the new edition, footnote 117), *Halichos Shlomo* (on *Tefilla* Ch. 4:25, footnote 78), *Va'aleihu Lo Yibol* (vol. 2, Y.D. 1), *Shu"t Igros Moshe* (Y.D. vol. 2:146 s.v. *u'mah* and Y.D. vol. 4:2), and *Yalkut Yosef* (*Issur V'Hetter* vol. 2, 84:21). Although it is known that Rav Shlomo Zalman Auerbach later reversed his lenient position, it was only in regard to specific insects that he acknowledged that their movement can actually be discerned, as opposed to his previously held conviction; however, he still ruled leniently regarding other potential insects that only appear to the naked eye as a dot.

Still, the bottom line is that using a magnifier or microscope to see something that *cannot* be seen at all by the naked eye would have no *halachic* bearing whatsoever, "*bein lehakel bein lehachmir.*" So, although Leeuwenhoek's impact on the world in various important areas is immeasurable, nevertheless, his *halachic* legacy remains—quite ironically—microscopic.

Postscript: Bubby Didn't Eat Bugs!

Although nowadays there sometimes seems to be a push to quickly classify certain widely-eaten food or drink items as *assur* due to finding some sort of potential insect issue, in this author's opinion, aside from the exhortation in *Pirkei Avos* to be "*Mesunin BaDin*, deliberate in judgment,"[17] it is also worthwhile to review an invaluable lesson that the *Gadol Hador*, Rav Moshe Feinstein imparted to us on this topic shortly before his *petirah*. Rav Moshe was asked to sign a *Kol Koreh* prohibiting a certain type of fruit due to a possible insect issue. Rav Moshe responded that on the contrary, in his opinion it may not be publicized that this fruit is prohibited, as aside from the fact that there were lenient opinions to rely upon (in that specific situation),[18] more importantly, "it is prohibited to

---

16 *Minchas Asher* (*Vayikra, Parashas Shemini* 15:5 s.v. *amnam* and 16:2; based on *Shu"t HaRadbaz* vol. 1:753 and *Bach* Y.D. end 84) and *Shu"t Machazeh Eliyahu* (vol. 1:91, 8) who brings proof to this from the *Chasam Sofer's* custom (*Minhagei Chasam Sofer* Ch. 10:18; see also *Shu"t Chasam Sofer* Y.D. 277 and *Mishnah Berurah* 473:42) regarding checking Maror on *Erev Pesach*. Rav Shmuel *Halevi* Wosner (*Shu"t Shevet Halevi* vol. 7:125, 2 s.v. *v'lo*) writes similarly, that a magnifying glass should be used if one's eyesight is not up to par, and it helps one see what someone with strong eyesight would be seeing. However, he reiterates, if while utilizing the magnifying glass one can see something indiscernible to the naked eye, it has no *halachic* relevance. This use of a magnifying glass to ascertain actual insects also seems to be the approach of renowned bug-checking expert, Rav Moshe Vaye (see his *Bedikas Hamazon Kehalacha* Ch. 3).

17 *Avos* (Ch. 1, Mishnah 1).

18 Another potential leniency (known as the *Shittas HaKreisi U'Pleisi*) is that perhaps an insect born inside a food item does not maintain the full *halachic*

spread rumors about earlier generations, who could not have possibly been stringent on these issues, as they were unaware of them."

Rav Moshe's thrust and main point was not that people from earlier generations were not culpable even though they may have been eating potential non-kosher; rather it was that even if it is assumed that the *halacha* here generally follows the more stringent opinion, nevertheless, we still may not publicize that certain issues are *assur*. Rav Moshe was teaching us that is preferable to rely on a lenient opinion, thus implying that previous generations had what to rely on as well, rather than assert that something is definitively *assur* and cast negative aspersions on previous generations, whom, without any doubt, were on a higher

---

status of a bug, and might be considered nullified. Several authorities tried to find other *hetterim*, including the *Aruch Hashulchan's* controversial take that since bugs are generally considered utterly disgusting, they are immediately nullified; and the *Kreisi U'Pleisi's* and *Avnei Nezer's* (*Shu"t* Y.D. 81:6) opinion, based on the minority opinion of several Rishonim, including the *Rashba* (*Shu"t* vol. 1:271) and *Rash M'Shantz* (*Terumos* Ch. 10, *Mishnah* 8), and cited by the *Tur* (Y.D. 100), that even a *beriyah* has a *din* of *bittul* if there is present 960 times the size of the insect. [However, it is important to note that the consensus among the Rishonim and Acharonim, including the *Shulchan Aruch* (Y.D. 100) and the main commentaries (ad loc.), as well as the *halacha lemaaseh*, is that a complete insect is never nullifiable.] In fact, many great *Poskim* and *Gedolim* over the generations worked tirelessly to find any sort of justification to allow the eating of many foods. In those days, especially in the summer, many foods, including basic wheat and grain, were extremely prone to insect infestation and the deplorable storage conditions did not help matters. These *Gedolim* include Rav Yonason Eibeshutz (*Kreisi U'Pleisi* Y.D. 100:2 and 4), Rav Shlomo Kluger (*Shu"t Tuv Taam V'Daas, Mahadura Telita'ei* vol. 1:160), the *Ksav Sofer* (*Shu"t* Y.D. 63), the *Imrei Baruch* (Y.D. beg. 100), the *Mishkenos Yaakov* (*Shu"t* Y.D. 30), and the *Aruch Hashulchan* (Y.D. 100:13–18). Others, including the *Yad Yehuda* (61, *Peirush Ha'aruch* 63:6), tried to give *eitzos* and potential solutions to lessen the odds of eating bugs. Their collective reasoning was (loose translation), "to find merit for Bnei Yisrael to save them on The Day Of Judgment, and Heaven forbid to say that all of Bnei Yisrael would stumble on such a great sin, as it is a near impossibility to find any food, especially in the summer days, that has no trace of any sort of insect, and it is almost impossible to properly check."

spiritual level than us, especially as they are at least one step closer to Har Sinai.¹⁹ Just some "food for thought."

---

19   See *Shu"t Igros Moshe* (Y.D. 4: end 2). Rav Shlomo Zalman Auerbach, as well, is known to have expressed similar sentiments (see *Shu"t Minchas Shlomo, Tinyana* 63:2 and *Halichos Shlomo* on *Moadim* vol. 2, *Pesach* Ch. 7: footnote 121). See also *Shu"t Minchas Asher* (vol. 3:49), who writes that although one may question each individual leniency, nonetheless, as many *Gedolei Poskim* and *Amudei Horaah* wrote to be *meikil*, there certainly collectively is what to rely upon after inspecting the item to the best of one's ability. Indeed, several years before he was *Rachmana l'tzlan* murdered by terrorists, Rav Eitam Henkin H"yd, wrote a *sefer* titled *Lachem Yihiyeh L'Achlah*, citing many leniencies, rationales, and *tzirufim* regarding insect infestation in produce so that the *Hamon Am*, who perhaps were not as stringent with bug checking as they could or should be, would have what to rely upon.

Chapter 29

The *Halachic* Discourse of Louis Pasteur: Is Wine Fine?

ALTHOUGH BEST KNOWN AS THE "father" of microbiology, bacteriology, and germ theory, as well as the discoverer of the rabies and anthrax vaccines, Dr. Louis Pasteur (1822–1895) is credited with a number of other innovations as well. Quite unknown to many of us, we all have him to thank for enabling us to safely drink wine and milk nowadays. You see, Dr. Pasteur also invented a process of heating up liquids that destroys bacteria and other germs lurking inside, thereby increasing shelf life and preventing these liquids (mainly milk and wine) from causing disease. This process later became widely known as "pasteurization," in his honor.

Hilchos Pasteur?

Aside from the health benefits of pasteurization, there potentially might be *halachic* benefits, as well. It is well known that there is a Biblical prohibition to benefit whatsoever from wine that was poured as a libation in idol worship (*Yayin Nesech*).[1] There is also a Rabbinic prohibition against drinking wine that was poured or touched by a non-Jew (*Stam Yaynam*), as a safeguard to prevent intermarriage and assimilation ("*chasnus*").[2] This proscription was extended to include wine that was

---

1   *Parashas Ki Sisa* (*Shemos* Ch. 34:12–15). See *Sefer Hachinuch* (ad loc. Mitzva 111).

2   Mishnah (*Avodah Zarah* 29b); see *Tosafos* (ad loc. s.v. *v'yayin*), based on the

The Halachic Discourse of Louis Pasteur: Is Wine Fine? **379**

Gemara later on (*Avodah Zarah* 36b), who explains that this decree is due to preventing intermarriage or "*chasnus.*" This is also how the *Tur, Shulchan Aruch*, and their main commentaries conclude (Y.D. 123:1). The prohibition of *Stam Yaynam* is one of the eighteen *Gezeiros* that Chazal established on that famous, fateful day when Beis Shamai overruled Beis Hillel. See Mishnah (*Shabbos* 13b) and accompanying Gemara (17b), as well as *Yerushalmi* (*Shabbos* Ch. 1, *Halacha* 4; 12a in the Friedman edition and 9b in the *Me'orei Ohr* edition). Although true *Stam Yaynam* is also *assur b'hana'ah* (see Gemara *Avodah Zarah* 30a-b), nonetheless, this only holds true regarding the *Stam Yaynam* of an actual idolator. The Gemara later teaches (*Avodah Zarah* 64b) that *Stam Yaynam* of a *Ger Toshav* (non-idol worshipping non-Jew), although forbidden to be drunk, is still *muttar b'hana'ah*. Practically, as taught by many of the Rishonim, the same classification applies to the wine of the average non-Jew nowadays (see *Shulchan Aruch, Rema* and their main commentaries to *Yoreh Deah* 123:1, 132:1, 133:1, 147:3, and 155:3, as well as the *Rema* and *Levush* to *Orach Chaim* 156: end 1 [although it should be noted that there are those who differentiate between practicing Christians and Muslims; on this topic, see the Chida's *Shiyurei Bracha* (Y.D. 123:1 and *Shiyarei Shirayim, Kuntress Acharon* ad loc. 1) and *Maris Ha'ayin* (*Likutim* 8, pg. 79a), *Pri Toar* (4:11), *Ben Ish Chai* (Year 2, *Parashas Balak* 1), *Shu"t Rav Pe'alim* (vol. 1, Y.D. end 28), *Shu"t Yabia Omer* (vol. 7, Y.D. 12:2 and 3), and *Yalkut Yosef* (*Kitzur Shulchan Aruch, Hilchos Yayin Nesech,* Y.D. 123:1); this ruling is mainly based on earlier Sefardic authorities, including the famous *shittah* of the *Rambam* regarding the status of *Yishmaelim* (*Hilchos Maachalos Assuros* Ch. 11:7 and *Shu"t HaRambam*, 5776 *Machon Yerushalayim* edition, vol. 1:149 and 262); see also *Rema* (Y.D. 146:5) and *Shu"t Ein Yitzchak* (O.C. 11), and conversely, *Pri Toar* (19: end 10), *Shu"t Tzitz Eliezer* (vol. 14: end 91), and *Shu"t Divrei Yatziv* (O.C. vol. 1:90)]. Even though the prohibition of *Stam Yaynam* is *Derabbanan*, the *Chochmas Adam* (75:1) avers that one who drinks it will have his *neshamah* uprooted from Gan Eden and will have no share in *Olam Habaah*. The Chida (*Shiyurei Bracha* Y.D. 123:2 s.v. *uv'emes*) writes similarly, adding that the violator will also be reincarnated as a donkey. Very strong exhortations, indeed. However, the *Ba'er Heitiv* (ad loc. 1, in the parenthesis) cites the *Chavos Yair* (*Shu"t* 183), that even so, one does not have to give up his life or limb (or even an ear) for this prohibition. It is worthwhile to read Rav Tzvi Hirsch Heller-Charif's fiery letter from over one hundred fifty years ago (*Chiddushei V'Shu"t Hara"tz Charif (Heller), Shu"t* 25) as to his efforts *"l'gdor geder v'laamod*

touched or poured by public Sabbath desecrators (*Mechalalei Shabbos B'farhesya*).³

However, there is an important exclusion to this rule: If the wine is cooked (*Yayin Mevushal*) then even if it was later touched or poured by a non-Jew,⁴ it does not gain the status of *Stam Yaynam*, and is still

---

b'peretz" to clean up the rampant laxity of his time regarding the prohibition of *Stam Yaynam*.

3   This is because Shabbos is the sign of and testament to Hashem having created the world in six days and rested on the seventh. Therefore, one who blatantly and publicly desecrates Shabbos is considered as if he is denying that Hashem created the world, and in that aspect is somewhat akin to an idolator. See, for example, *Rashi* (*Chullin* 5a s.v. *ela lav*), *Ran* (ad loc.), *Rambam* (*Hilchos Shabbos* Ch. 30:15), *Shulchan Aruch* (O.C. 385:3, Y.D. 2:5; 119:7; see also 124:8), *Shach* (*Nekudos Hakessef* beg. Y.D. 124), *Magen Avraham* (O.C. 306:29), *Pri Chodosh* (Y.D. 112:2), *Pri Megadim* (ad loc. S.D. 2), *Kitzur Shulchan Aruch* (72:2), and *Kaf Hachaim* (Y.D. 112:11). On the other hand, there are several *Poskim*, including the *Chasam Sofer* (*Shu"t* Y.D. 120) and the *Chazon Ish* (Y.D. 2:23 and 49:7), who maintain that this *chumrah* regarding wine touched by *Mechalalei Shabbos* is truly only a *kenass*, and not actually *m'din*, as "*chasnus*" should technically not apply to any sort of Jew. Rav Akiva Eiger (Y.D. 123, gloss to *Taz* 3) implies this way as well. There is much contemporary Rabbinic literature on how to properly define and classify modern day *Mechalalei Shabbos B'farhesya*, if they are included in this category, or perhaps have the exception of "*Tinokos Shenishbu*" (see *Rambam*, *Hilchos Mamrim* Ch. 3:1–3). Certainly, *lechatchilla* it would be preferred to ensure that wine being served to any sort of *Mechalel Shabbos* be *mevushal*, in order to avoid this *halachic* issue entirely.

4   There is an additional *shittah*, not cited by the *Rambam, Tur, Shulchan Aruch*, or main commentaries, that there are those who are even stringent regarding wine that a gentile *sees*, and especially regarding using it for *Kiddush*. Although certainly not the normative *halacha*, it seems the first mention of such an opinion is from Rav Nosson HaBavli in his *Taamei HaMitzvos* (cited by the *Darchei Teshuva* 123:2) calling this a "*Minhag Vasikin*" of "*Anshei Maaseh*," and is later cited approvingly by the *Shlah* (*Shaar Ha'Osiyos, Kedushas Ha'achilah* 106) and Rav Chaim Palaji (*Ruach Chaim*, Y.D. 131:2). See also *Yalkut Yosef* (*Kitzur Shulchan Aruch*, Y.D. 123:11), who refers to this view as "*Midas Chassidus*." Others seem to accept this as a Kabbalistic approach, albeit not the *halachic* approach. Come what may, it is told that the late Lubavitcher

permitted to be drunk.[5] There are several reasons advanced by the *halachic* authorities for this exception, among them:[6]

- Cooked wine is considered substandard and is no longer fit for a libation.
- Cooked wine is uncommon, and therefore was never considered part of the prohibition.
- Cooked wine's taste is inferior to uncooked wines, and is not considered "real" wine for this purpose.

Although *Yayin Mevushal* is *halachically* considered somewhat inferior for sacramental purposes (i.e. *Kiddush, Havdalah, Arba Kosos* etc.),[7]

Rebbe used to be very *makpid* on this and kept the wine bottle he was using at *farbrengins*, etc., covered, in case some of the non-Jewish cleaning staff would enter the Beis Midrash and see the wine.

5 See Gemara *Avodah Zarah* (30a), which relates the story of Shmuel and Abalet (a non-Jew) who drank (kosher) wine together, as it was *mevushal*, as well as explicitly ruled by Rava. This ruling is followed *lemaaseh* by *Rashi* (ad loc. s.v. *harei amru*), *Tosafos* (ad loc. s.v. *Yayin Mevushal*), *Rambam* (*Hilchos Maachalos Assuros* Ch. 11:9), *Tur* and *Shulchan Aruch* (Y.D. 123:3), and later authorities. However, Rav Akiva Eiger (ad loc. s.v. *v'af al gav*) further qualifies this leniency, that it is only referring to a Jew's cooked wine that a non-Jew touched, that is still permissible to be drunk, but not to a non-Jew's cooked wine, even if it is technically "kosher" (as the *lashon* used by the *Tur* and *Shulchan Aruch* is "*Yayin Mevushal* **shelanu** *shenaga bo goy*"). The *Bach* (ad loc.) and later, the *Chochmas Adam* (75:10) imply this way as well. Rav Tzvi Pesach Frank was known (*Shu"t Har Tzvi* Y.D. 111) to have practically ruled this way. This *shittah* should not be confused with the allowance of making kosher wine at a non-Jew's factory etc., which is permitted to be drunk, even if the non-Jew owns it; see *Yoreh Deah* 131 at length.

6 See *Rosh* (*Avodah Zarah* Ch. 2:13), *Rashba* (*Shu"t* vol. 4:149 and in *Toras Habayis, Bayis* 5 *Shaar* 3), *Meiri* (*Avodah Zarah* 29b-30a), *Knesses Hagedolah* (Y.D. 123, *Hagahos* on *Beis Yosef* 16), *Taz* (ad loc. 3), and *Sdei Chemed* (*Maareches Yayin Nesech*).

7 In fact, the *Rambam* (*Hilchos Shabbos* Ch. 29:14) writes explicitly that one may not make *Kiddush* on *Yayin Mevushal*, as the Gemara states (*Bava Basra* 97a) that one needs wine that is fit for a libation on the *Mizbe'ach* for *Kiddush*. The *Maggid Mishnah* (ad loc.) adds that this is the opinion of "*Kol HaGaonim*" as

nonetheless, in certain situations, especially with non-Jews present (e.g., serving as waiters), it becomes the preferred option.[8]

---

well. The *Panim Meiros* (*Shu"t* vol. 3:20) and Rav Avraham Azulai (*Hagahos Mahar"a Azulai on Levush* O.C. 272:7) even maintain that such wine is not even *Hagafen*, but rather *Shehakol lemaaseh*, an opinion originally cited by several Rishonim, including *Rashi* (*Shu"t Rashi* 88) and the *Rash* (both cited by *Tosafos, Bava Basra* 97a s.v. *eeleima*), the *Ri"tz Giyus* (*Hilchos Kiddush*), and even Rav Hai Gaon (both cited by the *Tur* O.C. 272:8). Although this is not the normative *halacha*, as many other Rishonim, including *Tosafos* (ibid.), the *Rosh* (*Bava Basra* Ch. 6:10), *Baal Ha'Itur* (*Hilchos Matzah U'Maror, Seder Arbah Kosos*), *Ran* (*Pesachim* 22a in the *Rif's* pagination s.v. *ain*) and *Agur* (381), argue, citing proof from the *Yerushalmi* (*Pesachim* Ch. 10, *Halacha* 1) that one may use "*Konditon*," a wine-based drink containing many other ingredients, including honey, mixed in, for *Kiddush* on Pesach, and *Yayin Mevushal* is certainly preferable to that. Although the *Tur* (O.C. 272:8) cites both sides with no clear conclusion, this is still the bottom line *halacha* as codified by the *Shulchan Aruch* and *Rema* (ad loc.), as well as the *Levush* (ad loc. 8), *Chayei Adam* (vol. 2, 6:7), and *Shulchan Aruch Harav* (O.C. 272:9), that one may indeed use *Yayin Mevushal* for *Kiddush*. See *Aruch Hashulchan* (O.C. 272:8 and 9) for a brief explanation and roundup of opinions on topic. Interestingly, the *Tashbetz* (vol. 1:85) maintains that even according to those who hold one may not make *Kiddush* on *Yayin Mevushal*, nonetheless one may still make *Havdalah* with it. See also *Shu"t Maharam Schick* (O.C. 84 s.v. *uv'prat*) who strongly defends the position that *Yayin Mevushal* is indeed *Hagafen*, arguing on the *Panim Meiros'* assertions. Practically, the *Elyah Rabba* (ad loc. 11), *Kitzur Shulchan Aruch* (47:6), and *Mishnah Berurah* (272:23), based on all of the above, conclude that with all other factors being equal, it is therefore preferable not to make *Kiddush* with *Yayin Mevushal* (but that its proper *bracha* is indeed *Hagafen*).

8   See *Shemiras Shabbos Kehilchasa* (vol. 2, Ch. 47:19, footnote 91) based on the *Mishnah Berurah* (ibid.), that with all other factors being equal, non-*mevushal* wine is preferred; implying that in a scenario where there might be potential issues of *Stam Yaynam* and *mevushal* wine is available, it is preferable not to come into problems with *Stam Yaynam*, and in order to prevent us from a *chashash* of *issur*, *Yayin Mevushal* then becomes the wine of choice, even for *Kiddush*.

Debate Heats Up

There is some debate among the authorities as to what level of cooking this wine needs in order to receive the coveted *mevushal* status.

The *Tur* and *Shulchan Aruch* simply state "*mishehirsiach al gabei ha'aish*, when it starts to boil on the fire,"[9] implying that the temperature reached must certainly be at least "*Yad Soledes Bo*," the degree of heat that when felt or touched causes one to draw back his hand for fear of getting burned[10] (as elucidated by the *Magen Avraham* regarding *Hilchos Shabbos*).[11]

Generally speaking, in other areas of *halacha*, we find that most *Poskim* are of the opinion that this level is reached at approximately 113°F (45°C).

However, several contemporary authorities understand the "*Yad Soledes Bo*" requirement in our case to be a higher temperature than that.[12] Accordingly and in any event, if this truly was the Gemara's

---

9 *Tur* and *Shulchan Aruch* (Y.D. 123:3).

10 This is known as *Shittas HaGaonim* (see *Shu"t Maaseh Gaonim* pg. 77), as cited by the *Raavad* (whose opinion is brought by the *Ramban* in his *Chiddushim* to *Avodah Zarah* (30a s.v. *matzasi*; see also *Shaarei Teshuva* 258; as cited in the *Beis Yosef* ad loc.), *Rosh* (ibid.), *Mordechai* (*Avodah Zarah* 817), *Sefer HaTerumah* (vol. 3, *Hilchos Avodah Zarah* 156), *Orchos Chaim* (vol. 2, Y.D. pg. 247:10; who concludes that the *ikar* follows the *shittah* of Rav Hai Gaon and the Gaonim), and *Biur HaGr"a* (Y.D. 123:7). This is also the basic understanding of the *Tur* and *Shulchan Aruch* (ad loc.), as well as that of the *Levush* (ad loc. 3), that once the wine is "*maaleh resichah al ha'aish*" it is considered *mevushal*. Several of the aforementioned Rishonim understand the "*resichah*" required here to be only somewhat of a slightly higher temperature than another case mentioned in the Gemara (*Shabbos* 40b) of *Shemen Mevushal*, cooked oil, which only needs to be "cooked" by being "*hufsheru*," defrosted (heating up performed at *poshrim*, lukewarm temperature), for one to have transgressed cooking it on Shabbos. Accordingly, the "*Yad Soledes Bo*" required for wine to be considered "cooked," would seemingly not be a much higher temperature. See next several footnotes.

11 *Magen Avraham* (O.C. 318:12).

12 Although Rav Shmuel *Halevi* Wosner (*Shu"t Shevet Halevi* vol. 2:51) among

intent with "*Yayin Mevushal*," then once wine is "cooked" at whichever exact temperature this is, one need not worry about a non-Jew touching or pouring said wine afterward.

However, this remains a big "if," as the *Shach*, quoting the *Rashba* and *Ran*, offers an alternate interpretation, as well as an important caveat: "*Mishehirsiach al gabei ha'aish*" is referring to the heat level when the wine's volume is noticeably reduced due to the cooking;[13] a much higher temperature than the *Shulchan Aruch* seemingly mandated sufficient.

---

others, understands the *Shittas HaGaonim* and Rishonim to be referring to the same "*Yad Soledes Bo*" mentioned in other areas of *halacha*, still Rav Yisrael Pesach Feinhandler (*Shu"t Avnei Yashpei* vol. 1:150) argues that the "*Yad Soledes*" requirement here must be a higher temperature than that mandated in other areas of *halacha*, as the full *lashon* is "*mishehirsiach **al gabei ha'aish**, when it starts to boil **on the fire**.*" 113°F can be attained even off the fire. He thus maintains that even according to the *Shittas HaGaonim*, "*Yad Soledes*" required here for *Bishul* is a much higher temperature. This also bears out from a famous, albeit brief, *teshuva* of Rav Moshe Feinstein (*Shu"t Igros Moshe* O.C. vol. 4:74, *Bishul* 3) who writes that the *shiur* of the "*Yad Soledes*" mentioned in *Hilchos Shabbos* that is 110°F (43°C), is only correct *lechumrah*, when we need to be stringent (i.e. tread cautiously to prevent potential Shabbos violation), yet in other cases, when we need to ascertain that something reached the correct temperature of "*Yad Soledes*" *l'kula*, to allow leniency, it is only at 160°F (71°C) when we are certain that it has reached "*Yad Soledes Bo*." Accordingly, although in his first *teshuva* on *Yayin Mevushal* (*Shu"t Igros Moshe* Y.D. vol. 3:31) he mentions that the "*Yad Soledes*" mandated by the *Shittas HaGaonim* is the same *shiur* detailed by the *Magen Avraham* in *Hilchos Shabbos* (ibid.), nonetheless, it stands to reason that this rationale should be viewed as Rav Moshe did regarding *Hilchos Shabbos*. Hence, *leshittaso*, although 110°F would be considered "*Yad Soledes*" *lechumrah*, nevertheless, *l'kula* it would need to be a much higher temperature, approximately 160°F. Additionally, the conclusions of several Rishonim that both *shittos*, of "*hirsiach*" and being reduced, are actually referring to the same temperature of *Bishul* (see next footnote), is more easily understood following the supposition that "*Yad Soledes*" mandated for *Yayin Mevushal* is a higher temperature than mandated in other areas of *halacha lechumrah*. Thanks are due to my *talmid*, R' Avraham Perton, for pointing out several of these invaluable sources.

13 *Rashba* (ibid.), and *Ran* (*Avodah Zarah* 10a in the *Rif's* pagination), as cited

- This understanding is cited as the basic *halacha* by several later authorities including the *Chochmas Adam* and *Kitzur Shulchan Aruch*, as well as most contemporary *Poskim*.
- Rav Moshe Feinstein, in several responsa, estimates this temperature to be approximately 165–175°F. He maintains that once the wine reaches this temperature while being cooked, it certainly starts being reduced, and is already considered *Yayin Mevushal*; ergo, we no longer have to worry about the *halachic* ramifications if a gentile would touch this wine.[14]

---

by the *Shach* (Y.D. 123:7) and later, the *Ba'er Heitiv* (ad loc. 3). This is also the *Ramban's* (ibid.) own *shittah*, based on his understanding of the *Yerushalmi* (*Avodah Zarah* Ch. 2: *Halacha* 6) that *Bishul* in this context requires an actual reduction in the wine's amount due to the cooking. The *Ritva* (*Avodah Zarah* ad loc.) mandates this as well, adding that perhaps when it is *"maaleh resichah al ha'or"* is a *siman* that the wine has started to reduce. This understanding is cited as the basic *halacha* by several later authorities including the *Chochmas Adam* (75:10) and *Kitzur Shulchan Aruch* (47:3). Yet, as several Acharonim point out (as well as can be seen from the *Beis Yosef* ad loc.), the *Rashba* and *Ran* do not seem to actually conclude with the more stringent *shittah*. Rather, after citing the more lenient opinion of the Gaonim, they addressed the fact that there is a more *machmir* opinion, that the wine needs to be reduced, but concluded that the *"Kabbalas HaGaonim Tachria,"* and as a possible solution opining that perhaps both opinions were referring to the same *shiur*, that any time wine is heated up there is a reduction in its measurement. The *Tashbetz* (*Shu"t* vol. 1: end 29 s.v. *ul'inyan*) as well, after citing both opinions, concludes similarly, that *"efshar shehakol echad, inyan echad, v'shiur echad."*

14 *Shu"t Igros Moshe* (Y.D. vol. 2:52, Y.D. vol. 3:31, Y.D. vol. 5:9, and E.H. vol. 4:108). Although in several of his responsa Rav Moshe writes that once the wine reaches 165°F, it is sufficient, see however, Rav Yisroel Belsky's *Shu"t Shulchan Halevi* (Ch. 25:4) who writes that the *ikar* in Rav Moshe's *shittah* is 175°F, as he himself indicates in other *teshuvos*. Interestingly, in all of his *teshuvos* on topic, Rav Moshe only refers to the heat level that is reached during pasteurization as sufficient to be considered *"bishul."* As flash pasteurization's application to the kosher wine industry only first started in 1985 (as detailed in a later footnote), and Rav Moshe passed away in 1986, he never once mentions the process of modern day pasteurization, or whether he would have deemed it sufficient to allow wine to be considered *mevushal*. Several years

There is, however, a third opinion, brought in the *Gilyon Maharsha*, *Darchei Teshuva* and others,[15] referred to as the *"shittah* of the Sefardic

> ago, this author asked Rav Mordechai Tendler, Rav Moshe's grandson and author of *Mesores Moshe*, his thoughts on the matter, and he agreed with this author's observations that based on Rav Moshe's *teshuvos* it would indeed be a *chiddush* to say that Rav Moshe allowed all aspects of the pasteurization process to be considered actual *bishul*, as opposed to how it is widely quoted in his name. On the other hand, a certain esteemed Rabbinic personality (who requested not to be named) later professed an opposing viewpoint to this author: that in Rav Moshe's eyes, the main factor contributing to declaring wine as *mevushal* was the heat level. [Indeed, according to historian Roger Horowitz in his recent book *Kosher USA: How Coke Became Kosher and Other Tales of Modern Food* (pg. 144), Rav Moshe's first *teshuva* on topic in 1966 (although curiously only published in a later volume of *Igros Moshe* than a later *teshuva* on topic) was in essence a sharp riposte and direct rejoinder to a Conservative rabbi's publicly maintaining a year earlier that pasteurization at 140°F was sufficient to render a wine *mevushal*. Moreover, in several of his *teshuvos* on the topic, Rav Moshe added that it was scientifically proven that once wine reaches 165°F, it starts reducing (at a slow rate), and if it is kept at this temperature for an hour (in standard vat pasteurization), it will lose over one-tenth of its volume.] Accordingly, Rav Moshe did not address any other potential related issues of pasteurization, as it seems there was no need to, as presumably it would not have affected his conclusion.

15   *Gilyon Maharsha* (Y.D. 115:1), *Darchei Teshuva* (123:15), and *Kaf Hachaim* (Y.D. 118:7; passage written by Rav Ovadiah Yosef) quoting several early Sefardic Acharonim, including the *Divrei Yosef* (vol. 3:845, 2), Chida (*Kikar La'aden* pg. 162a; citing the Maharam de Luzano), *Ikrei Hada"t* (*Ikrei Dinim*, Y.D. 13:13), *Knesses Hagedolah* (ad loc. 14), *Erech Hashulchan* (ad loc. 5), and Rav Chaim Palaji (*Ruach Chaim* 123:2). The *Ben Ish Chai* (Year 2, *Parashas Balak* 7) was also known to be *machmir* for this *shittah*, mandating "*bishul rav*," until the wine's taste changes akin to honey. This was also known to be the opinion of several Rishonim, including the *Meiri* (*Avodah Zarah* 30a, and not like he seemingly implies leniently in *Pesachim* 107a; who although citing four different *shittos*, including the aforementioned two and the more stringent opinions that the wine must thicken or become concentrated by a third due to cooking, nonetheless concludes that the proper *Bishul* requirement is "*mevushal ad shenishtana taamo*") and the *Ohr Zarua* (*Avodah Zarah* Ch. 2:155; also cited by the *Shiltei Hagiborim* on *Avodah Zarah* 10a; that it must be "*nada*

Acharonim," that in order to be truly considered cooked, this wine must really be so—meaning it has to reach its full boiling point. Even though water generally boils at 212°F (100°C), due to its alcoholic content (alcohol has a much lower boiling point than water) the average wine's boiling point is approximately 190–195°F.

- However, Rav Feinstein maintains that since this opinion is not brought in the *Shulchan Aruch* or its main commentaries, we are not required to follow it.[16]
- Conversely, other contemporary authorities do take this opinion into account.

This debate also influences the *halachic* ramifications of pasteurization. Wine producers are not eager to actually cook—let alone boil—their wine, as doing so drastically diminishes its quality and taste, and consequently, and more importantly to them, their profits. And that's where pasteurization comes into the picture. Since they often are required to pasteurize their wine anyway for health reasons, if it is also

---

b'birur shirsiach v'nisbashel bishul gamur"). The Maharam Schick (*Shu"t* O.C. 84 s.v. *uv'prat*) in his rebuttal to the *Panim Meiros'* position regarding *Yayin Mevushal* (as detailed in an earlier footnote), implies that he understood the requirement this way as well, writing that it is "*yayin mishtaneh taam legeri'usa.*" See also next footnote.

16 *Shu"t Igros Moshe* (Y.D. vol. 3: end 31). This is akin to the position of the *Shulchan Gavoah* (Y.D. 123:7), that 'the *Shiltei Hagiborim's shittah* is "*battlah da'ato eitzel kol hani derabvusa.*" On the other hand, Rav Ovadiah Yosef, wrote in *Kaf Hachaim* (Y.D. 118:7; as will be explained below) that he found that the *Rambam* in *Hilchos Issurei Mizbe'ach* (Ch. 6:9) holds that the meaning of "*bishul*" is that it must be cooked to the extent that its intrinsic taste changed. He posits that the same should apply by *Hilchos Stam Yaynam* as well. He then cites several of the aforementioned *Poskim* (in the previous footnote), concluding that certainly *lechatchilla* we should be *choshesh* for the *Rambam's* and the other *Poskim's* more stringent opinion, but *b'dieved*, "*ain lehachmir klal*" since the vast majority of authorities hold that simply heating it up is indeed sufficient. [Unbeknownst to many, but as mentioned in the introduction to the final volume of *Kaf Hachaim* (Y.D. vol. 2), at the behest of the *Kaf Hachaim's* son, Rav Moshe Sofer, Rav Ovadiah Yosef finished the last portion

considered *mevushal*, they can "kill two birds with one stone" and keep the quality (and their profit margins) intact.

Pondering Pasteurizing

Contemporary authorities are divided as to the validity of pasteurization being considered *mevushal*:

- Rav Moshe Feinstein held that the temperature of modern-day pasteurization (once it reaches at least 165–175°F) is sufficient to be considered *mevushal*. Rav Ovadiah Yosef, as well as several other *Poskim*, agree that this process satisfactorily meets this requirement. In fact, as Rav Yisroel Belsky notes, the general custom is to consider wine *mevushal* from 180°F, as it certainly steams by that point.[17]

---

of the tenth and final volume of *Kaf Hachaim* (*Hilchos Maachalei Akum*), basically following the author, Rav Yaakov Chaim Sofer's approach and style, but sometimes drawing his own conclusions as well.]

17 See Rav Ovadiah Yosef's *Shu"t Yabia Omer* (vol. 8, Y.D. 15) where he attempts to resolve all of the claims and concerns of the *machmirim*, yet still concludes that if one can be *machmir* and not have to rely upon the pasteurization process as actual *bishul*, then "*tavo alav bracha*." On the other hand, he refers to the *minhag* to be *meikil* with pasteurized wine (at approximately 80°C [176°F]) as "*yesodoso b'hararei kodesh*." [See also previous footnote for what Rav Ovadiah himself wrote in *Kaf Hachaim*, as well as *Me'or Yisrael* (vol. 3, pg. 346), *Shu"t Yabia Omer* (vol. 1, Y.D. 11:21 and vol. 9, O.C. 108:134), and *Yalkut Yosef* (*Kitzur Shulchan Aruch*, *Hilchos Yayin Nesech* 6). Interestingly, in his letter printed in *Nishmas Avraham* (Third edition, vol. 2-Y.D. pg. 67–68), Rav Ovadiah seems to have taken a more stringent position, only allowing such wine to be considered *mevushal b'dieved* and writes that when he originally gave *hashgacha* to Carmel Mizrachi Winery he refused to allow them to claim that the pasteurized wine was also considered *mevushal*, as he held that *lechatchilla* it was not. In his later *teshuvos*, however, he concludes "*sheyeish lismoch al zeh l'halacha ulemaaseh*."] See also Rav Yisroel Belsky's *Shu"t Shulchan Halevi* (Ch. 25:11), as well as Rabbi Yissachar Dov Eichorn's *maamar* in *Kovetz Yeshurun* (vol. 14; pg. 838–841), where he concludes that pasteurization is indeed sufficient to make the wine be considered *mevushal*. Rav Yaakov Kamenetsky implies this way as well; see *Emes L'Yaakov* on *Tur* and *Shulchan Aruch* (O.C.

- On the other hand, Rav Shlomo Zalman Auerbach,[18] Rav Yosef Shalom Elyashiv,[19] Rav Ben Tzion Abba-Shaul,[20] and Rav Menashe Klein[21] were unconvinced, as the vast majority of wine nowadays is pasteurized, and therefore cannot be considered uncommon, as cooked wine is supposed to be.[22]

Additionally, with the advent of flash pasteurization (a process performed extremely quickly—"in a flash"),[23] they assert that the

---

472: footnote 477). See also Rav Yosef Kapach's commentary on the *Rambam* (*Hilchos Brachos* Ch. 8:5, pg. 614) who proves that pasteurization should indeed be considered *mevushal*. He explains that the *Yerushalmi* in *Terumos* (Ch. 2) states that Rav Yochonon holds that the wine's needing reducing does not refer to its volume during the cooking process, but rather reducing its drinkability or quality. He maintains that this occurs during pasteurization, asserting as proof that authentic wine connoisseurs certainly prefer quality wine that was not cooked in the slightest. He adds that even according to the basic understanding it is not possible that during pasteurization the wine's volume would not get reduced, at least a minute amount, which should still satisfy that requirement. See also next footnote.

18 *Shu"t Minchas Shlomo* (*Kama* vol. 1:25). It is known that Rav Shlomo Zalman ruled extremely stringently in this manner, and even *b'shaas hadchak* or *hefsed merubah* (see *Va'aleihu Lo Yibol* vol. 2, Y.D. 5 and 6), yet nonetheless acknowledged that he was aware that the *"olam* is *noheg* to be *meikil."*

19 *Kovetz Teshuvos* (vol. 1:75 and 76).

20 *Shu"t Ohr L'Tzion* (vol. 2, Ch. 20:18, *Biurim* s.v. *v'yeish*).

21 *Shu"t Mishnah Halachos* (vol. 12:34–36). However, he was somewhat more lenient than the other *machmirim*, as he wrote *"devadai lechatchilla ain lishtoso chas v'shalom, v'gam ain lekadesh oh lehavdil alav, aval ain lehachmir bo k'she'avar b'dieved."*

22 On the other hand, see *Shu"t Avnei Nezer* (Y.D. 116:4), who maintains that we are not concerned that future generations might use *Yayin Mevushal* as part of idolatrous practice. He explains that we always exclusively follow the letter of Chazal's *takkanos*, and since at the time of the prohibition they were not *gozer* against *Yayin Mevushal*, it was never considered to have been, nor can be, included and proscribed. According to his understanding, a strong argument can be made that this issue should not make a *halachic* difference.

evaporated wine is recovered through sealed pipes and therefore is not actually noticeably reduced, and the taste ends up being not significantly altered. Moreover, nowadays, with the notable exception of true wine connoisseurs, the majority of wine drinkers cannot distinguish flash pasteurized wine from uncooked wine, neither by appearance nor by taste.[24] These authorities also take the stringent definition of

---

23 Known as HTST (high temperature short time) pasteurization by the trade, flash pasteurization has more potential to produce higher quality *mevushal* wine than the standard vat pasteurization. Scientists discovered that sterilization at high temperatures required far less time that at low temperatures. Vat pasteurization that took thirty minutes at 145°F could now be achieved in a few seconds at 185°F. According to historian Roger Horowitz in his recent book *Kosher USA: How Coke Became Kosher and Other Tales of Modern Food* (pg. 154–155), this technology was first modified and adapted from HTST equipment used for fruit juices, by winemaker Ernest Weir of Hagafen Cellars in California in 1985, and later by the Herzog family of Kedem (Royal) Wine. The result? A better quality *mevushal* wine whose taste was barely changed by the pasteurization process. This innovative flash pasteurizer for wine was even dubbed the *"mevushalatar"* at the time. Knowledge and exact techniques of each company's individual and exclusive pasteurization processes are proprietary and not shared publicly. Consider the testimonial of famed Israeli wine critic Daniel Renov ("A California Cult Winery (And Kosher, Too)"; *Haaretz*, August 23, 2008), that "nearly everyone knows that after a few months in bottle, most *mevushal* wines tend to offer cooked aromas and flavors, and too often remind one more of oxidized fruit compote than of fine wine. No one is quite sure how Hagafen winemaker Ernie Weir does it, but his are among the very few flash pasteurized wines to have escaped this fate, and his wines, frequently earning scores of ninety or above, tend to be rather long-lived. Some may think that shipping kosher wines to Israel is somewhat akin to selling ice to Eskimos, but in this case the Hagafen wines are a most welcome addition to local shelves."

24 As first proven by University of California-Davis graduate student (and current chief vinter of Teperberg winery in Israel) Shlomo "Shiki" Rauchberger's Cabernet Sauvignon *mevushal* (pasteurized) vs. non-*mevushal* taste tests performed in 1992, when a panel of judges could not tell nor taste the difference. Although many non-Jewish wineries did not and do not pasteurize at all, claiming that many can tell the difference in quality even with flash

mevushal into account and therefore maintain that pasteurized wine cannot possibly be deemed *mevushal* unless it is performed at a higher temperature and the wine actually bubbles and boils.[25] Although they do not all make the same arguments, nonetheless, these *Poskim* concur that the general pasteurization process as we know it does not adequately translate into actual *Yayin Mevushal*.

Remarkably, both the *Shemiras Shabbos Kehilchasa* and the *Nishmas Avraham* cite both sides of this dispute, with no *halachic* preference or conclusion.[26]

Other authorities, including the *Minchas Yitzchak*, the *Shevet Halevi*, Rav Moshe Sternbuch, and the *Avnei Yashpei*,[27] maintain a middle ground, albeit each via separate reasoning, that although standard modern-day flash pasteurization (performed at approximately 175–180°F) should not be considered cooking to actually permit consumption of wine touched by a non-Jew due to the issues raised, it nonetheless would be

---

pasteurization, nevertheless, after these taste tests were publicized, kosher pasteurized wine took off as a more upscale option than was previously perceived by the public.

25 For example, the Tzehlemer Rav, Rav Levi Yitzchak Greenwald, (cited in Rav Avraham Blumenkrantz's annual *Kovetz Hilchos Pesach*, e.g., 5766, pg. 784; 5777, pg. 535) was *machmir* for the heat level of pasteurization (but not the process), and maintained that the pasteurization needed to be performed at a higher temperature, at least 190°F—actual *resichah*, to be considered *mevushal*. Kedem wine, which was and is under his and currently his successor's *hashgacha*, ensures that when they state "*mevushal*" on the label, it meets his criteria of *mevushal*, and reaches at least 190°F during the pasteurization process. It is known that Rav Yosef Eliyahu Henkin (*Shu"t Gevuros Eliyahu* vol. 2-Y.D. 41 s.v. b'nogeya) was even more stringent, mandating complete "*bishul*" (presumably a full roiling boil), at a temperature of at least 220°F (104.44°C) to ensure wine reduction during the process.

26 *Shemiras Shabbos Kehilchasa* (vol. 2, Ch. 47:19) and *Nishmas Avraham* (Third edition, vol. 2-Y.D. 123:2).

27 *Shu"t Minchas Yitzchak* (vol. 7:61, 1), *Shu"t Shevet Halevi* (vol. 2:51 and vol. 7:234, 2), *Shu"t Teshuvos V'Hanhagos* (vol. 2:401), and *Shu"t Avnei Yashpei* (vol. 1:150).

considered as such to permit wine touched by a public Sabbath desecrator, as it is only a corollary of the original proscription.[28]

Places to Pasteur

Interestingly, nowadays, in America, where wine is more commonly pasteurized, most kosher wines are considered *mevushal*, generally via pasteurization, unless they specifically state that they are not, while throughout Europe and in Israel the opposite holds true: wines are commonly not considered *mevushal* unless they specifically state on the label that they are. A known exception to the American rule is Kedem wines, which are under the *hashgacha* of both the Tzehlemer Rav and the OU, and make sure that when they state *"Mevushal"* on the label, it meets the criteria of both what the Tzehlemer Rav and Rav Moshe Feinstein consider *mevushal* and reaches at least 190°F during the pasteurization process.

In Israel, a third classification might be printed on the label: *"Mevushal al yedei pistor,"* or *"Mevushal* via pasteurization," which is a easy way of letting the public be aware that depending on which opinion of contemporary *Poskim* he follows, said wine may or may not be drunk after being touched or poured by a non-Jew or public Sabbath desecrator.

---

28   Although Rav Shlomo Zalman Auerbach and other *machmirim* ruled stringently with this as well, on the other hand, *Halichos Shlomo* (*Mo'adim* vol. 2, *Pesach*, footnote 429 s.v. *ulam*) mentions an important qualification to Rav Shlomo Zalman's ruling. He held that regarding those who are not yet Shabbos observant, but are coming closer to *Yiddishkeit* and *Shemiras Torah U'Mitzvos* by attending Yeshivos and programs to learn more about their heritage, that their touch will no longer prohibit wine. On the other hand, Rav Moshe Feinstein is quoted (*Mesores Moshe* vol. 1, pg. 239:69) as expressing that although this is an interesting rationale, nevertheless, it is preferable to ensure that any wine these students might touch be *mevushal*. Rav Yaakov Kamenetsky (*Emes L'Yaakov on Tur and Shulchan Aruch*, pg. 312, footnote 56) also maintained in regard to those not yet Shabbos observant, that we should nonetheless be more stringent regarding wine they touch than pertaining to other potential *halachic* issues that may arise.

This puts the decision of how, when, and in what company to serve the wine squarely in the consumer's hands.

Not Out to Pasteur!

Although there is no clear-cut contemporary consensus to this "touchy" subject, I can imagine that if he were alive today, Dr. Pasteur would be amazed to find that his works are still being discussed and debated, not just in the halls of science and academia, but even in the hallowed halls of *Batei Midrashim* all over the world. *Hafoch Bah V'Hafoch Bah d'Kulah Bah!*[29]

---

29 *Avos* (Ch. 5, Mishnah 22). The author wishes to thank author and educator Rabbi Yair Hoffman, as his related article was the impetus for my interest and research on this topic.

Chapter 30

Chalav Yisrael: A Halachic History

"Cream" of the Crop?

IN HIS *HALACHIC* DISCUSSION OF the topic of *Chalav Yisrael*, the famed *Aruch Hashulchan* uncharacteristically relates a story, or more accurately, a sordid tale (paraphrased below):[1]

> A certain wealthy merchant, when away on business in the big city, would frequent a small store near his inn. Every morning for their "cuppa joe," he and the other guests would purchase some milk from this non-Jewish store owner, as it was well known for its creaminess. One day, the merchant decided to ask the storekeeper to reveal the secret of why his ultra-rich milk was so much tastier than the competition's. His answer stunned the merchant. Apparently, the storekeeper stocked up on fresh cow brains from the local non-kosher slaughterhouse and would cook them in milk, blending them together to make his famous "creamy milk." Realizing that he had been unwittingly drinking *treif* and *Bassar B'chalav* all this time,[2] the crestfallen merchant

---

1   *Aruch Hashulchan* (Y.D. 115:6).

2   Although the *halachic* consensus is that if one eats the Biblically prohibited *Bassar Neveilah* in milk there is no additional transgression of *Bassar B'chalav* [and not like the minority opinion of the *Bach* (Y.D. 87:1) and *Drishah* (ad loc. 2), who maintain that one is liable for an additional *Rabbinic* transgression of *Bassar B'chalav*], nonetheless, there is a large debate regarding

> undertook a regimen of teshuva, including pledging to always listen to the wise words of the Chachamim, especially regarding purchasing and drinking milk from a non-Jew.

The *Aruch Hashulchan* concludes his passage explaining that this warning message on the pitfalls of drinking unsupervised milk is especially important in America, as he heard that many non-Jews drink pig milk there, as it is so plentiful, implying that there is grave concern that they may have no qualms admixing such milk into their cows' milk sold commercially. Although this statement was written in the 1890s, and such a *metzius* seems unlikely in America of 2020 (due to strict government regulations prohibiting adulterating cows' milk with any other milk, along with contemporary societal norms that pigs' milk is deemed an anathema), nonetheless, there is an important lesson to be learned. But first some background is necessary.

Chalav Akum

As was discussed in previous chapters, the Mishnah in *Bechoros* teaches that "*hayotzei min hatamei, tamei*—anything that comes out from (or its basis is from) a non-kosher animal is deemed non-kosher." Hence, as the Gemara elucidates, milk from a non-kosher species shares a similar non-kosher status with its source animal. The flip side of this rule is "*v'hayotzei min hatahor, tahor*—anything that comes out of (or is derived from) a kosher animal is deemed kosher."[3] This is why milk that comes from a kosher species is also *halachically* considered kosher. However, there is an important qualification to this rule.

---

whether it still is considered *assur b'hana'ah*, and thus practically, if one may derive any benefit from this forbidden mixture or not. See the *Rambam's Peirush HaMishnayos* (*Kerisos* Ch. 3, end Mishnah 3, "*Nekudah Nifla'ah*"), *Dagul Mervavah* (Y.D. 87:1), *Pri Megadim* (*Pesicha* to *Bassar B'chalav* s.v. *ul'inyan chalav b'cheilev* and Y.D. 92 S.D. 10), *Shu"t Chasam Sofer* (Y.D. 92), *Kreisi U'Pleisi* (87:6), *Pischei Teshuva* (ad loc. 6), and *Yad Yehuda* (ad loc. *Peirush Hakatzer* 7).

3   Mishnah (*Bechoros* 5b) and following Gemara (ad loc. 6b). This is the general rule. As explained by the Gemara and commentaries, there are specific notable exceptions, such as honey and human's milk, due to varying reasons.

The Mishnah in *Avodah Zarah* instructs that certain food items produced by non-Jews are prohibited to be eaten or drunk, *even* if there seems to be no inherent kashrus issues with said products. The first item listed is milk that a non-Jew milked without a Jew watching the milking process. The Gemara explains that there is a *"chashash irbuv,"* or that we are concerned that the non-Jew will (quite possibly, imperceptibly) mix in some non-kosher milk into the kosher milk. This means that there is a full Rabbinic proscription against drinking *"Chalav Akum,* or Non-Jews' Milk,"[4] even though said milk presumably came from a kosher animal. The *Rambam* writes that if someone transgresses this and drinks *Chalav Akum*, he is liable to *Makkas Mardus*, lashes for rebelling against Rabbinic Law.[5]

---

4 Mishnah (*Avodah Zarah* 35b): "*V'Eilu devarim shel Ovdei Kochavim assurin, v'ein assurin issur hana'ah: chalav shechalvo Oveid Kochavim v'ein Yisrael ro'ahu....*" See also *Rif* (ad loc. 14b in his pagination), citing the *Yerushalmi*. It is important to note that as this is an actual *Gezeira*, *bittul* or nullification is not applicable. As Rav Shlomo Kluger (*Shu"t Tuv Taam V'Daas, Mahadura Telita'ei*, vol. 2:3) wrote to "*Maskil Echad*," we cannot simply rely that of the millions of gallons of milk produced worldwide the amount of possible non-kosher milk mixed in is negligible, as since *Chalav Akum* is a *Gezeiras Chazal*, it is immutable, and not dependent on actual volume of non-kosher milk potentially admixed. Hence, nullification in this case is not a valid avenue of leniency. In other words, while a Torah law, and even Rabbinic law, does have *bittul*, an actual *Gezeira* does not.

5 *Rambam* (*Hilchos Maachalos Assuros* Ch. 3:13 and 15). In a similar vein, the *Issur V'Hetter* (45: end 8) writes quite strongly, that anyone who drinks *Chalav Akum* is "*over al Lo Titosh Toras Imecha u'poretz hageder she'asu Rabboseinu hakadmonim, u'meikil b'maamaram shekol divreihem gachalei aish.*" The *Darchei Teshuva* (115: end 6 s.v. *v'ayen*) cites the *Radbaz* (*Shu"t* vol. 4:145; interestingly, this *teshuva* originally appeared in a stand-alone edition of *Shu"t HaRadbaz* originally printed in Livorno [Leghorn], Italy; which quite intriguingly, on its title page, boldly gives thanks to the local ruler, Ferdinando de' Medici, the Grand Duke of Tuscany, and only later was incorporated as vol. 4 in the series) and later, Rav Chaim Palaji (*Ruach Chaim* 129b) that unless in *sakana* (grave danger), one must spend all of his money to obtain permitted milk, in order not to transgress drinking the prohibited *Chalav Akum*.

The importance of being vigilant not to imbibe milk that is considered non-kosher, even if only on a Rabbinic level, cannot be overstated. Indeed, the *Rema* emphasizes that *Chalav Akum* causes "*Timtum Halev*" (clogs the heart on a spiritual level) and infuses negative character traits.[6] In fact, the *Pri Chodosh*, and later the *Aruch Hashulchan*, lament the low spiritual state of much of the youth in their days, and attribute it to their partaking of *Devarim Ha'Assurim M'Derabbanan*.[7]

Chalav Yisrael: Observant Jews

However, the rule of avoiding non-Jewish milk does not dictate that we are all required to rush out and become dairy farmers. Indeed, on the other hand, the next Mishnah continues that if a Jew simply observed the milk production of the non-Jew, then it is permitted for consumption.[8] The Gemara following cites a Beraisa that explains that if the Jew sat "*b'tzad edro*," at the side of the pen, or corral of the non-Jew at the time of the non-Jew's milking, then "we are not concerned."

The Gemara clarifies that although the rationale behind this *Gezeira* is that the non-Jew might mix in non-kosher milk, nonetheless, in this specific case, the Jew's presence on location, where he could technically

---

6   *Rema* (Y.D. 81:7), citing the *Ran* (*Avodah Zarah* 7b in the *Rif's* pagination) quoting the *Rashba*. Although they are at first referring to a baby nursing from a non-Jewess (a different type of "*Chalav Akum*," you might say), also citing the Midrash (*Shemos Rabbah*, 1:25) regarding Moshe Rabbeinu refusing to nurse from a non-Jewish wet-nurse (see also *Biur HaGr"a* ad loc. 31), which is not technically *halachically assur* in times of need, nonetheless, several Acharonim (ad loc.) draw a direct parallel to *Chalav Akum* and other food products that are Rabbinically prohibited, adding that partaking of them in one's youth may even cause detrimental effects in old age. Thanks are due to my father, renowned kashrus expert Rabbi Manish Spitz, for pointing out several of these sources.

7   *Pri Chodosh* (Y.D. 81:26) and *Aruch Hashulchan* (ad loc. 34). The *Aruch Hashulchan* writes that this is "*baduk u'menusah*," and concludes with an exhortation that "*yizharu me'od me'od*" with this *inyan*.

8   *Avodah Zarah* (39b): "*V'Eilu muttarin b'achilah: chalav shechalvo Oveid Kochavim v'Yisrael ro'ahu....*"

stand up or walk in at any time, creates a *"Mirsas,"* or a fear of getting caught adulterating the milk, which keeps the non-Jew in line, and thus ensures that the milk the Jew is drinking is one hundred percent fully kosher milk.[9] This is referred to as the permitted *Chalav Yisrael*, milk that a Jew either supervised the milking process, or was at least present at the time of the non-Jew's milking.

Rishonims' Rationales

Many Rishonim, including the *Mordechai*, *SMa"K*, and *Shaarei Dura*,[10] understand that the Gemara is informing us that unless the Jew is actually situated on location at the time of the non-Jew's milking, the milk has the status of *Chalav Akum*, and is prohibited, *even* if there are not any non-kosher animals present for the non-Jew to readily mix in their milk. In other words, they consider this to be a *Gezeiras Chazal*, hence always in effect. Therefore, in order to permit milk for consumption, a Jew must *always* be present when a non-Jew milks.

---

9 In the words of kashrus expert Rav Mordechai Kuber, "*Halachically*, we may presume that the non-Jew will not go to the trouble of adulterating the milk when aware that he might be observed. Chazal made the *Gezeira* against drinking *Chalav Akum* even though the concern of admixture is generally not that high, and when the equation becomes more stilted, there is no more *Gezeira*." As the *Tur* (Y.D. 115: end 1) notes, this *halacha* is only relevant if the non-Jew is aware that milk from a non-kosher animal is prohibited to Jews. Otherwise there would be no *Mirsas*, as an oblivious non-Jew would have no qualms adding in some tasty pig or camel milk.

10 *Mordechai* (*Avodah Zarah* 39b, 826 s.v. *ee d'leika*), *SMa"K* (end 223 s.v. *shelo le'echol chalav*), and *Shaarei Dura* (82). The *Shaarei Dura* also cites this understanding as *Rashi's shittah* (*Teshuvos Rashi* 152 and *Sefer Ha'Orah* vol. 2:83). *Tosafos* (*Avodah Zarah* 35a s.v. *lefi* and *Piskei Tosafos* ad loc. 84) implies this way as well. This also seems to be the understanding of the *Rashba* (*Shu"t* vol. 1: end 248), as he states that all of the Rabbinically prohibited food items produced by non-Jews listed by the Mishnah in *Avodah Zarah* (ad loc.), "*Gezeiros kavuos hein*, are set proscriptions," implying that they are always in effect, even when we are not actually concerned with the original reason for Chazal's *Gezeira*.

Most authorities follow this interpretation,[11] and in fact it is the *only* one cited by the *Beis Yosef* and *Rema* in their explanations of the *halacha*,[12] and they seem to have practically ruled this way when codifying the *halacha* in the *Shulchan Aruch*.[13] The *Rema* adds that *lechatchilla*, the Jew should be present at the start of the milking process, and optimally to inspect the milking pail to ensure that it does not contain any non-kosher milk (or its residue from previous milkings).[14]

On the other hand, there are several Rishonim, including the *Tashbetz*, his son, the *Rashbash*, the *Kaftor Vaferach*, and *Radbaz*, who understand the Gemara quite differently.[15] They take the Gemara's statement "that

---

11   See *Levush* (Y.D. 115:1), *Bach* (ad loc. s.v. *umashekasav*), *Prishah* (ad loc. 2), *Shach* (ad loc. 5 and 8), *Taz* (ad loc. 2 and 4), *Biur HaGr"a* (ad loc. 4), and *Ba'er Heitiv* (ad loc. 5 and 8).

12   *Beis Yosef* (Y.D. 115:1 s.v. *u'mashekasav v'hu*) and *Toras HaChatas* (81:6).

13   *Shulchan Aruch* (Y.D. 115:1) and *Toras HaChatas* (81:7). The *Tur* (ad loc.) also implies this way. This is because they all write that if the Jew is sitting outside (the barn) and knows that there are no non-kosher animals present, then it is permitted to drink that milk, even if he did not see the non-Jew's actual milking process (due to the *Mirsas*). This implies that the fact that there are no non-kosher animals present is not enough of a distinction by itself to permit the milk, without the Jew being present as well.

14   *Rema* (ad loc. 1). See also *Toras HaChatas* (ibid.) citing precedents from Rabbeinu Peretz in his *Hagahos* on the *SMa"K* (ibid. 1) and *Issur V'Hetter* (*Ha'aruch* 45:1). On the nuances between them, see *Darchei Moshe* (Y.D. 115:1), *Shach* (ibid. 8), *Minchas Yaakov* (ad loc. 12), and *Toras Ha'Asham* (ad loc. s.v. *mihu*). Several Rishonim, including the *Shaarei Dura* (end 81) and *SMa"G* (*Mitzvos Lo Sa'aseh* 132 s.v. *sha'alu*), relate a tale about a Yid whose daughter used to supervise the non-Jews' milking. One day, she arrived late and only viewed the tail-end of the milking. Although Rabbeinu Tam was upset about this occurrence, he nevertheless ultimately ruled it was permitted *b'dieved*, due to the *Mirsas* involved, as the non-Jews knew she would show up any minute. On the other hand, the Maharam M'Rothenburg (*Shu"t*, Prague edition 215) cites this story and *psak* differently, that she never arrived on time to properly observe the milking, and as such Rabbeinu Tam *prohibited* the milk as there was no *Mirsas*.

15   *Shu"t Tashbetz* (vol. 3:143; where he refers to this as a *safek Deoraysa*; and vol.

if there aren't any non-kosher animals in the non-Jew's pen, *Peshita*—it is obvious"—at face value, meaning that there is no inherent problem in such an eventuality. They maintain that as the prohibition of *Chalav Akum* was instituted to safeguard *Yidden* from unwittingly drinking non-kosher milk, if there aren't any non-kosher animals at hand for the

---

4, *Chut Hameshulash*: 32 from his grandson, who cites an additional *teshuva* of his grandfather's in which he explains that if there aren't any non-kosher animals present, it removes the *safek Deoraysa*, and thus the milk is permitted; cited briefly by the *Pischei Teshuva* Y.D. 115:3, and more at length by the *Yad Efraim* ad loc. 1), *Shu"t HaRashbash* (554), *Kaftor Vaferach* (Ch. 5, pg. 13 s.v. *v'chein mah*; citing the *Sefer Ha'Ittim* who was *meikil* but also quotes a "*yeish machmirin;*" he concludes "*v'al hakol ani omer baal nefesh shomer piv, im sheha'emes chaviv*"), and *Shu"t HaRadbaz* (vol. 4:75; old print 1147; see however the *Chida's Shu"t Yosef Ometz* 64, who seems to understand the *Radbaz* differently from a different *Teshuva* regarding yogurt—*Shu"t HaRadbaz*, vol. 5:2291). Additionally, the *Rabbanim* of Rome whom with the *Shaarei Dura* (ibid.) disagreed, held this way, as did the "*Yeish Mochichim*" whom the *Mordechai* (ibid.) disputed. The *Knesses Hagedolah* (Y.D. 115, *Hagahos* on the *Beis Yosef* 3) cites a similar *shittah* from the Maharash Algazi, and the *Orchos Chaim* (vol. 2, pg. 330) cites a *Tosefta* (which no longer seems extant in our editions) stating this outright. Rav Elazar Kahanow, Rosh Yeshivas Torah Vodaath (*Shu"t Zichron Betzalel* vol. 3, 94:25, 26, 27, and 31, and in the posthumously published *Pekudas Elazar*, Ch. "*Ofanei Hetter Chalav Akum*," 25, 26, 27, and 31) infers that this was also the opinion of the *Rivash* (*Shu"t* 394) and *Meiri* (*Avodah Zarah* 35b), similar to the *Tashbetz* (ibid.), that once the *chashash* of *Chalav Tamei* is removed, a non-Jew's milk should be permitted. Moreover, he points out, *Rashi*, in *Sefer HaPardes Hagadol* (255), explicitly rules this way as well, seemingly quite contradictory to what he wrote in *Teshuvos Rashi* and *Sefer Ha'Orah* (ibid.; as cited in a previous footnote). This discrepancy in *Rashi's shittah* was also noted by Rav Yaakov Breisch (*Shu"t Chelkas Yaakov*, original edition vol. 2: end 38; reformatted edition, vol. 2, Y.D. end 35 s.v. *hinei*), who wryly commented "*v'eini yode'a ad kamah anu yecholim lismoch al sifrei hakadmonim v'al hagirsa'os shebihem, hayotzim mei'chodosh al yedei melumadim.*" Interestingly, in a similar vein, several differing Acharonim cite the somewhat ambiguous related comments of the *Rambam* (ibid.) and/or *Issur V'Hetter* (45:7 and 47:6) as proof to either side of this *machlokes* as well.

non-Jew to have obtained and mixed in its milk, then such milk is also indeed permitted.

Piskei Peiros Ginosar

Although as mentioned previously, most authorities follow the first understanding of the Gemara, nonetheless, Rav Chizkiya Di Silva, the renowned *Pri Chodosh*, in the late 1600s, explicitly ruled in line with the latter approach and even extended the *hetter*, declaring that in Amsterdam in his day, the *minhag* was to drink non-Jews' milk even without specific Jewish supervision, as there were not any non-kosher animals to be found in the whole *city*.[16] He further expanded the *hetter* to include a situation where non-kosher milk is available, but much more expensive. In such a case, where the non-Jew would have to suffer a financial loss to adulterate his pure milk from a kosher animal with the milk of a non-kosher one, the *Pri Chodosh* rules that it is permitted to drink such milk. The *Pri Toar*, better known as the *Ohr Hachaim Hakadosh*, concurred with the *Pri Chodosh* on both counts, and likewise ruled leniently when it was unmistakably evident that there were not any non-kosher animals extant in the locale or if non-kosher milk was much more expensive.[17]

Several other *Poskim* followed this precedent,[18] and it became the de facto *minhag* in several cities, including Algiers,[19] but as the Chida asserted after delivering a lengthy defense of the *Pri Chodosh's* position,[20] that *"l'inyan halacha,"* unless a particular city has a specific custom to

---

16 *Pri Chodosh* (Y.D. 115:6 s.v. *haklal*).

17 *Pri Toar* (115:1 s.v. *ul'inyan* and 2). The *Kaftor Vaferach* (ibid.) actually made this same point several centuries earlier. On the other hand, the *Zivchei Tzedek* (115:13 and 14) cites this rationale, as well as the opposing *shittah*, and concludes that if the non-kosher milk is really four times the price of the kosher milk, as was the case of the *Pri Toar*, and *"koftzim alav lokchim"* [meaning there are those pressing the non-Jew to sell them non-kosher milk at that exorbitant price (perhaps as a "cure" for some ailment), so he would stand to lose a "king's ransom" if he would adulterate the kosher milk with it], only then may one be lenient.

be lenient, "*yeish lehachmir vaday*, they should certainly be stringent, as was the ruling throughout the Turkish Empire and Eretz Yisrael."[21]

---

18 Other authorities who ruled this way include the *Beis Lechem Yehuda* (Y.D. 115:1), *Yashiv Moshe* (*Shu"t* vol. 1:209), and the *Zechor L'Avraham* (Avigdor; *Shu"t* Y.D. 4; although citing both sides of the *machlokes* and writing that reliance on this leniency should depend on "*Minhag HaMakom*," he nonetheless concludes that certainly in Kushta, where there were no camels or pigs, "*min hadin muttar*"), the controversial *Shu"t Besamim Rosh* (36), and the *Mizmor L'Dovid* (Pardo; Y.D. 115 s.v. *sham daf* 248; although he at first questions the *Pri Chodosh's hetter*, as there is still a possibility that there might be non-kosher milk residue in the milking bucket, nonetheless, he ultimately concludes that as a mixture of milk from kosher and non-kosher animals is disgusting to them (as per the *Rashba* in *Toras Habayis Ha'aruch*, beg. *Shaar* 6), the non-Jews would certainly rinse out the milking bucket in between such milkings, and therefore "*yeish makom lehakel*"). [On the other hand, several *Poskim* reject the "disgusting theory," as even if so, the non-Jews could still sell it to unsuspecting Jews in order to make a profit. See *Shu"t Zera Avraham* (Y.D. 25, pg. 103a), *Shu"t Chokekei Lev* (Y.D. 32), *Zivchei Tzedek* (115:15) and *Kaf Hachaim* (ad loc. 16[b]).] The *Ikrei HaDa"T* (*Ikrei Dinim* 12:3) cites a long list of *Poskim* who followed the *Pri Chodosh's* precedent, concluding with the *Matteh Asher* (pg. 103: *anaf* 2 and 3) that this milk is *muttar*, especially as "*rov binyan v'rov minyan sevirei leih d'muttar, ach mishum chassidus...tov lehachmir.*"

19 See *Shu"t Tashbetz* (vol. 4, *Chut Hameshulash* ibid.), *Shu"t HaRashbash* (ibid.), and *Shu"t Beis Yehuda* (*Minhagei Kehillah Hakedosha Ar'jil* pg. 114b).

20 *Shiyurei Bracha* (Y.D. 115:1). Interestingly, he takes great umbrage at the audacity of a small *sefer* titled *Teshuvos HaGaonim U'Maaseh Rav* (pg. 15) that argued on the *Pri Chodosh*, pejoratively referring to him as a "tourist in Amsterdam who was unaware of the city's true *minhagim*." The Chida issued a sharp rejoinder, wondering how anyone could write thus about the "*Ma'or Hagadol*" who lived in Amsterdam for over fifteen years, concluding that the *Pri Chodosh's* testimony was certainly accurate, "*upashut.*"

21 The *Zivchei Tzedek* (115:12) cites both sides of the debate, concluding that the correct *psak* follows the Chida. Hence, only in a place where the actual set *minhag* was to be lenient may one be lenient; otherwise, one may not rely on the *Pri Chodosh's hetter*. He concludes that the *minhag* in Baghdad was indeed to be *machmir*, and that "no one would dare open their mouths to argue" and drink milk from a non-Jew, even if there were no non-kosher animals present.

Milking Mandate

On the other hand, the *Pri Chodosh's psak* was roundly and outright rejected by the majority of Acharonim, chief among them the *Beis Meir*,[22] *Teshuva Mei'ahava*,[23] *Chochmas Adam*,[24] *Chasam Sofer*,[25] *Tzemach Tzedek*,[26] and *Aruch Hashulchan*.[27] Aside from questioning how the *Pri*

The *Kaf Hachaim* (ad loc. 15) writes similarly, citing *Poskim* on both sides of the debate, and concluding with the Chida's assessment, adding *"u'mashma aval b'makom shekvar nahagu lehakel ain limchos."*

22 *Beis Meir* (Y.D. 115 s.v. *Pri Chodosh seif kattan* 6). He questions how the *Pri Chodosh* could have disregarded the majority of the Rishonim's understanding of the Gemara's teaching, as well as how it was possible to ascertain that an entire city would not have any non-kosher animals. On the other hand, as mentioned by the *Tashbetz's* grandson in *Chut Hameshulash* (ibid.), as well as the *Kaftor Vaferach* (ibid.), this dispensation was not referring to dogs, horses, or donkeys which no one actually milked, as their milk was considered disgusting, but rather camels. The *Chasam Sofer* (ibid.) also seemed to understand this as their opinion.

23 *Shu"t Teshuva Mei'ahava* (vol. 1, *Pesicha*, pg. 5a-b, end s.v. *v'chelki*). He avers that anyone who relies on the *Pri Chodosh* in this case is making two mistakes: 1. Not realizing that *"D'batlah daato negged kol HaPoskim."* 2. That his *hetter* was contingent upon the absence of non-kosher animals throughout an entire city, which is an impossibility, as every city contains horses, donkeys, and camels, *"ain mispar, v'omdim l'chalivah."*

24 *Chochmas Adam* (67:1, in the parenthesis). He declared *"v'keyvan shekol Gedolei Rishonim v'Acharonim ain echad sheyazkir hetter zeh, shema minah d'kulam kiblu aleihem k'hayeish machmirin...v'assur l'shanos."* On the other hand, as noted by Rav Elazar Kahanow (*Shu"t Zichron Betzalel* vol. 3, 94:45; and *Pekudas Elazar*, ibid. 45), this statement that *every* Rishon and Acharon agreed does not seem entirely accurate, as many Rishonim, several even listed by the *Chochmas Adam* himself, were indeed lenient, as detailed previously.

25 *Shu"t Chasam Sofer* (Y.D. 107; cited in *Pischei Teshuva* Y.D. 115:3).

26 *Shu"t Tzemach Tzedek* (*Hachadoshos*; Y.D. 74–76). He asserts that the *"minhag pashut bechol medinos eilu lehachmir...afilu yavo Eliyahu ain shomin lo levattalah."*

27 *Aruch Hashulchan* (Y.D. 115:5). He emphasizes the importance of keeping this *Gezeira* even when there is no non-kosher milk in the vicinity, bemoaning the fact that many unfortunately do not, stressing that *"Chamurim Divrei Sofrim*

Chodosh could have disregarded the mainstream understanding of the Gemara's teaching, they were also highly skeptical that it was possible to ascertain that an entire city did not contain any non-kosher animals. Moreover, Chazal did not necessarily specify their entire reasoning for any particular edict; sometimes even when the evident reason is not relevant there are other concealed reasons which may still apply. As such, they argued, the *takkanah* of *Chalav Yisrael* should still apply in full force, even when non-kosher animals are nowhere to be found.

Indeed, the great *Chasam Sofer*, in a far-reaching *teshuva* dated Tu B'Av 5594/1834, emphatically declared that for all Ashkenazim, the proscription of *Chalav Akum* is binding akin to a Biblical vow (*Karov L'Neder Deoraysa*), since "our forefathers accepted upon themselves to uphold it, even when there are no non-kosher animals extant."[28] He added, echoing Shlomo *HaMelech's* wise words in *Koheles* regarding a

---

M'Divrei Torah, v'Talmid Chacham she'asah kein, avono yissa," and concluding *"v'keyvan shnifsak l'issur b'Tur v'Shulchan Aruch v'kol Gedolei Acharonim, mi yachol l'ha'iz panav u'limalei taavas nafsho, v'shomer nafsho yirchak es atzmo mizeh."*

28 *Shu"t Chasam Sofer* (ibid.). He points out that all of the Rishonim whom the *Pri Chodosh* bases his lenient *psak* on were Sefardim, and when the *Pri Chodosh* was in Amsterdam he was part of the Sefardic Portuguese community. He cites proof from the many Ashkenazic Rishonim and Acharonim who understood the Gemara's classification of *Chalav Akum* to apply fully, even when non-kosher milk was not extant, as well as those who seemed to hold that *Chalav Tamei* was a *"Davar Sheb'minyan"* and thus much more stringent and even non-nullifiable [e.g., see *Shu"t Mahari M'Bruna* (78), and *Tiferes Yisrael* (*Kilayim* Ch. 9, Mishnah 2, *Yachin* 11); however, as detailed by the *Sdei Chemed* (*Asifas Dinim, Maareches Chalav Nochri* 1) this is not the *shittah* of *Rov Minyan U'Binyan* of Rishonim]. The *Chasam Sofer* concludes that however, one may make a *Zimun* with those who relied on the *Pri Chodosh's psak*, as he based it on his Sefardic *Mesoras HaPsak*, as well as due to the importance of *Shalom*. [Parenthetically, the *Pesach Dvir* (vol. 2, 196:2 s.v. *aval*) was so *machmir* with this *inyan*, he took the *Chasam Sofer* to task for allowing a *Zimun* with those who were *meikil*. Ultimately, he agreed *lemaaseh*, but only after finding other *sniffim lehakel*.]

"*poretz geder*," that one who transgresses this prohibition deserves to be bitten by a snake.[29]

This was the accepted common consensus, certainly since then,[30] that only true *Chalav Yisrael*, with a Jew on hand to supervise the milking process, was permitted to be drunk, period.[31]

"Chalav Companies"

However, starting in 1950 (5710), the *Gadol Hador*, Rav Moshe Feinstein, issued a groundbreaking *psak* in several *teshuvos* that forever changed the realm of *Chalav Yisrael* and its observance.[32] Rav Moshe noted that in his day in America, the federal government kept tight control on milk production to ensure that what was being sold as cow's milk was truly exclusively that.[33] To this end, the government assessed substantial fines on dairy companies caught adulterating their milk with that of other animals, and at times even closing them down.

As such, he made several *halachic* points:

- As the milk companies were compelled to follow the government's dictates at the cost of their own livelihoods, this strictly enforced "government supervision" was akin to the *Mirsas*, fear of getting caught adulterating the milk, that the Gemara teaches was perfectly acceptable to allow milk from a non-Jew to be drunk. Meaning, the fear of the consequences levied by the government for adulterating the milk is similar to that of the Jew sitting nearby the milking though not supervising the actual process.[34]
- We find precedent that "*yadea berurah*—knowing," is considered "*re'iyah*—seeing." As we know that due to the government's close monitoring of the dairy industry, the milk companies cannot mix in non-kosher milk without fear of reprisal, it is akin to an "*anan sahadi*, virtual witness," that they are not doing so, and sufficient proof that the kosher milk is indeed unadulterated.

---

29 *Koheles* (Ch. 10:8).

30   Other *Poskim* who ruled this way over the years, rejecting the *Pri Chodosh's psak*, include the *Me'il Shmuel* (*Shu"t* 12), *Minchas Yaakov* (*Soles L'Mincha* 81:6; "*v'anu nohagin lehachmir*"), *Maharshdam* (*Shu"t* Y.D. 52), *Matteh Yonason* (Y.D. 115:1), *Dvar Shmuel* (Abuhav; *Shu"t* 273), *Beis Dovid* (*Avodah Zarah* Ch. 2, *Mishnah* 6 s.v. *chalav*; he adds that the great Maharash Ayleon argued with the *Pri Chodosh* extensively at the time of his *psak*), *Noda B'Yehuda* (*Shu"t*, *Kama* Y.D. 36; he even refers to those who drink black coffee in mugs previously used with *Chalav Akum*, as "*Kalei Daas*"; on this brief *teshuva* see also *Shu"t Maharash Engel* vol. 7, *Kuntress Sheim M'Shmuel*, pg. 195), *Pele Yo'etz* (*Os Dalet*, *Divrei Chachamim*), *Tiferes Yisrael* (*Beis Kilayim*, Ch. 4 *Kilai Begadim*, 113; printed at the end of the original editions of *Tiferes Yisrael* on *Zeraim* vol. 1), *Pesach Dvir* (vol. 2, 196:2 s.v. *aval*; adding that the *minhag* in Izmir was always to be *machmir*), *Me'orei Ohr* (Wirmush; vol. 7, *Chullin daf* 105, end s.v. *chala bar chamra*), *Ksav Sofer* (*Shu"t* vol. 1, O.C. 22; who in a related topic does not even mention the *Pri Chodosh* as a *tzad lehakel*), *Noheg K'tzon Yosef* (*Inyan Issurim* 1, pg. 48; he adds that anecdotally, when he traveled to Amsterdam to print his *sefer* of *Peirushim* on *Selichos* (titled *Sefer Kaneh*) in 1712/5472 [a mere twenty years after *Sefer Pri Chodosh* was first published], the local *Av Beis Din* at the time was the famed Rav Tzvi Ashkenazi [whose landmark *Shu"t Chacham Tzvi* was first published that same year], and on his watch, the community was extremely *makpid* on ensuring that all milk was indeed *Chalav Yisrael*), Rav Shlomo Kluger (*Shu"t Tuv Taam V'Daas*, *Mahadura Telita'ei*, vol. 2:3), *Avnei Nezer* (*Shu"t* vol. 2, Y.D. 102:6), Rav Chaim Palaji (*Shu"t Chokekei Lev* Y.D. 30 and 31, and *Ruach Chaim* Y.D. 115, pg. 129a; although extensively citing both sides of the dispute, he ultimately concludes that it is prohibited; indeed in the latter *sefer* he uses extremely strong terms condemning those who are lenient), *Mincha Belulah* (Y.D. 115:1), *Sdei Chemed* (vol. 3, *Maareches Ches*, 131; briefly, and vol. 8, *Asifas Dinim*, *Maareches Chalav Nochri* 1; at length), *Melamed L'Ho'eel* (*Shu"t* vol. 2, Y.D. 33; citing that only "*kalei hadaas*" would be lenient, as *Haskamas HaPoskim* was against the *Pri Chodosh*), *Me'orei Ohr* (Schorr; *Kitzur Shulchan Aruch on Yoreh Deah*, 115:1), *Ba'er Chaim Mordechai* (*Shu"t* vol. 3:22), *Levushei Mordechai* (*Shu"t* Y.D. *Tinyana* 57; although he does give dispensation for children and *cholim*, based on the *Pri Chodosh* et al.), *Ohel Yehoshua* (*Shu"t* vol. 2:25; stating that "*shamaati b'birur*" that even chemical testing cannot discern less than two percent adulteration, hence there can be no true *Mirsas* simply relying that non-Jews will not admix, even with government supervision; adding a story of a *Talmid Chacham* in Berlin who witnessed a servant proudly adding horse's milk as a milk preservative),

Minchas Elazar (*Shu"t* vol. 4:25; who writes strongly that even if there is no other milk available there is absolutely no *hetter* to rely upon), and *Daas Sofer* (*Shu"t* vol. 1, Y.D. 36; concluding that certainly and especially those of Hungarian descent were beholden to follow his great-grandfather, the *Chasam Sofer's psak*). The *Divrei Chaim* of Sanz, citing his father-in-law, the *Baruch Taam*, is also widely quoted [see *Kuntress Darchei Chaim* (vol. 2:50) and *Shu"t Divrei Yatziv* (O.C. vol. 1:27, in the postscript)] as being extremely vigilant with this prohibition, stating a *mesorah* tracing back to Moshe Rabbeinu! The *Kitzur Shulchan Aruch* (38:13) also implies to be stringent, as he does not mention the *hetter* of no non-kosher animals present on the standard *halacha*, but rather simply if a Jew did not supervise a non-Jew's milking, "*assur*." The *Yad Yehuda* (99, *Peirush Ha'aruch* 22 s.v. *uvaguf hadin*) implies this way as well, as he refers to the prohibition of *Chalav Akum* as an "*Issur Derabbanan* that has an *Ikar Deoraysa*," due to the fact the reason for the prohibition is the concern that non-kosher milk, which is *assur M'Deoraysa*, will get mixed in with the kosher milk. Indeed, after citing a long list of *meikilim*, the *Darchei Teshuva* (ad loc. 6) cites an even longer list of *machmirim*, who reject the *Pri Chodosh's psak* out of hand.

31   Indeed, the *Pri Chodosh's* own brother-in-law, Rav Moshe Chagiz (*Shu"t Shtei Halechem* end 42 s.v. *kol*), while citing many honorifics about his esteemed brother-in-law: "*Rav v'atzum, baki, u'mumcheh l'rabbim, v'charif*," nevertheless continues, "*agav churfeih b'aizeh devarim b'chiburo lo dak, v'hichmir b'makom shehaya lo lehakel, v'heikel b'makom shehaya lo lehachmir, v'tafas daas yachid b'inyan chalvo shechalav goy v'ein Yisrael ra'ahu, **sheheikel bo neged Minhag Yisrael**.*" Parenthetically, the *Pri Chodosh's* "*charifkeit*" (sharpness) was a point of contention for many, especially the way he seemed to relate to the *psakim* of the *Shulchan Aruch*, and due to it, his *sefer* was actually banned throughout Egypt [see *Shu"t Ginas Veradim* (Y.D. 3:3)]. But as noted by the Chida in his *Sheim Hagedolim* (vol. 1, *erech Ches*, 3: *Moreinu Harav Rav Chizkiya Di Silva*), that after he was *niftar*, quite ironically, the *Pri Chodosh's* noted *talmid*, the Maharash Algazi, was elected Chief Rabbi of Mitzrayim, and served in that capacity for forty-five years, always following the *psakim* of his *Rebbi*, the *Pri Chodosh*. The Chida concludes that by his time (1770s), "all of the *Chachmei Yisrael* thirstily drink his [the *Pri Chodosh's*] words."

32   *Shu"t Igros Moshe* (Y.D. vol. 1:46 s.v. *u'mashekasav*, 47, 48, and 49). The bulk of these *teshuvos* are from 1954. Decades later, Rav Moshe revisited the topic and wrote several additional related *teshuvos* as well: *Shu"t Igros Moshe*

- Since the *takkanah* did not specifically require that a Jew watch the actual milking but rather to verify to the point of certainty that the milk has no non-kosher admixture, government regulation should be tantamount to this type of supervision.

Rav Moshe referred to this milk as "*Chalav Companies*," which later became collectively known as "*Chalav Stam*." Although not quite "*Chalav Yisrael*," as no Jews actually supervised the process, nevertheless, he averred that it was certainly not considered the prohibited *Chalav Akum*, but rather was fully permitted for kosher consumption. Rav Moshe added that many *Bnei Torah* and *Rabbanim* were drinking the "*Chalav Companies*," and *chas v'shalom* one should claim that they were acting contrary to *halacha*. He concluded that a "*baal nefesh*" (scrupulous individual) should be stringent, and that he himself personally was

---

(Y.D. vol. 2:35; Y.D. vol. 3:16 and 17; Y.D. vol. 4:5), and one to Rav Avraham Weinfeld, the *Lev Avraham*, which although dated 5716/1956, was first published in Rav Binyomin Forst's *Pischei Halacha* on *Hilchos Kashrus* (pg. 107) in 1984. As noted by Rav Doniel Neustadt in his *The Monthly Halachah Discussion* (pg. 150, footnote 136), "For unspecified reasons, this responsum was not published in *Igros Moshe*."

33   During Rav Moshe's lifetime, it seems that the Food and Drug Administration of the Department of Health and Human Services (FDA), aside from on-site inspectors at dairy plants, would apparently also take milk samples to test for specific fat contents and ascertain irregularities germane to adulteration with milk from different animals. For a handy chart comparing the fat content of the milk of various kosher and *treif* animals, all in easily readable German, see *Shu"t Melamed L'Ho'eel* (vol. 2, Y.D. 36; in the newer editions, the chart is translated into Hebrew).

34   It was neither Rav Moshe nor the *Chazon Ish* who first cited the rationale that government supervision creates a *Mirsas*. Such reasoning was used decades earlier in *Shu"t Matteh Yosef* (vol. 2:15), *Shu"t Melamed L'Ho'eel* (ibid.), and *Shu"t Ohel Yosef* (Y.D. 15:3; written by Rav Yosef Eliyahu Fried at the turn of the twentieth century in New York regarding milk for a *choleh* when there was no *Chalav Yisrael* available). Yet, they each utilized this principle as a *snif* to improve a specific *b'dieved* situation, rather than Rav Moshe's far-reaching application of the concept.

machmir as well,[35] but reiterated that it is perfectly acceptable for one to be lenient, especially in places where *Chalav Yisrael* was not readily available.[36] [37] [38]

---

35 *Shu"t Igros Moshe* (Y.D. vol. 1: end 47). See also *Kuntress Yad Dodi* (Y.D. Kashrus, Question 13), where his son Rav Dovid Feinstein, was recently quoted as stating that anyone who thought Rav Moshe drank *Chalav Stam* himself is mistaken. Rav Menashe Klein attested to this as well in the end of his first *teshuva* on topic (*Shu"t Mishnah Halachos* vol. 4: end 103 s.v. *u'va'emes*; adding that in his opinion, the main point of Rav Moshe's *teshuva* was simply to defend the masses who were already drinking it). In later *teshuvos* [e.g., *Shu"t Igros Moshe* (Y.D. vol. 2:35)], Rav Moshe advised *Bnei Torah* to be *makpid* as well, and ruled that schools and Yeshivos should make sure to only serve their students *Chalav Yisrael*, even if the student body was not *makpid* at home. He contends that part of proper *chinuch* is to show children the importance of following a stricter standard, even when *halacha* does not necessarily require one. Even so, later on (*Shu"t Igros Moshe* Y.D. vol. 3:16 s.v. *v'zeh*), Rav Moshe categorized being *makpid* not to drink *Chalav Stam* as a "*chumrah*," adding "*rak min haraui lehachmir l'baalei nefesh.*"

36 It goes without saying that Rav Moshe's *hetter* was meant for the USA, as there exists a legitimate fear of government inspection. However, in countries where there is no concern for government inspection or potential repercussions, it is quite obvious that there is no *Chalav Stam* hetter to rely upon. As pointed out by Rav Efraim Greenblatt (*Shu"t Rivevos Efraim* vol. 8:11, 1), there is no *Mirsas* in Mexico, as the standard way of life there involves "*shochad b'mamon*," bribery (including to government officials). Hence, there does not seem to be a *Chalav Stam* dispensation available south of the border.

37 As noted by Rabbi Yair Hoffman in his related article ("The Milk *Machlokes*," *Ami Magazine* Jan. 18, 2012/23 Teves 5772), Rav Moshe was not actually the first to rule leniently regarding *Chalav Stam* in America. That honor goes to Rav Dovid Leibowitz, Rosh Yeshivas Chofetz Chaim, in the 1930s, when he realized that the *Chalav Yisrael* milk producers of his day were unscrupulously watering down the milk in order to increase profits. To help rectify the untenable situation, he ruled that under such circumstances, drinking the local commercially produced milk would be permitted. [See Mishnah in *Kerisos* (8a) for a possible precedent for a similar ruling, when Rabbi Shimon ben Gamliel issued a non-accurate *drasha* in order to bring down the over-inflated prices

Several other *Gedolei Hador*, including the *Chazon Ish*, Steipler Gaon (their *shittah* will be discussed at length further in the chapter),[39] and Rav Yosef Eliyahu Henkin,[40] wrote similar assessments regarding "*Pikuach Memshalah*," or "Government Supervision" on the dairy companies, contending that it was sufficient to allow milk to be drunk. Other *Gedolim*, including Rav Yaakov Kamenetsky,[41] and later, Rav Ovadiah Yosef,[42] held that although preferable not to rely upon this dispensation, nevertheless *me'ikar din* it is correct and one may indeed be lenient in a pinch.

---

of *Kinei Yoldos* a hundred-fold. Thanks are due to Rav Mordechai Kuber for pointing out this important reference.]

38 It should be noted that although there are those who theorized [see for example *Shu"t Zichron Betzalel* (vol. 3, 94:63; and *Pekudas Elazar*, ibid. 63)] that Rav Moshe's *hetter* should also apply to purchasing milk from private farms, since if they are caught adulterating the milk, the large dairy companies who would consequently be fined would no longer purchase from them, nevertheless, Rav Moshe himself did not apply his *hetter* to such a case but rather ruled that there is no *Chalav Stam* leniency for milk coming from small private farms.

39 *Chazon Ish* (Y.D. 41:4 s.v. *v'amnam* and on *Maseches Avodah Zarah* 4:4). See also his brother-in-law, the Steipler Gaon's *Kraina D'Igresa* (vol. 2:123 s.v. *b'dvar hachalav*) and *Orchos Rabbeinu* (new edition; vol. 4, pg. 31–33:8, 10, and 12). However, they themselves were *makpid* to only drink milk from a private *frum* farm that was milked exclusively for them and supervised the entire time. From that milk they would have butter and cheese made. There is some debate as the parameters of the *Chazon Ish's* dispensation. This will be addressed later in the chapter.

40 *Teshuvos Ibra* (Ch. 3:43) and in the posthumously published *Shu"t Gevuros Eliyahu* (vol. 2-Y.D. 29); *teshuva* dated 5718/1958.

41 *Emes L'Yaakov* (on *Tur* and *Shulchan Aruch*, Y.D. 115:1 and footnote 45); *teshuva* dated 5712/1952. See also *Shu"t Shulchan Halevi* (Ch. 22:5, 1 s.v. *v'zechorani*).

42 Cited in *Yalkut Yosef* (*Issur V'Hetter* vol. 2, pg. 93, s.v. *gam Maran*). Rav Ovadiah himself, when visiting America, was still *makpid* to only drink *Chalav Yisrael*. His son, current Chief Rabbi of Israel Rav Yitzchak Yosef rules similarly (*Yalkut Yosef* ibid. 81:11 and *Kitzur Shulchan Aruch*, Y.D. 81:12).

Got Kosher Milk?

However, opposition was not long in coming. Many *Rabbanim*, mostly Chassidic and/or European, vehemently, vigorously, and vociferously objected to Rav Moshe's *hetter* in the strongest of terms. They maintained that as a *Gezeiras Chazal*, there is no basis for such dispensation, questioning the strength of government supervision on a practical level,[43] and asserting that the tenets of *Chalav Yisrael* must be kept as they have been for hundreds of years previously.

These *Rabbanim* included the Tzehlemer Rav,[44] Krasna Rav,[45] Rav Yonason Steif,[46] Rav Yisrael Veltz (Welcz),[47] Rav Eliezer Silver,[48] the

---

43 They maintain that practically, for a large dairy company, whose profits are in the millions, a small fine levied, even running into thousands of dollars, would not be sufficient to make them change their ways. Additionally, inspectors can also be cheated or bribed. However, it must be noted, that in his third full *teshuva* dedicated to this topic (*Shu"t Igros Moshe* Y.D. vol. 1:49), Rav Moshe does address this issue, defends his position, and maintains that in his opinion, it still creates the necessary *Mirsas*, even if *"lo mirsasi kuli hai."*

44 See *Shu"t Migdalos Merkachim* (Y.D. 28) and his brief *teshuva* printed in *Shu"t Lev Avraham* (74). It is well-known how much the Tzehlemer Rav tirelessly worked to upgrade the standards of kashrus in post-World War II America, especially in ensuring that *Chalav Yisrael* milk would be obtainable, including helping set up and give *hashgacha* to the famous J & J *Chalav Yisrael* dairy company. He wrote (*Shu"t Migdalos Merkachim* Y.D. 27) that in his opinion, it is worthwhile for a *mashgiach* to live in solitude on a farm, with no access to a *minyan* or other Jewish amenities, strictly to ensure the availability of *Chalav Yisrael* milk, even referring to it as *"ain lecha Mitzva gedolah m'zu."*

45 He wrote an entire *Kuntress* dedicated to this topic titled *Kavannas Halev*. See also his later *Shu"t Kavannas Halev* (Y.D. 9) and brief *teshuva* printed in *Shu"t Lev Avraham* (74).

46 See *Shu"t Mahari Shteif* (34) and brief *teshuva* printed in *Shu"t Lev Avraham* (74). Later known as the Vienner Rav, he was a *Dayan* in pre-World War II Budapest.

47 *Shu"t Divrei Yisrael* (vol. 2, Y.D. 15). He was a *Dayan* in pre-World War II Budapest.

48 An English translation of his *teshuva* was published in *Encyclopedia of Kashruth*

Satmar Rebbe,[49] the *Chelkas Yaakov*,[50] the *Lev Avraham*,[51] the Helmetzer Rebbe,[52] the Shopron Rav,[53] the Strasbourger Rav,[54] the Debreciner Rav,[55] the Sharmash Rav,[56] the *Minchas Yitzchak*,[57] the Lubavitcher Rebbe,[58] Rav Menashe Klein,[59] and Rav Moshe Sternbuch.[60] [61]

---

vol. 1: Jewish Milk in Accordance with Jewish Law (pg. 85–87). It is reported that when Rav Silver, *Rosh Agudas HaRabbanim* of the United States and Canada, would travel across North America by train, he would always make sure to take along a supply of his own *Chalav Yisrael* milk.

49 *Shu"t Divrei Yoel* (vol. 1, Y.D. 50:1 and 51).

50 *Shu"t Chelkas Yaakov* (original edition vol. 2:37 and 38; reformatted edition, vol. 2, Y.D. 34 and 35). He was the *Av Beis Din* of post-World War II Zürich.

51 *Shu"t Lev Avraham* (74).

52 *Taharas Yom Tov* (vol. 7, *Mahadura Tinyana*, pg. 33–49); also printing other *Teshuvos HaPoskim* on topic.

53 His brief *teshuva* was printed in *Shu"t Lev Avraham* (74).

54 *Shu"t Kinyan Torah B'Halacha* (vol. 1:38).

55 *Shu"t Ba'er Moshe* (vol. 4:52).

56 An English translation of his *teshuva* was published in *Encyclopedia of Kashruth vol. 1: Jewish Milk in Accordance with Jewish Law* (pg. 69–73).

57 See *Shu"t Minchas Yitzchak* (vol. 1:138; vol. 2:21; vol. 3:4, 10; and vol. 10:31, 15).

58 *Shaarei Halacha U'Minhag* on *Yoreh Deah* (10, pg. 37–38). He cites that the previous Rebbe, Rav Yosef Yitzchak Schneerson, held that *"Chalav Akum me'oreir sfeikos b'emunah."* An English translation of his original Yiddish *maamar* was published in *Encyclopedia of Kashruth vol. 1: Jewish Milk in Accordance with Jewish Law* (pg. 117–118).

59 *Shu"t Mishnah Halachos* (vol. 4:103). See also *Shu"t Mishnah Halachos* (vol. 9:155) in a related *teshuva* to Rav Shraga Feivel Schneebalg of Manchester (*Shu"t Shraga HaMeir* vol. 3:21, 1) agreeing with his stringent position regarding not feeding children *Chalav Akum*, with neither of them mentioning any sort of *Chalav Stam* dispensation.

60 *Shu"t Teshuvos V'Hanhagos* (vol. 1:441 and 480, and vol. 5:254).

61 Others authorities who wrote to be *machmir* include Rav Chaim Eliyahu Sternberg, Rosh Yeshivas Machzikei HaDas (an English translation of his

Rav Sholom Yehuda Gross, the Holminer Rav, and prolific author of numerous *sefarim*, wrote a book in English entirely dedicated to this topic, titled *Encyclopedia of Kashruth vol. 1: Jewish Milk in Accordance with Jewish Law*,[62] citing dozens of letters and *teshuvos* of *Poskim* through the years, all to stress the importance of exclusively drinking *Chalav Yisrael* to the American kosher consumer.[63] He relates that when he was

teshuva was published in *Encyclopedia of Kashruth vol. 1: Jewish Milk in Accordance with Jewish Law* pg. 87–92), Rav Henoch Padwa, *Av Beis Din* of London (*Shu"t Cheishev Ha'Eifod* vol. 2:72 s.v. *acharei*; he does not mention a *Chalav Stam* dispensation, but rather relying *b'shaas hadchak* on the fact that in the case he was discussing, the milking was performed electronically via automated systems), the *She'arim Metzuyanim B'Halacha* (38:12; who concludes that "*rov Acharonim svirei lei d'ain chiluk, d'gam meshum geder v'takkanah yeish bazeh*"), the *Beis Avi* (vol. 1, Y.D. 72, postscript; and vol. 4, E.H. 180:21; his *shittah* is discussed at length in following footnotes), Rav Shlomo Schneider (of Monticello; *Shu"t Divrei Shlomo* vol. 4:471), the *Maadanai Hashulchan* (*Shu"t Maadanei Melachim* 166; as opposed to many of the other *Rabbanim* listed above, he does not condemn the *meikilim*, but rather cites Rav Moshe and even implies that the *ikar din* followed him, nonetheless concludes "*nireh she'ain lismoch al zeh l'vad*"), Rav Shmuel *Halevi* Wosner (*Shu"t Shevet Halevi* vol. 5:59 s.v. *amnam* and vol. 6:110 s.v. *uv'Pri Chodosh* and *u'kvar*, concluding "*halacha b'zeh k'haChasam Sofer*"), and Rav Pinchas Meyers of The Hague (*Shu"t Nachlas Pinchas* vol. 1:1, 88; briefly, and *Shu"t Divrei Pinchas* vol. 1:50; at length).

62 Rav Gross also wrote a companion volume in English titled *Encyclopedia of Kashruth vol. 2: Cholov Akkum and Infant Formulas*, stressing the importance of not feeding infants formula produced from *Chalav Akum*. Written in 1980, featuring a strongly worded *teshuva* from the Debreciner Rav, the "spiritually contaminating formula" he was most concerned with (in his own words, "rant and rave so much about") was Similac. I am sure that nowadays, almost forty years later, Rav Gross appreciates the fact that there currently exists an array of brands of *Chalav Yisrael*-based infant formula, including J & J/Sunrise and Materna, and even the very same Similac is now widely available in America (as well as in Israel) in a *Mehadrin* version, produced with *Chalav Yisrael* milk under the *hashgacha* of the *Badatz Eidah Hachareidis*.

63 Interestingly enough, the very first *haskamah* printed in his *sefer* is from none other than Rav Moshe Feinstein!

stationed for a time in a small town in Pennsylvania, he traveled around to the local dairy farms to attempt to purchase *Chalav Yisrael* milk, and unwittingly stumbled upon a startling discovery: the local farmers admitted that pigs are a dire necessity in milk production because they oftentimes had to add in pigs' milk, which helps preserve the cows' milk and increase its palatable effect.[64] Rav Gross recounts that he received this alarming report from all of the small dairy farms throughout the state, and adjacent ones as well, noting that they served a large portion of New York City and its suburbs. He writes that he could not sleep at night after this shocking discovery, and made it his mission to publicize this information, adding that it is self-evident that this is the main reason he published the book despite the staggering expenses involved.

The *Chazon Ish's Shittah*

Interestingly, several of the aforementioned *Rabbanim* seemed to take issue with "the American Rabbi" who had the temerity to suggest such a dispensation[65] (obviously those who did not realize the greatness

---

64 The *Chelkas Yaakov* (ibid. s.v. *v'sipeir*) relates a similar story from Rav Moshe Soloveitchik of Switzerland, that he met a girl bringing milk down the mountains on a hot day, and when he questioned how it doesn't spoil, she revealed that she adds in donkey milk, which extends its shelf-life. She apparently had no qualms about doing this, even though the milk industry in Switzerland was regulated via government supervision.

65 As noted earlier in this chapter, many of the *Rabbanim* opposed to Rav Moshe's *hetter* were European or recent immigrants from Europe and/or Chassidic. This is an important detail. There is a fascinating and quite telling postscript in a related *teshuva* from Rav Yitzchak Isaac Liebes, originally from Poland, and later settled in the Bronx, New York. The bulk of the *teshuva* (*Shu"t Beis Avi* vol. 1, Y.D. 72), written in Poland, is regarding finding a *hetter* for consuming commercial powdered milk sent to Europe from America, to aid in the recovery of weak, sick people recuperating from typhus. Yet, in his postscript, added years later when he was already settled in the Bronx, Rav Liebes notes that throughout much of Europe *"nispashtu Minhagei Gedolei Ashkenaz, u'mechuyavim anachnu leileich bechol davar al pi kabbalasam, k'mo shekasav HaChasam Sofer,"* that as the *Chasam Sofer* declared, they always followed the *mesorah* of the *Gedolei Ashkenaz*. Yet, America, is *"shonah hadavar legamri,"* an

of Rav Moshe), but had a harder time coming to terms with the *Chazon Ish's* utilization of a similar *hetter*.⁶⁶ Various rationales were suggested to justify his *shittah*, including that he meant his *hetter* exclusively on a theoretical level.⁶⁷ Although there are differences between his understanding and Rav Moshe's,⁶⁸ and although he may not have meant

---

entirely different "kettle of fish," as many *Gedolei Rabbanim*, originally from Lita (Lithuania), permitted milk based on government supervision. As the *Chasam Sofer's* ruling was based mostly on Ashkenazic "*Kabbalas Avoseinu*," in contrast, the first Jewish community in America was of Sefardic (Portuguese) origin [the same community that the *Pri Chodosh* was a part of in Amsterdam]. Over the years, as different communities expanded and grew throughout the United States, there was an amalgamation of sorts of *minhagim*. Hence, he points out, it is not a contradiction nor an anathema that *Rabbanim* of Lithuanian extraction in America would rule somewhat more leniently regarding finding a possible dispensation for commercially produced milk than would those in or from Europe, for whom the *Chasam Sofer's* ruling on topic was the final word for generations. Rav Liebes concludes that he personally does not agree with the *Chalav Stam hetter*, as "*anachnu m'bnei b'neihem shel Gedolei Ashkenaz, Minhag Avoseinu B'Yadeinu*," yet asserts that it certainly may be added as a *snif* to allow powdered milk, even according to those *makpid* on *Chemas Akum* (both discussed at length later in this chapter).

66 *Chazon Ish* (Y.D. 41:4 s.v. *v'amnam* and on *Maseches Avodah Zarah* 4:4). In the next paragraph (s.v. *u'mashekasav HaChasam Sofer*), the *Chazon Ish* raises several difficulties with the *Chasam Sofer's* proofs to his position, calling them "*devarim temuhim me'od*," and seemingly concludes akin to the *Pri Chodosh's shittah*. Rav Moshe Feinstein (*Shu"t Igros Moshe* Y.D. vol. 1:49 s.v. *v'ayen* and *ulefi zeh*) as well, raised several concerns with the *Chasam Sofer's* proofs, especially how he cites *Rashi's shittah*.

67 For example, see *Shu"t Divrei Yisrael* (ibid.), *Shu"t Kinyan Torah B'Halacha* (ibid.), *Shu"t Chelkas Yaakov* (ibid. 38 or 35, depending on edition), and *Shu"t Teshuvos V'Hanhagos* (ibid.). This author has heard several other theories floated over the years. See next footnote.

68 There are different theories opined to explain the words of the *Chazon Ish*, including that this specific passage in his *sefer* was only meant for *lomdus* purposes as he uses the terminology '*yeish makom lomar*'; or that since he seems to favor the *shittah* of the *Pri Chodosh* over the *Chasam Sofer*, his writing is irrelevant because "we *pasken* like the *Chasam Sofer*." [Several *Poskim*, including

it as a sweeping general dispensation, nonetheless, history has since proven that the *Chazon Ish* did practically stand by his *hetter* of *Pikuach Memshalah* on milk, and as attested to by his brother-in-law, the Steipler Gaon, ruling in specific cases when *Chalav Yisrael* was unavailable, that *bochurim* who needed it should drink it.[69]

---

the *Daas Sofer* (*Shu"t* vol. 1, Y.D. 36 and 37) and *Chelkas Yaakov* (*Shu"t* ibid.) (see also *Likutei He'aros V'Sefer HaYovel L'Maran HaChasam Sofer* from 5750; end 29) do attempt to resolve the *Chazon Ish's* difficulties with the *Chasam Sofer's* position. Rav Shmuel *Halevi* Wosner writes that the *Chazon Ish's kushyos* notwithstanding, the *halacha* still follows the *Chasam Sofer*. See next footnote.] An additional theory was that the *Chazon Ish* was only referring to powdered milk (which will soon be addressed in this chapter at length). Several of the aforementioned *Poskim* wrote that when they spoke or wrote to the *Chazon Ish* or Steipler Gaon, they maintained that the *hetter* was only meant for children, nursing mothers, or *b'shaas hadchak mamash*, whereas Rav Moshe wrote that his *hetter* was for all. On the other hand, and as opposed to the *Chazon Ish's* preference for the *Pri Chodosh's shittah*, Rav Moshe wrote that this *hetter* was also in effect according to the *shittah* of the *Chasam Sofer*, but also concluded that nonetheless "*baal nefesh yachmir*," a qualification the *Chazon Ish* did not actually write in his treatment of the subject. This author finds it interesting that in his original *teshuvos* on topic (*Shu"t Teshuvos V'Hanhagos* vol. 1), Rav Moshe Sternbuch differentiated between the *shittos* of Rav Moshe and the *Chazon Ish*. Yet, in his later *teshuvos* (ibid. vol. 5), Rav Sternbuch places both of their *shittos* together, as ruling leniently regarding milk produced under *Pikuach Memshalah*, akin to the *Yalkut Yosef's* (*Kitzur Shulchan Aruch*, Y.D. 81:12) presentation of their *shittos*.

69   See the Steipler Gaon's *Kraina D'Igresa* (vol. 2:123 s.v. *b'dvar hachalav*), *Orchos Rabbeinu* (new edition; vol. 4, pg. 31–33:8, 10, and 12), and *Shu"t Shevet Halevi* (vol. 5:59 s.v. *amnam* and vol. 6:110 s.v. *uv'Pri Chodosh* and *u'kvar*). Rav Wosner writes that he personally argued with the *Chazon Ish* about this topic, asserting that in his opinion, "*hagam d'harayos ainam machriyos, mikol makom halacha b'zeh k'haChasam Sofer*." It is important to note that it turns out that the stories with the *Chazon Ish* ruling leniently for *bochurim* with powdered milk were "*maasim shehayu*" due to the government rationing in place in the years of austerity following the founding of the modern State of Israel, but was no means due to the fact that it was powdered milk. Aside from the *Chazon Ish's* (Y.D. 41:4 s.v. *avkas chalav*) sharply worded contention

Indeed, both Rav Yosef Eliyahu Henkin and Rav Yaakov Kamenetsky cited precedent from the *Chazon Ish* in their respective *teshuvos* on topic, while Rav Wosner wrote that when he was younger, he personally argued with the *Chazon Ish* about his lenient ruling.[70]

Only Kosher Cheese, Please

It is imperative to be aware that any possible dispensation for *Chalav Stam* does not include cheese. This is because aside from the proscription of *Chalav Akum*, there is a completely separate *Gezeira* prohibiting eating *Gevinas Akum*. As an earlier Mishnah in *Avodah Zarah* teaches, cheese produced by non-Jews, or *Gevinas Akum*, is prohibited for consumption, even though technically speaking cheese can only be produced utilizing milk from a kosher animal.[71] Although the subsequent Gemara offers several different potential reasons for this proscription, the conclusion of the Gaonim is that even in a scenario where none of them seem to apply, this *Gezeira* is nonetheless equally and unequivocally binding. This rule is duly codified as *halacha lemaaseh*.[72] [73] [74] Practically, many authorities maintain that in order for cheese, even

---

that there is no *halachic* difference between regular milk and powdered milk, in the recently published *Genazim V'Shu"t Chazon Ish* (vol. 1, pg. 383–392), the original (lenient) *teshuva* of Rav Tzvi Pesach Frank regarding powdered milk was reprinted along with the *Chazon Ish's* actual *he'aros* on it (also recently reprinted in *Shu"t V'Chiddushim Chazon Ish* 148), leaving no room for ambiguity in the *Chazon Ish's* stringent position. This will be discussed further on in the chapter.

70 *Teshuvos Ibra* (Ch. 3:43), *Shu"t Gevuros Eliyahu* (vol. 2-Y.D. 29), *Emes L'Yaakov* (on *Tur* and *Shulchan Aruch*, Y.D. 115:1), and *Shu"t Shevet Halevi* (vol. 5:59 s.v. *amnam* and vol. 6:110 s.v. *u'kvar*).

71 Mishnah (*Avodah Zarah* 29b) and Gemara (ad loc. 35b). According to the *Yerushalmi* (*Shabbos* Ch. 1, *Halacha* 4; 12a in the Friedman edition and 9b in the *Me'orei Ohr* edition), the prohibition of *Gevinas Akum* is one of the eighteen *Gezeiros* that Chazal established on that famous, fateful day when Beis Shamai overruled Beis Hillel. On the other hand, it is noticeably absent from the *Talmud Bavli's* list of these *Gezeiros* (see *Shabbos* 17b and *Avodah Zarah* 36a-b).

72 *Avodah Zarah* (ad loc. 34b-35b). These reasons include: that non-Jews may produce the cheese using non-kosher enzyme catalysts, for example, setting it using non-kosher calf stomach lining (rennet) to curdle the milk and turn it into cheese ("*Maamid B'Or Keiva Neveilah*"); non-kosher milk getting stuck in its nooks, crannies, and crevices ("*gumos*"); they may shine or grease it with lard; it might contain *Yayin Nesech*-based vinegar, or "*Sraf Orlah*," or unknowingly, snake venom in its make-up. [The snake venom issue is a *chashash* of *Giluy*; meaning as the milk is uncovered and left unsupervised during cheese production, a snake may have poisoned it, surreptitiously injecting it with his venom. For more on *Giluy*, see *Mishnayos Terumos* (Ch. 8, Mishnah 4), Gemara *Avodah Zarah* (30a-b), and *Chullin* (9b-10a).] Whatever the reason, the *halacha* states that even if none of them technically apply, the *Gezeira* is binding and immutable. Many add that *Gevinas Akum* is considered a *Davar Sheb'minyan*. See *Rif* (*Avodah Zarah* 13a in his pagination), *Rambam* (*Hilchos Maachalos Assuros* Ch. 3:14 and 15), *SMa"G* (*Mitzvos Lo Sa'aseh* 132, pg. 45b), *SMa"K* (end 223, s.v. *shelo le'echol Gevinos shel Akum*), Rabbeinu Peretz (*Hagahos* ad loc. 1), *Ramban* (*Chiddushim* to *Avodah Zarah* 35a s.v. *v'Rabbeinu*), *Rashba* (*Toras Habayis*, *Bayis* 3 *Shaar* 6, pg. 90b), *Ohr Zarua* (*Avodah Zarah* 186 and 197), *Shaarei Dura* (end 81), *Tur* (Y.D. 115:2), *Hagahos Ashri* (*Avodah Zarah* Ch. 2:26 and 40 s.v. *maaseh* and *Yisrael*), *Radbaz* (*Shu"t* vol. 5:2291), *Toras HaChatas* (81:1), *Shulchan Aruch* (Y.D. 115:2), *Rema* (ad loc. 2), *Levush* (ad loc. 2), *Shach* (ad loc. 19), *Taz* (ad loc. 10), *Biur HaGr"a* (ad loc. 13), *Chochmas Adam* (67:7), *Kitzur Shulchan Aruch* (38:14), and *Aruch Hashulchan* (Y.D. 115:16). The *halacha* does not follow the minority opinion of Rabbeinu Tam (see *Tosafos* in *Avodah Zarah* 35a s.v. *lefi*; also cited at length in *Shaarei Dura* beg. 78) and Maharam M'Rothenburg (*Shu"t*, Prague edition 216), who seem to permit leniency in a scenario where all of the reasons given by the Gemara are ruled out and the non-Jew made the cheese for his own personal (non-commercial) use. [See *Beis Yosef* (Y.D. 115:2 s.v. *v'da*). It is important to note that several Rishonim who cite Rabbeinu Tam's *hetter* and related *maaseh shehaya* where he ruled leniently, including the Maharam M'Rothenburg, *Ohr Zarua*, and *Hagahos Ashri*, conclude that this dispensation was only relevant *b'dieved* or *b'makom hefsed merubah*; certainly not *lechatchilla*.] However, based on Rabbeinu Tam's *hetter*, the *Rema* (ibid.) adds a slight qualification, that if there is a community that can ascertain that it has a long standing tradition "*mei'kadmonim*" permitting it, they may continue consuming such cheese. In his *Toras HaChatas* (ibid.), the *Rema* mentions two locales that in his time (mid-1500s) were lenient regarding consuming local non-Jewish cheese that was produced

utilizing plant-based enzymes—Narvona/Narbonne (in Southern France; as first mentioned by *Tosafos* ad loc. s.v. *chada*) and Italy; however, regarding all others he rules unequivocally: *"assur lifrotz geder."* On the other hand, the *Beis Yosef* (ad loc. end 2) rejects any dispensation for the *"Bnei Italia,"* arguing that the *hetter* they espoused did not actively fit Rabbeinu Tam's *shittah*, as it seems he was only concerned with *Giluy*, which does not seem to be the practical reason for the proscription (see *Yoreh Deah* 116:1). However, the *Bach* (ad loc. s.v. *kasav Beis Yosef*) defends their *minhag*, maintaining that it is indeed based on several other Rishonim's understanding of Rabbeinu Tam's position. The *Rashal* (*Amudei Shlomo* on the *SMa"G* ibid. and in his commentary on the *Shaarei Dura* ibid. 2) maintains that Rabbeinu Tam only intended to permit cheeses in specific situations which comprised a combination of mitigating factors: both a manifest *Mirsas*, in addition to a milieu where *Giluy* was not a concern. In such a case, since cheese can only be made from kosher milk, Rabbeinu Tam allowed leniency. See also Rav Shlomo Zalman Auerbach's explanation of the dynamics of this *shittah* in his *Shu"t Minchas Shlomo* (*Tinyana* 100:1). However, it is important to note that although in today's world of advanced food technology much of the rennet used is artificial, nonetheless Chazal's reasons still apply. In a related article titled "How Do We Make Kosher Cheese?" (accessible at: http://rabbikaganoff.com/how-do-we-make-kosher-cheese/), Rav Yirmiyohu Kaganoff shares a curiosity: "While researching information for this article, I discovered a forty-year-old article describing how one manufactures cheddar cheese (by the way, the origin of the name is that this cheese was originally developed in Cheddar, a village in England), which reports that the cheese was made by adding calf stomach rennet to the milk so that it curds, heating the curd, going through several processes to carefully remove "every scrap" of whey, pressing the curd and then plunging it into hot water briefly to form a thin rind, and then greasing the rind with *pure lard* to keep the shape and thicken the rind. Thus, three of the reasons mentioned by the *Gemara* to prohibit cheese were very much applicable to this cheese—the use of non-kosher rennet; the use of lard; and the remaining uncurded milk in the cheese which could contain adulterated milk, were it not processed so carefully to remove it all." Indeed, the OU notes (in several online articles) that in mainland Europe, the prevalent practice in cheesemaking is still to use animal rennet. Furthermore, lipase, an enzyme added to some cheeses to hasten the breakdown of fat and endow a more powerful flavor, is almost always animal-derived (lipase is extracted from the tongues of domesticated animals). For example, Romano cheese is usually treated with goat, lamb, or kid lipase, and blue cheese often contains calf lipase. On the other hand, in the United States and in England, microbial (artificial) rennet is typically utilized, and many varieties of Portuguese hard cheese are coagulated with thistle flower. Nevertheless, as Chazal banned all cheese made without onsite rabbinical supervison irrespective of the presence of animal rennet, even if the rennet is derived from kosher sources such as microbial or thistleflower rennet, that non-Jewish cheese still remains forbidden as *Gevinas Akum*. See next footnote.

73   In the words of the *Shaarei Dura* (end 81) "*V'horu HaGaonim shehagevinos shel Nochrim assurim, bein shehaamidu osan b'dvar hetter u'vain shehaamidu osan b'dvar issur, shene'essru kulan. V'afilu b'makom d'leika taam issur, gazrinan atu makom sheyeish bo taam issur.*" The *Rambam* (*Hilchos Maachalos Assuros* Ch. 3:14; see also *Kessef Mishneh* ad loc.) wrote similarly, as did the *Ritzba* (cited in *Shiltei Hagiborim* on the *Mordechai* ibid. *Haghah*), and *Ramban* (ibid.), and is duly codified as halacha by the *Tur* and *Shulchan Aruch* (Y.D. 115:2; see also *Beis Yosef* ad loc.). See also *Drishah* (ad loc. 3), *Prishah* (ad loc. 8), *Biur HaGr"a* (ad loc. 13), and *Chochmas Adam* (53:38). Interestingly, neither the Mishnah nor Gemara attempted to find a loophole or dispensation given specific circumstances to allow *Gevinas Akum*, even though cheese can only be produced using milk of a kosher animal (indeed, the *Tanna* Rabbi Yehoshua evaded explaining why Chazal were *gozer* on *Gevinas Akum*; later revealed by the Gemara that Chazal did not want people theorizing and rationalizing what the proper motivation for the proscription was and attempting to overturn it). Thus, as cheese should seemingly have a built-in *hetter* as it ostensibly is manufactured from kosher sources, but instead, quite conversely, Chazal were *gozer* against consuming it [due to whichever various reason offered by the Gemara, or alternatively attributable to all of them, as the majority of non-Jewish cheese would be found problematic on account of at least one of the potential issues raised], perhaps shows that they intended for this proscription to be all-encompassing. In other words, it seems that as opposed to the *din* of *Chalav Akum*, wherein the parameters of Chazal's intent regarding their *Gezeira* was debated by Rishonim, thus potentially allowing room for possible dispensation in specific cases where the reason for the *Gezeira* is not applicable, on the other hand, regarding *Gevinas Akum*, aside from the *Daas Yachid* of Rabbeinu Tam (and possibly the Maharam M'Rothenburg), the other Rishonim understood from the Gemara, as well as the Gaonim, that Chazal established its strictures with no avenue for leniency. Hence, *lemaaseh*, *Gevinas Akum* is categorically *assur*, period.

when commercially produced, to be rendered kosher, it must be owned or manufactured by a Jew, meaning he must actually take an active part in the cheesemaking procedure, i.e., personally adding in the rennet.[75]

---

74 However, there is some *halachic* debate regarding a case where a Jew supervised the cheesemaking process but did not witness the actual milking, whether such cheese is *muttar b'dieved* or only *b'hefsed merubah*, or even outright *assur*. See *Rema* (Y.D. 115: end 2), *Taz* (ad loc. 11), *Shach* (ad loc. 22), *Chochmas Adam* (67:7), *Aruch Hashulchan* (ad loc. 19), and for a contemporary view at length, *Shu"t Igros Moshe* (Y.D. vol. 3:16; who maintains that nowadays this may even be *muttar lechatchilla* as it may be considered a *"chumrah al chumrah"*). The practical applications, parameters, and nuances of *Gevinas Akum* vis-à-vis *Gevinas Yisrael* are discussed in *Yoreh Deah* (115:2).

75 *Shach* (Y.D. 115:20 and 21), *Taz* (ad loc. 11), *Pri Chodosh* (ad loc. 15; although he qualifies it somewhat), *Ba'er Heitiv* (ad loc. 14), *Beis Meir* (*Chiddushim* ad loc.; although he cites the *mashmaos* of the *Rashba* who seems to be *meikil* and concludes *tzarich iyun*), *Imrei Baruch* (*Hagahos* ad loc.), *Chochmas Adam* (67:7; although he does also cite the dissenting opinion in parenthesis), and *Kitzur Shulchan Aruch* (38:14). The *Shach* explains one of the reasons for his added provision regarding cheese. When discussing *Chalav Akum*, the Mishnah refers to it is *"chalav shechalvo Oveid Kochavim v'ein Yisrael ro'ahu,"* meaning its inherent problem is that a Jew did not supervise the milking, implying that if a Jew did so, it would be permitted. Yet, regarding *Gevinas Akum*, the Mishnah simply prohibits "the cheese of gentiles," with no mention of supervision, implying that Jewish supervision is not a mitigating factor, and would not be sufficient to permit its consumption. The OU reports (in an online article titled "Say Cheese!," accessible at https://oukosher.org/blog/consumer-kosher/say-cheese/) that their standard of *hashgacha* is to insist that their rabbinic field representatives supervise all kosher cheese productions and add the rennet as well. They explain that in modern cheese facilities, rennet is often not added manually. Rather, it is dosed into cheese vats via automated rennet feeders. In such cases, the rabbinic field representatives activate the rennet feeders for each vat of cheese produced. Indeed, the policy of most major reputable kashrus organizations is to require this as well. However, they qualify that cheese produced in Jewish-owned plants is automatically considered *Gevinas Yisrael*, thereby alleviating the need for full-time rabbinic supervision or involvement.

At the very least, following the dissenting opinion, the process must be under direct Jewish supervision to be considered kosher cheese.[76]

Butter Battle

On the other hand, there is a known exception to the non-Jewish dairy decrees—butter. As butter manufactured by a non-Jew is not mentioned as part of any *Gezeiras Chazal* throughout *Shas*, does not fit any of the possible reasons for non-Jewish cheese's prohibition, and can only be produced utilizing the milk of a kosher animal, non-Jewish butter is essentially permitted to be eaten.[77] Although there was an early

---

[76] Following the more lenient *psak* of the *Rema* (ad loc. 2), *Minchas Yaakov* (81:3; citing proof the *Rambam's Peirush HaMishnayos*, *Avodah Zarah*, Ch. 2, Mishnah 5), *Noda B'Yehuda* (*Shu"t Tinyana* O.C. 37), *Pri Toar* (115: end 7), *Gilyon Maharsha* (ad loc. s.v. *v'hu hadin*), *Aruch Hashulchan* (ad loc. 19), and *Kaf Hachaim* (ad loc. 32), who maintain that this indeed sufficient, even regarding cheesemaking. The *Shulchan Aruch Harav* (O.C. 307:38) and *Mishnah Berurah* (ad loc. 79 and *Shaar Hatziyun* 90) imply this way as well. See also *Ikrei HaDa"T* (*Ikrei Dinim* 12:4) at length. The *Pischei Teshuva* (ad loc. 6) presents both sides of the *machlokes* without a clear ruling. However, Rav Moshe Feinstein states in several places (see *Shu"t Igros Moshe* Y.D. vol. 1:50 and vol. 3:16 s.v. *umitzad*), that the Acharonim clearly ruled like the *Rema*, and ergo, supervising the cheesemaking process is deemed sufficient. It is recorded that during the Israeli days of austerity post-World War II, when faced with a problematic situation regarding imported cheeses produced via powdered rennet, the *Chazon Ish* (*Shu"t V'Chiddushim Chazon Ish* 143–147) requested that the powder be tested for *taaruvos issur*. If the tests proved negative, he would then allow reliance on the *meikil shittah*, as it was considered a *shaas hadchak*. Otherwise, he expressed preference for the more stringent opinion.

[77] See *Rambam* (*Hilchos Maachalos Assuros* Ch. 3:15–16) and main commentaries, *Rashba* (*Toras Habayis* ibid. and *Shu"t* vol. 1:110; who is stringent with all *Chemas Akum*), *Rabbeinu Peretz* (*Hagahos* on the *SMa"K* ibid. end 1; who concludes "*ain bah shum issur*"), *Mordechai* (*Avodah Zarah* Ch. 2:826 s.v. *mipnei*), *Shu"t Maharil* (35; he rules stringently as well), *Shaarei Dura* (78; at length), *Toras HaChatas* (81:1–4), *Tur*, *Bach*, *Beis Yosef*, *Shulchan Aruch*, *Rema*, and *Levush* (Y.D. 115:3) and main commentaries, including the *Shach* (ad loc. 27), *Taz* (ad loc. 12), *Biur HaGr"a* (ad loc. 17), *Chochmas Adam* (67:7), *Kitzur Shulchan Aruch* (38:15), and *Aruch Hashulchan* (Y.D. 115:25–28), on the *ikar*

machlokes regarding its use, nonetheless, as the *Chochmas Adam* noted, the general *minhag* throughout Ashkenaz was traditionally to be lenient with consuming *Chemas Akum*.[78] On the other hand, it is important to

---

machlokes and *psak lemaaseh*. Aside from whether *Chemas Akum* is permitted, there is an additional *machlokes* whether the dispensation applies exclusively to raw butter that a Jew later cooks (*Shittas HaRambam*) or even to butter that was already cooked by a non-Jew as well. The butter bottom line is that basically, the *halacha* follows the lenient *minhag* of *Bnei Bavel* and not *Bnei Eretz Yisrael*, but would also depend on *minhag hamakom* [although the *Pri Chodosh* (ad loc. 21 and 22 is lenient with this as well, stating *"b'rov ha'olam nohagin bah hetter"*; see also *Shu"t Noda B'Yehuda* (*Tinyana* Y.D. 66; who takes a strong contrary position to the *Pri Chodosh*), *Chochmas Adam* (ibid.), *Pischei Teshuva* (Y.D. 115:6), and on a more contemporary note, *Shu"t Levush Mordechai* (22; from Rav Moshe Mordechai Epstein, in a *teshuva* to Rav Yitzchak Isaac *Halevi* Herzog, then Chief Rabbi of Dublin)]. On the other hand, and quite interestingly, *Rashi* (*Avodah Zarah* 35a s.v. *lefi* and 35b s.v. *leika*) seems to hold that the cream that was separated from the milk (*"Nisyuvei D'Chalva,"* which is technically needed in order to make butter) still has a *chashash* of *Gevinas Akum*. Hence, as opposed to the vast majority of *Poskim*, it seems that he might be of the opinion that *Chemas Akum* should be included in the category of the prohibited *Gevinas Akum*. [For more on the topic of the *halachic* status of *Nisyuvei D'Chalva*, see *Tur* and *Shulchan Aruch* (Y.D. 87:8) and *Shach* (Y.D. 81:12–14).] As an interesting counterpoint to the mainstream *psak*, the *Hagahos Maimoniyos* (*Hilchos Maachalos Assuros* Ch. 3:15, *Os Lamed*) citing the *Agur* (*Hilchos Bishul Akum*, 1296), the *Beis Yosef* (115:3 s.v. *v'kasav*) citing the *SMa"G* (*Lo Sa'aseh* 132), and later the Vilna Gaon (*Biur HaGr"a* ad loc. end 17), mention a *girsa* in the *Yerushalmi* (*Shabbos* ibid.) that includes *Chemas Akum* as one of the famous eighteen *Gezeiros Chazal* mentioned earlier. If deemed accurate, the whole butter *hetter* would be moot. However, as the Vilna Gaon (ibid.) concludes *"amnam b'Yerushalmi shelanu ain kasuv v'chemoseihem,"* and practically, the *Poskim* do not take this possible *girsa* into account.

78 *Chochmas Adam* (67:9). Also cited in *Me'orei Ohr* (*Kitzur Shulchan Aruch* on *Yoreh Deah*, 115: end 2). Indeed, the *Pri Chodosh* (ad loc. 21) earlier stated *"v'chein b'rov ha'olam nohagin bah hetter."* More contemporarily, as noted by Rav Yosef Eliyahu Henkin (*Teshuvos Ibra* and *Shu"t Gevuros Eliyahu* ibid.) in his brief *teshuva* on topic, *"v'chemah yoseir kal mei'chalav."* In a related *teshuva*, the *Pri Megadim* (*Shu"t Megidos* 91) permitted Jews to commercially deal and sell *Chemas Nochri*, even if they themselves were *makpid* not to eat it, as it

note that several locales did not accept this *hetter* and exhortations to the masses to beware of *"ziyuf"*, fraudulent versions of "butter" containing non-kosher supplements, abound in the works of the Acharonim.[79] However, as noted in several recent reports by the OU,[80] as well as the OK and EarthKosher,[81] butter has of late been increasingly produced with cream recovered from whey (the milk-based fluid that remains behind after milk coagulates into cheese),[82] rather than exclusively

---

is not considered intrinsically *assur*. [On the topic of the permissibility of selling *Issurei Derabbanan*, see *Tur* and *Shulchan Aruch* (Y.D. 117:6), *Beis Hillel* (Y.D. 84:2), *Darchei Teshuva* (117:60), and *Kaf Hachaim* (ad loc. 77).] This is somewhat similar to the *Rema's* (Y.D. 115: end 1) ruling that *Chemas Nochri* will certainly not *assur keilim*.

79 See *Bach* (Y.D. 115:3 s.v. *u'mashekasav sheharei*; citing the *Tashbetz*), *Pri Toar* (ad loc. 8), Chida (*Shu"t Chaim Sha'al* vol. 1:43; citing the *Radbaz*), *Chochmas Adam* (ibid.), *Ikrei Dinim* (*Ikrei HaDa"T* 12:19; citing testimony from several *Poskim* but concluding that in Florence they were lenient, as camels were not common in Italy), *Zivchei Tzedek* (ad loc. 32 and 33; maintaining that it was indeed an issue, but the local *frum* Baghdadi storekeepers were experts in recognizing "fake butter"), *Kitzur Shulchan Aruch* (38: end 15), *Aruch Hashulchan* (ad loc. 27), *Darchei Teshuva* (ad loc. 20), and *Kaf Hachaim* (ad loc. 41 and 45). On this topic, see also *Shu"t Yabia Omer* (vol. 9, O.C. 85:19) and *Kovetz M'Beis Levi* (on *Yoreh Deah*, pg. 80).

80 See https://oukosher.org/blog/articles/if-you-think-all-butter-is-kosher-youre-whey-out-of-line/, https://oukosher.org/btus/2016/08/18/whey/, https://oukosher.org/blog/consumer-kosher/spread-word-not-butters-created-equal-kosher/, and most recently, the Shavuos 5778 edition of the OU's *Daf HaKashrus* ("The Kashrus of Butter: Much More Than Meets the Eye"). Thanks are due to Rav Yisroel Reisman, Rosh Yeshivas Torah Vodaath, for pointing out the latter source.

81 See http://www.ok.org/kosherspirit/winter-2012/consumer-questions-4/, as well as Rav Zushe Yosef Blech's enlightening article, accessible at: http://certified.earthkosher.com/kosher-certification-butter/.

82 Aside from the kashrus issues inherent in whey production, there is also a contemporary *machlokes* whether or not whey might be considered the prohibited *Gevinas Akum*. See *Shu"t Igros Moshe* (Y.D. vol. 3:17) and *Shu"t Shevet Halevi* (vol. 4:86). Even if whey would be considered milk, using it as a basis

Chalav Yisrael: A Halachic History   425

with the traditional and less-kashrus sensitive sweet cream, as well as with starter distillate, and often incorporating cultures. Since the dairy companies are still allowed to label the product "100% Grade A butter" and even sometimes "100% Grade AA butter" (if the butter meets the organoleptic threshold for this requirement), it no longer seems simple or recommended to rely on purchasing commercially produced butter with no specific *hashgacha* and assume that it does not contain any inherent kashrus issues. In other words, even if one would generally rely on *Chalav Stam*, it seems that nowadays it would be prudent to ensure that one's butter has a proper *hashgacha*.

However, it is important to note that while commercially manufactured butter with kosher certification is guaranteed to contain only kosher cream, it likely contains whey cream as well as starter distillate, and may no longer qualify for the *Chalav Yisrael* butter exemption. Practically, this means that if one is *makpid* on *Chalav Yisrael*, he should be aware that nowadays butter requires *Chalav Yisrael* certification to ensure that all ingredients exclusively come from *Chalav Yisrael* sources.

---

for butter would technically invalidate the butter dispensation. This is because it would not be the classic butter that was not included in any *Gezeira* due to its unique properties, but rather a dairy item later produced from a milk by-product, which would have been included at least in the *Chalav Akum Gezeira* (but nowadays could still technically qualify as *Chalav Stam*, just not the *Chalav Yisrael* butter exemption). [See for example *Shu"t Mishpetei Uziel* (vol. 1, Y.D. 7). On the other hand, the *Chasam Sofer* (*Shu"t* Y.D. 79) allows leniency in this case *b'dieved*, that one may rely on this whey-based butter being considered traditional butter to the extent that *keilim* would not need to be *kashered*, etc. He adds that this is in no way a *hetter* to purchase such non-Jewish "butter" *lechatchilla*.] In the aforementioned *Daf HaKashrus*, Rav Yisroel Belsky is cited as asserting the same regarding butter containing starter distillate, as this is a separate *Chalav Stam* ingredient added to butter, and is not exempted from *Chalav Yisrael* requirements. Hence, even with kosher certification, due to these ingredients and additives, commercially produced butter may no longer be presumed to warrant a *Chalav Yisrael* butter exemption, as it may not be considered true "butter," but rather quite possibly, a *Chalav Stam* milk by-product.

Taking a Powder?

Over the years, other dairy products were discussed and debated by authorities to decide whether or not they can be included in the purview of the basic butter *hetter*.[83] But the item that set off another *machlokes* in the 1950s that still has ramifications today is powdered milk. Powdered milk, essentially ultra-concentrated milk without the actual liquid "milk," is dehydrated milk that is turned into a base powder. When water is later added to the powder, it rehydrates, reconstituting into watery "milk." This process extends the milk's shelf life

---

83 For example, "soft cheeses," such as ricotta, yogurt, leben, and *"shmetinin,"* the layer of fat skimmed off the top of milk. See *Shu"t HaRadbaz* (vol. 5:2291), *Pri Chodosh* (Y.D. 115:21), the Chida's *Shu"t Yosef Ometz* (64), *Shu"t Chaim Sha'al* (vol. 1:43), and *Shiyurei Bracha* (Y.D. 115:5), *Shu"t Chokekei Lev* (Y.D. 38), *Chochmas Adam* (53:38 and 67:3), *Shu"t Tzemach Tzedek* (*Hachadoshos*; Y.D. 75), *Shu"t Chasam Sofer* (Y.D. 79), *Shu"t Maharsham* (vol. 3:164), *Zivchei Tzedek* (115:34–36), *Aruch Hashulchan* (ad loc. end 16, 17 and 28), *Darchei Teshuva* (ad loc. 39), *Kaf Hachaim* (ad loc. 46 and 49–51), *Shu"t Seridei Aish* (new edition; vol. 2, Y.D. 25), *Shu"t Mishpetei Uziel* (vol. 1, Y.D. 7), *Shu"t Igros Moshe* (Y.D. vol. 3:17), *Shu"t Ba'er Moshe* (vol. 4:52), *Shu"t Shevet Halevi* (vol. 4:86), *Shu"t Mishnah Halachos* (vol. 4:103, 1–9), and *Yalkut Yosef* (*Issur V'Hetter* vol. 2, 81:23–25). Regarding cream cheese, see *Shu"t Igros Moshe* (Y.D. vol. 1:50 s.v. *uvadavar cream cheese*); regarding cottage cheese, see *Shu"t Igros Moshe* (Y.D. vol. 2:48), at length, in a *teshuva* to Rav Shimon Schwab of KAJ. According to Rabbi Dovid Cohen, Administrative Rabbinical Coordinator for the cRc Chicago (in an article accessible at: http://www.crcweb.org/kosher_articles/gevinas_yisroel_acid_cheese.php), the accepted custom in the United States is to follow the lenient opinion, which argues that acid-set cheeses (such as cottage cheese) were never included in the *Gezeirah* because those cheeses curdle without rennet (and sometimes without the addition of any coagulant at all), such that there's no reason to be concerned that *neveilah* rennet will be used. He further reports that it is likely that this custom is based on a ruling by Rav Yosef Eliyahu Henkin to that effect. Although the ruling wasn't given in writing, it was reported by Rav Gedalia Dov Schwartz, from Rabbi Shraga Feivel Greenstein (from Newark), who transmitted it from his *Rebbi*, Rav Henkin *zt"l*. Likewise, the OU (in several online articles), citing Rav Yisroel Belsky, credits this custom to Rav Henkin as well. However, it is known that the Star-K (in an article titled "Eating Her Curds? No Way!;"

exponentially, enabling it to withstand long-term storage, while taking up a fraction of the storage space needed for actual milk. It needs no refrigeration and is considered non-perishable.

Rav Tzvi Pesach Frank (d. 1960), the longtime and venerated Chief Rabbi of Yerushalayim, ruled that powdered milk, which in his time was a recent technological innovation, was *halachically* akin to butter. Since the milk was entirely changed from its original form, and was only produced from the milk of kosher animals, it would therefore be excluded from the prohibited categories of *Chalav Akum* or *Gevinas Akum*. He explains that although it is technically possible to produce milk powder from non-kosher animals' milk, it is highly unlikely, as the yields are poor, much more expensive, and there would be no reason to do so.[84] In other words, practically, it is just not done. Rav Frank reasoned that the prohibition of *Chalav Akum* was limited to milk and its by-products available in the days of Chazal which could easily be produced from non-kosher milk. Since powdered milk did not exist in those days, and we are certain that it is of bovine origin, especially as it is also produced

---

accessible at: https://www.star-k.org/articles/kashrus-kurrents/609/eating-her-curdsno-way/) takes a stricter position, and holds that a *mashgiach* is required to add the acid to cottage cheese, as was intimated by Rav Moshe (at least *lechatchilla*), that the *halachic* status of *Gevinas Akum* should apply to cottage cheese as well.

84   *Shu"t Har Tzvi* (Y.D. 103 and 104). Rav Frank cites precedent from the *Ritva* (*Avodah Zarah* 35b), regarding the Gemara's (ibid.) discussion of *Gevinas Akum*, that technically speaking cheese can only be made using milk of a kosher animal. The *Ritva* points out that technically cheese *can* be made from milk of non-kosher animals, but the cheese yield is poor and not worth the effort. Thus, although it is theoretically possible to make cheese or butter from non-kosher milk, the *halacha* does not require one to be concerned about this. The same can be said of powdered milk. As Rav Yirmiyohu Kaganoff writes (www.rabbikaganoff.com/chalav-yisrael-and-powdered-milk/), "It is indeed noteworthy that while researching milk and cheese made the world over, I discovered cheeses made from the milk of cows, sheep, goats, water buffalo, and yak—all of them kosher species. I also found places where milk from several non-kosher mammals, such as donkeys, mares, and camels, are

under government supervision, it is permitted for consumption, even without specific Jewish supervision.

On the other hand, the *Chazon Ish* sharply rejected this *hetter*, maintaining that there is neither *halachic* nor qualitative difference between powdered milk and regular milk. He maintains that butter is made utilizing a specific process (churning), which affects milk from a kosher animal, as opposed to milk from a non-kosher animal. However, powdered milk is made by dehydrating milk, and in his words, "any liquid can be dehydrated and rehydrated." As such, in his opinion there is no more dispensation for powdered milk that for any other milk that is not *Chalav Yisrael*.[85]

Many *Poskim*, including several of those who did not accept Rav Moshe's *hetter*, nonetheless concurred with Rav Tzvi Pesach's *psak*, ruling likewise, and permitting powdered milk for consumption, even if not actually *Chalav Yisrael*.[86] In fact, this *hetter* is more widely followed throughout Europe and in Eretz Yisrael than Rav Moshe's "*Chalav Stam Hetter*."[87] Indeed, the Israeli Chief Rabbinate grants *hashgacha*

---

consumed. But I did not find a single populace making cheese from the milk of a non-kosher species, verifying the *Ritva's* observation that it is simply not worthwhile to make cheese from the milk of non-kosher species."

85 *Chazon Ish* (Y.D. 41:4 s.v. *avkas chalav*). See also *Genazim V'Shu"t Chazon Ish* (vol. 1, pg. 383–392), which prints the original (lenient) *teshuva* of Rav Tzvi Pesach Frank along with the *Chazon Ish's* actual *he'aros* on it, leaving no room for ambiguity in the *Chazon Ish's* stringent position. His comments were also recently reprinted in *Shu"t V'Chiddushim Chazon Ish* (148).

86 See *Shu"t Zekan Aharon* (vol. 2, Y.D. 44), *Shu"t Yaskil Avdi* (vol. 5, Y.D. 9), *Shu"t Dvar Yehoshua* (Y.D. 17), *Shu"t Beis Avi* (vol. 1, Y.D. 72), *Shu"t Tzitz Eliezer* (vol. 16:25; in a *teshuva* to Rav Ovadiah Yosef), *Shu"t Eimek Halacha* (vol. 56; permitting only in conjunction with a chemical test to rule out non-kosher milk), *Shu"t Mishnah Halachos* (vol. 13:104), *Yalkut Yosef* (*Issur V'Hetter* vol. 2, 81:14), and *Shu"t M'Tzion Teitzei Torah* (284, pg. 223–226). See also *Shu"t Gevuros Eliyahu* (vol. 2-Y.D. 30 s.v. *ul'inyan*).

87 Case in point: It is worthwhile to read Rav Yirmiyahu Cohen, former *Dayan* in Antwerp and later *Av Beis Din* of Paris' extensive recent *teshuva* to the heads of the OU (*Shu"t Veheirim Hakohen* vol. 5:69; dated 5771), asking them not to

on products with the distinction of containing *"Avkas Chalav Nochri,"* although they officially will not certify as kosher products containing *Chalav Stam* (such as Häagen-Dazs ice cream).

On the other hand, many authorities agreed with the *Chazon Ish's* assessment,[88] and currently, no *Mehadrin* kashrus agency or *Badatz* in Eretz Yisrael will grant *hashgacha* on products containing powdered

---

start importing *Chalav Stam* products to France. He explains at length that that *hetter* was never widely accepted there, as opposed to the powdered milk *hetter*, which is commonly used by the French *Consistoire* and local *hashgachos* in their supervision of dairy products.

88 *Shu"t Divrei Yisrael* (vol. 2, Y.D. 15 s.v. *b'inyan avkas*), *Shu"t Minchas Yitzchak* (vol. 4:12, 2 and 3), *Shu"t Ba'er Moshe* (vol. 4:51), Rav Yonason Steif (in a *teshuva* published in *Shu"t Zahav Shi"va* 26; the author, Rav Dovid Gross, former Dayan in Pressburg, concurs in *teshuva* 27), *She'arim Metzuyanim B'Halacha* (38:12 s.v. *v'avak chalav*), *Shu"t Tiferes Tzvi* (Kornmehl; vol. 2:35; he maintains that if we can ascertain that it is impossible to make powdered milk out of non-kosher milk, then it should be *muttar*, otherwise *assur*), *Shu"t Mishpatecha L'Yaakov* (34), *Shu"t Shevet Halevi* (vol. 5:59 s.v. *amnam*), *Shu"t Teshuvos V'Hanhagos* (vol. 2:237), and *Shu"t Maamar Mordechai* (of Rav Mordechai Eliyahu; vol. 1, Y.D. 4:5). The *Chelkas Binyomin* (Y.D. 115:1, Biurim s.v. *chalav shechalvo*) offers an additional rationale why in his opinion the *Chazon Ish* was correct and not Rav Frank. He states that milk that was turned into butter or cheese is essentially changed in the process and cannot revert back to milk; yet, powdered milk is simply dehydrated milk. Add hot water and presto, it reverts right back to milk with no actual change taking place. However, in this author's estimation, that logic alone is not sufficiently compelling. First of all, regarding non-kosher *Or Hakeiva* (stomach lining) that is completely dried out (like wood) but can revert back to its original form via cooking, there is a *machlokes* Acharonim whether its *halachic* status as not kosher is reconstituted as well, even though referring to actual *Issurei Deoraysa* of *Neveilah* and *Bassar B'chalav* [see *Pischei Teshuva* (Y.D. 87:21]. Hence, to assert that regarding the much-less-strict powdered milk there is no avenue available for similar dispensation seems to this author somewhat pretentious. Also, although certainly a valid point vis-à-vis butter being changed to the point of no return, powdered milk does not actually revert to its original form when hot water is added. It does become a whitish milk-like liquid, but of much lower quality, both in taste and substance, than the

milk unless it is supervised powdered milk and actually *Chalav Yisrael*. In fact, *milchig* Materna, and now Similac, baby formulas are widely available in Eretz Yisrael under *hashgacha* from the *Badatz Eidah Hachareidis*, exclusively utilizing *Chalav Yisrael* powdered milk in its makeup.[89]

Keilim Clash

There is an additional common *hetter* regarding *Chalav Stam* that many make use of: that of *keilim*, or utensils. Although the *Rema* rules that *Chalav Akum* also *assurs* the utensils it was cooked in, akin to other non-kosher items (meaning, "it *treifs* up the pot"), even though there is only a *safek* that non-kosher milk was added to the kosher milk,[90] nevertheless, many *Poskim* maintain that this regulation does not apply regarding *Chalav Stam*.[91] Meaning, although many may have been

---

original milk. Hence, it seems that his comparison is not exact. [For a possible *halachic* precedent, see Mishnah in *Nida* (Ch. 7:1) regarding the need for exact reconstitution of liquids that were dried out, as it pertains to the *Tamei* status of *Zov, Rok, Neveilah*, and arguably *Meis*.] Indeed, Rav Shlomo Zalman Auerbach (*Shu"t Minchas Shlomo, Kama* vol. 1:4, 3 s.v. *gam*) maintains that powdered milk is essentially considered milk-flavored water (regarding the *inyan* of *chiyuv malkos*); it is only regarding *dinei bittul* that it is categorized as milk, as this issue depends on *taam*, and powdered milk tastes like milk, not water. Thanks are due to Rav Mordechai Kuber and Rabbi Nissim Abrin for pointing out several of the above *mareh mekomos*.

89 See the *Badatz Eidah Hachareidis'* recent *Madrich HaKashrus* (5778; vol. 1— *L'Chag HaPesach*, pg. 22–23). The term "*Mehadrin*" used throughout this chapter is referring to a stricter standard of kashrus utilized in Israel; not to be confused with the American *Chalav Yisrael* dairy company of the same name.

90 *Rema* (Y.D. 115:1), citing the *Rashba* (*Shu"t* 143). Additionally, as mentioned previously, the *Noda B'Yehuda* (*Shu"t, Kama* Y.D. 36) referred to those who drink black coffee in mugs previously used with *Chalav Akum*, as "*Kalei Daas*," the *Pri Chodosh's hetter* notwithstanding.

91 See *Shu"t Mahari M'Bruna* (78), *Shu"t Avnei Nezer* (vol. 2, Y.D. 102:3), *Shu"t Ha'Elef Lecha Shlomo* (Y.D. 191), and *Darchei Teshuva* (115:18; citing several other Acharonim, mainly *b'makom hefsed merubah*). These *Gedolei* Acharonim maintain that if there is any sort of *hashgacha* or way to ensure that the milk does not have any non-kosher additives, or even if no non-kosher animals

hesitant to fully rely on Rav Moshe's *hetter* to actually drink *Chalav Stam*, on the other hand, they are not that *makpid* on its *bliyos*, imparted taste that the milk may have transferred to its containment vessels.

Interestingly, several *Poskim* who came out strongly against Rav Moshe's dispensation nonetheless ruled more leniently regarding *Chalav Stam*-infused *keilim*, and especially if said milk used was powdered milk.[92] Conversely, and perhaps seeming somewhat paradoxical, in a later *teshuva*, Rav Moshe himself wrote that in his opinion, if one is *makpid* on *Chalav Yisrael*, he should also be *makpid* on its *keilim*.[93]

---

are present anywhere near the milking, and although not technically meeting the criteria of actual *Chalav Yisrael*, nonetheless, such milk is not considered full-fledged *Chalav Akum*, and ergo, will not *assur* the *keilim*. [Additionally, we find regarding *Chalav Akum*, that several *Poskim* attribute somewhat more lenient qualities to it than with other *Issurim*. For example, see *Pri Megadim* (Y.D. 97, E.A. end 1) concerning *Chanan B'Shaar Issurim*, and Rav Akiva Eiger (Y.D. 121:1 s.v. *ela*) who maintains that milk is considered "*Heteira Bala*."] On a more contemporary note, Rav Yosef Eliyahu Henkin (*Teshuvos Ibra* and *Shu"t Gevuros Eliyahu* ibid.), Rav Yaakov Kamenetsky (*Emes L'Yaakov* ibid. and *Shu"t Shulchan Halevi* Ch. 22:5, 1 s.v. *v'zechorani*), and Rav Ovadiah Yosef (*Shu"t Yechaveh Daas* vol. 4:42), all maintain that even those who are *machmir* not to drink *Chalav Stam*, may certainly rely on *keilim*, especially if they cannot be *kashered*. See next footnote.

92 *She'arim Metzuyanim B'Halacha* (ibid.) and *Shu"t Beis Avi* (vol. 4, E.H. 180:21). See also *Shu"t Minchas Yitzchak* (vol. 2:12, 3; regarding powdered milk), *Shu"t Migdalos Merkachim* (Y.D. 29), *Shu"t Mahari Shteif* (34), and *Shu"t Chelkas Yaakov* (updated edition; vol. 1, O.C. 199:3; regarding powdered milk), all of whom ruled more leniently with *keilim*, and especially *b'shaas hadchak*.

93 *Shu"t Igros Moshe* (Y.D. vol. 2: end 31 s.v. *v'hinei*). Rav Yisroel Belsky (*Shu"t Shulchan Halevi* ibid.) wrote similarly, that if one is *machmir* with *Chalav Stam*, he should likewise be *machmir* with its *keilim*, adding that Rav Yosef Shalom Elyashiv also ruled this way. See also *Shu"t Maadanei Melachim* (167), who wrote to be *machmir* with *keilim* unless there was some sort of Jewish supervision at the actual milking. Several Chassidic groups, including Chabad, are known to be very *machmir* regarding *keilim* as well.

Rav Moshe's *Hetter* Revisited

In any event, most mainstream American kashrus agencies currently do grant *hashgacha* to *Chalav Stam* products, based on Rav Moshe's *hetter*. Yet, in December 2008, the OU released a report titled "Rav Moshe ZT"L's *Heter* of *Cholov Stam* Revisited."[94] In it, they revealed a disconcerting discovery. Apparently, the FDA stopped testing for adulteration of milk, but rather exclusively for bacteria count and the presence of antibiotics. In other words, federal government inspectors currently do not in any way test milk to determine the source animals, nor do they even see the milking animals.[95]

On the other hand, they reported that the farms *are* uniformly inspected by state inspectors (as opposed to federal inspectors) for non-kosher animals, and the dairy plants' inspectors work with the farm inspectors' data, as they track the intake and output of all milk at dairies. Hence, the correlation of data between the farm and dairy inspections extends the farm inspection's efficacy to the dairies, which in their opinion, engenders sufficient grounds for a *Mirsas hetter* of government inspection.

Ironically, this means that the current *Chalav Stam hetter* commonly being used in America, relying on *state* inspectors at farms ostensibly following Rav Moshe's *psak*, is actually technically the total reverse of Rav Moshe's *hetter*, which actually relied on *federal* inspections at dairy factories and not farms.

The report concludes: "As evidenced by the above *psak* and research, the OU continues to pave the way in kashrus technical data and to

---

94   Accessible at: https://oukosher.org/blog/consumer-kosher/rav-moshe-ztls-heter-of-cholov-stam-revisited/.

95   The FDA's current actual form for Milk Plant Inspection can be accessed at: https://www.fda.gov/downloads/AboutFDA/ReportsManualsForms/Forms/FoodForms/UCM053453.pdf.
    Note that there is no inspection performed for milk adulteration. However, the OU maintains that although the FDA does not check to see if any non-kosher milk was added, based on the other tests they do, they can indicate immediately if any non-kosher was placed into the cow's milk.

service those in Klal Yisrael who wish to rely on Rav Moshe's *heter* concerning *Chalav Stam*."

Assisting DA

Another area of concern regarding our milk is that of surgical remediation of DA (displaced abomasum), a condition on the increase, pertaining almost exclusively to dairy cows.[96] This is referring to when a cow's abomasum, her fourth stomach, gets displaced and filled with fluid and gas. One of the main treatments for this condition is by surgically placing the abomasum back into its normal position. Several *Poskim* were concerned that this surgery may possibly render the cow a *treifa*, non-kosher. If so, it will affect its milk's status, rendering it not kosher as well.[97]

Although Rav Yisroel Belsky wrote extensively on this topic, maintaining that in no way should the DA surgical procedure render a cow non-kosher,[98] *Chalav Yisrael* companies came up with a practical solution: to avoid the issue altogether. Most *Chalav Yisrael* companies in America do

---

[96] As detailed in Rabbi Yair Hoffman's related article "The Milk *Machlokes*" (*Ami Magazine* Jan. 18, 2012/23 Teves 5772).

[97] As the milk of an animal from a kosher species that is rendered non-kosher is considered non-kosher as well, although *M'Derabbanan*. See *Rambam* (*Hilchos Maachalos Assuros* Ch. 3:6) and *Tur* and *Shulchan Aruch* (Y.D. 81:1).

[98] *Shu"t Shulchan Halevi* (*Chelek Birurei Halacha* 16–17). This issue is also discussed in *Shu"t Shevet Halevi* (vol. 9:154–155) and *Shu"t Chayei Halevi* (vol. 4:44), as well as *Kovetz B'Nesiv Hachalav* (vol. 1, Tishrei 5763; *Mador Chalav Treifos*; with *teshuvos* from Rav Shmuel *Halevi* Wosner (reprinted from his *Shu"t* ibid.), Rav Yaakov Meir Stern, Rav Shmuel Eliezer Stern, and Rabbi Dov Landau). However, it is important to note that even if one would theoretically consider a cow not kosher due to this surgery, according to the vast majority of *Poskim* this would not affect one's ability to drink milk, as its milk is surely *battel*. See *Shulchan Aruch*, *Rema*, and main commentaries (Y.D. 81:2), as well as on a more contemporary note, *Shu"t Har Tzvi* (Y.D. 36), *Shu"t Teshuvos V'Hanhagos* (vol. 5:245), *Kovetz Teshuvos* (vol. 1:72), *Shu"t Mishnah Halachos* (vol. 16:7 and 137), and *Minchas Asher* (*al HaTorah, Parashas Mishpatim* 43:4). On the other hand, due to the current *chashashos* of the abundance of dairy

not own their own entire farm, but rather use a particular portion of a specific farm's area for their supervised milking. If their staff realizes that a cow is suffering from DA and requires surgery, they simply segregate that cow from the kosher herd, transferring it over to the general populace for the regular (non-*Chalav Yisrael* runs of) milking. Hence, by purchasing *Chalav Yisrael* milk in America, one is also circumventing this potential concern entirely. In Eretz Yisrael, where relocating cows to non-Jewish farms is not a viable option, *Mehadrin* kashrus agencies officially ensure that such surgeries are only performed under direct supervision of *mashgichim*.[99]

Israel Issues

This may come as a surprise to readers, but the basic level of standards of *Chalav Yisrael* in Israel is not actually on par with *Chalav Yisrael* in America. This is because in America, *Chalav Yisrael* accounts for a mere fraction of a percent of milk produced nationwide. As such, to certify milk as *Chalav Yisrael*, there needs to be constant supervision at the milkings with on-site *mashgichim* during the *Chalav Yisrael* runs to ensure that it stays separate from the general milkings performed on the farms.[100]

Yet, in Eretz Yisrael, many farms are owned by Jews, but the milking is performed entirely by non-Jewish farmhands. Is this considered *Chalav Yisrael*, as it is technically Jewish-owned milk? Or not, as the Jew is

---

cows that might be *treifos*, it is rumored that Rav Herschel Schachter, Rosh Yeshivas Rabbeinu Yitzchak Elchanan (YU) and current Chief *Posek* for the OU, stopped drinking *all* milk as a personal stringency. An enlightening review of the topic of DA cows in English is accessible on the OU's website: https://oukosher.org/blog/consumer-kosher/milk-from-a-possibly-treif-cow/.

99 *Kovetz B'Nesiv Hachalav* (ibid. *Mador Va'adas Mehadrin*, pg. 105–106).

100 See Rav Avraham Rubin's *Shu"t Naharos Ayson* (vol. 2:33) for a guide to proper *hashgacha* for *Chalav Yisrael* on non-Jewish farms. Interestingly, in an article published in a recent *Kuntress Shvil Hachalav* (2018), Rabbi Zev Weitman, Rabbi of Tnuva, defends the standards of *Chalav Yisrael* milk produced in Israel vis-à-vis its American counterparts. He asserts that in his opinion, one cannot compare milk produced by non-Jews in America with all of its

not actively involved with the milking process at all? The *Shaarei Dura* cites a ruling from Rabbeinu Tam, which is later codified as *halacha* by the *Rema*,[101] that a non-Jewish servant or maid living in a Jew's house is permitted to milk the Jew's cow for him, even if the Jew does not see the actual milking process. This is due to the *Mirsas* involved, as it is certain that she is serving her Jewish master kosher milk. Is this precedent similar to the Israeli farms' facts on the ground?

Rav Yosef Shalom Elyashiv, in a *teshuva* written by his noted *talmid*, Rav Yosef Efrati, ruled that this exact scenario does not fit into the criteria of Rabbeinu Tam's *hetter*. Yet, he asserts that if in such a case a *mashgiach* is present several times a week during the milking, in addition to the workers' fear of the Jewish owner (even if he is not *Shomer Shabbos*)[102] firing them if they get caught adulterating the milk, it would

---

underlying issues and the *halachic* strictures necessitated, with that of (non-religious) Jews in Israel that happens to be processed by non-Jewish workers.

101 *Shaarei Dura* (82), citing a ruling from Rabbeinu Tam to Rav Eliezer M'Shantz. The *Issur V'Hetter* (45:8) also cites this ruling. The *Rema* (Y.D. 115:1; see also *Toras HaChatas* 81:8 and *Darchei Moshe* Y.D. 115:1) rules this way *lemaaseh* [see also *Shach* (ad loc. 13) who clarifies his intent]. Interestingly, the *Shaarei Dura* notes that even though this is the *halacha*, nevertheless he adds that it is a "*davar mechuar laasos kein lechatchilla.*"

102 Rav Efrati explains (*Shu"t Yissa Yosef* ad loc. s.v. *ela d'efshar*) that in his opinion, although the owners of these dairy plants are not *Shomer Shabbos*, and do not particularly care about kashrus, nonetheless, they are concerned with milk quality. Hence, if the non-Jewish workers are caught adulterating the milk in any manner, fines will be levied on the plant, and the owner will certainly fire those workers. As such, although there may not be a true *Mirsas* due to the prohibition as was defined by the Gemara, but in his opinion, there still exists a similar *Mirsas* of the factory owner firing the non-Jewish workers for noncompliance. On the other hand, a certain esteemed Rabbinic personality (who requested not to be named) professed an opposing viewpoint to this author. He explained that if the *Mirsas* is truly based exclusively on milk quality, then in a scenario where the fat content of the cows' milk came out low, then supplementing it with twenty-five percent pigs' milk would do wonders to bring it up to the norm. Hence, it is reasonable to assume that a non-*Shomer Shabbos* dairy plant owner who has no interest in kashrus, but rather

then constitute "*Chalav Yisrael L'Mehadrin*,"[103] especially if there are also video cameras present as a preventive measure.[104] Rav Shmuel *Halevi* Wosner agreed with this logic as well.[105] Much of the *Chalav Yisrael* (or "*Mehadrin*") milk currently produced in Israel relies upon this ruling of the *Gedolim*.[106]

---

in making money due to milk quality, would seemingly not have too many qualms if the non-Jewish worker decided to adulterate the milk to enhance its quality.

103 *Shu"t Yissa Yosef* (vol. 2, Y.D. vol.1:13). This *teshuva* was first published in *Kovetz B'Nesiv Hachalav* (vol. 1, Tishrei 5763).

104 The issue of how video cameras are viewed by *halacha*, especially in enabling milk to be considered *Chalav Yisrael*, is a recent topic of debate. Several *Poskim* allow its use as an aid to create a *Mirsas* so the non-Jews realize that they are always being watched, while other authorities reject its use entirely, since it can be easily tampered with and they do not consider its use as a *mashgiach* being physically present at the milking. On the other hand, others view it as a boon for granting proper *hashgacha*—provided that the film is continuously being monitored by a Jew in real-time, meaning that the supervision is being performed remotely via video camera. There does not seem to be a clear-cut consensus on the topic. Aside from Rav Elyashiv's view cited above, see *Shu"t Teshuvos V'Hanhagos* (vol. 5:255 and vol. 6:176), *Shu"t Eimek Hateshuva* (vol. 9:85), *Shu"t Chayei Halevi* (vol. 6:116), *Kovetz B'Nesiv Hachalav* (vol. 1, Tishrei 5763, pg. 54; *teshuva* from Rav Mordechai Gross), *Kovetz Shaarei Horaah* (vol. 1, pg. 100; *teshuva* from Rav Shmuel Eliezer Stern), and *Kovetz Ohr Yisroel* (vol. 63; Tishrei 5772; *teshuvos* from Rav Mordechai Gross, Rav Menachem Meir Weissmandl, Rabbi Dov Landau, and a letter from the *Shevet Halevi*). There is an excellent round-up of opinions and positions presented in Rabbi Yaakov Skoczylas' recent *Ohel Yaakov* on *Hilchos Maachalei Akum* (pg. 251–256), as well as R' Zvi Ryzman's *maamar* titled "*Matzleimos Video B'Halacha*" (*Ratz Katzvi, Actuali B'Halacha* vol. 2:14, 2).

105 *Shu"t Shevet Halevi* (vol. 9:165) and *Shu"t Yissa Yosef* (vol. 2, Y.D. vol.1:14). This *teshuva* was also printed in *Kovetz B'Nesiv Hachalav* (ibid.). The Steipler Gaon is also quoted as holding similarly (*Orchos Rabbeinu*, new edition, vol. 4, pg. 32–33:10). However, in a *haskama* to his *talmid*, Rav Moshe Shaul Klein's *sefer Sheilas Moshe* (*Shaarei Issur V'Hetter, B'Inyanei Chalav Akum*), Rav Wosner indicated that he later retracted his lenient position regarding video cameras.

106 See *Kovetz B'Nesiv Hachalav* (vol. 1, Tishrei 5763), "*Mador Va'adas Mehadrin*,"

On the other hand, in a recent *Madrich HaKashrus*,[107] the *Badatz Eidah Hachareidis* writes that they only grant *hashgacha* to farms that are entirely *Shomer Shabbos*, and do not rely on the use of video cameras at all, even as an aid, but rather exclusively use *mashgichim*. Hence, the kosher consumer should be aware that there exist varying standards for considering milk *Chalav Yisrael* or *Mehadrin* in Eretz Yisrael itself, which at the same time is somewhat divergent from the stricter standards used as *Chalav Yisrael* in America, where it is mainly being produced commercially on non-Jewishly owned farms with *mashgichim temidi'im*.

Dairy Delights?

Practically, based on Rav Moshe's *hetter*, starting back when it was a hardship to procure *Chalav Yisrael* milk, right up to nowadays when it is easily obtainable in most metropolitan areas,[108] most leading mainstream kashrus organizations in the United States grant kosher certification on milk and dairy products that are or contain *Chalav Stam*.[109]

---

especially pg. 105 and 106 detailing the prevailing "*Mehadrin*" standards; also featuring *Michtavei Bracha* from Rav Elyashiv and Rav Wosner. To the best of this author's knowledge, the only major *hashgacha* in Israel that was *makpid* on *Chalav Yisrael* mandating a *mashgiach temidi* on-site at all milkings, was that of Rav Moshe Yehuda Leib Landau of Bnei Brak.

107 *Madrich HaKashrus* (5778; vol. 1—*L'Chag HaPesach*, pg. 22–23 and 40–43). The *Badatz* adds that there are 1,473,812,194 liters of milk produced annually at over 800 farms throughout Israel; of them, they write that they only grant *hashgacha* to 180 of them, all of whom are *Shomer Shabbos*. More recently, with Tara Milk now under their *hashgacha*, although their farms are not strictly *Shomer Shabbos*, the *Badatz* writes that they instituted numerous alternative safeguards.

108 Yup, gone are the halcyon days of my youth, when *Chalav Yisrael* milk was shipped down frozen to Miami once a week, arriving past its due date, and spoiling immediately upon opening.

109 Including the American "Big Five" kashrus agencies, at least on some level. The OU, Kof-K, and cRc Chicago grant *hashgacha* on *Chalav Stam* products. The OK does as well on commercial products, but not on their catering and food services. The Star-K is officially *makpid* on *Chalav Yisrael*, but their

Conversely, many smaller, and especially Chassidic, *Vaadei Kashrus* do not, rather ensuring that dairy products under their supervision are indeed *Chalav Yisrael*.[110] As mentioned previously, in Israel, milk can only be considered "*Mehadrin*" or under *hashgacha* of a *Badatz* if it is fits their criteria of *Chalav Yisrael*.

Yet, although we can safely assume that the milk on the supermaket shelf is, as it claims, unadulterated cow's milk, it is important to note that in his later *teshuvos*, Rav Moshe wrote that optimally, one should only rely on his *hetter* of *Chalav Stam* when *Chalav Yisrael* was not readily available or when *Chalav Yisrael* milk was prohibitively more expensive.[111] This, coupled with the drastically changed conditions in the milk industry from the time of his initial *psak*, from DA cows to FDA reports, as well as the relatively widespread availability and abundance of *Chalav Yisrael* milk and dairy products nowadays, leads many to be more *makpid* with milk than they may have been in the past.

---

secondary affiliate *hashgacha*, Star-D, is not. Across the pond, the largest European kashrus agency, *London Beis Din* (KLBD), also grants *hashgacha* on *Chalav Stam* products.

110 Including CRC—*Hisachdus HaRabbanim*, New Square Kashrus, the Tzehlemer Rav, Volover Rav, Nirbater Rav, and Rav Menachem Meir Weissmandl. In England, Kedassia, Manchester Beis Din, and Igud Rabbanim—Rav Osher Yaakov Westheim, are *makpid* to only grant *hashgacha* on *Chalav Yisrael* dairy products.

111 This *psak* was echoed by several other *Poskim*, including Rav Elazar Kahanow (*Shu"t Zichron Betzalel* vol. 3, 94:58 and *Pekudas Elazar*, ibid. 58) and Rav Efraim Greenblatt (*Shu"t Rivevos Efraim* vol. 8:11, 1). See also *Kuntress Yad Dodi* (Y.D. *Inyanei Kashrus*, Question 11), where his son, Rav Dovid Feinstein, gives several guidelines on the nuances of observing *Chalav Yisrael* vis-à-vis *Chalav Stam*.

Chapter 31

Kashering Teeth?!

AROUND EIGHTY YEARS AGO, a relatively unknown young *avreich* (*kollel yungerman*) living in Eretz Yisrael wrote a very detailed and extensive *halachic* query to the *Gadol Hador* of the time, the renowned *Chazon Ish*, Rav Avraham Yeshaya Karelitz, regarding a personal pressing issue. Apparently, this young Talmudic scholar had gold crowns on his teeth, and wanted to clarify their *halachic* status in relation to Pesach. It is well known that metal utensils used for *chometz* year-round need to be *kashered* to be fit for Pesach use, generally by dipping them into a vat of boiling water.[1] The problem here is that metal crowns fitted over bad teeth are actually embedded in the mouth, so that would seem to rule out the boiling water. Would he have to forego hot food the entire Pesach?

This question is not only relevant to crowns, but to fillings, implants, braces, and bridges as well. What is one to do?

Nothing but the Tooth…

Now, by your G-d-given set of choppers, all agree that these natural teeth do not need to be *kashered* in order to render them suitable for use on Pesach, as they are considered part and parcel of the body. Furthermore, the material of which they are fashioned (enamel) is not considered *halachically* absorbent. That is why nothing more than a thorough cleaning (brushing and flossing) on Erev Pesach after eating one last bite of *chometz*, is necessary to have a *kosher l'Pesach* mouth.

---

1   See *Tur* and *Shulchan Aruch* (O.C. 451 and 452) at length.

Denture Divergence?

However, to resolve the issue of crowns and implants, we must first digress to a more common concern: dentures and false teeth, which were first addressed by *halachic* authorities a generation or two earlier.

Many *halachic* authorities of the previous generations maintained that there was no need to *kasher* dentures between eating hot meat and hot milk due to a variety of reasons,[2] including:

- The makeup of dentures is similar to natural teeth and they are also considered *halachically* nonabsorbent.
- Most people do not generally eat food while it's piping hot, which inhibits any actual absorption into the false teeth.
- By the time the food is eaten, it is already considered a *kli shlishi* (or at the very least a *kli sheini*, meaning at least twice removed from being cooked on the fire, and not considered *halachic* cooking), which according to most authorities hinders the food's ability to be absorbed in the false teeth.

---

2   Including the *Sheilas Shalom* (*Shu"t Tinyana* 195; cited in *Darchei Teshuva* 89:11), the Maharsham (*Shu"t* vol. 1:197), *Melamed L'Ho'eel* (*Shu"t* vol. 1-O.C. 93), *Kaf Hachaim* (Y.D. 89:22), *Zekan Aharon* (*Shu"t* vol. 2, Y.D. 51), *Mei Be'er* (*Shu"t* 24), *Chemdas Efraim* (*Shu"t* Y.D. 13), *Tzur Yaakov* (*Shu"t* 188), Rav Moshe Feinstein (*Shu"t Igros Moshe* O.C. vol. 1, end 5), Rav Yaakov Kamenetsky (*Emes L'Yaakov* on *Tur* and *Shulchan Aruch*, O.C. 451, footnote 441), *Minchas Yitzchak* (*Shu"t* vol. 8:37), *Mishnah Halachos* (*Shu"t* vol. 3:56; vol. 4:68 and 93; vol. 12:13), Rav Yisrael Yaakov Fischer (*Shu"t Even Yisrael* vol. 9:68, footnote 1), *Beis Avi* (*Shu"t* vol. 2:96), Rav Ovadiah Yosef (*Shu"t Yabia Omer* vol. 3, O.C. 24:7 and *Shu"t Yechaveh Daas* vol. 1:8), *Yalkut Yosef* (*Issur V'Hetter* vol. 3, 89:12), and the *She'arim Metzuyanim B'Halacha* (vol. 1:46, 5). However, the *Darchei Teshuva* himself concludes that if at all possible, it is worthwhile to procure a separate set of dentures, one for eating dairy and one for eating meat. It is widely rumored that the Rebbe Rashab of Lubavitch followed this stringency, utilizing three separate pairs of dentures: one each for milk, meat, and for Pesach; however, this account is disputed (see *Otzar Minhagei Chabad* vol. 2, pg. 65:22). In any event, as written above, *halachically* speaking, separate dentures are most definitely not required.

In other words, relating to the issue of *Bassar B'chalav*, dentures are deemed not to be considered an actual utensil that requires *kashering*, but rather similar to genuine teeth themselves, sharing the same relevant *halachos*.

A Pesach Pair?

Several authorities maintain that the very same ruling would apply for Pesach, and rule that a thorough cleaning of the false teeth prior to Pesach would be sufficient.[3]

Yet, other authorities, including the famed Maharsham, assert that one must be more stringent regarding Pesach, and rule that one must at least perform an *Iruy Roschin*, pour boiling hot water over the dentures, to be suitable for Pesach use.[4] It must be noted though, that *Iruy* is a lesser form of *kashering* and is usually not considered an acceptable process for utensils.

This is all relevant to our discussion, as the issue is: How do we define these crowns, fillings, implants, and braces, et al.? If we were to follow the Maharsham's ruling and necessitate *Iruy* before Pesach, how can we accomplish this, if they have since become a part of us?

---

3 The *Sdei Chemed* (*Maareches Chometz U'Matzah* 4:23) cites both sides of this dispute without coming to a clear consensus. Those who are lenient include the *Rava"z* (*Shu"t* 10), *Mayim Chaim* (*Shu"t* O.C. 177), *Beis Yitzchak* (*Shu"t* Y.D. vol. 1:43, 2), *Beis Ha'Otzar* (cited in *Sdei Chemed* ibid.), *Melamed L'Ho'eel* (ibid.), and *Beis Yisrael* (*Shu"t* O.C. 85). The *Yad Yitzchak* (*Shu"t* vol. 3:78) maintains that *Irui U'Milui* with cold water for three days while switching the water after every twenty-four hours is sufficient.

4 *Shu"t Maharsham* (ibid.). Others who rule stringently include the *Sheilas Shalom* and *Tzur Yaakov* cited above. As mentioned above, the *Sdei Chemed* did not rule conclusively. Several contemporary authorities as well, rule stringently, and maintain that at least *lechatchilla* one should try to perform *Iruy* on his dentures before Pesach, including Rav Moshe Sternbuch (*Shu"t Teshuvos V'Hanhagos* vol. 2:211, 7), and the *Minchas Chein* (*Shu"t* vol. 1, O.C. 28, Ch. 3:3). Rav Yaakov Kamenetsky (*Emes L'Yaakov* ibid.) was also known to be more stringent with this issue regarding Pesach.

Pagum Protection

In his writing, our young scholar offered and rejected various rationales, until finally hitting upon what he felt was the proper *halachic* solution, echoing the words of the great *Chasam Sofer* and his son, the *Ksav Sofer*.[5] They maintained that when bits of meat would be left inside the mouth (i.e., stuck between the teeth), the combination of the salivary juices, natural heat, and chemical reactions taking place in the oral cavity greatly accelerates the digestive process and renders that "meat" *pagum*, repulsive and utterly inedible, and resulting in its losing its status of "meat."[6] This *avreich* extrapolated that the same underlying principle would apply by implants (and even dentures) as well, and thereby negates the need for *kashering*, as any possible absorbed taste or flavor of *chometz* would long ago have been considered *pagum* and thus negligible.

Although he did qualify his resolution, stating that it is proper not to eat any *chometz* within twenty-four hours before Pesach, and to drink a

---

5   *Chasam Sofer* (commentary on Gemara *Chullin* 105a s.v. *bassar shebein*), *Ksav Sofer* (Glosses to *Shulchan Aruch* Y.D. 89).

6   This *halachic* ruling of the *Chasam Sofer* and *Ksav Sofer* regarding the "*pagum*-making" ability of the oral cavity also affects a different aspect of *halacha*: tiny bits of meat stuck between the teeth which later get swallowed. Although some, including the *Badei Hashulchan* (Y.D. 89:13), opine that in such a case one must wait an additional full six hours from the time that the minuscule morsels of meat were swallowed, nevertheless, the vast majority of contemporary authorities maintain that a simple *kinuach* and *hadacha*, without a new waiting period, are certainly sufficient, especially as the renowned *Hafla'ah* (Glosses to *Shulchan Aruch* ad loc. *Chiddushim* 1) explicitly ruled this way (and not as some mistakenly quote him). Many of them wrote that they are following the precedent of the *Chasam Sofer* and *Ksav Sofer*, and aver that at the time of swallowing, due to the conditions inside the mouth, those tiny bits of meat have long since lost their *halachic* status as such, and are already considered *pagum*. See *Machatzis Hashekel* (ad loc. 2 s.v. *mishum*), *Shu"t Zekan Aharon* (vol. 2, Y.D. 51), *Shu"t Beis Avi* (vol. 2: 96), *Shu"t Even Yisrael* (vol. 9:68, footnote 1), *Rayach Habosem* (on *Bassar B'chalav*, Ch. 3, Question 33; citing the *Ba'er Moshe*), *He'aros B'Maseches Chullin* (pg. 403; *Psak* of Rav Yosef Shalom Elyashiv; also personally confirmed by his noted *talmid*, Rav Nochom Eisenstein), *Kashrus*

Kashering Teeth?! 443

hot cup of water (hotter than usual) prior to the onset of Pesach, still, he felt that even so, a proper oral cleaning would be *halachically* sufficient.

A "Crowning" Achievement

So, what was the name of our erudite scholar? None other than Rav Shlomo Zalman Auerbach, later to become the *Gadol Hador* in his own right! His letter actually turned out to be one of his most famous published *halachic* rulings in his three-volume collection of responsa, *Shu"t Minchas Shlomo*.[7] Several other contemporary authorities echo Rav Shlomo Zalman's sound reasoning in their own applicable rulings.[8] And although the *Chazon Ish* never actually replied in writing to his letter, it is known that he accepted Rav Shlomo Zalman's ruling as *halacha*, and did not mandate any sort of *kashering* for dentures, crowns, or implants.[9] In fact, when later asked why he never sent an official response, the *Chazon Ish* replied that "the author asked my opinion, but after such a complete and articulate take on the situation, what can I possibly add?"[10]

---

in the Kitchen Q & A (*Teshuvas* Rav Chaim Kanievsky; pg. 209), *Sefer Hakashrus* (Ch. 10, footnote 68; citing Rav Moshe Halberstam), *Ohel Yaakov* (on *Hilchos Issur V'Hetter*, revised edition; 89:15; citing Rav Chaim Pinchas Scheinberg and Rav Avigdor Nebenzahl), *Kuntress Shu"t Ketzaros B'Inyanei Issur V'Hetter* (pg. 16; citing Rav Yisrael Zev Gustman, Rav Ezriel Auerbach, and Rav Mattis Deutsch), *Shu"t Maadanei Melachim* (82), *Shu"t Eimek Hateshuva* (vol. 6:310), *Shu"t M'Tzion Teitzei Torah* (180, pg. 144–145), *Shu"t Shulchan Halevi* (Ch. 22:10, 2 s.v. *mihu*), *Shu"t Chayei Halevi* (vol. 5:60, 5), and *Megillas Sefer* (on *Bassar B'chalav*, 89 ad loc.). This was also the personal ruling that *Mori v'Rabi* Rav Yaakov Blau of the *Eidah Hachareidis* told this author.

7   *Shu"t Minchas Shlomo* (vol. 2:46; *Tinyana* 50). It is also cited decisively in his name by several later *sefarim* including *Nishmas Avraham* (vol. 2, Y.D. 89:2), *Halichos Shlomo* (Moadim vol. 2, Ch. 12:12, footnote 14), and *Shalmei Moed* (pg. 137, Ch. 72, end footnote 75).

8   Including the *Zekan Aharon*, the *Beis Avi*, and the *Even Yisrael* (cited in a previous footnote).

9   *Orchos Rabbeinu* (vol. 2, *Hilchos Pesach*, pg. 27:25).

10 This conclusion is brought in *Shalmei Moed* (pg. 134, Ch. 72, footnote 74), quoting Rav Shmuel Greineman.

Postscript: Other Opinions on Dentures

Many other contemporary *halachic* authorities, including the Steipler Gaon, Rav Tzvi Pesach Frank, Rav Yosef Shalom Elyashiv, Rav Ben Tzion Abba-Shaul, the Pupa Rebbe, the *Yesodei Yeshurun*, and Rav Nissim Karelitz,[11] followed Rav Shlomo Zalman's precedent, and ruled accordingly, that dentures do not need any sort of *kashering* for Pesach.

However, it must be noted that this lenient Pesach ruling of Rav Shlomo Zalman regarding dentures is not universal, as several contemporary authorities, including Rav Moshe Sternbuch and Rav Noach Isaac Oelbaum, do rule stringently, and maintain that at least *lechatchilla* one should try to perform *Iruy* on his dentures before Pesach. Rav Yaakov Kamenetsky was also known to be more stringent in this issue regarding Pesach.[12]

Additionally, several other authorities agree that although *me'ikar hadin* one is not required to perform *Iruy* on false teeth, they still feel that nevertheless it is preferable if at all possible to try and do so, unless one is concerned that the *Iruy* will ruin or warp them. These *Poskim* include Rav Shmuel *Halevi* Wosner, the *Tzitz Eliezer*, Rav Menashe Klein, the *Beis Avi*, and Rav Ovadiah Yosef. This is also the opinion of the *Badatz Eidah Hachareidis*, as cited in their annual *Madrich HaKashrus*.[13]

This author continually finds it fascinating that even the small details of life that most of us rarely think about—such as teeth, dentures, crowns, or braces—have already been addressed in the purview of *halacha*.

---

11 Steipler Gaon (*Orchos Rabbeinu* ibid.), the *Har Tzvi* (cited in *Chok L'Yisrael* vol. 4:36), Rav Yosef Shalom Elyashiv (cited in *Ashrei Ha'Ish* O.C. vol. 3, pg. 349:24), Rav Ben Tzion Abba-Shaul (*Shu"t Ohr L'Tzion* vol. 3, Ch. 10:15), Rav Nissim Karelitz (*Chut Shani* on *Hilchos Pesach*, pg. 113–114), the Pupa Rebbe (*Kelach Shel Eizov* 23), and the *Yesodei Yeshurun* (vol. 6, pg. 164).

12 *Shu"t Teshuvos V'Hanhagos* (vol. 2:211, 7), *Shu"t Minchas Chein* (vol. 1, O.C. 28, Ch. 3:3), *Emes L'Yaakov* (ibid.).

13 *Shu"t Shevet Halevi* (vol. 1:148; vol. 4:74 and *Kovetz Moriah* #99, Iyar 5751, pg. 89–90), *Shu"t Tzitz Eliezer* (vol. 9:25), *Shu"t Mishnah Halachos* (vol. 4:68), *Shu"t Beis Avi* (ibid.), *Shu"t Yabia Omer* (ibid. 10), and the *Badatz Eidah Hachareidis' Madrich HaKashrus* (5771; pg. 44, Ch.10:2 and 3).

Addendum

Additions

Locusts (Chapter 1, Footnote 9)

ANOTHER RISHON WHO DISCUSSED THE *minhag* of eating locusts, and allowing those with a *mesorah* to continue to partake of them (albeit stating that the *minhag* in his locale was not to partake of them), was Rav Tzemach Duran, grandson of the *Tashbetz* and Rav of Algiers in the mid-1400s (*Shu"t Yachin U'Boaz*, vol. 1:64; see also the comment of his grandson, Rav Tzemach, explaining how the *mesorah* works for those who have it; citing the Jewish communities of Tunisia and Djerba as examples of places that commonly ate locusts based on their *mesorah*).

Aside from Rav Yitzchak Ratzabi, another famous contemporary Yemenite Rabbi who was of the opinion that the rest of world-Jewry can and should rely on their *mesorah* to permit eating locusts was Rav Yosef Kapach, in a brief article published in *Hamodia* (5 Adar I 5719/ February 16, 1959; accessible at: http://halachicadventures.com/wp-content/uploads/2009/09/21.jpg). See also *Masorah L'Yosef* (vol. 9, pg. 77–85), "*Achilas Chagavim L'Bnei Ashkenaz L'Daas Rav Yosef Kapach*," citing a letter from Rav Kapach dated Elul 5759, where he reasserts his position, referring to eating locusts as "*mesoras emes nafutza mei'az Moshe Rabbeinu*," a true *mesorah* dating back to the time of Moshe Rabbeinu.

On the other hand, aside from the many (non-Yemenite) Rabbanim listed previously (pp. 6–7, end footnote 9) who did not accept this position, and prohibited locust consumption for those without a *mesorah*, Rav Ovadiah Yosef did as well, in a handwritten letter from

Rav Ovadiah's personal assistant dated 30 Sivan 5762 (accessible at: halachicadventures.com/wp-content/uploads/2013/03/rav-ovadia-chagavim.pdf). Rav Ovadiah, however conceded that if one would cook such locusts, in his opinion it would not actually "*treif* up" the *kli*, and the pot would not need to be *kashered*.

Waiting Periods after Eating Meat before Dairy (Chapter 4, Page 36)

Although waiting six hours is indeed the most common *minhag*, nonetheless, most contemporary *Poskim* are of the opinion that this is not obligatory for children, following the lead of several Rishonim, including the *Terumas Hadeshen* (*Leket Yosher* vol. 1, pg. 69 s.v. *v'nahag*; thanks are due to Rabbi Avromy Kaplan for pointing this out) and the *Meiri* (*Chullin* 105a), who briefly mention that children are not mandated to keep the full waiting period. Several authorities, including the *Chelkas Yaakov* (*Shu"t* vol. 2:88–89 and vol. 3:147), Rav Yaakov Kamenetsky (*Emes L'Yaakov on Tur and Shulchan Aruch*, Y.D. 89, footnote 36), and Rav Nissim Karelitz *Chut Shani* (*Shabbos* vol. 4, end 343, pg. 309–310), maintain that young children need only wait an hour, and only once they reach nine years old should they start waiting longer. Rav Ovadiah Yosef (*Shu"t Yechaveh Daas* vol. 3:58) is more lenient, ruling that children only need to start waiting the full amount from a year before their Bar or Bas Mitzvah.

Other *Poskim*, including the Debreciner Rav (*Shu"t Ba'er Moshe* vol. 8:36, 5), Rav Yosef Shalom Elyashiv (cited in *Piskei Halachos* pg. 53:4–5), and Rav Moshe Sternbuch (*Shu"t Teshuvos V'Hanhagos* vol. 1:434) prefer a staggered approach. Once a child reaches age two-three, he should wait an hour. When he turns five-six, he should wait three hours, and from age nine-ten, he should wait the full six hours.

Others, including the Ponovezh Rosh Yeshiva Rav Elazar Menachem Mann Shach (*Michtavim U'Maamarim* vol. 4:332), Rav Shlomo Zalman Auerbach (cited in *Va'aleihu Lo Yibol* vol. 2, pg. 64:3 and *Maadanei Shlomo on Dalet Chelkei Shulchan Aruch* pg. 241–242), and Rav Shmuel Halevi Wosner (*Shu"t Shevet Halevi* vol. 4:84 and *Kovetz M'Beis Levi* vol. 9, pg. 23:9 and vol. Y.D. pg. 36:13, footnote 14) maintain that there is no specific set age, but rather depends on each individual child, his needs, and specific situation. All agree that the child should be educated and trained to gradually wait longer, building up to the full waiting period. See also *Shu"t She'aris Yisrael* (Y.D. 3), *Shu"t Eimek Hateshuva* (vol. 6:314), and *Shu"t Shulchan Halevi* (Ch. 22:10, 3).

Many stress that this leniency for children is only applicable to real food or milk, as they are satiating and nutritional, as opposed to *milchig* candies and chocolates, etc., which are decidedly not, and for which no dispensation should be given. See *Shu"t Yabia Omer* (vol. 1, Y.D. 4 and vol. 3, Y.D. 3), *Shu"t Maadanei Melachim* (83:2), and *Chinuch Habanim L'Mitzvos* (*Tzorchei Kattan* 47 and footnote 183).

On the other hand, and contrary to all the above, there is the minority noteworthy opinion of the Steipler Gaon (*Orchos Rabbeinu*, new edition, vol. 4, pg. 25:2) who held that all minors should still keep the full six hours. His son, Rav Chaim Kanievsky holds this way as well (cited in *Moadei HaGra"ch* vol. 1:189–190). As with all *inyanei halacha*, one should ask his personal local *halachic* authority for guidance as to which opinion he should follow.

Barton's Candy (Page 107, Footnote 16)

As mentioned previously, Barton's was famous (and perhaps a bit infamous) for their strict adherence to *halacha*. In fact, that very fact—that a wildly successful and highly popular American confection company with dozens of stores nationwide was devoted to *Shemiras Shabbos* and strict kashrus—was deemed such an anomaly that it was the subject of a thorough article in one of the most popular mainstream periodicals of the day, *Commentary Magazine* (May 1952; accessible at https://www.commentarymagazine.com/articles/from-the-american-scene-orthodox-sweets-for-heterodox-new-york/). Thanks are due to historian Roger Horowitz for providing this fascinating article.

Alternative Kosher "Gelatin" (Page 108, Footnote 17)

According to a book on seaweed production, *The Biology of Seaweeds*, the vast majority of agar-agar gelatin used to be produced in Japan, and only after World War II did it take off in America, from around 1947. Hence, it is plausible that a comment from 1952 (in the aforementioned

Commentary Magazine feature on Barton's) that "science has recently found a way to produce vegetable gelatin," was likely referring to agar-agar gelatin being sourced from American factories at the time. Since then, agar-agar gelatin has remained a popular vegetable-based alternative to authentic gelatin in confections.

On the other hand, kosher fish gelatin only became a viable option in 1993, when Rabbi Dovid Holzer of Miami Beach perfected and later patented (US Patent No. 5,484,888) a process to extract high-yield gelatin from kosher fish skins. His company, Food Industry Technology (FIT), became the first to commercialize and supply kosher fish gelatin. Nowadays, fish gelatin is the most commonly used gelatin in candies, gummies, and confections for the kosher consumer.

The OU's Stance on Lab-Grown Meat (Page 101, Footnote 7)

Rabbi Menachem Genack, Rabbinic Administrator and CEO of the OU, first publicized the OU's change of policy and current classification of lab-grown meat as actual "meat" (and hence required to be kosher-*shechted*-sourced) in an "OU & You" video on Kosher.com ("Is Lab-Grown Meat Pareve?"; accessible at: https://www.kosher.com/shows/video/297/is-lab-grown-meat-parve) in mid-2018. Indeed, in a recent *teshuva* distributed at the December 2019 annual AKO (Association of Kashrus Organizations) meeting, Rabbi Genack notes that although Rav Herschel Schachter (Rosh Yeshivas Rabbeinu Yitzchak Elchanan/YU and current Chief *Posek* for the OU) maintains that the classification of "meat" can only be applied to that which is naturally born, nonetheless, both Rav Mordechai Gross of Bnei Brak (*Av Beis Din* of *Chanichei Yeshivos*) and Rav Asher Weiss (the renowned *Minchas Asher*), rule that lab-grown meat is considered a true meat. In his *teshuva*, Rabbi Genack ultimately concurs to the latter approach and *psak*, concluding this way as well, and setting OU policy accordingly.

The Impossible Burger (Page 129, Footnote 52)

Indeed, the plant-based Impossible Burger has proven to be a tremendous hit, rolling out a popular 2.0 version in late 2019, and even being sold at national restaurant chains. However, success has spawned competition: prototype 3D-printed veggie burgers, as well as Beyond Meat's "Beyond Burger," certified kosher by the OK. According to Cnet.com, "The Beyond Burger looks similar to the Impossible Burger in terms of color and consistency, but the Beyond Burger uses different ingredients. The main protein source in a Beyond Burger is pea protein (along with mung beans and brown rice; as opposed to the Impossible Burger's soy protein and soy leghemoglobin to make it "bleed"), and its red color comes from beets. The beet juice is what gives the Beyond Burger the same "bleeding" effect as the Impossible Burger."

In sum, innovative "great taste, plant-based" meat alternative "products like those from Impossible Foods and Beyond Meat have the potential to impact a few pertinent things: human health, environmental sustainability, and global resources," as well as offering a cutting-edge and tasty (and unanimously pareve), yet less *halachically* problematic "meat" solution than does stem-cell meat.

Rav Nosson M'Romi (the *Aruch*) and *Rashi's* Relationship (Page 207, Footnote 3)

See also *Teshuvos Rashi* (41), where *Rashi* sends the *Aruch* and his brothers a complicated *halachic* query regarding a *bris* on *Rosh Hashanah*.

The Importance of *Mayim Acharonim* (Page 319, Footnote 31)

Indeed, in telling the tale of the nefarious and thieving innkeeper, aptly named Kidor (*Yoma* 83b), who ultimately murders his wife after his ruse was discovered due to him not washing *Mayim Acharonim*, Chazal wryly comment, "*Mayim Acharonim hargu us hanefesh*," a person was killed due to (not washing) *Mayim Acharonim*. Thanks are due to my *talmid*, R' Gavi Geffen, for pointing this out.

Overnight Onions (Page 225, Footnote 3)

As mentioned previously, it is well known that the *Rambam* seems not to have been concerned with the issue of *Ruach Ra'ah* at all. Nonetheless, Rav Tzadok Hakohen M'Lublin (*Tiferes Tzvi* on Y.D. 116) asserts that practically, we cannot simply rely on the *Rambam's* expertise as a doctor to avoid this spiritual danger, and we therefore must still remain vigilant with spiritual dangers. Yet, he nonetheless concludes, citing "*Morei HaHora'ah*," that "*b'makom Mitzva ul'tzorech Shabbos V'Yom Tov*," regarding a Mitzva or Shabbos or Yom Tov need, we can be *meikil*, as it states in *Koheles* (Ch. 8:5): "*Shomer Mitzva lo yeida davar ra*." [See *Rema* (O.C. 455) for a precedent for this.] The *Yaskil Avdi* (*Shu"t* vol. 8, Y.D. 14:4, 2) rules this way *lemaaseh*, that certainly eggs or onions left overnight that were intended for *Seudas Shabbos*, may still be used due to this dictum.

As mentioned previously (page 228, footnote 8), there are several authorities who were more lenient regarding peeled overnight eggs, due to *Rashi* and others' omission of it from the prohibited criteria [see *Rashi* (ad loc. s.v. *she'avar*), *Tashbetz* (*Chiddushei Rashbatz* ad loc.), *Rashash* (ad loc.), *Ben Yehoyada* (ad loc.), *Ben Ish Chai* (ibid.), *Shu"t Igros Moshe* (Y.D. vol. 3:20 s.v. *v'gam ayin Rashi*), and *Shu"t Yaskil Avdi* (vol. 7, O.C. 44:4) on this topic]. Moreover, there is some debate among several later *Poskim* about what type of peeled eggs are intended for inclusion in the prohibition, cooked eggs or raw eggs. Indeed, although the common custom is to be stringent with both types of overnight eggs, the *Chazon Ish* (cited in *Orchos Rabbeinu* vol. 1, pg. 210:16) was known to be lenient with raw eggs left out, sufficing with a simple cover.

As the *Tzitz Eliezer* (*Shu"t* vol. 18:46) notes, there will always be a *sfek sfeika* to permit eggs *b'dieved*, as whichever type of egg one peels that was left overnight—raw or cooked—it is always possible that *Ruach Ra'ah* is actually exclusive to the other type. Practically, factoring that in, along with this prohibition's lacuna among many of the classic codifiers [in the words of the *Yad Meir* (*Shu"t* 19; cited in *Darchei Teshuva* 116:74), "*Shelo b'chinam hishmitu HaTur V'HaMechaber v'chol HaPoskim din zeh, ki mei'HaYerushalmi mashma d'ain b'zeh issur m'tzad Ruach Ra'ah b'zman hazeh' al kein yafeh minhagan shel Yisrael she'ain nizharim, lo b'shum kaluf, v'lo b'beitzah klufa*"], the Maharam M'Rothenburg and other Rishonim's *shittah* of *Ruach Ra'ah* not being prevalent nowadays, plus the opinions who exclude eggs altogether from the prohibition, should assuredly allow room for leniency, especially *l'kavod Shabbos*, as per the *psak* of Rav Tzadok Hakohen M'Lublin and the "*Morei HaHora'ah*."

Coca-Cola and Rav Pardes (Chapter 20, Pages 263–268)

As mentioned previously, it seems that Rav Pardes later accepted Rav Geffen's findings that glycerin was present in Coca-Cola in the early 1930s, but ruled that anyway, in his opinion, Coke would still be kosher and was permitted to be drunk. Rav Pardes' *teshuva* on the topic, which was published posthumously in a collection of his writings titled *Avnei Shmuel* (*Birurei Halacha* 20), as well as his *rebbi's*, Rav Yehuda Leib Graubart of Toronto's *teshuva* addressed to Rav Pardes (*Shu"t Chavalim B'Ne'imim* vol. 5:17; published posthumously in 1938), were both originally published in the July 1936 issue of *HaPardes* journal in response to a learned question—in English (!)—posed by the prestigious physiologist and chemist, Dr. David Israel Macht of Baltimore, titled "The Problem of Glycerin." In response to his query, both Rav Pardes' and Rav Graubart's responsa permitting it were published. This confirms that even after Rav Geffen proved animal-sourced glycerin *halachically* problematic regarding Coke in 1935 and had it substituted in Coke's formula, nonetheless, in 1936, Rav Pardes still "stuck to his guns," and maintained that even with such glycerin as an ingredient, Coke would still be considered kosher.

However, this does not mean that Rav Pardes did not acknowledge Rav Geffen's Coke kashrus contribution. In the July 1942 issue of *HaPardes*, Rav Pardes printed a scathing diatribe against chemist Dr. Abraham Goldstein, his OK Laboratories, and his *Kosher Food Guide*, who declared over the years that several food products that Rav Pardes gave his authorization to were not truly kosher. One of his contentions with Dr. Goldstein "and his ignorance," was that Dr. Goldstein maintained even at that time (seven years after Rav Geffen persuaded Coke to substitute the animal-based glycerin with that of vegetable origin), that Coca-Cola (as well as Pepsi-Cola) was not kosher, as it contained animal-based glycerin. In his rejoinder, Rav Pardes related that "truthfully, these drinks were exclusively produced with only kosher ingredients," following a position that he personally held was not necessary, but was nonetheless adhered to by Coca-Cola, as per Rav Geffen's instruction.

Chodosh and Yoshon (Chapter 25, Pages 335–337)

The *Moshav Zekeinim al HaTorah* (*Vayikra* Ch. 23:14) cites the fascinating and novel *shittah* of one of the eminent French *Baalei HaTosafos*, Rav Shlomo M'Dreux, who permitted drinking beer the entire winter, even in a country where new grain was not planted prior to Pesach. His reasoning was that since most of the world planted their new grain before Pesach, one may rely on the *rov*, even in a sealed country that did not. Interestingly, this author has not seen this *shittah* cited or discussed elsewhere. Thanks are due to Rabbi Pesach Feldman for pointing this out.

Aside from the *Lechem Mishneh* and *Pnei Yehoshua*, there were other authorities who agreed with their *chodosh* beer *hetter* (page 335, footnote 19), including Rav Aviezri Zelig Auerbach, Rav of Bouxwiller, Alsace, France, in the mid-1700s, and grandfather of the *Nachal Eshkol*, Rav Tzvi Binyamin Auerbach. In his recently printed *Shu"t Olilos Aviezer* (8; published in 2014 by *Machon Shomrei Mishmeres Hakodesh* as part of *Shu"t Nachal Eshkol*), he penned an extensive *teshuva* defending this position, maintaining that even beer produced from *chodosh* grain may be drunk.

In Rav Yerachmiel Fried's recent *Maadanei Shlomo* (on *Dalet Chelkei Shulchan Aruch*, pg. 255–256), he recounts that when he first moved to Dallas as Rosh Kollel of DATA decades ago, he was in a quandary. As a *talmid* of Rav Aharon Soloveitchik, Rosh Yeshivas Brisk Chicago, who was extremely *makpid* with *yoshon* even in *Chutz La'aretz*, Rav Fried was careful to eat only *yoshon* products. Yet, in Dallas at the time, *yoshon* items were not at all available. He relates that Rav Shlomo Zalman Auerbach told him that as the majority of Bnei Torah in America were not *makpid* with keeping *yoshon* at the time, it is as if he did not accept the *minhag* to be *machmir* upon himself in a situation where *yoshon* was not obtainable. Rav Shlomo Zalman advised him to be *mattir neder*, which he did. Yet, Rav Fried adds parenthetically that it caused him great distress that he needed to be *mattir neder* and give up on his long-standing custom of exclusively eating *yoshon* in *Chutz La'aretz*.

Gedolims' Reliance on "Chalav Stam" (Chapter 30, Page 410)

It has recently come to light that Rav Shlomo Zalman Auerbach held of the *hetter* of *"Chalav Stam" me'ikar hadin* as well, ruling that those in *Chutz La'aretz* who are living in areas where it is difficult to obtain *Chalav Yisrael*, is considered *shaas hadchak*, and (paraphrasing the Gemara in *Brachos* 9a regarding Rabbi Shimon bar Yochai), "*u'kdai hu Rav Moshe zt"l lismoch al hetteiro zeh b'shaas hadchak.*" See Rav Yerachmiel Fried's recent *Maadanei Shlomo* (on *Dalet Chelkei Shulchan Aruch*, pg. 243–244).

Kosher Soap (Chapter 6, Pages 66–68)

Soap had traditionally been produced with animal fats, thus posing a potential problem for the kosher consumer (at least *lechatchilla*; as it is processed with a strong alkali such as sodium hydroxide, the finished product should be rendered *pagum*). This changed in the mid-1800s, when Israel Rokeach of Kovno opened the first factory that mass produced kosher soap, sourced from coconut oil. A true innovator, Mr. Rokeach devised a method of imprinting the Hebrew word "kosher" in blue or red dye penetrating through each bar of soap, thus enabling the designation of separate bars of soap for *milchigs* and *fleishigs*, and earning the personal *hashgacha* of the *Gadol Hador*, Rav Yitzchak Elchanan Spektor.

Although the *halacha* (Y.D. 89:4; see *Rema*, *Levush*, and main commentaries) requires noticeably different designated cutlery and placemats, etc., for dairy and meat, Mr. Rokeach's color-coded soaps are credited with launching the widespread "tradition" of using specifically blue for *milchigs* and red for *fleishigs* on everything food related, from labels to dishtowels.

Fleeing pogroms, Mr. Rokeach moved his soap enterprise to New York in 1890. In the ensuing years, his company, I. Rokeach and Sons, grew into one of the world's largest kosher food manufacturers. Known as a tremendous *Baal Tzedaka*, Mr. Rokeach was one of the founders of the kosher Beth Moses Hospital, today known as Maimonides Medical Center, as well as three settlements in Israel.

Interestingly, history has proven that he was not the first to manufacture kosher soap in America. As per an ad in *The Occident* (April 02, 1866), that title seems to go to Hammerschlag & Amram of Philadelphia, who "commenced the manufacture of Kasher Soap, which has been long a great desideratum to religious households."

Appendix
The Evolution of "Kosher" Gelatin in America

ALTHOUGH TOUCHED UPON PREVIOUSLY (chapter 9, pages 104–108), American kosher gelatin production's fascinating and divisive *halachic* history deserves a more comprehensive treatment due to its impact on kosher certification, even until today. As noted, gelatin, the translucent and flavorless gelling agent that makes marshmallows and gummy bears gummy, is derived from collagen obtained from various animal by-products, mainly the bones and skin of cows and/or pigs.

In the 1920s and 30s, "kosher" gelatin was all the rage, as it was a cheap and easy-to-make dessert.[1] Jell-O brand gelatin, although not actually certified at the time by any Rabbinic authority, was widely considered kosher. Aside from taking out Yiddish ads in the main Jewish periodicals of the day, Jell-O also published promotional booklets specifically targeting the Jewish consumer, including *At Grandmother's* (in Yiddish, 1924) and *Tales and Legends of Israel* (in English, 1933). Unbelievably, these

Yiddish Jell-O ad from the 1920s

---

1   As detailed at length in historian Roger Horowitz's *Kosher USA: How Coke Became Kosher and Other Tales of Modern Food* (Chapter 3, "The Great Jell-O Controversy").

booklets coupled Biblical stories and moral lessons with promoting a general market food product, certainly a novelty at the time.

In the January 1932 issue of *HaPardes*, the journal's editor, Rav Shmuel Aharon Pardes published a *teshuva* permitting Junket, which essentially is dried-out and ground-up rennet[2] from non-*shechted* cows, used as a thickening agent in preparing food. He based his leniency on the *psak* of the *Rema* regarding *Or Hakeiva*, the stomach lining of a cow.[3] If it is dried up "like wood," the *Rema* rules that one may use it for cheese processing, and it is not considered a violation of the *halachos* of *Bassar B'chalav*. Not a simple topic, later authorities caution not to rely on this *psak lechatchilla*, and there is question whether this ruling would also apply to actual meat, as well as if it can be "re-awakened" via cooking to become once again prohibited.[4]

Rav Pardes writes that he spoke with Rav Eliezer Silver about this topic, but reports that Rav Silver was uneasy about accepting this product as kosher. Since Junket was being produced exclusively for the purpose of being part and parcel of actual food, as opposed to an aid in cheese production as was the case of the *Rema*, he thought that perhaps such leniency was overreaching.

In his *teshuva*, Rav Pardes continues that he replied with a precedent from an earlier *teshuva* of the *Gadol Hador*, Rav Chaim Ozer Grodzenski (dated March 1912),[5] allowing the use of non-kosher wine sediments as part of the process of producing "citron salt" (presumably calcium citrate). Since during this process, chemically, any non-kosher wine residue is entirely destroyed and converted into something that "even a dog would not eat," and hence considered "*Panim Chadoshos*, akin to

---

2   Rennet is a complex set of enzymes produced in the stomach of ruminant animals; essentially the stomach lining. It is what curdles milk into cheese.

3   *Rema* (Y.D. 87: end 10), ruling like the *Shibolei Leket* (vol. 2:34).

4   See commentaries of the *Shach*, Rav Akiva Eiger, *Pischei Teshuva*, and *Pri Megadim*, et al. ad loc.

5   Published as *Shu"t Achiezer* (vol. 1, Y.D. 11).

a brand new entity," it is essentially permitted, even if it would be later used as part of a *taaruvos* in a different edible item.⁶

A second precedent he cites is the *shittah* of the *Yad Yehuda*. The *Yad Yehuda* maintains that there should not be any difference regarding dried-out *Or Hakeiva* between skins and flesh, nor milk and meat or *treif*, that if truly dried-out "like wood," all would be permitted. [This interpretation argues on earlier authorities, including the *Noda B'Yehuda* and *Pri Megadim*, who understood the *Rema's hetter* to be exclusively pertaining to *Or*, skin, *halachically* considered extraneous and inedible, and not actual meat].⁷

A third precedent Rav Pardes cites is that of Rav Yehuda Leib Tsirelson's, Chief Rabbi of Bessarabia, in a *teshuva* published in his *Shu"t Atzei Halevanon* in 1922 (dated 1910), outright permitting using ground-up dried-out rennet powder from non-*shechted* cows to produce cheese (*Käselabpulver*). Rav Tsirelson felt strongly about this *hetter*, as in his *sefer*, he printed an anonymous opposing *teshuva* (this author discovered that it was penned by Rav Zalman Prager of Kishinev in 1911), and devoted a second *teshuva* defending his lenient position.⁸

---

6   The source for this leniency is the opinion of Rabbeinu Yonah, cited by the *Rosh* in *Brachos* (Ch. 6:38) regarding the status of musk. Accordingly, as during the process of producing gelatin the original bones are completely destroyed by the various acids et al. and the inedible gelatinous results bear no resemblance, not even by taste nor form to the original, it would therefore be considered a completely new item.

7   *Yad Yehuda* (Y.D. 87, *Peirush Ha'aruch* 24), *Shu"t Noda B'Yehuda* (*Kama* Y.D. 26), and *Pri Megadim* (ibid.). The *Maharsham* (*Shu"t* vol. 3:347) seems to understand this *halacha* akin to the *Yad Yehuda*, that if *cheilev* (tallow) would be dried out and "*nifgam ad shenifsal mei'achilas kelev*," it would be allowed to be used for lighting a pipe. However, he does not discuss the permissibility of using this *hetter* in preparing actual edible food.

8   *Shu"t Atzei Halevanon* (Y.D. 43–45). Rav Prager's *teshuva* was originally published in the *Shaarei Torah* journal (*Choveret* 12, *Chelek* 6:100; 1922; Rav Tsirelson's were originally published in this journal as well). However, and seemingly unreported in America, Rav Prager actually issued a fiery rejoinder to Rav Tsirelson's second *teshuva*, titled "*Devarim al Michonam*," in a later issue

Rav Pardes also later received a *teshuva* permitting gelatin from his former *rebbi*, Rav Yehuda Leib Graubart, at the time Chief Rabbi of Toronto, dated January, 1933, asserting a similar permissibility as ruled by Rav Tsirelson.[9] This permissive ruling was further endorsed when Rav Chaim Ozer Grodzenski penned a famous *teshuva* in May, 1936, specifically regarding gelatin, directly permitting "gelatin produced from hard cows' bones."[10]

Based on the above strong rabbinic precedents, it seems that Rav Silver acquiesced to Rav Pardes' lenient ruling regarding rennet, gelatin, and Junket. All share a similar *hetter*—all are animal-based products that were dried out and chemically processed into a different item.

Indeed, in the years following, other purportedly kosher gelatins reached the market, but this time with a *hashgacha*, including "Kojel," manufactured by Kosher Desserts, Inc., under the *hashgacha* of Rav Yehuda Leib Seltzer, *Menahel* of the *Agudas HaRabbanim*. Although there was some mention of gelatin in rabbinic literature on both sides of the debate in the following years,[11] nonetheless, until the late

---

of the *Shaarei Torah* journal (vol. 7, *Kuntress* 12:145; 1923). He argued that the cheese production of the time using this rennet did not actually fit into any of the *halachic* precedents and leniencies cited. He stressed that cheesemakers under *hashgacha* would certainly not rely on using such rennet processed from *neveilos u'treifos*, asserting that anyone who would rule leniently, "*batla daato*, his opinion is irrelevant (nullified)."

9   Published in his *Shu"t Chavalim B'Ne'imim* (vol. 4:23).

10 This *teshuva* was published as *Shu"t Achiezer* (vol. 3:33, 5). It was addressed to Rav Yosef Konvitz (son-in-law of the *Ridbaz*), who later wrote his own *teshuva* permitting it as well—*Shu"t Divrei Yosef* (vol. 2:6). Other famous *Poskim* of the time who permitted gelatin produced exclusively from bovine bones include Rav Simcha Zelig Rieger, *Dayan* of Brisk (responsum dated 5698/1938 but only first published in *Kovetz Moriah* (Elul 5775; issue 400-402, pg. 76-77), and Rav Moshe Nosson Nota Lemberger (*Shu"t Ateres Moshe* Y.D. vol. 1:42-43).

11 See for example, Rav Dovid Tzvi Hoffman's *Shu"t Melamed L'Ho'eel* (vol. 2, Y.D. 35), Rav Yitzchak Burstein's *Shu"t Metaamei Yitzchak* (vol. 2:24-25), Rav

1940s, it appears that this lenient ruling was not strongly contested in America, perhaps with the exception of Dr. Abraham Goldstein and his son George.

Dr. Goldstein, a noted chemist who headed the OK Labs and authored the *Kosher Food Guide* (which his son took over after his death in 1944), publicly maintained that any food item whose origins lie in a non-kosher source may not be considered kosher, no matter how "changed" it may currently appear. His strongly held views (correct or not) caused him to be at loggerheads with Rav Pardes over quite a few issues over the years. Already in 1936, Jell-O gelatin was described in the *Kosher Food Guide* as "absolutely *trefa*...as the gelatin contained in the product is derived from *trefa* bones and parts of skins, as for instance the skins of hams, etc."[12] He also noted that there was "unfortunately no kosher animal gelatin produced."[13] Yet, at the time, Dr. Goldstein was shunned

---

Shlomo Zalman Weisberg's *Shu"t Sha'al Shlomo* (6), Rav Elazar Meir Preil's *Shu"t Hama'or* (vol. 2:23–24), Rav Avraham Moshe Karpel's *Chiddushei R"AM* (25), Rav Chaim Yitzchak Yerucham's *Shu"t Birkas Chaim* (17), and Rav Nissan Telushkin's *Taharas Mayim* (Ch. 61).

12 However, Dr. Goldstein was not the first learned American Orthodox chemist to oppose gelatin consumption. That distinction most likely goes to prestigious physiologist and chemist, Dr. David Israel Macht of Baltimore. In the September 5, 1914 issue of *The Medical Record* ("Detection of Gelatin in Ice Cream"), Dr. Macht describes the experiments he conducted on "all ice-creams available in the market, and was surprised to find that almost all" gave a positive reaction, "thus pointing to the presence of gelatin." He gives several reasons why he was conducting such experiments, including that "some people, as for instance Orthodox Hebrews, regard such ice-creams as not kosher and prohibited by the Jewish Dietary laws." See also his related article in the *Jewish Forum* (vol. 14, issue 1) from 1931, titled "Ice Cream, Sour Cream, and Gelatin."

13 In other words, although nowadays easily obtainable, at the time there was no fully-kosher gelatinous alternative available. According to *The Biology of Seaweeds*, the vast majority of agar-agar (seaweed) vegetable gelatin used to be produced in Japan, and only became available in America after World War II, starting around 1947. Although Rav Nochum Tzvi Kornmehl of Barton's

by many rabbinic organizations due to his vociferous positions, coupled with his lack of rabbinic training or authority.

Indeed, in the January 1948 issue of *HaPardes*, in response to Dr. Goldstein and his son's challenge regarding gelatin, as part of a sharply worded rejoinder, Rav Pardes republished Rav Chaim Ozer's famous *teshuva* permitting "gelatin produced from hard cows' bones," as well as stating that Rav Graubart also permitted it. Rav Pardes concluded reiterating his utmost approval of Rav Seltzer and his *hashgacha* on gelatin (which he previously did in the August 1942 issue), asserting that it was certainly kosher, without a single reason or notion for doubt.

All of this changed in the early 1950s. In 1951, Jello-O brand gelatin actually became certified as kosher "without reservation," by Rabbis Shmuel Baskin and Shimon Winograd of the *Agudas HaRabbanim*, along with receiving a public endorsement from Rav Seltzer.[14] "Announcements were broadcast over the radio, publicized in newspapers, and published in advertising circulars."

However, soon after, and as discussed previously (chapter 9, footnote 15), after ascertaining the true state of affairs of gelatin production of the time, which utilized not only non-*shechted* bovine (cow) hides, but

---

Candy managed to produce kosher-slaughtered bovine-derived gelatin in the 1950s–60s for their confections, yet, it was not until 1991 when Rav Shimon Eider founded "Kolatin Real Kosher Gelatin," that gelatin produced from 100% *Glatt* kosher cow hides became widely available. Kosher fish gelatin only became a viable option in 1993, when founder of Food Industry Technology (FIT), Rabbi Dovid Holzer of Miami Beach, perfected, and actually patented, a process to extract high yield gelatin from kosher fish skins. Nowadays, kosher fish gelatin is the gelatin most commonly used in products for the strictly kosher consumer.

14   The Atlantic General Division of General Foods Corporation published a booklet titled "Atlantic Gelatin is Kosher and Pareve," featuring a study and responsum by Rabbis Baskin (later author of *Olas Shmuel*) and Winograd, in both English and Hebrew, followed by an approbation from Rav Seltzer, also in English and Hebrew.

also porcine (pig) hides,[15] the *Rosh Agudas HaRabbanim*, Rav Eliezer Silver, publicized a strongly-worded letter critical of the *hechsher* certifying Jell-O, Junket, and rennet, as well as listing over twenty-five well-known *Rabbanim* and *Poskim* of the time who agreed with his stringent position. In it, Rav Silver exclaimed that he was originally misled, as there were several important points overlooked by the *mattirim* (he referred to them as "struck with blindness, using weak inferences, and rationales pulled out of thin air...in order to permit items that the masses wonder about," meaning, they wonder how can such be permitted), including whether said original item was intended for the purpose for which it was actually being produced.

He explained that Rav Chaim Ozer's original permissive *teshuva* regarding non-kosher wine sediments being utilized in the production of "citron salt" was conditioned on the fact that this is not the main purpose of wine or even its sediments, but rather an additional use from its remnants. Additionally, only the *bliyos* (absorption) of wine

---

15 According to historian Roger Horowitz, this "innovation" in gelatin manufacture is due to the invention of the mechanized pork skinner by Townsend Engineering in 1947. He estimates that by the 1970s, fully 70 percent of American-produced gelatin came from pork sources. This estimation certainly holds true today. In fact, the OU maintains that presently, porcine-sourced gelatin accounts for almost 90 percent (!) of American gelatin production. *Kosharot* reports that currently worldwide, 44 percent of gelatin is porcine, 28 percent is sourced from non-kosher-slaughtered bovine hides, 27 percent is from non-*shechted* bovine bones, and only 1 percent is produced from kosher fish and kosher-slaughtered cows. In Rav Yirmiyahu Cohen, *Dayan* in Antwerp and later *Av Beis Din* of Paris' *Shu"t Veheirim Hakohen* (vol. 2:31), he details at length the processes of two types of dedicated gelatin lines from a plant in Belgium—one using only dried-out bones, and the other utilizing skins and fresh bones, etc., from *neveilos*. He concludes that although "we personally do not rely on either one" as kosher gelatin, nevertheless, he notes that the production line of gelatin processed exclusively out of dried-out bones is exactly as Rav Chaim Ozer described in his *teshuva*. Although evidently no longer extant in America, it is worth mentioning that such gelatin production still does exist.

in the sediments are actually prohibited; once that is destroyed in the chemical process, the remainder can be used as part of a mixture of a new product. On the other hand, regarding gelatin, by the 1950s, there were entire factories devoted to utilizing all of the bovine (and worse, porcine) parts—straight from the slaughterhouse—by breaking them down and turning their essence into gelatin.

Hence, Rav Silver asserted, not only would this be considered the actual original item intended for this specific purpose, but it also never truly became a *"Panim Chadoshos,"* as the collagen used for gelatin was inherently contained inside of it the entire time. Ergo, in his opinion, it by no means ever became *pagum* (foul and inedible), but rather "fit to be eaten," and hence, prohibited, if the source material was not kosher.[16] [Also, the *Yad Yehuda* quoted earlier actually qualified his permissive stance in one specific situation—prohibiting "dried-out-as-wood" cow stomach lining that became "re-awakened" via cooking, thus reverting to its original status and now "edible"—all of which would seem to fit gelatin production of the time.]

Rav Silver's assessment also is born out from Rav Chaim Ozer's famous permissive gelatin *teshuva* from 1936. As aside from his writing that his leniency with this dried-out ground-up powder only applied regarding hard bovine bones or bones that were dried out like wood, with absolutely no mention of hides[17] or flesh, and certainly not pork,

---

16   Many later *poskim* agreed with this assessment. Interestingly, it was first made decades prior by Rav Binyomin Aryeh Weiss, *Av Beis Din* of Czernowitz (*Shu"t Even Yikara* vol. 2:140), who makes this distinction in the *shittos* of Rishonim regarding honey manufactured by a non-Jew. It is cited in *She'arim Metzuyanim B'Halacha* (47:5), who adds that accordingly, gelatin would certainly be prohibited.

17   However, history has since proven that in a different (and apparently not well-known) *teshuva* addressed to Rav Pardes (printed in his posthumously published *Avnei Shmuel*, and later in *Igros R' Chaim Ozer*, vol. 1:341), Rav Chaim Ozer actually permitted gelatin processed from bovine hides as well, but exclusively those that were *"nifsalim mei'ochel adam, k'mo oros me'ubadim b'shvil na'alayim,* completely invalidated from the ability to be edible, such as

he also wrote that these bones were a waste product (*passul*), and their future use as an ingredient helping stabilize a mixture could never lead to an *Issur Deoraysa*, implying that there will be a ratio of 1:60 against it in the final product.[18] As Rav Silver noted, this decidedly did not seem to be the case in America in the 1950s, where the ground-up powder was being mass produced as gelatin, not only instrumental in thickening and stabilizing new food items, but more importantly, used as the core ingredient and basis of delicious desserts.

In Rav Silver's unambiguous words, "If Rav Chaim Ozer would have seen this gelatin production, he would certainly have prohibited it outright."[19] Rav Silver emphatically concluded that all such animal-based products, including gelatin, Junket, and rennet, must be kosher sourced to truly be considered kosher.

In fact, this debate became the hot topic of the day. Indeed, there was a screaming headline and article published in the *Hama'or* journal in December 1951, "*Shaaruriya M'Saviv L'Gelatin*, Disaster Regarding Gelatin," urging everyone to publicly protest this abomination of "*bassar chazir u'neveilah nimkar b'pumbi b'tur kosher*, pig meat and *neveilos* publicly being sold as kosher," and everyone buying it!

Aside from storms of protest from the *Kosher Food Guide*, well-known *Rabbanim* started getting involved, publishing *maamarim* to clarify the underlying *halachic* concerns inherent in Jell-O's consumption. For example, Rav Nochum Tzvi Kornmehl of Albany, highly regarded

---

processed hides used as shoe leather." He also reiterated that the final gelatin product is for use as part of a mixture to help it become thicker and less "liquidy," and does not impart any taste whatsoever.

18 The precedent Rav Chaim Ozer cites for this ruling is *Shu"t Rabbi Akiva Eiger* (vol. 1:207; quoted in *Pischei Teshuva* Y.D. 87:19), discussing a similar case of probable *bittul* issue in a manufacturing process. Rav Eiger rules leniently in his scenario as there assuredly is always *shishim k'negged* the amount of potential *issur* being placed in the *taaruvos*.

19 Rav Moshe Feinstein was also quoted as asserting similarly in the recently published *Mesores Moshe* (vol. 2, pg. 186:46): "*D'hayom gam ha'Achiezer yodeh, dehalo osim mei'oros im bassar.*"

mashgiach for the famous Barton's Candy, and expert in candy and gelatin production, wrote an extensive *teshuva* on gelatin production methods of the day, published in the December 1951 issue of *HaPardes*.[20] His conclusion was that although gelatin produced from dried-out non-kosher-slaughtered bovine bones or hides may be considered "bottom-level" kosher (although he maintains that they would not be), "it certainly would behoove any G-d-fearing Jew who is concerned with kashrus not to rely on such, but rather work with factories that produce gelatin from kosher-slaughtered cattle, as this is a viable alternative that will also make a *Kiddush Hashem*."

It seems that their words had an impact, and indeed, in the wake of Rav Silver's proclamation and ensuing public outrage, toward the close of 1951, the *Agudas HaRabbanim* summoned the rabbis granting Jell-O supervision to a special assembly. By the end of this meeting, all three certifying rabbis were forced into withdrawing their *hashgacha* and endorsements on Jell-O. However, only Rav Seltzer's retraction remained. Several months later, Rabbis Baskin and Winograd retracted their retraction, and recertified Jell-O.

But the public pressure for their "passing off non-kosher as kosher" did not abate.[21] The March 1952 issue of the *Hama'or* journal contained

---

20 This *teshuva* was later republished as part of his "*Kuntress B'Inyan HaGelatin*" in his *Shu"t Tiferes Tzvi* (vol. 1).

21 Indeed, the public kashrus battle over Jell-O in America eerily mirrored a concurrent political one: the trial, conviction, and subsequent execution of the "Atomic Spies," Julius and Ethel Rosenberg, between 1951 and 1953. As the main evidence for the prosecution directly hinged upon a box of Jell-O cut in half, claiming it was used as a signal for "passing atomic secrets," Jell-O, itself crossing the borderline between kosher and *treif*, became a symbol of subversion and disloyalty. According to several recent accounts, as at the same time Jell-O was being publicly outed as not-kosher masquerading as kosher, it became a signifier for the Rosenbergs themselves: non-assuming Jewish parents who were deemed covert enemy agents, transferring American nuclear secrets to the Soviet Union. To American Jews Jell-O signified *treif*; to the jury in the Rosenberg case it signified guilt.

an extensive *teshuva* by the esteemed Professor Yisrael Mordechai (I.M.) Rabinowitch, Director of the Metabolism and Toxicology Department at Montreal General Hospital, and widely considered the "father of clinical chemistry in Canada." Prof. Rabinowitch dissected the permissive rabbis' *teshuva* permitting Jell-O, proving that it was not only inaccurate from a *halachic* perspective, but also from a scientific standpoint. Of his points, he convincingly argued that the gelatin process does not destroy the source animal's essence, but rather, preserves and even enhances it while obtaining its collagen.

The July 1952 issue of *HaPardes* was devoted exclusively to the topic of the permissibility of gelatin. The title page had a note recounting the stormy meeting of the *Agudas HaRabbanim* months prior, when the disagreement on the *halachic* viability and kashrus of gelatin transpired. The journal's editor at the time (and later, author of *Shalmei Simcha*), Rav Simcha Elberg (Rav Pardes passed away in 1956 after being severely ill for seven years, so it seems he was not part of this later gelatin controversy), added that the journal does not take sides in any debate, but rather allows all to partake in "legitimate arguments to reach the truth."

In this issue, Rav Seltzer, who endorsed Jell-O and certified Kojel, led off with a (rather unconvincing, in this author's opinion) response to Rav Silver's strongly worded attack, but it seems his rationale was contrived. Rav Seltzer resorts to saying that his ruling permitting gelatin was based on the rulings of three Torah giants of the previous generation: Rav Chaim Ozer, Rav Tsirelson, and Rav Graubart—all of whom he claimed must have permitted not only bovine bones, but also their hides in gelatin production, adding that one cannot assume that these bones were cleaned before processing. He also made a novel, and perhaps overreaching, inference in the *Rambam*'s words regarding extraneous animal parts,[22] claiming that the *Rambam* must have been referring to actual flesh of *neveilos* being permitted Biblically as well, as otherwise there is no "*chiddush*," as bones and skin are not truly edible.[23]

---

22 *Rambam (Hilchos Maacholos Assuros* Ch. 4:18).

23 Rav Seltzer's *teshuva* was later published in his *Shu"t V'Zos L'Yehuda* (O.C. 26).

However, in light of the strength of the opposition, this defense did not seem to impress the masses. The very next *teshuva* in the journal was from Rav Yosef Eliyahu Henkin, who prohibited such gelatin outright, unless exclusively produced with hard bovine bones, which was no longer the common process at the time.[24] This *teshuva* is in addition to a clarification to "Publicize the Truth" that Rav Henkin published in the November 1951 issue of *HaPardes*. In this quarter-page column, he stated that he was publicly reiterating that the only non-*shechted* animal-based gelatin he permitted was gelatin that was produced from dried-out bovine bones, and certainly not hides or flesh.

The last *teshuva* in the aforementioned issue was from the *HaPardes* editor, Rav Simcha Elberg, who tried to remain "pareve," maintaining that gelatin processed from dried-out bones should be allowed, yet concurring that it is not a simple matter to permit gelatin produced from hides, and certainly not from the flesh of non-kosher animals. He concludes with a thought that perhaps, "not to get embroiled in a potential stumbling-block, it is worthwhile to prohibit all types of gelatin and similar products that are not sourced from kosher-slaughtered animals."

However, the biggest point of contention with gelatin production of the day was that, as mentioned previously, much of it, by that time, was porcine sourced. Although truthfully, many were probably previously unaware regarding the non-kosher cow hides commonly used in gelatin production, but certainly the masses were not willing to stomach pig-based gelatin considered as kosher, with a *hashgacha*, yet.[25] Even those

---

24 This *teshuva* was originally printed in the *Hamsiloh* journal in February 1938, and later in his *Eidus L'Yisrael* (pg. 177), as well as his posthumously published *Shu"t Gevuros Eliyahu* (vol. 2-Y.D. end 16–23).

25 Especially as the *Rambam* (*Hilchos Maacholos Assuros* Ch. 4:21) ruled that the hides of domesticated pigs have the *halachic* status of actual pork, are considered edible, and are most definitely not kosher. Thus, even those who argue that gelatin produced from the hides or bones of non-*halachically shechted* cattle is still *me'ikar hadin* kosher have a harder time defending that position in regard to porcine gelatin.

ruling leniently, including Rav Seltzer, did not mention porcine gelatin in his defense, but rather, just non-kosher-slaughtered bovine flesh.[26]

In response to the *HaPardes* gelatin issue, aside from publishing a *teshuva* opposing such gelatin in the rival *Hama'or* journal, as well as in English in the *Kosher Food Guide*, noted author and wordsmith Rav Chaim Bloch wrote an entire *sefer* devoted exclusively to attacking those who would grant *hashgacha* to non-kosher-sourced gelatin. This work was provocatively titled *"Me'ashrim To'im U'Mat'im,"* literally meaning "Those Who Grant (or affirm) are Mistaken and Misleading Others," specifically referring to those giving *hashgacha* to such gelatin. In it, he prints several *teshuvos* from Rav Ben Tzion Chai Uziel, the first Sefardic Chief Rabbi of Israel, confirming that any non-kosher-sourced gelatin is indeed non-kosher. Rav Bloch also notes that Rav Seltzer's response was rather tepid, and although presenting the non-compelling rationale that the *Rambam*'s leniency included bovine flesh, nowhere did Rav Seltzer mention pork in his *teshuva*. Meaning, as Rav Seltzer was specifically writing to answer Rav Silver's attacks, which the main point of contention was that he, as well as Rav Chaim Ozer, was misled as to current porcine-based gelatin production, how did that core detail slip by without being addressed?[27]

---

26 However, in Rav Pardes' posthumously published responsum regarding gelatin (*Avnei Shmuel*, *Birurei Halacha* 19), while citing precedence from his earlier Junket *teshuva* (from 1931), he also acknowledged that gelatin may be produced from hides and bones of non-kosher animals, including pigskin. Although there is only one mention of this detail in the entire four-page responsum, it is feasible that he did not want such a fact to be published publicly (as Rabbis Baskin and Winograd originally attempted as well). Also, as he noted, he was not actually granting the *hashgacha* on the product, but rather merely "attempting to find a leniency to permit its consumption for those asking his opinion, as many were already eating it." There is quite a fine line between that and actively granting non-kosher-sourced gelatin a full *hashgacha*, as Rabbis Seltzer, Baskin, and Winograd did.

27 As attested to by Rabbis Baskin and Winograd in their later responsum defending their actions after being forced to give up their *hashgacha* on Jell-O, the truth is that aside from briefly endorsing Jell-O, Rav Seltzer's own

Rav Bloch pours on the rhetoric, adding that when he was interred in a World War I POW camp (after being drafted, he served as a chaplain in the Austro-Hungarian army), at one point, all the starving prisoners had to eat was ground-up pig bones' powder, and they had to ask a *halachic* question and force themselves to eat it just to survive. So how can it be that "the so-called rabbis" in America are deeming such items as "kosher"?! He avers that "one would require psycho-analysis in order to understand how a rabbi could permit the skin of pigs."

Around the same time, a rival journal to *HaPardes*, *Kovetz Kerem*, under the editorship of the renowned Rosh Yeshiva, Rav Chaim Zimmerman, devoted an issue to the topic.[28] First bemoaning that the *HaPardes* journal has "lost its way" and declaring that it no longer speaks for Orthodox Jewry, it then singled out gelatin as one of their main contentions. To drive their point home, they republished Rav Silver's scathing responsum, using many honorifics and a giant bolded headline, including the twenty-five respected rabbis who concurred with him, and followed by an extensive *maamar* by Rav Silver's son-in-law, Rav Yehuda Gershuni, who was widely regarded as an *iluy* (genius), proving his points.

---

personal *hashgacha* was not actually granted to porcine gelatin. In fact, Rabbis Baskin and Winograd bitterly lamented that Rav Seltzer still gave *hashgacha* on Kojel, which at the time was sourced from bovine *neveilos* and *treifos* and not pork, yet, did not seem to be contested. They questioned the *halachic* differentiation between the two and concluded with a rhetorical question: If they can convince Jell-O to switch their source of gelatin from pig-skins to cow *neveilos* and *treifos*, would their *hashgacha* then be acceptable? Come what may, nowadays, and for at least the last several decades, Kojel has been widely known for exclusively being vegetable sourced—from agar-agar (seaweed)—and truly kosher. Indeed, Kojel even made PETA's list of acceptable kosher gelatin alternatives.

28 *Kovetz Kerem* (Year 2: vol. 1; Tishrei 5713). Rav Silver's *teshuva* was also reprinted as part of the "*Kuntress B'Inyan HaGelatin*" in Rav Kornmehl's *Shu"t Tiferes Tzvi* (vol. 1). Another *teshuva* he wrote on the topic, addressed to Rav Zelig Reuven Bengis of the *Eidah Hachareidis* in Yerushalayim, was reprinted in *Kovetz Yeshurun* (vol. 12, pg. 241).

Ultimately, by mid-1952, due to the unrelenting public pressure, Rabbis Baskin and Winograd bowed out for good from certifying Jell-O. However, they wrote a *teshuva* in defense of their actions, published in the *Hama'or* journal in August 1952, explaining why they felt that there should not have been an issue with certifying non-kosher-sourced gelatin, even gelatin produced from pig-skins. This responsum is immediately followed by an editor's note explaining where they went wrong, and once again asserting that there really is no basis for such leniency.

It is believed that this public censure helped spur the "gelatin turnaround" for mainstream Orthodox Judaism. Proof of this, perhaps, is that although gelatin was on the table again in the October 1952 issue of *HaPardes*, featuring two *teshuvos* from Rav Pinchas Mordechai Teitz from Elizabeth, New Jersey, as well as a response from Rav Elberg, nonetheless, both of them strongly questioned the permissibility of gelatin, concluding that certainly there is no allowance for porcine gelatin, asserting that "anyone who thinks so is mistaken, as the rule of *Panim Chadoshos* can only work to remove an *issur* from a product that is inherently kosher." [Meaning, a cow is essentially a kosher animal, and even if not slaughtered properly, it is still a kosher animal, it just cannot be eaten because it became a *neveilah*.] On the other hand, a pig, which is a non-kosher animal, even if chemically dried out, its essence is still non-kosher.[29]

Indeed, the next time gelatin makes an appearance in *HaPardes*, it is over a year later, in the January 1954 issue, with a *teshuva* by Rav Moshe Feinstein regarding gelatin produced from kosher-slaughtered hides, discussing whether it is considered *fleishig* or pareve. There was one later feature in *HaPardes* in the September 1955 issue, by the venerated Rav Yechezkel Abramsky, former head of the *London Beis Din*, who had just retired to Yerushalayim, in which he argues (as Rav Henkin and Rav Chaim Ozer et al. did previously) that gelatin produced from dried bovine bones is still technically kosher, as opposed to hides or flesh,

---

29 Rav Elberg republished all of his gelatin *teshuvos* together as an extensive *Kuntress* on gelatin in *Avnei Shmuel*, which he compiled and edited.

which he defines as non-kosher. Yet, he concludes that since people will get confused and wonder how non-kosher animals can produce kosher gelatin, it is preferable to consider all non-kosher-slaughtered animal-based gelatin non-kosher as well, even if not necessarily actually non-kosher.[30]

To sum up the matter, it seems that the parallels and precedents used by Rabbis Pardes and Seltzer back in 1931 for permitting Junket, rennet, and gelatin did not hold up to the test of actual mass gelatin production as it was performed in America in 1952. Indeed, a scant five years after Rav Pardes wrote assuredly that gelatin under *hashgacha* was definitively kosher, even his own journal "turned around 180 degrees," and only kosher-sourced gelatin was discussed in it as being truly kosher.

In fact, upon researching how non-kosher-slaughtered animal-based gelatin was perceived in the decades following, this author discovered several explicit examples of how the tide had turned and mainstream American Orthodox public opinion was now that this gelatin was indeed considered "*treif*," notwithstanding that there were and are several individual rabbis who continued to grant *hashgacha* to such animal-based gelatin:[31]

---

30 Both of these *teshuvos* were later reprinted in the authors' respective *sefarim*—*Shu"t Igros Moshe* (Y.D. vol. 1:37) and *Chazon Yechezkel* (*Zevachim*, *Shu"t* 5; also printed in the preface to *Shu"t Tzitz Eliezer* vol. 4).

31 Indeed, for many years now, Jell-O brand gelatin products have sported a small "K" on the label to mark it as kosher. Parent company Kraft Foods has for years professed that Jell-O "is certified as kosher by a recognized Orthodox rabbi. Jell-O is also Pareve, and can be eaten with either a meat meal or a dairy meal." For those who request more information, it is reported that they send a fact sheet with a copy of "The Halachic Basis of Our Kashruth Certification of Atlantic Gelatin and the General Foods Products Containing This Gelatin" by Rabbi Yehuda Gershuni and Rabbi David Telsner. The upshot of this "responsum" is that since the collagen has been taken apart by chemical digestion and a new substance has been produced, "it meets the specifications of the Orthodox Dietary Laws and is Kosher and Pareve." [This author cannot adequately explain how this position is in line with Rav Gershuni's fiery *teshuva* from 1952 opposing those who granted such gelatin *hashgacha*,

In 1964, the *Noam* journal printed Rav Kornmehl's query for Barton's Candy (discussed previously, page 107, footnote 16) regarding kosher-slaughtered bovine gelatin—whether it was considered pareve or *fleishig*—along with the extensive replies from Rav Moshe Feinstein and Rav Aharon Kotler, as well as Rav Yitzchak Flakser of the *Vaad HaRabbanim* of the *Agudas Yisrael* in Yerushalayim. All decisively maintain that gelatin sourced from non-*shechted* animals is not kosher.[32]

---

except to surmise that perhaps he later felt that if people were going to eat it anyway, he should at least give them something to be *somech* on, not to be considered blatant transgressors.] There is a telling article that this author has discovered, penned by a non-Jew, titled "The Gelatin Question: Some Gelatin Passed off as Kosher," about how dismayed he was, and the lengths he had to go, just to get a straight answer as to how "kosher" his Jell-O truly was. His response upon finding out the "amazing conclusion" that "kosher" Jell-O gelatin "could be made from ANY animal," including pork, was that "by this deceitful line of reasoning, one could conceivably start with MANURE and get a certified 'kosher' product." There is even an online petition (remarkably, started by non-Jews) to convince Kraft Foods to stop sourcing their Jell-O with "the remains of unclean animals." Interestingly, this campaign may have been partially successful. In recent years, a variety of Jell-O brand pudding products have been sporting mainstream *hashgachos*: the OK in the United States and the COR in Canada. The secret to this interesting outcome (as confirmed by the certifying agencies) is that although produced by Jell-O brand, these pudding snacks (as opposed to their gel-based snacks) do not actually contain gelatin.

32   Rav Moshe and Rav Flakser concluded that gelatin produced from *shechted* cattle is considered pareve, a *psak* that the OU and other kashrus organizations follow. On the other hand, Rav Aharon maintained that it remains sort of *fleishig*; not that eating it would mandate a waiting period, but rather not to mix such gelatin with dairy unless there is a 60:1 ratio against it in the mixture. Rav Aharon adds a salient point. He maintains that the fact that one intends to use gelatin as a food item makes it considered "*Achshevei.*" This means that one's intention to eat it, although currently inedible, would *halachically* return it to its original status, reconsider it a food item, and thus, in the case of non-kosher-sourced gelatin, be rendered *treif*. In the case of kosher-*shechted* gelatin, he maintains it would maintain a "somewhat *fleishig*" status. For examples of how "*Achshevei*" might work, see *Rosh* (*Pesachim*,

In 1966, the *Noam* journal published a brief *teshuva* from Dayan Aryeh Leib Grossnas of the *London Beis Din* (author of *Shu"t Lev Aryeh*), regarding gelatin sourced from Chrome Leather. His reply was that although animal-based gelatin is commonly considered *treif* (and briefly citing the debate from the previous decade), nonetheless, if it is produced after it was already fashioned into leather, all would agree it is acceptable.[33] He concludes that this topic is purely academic, as gelatin sourced from Chrome Leather was at the time processed under *hashgacha* and sourced from kosher-slaughtered cows.

In 1970, Rav Shmuel Tuvia (Tibor) Stern of Miami Beach (known for his controversial kosher certification of Hebrew National meats) wrote a responsum prohibiting all animal-based gelatins not sourced from kosher-slaughtered animals.[34]

In April 1972, Dayan Gavriel Krausz of the *Manchester Beth Din* published a pamphlet on the permissibility of animal-based gelatin (originally a lecture delivered to the Association of Orthodox Jewish Scientists), titled "Kashrus, Food, and Chemicals." He concluded that it is forbidden to eat, but offered leniency in certain cases of medication containing gelatin, especially if it has an unpleasant taste or is tasteless.[35]

Ch. 2: end 1), *Taz* (O.C. 442:8), *Minchas Chinuch* (Mitzva 261:5), and *Shu"t Shaagas Aryeh* (75). All of these gelatin *teshuvos* were later published in 1966 in Rav Kornmehl's own "*Kuntress B'Inyan HaGelatin*" in his *Shu"t Tiferes Tzvi* (vol. 1), as well as in the authors' respective *sefarim—Shu"t Igros Moshe* (Y.D. vol. 2:27) and *Shu"t Mishnas Rabbi Aharon* (16–17).

33 Rav Grossnas later devoted a *kuntress* to this topic (presumably a volume of his *Hotzaas Bais Din Tzedek London V'Hamedina*). Others who made a similar assessment include Rav Chaim Ozer Grodzenski (in his little-known *teshuva* to Rav Pardes ibid.), Rav Moshe Feinstein (*Shu"t Igros Moshe* Y.D. vol. 2:23), and Rav Menashe Klein (*Shu"t Mishnah Halachos* vol. 19:94). On the other hand, the *Minchas Yitzchak* (*Shu"t* vol. 5:5) is stringent even in this case, since even after being processed into shoe leather it can still be "re-awakened" as fully functional gelatin.

34 Published in his *Shu"t Hashavit* (vol. 3, Y.D. 3).

35 Many other recent *Poskim* made this distinction for a *choleh* as well, especially

In the May 1973 issue of the *Hama'or* journal, Rav Shmuel Dovid Munk of Haifa (author of *Shu"t Pe'as Sadecha*) discussed the permissibility of an artificial salt (for one who cannot eat real salt) that may contain an animal-based ingredient that has gone through a chemical change, in minute amounts. There is an editorial note cautioning not to glean from this topic that the author would be of the opinion that animal-based gelatin is kosher, and briefly delineates significant differences between the issues.

The September 1973 issue of *Hama'or* journal published a letter from Gedalia Schwartz of Los Angeles, in which he decried the current situation where a certain anonymous "rabbi" permitted the mixing of non-*shechted* animal-based gelatin into the local milk. He felt the need to publicize this to raise awareness of the gravity of the situation, asserting that it is decidedly not kosher.

This gelatin debate and its ultimate resolution signified a turning point in America's kosher industry for several reasons. *Rabbanim* realized the need to take into account the complexity of modern food production when granting a *hashgacha*, recognizing that it may not necessarily suffice to rely upon *halachic* precedents discussing food production methods from the *"Alter Heim."*

Another upshot is that since this era, when the most respected American *Rabbanim* of the time issued the widely accepted ruling that true kosher gelatin must be kosher sourced, as far as this author is aware, all major mainstream American kashrus agencies, even nowadays, consider all other animal-based gelatin as non-kosher.[36] Although

---

regarding a pill or caplet containing gelatin, which is not actually "eaten," but rather swallowed. See, for example *Shu"t Melamed L'Ho'eel* (vol. 2-Y.D. 34–35), *Chazon Ish* (O.C. 116:8 s.v. tabla'os), *Shu"t Shevet Halevi* (vol. 7:135), *Shu"t Sdei Elchanan* (vol. 2:12), *Kovetz Teshuvos* (vol. 1:73), *Emes L'Yaakov* (on *Tur* and *Shulchan Aruch*, Y.D. 84, footnote 33), *Shu"t Tzitz Eliezer* (vol. 10:25, 2), and *Nishmas Avraham* (vol. 2, Y.D. 84:2).

36 However, contrary to the accepted mainstream norm described above, and similar to the Israeli Chief Rabbinate's former position (see following

the Israeli Chief Rabbinate does maintain a bottom-line kosher designation of *"kosher l'ochlei gelatin,"*[37] on the other hand, no *Badatz* in

---

footnote), there are several American Orthodox rabbis who profess a nuanced approach, and currently certify non-*shechted* bovine-based gelatin as kosher while rejecting porcine-sourced gelatin. Rabbis who maintain this minority position include Rabbi David I. Sheinkopf (Kosher Supervisory Services), grandson of Rav Seltzer and author of *Gelatin in Jewish Law*, and Rav Aryeh Ralbag, whose *hashgacha*, the Triangle-K, maintains a designation of "Triangle-K-Contains Gelatin" for products "that have been kosher certified by Triangle-K but contain (bovine) gelatin."

37 This is presumably due to the more permissive rulings (at least *mei'ikar hadin*) of several highly regarded *Poskim*, including longtime Chief Rabbi of Yerushalayim Rav Tzvi Pesach Frank (*Shu"t Har Tzvi* Y.D. 83), Rav Eliezer Yehuda Waldenberg (preface to *Shu"t Tzitz Eliezer* vol. 4 and vol. 20:34), Rav Ben Tzion Abba-Shaul (*Shu"t Ohr L'Tzion* vol. 1, O.C. 34, pg. 90), and former Sefardic Chief Rabbi Rav Ovadiah Yosef (*Shu"t Yabia Omer* vol. 8, Y.D. 11). According to an article on the OU website from 2005 titled "What is Kosher Gelatin Revisited," "Non-*Mehadrin hashgachos* in Israel relied on the lenient opinion and allowed gelatin from non-slaughtered beef bones into certified yogurt products. This situation bothered *Gedolei HaPoskim* in Eretz Yisrael, and after many years of behind-the-scenes work, they were finally able to convince the *hashgachos* to stop this practice." This is further confirmed by former Sefardic Chief Rabbi Rav Eliyahu Bakshi-Doron in a *maamar* published on topic in 2003 (*Techumin* vol. 23). He writes that the *Rabbanut* used to give *hashgacha* on products containing non-*shechted* bovine-bone gelatin, but attests that *"k'yom, B'Siyatta D'Shmaya,"* they only accept gelatin sourced from *"beheimos kesheiros, she'ain bo kol chashash."* However, this change of policy may have likely resulted due to practical reasons. In 2006, a lawsuit for 12.3 billion NIS was filed against Strauss-Elite and the *Rabbanut*, claiming that they misled consumers as to the ingredients in their favorite yogurts and dairy puddings. It turns out that it was only in 2003 when it was revealed that these yogurts, etc., contained gelatin sourced from *neveilos u'treifos*, resulting in a public hue and cry. Part of their contention was that in the years preceding, divergent statements from the *Rabbanut* were publicly presented as to their standards of kosher gelatin, as well as whether dairy products under their *hashgacha* contained such gelatin. To partially alleviate the situation, in 2004, Strauss established a separate dedicated line for *Mehadrin* versions of these

Eretz Yisrael or *Mehadrin hashgacha* worldwide would consider bona fide animal-gelatin kosher unless it is produced from properly *shechted* kosher animals.[38] [39]

The next time you sit down to enjoy jello for dessert, appreciate the long and arduous journey that was traveled to ensure that your gelatinous treat is truly kosher.

---

products. Come what may, according to Rav Chagai Bar-Giora, Director of the Department of Industry and Manufacturing of the Chief Rabbinate (via personal communication on February 23, 2020), nowadays the designation of *"kosher l'ochlei gelatin,"* is used exclusively for certifying non-prescription medicines and vitamins. However, he assures that the *Rabbanut* does not currently accept nor grant *hashgacha* to actual food products containing gelatin unless it is properly kosher-sourced.

[38] Following the many contemporary *Poskim* who ruled this way, including the *Chazon Ish* (Y.D. 12:7), *Minchas Yitzchak* (*Shu"t* vol. 5:5), Rav Yosef Shalom Elyashiv (*Kovetz Teshuvos* vol. 1:73, 3), Rav Shmuel *Halevi* Wosner (*Shu"t Shevet Halevi* vol. 7:135), Rav Moshe Sternbuch (*Shu"t Teshuvos V'Hanhagos* vol. 2:381), Rav Menashe Klein (*Shu"t Mishnah Halachos* vol. 3:111), and Rav Yechezkel Roth (*Shu"t Eimek Hateshuva* vol. 3:67).

[39] With the exception of fish gelatin, which although not requiring *shechita*, would still need to be sourced from kosher fish (i.e., have fins and scales). As mentioned previously, nowadays fish gelatin is the most commonly used gelatin in candies, gummies, and confections for the strictly kosher consumer.

Index

A

Achshevei 106, 471

Ain Mevattlin Issur Lechatchilla 69, 88, 257–58

almond milk 362–64, 366

angels 20–23, 100, 372

Aver Min Hachai 100, 102, 111–12

B

baal nefesh 39, 333, 336, 342, 344, 400, 408, 416

Bach's hetter 337–39, 341–42, 347

bagels 84, 95, 297, 304, 307

Bal Tashchis 8, 272, 330

Bal Tosif 4, 138

Barton's 107, 447–48, 459, 464, 471

Bassar B'chalav 1, 3, 5, 11, 14, 16–17, 19–21, 23, 25, 27, 35–36, 42, 44–45, 48, 51–53, 58, 60–62, 64, 69, 73–75, 77–79, 93–94, 113, 123, 124, 137, 259, 273–76, 356, 362–63, 366, 394–95, 429, 441–43, 456

Bassar Min Hachai 102, 111, 116

bassar shenisalem min ha'ayin 156

battel b'rov 157, 267, 330, 353

battel b'shishim 60, 88, 119–21, 125, 257

beer 335–37, 349, 452

beheimos 133, 136, 144, 150, 474

bentching 28, 28–29, 310, 318–22

Beyond Burger 449

Bilaam 32–34

Bishul Akum 217, 219–24, 296–97, 300–3, 306, 358, 423

Bishul Yisrael 217–19, 221–24, 303–6

biskugies 273

bison 134, 136, 138, 142–44

bittul 86, 159, 263, 376, 396, 430, 463

bliyos 61, 71, 75, 90, 131, 262, 340, 431, 461

bochurim 194, 197, 200, 201, 272, 416
bones 104–9, 113, 114, 200–5, 455, 457–69, 474
bourekas 275
braces 439, 441, 444
Bris Seudah 83
buffalo 101, 133–34, 137–39, 142–44, 427
bullseye 28, 269, 274
butter 20, 94–96, 360, 364, 366, 410, 422–29

C

cake 232, 275–76, 295–97, 327, 332
cannabis 364
carbon dioxide 130, 288
cereal 219, 241, 246, 249, 302–306, 350
Chalav Akum 395–98, 400, 404, 406–8, 412–13, 417, 420–21, 425, 427, 430–31
Chalav Companies 405, 408
Chalav Stam 349, 408–10, 412–13, 415, 417, 425, 428–33, 437–38, 453
Chalav Yisrael 349–50, 394, 397–98, 404–6, 408–14, 416, 425, 428, 430, 430–31, 433–34, 436–38, 453
challah 176, 242, 271, 298, 300–1, 326, 331, 334

Chamira Sakanta Mei'Issura 85–86
Chashad 361–62
chasnus (intermarriage) 289, 378–80
Chassidei Umos Ha'Olam 206
Chatichah Hareuyah L'Hischabed 22, 145, 156–58, 164–65, 351, 353–58
chayos 133, 136
Chazara 189–91, 194–96, 198, 201–5
cheesecake 25, 28, 269, 271, 275–77
cheilev 133, 136, 395, 457
Chemas Akum 415, 422–23
chicken bones 201, 201–4
chodosh 59, 325–50, 400, 452
choleh 13, 105, 113, 114, 169–70, 250, 408, 472
cholent 60, 72, 88, 187–91, 194–5, 207, 224
chometz 73, 125, 210–14, 216, 235–39, 241, 243, 245, 247–48, 260, 263, 265, 326, 439, 441–42
Chutz La'aretz 55, 224, 325, 328–36, 338, 338–40, 343–49, 350, 452–53
clone 109, 116, 118
clothes 76
Coca-Cola 69, 124–26, 205, 256, 258, 261, 261–66, 268, 451–52

coffee 12, 17, 44, 76, 175, 268, 367, 406, 430
cookies 273, 275, 294–97, 307, 350
corn 236–37, 241–42, 244, 246, 252, 253
corn flour 249
corn syrup 263
cottage cheese 426–27
cottonseed oil 240–41, 253
crackers 58, 299, 302–3, 327
cream cheese 5, 83–84, 426
Crimson Tide 281, 285, 287
crowns 439–41, 443–44

D

daato lehachzir 195–96
Dagon 180
dairy bread 28, 269, 272–74, 276
davar charif 233–34
Davar HaMaamid 120–23, 132
Davar Sheyesh Lo Mattirin 165
dentures 440–44
deplume 355–56
detergent 66, 68–69
devarim shebekedusha 32
dishwashers 59, 61, 63–71, 233, 256
diyuk 3, 5, 7–8, 12–13, 26, 37, 313
doreis 135
doughnuts 300–1

E

eggs 67, 114, 165, 225–33, 296, 365, 450
enzyme modified cheese 58
esrog 5, 150, 208, 338, 368, 372

F

FDA 129, 408, 432, 438
fins and scales 133, 178, 182, 475
five steps (of serving cholent on Shabbos) 189
flash pasteurization 385, 389–91
forks 10, 25
french fries 219–22, 358

G

garlic powder 230–31
Garuf V'Katum 190–91, 193–94, 196
gelatin 104–10, 205, 268, 447–48, 455, 457–75
German custom 40
Gevinas Akum 417–18, 420–21, 423, 424, 427
Giddulei Issur 117
Gid Hanasheh 145, 148, 150
Gidulei Gedulim 117
Giluy 418–19
glycerin 125, 257, 261–62, 265–67, 451
Golem 102–3, 118, 178

H

Hachnassas Orchim 352–53
hadacha 8, 22, 25, 35, 43–44, 50–51, 85, 170, 442
Hagafen Cellars 390
hana'ah 3–4, 100, 379, 395–96
handwashing 7, 9, 11, 25, 50, 287, 308, 310–14
hard bones 106
hard cheese 28–29, 39, 47–49, 51–58, 420
hashlachas kiseim 290
hefsed merubah 157, 158, 164, 352, 354–55, 389, 418, 421, 430
Heiliger Sand 47
hekker 11, 16–21, 88, 100, 103, 273
hermetically sealed 230
hindquarters 146–47

I

Ikar and *Tafel* 277
Impossible Burger 129, 448–49
insects 369–72, 374–75
Iruy 441, 444
Israel issues 434

J

Jell-O 105, 455, 459, 461, 463–65, 467–71
J & J 411, 413

K

Kabbalah 26, 180
Kansas City *Takkanah* 155
kashering 76, 90, 146, 167, 169, 171–72, 174, 439, 441–44
kavua 144, 156, 158–64
Kavua Deoraysa 158–60
Kavua Derabbanan 158–61
kavush k'mevushal 131–32
Kedem Wine 391–92
k'eyn tura 274
kinuach 7–8, 22, 25, 35, 43, 50–51, 85, 442
kitniyos 210–217, 235–45, 247–55, 263
kli sheini 65, 440
Kojel 458, 465, 468
Kolatin 107, 460
Korban Omer 325, 333, 335, 339
Korbanos 99, 166–67, 173, 175, 271
koy 134

L

L'chvod Orchim 352
lelafos bo es hapas 218–21, 223, 304–5
Lifnei Iver 336
liver 169
locust 5–7, 445–46
lox and cream cheese 5, 83–84
L'tzorech Mitzva 197, 200

M

maachal Ben Derosoi 190, 194, 203

Maaseh Avos Siman L'Banim 24, 145, 351
magnifying glass 111, 368, 371–73, 375
Maris Ayin 16, 18, 21–22, 100, 102–3, 126–28, 216, 360–67
Maxwell House 268
maya b'alma 110–12, 119
Maygis 189, 191, 194–95, 198–99
Mayim Acharonim 10, 26, 282, 308–22, 449
meat and fish 84, 86–87, 89–90
Mechalel Shabbos B'farhesya 380
mechuar hadavar 126, 262, 266–67
mechusar maaseh gadol 356
melicha 132, 168, 171–72
Meraglim 31–32
mesorah 5–7, 130, 135–38, 140–43, 150, 152, 188, 249, 251, 254, 328, 407, 414, 445
microscope 111, 368, 371–72, 375
microscopic 103, 110–12, 115–16, 281, 284, 372, 375
mikva 283–85
milk allergy 17–18
milk and fish 84, 91–94
Minhag Baghdad 95–96
Mirsas 398–99, 405–6, 408–9, 411, 419, 432, 435–36
miut hamatzui 369–70

Mizbe'ach 167, 175, 271, 310–11, 381, 387
munn 34, 100
Muscovy Duck 140–41

N

Nat Bar Nat 60–64, 71, 233
Netillas Yadayim 9, 281–86, 292–93, 314–16, 319
Netilla Teikef L'Bracha 321
New World food item 244, 253–54
nikkur 146–48, 152
Nireh L'Einayim 115
non-Jew's nullification 125, 260
noodles 302
Nosein Taam 60, 234, 259

O

ochlei gelatin 107, 474–75
Ochlei Kitniyos 250–51
Oleh al Shulchan Melachim 218–22, 301–5
one hour 13–14, 26–27, 36, 40, 42, 50–51
oral cavity 35, 442
Or Hakeiva 105, 429, 456–57
or shuman avaz 355, 358
overnight onions 227, 449

P

pagum 66–69, 71, 233, 267, 442, 462
palate cleansing 4, 7, 25, 28, 30, 50

pancakes 297–98
panim chadoshos 104, 106, 456, 462, 469
parperes 219, 223, 305
parush 156, 158, 160, 162
Pas Akum 289, 291, 295, 302, 326
Pas Palter 23, 219, 289–94, 297, 301, 304, 326
pasteurization 378, 385–92
Pas Yisrael 23, 290–95, 297, 302–3
peanuts 236–38, 252–53
Pikuach Memshalah 410, 416
pizza 51–52, 57–58, 327
plata 193–94, 196
poretz geder 36, 213, 236, 405
pork 109, 127, 461–62, 466–68, 471
potato 129, 187, 206–10, 214–16, 219–24, 236–38, 242, 252–53, 263, 301, 304, 358
potato chips 219, 221–24
potato flour 214–16, 237
powdered milk 414–17, 426–31
pretzels 297, 300, 327
Pri Chodosh's hetter 216, 402, 430
Proctor and Gamble 262

Q
quinoa 214, 235–36, 242–55

R
ransom 47, 401
rechitza 7, 9, 22, 25, 50
re'iyah 372
restaurant 128, 147, 217–18, 301, 367, 449
Reviis 315–16, 318
rice 208–9, 211–12, 222, 246, 249, 290, 449
Rosenberg trial 464
Ryvita 299, 302

S
sakana 18, 84–88, 91–93, 114, 227, 288, 311, 314, 396
sandfish lizard 183–84
S'dom Salt / *Melach S'domis* 308–14, 317
Sefer Yetzira 23, 99–100, 102–4, 109, 118
seltzer 287–88
seudasa chada 26
sfek sfeika 71, 164–65, 217, 228, 331–32, 333, 347, 450
sha'os zmanios 39, 40–41
shawarma 355, 357–358
shechita 101–3, 142, 144, 155, 370, 475
She'eilas Chalom 319
Shehiya 189–90, 193, 198, 204
Sheviis 117–18
shinui 272–73, 276, 286
Shiur Melicha 168

Shmetinin 94–95, 426
Shnei Keilim Shenagu 72–73, 78, 79, 489
shomer 16, 19–21, 100
Shtei Halechem 270, 407
silk 364
Similac 413, 430
six hours 13, 24, 26, 35–42, 44–45, 48, 51–55, 57–58, 442, 446–447
soap 66–67, 265
Sof Zman 33
Stam Yaynam 378–80, 382, 387
Stella D'oro 294
stem-cell 97, 99, 110–12, 115, 122, 129, 449
Stincus Marinus 177–84
sugar 132, 146, 166, 172–77, 229–231, 246, 263, 271, 311
sulfuric acid 104
Swamp Chicken 135

T

taaruvos 3, 38, 88, 91, 105, 107, 123, 124, 156, 159–60, 164, 259, 260, 265, 273, 286, 336, 356, 358, 422, 457, 463
Taaruvos Chanuyos 158–59, 161
Tartuffel 207
tavlin 231
teeth 34–36, 170, 187, 271, 439–42, 444

Tefilla B'Tzibbur 33, 292, 293
Tefilla B'Zmana 33
Teisha Chanuyos 158
teva 87
three hours 40–43, 45, 446
three o'clock 155–56, 160, 163
Timtum Halev 397
To'ameha 189, 204
tongue 20, 22, 419
treibbering 146–47
turkey 84, 128, 140–41
Tzaar Baalei Chaim 34
tzara'as 84, 92
tzliyah 132, 169
tzuras hapas 289, 295–303

U

umtzah 169–71
universal *minhag* 345, 346, 349
USDA 129

V

vinegar 35, 266, 370, 372, 418

W

wafers 298–99, 302
waiting period 4, 13–14, 26–27, 34–35, 44, 48–51, 53, 57, 442, 446–47, 471
women 13–14, 149, 152, 312, 317–18
Worcestershire sauce 89

Y

Yad Soledes Bo 194, 383–84
Yayin Mevushal 380–82, 384–85, 387, 389, 391
Yayin Nesech 378–81, 388, 418
yellow cheese 51–58
yoshon 325–27, 329–30, 332, 335–36, 341, 343–44, 347–51, 452–53
Yotzei 112–16, 209, 270, 329

Z

zebu 133–34, 137–39, 142–44
Zeh V'Zeh Gorem 121–23, 132
Zohar 26–27, 29–30, 40, 48–50, 282, 314, 344

Contributors

WE WOULD LIKE TO TAKE the opportunity to thank the following people worldwide for their contributions in helping finance this *sefer*. Without the efforts and support of these individuals and their families, the publication of this *sefer* would not have been possible.

Patrons
    Bernard and Susan Hutman
    Gamliel and Terri Kagan
    Reuven Chaim and Shira Yael Klein
    Yitzchak and Toby Oratz
    Howard and Dena Seif
    Rabbi Manish and Rochel Spitz
    Yisroel Meir Wachs
    Yitzchok Weinberg

Benefactors
    Gary and Sharon Glogower
    David and Rivka Herzog
    Drs. Robert and Nilza Karl
    Shlomo and Naomi Radner
    David J. and Sarah Wayntraub

Sponsors
    Anonymous
    Avrom and Ellen Baker

Rabbi Yaakov and Faygie Bienenfeld
Shmuel Botnick and Duvi Sklarz
Leonard and Pamela Cohen
Ira and Tmima Gross
Zev and Naomi Handler
Henry and Shoshana *a"h* Kagan
Charles Z. and Sara Kalchman
Ahron and Esty Lieberman
Binyomin and Brochi Radner
Moishe and Gitty Radner
Rabbi and Mrs. Avraham Rockmill
Harry and Amy Rothenberg
David and Randi Sultan
Rabbi and Mrs. Yakov Vann
Mr. and Mrs. Menashe Weiss

Supporters

Anonymous
Dr. and Mrs. Shlomo Adler
Akiva and Emmy Attar
Binyomin and Chaya Sara Auerbach
David and Ruth Binter
Michael and Sara Carter
Yossi and Adina Elefant
Shmuel and Sara Farekas
Elazar and Chani Flam
Gedaliah and Sarah Fineman
Shamai Forster
Rabbi and Mrs. Yitzchok Dovid Frankel
Daniel and Jessica Freedman
Pinchas and Rivka Garfunkel
Shaul and Rivkie Geller
Nisan and Gilan Gertz
Yehuda and Basya Goldman
Rabbi and Mrs. Yonason Goldson

William and Robin Graff
Ephraim and Malka Guttentag
Asher and Aura Haft
Shloimie Hammer
Daniel and Margaret Herssein
Ari and Shaindy Hollander
Rabbi Aver and Chavi Jacobs
Charles Jaffe
Dov and Tammi Jeremias
Gershon and Yael Kagan
Shragi and Eva Kahana
Zevi and Sabina Kaufman
Rabbi and Mrs. Leib Kelman
Yehuda Klein
Avi and Devorah Kolko
Elisheva Krevsky
Yechiel Mechel Langner
Danny and Blimy Lemberg
Yitzchok Lewis
Dovid Lichtenstein
Rabbi Yaacov Tzvi and Rochel Lieberman
Sandra Lieberman and Yonason Shapiro
Tova Lieberman
Rabbi and Mrs. Yaakov Luban
Moshe and Rachel Machuca
Binyomin and Penina Medetsky
Tzvi and Rivka Mitzman
Rabbi Yitzchak and Talia Mizrahi
Rafael and Ella Mor
Dovid and Sara Perlman
Yitzchok and Miriam Portnoy
Abbish and Estie Rand
Rabbi and Mrs. Shaya Richmond
David and Stacey Rubin
Moshe and Devora Rubin

Shabsi and Leah Rubin
Joel and Zeesy Schnur
Yehoshua and Elkie Shalet
Rabbi Elchanan and Sara Shoff
Bernard and Ruth Spitz
Rabbi and Mrs. Lawrence Teitelman
Nussen and Etty Tenenbaum
Rabbi and Mrs. Daniel Yaakov Travis
Tsachi and Miriam Treuhaft
Seth and Aliza Trevino
Ari and Miryam Wasserman
Keith and Jessica Wasserstrom
Motty and Sarili Weinstock
Eli and Tamar Weiss
Shlomo and Shelly Weiss
Zvi Wilamowsky
Michael and Susanne Wimpfheimer

Donors

Anonymous
Moshe and Hadassah Baker
Leib and Devorah Bolel
Yitzchak and Rivka Botton
Rabbi and Mrs. Tanchum Cohen
Moses Fridman
Yehuda and Tali Greenberg
Yitzchok and Yonina Grossberg
Dovid and Talia Kanter
Cheskel Lefkowitz
Yoav and Dina Marer
Aaron and Shaindy Muller
Yehuda Roth
Rabbi Yaakov Asher and Vanina Sinclair
Yisroel and Draizel Strauss
Ephraim and Dena Terebelo

Michael Volpo
Rabbi and Mrs. Dovid Weinberger
Yehuda and Hennie Zolty

We thank them for their generosity and pray that Hashem will grant them the ability to continue contributing to the dissemination and support of Torah throughout the world for many years to come.

About the Author

ORIGINALLY FROM MIAMI BEACH, FLORIDA, Rabbi Yehuda Spitz is a product of Yeshiva Gedolah Ateres Mordechai of Greater Detroit as well as Yeshivas Mir in Yerushalayim. He studied *horaah* under the guidance of Rav Yosef Yitzchok Lerner at Beis Midrash L'Horaah Toras Shlomo, as well as Rav Yonason Wiener of the She'aris Yisrael Beis Din, and received *Semicha* from leading authorities Rav Moshe Halberstam, *zt"l*, Rav Moshe Sternbuch, and Rav Zalman Nechemia Goldberg, *zt"l*, as well as a *hetter horaah* from Rav Yaakov Blau, *zt"l*, of the *Badatz Eidah Hachareidis*. He has published an award-winning *kuntress* on the topic of *Shnei Keilim Shenagu*, and his recent *halacha sefer*, *M'Shulchan Yehuda*, is currently entering its third printing.

Rabbi Spitz has served as *Rosh Chaburah* and *Shoel U'Meishiv* of the Ohr Lagolah Halacha Kollel at Yeshivas Ohr Somayach in Yerushalayim since 2007. A prolific writer on *halachic* topics, he authors a popular longstanding contemporary *halacha* column titled "Insights into Halacha" for Ohr Somayach's website: http://ohr.edu/this_week/insights_into_halacha/.

Noted for their comprehensive portrayal, Rabbi Spitz's diverse and fascinating in-depth *halacha* articles have been featured in many major international Jewish publications, including *Yated Ne'eman*, *Hamodia*, *Mishpacha/Kolmus*, *Ami Magazine*, *Kashrus Magazine*, and *OHRNET*, as well as popular Jewish websites such as Matzav.com, VINNews, Kashrut.com, DINonline, Jerusalem Kosher News, and many others. The diverse global readership (articles are reprinted across the globe, featured in popular *parashah* compilations, and have been translated into several languages—from South Africa to Australia, London to New York, Denver, Toronto, Dallas, Baltimore, Mexico, Brazil, Israel, and even Poland) is apparent in the tremendous volume of correspondence Rabbi Spitz receives.

Rabbi Spitz has also published *halachic maamarim* in several prestigious journals, including *Moriah*, *Ohr Yisroel*, *Kovetz Eitz Chaim*, *Techumin*, *Kovetz Mah Tovu Ohalecha Yaakov*, *Peninei HaGivah*, the *(RJJ) Journal of Halacha and Contemporary Society*, and the *Rambam Maimonides Medical Journal*, for which he has reviewed as well.

Rabbi Spitz lives with his wife, Miriam, a renowned educator and lecturer in her own right, and family in Givat Zev, Israel. He can be reached at yspitz@ohr.edu.

MOSAICA PRESS
BOOK PUBLISHERS
Elegant, Meaningful & Bold

info@MosaicaPress.com
www.MosaicaPress.com

The Mosaica Press team of acclaimed editors and designers is attracting some of the most compelling thinkers and teachers in the Jewish community today. Our books are available around the world.

HARAV YAACOV HABER
RABBI DORON KORNBLUTH